Companion Reader on VIOLENCE AGAINST WOMEN

on or before the last
...low.
...114 or
...

Companion Reader on
VIOLENCE AGAINST WOMEN

EDITORS

Claire M. Renzetti
University of Kentucky

Jeffrey L. Edleson
University of Minnesota

Raquel Kennedy Bergen
Saint Joseph's University

⑤SAGE

Los Angeles | London | New Delhi
Singapore | Washington DC

Los Angeles | London | New Delhi
Singapore | Washington DC

FOR INFORMATION:

SAGE Publications, Inc.
2455 Teller Road
Thousand Oaks, California 91320
E-mail: order@sagepub.com

SAGE Publications Ltd.
1 Oliver's Yard
55 City Road
London EC1Y 1SP
United Kingdom

SAGE Publications India Pvt. Ltd.
B 1/I 1 Mohan Cooperative Industrial Area
Mathura Road, New Delhi 110 044
India

SAGE Publications Asia-Pacific Pte. Ltd.
33 Pekin Street #02-01
Far East Square
Singapore 048763

Acquisitions Editor: Kassie Graves
Editorial Assistant: Courtney Munz
Production Editor: Kelle Schillaci
Copy Editor: Diana Breti
Typesetter: C&M Digitals (P) Ltd.
Proofreader: Joyce Li
Indexer: Diggs Publication Services
Cover Designer: Candice Harman
Marketing Manager: Katharine Winter
Permissions Editor: Adele Hutchinson

Printed in the United States of America

Library of Congress Cataloging-in-Publication Data

Companion reader on violence against women / editors Claire M. Renzetti, Jeffrey L. Edleson, Raquel Kennedy Bergen.

p. cm.
Includes bibliographical references and index.

ISBN 978-1-4129-9649-5 (pbk.)

1. Women—Crimes against. 2. Abused women. 3. Marital violence. 4. Sex discrimination against women. I. Renzetti, Claire M. II. Edleson, Jeffrey L. III. Bergen, Raquel Kennedy.

HV6250.4.W65C653 2012
362.88082—dc22
2010051203

This book is printed on acid-free paper.

11 12 13 14 15 10 9 8 7 6 5 4 3 2 1

Contents

Introduction

Claire M. Renzetti, Jeffrey L. Edleson, & Raquel Kennedy Bergen

The second edition of the *Sourcebook on Violence Against Women* is intended to provide a comprehensive overview of the major concepts, theories, and methodologies in this ever-growing field, along with a discussion of some of the controversies and challenges confronting violence against women researchers and practitioners and the cutting-edge work being undertaken to address them. As we note in the Preface to that volume, however, given the vast amount of work that has been done and that is currently under way, it is impossible to cover all the topics from all competing perspectives and still keep the book manageable in size. In offering this companion reader, we hope to address some of the issues that are not included in the *Sourcebook*. Indeed, one of our goals here is to draw on the expansive literature in the violence against women field published by Sage Publications in recent years, to expose students, researchers, practitioners, and instructors to research on issues and problems not often covered in standard textbooks and which we could not include, for various reasons, in the *Sourcebook*, or which were covered in only a cursory way. In this volume, readers will find, for example, articles on same-sex intimate partner violence (McClennen) and services for LGBT victims of sexual violence (Todahl et al.), human trafficking (Logan, Walker, & Hunt), international parental child abductions in which domestic violence is a central factor (Shetty & Edleson), wartime violence against women (Borer), and violence against women during natural disasters (Fisher).

Many of these articles also encompass our second goal in compiling this reader: to draw further attention to the global dimensions of violence against women and the importance of taking into account political, economic, and cultural differences across diverse groups of people, especially those who are marginalized in some way. Consequently, readers will find articles based on research conducted in Asia (Andersson et al.; Fisher; Rani & Bonu), South Africa (Borer), and Latin America (Cole & Phillips). As well, several articles look at the impact of intersecting inequalities such as race/ethnicity (Ferraro) and poverty (Goodman et al.), while others focus on such marginalized groups as immigrant women (Erez, Adelman, & Gregory), incarcerated women (McDaniels-Wilson & Belknap), and street-level sex workers (Dalla, Xia, & Kennedy).

The *Sourcebook* gives a broad overview of research and programming in the field of violence against women, but we also wanted to provide more specific applications of some of the concepts and ideas presented in those chapters. In this volume, for example, Campbell, Dworkin, and Cabral apply the ecological model, discussed in Chapter 1 of the *Sourcebook*, to the study of sexual assault. Adams and her colleagues discuss the development of a measure of one type of intimate partner violence, economic abuse. Andersson et al. demonstrate how to collect reliable data on a highly sensitive topic from a population not used to participating in research, while simultaneously ensuring both the research participants' and the researchers' safety. And Bloom et al. illustrate the mutual benefits that accrue when researchers and practitioners engage in partnerships and collaborations.

In short, the 21 articles included in this reader are designed as companion pieces to the chapters in the second edition of the *Sourcebook*. But the volume may also be used as a stand-alone text by those who are researching specific topics, conducting trainings—for instance, on diversity issues—or teaching advanced courses (e.g., international social work) that require a more concentrated focus on particular topics and less breadth than the *Sourcebook* provides. In any case, we hope that this book advances knowledge about the many facets of violence against women and serves as inspiration to those working in the field or contemplating such work, as they undertake research, study, or practice.

PART I

Theoretical and Methodological Issues in Researching Violence Against Women

CHAPTER 1

An Ecological Model of the Impact of Sexual Assault on Women's Mental Health

Rebecca Campbell, Emily Dworkin, and Giannina Cabral

The impact of sexual assault on women's mental health has been extensively studied and has been the subject of multiple prior reviews (Briere & Jordan, 2004; Chivers-Wilson, 2006; Ellis, 1983; Goodman, Koss, & Russo, 1993; Koss, 1993; Koss, Bailey, Yuan, Herrera, & Lichter, 2003; Koss et al., 1994; Kilpatrick & Acierno, 2003; Kilpatrick, Amstadter, Resnick, & Ruggiero, 2007; Resick, 1993; Rogers & Gruener, 1997). The reviews from the early 1990s are remarkably consistent with more recent syntheses of the literature: rape is one of the most severe of all traumas, causing multiple, long-term negative outcomes. Between 17% and 65% of women with a lifetime history of sexual assault develop posttraumatic stress disorder (PTSD; Clum, Calhoun, & Kimerling, 2000; Kilpatrick et al., 1989; Kilpatrick & Resnick, 1993; Kilpatrick, Saunders, Veronen, Best, & Von, 1987; Rothbaum, Foa, Riggs, Murdock, & Walsh, 1992). Many

(13%–51%) meet diagnostic criteria for depression (Acierno et al., 2002; Becker, Skinner, Abel, Axelrod, & Treacy, 1984; Burnam et al., 1988; Clum et al., 2000; Dickinson, deGruy, Dickinson, & Candib, 1999; Frank & Anderson, 1987; Golding, 1996; Kilpatrick et al., 1987; Winfield, George, Swartz, & Blazer, 1990). Most sexual assault victims develop fear and/or anxiety (73%–82%; Frank & Anderson, 1987; Ullman & Siegel, 1993), and 12% to 40% experience generalized anxiety (Siegel, Golding, Stein, Burnam, & Sorenson,1990; Winfield et al., 1990). Approximately 13% to 49% of survivors become dependent on alcohol, whereas 28% to 61% may use other illicit substances (Frank & Anderson, 1987; Ullman, 2007; Ullman & Brecklin, 2002a). It is not uncommon for victims to experience suicidal ideation (23%–44%; Frank & Stewart, 1984; Frank, Turner, Stewart, Jacob, & West, 1981; Kilpatrick et al., 1985; Petrak, Doyle,

Campbell, R., Dworkin, E., & Cabral, G. (2009). An ecological model of the impact of sexual assault on women's mental health. *Trauma, Violence, & Abuse, 10*, 225–246.

Williams, Buchan, & Forster, 1997), and 2% to 19% may attempt suicide (Davidson, Hughes, George, & Blazer, 1996; Frank et al., 1981; Kilpatrick et al., 1985).

KEY POINTS OF THE RESEARCH REVIEW

- The negative mental health sequelae of sexual assault stems from multiple factors, not just characteristics of the victim. Aspects of the assault itself, postassault disclosures and help seeking, and sociocultural norms help shape the way in which this trauma affects women's psychological well-being.
- Women's victimization is cumulative, and the response from the social world is cumulative, both of which affect how any one incident of sexual violence will affect women's mental health.
- Self-blame has been studied from both individual-level and extra-individual perspectives, and we conceptualize it as a meta-construct that develops from and is shaped by multiple levels in the ecological system.

Though there is little disagreement that sexual assault is highly detrimental to women's mental health, how to conceptualize that harm has been the subject of debate. A trauma response theoretical model has been proposed as a useful conceptual framework for guiding research and intervention (Goodman et al., 1993; Herman, 1992), though concerns have been raised that the clinical diagnosis of PTSD risks pathologizing victims (Berg, 2002; Gilfus, 1999) as well as perpetuating ethnocultural biases (Marsella, Friedman, & Spain, 1999; Wasco, 2003). Framing the impact of sexual assault solely within a PTSD framework would indeed be limiting, and hence, violence

against women scholars have advocated for ecologically informed trauma models of rape recovery (Koss & Harvey, 1991; Neville & Heppner, 1999). Sexual assault does not occur in social and cultural isolation: we live in a rape-prone culture that propagates messages that victims are to blame for the assault, that they caused it and, indeed, deserve it (Buchwald, Fletcher, & Roth, 1993; Burt, 1998; Lonsway & Fitzgerald, 1994; Sandy, 1998). Victims are faced with negotiating postassault help seeking and, ultimately, their pathway to recovery within multiple hostile environments. If survivors turn to their family and friends for social support, how will they react, as they, too, have been inundated with these cultural messages? If victims turn to formal systems, such as the legal, medical, and mental health systems, they may face disbelief, blame, and refusals of help instead of assistance. The trauma of rape extends far beyond the actual assault, and society's response to this crime can also affect women's well-being.

The purpose of this review is to examine the psychological impact of adult sexual assault through an ecological theoretical perspective to understand how factors at multiple levels of the social ecology contribute to the deleterious mental health effects that have been so consistently reported in the literature. The utility of an ecological framework is that it can suggest multiple strategies, at multiple levels of analysis, for alleviating the psychological harm caused by sexual assault. We will begin with a brief discussion of the different ecological theories that have been utilized in violence against women research. Since Koss and Harvey (1991) and Neville and Heppner (1999) first called for more ecologically informed research on psychological sequelae and recovery, numerous studies have been conducted on the relationships between extraindividual level factors and mental health outcomes. Our review will synthesize this developing literature to identify positive, negative, and still inconclusive findings regarding the relationships between individual, assault, and ecological factors and survivors' psychological distress.

Ecological Theories in Violence Against Women Research

There are multiple ecological theories evolving in the social sciences, and it is beyond the scope of this article to explore each one (see McLaren & Hawe, 2005 for a review). In violence against women scholarship, two specific approaches have been drawn on to inform research, prevention, and treatment. First, from community psychology, Kelly's (1966, 1968, 1971) ecological theory posits that the functions of individuals and community organizations are interdependent and that individuals have differential patterns of experiences given different ecological settings. Ecological settings consist of person constructs, which are individual characteristics such as race/ethnicity, gender, and beliefs and attitudes; events, which refer to the specific problem(s) that prompts an individual to need assistance and/or seek help and instigates a community help-system network to respond; and environments, which include structural features of a community (e.g., resources), functional features (e.g., service delivery processes), as well as the attitudes and values of the community as a whole (Kelly, Ryan, Altman, & Stelzner, 2000). Koss and Harvey (1991) and Harvey (1996) adapted these ideas to propose an ecological model of rape recovery, and Campbell and colleagues have used this model in empirical research to evaluate how the legal, medical, and mental health systems respond to victims' needs and how those system experiences affect victims' psychological, physical, and sexual health outcomes (Campbell, 1998; Campbell et al., 1999; Campbell et al., 2001; Campbell, Sefl, & Ahrens, 2004).

Second, from developmental psychology, Bronfenbrenner's (1979, 1986, 1995) ecological theory of human development has similar conceptual foundations in its premise that human development occurs through constantly evolving interactions between individuals and their multiple, interconnected environmental contexts. Bronfenbrenner's model subdivides environmental influences into multiple levels reflecting the relative size, immediacy of interaction, and degree of formality/informality of the environmental setting. The individual level comprises bio-psycho-social characteristics of the person; the microsystem focuses on direct interpersonal interactions between individuals and members of their immediate environment such as families, friends, and peers; the mesosystem reflects interconnections and linkages between individuals and between individuals and systems; the exosystem includes organizations and social systems (e.g., legal, medical, and mental health); the macrosystem includes societal norms, expectations, and beliefs that form the broader social environment; and the chronosystem encompasses the changes that occur over time between persons and their multiple environments. Bronfenbrenner's conceptualization shaped the theoretical models created by Heise (1998) and White and Kowalski (1998) to explain the underlying causes of violence against women and risk factors for perpetration. Similarly, Grauerholz's (2000) model of sexual revictimization examines how personal, interpersonal, and sociocultural factors contribute to child sexual abuse survivors' increased risk for subsequent sexual victimization later in life. Both the Centers for Disease Control and Prevention (CDC; 2004) and the World Health Organization (WHO; Jewkes, Sen, & Garcia-Moreno, 2002; Krug, Mercy, Dahlberg, & Zwi, 2002) have adapted this approach to develop multilevel models for the prevention of gender-based violence.

As noted previously, Neville and Heppner (1999) also extended Bronfenbrenner's model to explain how sexual assault affects women's well-being and recovery processes, which they termed CIEMSAR: culturally inclusive ecological model of sexual assault recovery. The fundamental premise of their model is that sexual assault survivors' mental health is shaped by many factors, not just the assault itself or preexisting individual characteristics. With each disclosure and interaction with the social world, victims are given explicit and implicit messages about how they are to make sense of this crime and apportion blame. We, too, have chosen to adapt Bronfenbrenner's model. To set the stage for our empirical review, we will describe Neville and Heppner's model in detail, highlighting similarities and differences to the model we developed from our analysis of the literature (Figure 1.1).

First, at the individual level of analysis, characteristics of the victim could certainly influence the recovery process. Neville and Heppner's (1999) model examined age, race/ethnicity, and social class as sociodemographic correlates of postassault psychological distress; to that base, our model includes additional demographic features recently examined in the literature such as education, marital status, employment status, and income. Neville and Heppner noted race/ethnicity can be conceptualized at multiple levels of the social ecology, but that most research on postassault sequelae has not conceptualized race/ethnicity from a sociocultural perspective. In other words, racial differences have been examined without a full exploration of cultural identity. We concur with this analysis and followed the convention established by Neville and Heppner to discuss race/ethnicity at both the individual level of analysis and the macrolevel of

analysis, depending on the way in which this construct was conceptualized in the particular study. Also at the individual level, our model considers the role of personality characteristics, preexisting mental health conditions, and biological/genetic factors in victims' postassault distress, which were not examined in Neville and Heppner's model. Finally, victims' coping processes are also influential in recovery, although it is unclear at which level of analysis this construct best fits (e.g., coping by mobilizing social support reflects an interaction of individual and microsystem processes). We follow Neville and Heppner's precedent and place this construct at the individual level, as it reflects the choices and propensities of the survivors, but explore it "last" in the individual processes as a way of symbolizing its interconnections to the higher levels in the model (i.e., microsystems).

Second, characteristics of the assault itself affect women's psychological well-being. Neville and Heppner (1999) examined how the victim-offender relationship and the severity of injury differentially affect victims' distress. In addition to those factors, our model explores the roles of threats to kill the victim, weapon use, assault

Figure 1.1 An Ecological Model of the Impact of Sexual Assault on Women's Mental Health

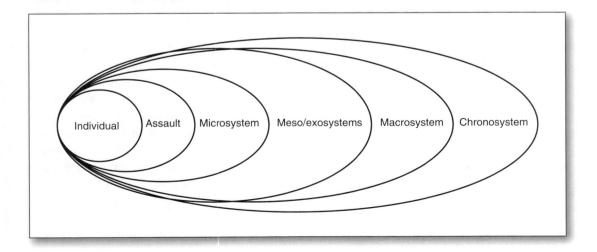

force or violence, and substance use at the time of the assault in relation to victims' postassault psychological sequelae, which has been a growing area of inquiry in recent years.

Third, at the microsystem level, our model explores the impact of disclosures to informal sources of support (e.g., family and friends) on victims' postassault psychological distress. Neville and Heppner (1999) conceptualized social support as the mesosystem level, but we have elected to reframe this construct as a microsystem process (when that support is specifically from family, friends, or peers). Bronfenbrenner (1979) defined the microsystem as the face-to-face interactions and interrelations between individuals and others in their immediate setting; because the provision of (or denial of) social support occurs through direct interactions with family, friends, or peers, we conceptualized this as a microsystem process. Since Neville and Heppner's model was developed, research on social support has flourished, and we can now refine the model in light of this new empirical knowledge base.

Fourth, although Bronfenbrenner's original model separates mesosystems (i.e., processes that contribute to linkages between systems and/or other individuals in the ecological environment) from exosystems (i.e., formal systems with which individuals may or may not have contact), our analysis of the extant literature on postassault sequelae suggests that empirically based distinctions between these levels are not yet warranted, which is consistent with Neville and Heppner's (1999) model. For example, victims may seek assistance from a rape crisis center (RCC), which could be conceptualized as a formal help resource (i.e., exosystem) and in the process of helping the survivors, RCC staff may help establish connections with other formal systems (such as the legal or medical systems) and/or work with survivors to help them access more informal supports in their lives (i.e., mesosystems). Therefore, we distinguish our combined meso/exosystem level from the prior microsystem level by whether the interactions take place between informal supports (microsystem) versus formalized supports (meso/exosystem).

Fifth, as noted previously, race/ethnicity can be conceptualized at the macrolevel of analysis when explored from a sociocultural perspective to understand the cultural identity and its role in rape recovery. Victims' postassault distress is also influenced by the rape-prone culture in which we live, which remains highly acceptant of rape myths and stereotypes that women are to blame for their own victimization (Rozee & Koss, 2001).

Sixth, the chronosystem was not included in Neville and Heppner's (1999) original model, but we have incorporated it to reflect Bronfenbrenner's idea that person-environment interactions are reciprocal and change over time. There are normative transitional events (e.g., school changes) and nonnormative events (e.g., sexual assault) that shape how individuals interact with their environments and how their environments respond to them. The chronosystem examines the cumulative effects of multiple sequences of developmental transitions over the life course. Therefore, a history of sexual assault and other victimizations across the lifespan would influence the recovery process at each victimization (if more than one is experienced). Neville and Heppner conceptualized sexual revictimization as an individual-level variable, but we view it as an historical lifespan factor that shapes how other levels in the model affect a recent victimization.

Finally, Neville and Heppner (1999) conceptualized self-blame as a macrolevel phenomenon, informed by Ward's (1995) analysis that women internalize societal rape myths, which leads to negative self-appraisals. We concur that societal rape myths contribute to internalized self-blame, but since the development of Neville and Heppner's original model, multiple empirical studies have established that survivors encounter a great deal of victim blaming in their interactions with both formal and informal systems (e.g., Filipas & Ullman, 2006). In addition, some victims, particularly racial/ethnic minorities, are more likely to be subjected to victim-blaming treatment (e.g., Campbell et al., 2001). Survivors of certain types of assault, such as acquaintance/date rape and those who have been sexually revictimized, are also more susceptible to being blamed for the assault (e.g., Arata, 1999; Filipas & Ullman, 2006). In view of these findings, we argue that self-blame transcends any one level of the model, as it stems from individual, assault, micro-, meso/exo-, macro-, and chronosystem-level processes. Therefore, we conceptualize self-blame as a meta-construct that results from interactions across all levels of the social ecology (Figure 1.2).

An Ecological Model of the Impact of Sexual Assault on Women's Mental Health

In our review, we focused on empirical studies of adult sexual assault, which is often operationalized in research as assaults that occurred at age 14 or older (Koss, Gidycz, & Wisneiwski, 1987). Age 14 is also the developmental demarcation identified by Burnam et al. (1988) for significantly different postassault mental health outcomes. As such, our review does not include

studies of childhood sexual abuse (only), but would include studies of victims who were sexually victimized multiple times in their lives, provided that one of the assaults clearly occurred in adulthood (as defined above). Studies that assessed lifetime sexual victimization but did not distinguish whether there was an assault sustained during adulthood (as defined above) were not included in this review (though we note that the substantive findings from these studies do not differ from those that met our inclusion criteria). Similarly, studies of criminal victimization were not reviewed unless subgroup analyses were available that separated victims of sexual assault from victims of other types of crimes. Because sexual assault is one form of intimate partner violence (Campbell & Soeken, 1999; Cole, Logan, & Shannon, 2005; Eby, Campbell, Sullivan, & Davidson, 1995), we searched the domestic violence/intimate partner violence literature as well to ensure that studies of intimate partner sexual assault were also included. Because our goal was to develop a model of mental health impact (not physical or sexual health impact), to be included in this review, a study must have

Figure 1.2   Self-Blame as a Meta-Construct That Stems From All Levels in the Ecological Model

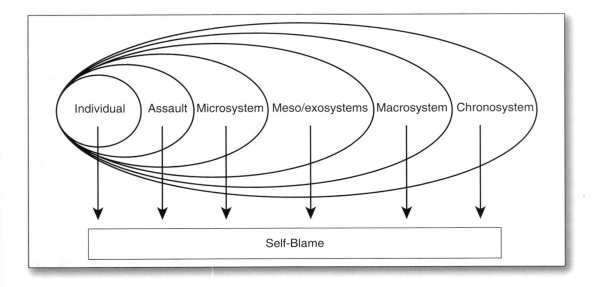

empirically examined a link between at least one of the factors in the ecological model described above and a psychological health outcome such as PTSD, depression, fear/anxiety, general psychological distress, suicidality, and/or substance use (see Table 1.1).

Table 1.1	Key Findings: The Impact of Multilevel Ecological Factors on Sexual Assault Victims' Psychological Sequelae

Ecological Level	**Major Findings**
Individual-level factors (victim and assault characteristics)	Mixed findings on the impact of sociodemographic variables (i.e., age, race, income, education, employment), assault characteristics (i.e., victim-offender relationship, injury, alcohol use), and biological factors (i.e., cortisol levels) on postassault well-being.

Personality traits such as neuroticism predict PTSD among sexual assault survivors.

Poorer preassault mental health predicts multiple negative outcomes, such as depression and anxiety.

Avoidance coping strategies predict multiple negative outcomes, such as longer recovery time, depression, and PTSD.

Perceived life threat during assault and perceived dangerousness of assailant predict negative outcomes, such as depression, anxiety, and PTSD symptomatology. |
| Microsystem factors | Positive social reactions and support from informal providers (e.g., family, friends, significant others) predicts less mental distress postassault.

Negative social reactions from informal support providers predicts multiple negative outcomes such as depression, anxiety, and posttraumatic stress. |
| Meso/exosystem factors | Legal System: secondary victimization (i.e., victim blaming, minimal help) predicts higher symptomatology such as PTSD and depression.

SANEs, rape crisis centers, and other community mental health programs help mitigate the negative effects of other medical systems (e.g., E.R.) and predict less mental health distress post assault. |
Macrosystem factors	The rape-prone culture, institutionalized racism, cultural differences in responding to rape, and acceptance of rape myths create a difficult sociocultural context for sexual assault survivors to recover.
Chronosystem factors	Cumulative trauma and revictimization over the lifetime predicts negative outcomes such as depression, anxiety, and PTSD.
Self-blame: Multilevel meta-construct	Self-blame is associated with PTSD and depression at the individual level. At the micro and meso/exo levels, receiving blame exacerbates self-blame and is associated with PTSD symptomatology. At the macro level, internalized sociocultural beliefs affect victims' self-blame. At the chronosystem level, victims of cumulative trauma have been found to have greater self-blame and higher levels of trauma.

Individual-Level Factors

1. Sociodemographic variables. Several sociodemographic variables have been studied in relation to postassault sequelae. Most studies have not found racial/ethnic differences in postassault distress; specifically, no difference has been found for PTSD (e.g., Campbell et al., 1999; Elliott, Mok, & Briere, 2004; Ullman & Brecklin, 2002a; Ullman, Filipas, Townsend, & Starzynski, 2006), depression (Elliott et al., 2004; Frank & Stewart, 1984; McFarlane et al., 2005; Wyatt, 1992), fear/anxiety (McFarlane et al., 2005; Wyatt, 1992), or general distress (Kilpatrick, Veronen, & Best, 1984). Studies of lifetime victimization have reported that Hispanic and non-Hispanic women do not differ in depression, substance use/dependence, phobia, panic, or obsessive-compulsive disorder (Burnam et al., 1988), and White and non-White women do not differ in suicidal ideation/attempts (Ullman & Brecklin, 2002b). However, one study with a small number of African American participants found that African American women were more likely than White women to be anxious after sexual assault (Burge, 1988), and a second study of intimate partner sexual assault victims identified that Hispanic women had significantly higher levels of PTSD than African American and White women (McFarlane et al., 2005). Ruch and Chandler (1983) defined trauma as the general effect of the assault on victims' lives, and under that definition, they found that White women were more traumatized than racial/ethnic minority survivors.

With respect to victims' age, several studies have found that older survivors experience increased depression and general trauma (Frank & Stewart, 1984; Ruch & Chandler, 1983; Ruch & Leon, 1983); however, younger age has been found to predict PTSD and depression (Elliott et al., 2004) and older victims have been found to have fewer PTSD symptoms when assaulted by relatives (Ullman et al., 2006). Several studies found no effect of age on distress (Bownes, O'Gorman, & Sayers, 1991; Campbell et al., 1999; Kilpatrick et al., 1984; Kramer & Green, 1991; Ullman & Filipas, 2001b).

In the examination of income level, marital status, and employment status with postrape distress, most studies that attempted to relate these variables with specific postrape diagnoses have not found an association (e.g., Bownes et al., 1991; Campbell et al., 1999; Mackey et al., 1992; Ullman & Brecklin, 2002a; Ullman & Filipas, 2001b). However, when these variables are studied in relation to more general indices of trauma or stress, associations have been found. One study found that victims who were "economically stressed" were less likely to report that they were "recovered" from the assault months or years afterward (Burgess & Holmstrom, 1978), a single study found that being married was related to increased trauma (Ruch & Chandler, 1983), and a similar study identified that being unemployed was related to postassault trauma two weeks after assault (Ruch & Leon, 1983). Furthermore, Ullman and Brecklin's (2002b) study of lifetime victimization indicated that those who were employed or married experienced less suicidal ideation, but no difference was found for suicide attempts.

The relationship between education and postassault distress is also unclear. Two studies reported that less education is related to PTSD (Burge, 1988; Ullman & Brecklin, 2002a): one identified that higher education predicted lowered levels of PTSD (Ullman & Filipas, 2001b), and one found that a lack of a college education was related to suicide attempts (Ullman & Brecklin, 2002b). However, an equivalent number of studies have found no effect of education on posttraumatic stress (Campbell et al., 1999; Ullman et al., 2006) or depression (Frank & Stewart, 1984). Studies of lifetime victimization have found that depression, substance abuse, phobia, panic disorder, obsessive-compulsive disorder, and suicidal ideation do not differ based on level of educational attainment (Burnam et al., 1988; Ullman & Brecklin, 2002b).

2. Personality factors. Few studies have been conducted on the relationship between personality factors and postassault psychological distress.

Researchers commonly conceptualize personality using the Five-Factor Model, which consists of five dimensions: openness, conscientiousness, extraversion, agreeableness, and neuroticism. Cox, MacPherson, Enns, and McWilliams (2004) reported that neuroticism (including traits such as anxiety, impulsiveness, hostility, and depression; John & Srivastava, 1999) was found to predict PTSD, and that the self-criticism, an additional personality variable, also predicted PTSD.

3. Preexisting mental health conditions. Several studies have identified that preexisting mental health conditions are positively related to postassault mental health sequelae. Victims who had attempted suicide preassault experienced significantly more postassault depression and anxiety (Frank et al., 1981), and preexisting mental health diagnosis and substance abuse problems were positively associated with postassault trauma (Frank & Anderson, 1987; Ruch & Chandler, 1983; Ruch & Leon, 1983). Preassault depression and suicidal history significantly predicted depression levels 4 months post assault (Atkeson et al., 1982). Anxiety attacks and obsessive-compulsive symptoms also predicted depression at 8 and 12 months. Psychiatric treatment history before the sexual assault predicted depression at a year post assault (Atkeson et al., 1982). Conversely, several studies have not found that prerape psychopathology predicts postrape distress (Bownes et al., 1991; Frank et al., 1981; Frank & Stewart, 1984; Kilpatrick et al., 1984). However, these studies examined psychiatric history generally (e.g., visits to psychiatrist, psychiatric hospitalization), suggesting that although prerape psychiatric history overall may not be associated with postrape symptomatology, more specific mental health variables (e.g., diagnoses) may be associated with postassault distress.

4. Genetic and biological factors. To date, no studies have examined genetic factors as predictors of postrape distress, but several biological factors have been examined in a limited body of work.

Normally, in reaction to stress, the body reacts by releasing hormones such as cortisol (Chivers-Wilson, 2006). However, traumatic events such as sexual assault seem to alter cortisol response, possibly contributing to PTSD (Yehuda, 2006). Among adult rape victims, cortisol levels immediately after the assault have been alternately identified as a positive correlate of PTSD (Resnick, Yehuda, & Acierno, 1997) and unrelated to PTSD (Resnick, Yehuda, Pitman, & Foy, 1995). Some have theorized that sexual assault survivors who develop PTSD may have abnormally low cortisol levels due to a history of sexual victimization (Resnick et al., 1997), which may function to maintain the stress response, contributing to PTSD (Shalev & Sahar, 1998). MHPG (3-Methoxy-4-Hydroxyphenylglycol), a metabolite of norepinephrine (a stress hormone), has also been found to contribute to PTSD (Yehuda, Resnick, Schmeidler, Yang, & Pitman, 1998). Survivors of sexual assault without PTSD showed associations between MHPG and cortisol, suggesting that these responses are coordinated in an adaptive response to trauma (Yehuda et al., 1998).

5. Coping responses. Finally, victims' coping responses affect their postassault psychological health. As noted previously, coping is a "transitional" construct that includes both individual-level and situational factors (Roth & Cohen, 1986). Survivors may use approach strategies (i.e., emotional or cognitive activity oriented toward the threat) and/or avoidance strategies (i.e., emotional or cognitive activity oriented away from the threat) for any given situation and at any given point in time during their recovery process. Survivors may use a consistent coping orientation over time to deal with stress, but this orientation may change depending on the availability of resources (e.g., personal resources and/or support in the environment). For example, Ullman and colleagues have found that rape survivors who receive negative social support are more likely to use avoidance coping and have increased PTSD symptomatology (Ullman, 1996c; Ullman,

Townsend, Filipas, & Starzynski, 2007). Therefore, coping can be explained as an underlying orientation toward stress that can be influenced by time, situation/context, and environmental support.

The empirical research on sexual assault survivors' coping distinguishes between maladaptive or adaptive recovery strategies. Maladaptive approaches involve some level of avoidance, such as staying at home, withdrawal, disengagement, and substance abuse, which are associated with longer recovery time and higher levels of depression, anxiety, fear, and PTSD (Burgess & Holmstrom, 1979; Gutner, Rizvi, Monson, & Resick, 2006; Frazier & Burnett, 1994; Frazier, Mortensen, & Steward, 2005; Meyer & Taylor, 1986; Santello & Leitenberg, 1993; Ullman et al., 2007). Adaptive strategies, such as expressing emotions, seeking social support, and reducing stress, have been found to be related to faster recovery and less depression, anxiety, fear, and PTSD (Burgess & Holmstrom, 1979; Frazier & Burnett, 1994; Frazier et al., 2005; Gutner et al., 2006; Meyer & Taylor, 1986; Valentiner, Foa, Riggs, & Gershuny, 1996). However, several studies have found mixed findings regarding coping and postassault distress. For example, Valentiner et al. (1996) reported that seeking social support was not associated with PTSD severity, and instead, the actual type of support received by survivors predicted adjustment. Furthermore, Ullman (1996a, 1996b, 1996c) found that approach strategies such as joining a support group and going to a therapist were actually related to more distress. It has also been suggested that avoidance can be beneficial for recovery. Frazier and Burnett (1994) found that avoidance strategies such as keeping busy and suppressing negative thoughts were related to less distress. This finding is also consistent with Roth and Cohen's (1986) theory that the use of avoidance immediately after a stressful life event may be helpful to adjustment. These mixed findings suggest that perhaps coping strategies should be examined in relation to the context in which they are used (i.e., microsystem influences).

Assault-Related Factors

Numerous studies have investigated how characteristics of the assault itself affects victims' postassault distress. With respect to victim-offender relationship, most studies have found that experiencing rape perpetrated by a stranger is not associated with differential levels of post-rape symptomatology (e.g., Arata & Burkhart, 1996; Campbell et al., 1999; Frank, Turner, & Stewart, 1980; Kilpatrick et al., 1984; Kramer & Green, 1991; Mackey et al., 1992; Riggs, Kilpatrick, & Resnick, 1992; Ullman & Filipas, 2001b), but some studies have reported that surviving stranger rape was associated with increased PTSD (Bownes et al., 1991; Ullman et al., 2006), depression (Ellis, Atkeson, & Calhoun, 1981) and general trauma (Ruch & Chandler, 1983). Ellis and colleagues (1981) reported that stranger rapes tended to be more violent and invasive than nonstranger rapes and suggested that this may contribute to findings of increased postrape symptomatology. Sexual assault by a partner has been found to be a significant predictor of PTSD (Temple, Weston, Rodriguez, & Marshall, 2007; Ullman et al., 2006), although when compared to other types of assailants, there was no difference in depression (Koss, Dinero, Seibel, & Cox, 1988; Riggs et al., 1992) or anxiety (Koss et al., 1988). Some have suggested that the perceived dangerousness of the assailant (rather than simpler stranger/nonstranger distinction) may be related to the severity of PTSD symptoms (Cascardi, Riggs, Hearst-Ikeda, & Foa, 1996).

Many studies report that injury incurred as a result of sexual assault is related to postassault PTSD, depression, and anxiety (e.g., Bownes et al., 1991; Sales, Baum, & Shore, 1984), but many have not found a relationship between psychological distress and injury (Campbell et al., 1999; Kilpatrick et al., 1984; Ullman & Filipas, 2001b). One study identified that threats to kill the victim did not affect postrape depression or anxiety (Frank et al., 1980), but Sales et al. (1984) reported that threats to kill predicted depression and anxiety immediately after the assault. Most examinations of postrape distress have not found an effect for weapon use (Campbell et al., 1999; Frank et al., 1980; Kilpatrick et al., 1984; Sales et al., 1984), although one study identified that victims with PTSD had experienced more weapon use than those without PTSD (Bownes et al., 1991). However, this sample differed from those that found no weapon effect, in that all victims had reported the rape to the police. Although most attempts to associate assault force or violence with postassault distress have found that these variables are positively related (Bownes et al., 1991; Sales et al., 1984; Ullman & Siegel, 1993), others have found that violence/force does not predict postassault depression and anxiety (Atkeson et al., 1982) or general postassault distress (Kilpatrick et al., 1984).

A limited number of studies have assessed the relationship of victim substance use before or during sexual assault to postassault distress. These studies have not found an association between substance abuse and posttraumatic symptoms (Arata & Burkhart, 1996; Campbell et al., 1999; Resnick et al., 1997; Schwartz & Leggett, 1999). The relatively high level of perpetrator violence and relatively low level of victim resistance that are common among substance-facilitated rapes (Ullman, Karabatsos, & Koss, 1999) could contribute to postassault symptomatology; therefore, the mental health outcomes of substance-facilitated rapes should be further examined.

Microsystem Factors

Although several studies have investigated sexual assault survivors' disclosure processes (Ahrens, 2006; Ahrens, Campbell, Ternier-Thames, Wasco, & Sefl, 2007; Fisher, Daigle, Cullen, & Turner, 2003; Golding, Siegel, Sorenson, Burnam, & Stein, 1989; Ullman & Brecklin, 2003) and the positive and negative social reactions they receive from both formal and informal support providers (Ahrens et al., 2007; Golding et al., 1989; Sudderth, 1998; Ullman, 2000), fewer studies

have actually examined how these social reactions affect mental health outcomes such as depression and PTSD. Overall, this literature suggests that social support from family, friends, and intimate partners facilitates sexual assault survivors' recovery. The availability of family and friends, living with family, and feeling close to family members are related to better adjustment (Burgess & Holmstrom, 1979; Kramer & Green, 1991; Ruch & Chandler, 1983; Ruch & Leon, 1983; Sales et al., 1984). Positive social reactions from family and friends are related to less psychological distress (Campbell, Ahrens, Sefl, Wasco, & Barnes, 2001; Coker et al., 2002), and similarly, in studies that did not differentiate between informal and formal sources of support, positive social support was also related to lower symptomatology (Atkeson et al., 1982; Thompson et al., 2000). Negative social reactions from family, friends, and peers have consistently been found to be related to increased anxiety, depression, and PTSD (Borja, Callahan, & Long, 2006; Campbell et al., 2001; Davis, Brickman, & Baker, 1991; Moss, Frank, & Anderson, 1990). Studies that have measured both informal and formal sources of support together substantiate this effect (Ullman, 1996a, 1996b, 1996c; Ullman & Filipas, 2001a; Ullman, Townsend, Filipas, & Starzynski, 2007).

Interestingly, it appears that negative social reactions have a stronger detrimental effect on survivors' mental health than positive social reactions have for bolstering well-being (Borja et al., 2006; Campbell et al., 2001; Fowler & Hill, 2004; Ruch & Leon, 1983). It may be that negative social reactions are more salient for survivors' recovery because survivors are more likely to first disclose to family and friends (Ahrens et al., 2007; Filipas & Ullman, 2001; Starzynski, Ullman, Filipas, & Townsend, 2005), and they likely expect sympathetic reactions from these people. If survivors receive unexpected negative reactions from family and friends, it may be particularly upsetting. However, the direction of causality between psychological distress and social support is unresolved. For example, Starzynski et al. (2005) found that increased levels of distress symptoms predicted seeking social support from both informal and formal support providers. In addition, what happens in one instance of seeking support has implications for further help seeking and distress. Ahrens et al. (2007) revealed that when initial disclosures were negative, victims refrained from further disclosures and were less likely to seek further help, which was associated with higher self-reported distress. These findings emphasize the need for longitudinal studies of victims' recovery process to examine the temporal relationships between social support and postassault psychological sequelae.

Meso/Exosystem Factors

Sexual assault victims have extensive postassault needs and may turn to multiple formal social systems for assistance: approximately 26% to 40% of victims report the assault to the police and pursue prosecution through the criminal justice system, 27% to 40% seek medical care and medical forensic examinations, and 16% to 60% obtain mental health services (Campbell et al., 2001; Ullman, 1996a, 1996b, 2007; Ullman & Filipas, 2001a). If victims are able to receive the services they need and are treated in an empathic, supportive manner, then social systems can help facilitate recovery. Conversely, if victims do not receive needed services and are treated insensitively, then these systems can magnify victims' feelings of powerlessness, shame, and guilt. Postassault help-seeking from formal social systems can become a "second rape," that is, a secondary victimization to the initial trauma. These experiences of secondary victimization can have a negative impact on victims' psychological well-being (Campbell et al., 1999; Campbell et al., 2001; Campbell & Raja, 1999, 2005).

The Legal System. Throughout their contact with legal system, victims are asked to recount the assault many times. During this questioning, they are often asked victim-blaming questions

about what they were wearing, their prior sexual history, and whether they responded sexually to the assault (Campbell, 2005, 2006; Campbell & Raja, 2005). In self-report characterizations of their psychological health, rape survivors indicate that as a result of their contact with legal system personnel, they felt bad about themselves (87%), guilty/self-blaming (73%), depressed (71%), violated (89%), distrustful of others (53%), and reluctant to seek further help (80%; Campbell, 2005; Campbell & Raja, 2005). The harm of secondary victimization is also evident on objective measures of PTSD symptomatology. In a series of studies on victim/police contact, Campbell and colleagues found that low legal action (i.e., case did not progress/was dropped) and high secondary victimization were associated with increased PTSD symptomatology (Campbell et al., 2001; Campbell & Raja, 2005). In tests of complex interactions, Campbell et al. (1999) identified that the victims of nonstranger rape whose cases were not prosecuted and who were subjected to high levels of secondary victimization had the highest PTSD of all—worse than those who chose not to report to the legal system at all.

The Medical System. Sexual assault victims may also seek help from the medical system for injury detection and care, medical forensic examination, screening and treatment for sexually transmitted infections (STIs), pregnancy testing, and emergency contraception. Although most victims are not physically injured to the point of needing emergency care (Ledray, 1996), traditionally, police, rape crisis centers, and social service agencies have advised victims to seek treatment in hospital emergency departments (EDs) for a medical forensic exam (Martin, 2005). During this medical care, doctors and nurses ask victims similar questions as do legal personnel regarding their prior sexual history, sexual response during the assault, manner of dress, and what they did to "cause" the assault. Medical professionals may view these questions as necessary and appropriate, but rape survivors find them upsetting (Campbell & Raja, 2005). Comparative studies suggest that victims encounter significantly fewer victim-blaming questions and statements from medical system personnel relative to legal professionals (Campbell, 2005, 2006; Campbell et al., 1999; Campbell et al., 2001; Campbell & Raja, 2005), but this still has a demonstrable negative impact on victims' mental health. Campbell (2005) found that as a result of their contact with ED doctors and nurses, most rape survivors stated that they felt bad about themselves (81%), guilty (74%), depressed (88%), violated (94%), distrustful of others (74%), and reluctant to seek further help (80%; see also Campbell & Raja, 2005). Victims who do not receive basic medical services rate their experiences with the medical system as more hurtful, which has been associated with higher PTSD levels (Campbell et al., 2001; Campbell & Raja, 2005). Specifically, nonstranger rape victims who received minimal medical services but encountered high secondary victimization had significantly higher levels of PTSD symptoms than victims who did not seek medical services at all (Campbell et al., 1999).

The Mental Health System. Few studies have examined if and how sexual assault victims benefit from community-based mental health system services.[1] In general, victims tend to rate their experiences with mental health professionals positively and characterize their help as useful and supportive (Campbell et al., 2001; Ullman, 1996a, 1996b). Whether positive satisfaction results in demonstrable mental health benefit is largely unknown although Campbell et al. (1999) found that community-based mental health services were particularly helpful for victims who had had negative experiences with the legal and/or medical systems. Victims who encountered substantial difficulty obtaining needed services and experienced high secondary victimization from the legal and medical systems had high PTSD symptomatology; but among this high-risk group of survivors, those who had been able to obtain mental health services had significantly lower PTSD, suggesting that there may have been some benefit from receiving such services. In this same sample, however, 25% of women who received postassault mental health services rated this contact as hurtful and 19% characterized it as severely hurtful (Campbell et al., 2001).

The Advocacy Community. Sexual assault victims may also seek help from rape crisis centers (RCCs) or domestic violence shelter programs. One of the key roles RCC staff fulfill is to help victims negotiate their contact with the legal and medical systems (i.e., mesosystemic processes). Sexual assault survivors who have the assistance of an RCC advocate during their contact with the legal and medical systems are significantly less likely to experience secondary victimization and also report significant less emotional distress after their system contact (Campbell, 2006). RCCs also provide direct services (i.e., exosystemic processes) to survivors, such as individual and group counseling (Campbell & Martin, 2001). Wasco et al. (2004) and Howard et al. (2003) compared self-reported PTSD symptoms pre- and postcounseling among victims receiving RCC counseling services and found significant reductions in distress levels and self-blame over time and increases in social support, self-efficacy, and sense of control. Because these studies did not examine the content of services or include comparison groups, it is unclear whether these observed improvements are attributable to the services provided.

Macrosystem Factors

Although there has been extensive research on how individual level, microsystem, and mesosystem factors impact rape survivors' well-being, the research on macrosystem factors is very limited. As noted previously, race/ethnicity can be conceptualized at multiple levels of analysis. Whereas many studies have examined racial/ethnic differences in rape recovery, fewer have examined sociocultural identity in post-rape recovery. For example, Neville, Heppner,

Oh, Spanierman, and Clark (2004) examined the self-esteem of African American and White college rape survivors, and although they did not find any differences in the postrape symptoms, self-blame and coping experienced by these survivors, they did find differences in their cultural attributions. African American women were more likely to internalize the "Jezebel" image as to why they were sexually assaulted. Engaging in these cultural blame attributions (e.g., "African American women are not valued in this society") was related to greater self-blame attributions and, in turn, related to lower self-esteem among African American women. These findings are reminiscent of Wyatt's (1992) findings that African American rape survivors were more likely to feel that they are at risk for being victimized and sexually assaulted than their White counterparts. Similarly, Lefley, Scott, Llabre, and Hicks (1993) found that among Hispanic, White, and African American rape survivors, Hispanics were more likely to be blaming and punitive toward themselves and other victims, whereas the White rape survivors were least punitive (see also Williams & Holmes, 1982). Not surprisingly, Hispanic rape survivors had the highest psychological distress and White rape survivors the least. Luo (2000) explored cultural-specific beliefs about rape among Chinese marital rape survivors and found that Chinese rape survivors had similar symptoms to those reported in the Western literature (e.g., fear, anxiety, self-blame, depression, loss of self-esteem), but her qualitative findings suggest that specific Chinese cultural beliefs such as collectivism, a strong emphasis of family honor, and a focus on female virginity have a strong negative impact on recovery.

Research on sexual assault has yet to take into account fully how the rape-prone culture in which we live not only condones male violence against women but also negatively affects the recovery of sexual assault survivors (Rozee & Koss, 2001). To date, most research on social factors, such as rape myth acceptance, has been primarily conducted with participants who have not been sexually assaulted (see Lonsway & Fitzgerald, 1994 for a review). Harned's (2005) qualitative study found that victims of date/partner rape blamed themselves because their experiences did not fit the typical rape stereotype (i.e., violent stranger rape). Likewise, women often reported that they cared about the perpetrator and thus did not believe he had meant to cause them harm. Harned (2005) argued that these beliefs signify the impact of rape myths on female victims and teaches them to blame themselves for the assault while taking away the responsibility from the perpetrator's actions. Similarly, Peterson and Muehlenhard (2004) reported that sexual assault survivors who were high in rape myth acceptance were less likely to acknowledge that what had happened to them was, indeed, sexual assault. High rape myth acceptance appears to decrease the likelihood that victims will disclose the assault and seek support (Botta & Pingree, 1997; Moor, 2007).

Chronosystem Factors

The primary chronosystem factor that may affect victims' recovery outcomes is their prior history of victimization throughout the lifespan. *Revictimization* is generally defined as the experience of sexual victimization in both childhood and adulthood (Messman-Moore & Long, 2003). A recent review of the literature identified that two of every three women who reported sexual victimization had been assaulted more than once (Classen, Palesh, & Aggarwal, 2005). Many studies have found that revictimization is more strongly associated with negative psychological outcomes (e.g., depression, suicide attempts, PTSD, anxiety) than a single sexual assault alone (Arata, 2002; Classen et al., 2005; Follette, Polusny, Bechtle, & Naugle, 1996; Messman-Moore, Long, & Siegfried, 2000; Miner, Flitter, & Robinson, 2006). Multiple sexual assaults may have a cumulative effect, increasing the severity of psychological sequelae with each assault (Nishith, Mechanic, & Resick, 2000). These distress outcomes may increase an individual's vulnerability to additional assaults, which may in turn exacerbate the existing psychological distress (Grauerholz, 2000; Messman-Moore & Long, 2003).

In addition, sexual assault is not the only form of violence women experience in their lifetimes, as physical and emotional abuse in childhood and in adult intimate partner relationships are highly prevalent (Pimlott-Kubiak & Cortina, 2003). Even though the focus of this review is the impact of sexual assault on women's mental health, we cannot define the scope of inquiry so narrowly that it bears little resemblance to the lived experiences of survivors. Other victimizations (prior or concurrent) undoubtedly affect how survivors respond to a subsequent sexual victimization. For example, in a sample of battered women, Campbell and Soeken (1999) summed how many sexual assaults women had endured in their lifetimes (childhood sexual assault, nonintimate partner adult sexual assault, and intimate partner adult sexual assault) and found that more assaults were associated with increased levels of depression. Other researchers have substantiated that sexual assault within intimate partner violence is associated with increased depression, PTSD, and anxiety, above that explained by physical violence alone (Bennice et al., 2003; Cole et al., 2005). Campbell, Greeson, Bybee, and Raja (2008) examined the cumulative impact of experiencing childhood sexual abuse, adult sexual assault, intimate partner violence, and sexual harassment on women's levels of PTSD symptomatology, and indeed, the women who experienced all four forms of violence at the highest levels were significantly higher on self-report distress than those who endured fewer forms at lower levels.

Although revictimization and/or other victimization experiences are often conceptualized as individual-level factors that affect survivors' mental health, Grauerholz (2000) convincingly argued that revictimization itself is an ecological phenomenon (see also Heise, 1998; Jewkes et al., 2002; White & Kowalski, 1998). For example, for victims of childhood sexual abuse, their postassault distress would be determined by aspects of the child, the assault sustained, informal support, formal systems, and sociocultural factors. If victims of childhood sexual abuse are then revictimized in adolescence, the postassault sequelae from that victimization would include the experiential vestiges of the prior victimization (and multilevel factors that contributed to postassault distress at that time, i.e., a chronosystem effect). In addition, the model would "repeat" itself in the context of the new victimization—new interactions in the ecology would shape the distress experience from the most recent assault (also a chronosystem effect). Women's victimization is cumulative and the response from social world is cumulative, and so it is little wonder then that the mental health consequences of revictimization are so severe.

Self-Blame as a Multilevel Meta-Construct

Self-blame has been studied as from both individual-level and extraindividual perspective, and therefore we conceptualize self-blame as a meta-construct that develops from and is shaped by multiple levels in the ecological system (see Figure 1.2). At the individual level, Janoff-Bulman (1979) identified two types of self-blame: characterological self-blame, which she theorized would be maladaptive because it involves blaming one's own character for the negative event; and behavioral self-blame, which involves blaming one's actions for the event. This latter type of self-blame may actually be adaptive because it enhances perceived control and the belief that future rapes can be avoided. Empirical support for Janoff-Bulman's model has been mixed. General self-blame has been found to be associated with PTSD and depression (Boeschen, Koss, Figueredo, & Coan, 2001; Filipas & Ullman, 2006; Frazier, 1990; Frazier & Schauben, 1994; Meyer & Taylor, 1986; Ullman, Townsend, Filipas, & Starzynski, 2007; Wyatt, Newcomb, & Notgrass,

1991). Some studies have found that characterological self-blame is indeed more harmful and behavioral self-blame can protect against distress (Hill & Zuarta, 1989; Koss & Figueredo, 2004; Koss, Figuerdo, & Prince, 2002), but others suggest that behavioral self-blame is more detrimental (Frazier, 2003; Frazier et al., 2005). Maladaptive coping strategies have also been linked with higher levels of self-blame and PTSD symptomatology (Filipas & Ullman, 2006; Frazier et al., 2005).

Yet, survivors' self-blame comes both from internal and external forces, as multiple ecological factors directly contribute to victims' negative attributions. For example, certain assault characteristics (e.g., greater severity of the assault, using alcohol/drugs) contribute to increased self-blame and thereby more postassault distress (Koss et al., 2002; Wyatt et al., 1991). Starzynski et al. (2005) reported that survivors with higher behavioral self-blame were less likely to reach out to both informal and formal support providers, perhaps out of concern that they would receive more criticism of their behavior or choices. Such apprehension may be warranted, as negative social reactions from informal supports have consistently been found to be associated with increased self-blame (Ahrens, 2006; Littleton & Breitkopf, 2006; i.e., a micro-system effect). Ullman and colleagues have documented univariate relationships between negative social reactions, self-blame, and PTSD symptoms, but in multivariate analyses, self-blame did not mediate the effect of negative social reactions on symptoms.

At the meso/exosystem level, Campbell and colleagues have documented in multiple studies that survivors often encounter victim-blaming treatment from legal and medical system personnel, and not surprisingly, survivors state that they do start to blame themselves more for the assault (Campbell, 2005, 2006; Campbell et al., 2001). In recent years, the emergence of community interventions, such as Sexual Assault Nurse Examiner (SANE) programs, have made a positive systemic effort to curb victim blaming and provide empowering postassault care to survivors (Campbell, Patterson, & Lichty, 2005). Interestingly, rape victims who received postassault care in a SANE program did not indicate that this model of care exacerbated their self-blame (Campbell, Patterson, Adams, Diegel, & Coats, 2008). At the macro-system level, Long, Ullman, Starzynski, Long, and Mason (2007) reported that less educated and older African American women tended to blame themselves more for the rape than younger, more educated African American women. The authors suggest that less educated African American women may have fewer resources to help counter the negative views about themselves (e.g., rape myth education) compared to college-educated women. The finding that older women blamed their behavior more than younger women may be because of their lack of exposure to sexual assault education and the nature of culture in which they were raised, which was more accepting of violence against African American women. A chronosystem effect has also been supported such that victims of repeated sexual assault have more self-blame, societal blame, and higher levels of trauma symptoms (Arata, 1999; Filipas & Ullman, 2006). Although we suspect it would be challenging to disentangle empirically the sources, levels, and relative impact of victims' self-blame, the extant literature clearly indicates that self-blame is fed and nurtured along an often destructive path by multiple people, settings, and cultures over time.

Conclusions and Future Directions

In this review, we extended the work of Neville and Heppner (1999) to examine how multilevel ecological factors affect sexual assault victims' psychological sequelae. Our analysis indicates that the mental health consequences of rape are caused by multiple factors beyond characteristics of the victim or the assault. Indeed, many studies found no relationship between sociodemographic variables and postassault distress. Survivors' preassault mental health may affect the recovery process, but because prior research has not assessed prior victimizations in relation to preexisting mental health, it is difficult to know what these findings actually reflect. An emerging field of study suggests biological processes are important in recovery, but why women have different cortisol levels (and thereby different degrees of posttraumatic symptomatology), and whether cortisol levels vary by victimization history, is not yet understood. The degree of violence and threat in the assault itself affects women's mental health outcomes to some extent, but whether the offender is a stranger or known person is not consistently predictive of victims' psychological outcomes. Overall, it would be difficult to predict fully women's postassault sequelae only from individual or assault characteristics.

Research findings are more consistent at the micro-, meso/exo-, macro-, and chronosystem levels. Receiving social support from family, friends, and peers is helpful, but these positive reactions may not be as powerful as unexpected negative reactions. This is not to say that positive social support is unimportant; rather, the findings suggest that negative reactions are more central to the prediction of depression and PTSD severity. If victims seek help from the legal system, it is probable that their cases will not be prosecuted, and the treatment they receive from legal system personnel will likely leave them feeling blamed, doubted, and judged, which, not surprisingly, is associated with increased PTSD symptomatology. If survivors seek medical care for a forensic examination and evaluation and management of sexually transmitted infections and pregnancy, they will typically encounter fewer difficulties obtaining needed assistance (relative to legal system contact) but may still be treated in ways that exacerbate their postassault distress. By contrast, community mental health services and rape crisis center advocacy can buffer these negative effects. Although empirical research on macrosystem factors is limited, institutionalized racism and pervasive rape myths contribute to societal acceptance of sexual assault, which creates a more difficult social context for victims to negotiate their recoveries. Cumulative trauma, a manifestation of the chronosystem, is highly detrimental to women's well-being.

A critical next step in the development of an ecological model of rape recovery is to examine interactions across different levels of the social ecology. For example, what individual or assault characteristics, in conjunction with what kinds of coping strategies, are associated with more positive or negative psychological outcomes? Then, adding the next layer of conceptual complexity, how do these individual-level features play out in different postassault help-seeking experiences? It may be that some survivors are more likely to have negative experiences with formal social systems, such as the legal and medical systems, and this contact may be more or less detrimental to some survivors than others— although such findings would not excuse any victim-blaming treatment from social system personnel. Similarly, how these individual and extraindividual factors co-occur for women who have been repeatedly sexually victimized throughout the lifespan are essential to examine. It is not difficult to imagine that negative informal or formal help-seeking experiences in an earlier assault would curb later help seeking for a subsequent assault and compound victims' psychological distress. We suspect that the mixed findings in the literature regarding individual and assault characteristics may be due not only to methodological differences across studies, but may also reflect unexamined cross-level interactions.

Although the literature on postassault recovery has advanced rapidly since Neville and Heppner's review, sexual assault survivors are a heterogeneous population and we still know very little about the recovery processes of many subgroups of survivors. Prevalence research suggests that women with disabilities (e.g., mobility/visual/hearing impairments, mental/emotional disabilities, cognitive/developmental disabilities, and/or chemical dependency) are at disproportionately high risk for being sexually assaulted (e.g., as many as 85% of women with disabilities have been raped; Elman, 2005), but how their recovery process unfolds is largely unknown. Similarly, the experiences of lesbian, bisexual, and transgendered survivors, elderly women, and immigrant women are largely missing in the literature. For this review, we made concerted effort to find research on sexual assault within intimate partner violence (IPV), and this work indicates that the combined effect of IPV and sexual assault is highly detrimental to women's mental health, but these survivors are understudied in both the IPV and sexual violence literatures. There is also a pressing need to examine specific cultural factors to understand how women from different racial/ethnic backgrounds are affected by mainstream and culture-specific beliefs and norms.

A key advantage of an ecological model of mental health impact is that it can suggest multiple strategies for intervention. Although individual and assault characteristics are difficult, if not impossible, to modify in their own right, it is possible to address myths and stereotypes about sexual assault and its victims, which could have positive effects on victims' recoveries. Public education efforts must emphasize that women's experiences of rape are usually not "stereotypical rapes" (i.e., violent stranger assaults). There is no universal experience of rape: all kinds of women may be victimized, and women may exhibit markedly diverse responses to this traumatic crime. At the microsystem level, rape awareness programs need to provide information for informal support providers about the varied reactions survivors may exhibit. In addition, such programs should emphasize to informal support providers that positive reactions such as emotional support and tangible aid are helpful for recovery, and negative reactions, such as egocentrism and blame, may overshadow any positive efforts. At the meso/exosystem level, there are many promising intervention models for improving the community response to rape. Emerging data suggest that sexual assault nurse examiner (SANE) programs and sexual assault response teams (SARTs) significantly improve the provision of consistent, victim-centered medical and crisis intervention services, and simultaneously increase rates of successful prosecution (see Campbell, Patterson, & Lichty, 2005 for a review). In addition, restorative justice programs for sexual assault provide a mechanism outside of the traditional criminal justice system to address victims' needs (see Koss, 2006; Koss & Achilles, 2008 for reviews). Rape crisis center services are beneficial to victims, and increasing the availability and accessibility of these programs to more survivors may also contribute to more consistently positive postassault help-seeking experiences (Campbell, 2006). Intervening at the macrosystem level may be the most difficult, but the comprehensive models developed by the CDC (2004) and WHO (Jewkes, Sen, & Garcia-Moreno, 2002) outline strategies for working with multiple systems and settings; specifically, they suggest using a wide variety of tactics, such as policy change, organizational change, systems advocacy, media campaigns, and rape awareness/prevention education, to create broad-based systemic change. Similarly, efforts that focus on the prevention of sexual assault reduce the likelihood of multiple victimizations in women's lifetimes, thereby curbing negative chronosystem effects. Both Kelly's and Bronfenbrenner's ecological theories emphasize that changes at any one level of the social ecology can have extended effects at other levels. As a result, there are many feasible approaches to improving the societal response to rape victims and addressing their postassault recovery needs.

Implications for Practice, Policy, and Research

- At the individual level, public education efforts must emphasize that women's experiences of rape are not universal. All women can be victimized, and they are likely to respond in diverse ways. Education efforts must also stress that survivors' experience of rape are usually not "stereotypical rapes" (i.e., stranger rape).

- At the microsystem level, rape awareness programs need to provide information for informal support providers about the varied reactions survivors may exhibit. These programs should also emphasize to informal support providers that positive reactions such as emotional support and tangible aid are helpful for recovery, and negative reactions, such as egocentrism and blame, may overshadow any positive efforts.

- At meso/exosystem level, promising programs such the sexual assault nurse examiner (SANE) programs and sexual assault response teams (SARTs) can help improve the provision of consistent, victim-centered medical and crisis intervention services and may increase rates of successful prosecution. Likewise, increasing the availability and accessibility of rape crisis centers to more survivors may contribute to more consistent positive postassault help-seeking experiences.

- Although intervening at the macrosystem level is most difficult, comprehensive intervention models may help reach multiple ecological systems and settings. Comprehensive models should use a wide variety of strategies, such as policy change, organizational change, systems advocacy, media campaigns, and rape awareness/prevention education to create broad-based systemic change. Making changes within these systems may help improve the community's response to rape and eventually change our culture to support survivors and hold perpetrators accountable.

- Efforts that focus on the prevention of sexual assault reduce the likelihood of multiple victimizations in women's lifetimes, thereby curbing negative chronosystem effects.

- Future research should also consider using an ecological approach to understand sexual assault survivors' postassault psychological experiences. Specifically, research should attempt to understand how variables at the multiple ecological levels interact to impact mental health outcomes.

Note

1. We distinguish community-based mental health services, such as the services provided by psychiatrists, psychologists, or social workers in private or public clinic settings, from the therapies available to victims who participate as research subjects in randomized control treatment (RCT) outcome studies (e.g., Foa, Rothbaum, Riggs, & Murdock, 1991; Krakow et al., 2001; Resick et al., 2008; Resick, Nishith, Weaver, Astin, & Feuer, 2002). These treatment outcome studies consistently find that their evidence-based practices are associated with decreased psychological distress symptomatology.

References

Acierno, R., Brady, K., Gray, M., Kilpatrick, D. G., Resnick, H., & Best, C. L. (2002). Psychopathology following interpersonal violence: A comparison of risk factors in older and younger adults. *Journal of Clinical Geropsychology, 8,* 13–23.

Ahrens, C. (2006). Being silenced: The impact of negative social reactions on the disclosure of rape. *American Journal of Community Psychology, 38,* 263–274.

Ahrens, C., Campbell, R., Ternier-Thames, K., Wasco, S., & Sefl, T. (2007). Deciding whom to tell: Expectations and outcomes of rape survivors' first disclosures. *Psychology of Women Quarterly, 31,* 38–49.

Arata, C. M. (1999). Coping with rape: The roles of prior sexual abuse and attributions of blame. *Journal of Interpersonal Violence, 14,* 62–78.

Arata, C. M. (2002). Child sexual abuse and sexual revictimization. *Clinical Psychology: Science and Practice, 9,* 135–164.

*Arata, C. M., & Burkhart, B. R. (1996). Post-traumatic stress disorder among college student victims of acquaintance assault. *Journal of Psychology & Human Sexuality, 8,* 79–92.

*Atkeson, B. M., Calhoun, K. S., Resick, P. A., & Ellis, E. M. (1982). Victims of rape: Repeated assessment of depressive symptoms. *Journal of Consulting and Clinical Psychology, 50,* 96–102.

Becker, J. V., Skinner, L. J., Abel, G. G., Axelrod, R., & Treacy, E. C. (1984). Depressive symptoms associated with sexual assault. *Journal of Sex and Marital Therapy, 10,* 185–192.

*Bennice, J. A., Resick, P. A., Mechanic, M., & Astin, M. (2003). The relative effects of intimate partner physical and sexual violence on post-traumatic stress disorder symptomatology. *Violence and Victims, 18,* 87–94.

Berg, S. H. (2002). The PTSD diagnosis: Is it good for women? *Affilia, 17,* 55–68.

*Boeschen, L. E., Koss, M. P., Figueredo, A. J., & Coan, J. A. (2001). Experiential avoidance and posttraumatic stress disorder: A cognitive mediational model of rape recovery. *Journal of Aggression, Maltreatment & Trauma, 4,* 211–245.

*Borja, S. E., Callahan, J. L., & Long, P. J. (2006). Positive and negative adjustment and social support of sexual assault survivors. *Journal of Traumatic Stress, 19,* 905–914.

Botta, R. A., & Pingree, S. (1997). Interpersonal communication and rape: Women acknowledge their assaults. *Journal of Health Communication, 2,* 197–212.

*Bownes, I. T., O'Gorman, E. C., & Sayers, A. (1991). Assault characteristics and posttraumatic stress disorder in rape victims. *Acta Psychiatrica Scandinavia, 83,* 27–30.

Briere, J., & Jordan, C. E. (2004). Violence against women: Outcome complexity and implications for assessment and treatment. *Journal of Interpersonal Violence, 19,* 1252–1276.

Bronfenbrenner, U. (1979). *The ecology of human development: Experiments by nature and design.* Cambridge, MA: Harvard University Press.

Bronfenbrenner, U. (1986). Ecology of the family as a context for human development: Research perspectives. *Developmental Psychology, 22,* 723–742.

Bronfenbrenner, U. (1995). Developmental ecology through space and time: A future perspective. In P. Moen, G. H. Elder, Jr., & K. Luscher (Eds.), *Examining lives in context: Perspectives on the ecology of human development* (pp. 619–647). Washington, DC: APA Books.

Buchwald, E., Fletcher, P., & Roth, M. (Eds.). (1993). *Transforming a rape culture.* Minneapolis, MN: Milkweed.

*Burge, S. K. (1988). Post-traumatic stress disorder in victims of rape. *Journal of Traumatic Stress, 1,* 193–210.

*Burgess, A. W., & Holmstrom, L. L. (1978). Recovery from rape and prior life stress. *Research in Nursing and Health, 1,* 165–174.

Burgess, A. W., & Holmstrom, L. L. (1979). Adaptive strategies and recovery from rape. *American Journal of Psychiatry, 136,* 1278–1282.

Burnam, M. A., Stein, J. A., Golding, J. M., Siegel, J. M., Sorenson, S. B., Forsythe, A. B., et al. (1988). Sexual assault and mental disorders in a community population. *Journal of Consulting and Clinical Psychology, 56,* 843–850.

Burt, M. R. (1998). Rape myths. In M. E. Odem & J. Clay-Warner (Eds.), *Confronting rape and sexual assault* (pp. 129–144). Lanham, MD: Rowman & Littlefield.

Campbell, J. C., & Soeken, K. L. (1999). Forced sex and intimate partner violence: Effects on women's risk and women's health. *Violence Against Women, 5,* 1017–1035.

Campbell, R. (1998). The community response to rape: Victims' experiences with the legal, medical, and mental health systems. *American Journal of Community Psychology, 26,* 355–379.

*Campbell, R. (2005). What really happened? A validation study of rape survivors' help-seeking experiences with the legal and medical systems. *Violence & Victims, 20,* 55–68.

*Campbell, R. (2006). Rape survivors' experiences with the legal and medical systems: Do rape victim advocates make a difference? *Violence Against Women, 12,* 1–16.

*Campbell, R., Ahrens, C., Sefl, T., Wasco, S. M., & Barnes, H. E. (2001). Social reactions to rape victims: Healing and hurtful effects on psychological and physical health outcomes. *Violence & Victims, 16,* 287–302.

Campbell, R., Greeson, M. R., Bybee, D., & Raja, S. (2008). The co-occurrence of childhood sexual abuse, adult sexual assault, intimate partner violence, and sexual harassment: A mediational model of PTSD and physical health outcomes. *Journal of Consulting and Clinical Psychology, 76,* 194–207.

Campbell, R., & Martin, P. Y. (2001). Services for sexual assault survivors: The role of rape crisis centers. In C. Renzetti, J. Edleson, & R. Bergen (Eds.), *Sourcebook on violence against women* (pp. 227–241). Thousand Oaks, CA: Sage.

*Campbell, R., Patterson, D., Adams, A. E., Diegel, R., & Coats, S. (2008). A participatory evaluation project to measure SANE nursing practice and adult sexual assault patients' psychological well-being. *Journal of Forensic Nursing, 4,* 19–28.

Campbell, R., Patterson, D., & Lichty, L. F. (2005). The effectiveness of sexual assault nurse examiner (SANE) program: A review of psychological, medical, legal, and community outcomes. *Trauma, Violence, & Abuse: A Review Journal, 6,* 313–329.

Campbell, R., & Raja, S. (1999). The secondary victimization of rape victims: Insights from mental health professionals who treat survivors of violence. *Violence & Victims, 14,* 261–275.

*Campbell, R., & Raja, S. (2005). The sexual assault and secondary victimization of female veterans: Help-seeking experiences in military and civilian social systems. *Psychology of Women Quarterly, 29,* 97–106.

Campbell, R., Sefl, T., & Ahrens, C. E. (2004). The impact of rape on women's sexual health risk behaviors. *Health Psychology, 23,* 67–74.

*Campbell, R., Sefl, T., Barnes, H. E., Ahrens, C. E., Wasco, S. M., & Zaragoza-Diesfeld, Y. (1999). Community services for rape survivors: Enhancing psychological well-being or increasing trauma? *Journal of Consulting and Clinical Psychology, 67,* 847–858.

*Campbell, R., Wasco, S. M., Ahrens, C. E., Sefl, T., & Barnes, H. E. (2001). Preventing the "second rape": Rape survivors' experiences with community service providers. *Journal of Interpersonal Violence, 16,* 1239–1259.

*Cascardi, M., Riggs, D. S., Hearst-Ikeda, D., & Foa, E. B. (1996). Objective ratings of assault safety as predictors of PTSD. *Journal of Interpersonal Violence, 11*(1), 65–78.

Centers for Disease Control and Prevention. (2004). *Sexual violence prevention: Beginning the dialogue.* Atlanta, GA: Author.

Chivers-Wilson, K. A. (2006). Sexual assault and posttraumatic stress disorder: A review of the biological, psychological, and sociological factors and treatments. *McGill Journal of Medicine, 9,* 111–118.

Classen, C. C., Palesh, O. G., & Aggarwal, R. (2005). Sexual revictimization: A review of the empirical literature. *Trauma, Violence, and Abuse, 6,* 103–129.

Clum, G. A., Calhoun, K. S., & Kimerling, R. (2000). Associations among symptoms of depression and posttraumatic stress disorder and self-reported heath in sexually assaulted women. *Journal of Nervous and Mental Disease, 188,* 671–678.

*Coker, A. L., Smith, P. H., Thompson, M. P., McKeown, R. E., Bethea, L., & Davis, K. E. (2002). Social support protects against the negative effects of partner violence on mental health. *Journal of Women's Health & Gender-Based Medicine, 11,* 465–476.

Cole, J., Logan, T., & Shannon, L. (2005). Intimate sexual victimization among women with protective orders: Types and associations of physical and mental health problems. *Violence and Victims, 2,* 695–715.

*Cox, B. J., MacPherson, P. S. R., Enns, M. W., & McWilliams, L. A. (2004). Neuroticism and self-criticism associated with posttraumatic stress disorder in a nationally representative sample. *Behavior Research and Therapy, 42,* 105–114.

Davidson, J. R., Hughes, D. C., George, L. K., & Blazer, D. G. (1996). The association of sexual assault and attempted suicide within the community. *Archives of General Psychiatry, 53,* 550–555.

*Davis, R. C., Brickman, E., & Baker, T. (1991). Supportive and unsupportive responses of others to rape victims: Effects on concurrent victim adjustment. *American Journal of Community Psychology, 19,* 443–451.

Dickinson, L. M., deGruy, F. V., Dickinson, W. P., & Candib, L. M. (1999). Health-related quality of life and symptom profiles of female survivors of sexual abuse in primary care. *Archives of Family Medicine, 8,* 35–43.

Eby, K. K., Campbell, J. C., Sullivan, C. M., & Davidson, W. S., II. (1995). Health effects of experiences of sexual violence for women with abusive partners. *Health Care for Women International, 16,* 563–576.

*Elliott, D. M., Mok, D. S., & Briere, J. (2004). Adult sexual assault: Prevalence, symptomatology, and sex differences in the general population. *Journal of Traumatic Stress, 17,* 203–211.

Ellis, E. M. (1983). A review of empirical rape research: Victim reactions and response to treatment. *Clinical Psychology Review, 3,* 473–490.

*Ellis, E. M., Atkeson, B. M., & Calhoun, K. S. (1981). An assessment of long-term reaction to rape. *Journal of Abnormal Psychology, 90,* 263–266.

Elman, R. A. (2005). *Confronting the sexual abuse of women with disabilities.* VAWNet Document, National Online Resource Center on Violence

Against Women, Minneapolis: University of Minnesota. Retrieved from http://www.vawnet.org/SexualViolence/Research/VAWnetDocuments

Filipas, H. H., & Ullman, S. E. (2001). Social reactions to sexual assault victims from various support sources. *Violence & Victims, 16,* 673–692.

Filipas, H. H., & Ullman, S. E. (2006). Child sexual abuse, coping responses, self-blame, PTSD, and adult sexual revictimization. *Journal of Interpersonal Violence, 21,* 652–672.

Fisher, B. S., Daigle, L. E., Cullen, F. T., & Turner, M. G. (2003). Reporting sexual victimization to the police and others. *Criminal Justice and Behavior, 30,* 6–38.

Foa, E. B., Rothbaum, B. O., Riggs, D. S., & Murdock, T. B. (1991). Treatment of posttraumatic stress disorder in rape victims: A comparison between cognitive-behavioral procedures and counseling. *Journal of Consulting and Clinical Psychology, 59,* 715–723.

Follette, V. M., Polusny, M. A., Bechtle, A. E., & Naugle, A. E. (1996). Cumulative trauma: The impact of child sexual abuse, adult sexual assault, and spouse abuse. *Journal of Traumatic Stress, 9,* 25–35.

*Fowler, D. N., & Hill, H. M. (2004). Social support and spirituality as culturally relevant factors in coping among African American women survivors of partner abuse. *Violence Against Women, 10,* 1267–1282.

*Frank, E., & Anderson, B. P. (1987). Psychiatric disorders in rape victims: Past psychiatric history and current symptomatology. *Comprehensive Psychiatry, 28,* 77–82.

*Frank, E., & Stewart, B. D. (1984). Depressive symptoms in rape victims: A revisit. *Journal of Affective Disorders, 7,* 77–85.

*Frank, E., Turner, S. M., & Stewart, B. D. (1980). Initial response to rape: The impact of factors within the rape situation. *Journal of Behavioral Assessment, 2,* 39–53.

Frank, E., Turner, S. M., Stewart, B. D., Jacob, M., & West, D. (1981). Past psychiatric symptoms and the response to sexual assault. *Comprehensive Psychiatry, 22,* 479–487.

Frazier, P. (2003). Perceived control and distress following sexual assault: A longitudinal test of a new model. *Journal of Personality and Social Psychology, 84,* 1257–1269.

Frazier, P. A. (1990). Victim attributions and post-rape trauma. *Journal of Personality and Social Psychology, 59,* 298–304.

Frazier, P. A. (1991). Self-blame as a mediator of postrape depressive symptoms. *Journal of Social and Clinical Psychology, 10,* 47–57.

*Frazier, P. A., & Burnett, J. W. (1994). Immediate coping strategies among rape victims. *Journal of Counseling and Development, 72,* 633–639.

*Frazier, P. A., Mortensen, H., & Steward, J. (2005). Coping strategies as mediators of the relations among perceived control and distress in sexual assault survivors. *Journal of Counseling Psychology, 52,* 267–278.

Frazier, P. A., & Schauben, L. J. (1994). Causal attributions and recovery from rape and other stressful life events. *Journal of Social and Clinical Psychology, 13,* 1–14.

Gilfus, M. E. (1999). The price of the ticket: A survivor-centered appraisal of trauma theory. *Violence Against Women, 5,* 1238–1257.

Golding, J. M. (1996). Sexual assault history and limitations in physical functioning in two general population samples. *Research in Nursing & Health, 19,* 33–44.

Golding, J. M., Siegel, J. M., Sorenson, S. B., Burnam, M. A., & Stein, J. A. (1989). Social support sources following sexual assault. *Journal of Community Psychology, 17,* 92–107.

Goodman, L. A., Koss, M. P., & Russo, N. F. (1993). Violence against women: Physical and mental health effects. Part I: Research findings. *Applied and Preventative Psychology, 2,* 79–89.

Grauerholz, L. (2000). An ecological approach to understanding sexual revictimization: Linking personal, interpersonal, and sociocultural factors and processes. *Child Maltreatment, 5,* 5–17.

*Gutner, C. A., Rizvi, S. L., Monson, C. M., & Resick, P. A. (2006). Changes in coping strategies, relationship to perpetrator, and posttraumatic distress in female crime victims. *Journal of Traumatic Stress, 19,* 813–823.

*Harned, M. (2005). Understanding women's labeling of unwanted sexual experiences with dating partners, *Violence Against Women, 11,* 374–413.

Harvey, M. R. (1996). An ecological view of psychological trauma and trauma recovery. *Journal of Traumatic Stress, 9,* 3–23.

Heise, L. L. (1998). Violence against women: An integrated, ecological framework. *Violence Against Women, 4*, 262–290.

Herman, J. L. (1992). Complex PTSD: A syndrome in survivors of prolonged and repeated trauma. *Journal of Traumatic Stress, 5*, 377–391.

Hill, J. L., & Zuarta, A. J. (1989). Self-blame attributions and unique vulnerability. *Journal of Social & Clinical Psychology, 8*, 368–375.

*Howard, A., Riger, S., Campbell, R., & Wasco, S. M. (2003). Counseling services for battered women: A comparison of outcomes for physical and sexual abuse survivors. *Journal of Interpersonal Violence, 18*, 717–734.

Janoff-Bulman, R. (1992). *Shattered assumptions: Towards a new psychology of trauma.* New York: The Free Press.

Jewkes, R., Sen, P., & Garcia-Moreno, C. (2002). Sexual violence. In E. G. Krug, L. L. Dahlberg, J. A. Mercy, A. B. Zwi, & R. Lozano (Eds.), *World report on violence and health* (pp. 147–181). Geneva: World Health Organization.

John, O. P., & Srivastava, S. (1999). The Big Five trait taxonomy: History, measurement, and theoretical perspectives. In L. A. Pervin & O. P. John (Eds.), *Handbook of personality: Theory and research* (pp. 102–138). New York: Guilford Press.

Kelly, J. G. (1966). Ecological constraints on mental health services. *American Psychologist, 21*, 535–539.

Kelly, J. G. (1968). Towards an ecological conception of preventive interventions. In J. W. Carter, Jr. (Ed.), *Research contributions from psychology to community mental health* (pp. 75–99). New York: Behavioral Publications.

Kelly, J. G. (1971). Qualities for the community psychologist. *American Psychologist, 26*, 897–903.

Kelly, J. G., Ryan, A. M., Altman, B. E., & Stelzner, S. R. (2000). Understanding and changing social systems: An ecological view. In J. Rappaport & E. Seidman (Eds.), *Handbook of community psychology* (pp. 133–160). New York: Plenum Press.

Kilpatrick, D. G., & Acierno, R. (2003). Mental health needs of crime victims: Epidemiology and outcomes. *Journal of Traumatic Stress, 16*, 119–132.

Kilpatrick, D. G., Amstadter, A. B., Resnick, H. S., & Ruggiero, K. J. (2007). Rape-related PTSD: Issues and interventions. *Psychiatric Times, 24*, 50–58.

Kilpatrick, D. G., Best, C. L., Veronen, L. J., Amick, A. E., Villeponteaux, L. A., & Ruff, G. A. (1985). Mental health correlates of criminal victimization: A random community survey. *Journal of Consulting and Clinical Psychology, 53*, 866–873.

Kilpatrick, D. G., & Resnick, H. S. (1993). PTSD associated with exposure to criminal victimization in clinical and community populations. In J. R. T. Davidson & E. B. Foa (Eds.), *PTSD in review: Recent research and future directions* (pp. 113–143). Washington, DC: American Psychiatric Press.

Kilpatrick, D. G., Saunders, B. E., Amick-McMullan, A., Best, C. L., Veronen, L. J., & Resnick, H. S. (1989). Victim and crime factors associated with the development of crime-related post-traumatic stress disorder. *Behavior Therapy, 20*, 199–214.

Kilpatrick, D. G., Saunders, B. E., Veronen, L. J., Best, C. L., & Von, J. M. (1987). Criminal victimization: Lifetime prevalence, reporting to police, and psychological impact. *Crime & Delinquency, 33*, 479–489.

*Kilpatrick, D. G., Veronen, L. J., & Best, C. L. (1984). Factors predicting psychological distress among rape victims. In C. R. Figley (Ed.), *Trauma and its wake* (pp. 113–141). Bristol, PA: Brunner/Mazel.

Koss, M. P. (1993). Rape: Scope, impact, interventions, and public policy responses. *American Psychologist, 48*, 1062–1069.

Koss, M. P. (2006). Restoring rape survivors: Justice, advocacy, and a call to action. *Annals of the New York Academy of Sciences, 1087*, 206–234.

Koss, M., & Achilles, M. (2008). *Restorative justice responses to sexual assault.* Retrieved March 3, 2008, from http://www.vawnet.org

Koss, M. P., Bailey, J. A., Yuan, N. P., Herrera, V. M., & Lichter, E. L. (2003). Depression and PTSD in survivors of male violence: Research and training initiatives to facilitate recovery. *Psychology of Women Quarterly, 27*, 130–142.

*Koss, M. P., Dinero, T. E., Seibel, C. A., & Cox, S. L. (1988). Stranger and acquaintance rape: Are there differences in the victim's experience? *Psychology of Women Quarterly, 12*, 1–24.

Koss, M. P., & Figueredo, A. J. (2004). Cognitive mediation of rape's mental health impact: Constructive replication of a cross-sectional model in longitudinal data. *Psychology of Women Quarterly, 28*, 273–286.

Koss, M. P., Figueredo, A. J., & Prince, R. J. (2002). A cognitive mediational model of rape recovery: Preliminary specification and testing in cross-sectional data. *Journal of Consulting and Clinical Psychology, 70,* 926–941.

Koss, M. P., Gidycz, C. A., & Wisniewski, N. (1987). The scope of rape: Incidence and prevalence of sexual aggression and victimization in a national sample of higher education students. *Journal of Consulting and Clinical Psychology, 55,* 162–170.

Koss, M. P., Goodman, L. A., Browne, A., Fitzgerald, L. F., Keita, G. P., & Russo, N. F. (1994). *No safe haven: Male violence against women at home, at work, and in the community.* Washington, DC: American Psychological Association.

Koss, M. P., & Harvey, M. R. (1991). *The rape victim: Clinical and community interventions.* Thousand Oaks, CA: Sage.

Krakow, B., Hollifield, M., Johnston, L., Koss, M., Schrader, R., Warner, T. D., et al. (2001). Imagery rehearsal therapy for chronic nightmares in sexual assault survivors with posttraumatic stress disorder: A randomized control trial. *Journal of the American Medical Association, 296,* 537–545.

*Kramer, T. L., & Green, B. L. (1991). Posttraumatic stress disorder as an early response to sexual assault. *Journal of Interpersonal Violence, 6,* 160–173.

Krug, E. G., Mercy, J. A., Dahlberg, L. L., & Zwi, A. B. (Eds.). (2002). *World report on violence and health.* Geneva: World Health Organization.

Ledray, L. (1996). The sexual assault resource service: A new model of care. *Minnesota Medicine, 79,* 43–45.

*Lefley, H. P., Scott, C. S., Llabre, M. & Hicks, D. (1993). Cultural beliefs about rape and victim's responses in three ethnic groups. *American Journal of Orthopsychiatry, 63,* 623–632.

Littleton, H., & Breitkopf, C. R. (2006). Coping with the experience of rape. *Psychology of Women Quarterly, 30,* 106–116.

Long, L. M., Ullman, S. E., Starzynski, L. L., Long, S. M., & Mason, G. E. (2007). Age and educational differences in African American women's sexual assault experiences. *Feminist Criminology, 2,* 117–136.

Lonsway, K. A., & Fitzgerald, L. F. (1994). Rape myths: In review. *Psychology of Women Quarterly, 18,* 133–164.

*Luo, T. (2000). "Marrying my rapist?!" The cultural trauma among Chinese rape survivors. *Gender & Society, 14,* 581–597.

*Mackey, T., Sereika, S. M., Weissfeld, L. A., Hacker, S. S., Zender, J. F., & Heard, S. L. (1992). Factors associated with long-term depressive symptoms of sexual assault victims. *Archives of Psychiatric Nursing, 6,* 10–25.

Marsella, A. J., Friedman, M. J., & Spain, E. H. (1999). Ethnocultural aspects of posttraumatic stress disorder: An overview of issues and research directions. In A. J. Marsella, M. J. Friedman, E. T. Gerrity, & R. M. Scurfield (Eds.), *Ethnocultural aspects of post-traumatic stress disorder: Issues, research, and clinical applications.* Washington, DC: American Psychological Association.

Martin, P. Y. (2005). *Rape work: Victims, gender, and emotions in organization and community context.* New York: Routledge.

*McFarlane, J., Malecha, A., Watson, K., Gist, J., Batten, E., Hall, I., et al. (2005). Intimate partner sexual assault against women: Frequency, health consequences, and treatment outcomes. *Obstetrics and Gynecology, 105,* 99–108.

McLaren, L., & Hawe, P. (2005). Ecological perspectives in health research. *Journal of Epidemiology and Community Health, 59,* 6–14.

Messman-Moore, T. L., & Long, P. J. (2003). The role of childhood sexual abuse sequelae in the sexual revictimization of women: An empirical review and theoretical reformulation. *Clinical Psychology Review, 23,* 537–571.

Messman-Moore, T. L., Long, P. J., & Siegfried, N. J. (2000). The revictimization of child sexual abuse survivors: An examination of the adjustment of college women with child sexual abuse, adult sexual assault, and adult physical abuse. *Child Maltreatment, 5,* 18–27.

*Meyer, C. B., & Taylor, S. E. (1986). Adjustment to rape. *Journal of Personality and Social Psychology, 50,* 1226–1234.

Miner, M. H., Flitter, J. M. K., & Robinson, B. E. (2006). Association of sexual revictimization with sexuality and psychological function. *Journal of Interpersonal Violence, 21,* 503–524.

Moor, A. (2007). When recounting the traumatic memories is not enough: Treating persistent self-devaluation associated with rape and victim-blaming myths. *Women & Therapy, 30,* 19–33.

*Moss, M., Frank, E., & Anderson, B. (1990). The effects of marital status and partner support on rape trauma. *American Journal of Orthopsychiatry, 60,* 379–391.

Neville, H. A., & Heppner, M. J. (1999). Contextualizing rape: Reviewing sequelae and proposing a culturally inclusive ecological model of sexual assault recovery. *Applied & Preventative Psychology, 8,* 41–62.

*Neville, H. A., Heppner, M. J., Oh, E., Spanierman, L. B., & Clark, M. (2004). General and culturally specific factors influencing black and white rape survivors' self-esteem. *Psychology of Women Quarterly, 28,* 83–94.

Nishith, P., Mechanic, M. B., & Resick, P. A. (2000). Prior interpersonal trauma: The contribution to current PTSD symptoms in female rape victims. *Journal of Abnormal Psychology, 109,* 20–25.

Peterson, Z. D., & Muehlenhard, C. L. (2004). Was it rape? The function of women's rape myth acceptance and definitions of sex in labeling their own experiences. *Sex Roles, 51,* 129–144.

Petrak, J., Doyle, A., Williams, L., Buchan, L., & Forster, G. (1997). The psychological impact of sexual assault: A study of female attenders of a sexual health psychology service. *Sexual and Marital Therapy, 12,* 339–345.

Pimlott-Kubiak, S., & Cortina, L. M. (2003). Gender, victimization, and outcomes: Reconceptualizing risk. *Journal of Consulting and Clinical Psychology, 71,* 528–539.

Resick, P. A. (1993). The psychological impact of rape. *Journal of Interpersonal Violence, 8,* 223–255.

Resick, P. A., Galovski, T. E., Uhlmansiek, M., Scher, C. D., Clum, G. A., & Young-Xu, Y. (2008). A randomized control trial to dismantle components of cognitive processing therapy for posttraumatic stress disorder in female victims of interpersonal violence. *Journal of Consulting and Clinical Psychology, 76,* 243–258.

Resick, P. A., Nishith, P., Weaver, T. L., Astin, M. C., & Feuer, C. A. (2002). A comparison of cognitive-processing therapy with prolonged exposure and a waiting condition for the treatment of chronic posttraumatic stress disorder in female rape victims. *Journal of Consulting and Clinical Psychology, 70,* 867–879.

*Resnick, H. S., Yehuda, R., & Acierno, R. (1997). Acute post-rape plasma cortisol, alcohol use, and PTSD symptom profile among recent rape victims. *Annals New York Academy of Sciences, 821,* 433–436.

Resnick, H. S., Yehuda, R., Pitman, R. K., & Foy, D. W. (1995). Effect of previous trauma on acute plasma cortisol level following rape. *American Journal of Psychiatry, 152,* 1675–1677.

*Riggs, D. S., Kilpatrick, D. G., & Resnick, H. S. (1992). Long-term psychological distress associated with marital rape and aggravated assault: A comparison to other crime victims. *Journal of Family Violence, 7,* 283–296.

Rogers, C., & Gruener, D. (1997). Sequelae of sexual assault. *Primary Care Update for OB/GYNs, 4,* 143–146.

Roth, S., & Cohen, L. J. (1986). Approach, avoidance and coping with stress. *American Psychologist, 41,* 340–347.

Rothbaum, B. O., Foa, E. B., Riggs, D. S., Murdock, T., & Walsh, W. (1992). A prospective examination of posttraumatic stress disorder in rape victims. *Journal of Traumatic Stress, 5,* 455–475.

Rozee, P. D., & Koss, M. P. (2001). Rape: A century of resistance. *Psychology of Women Quarterly, 25,* 295–311.

*Ruch, L. O., & Chandler, S. M. (1983). Sexual assault trauma during the acute phase: An exploratory model and multivariate analysis. *Journal of Health and Social Behavior, 24,* 174–185.

*Ruch, L. O., & Leon, J. J. (1983). Sexual assault trauma and trauma change. *Women & Health, 8,* 5–21.

*Sales, E., Baum, M., & Shore, B. (1984). Victim readjustment following assault. *Journal of Social Issues, 40,* 117–136.

Sandy, R. R. (1998). The socio-cultural context of rape: A cross cultural study. In M. E. Odem & J. Clay-Warner (Eds.), *Confronting rape and sexual assault* (pp. 93–108). Wilmington, DE: Scholarly Resources.

*Santello, M. D., & Leitenberg, H. (1993). Sexual aggression by an acquaintance: Methods of coping and later psychological adjustment. *Violence and Victims, 8,* 91–104.

*Schwartz, M. D., & Leggett, M. S. (1999). Bad dates or emotional trauma? The aftermath of campus sexual assault. *Violence Against Women, 5,* 251–271.

*Shalev, A. Y., & Sahar, T. (1998). Neurobiology of the posttraumatic stress disorder. In A. Levy, E. Grauer, D. Ben-Nathan, & E. R. de Kloet (Eds.), *New frontiers in stress research: Modulation of brain function* (pp. 235–248). Newark, NJ: Harwood Academic.

Siegel, J. M., Golding, J. M., Stein, J. A., Burnam, M. A., & Sorenson, S. B. (1990). Reactions to sexual assault: A community study. *Journal of Interpersonal Violence, 5,* 229–246.

*Starzynski, L. L., Ullman, S. E., Filipas, H. H., & Townsend, S. M. (2005). Correlates of women's sexual assault disclosure to informal and formal support sources. *Violence & Victims, 20,* 417–432.

Sudderth, L. K. (1998). "It'll come right back at me": The interactional context of discussing rape with others. *Violence Against Women, 4,* 572–594.

*Temple, J. R., Weston, R., Rodriguez, B. F., & Marshall, L. L. (2007). Differing effects of partner and nonpartner sexual assault on women's mental health. *Violence Against Women, 13,* 285–297.

*Thompson, M. P., Kaslow, N. J., Kingree, J. B., Rashid, A., Puett, R., Jacobs, D., et al. (2000). Partner violence, social support, and distress among inner-city African American women. *American Journal of Community Psychology, 28,* 127–143.

*Ullman, S. E. (1996a). Do social reactions to sexual assault victims vary by support provider? *Violence & Victims, 11,* 143–156.

*Ullman, S. E. (1996b). Correlates and consequences of adult sexual assault disclosure. *Journal of Interpersonal Violence, 11,* 554–571.

*Ullman, S. E. (1996c). Social reactions, coping strategies, and self-blame attributions in adjustment to sexual assault. *Psychology of Women Quarterly, 20,* 505–526.

Ullman, S. E. (2000). Psychometric characteristics of the social reactions questionnaire: A measure of reactions to sexual assault victims. *Psychology of Women Quarterly, 24,* 169–183.

Ullman, S. E. (2007). Mental health services seeking in sexual assault victims. *Women & Therapy, 30,* 61–84.

*Ullman, S. E., & Brecklin, L. R. (2002a). Sexual assault history, PTSD, and mental health service seeking in a national sample of women. *Journal of Community Psychology, 30,* 261–279.

Ullman, S. E., & Brecklin, L. R. (2002b). Sexual assault history and suicidal behavior in a national sample of women. *Suicide and Life-Threatening Behavior, 32,* 117–130.

Ullman S. E., & Brecklin, L. R. (2003). Sexual assault history and health-related outcomes in a national sample of women. *Psychology of Women Quarterly, 27,* 46–57.

Ullman, S., & Filipas, H. H. (2001a). Correlates of formal and informal support seeking in sexual assault victims. *Journal of Interpersonal Violence, 16,* 1028–1047.

*Ullman, S. E., & Filipas, H. H. (2001b). Predictors of PTSD symptom severity and social reactions in sexual assault victims. *Journal of Traumatic Stress, 14,* 369–389.

*Ullman, S. E., Filipas, H. H., Townsend, S. M., & Starzynski, L. L. (2006). The role of victim-offender relationships in women's sexual assault experiences. *Journal of Interpersonal Violence, 21,* 798–819.

Ullman, S. E., Karabatsos, G., & Koss, M. P. (1999). Alcohol and sexual assault in a national sample of college women. *Journal of Interpersonal Violence, 14,* 603–625.

*Ullman, S. E., & Siegal J. M. (1993). Victim-offender relationship and sexual assault. *Violence and Victims, 8,* 121–134.

*Ullman, S. E., Townsend, S. M., Filipas, H. H., & Starzynski, L. L. (2007). Structural models of the relations of assault severity, social support, avoidance coping, self-blame, and PTSD among sexual assault survivors. *Psychology of Women Quarterly, 31,* 23–37.

*Valentiner, D. P., Foa, E. B., Riggs D. S., & Gershuny, B. S. (1996). Coping strategies and posttraumatic stress disorder in female victims of sexual and nonsexual assault. *Journal of Abnormal Psychology, 105,* 455–458.

Ward, C.A. (1995). *Attitudes toward rape: Feminist and social psychological perspectives.* London: Sage.

Wasco, S. M. (2003). Conceptualizing the harm done by rape: Applications of trauma theory to experiences of sexual assault. *Trauma, Violence, and Abuse, 4,* 309–322.

*Wasco, S. M., Campbell, R., Howard, A., Mason, G., Schewe, P., Staggs, S., et al. (2004). A statewide evaluation of services provided to rape survivors. *Journal of Interpersonal Violence, 19,* 252–263.

White, J. W., & Kowalski, R. M. (1998). Male violence toward women: An integrated perspective. In R. G. Geen & E. Donnerstein (Eds.), *Human aggression: Theories, research, and implications for social policy* (pp. 203–228). San Diego, CA: Academic Press.

*Williams, J. E., & Holmes, K. A. (1982). In judgment of victims: The social context of rape. *Journal of Sociology and Social Welfare, 9,* 154–169.

Winfield, I., George, L. K., Swartz, M., & Blazer, D. G. (1990). Sexual assault and psychiatric disorders among a community sample of women. *American Journal of Psychiatry, 147,* 335–341.

*Wyatt, G. E. (1992). The sociocultural context of African American and white American women's rape. *Journal of Social Issues, 48,* 77–91.

Wyatt, G. E., Newcomb, M., & Notgrass, C. M. (1991). Internal and external mediators of women's experiences. In A. W. Burgess (Ed.), *Rape and sexual assault* (Vol. 3, pp. 29–55). New York: Garland.

Yehuda, R. (2006). Advances in understanding neuroendocrine alterations in PTSD and their therapeutic implications. *Annals of the New York Academy of Science, 1071,* 137–166.

*Yehuda, R., Resnick, H. S., Schmeidler, J., Yang, R. K., & Pitman, R. K. (1998). Predictors of cortisone and 3-methoxy-4hydroxyphenylglycol responses in the acute aftermath of rape. *Biological Psychiatry, 43,* 855–859.

*Indicates article included in empirical review.

CHAPTER 2

The Capabilities Approach and Violence Against Women

Implications for Social Development

Loretta Pyles

Social development approaches, welfare policies, and antipoverty strategies have often been premised on the idea that an increase in income or the material wealth of households is the best means to end poverty and thus the primary goal of social development. Neoliberal growth-oriented strategies of capital accumulation, privatization, and investment in developing countries with cheap labor markets are similarly focused on materialist underpinnings, often ignoring human well-being and human rights.

Many approaches to social development ignore the idea that how people live their lives and the kinds of services and institutions that they have access to are potentially just as important as, and tied in to, their annual income. Poor and low-income individuals are at risk and have low functioning not just because they have no money, but because they may lack certain freedoms or capabilities (Sen, 1999). Poor and impoverished women who are victims of violence and abuse in their isolation are especially vulnerable in the sense that they have less freedom and access to institutions. Unfortunately, social development approaches have rarely incorporated the unique realities of poor women into their blueprints, particularly the special concerns of women who are victims of violence. Though the Millennium Development Goals of the United Nations are appropriately concerned with gender equality and the empowerment of women, their indicators on these issues are not explicitly focused on violence against women. This is the case despite the evidence that violence against women and girls clearly has an adverse impact on women's economic and overall well-being (Pyles, 2006a; Raphael, 2000; Tolman and Rosen, 2001).

The capabilities perspective offers an alternative to development theories and policies

Pyles, L. (2008). The capabilities approach and violence against women: Implications for social development. *International Social Work, 51*, 25–36.

traditionally grounded in such materialism. The capabilities approach, as articulated by Sen (1999), Nussbaum (2000), and the United Nations Development Programme (UNDP; 1999), is based on the notion that human freedom and access to opportunities are central to social development. Given that women represent the largest number of individuals living in poverty and that they are vulnerable to violence and other inequalities that exacerbate their vulnerabilities, the capabilities approach offers a social development framework that can incorporate these realities. After clarifying the capabilities approach, I review the literature on the economic aspects of violence against women. I show how the capabilities approach, especially the work of Nussbaum (2000), offers new insights into understanding both violence against women and social development.

Capabilities Approach

The 1998 Nobel prize–winning economist Amartya Sen (1999) argues that while providing primary goods to a society, as proposed by the philosopher John Rawls, is an important moment in economic thinking, what use one makes of these primary goods "depends crucially on a number of contingent circumstances, both personal and social" (1971: 70). These circumstances, or "diversities and heterogeneities," as Sen calls them, include personal heterogeneities, environmental diversities, variations in social climate, differences in relational perspectives, and distribution within the family. People's abilities to activate these primary goods vary. Sen (1999: 73) thus emphasizes the importance of looking into "the *actual living* that people manage to achieve." This emphasis on securing a real opportunity for every individual to achieve functioning—what the person can succeed in doing with the primary goods at one's command—is the basis of the philosophy of the capabilities approach (Gotoh, 2001).

Many theories of welfare hold the position that positive outcomes, such as working in the formal wage-labor sector or achieving an income above the poverty line, contribute to well-being. The capabilities approach asserts that processes and human relationships are, in and of themselves, valuable and also valuable insofar as they have a positive impact on material well-being outcomes. According to the capabilities approach, equality of opportunity is what matters most for well-being (Pressman and Summerfield, 2000). Sen has focused on "what is of intrinsic value in life, rather than on the goods that provide instrumental value or utility" (Pressman and Summerfield, 2000: 97). While a utilitarian measure of human welfare would indicate that people are worse off if their standard of living is lower, the capabilities approach shows that with greater freedom and choice, welfare may increase. Poverty is viewed as a deprivation of basic liberties as opposed to just low income (Sen, 1999). Income is not necessarily an end in itself but a means to an end. The end is to increase the functioning and capabilities of people, so that an adequate measure of welfare ought to measure these capabilities.

The United Nations Human Development Index (HDI) is an example of a way to measure development not based on income alone, but incorporating other valued aspects of human life. The HDI is a "weighted average of income adjusted for distribution and purchasing power, life expectancy and literacy and education. It is expressed in terms of deprivation from what is potentially achievable" (Pressman and Summerfield, 2000: 101).

The basic capabilities advocated for by Sen (1999: 126) are "the ability to be well nourished, to avoid escapable morbidity or mortality, to read and write and communicate, to take part in the life of the community, to appear in public without shame." Nussbaum (2000), who broadens Sen's capabilities, incorporating more explicitly feminist concerns, articulates 10 central human capabilities: life; bodily health; bodily integrity; senses, imagination, and thought;

emotions; practical reason; affiliation; other species; play; and control over one's environment. Clearly, these perspectives reflect a different view of economic development compared with the traditional goals of achieving a certain income or owning property. To better grasp the idea of capabilities, it is important to understand the centrality of the concept of freedom.

Freedom as the Means and End

Freedom, liberties, agency, and choice are central tenets of the capabilities approach. According to Sen (1999), there are two aspects of freedom: the processes that allow freedom of actions and decisions; and the opportunities that people have, given their particular personal and social situations. Freedom is both the primary end and principal means of development. Sen also describes this dual function as the constitutive role and the instrumental role, respectively. He (1999) advocates for five basic instrumental freedoms: political freedoms (i.e., civil rights and other aspects of democratic processes); economic facilities (i.e., access to credit and other distributional considerations); social opportunities (i.e., access to education and health care); transparency guarantees (i.e., societal preventions of corruption and financial irresponsibility); and protective security (i.e., a social safety net providing income supplements and unemployment benefits). All of these instrumental freedoms are interconnected in their ability to help facilitate the ends of development.

It is critical to grasp the distinction between functioning and capabilities. A functioning is what people actually do, whereas a capability is what they are able to do given the personal and social situation. If one has the capability of being able to eat, one can still always choose to fast. Thus, the capability may not necessarily translate into a functioning. Women may choose to stay home with their children and/or do informal work rather than engage in the formal economic sector. But providing them with the capability to

choose to work in the formal sector (in a way that is safe and facilitates economic self-sufficiency) is the responsibility of society. So, under the capabilities approach, people should have the freedom to choose and self-determine their lives. The capabilities approach is ultimately congruent with social work perspectives on social justice, empowerment, and self-determination (Gutierrez and Lewis, 1994; Hill, 2003; Morris, 2002).

Violence Against Women and Economics

Violence against women affects the ability of women to achieve full functioning in the world. I define violence against women as physical, sexual, and emotional violence against women and girls by intimates, acquaintances, or strangers. Like many researchers, I view it as a patriarchal mechanism for controlling women, defined particularly by the use of power, force, manipulation, and isolation. In this section, I will discuss the ways in which violence against women tends to affect poor adult women. First, I will explain how violence limits women's access to certain institutions; then, I will discuss the effects of violence on the physical and emotional well-being of women; and finally, I will articulate the explicit ramifications of abuse on the economic well-being of women.

Violence as a Limit to Women's Access to Institutions

Women who have been victimized by an intimate partner or a stranger often experience fear, shame, and isolation. People who abuse women may use the tactic of isolation by deliberately isolating them from friends, family, work, and social institutions. These abusers often perceive connections with others in the community as a threat to their system of power and control. Women tend to be cut off from law enforcement, courts, healthcare systems, and other sources of social support. According to Sullivan (1991: 42),

> It has been suggested that a critical reason so many women remain with or return to their assailants is a lack of access to community resources, specifically, housing, legal assistance, employment, education, finances, childcare and social support systems.

This isolation from such social support is so pervasive that the most common form of intervention with survivors of violence is advocacy services (Schechter, 1982). The purpose of such advocacy services is "to enhance the quality of women's lives by improving their access to community resources and increasing the social support available to them" (Bybee and Sullivan, 2002: 105). Furthermore, because of the nature of the isolation associated with a problem such as violence against women and the fact that it is understood as a community rather than individual problem, many communities have developed community response teams to violence consisting of representatives of various institutions in the community. Cheers et al. studied family violence in an Australian indigenous community, and they argue for "an innovative, holistic and multifaceted community development response [that] addresses the economic, social and structural issues relating to family violence" (2006: 59).

Violence Affecting Women's Health and Mental Health

Women who have been assaulted or battered may be dealing with the realities of post-traumatic stress disorder (PTSD), anxiety, depression, and other physical health problems (Plichta, 1996). Tolman and Rosen (2001) found that women who experienced domestic violence in the past year reported three times as many mental health disorders as their non-abused counterparts. Sullivan and Bybee (1999) found that when

abuse in an intimate relationship ceased, the victim's physical health improved. Nasir and Hyder (2003) identified domestic violence among pregnant women in developing countries as a significant global health issue. The main risk factors in their research were identified as belonging to a low-income group, little education in both partners, and unplanned pregnancy.

Many survivors of violence must cope with memories of traumatic events, thoughts of suicide, and the effects of physical injuries. From a study by Raphael and Tolman (1997: 10), a research participant describes her experience:

> I have trouble at work as a result of past domestic violence. . . . I worry that I am always missing something. I am always watching for an attack so I am on guard all the time and I am not really listening. I am always needing to ask for clarification and that angers people on the job.

The ongoing effects of violence—physical and emotional—can be barriers to women's ability to engage in the community, get vocational training and education, and work in both formal and informal sectors.

Violence Affecting Women's Ability to Generate Income

Economic abuse is an aspect of violence that some women report having experienced (Raphael and Tolman, 1997). This kind of abuse may include behaviors such as isolating women from financial resources or preventing them from working. Many battered women do not have ready access to cash, checking accounts, or charge accounts. Studies show that an abuser may directly interfere with a woman's attempts to work or attend school by harassing her at work, disabling the family car, destroying her books or clothes, giving her visible wounds, or reneging on child-care commitments at the last minute (Raphael and Tolman, 1997). Other research has focused on how violence from an intimate partner affects women's alternative resource-generating strategies, including participation in the informal and illegal economies (Pyles, 2006b).

Violence appears to be a direct contributing factor to the poverty levels of women. Women who have left abusive relationships may find themselves with multiple barriers to employment in the formal sector, such as transportation, child care, and other ongoing safety issues (Sullivan, 1991). Thus, it has been reported that many women stay in abusive relationships for economic reasons (Sullivan, 1991).

Capabilities and Women

The work on capabilities conducted by Nussbaum (2000) expands Sen's original ideas and represents an important voice for advocating for the capabilities of women. Many of these ideas emerge from empirical evidence that exists internationally, particularly in developing countries. There are three additional concepts that are critical for understanding the capabilities approach and how it is useful for capturing the phenomenon of violence against women. In this section, I will review the concepts of missing women/household inequality, caring labor, and bodily integrity in more detail, as they are particularly important components of an expanded understanding of poverty alleviation.

Missing Women and Household Inequality

Sen (1992, 1999) has identified the high mortality rates of women across the world, a reflection of a capability deprivation for women. While women in Europe and North America tend to outnumber men, this is not the case in many developing countries. The explanation of this can be discovered by looking into the experiences of females in developing countries, especially female children. While female infanticide

does exist, the larger problem appears to be the neglect of female health and nutrition. "There is indeed considerable direct evidence that female children are neglected in terms of health care, hospitalization and even feeding" (Sen, 1999: 106). Sen estimates that 100 million women worldwide are missing in this sense.

Closely linked to the phenomenon of missing women, that is, women who have died prematurely in developing countries as a result of inadequate health care and education, Sen has acknowledged the phenomenon of household inequality (Sen, 1999). Household inequality is the idea that there are domestic power imbalances that need to be accounted for in assessing economic well-being. Because of such domestic hierarchies women do not have full access and opportunity to achieve capabilities. In fact, Iversen (2003: 97) remarks, "domestic hierarchies can deform individual preferences," forcing women to adapt their preferences and make choices about their lives that they would not make if they had true equality of opportunity.

Caring Labor

Scholarly inquiry into the nature of women's care work, that is, the often unpaid or underpaid caretaking of children, older adults, and families, has revealed some of the complexities of this phenomenon. Multidisciplinary thinkers have argued about the inequities that exist for women doing care work and how philosophers such as Rawls have ignored this aspect of women's realities (Okin, 1989). More recently, UNDP has incorporated the concept of "caring labor" as a critical element of social development (UNDP, 1999).

Because women worldwide spend two-thirds of their working hours on unpaid work and men spend one-quarter (most unpaid work is spent on caring work), women certainly have a lot to gain from an increased attention given to this reality (UNDP, 1999). For women in abusive relationships, commitments to care work may put them further in harm's way. Duties to care for children and husbands can influence the choices women make to report the violence they experience as well as to stay in or leave abusive relationships.

Bodily Integrity

While Sen (1999) has certainly been attuned to the unique situation of women and the necessity for increased attention to women's vulnerable position in order to enhance their capabilities, he has not proactively addressed the issue of violence against women. Nussbaum (2000), however, does take a proactive stance in her work on capabilities and one of the critical themes reflective of this is her recognition of violence against women as a capability deprivation. She calls this capability "bodily integrity." Nussbaum (2000: 78) defines the capability of bodily integrity as being able to move freely from place to place; having one's bodily boundaries treated as sovereign, that is, being able to be secure against assault, including sexual assault, child sexual abuse, and domestic violence; having opportunities for sexual satisfaction and for choice in matters of reproduction.

The reason for setting forth this capability is to recognize the community's responsibility to provide the social conditions (laws, interventions, etc.) that enable this capability in the case of women who experience lack of bodily integrity as a capability deprivation. This is crucial, as bodily integrity is an important freedom in its own right as well as a means to further freedoms and economic opportunities. According to the capabilities approach, the government, via its social policies, is ultimately responsible for delivering "the *social basis of* these capabilities" (Nussbaum, 2000: 81).

Implications for Social Development

It should be clear from the above discussion that there are complex ramifications to the problem of violence against women, including adverse effects on individual well-being and the ability of women to access social institutions, including the labor market. The capabilities approach identifies violence against women as a capability deprivation, arguing that social policies ought to provide social structures necessary to achieve capabilities, including bodily integrity. It is also the case that the capabilities approach sheds an important light on the problem of violence against women. Traditional interventions in violence against women, such as empowerment, strengths, or medical models, have often failed to address the deeper poverty and social development issues that accompany violence against women (Pyles, 2006a).

The limitation of the capabilities approach is that theorists tend to overlook how to implement the theory or discuss practice methods for actualizing its vision. Thus, it is important for scholars and practitioners in fields such as social work, education, business, public health, and other applied disciplines to contribute to this dialogue. In this section, I offer suggestions for social development practice as well as social research.

Social Development Practice

It would seem that a critical question concerning the articulation of a social development approach is how the approach can be actualized in practice. Promoting instrumental freedoms is an essential component of the development of women who are vulnerable to violence. Thus, this may include addressing political freedoms, social opportunities, and the protective security of women and their families. Historically, some of these activities have fallen under the purview of social workers and other social development practitioners. For example, social workers advocate for a minimum safety net of welfare and/or unemployment benefits.

Increasing the social networks of individuals and promoting access to services are important steps in the advancement of instrumental freedoms.

However, these traditional social work skills must be supplemented by the skills of organizing and policy advocacy. While it is the case that some social workers possess such skills, social development specialists and community organizers can offer their expertise in the areas of organizing and advocacy. When communities lack such skills, it may be necessary to partner with union organizers, feminist organizers, and other activists. It is not necessary to reinvent the wheel of community organizing and mobilization. Established, successful methods are well documented in the areas of planning, organizing, and advocacy. Concomitant activities may include the promotion of social capital, civic engagement, and democratic participation of women (Gutierrez and Lewis, 1994; Putnam, 2000). Women's support groups, grassroots political coalitions, and the promotion of women candidates are examples of democratizing activities that can enhance political freedoms and social opportunities.

Access to job development, micro-loans, and higher education are essential strategies for developing the economic facilities for women who are surviving violence (Pyles, 2006a). Providing supportive services for women working in both the formal and informal sectors will enhance the capabilities of women, especially those living with violence. These supports may include child care, support groups, legal advocacy, and other supplements to allow them to be successful in their work (Sullivan, 1991).

A vital component of social development involves not only economic and social development strategies, but also safety net assurances for the most vulnerable populations. Promoting the right to protective security measures such as a welfare safety net can be achieved through policy advocacy. Additionally, practitioners can advocate for unemployment and disability benefits for women who are forced to leave their jobs due to domestic or sexual violence. Thus, it is incumbent upon social workers and other social development practitioners to advocate for such policies, emphasizing a capabilities discourse.

Social Development Research and Policy

More research should continue to be conducted on the effects of violence on women's capabilities. Like the United Nations human development initiatives, social researchers investigating development practices and outcomes may be well served to consider measuring social development progress on a capabilities scale.

Though studies have been effected that are concerned with how violence affects the abilities of women to maintain employment and access supports, studies could explore how violence influences women's access to social institutions and political participation. Studies that correlate experiences with violence and access to social institutions and political participation would enhance the knowledge base of social development specialists. In addition to qualitative and exploratory studies, research could be conducted utilizing secondary data analysis to inquire into the association of women's social and political participation (such as voter turnout and other forms of political participation), rates of violence against women, and the availability of prevention and intervention programs.

There is a paucity of research published in social work journals that is concerned with the efficacy of community organizing strategies as well as social development programs. Evidence-based practice studies of micro-enterprise programs for battered women, job development endeavors in urban and rural areas, and the effects of political participation on the well-being of communities are just a few ideas of endeavors that could be assessed. With greater knowledge of what works and what does not work, practitioners and community members will be more able to actualize the ideals of the capabilities approach, including the safety and economic well-being of female survivors of abuse.

References

Bybee, D. I. and C. M. Sullivan (2002) "The Process through which an Advocacy Intervention Resulted in Positive Change for Battered Women over Time," *American Journal of Community Psychology* 30(1): 103–32.

Cheers, B., M. Binell, H. Coleman, I. Gentle, G. Miller, J. Taylor and C. Weetra (2006) "Family Violence: An Australian Indigenous Community Tells Its Story," *International Social Work* 49(1): 51–63.

Gotoh, R. (2001) "The Capability Theory and Welfare Reform," *Pacific Economic-Review* 6(2): 211–22.

Gutierrez, L. and Lewis, E. (1994) "Community Organizing with Women of Color: A Feminist Approach," *Journal of Community Practice* 1(2): 23–44.

Hill, M. T. (2003) "Development as Empowerment," *Feminist Economics* 9(2–3): 117–35.

Iversen, V. (2003) "Intra-household Inequality: A Challenge for the Capability Approach?" *Feminist Economics* 9(2–3): 93–115.

Morris, P. M. (2002) "The Capabilities Perspective: A Framework for Social Justice," *Families in Society* 83(4): 365–74.

Nasir, K. and A. Hyder (2003) "Violence against Pregnant Women in Developing Countries: Review of Evidence," *European Journal of Public Health* 13(2): 105–7.

Nussbaum, M. (2000) *Women and Human Development: The Capabilities Approach.* Cambridge: Cambridge University Press.

Okin, S. M. (1989) *Justice, Gender and the Family.* New York: Basic Books.

Plichta, S. B. (1996) "Violence and Abuse: Implications for Women's Health," in M. M. Falik and K. S. Collins (Eds.), *Women's Health: The Commonwealth Fund Study,* pp. 237–72. Baltimore, MD: The Johns Hopkins University Press.

Pressman, S. and G. Summerfield (2000) "The Economic Contributions of Amartya Sen," *Review of Political Economy* 12(1): 89–113.

Putnam, R. D. (2000) *Bowling Alone: The Collapse and Revival of American Community.* New York: Simon & Schuster.

Pyles, L. (2006a) "Toward Safety for Low-income Battered Women: Promoting Economic Justice Strategies," *Families in Society: The Journal of Contemporary Human Services* 87(1): 63–70.

Pyles, L. (2006b) "Economic Well-Being and Intimate Partner Violence: New Findings about the Informal Economy," *Journal of Sociology and Social Welfare* 33(3): 101–26.

Raphael, J. (2000) *Saving Bernice: Battered Women, Welfare and Poverty.* Boston, MA: Northeastern University Press.

Raphael, J. and R. Tolman (1997) "Trapped by Poverty, Trapped by Abuse: New Evidence Documenting the Relationship between Domestic Violence and Welfare." Available online at http://www.ssw.umich.edu/trapped/pubs_trapped.pdf (accessed 16 February 2003).

Rawls, J. (1971) *A Theory of Justice.* Cambridge, MA: Harvard University Press.

Schechter, S. (1982) *Women and Male Violence: The Visions and Struggles of the Battered Women's Movement.* Boston, MA: South End Press.

Sen, A. (1992) "Missing Women," *British Medical Journal* 304: 586–7.

Sen, A. (1999) *Development as Freedom.* New York: Knopf.

Sullivan, C. M. (1991) "The Provision of Advocacy Services to Women Leaving Abusive Partners: An Exploratory Study," *Journal of Interpersonal Violence* 6(1): 41–54.

Sullivan, C. M. and D. I. Bybee (1999) "Reducing Violence Using Community-Based Advocacy for Women with Abusive Partners," *Journal of Consulting and Clinical Psychology* 67(1): 43–53.

Tolman, R. M. and D. Rosen (2001) "Domestic Violence in the Lives of Women Receiving Welfare: Mental Health, Substance Dependence, and Economic Well-Being," *Violence Against Women* 7(2): 141–58.

United Nations Development Program (UNDP) (1999) *Human Development Report.* New York: Oxford University Press.

CHAPTER 3

Collecting Reliable Information About Violence Against Women Safely in Household Interviews

Experience From a Large-Scale National Survey in South Asia

Neil Andersson, Anne Cockcroft, Noor Ansari, Khalid Omer,
Ubaid Ullah Chaudhry, Amir Khan, and LuWei Pearson

There is good evidence that violence against women, especially in the domestic setting, is a common problem in both developed and developing countries (Garcia-Moreno, Jansen, Ellsberg, Heise, & Watts, 2006; Krug, Dahlberg, Mercy, Zwi, & Lozano, 2002; Watts & Zimmerman, 2002), and it is recognized as a serious public health problem (Campbell, 2002; Heise, Raikes, Watts, & Zwi, 1994; Krantz, 2002). But research into violence against women is not easy. Even the

definition of what constitutes violence against women varies from place to place and between researchers, making comparisons between studies difficult (Piispa & Heiskanen, 2005; Schwartz, 2000). Researchers have used various survey methods to measure the prevalence and incidence of different forms of violence against women, involving samples representing the adult female population of regions or whole countries (e.g., Ellsberg, Pena, Herrera, Liljestrand, & Winkvist,

Andersson, N., Cockcroft, A., Ansari, N., Omer, K., Chaudhry, U. U., Khan, A., & Pearson, L. (2009). Collecting reliable information about violence against women safely in household interviews: Experience from a large-scale national survey in South Asia. *Violence Against Women, 15,* 482–496.

AUTHOR'S NOTE: This study was undertaken with financial support from the UK Department for International Development (DFID). We thank Roohi Metcalfe for her support throughout the study, the members of the field teams for their committed work, and all the women who bravely and generously shared their experiences with us.

1999; Fanslow & Robinson, 2004; Garcia-Moreno et al., 2006; Jewkes, Penn-Kekana, Levin, Ratsaka, & Schrieber, 2001; Johnson, 1996; Tjaden & Thoennes, 2000). Because the data collection method can make a big difference to the prevalence of violence found in a population, comparisons between surveys in different places and over time are unreliable unless the surveys used similar methods (Posselt, 2005; Rand & Rennison, 2005).

Surveys of violence against women present particular methodological and ethical challenges, and several authors have reviewed these and offered pointers for conducting such surveys (Ellsberg & Heise, 2002; Ellsberg, Heise, Pena, Agurto, & Winkvist, 2001; Jewkes, Watts, Abrahams, Penn-Kekana, & Garcia-Moreno, 2000). The World Health Organization (WHO) has developed guidelines for ethics in surveys on violence against women (WHO, 2001), which extend overall ethical guidelines for research involving human subjects (Council for International Organizations of Medical Science, 1991). Among the most important concerns about surveys are underreporting of violence and the physical and emotional risks for respondents and interviewers. There is evidence that women are more likely to disclose sexual assault to a female interviewer (Sorenson, Stein, Siegel, Golding, & Burnham, 1987), and the interview context and setting, including training and support of interviewers, can make a big difference to violence disclosure rates (Ellsberg et al., 2001). Ensuring privacy of the interview is crucial, both to minimize under-reporting—shown to be more likely if someone else is present (Walby & Myhill, 2001)—and to protect the safety of the respondent and interviewer (Ellsberg et al., 2001; WHO, 2001). A further ethical consideration is that the findings should be used to support efforts to reduce the level of violence against women, thus balancing the real risks of the survey with potential benefits (Ellsberg & Heise, 2002; Jewkes et al., 2000; WHO, 2001).

We developed a practical approach in a large, nationally representative household survey of violence against women in Pakistan to deal with these concerns, especially to minimize underreporting and to ensure physical and emotional safety of the women respondents and interviewers. In designing and implementing the survey on this sensitive topic, we built on our experience of undertaking large-scale household surveys throughout Pakistan (Cockcroft et al., 2003) and of a study about access to justice for women in Karachi, Pakistan, in which we piloted methods for allowing women to disclose privately sensitive issues in the context of a household survey within an extended family setting (Mhatre, Andersson, Ansari, & Omer, 2002). We also used lessons from a survey of women's experience and reporting of sexual violence that we undertook in Johannesburg, South Africa (Andersson & Mhatre, 2003). A separate article will describe the efforts we made to ensure use of the findings to inform and encourage programs to reduce violence against women in Pakistan.

Background to the Survey in Pakistan

It is generally believed that rates of violence and other forms of abuse against women in Pakistan are high. But there is little quantitative evidence from representative samples of women. Civil society groups and bodies such as the Human Rights Commission for Pakistan have typically collected and reviewed reports from the press and cases reported to official bodies such as the police (Niaz, 2003). A study of 150 married women attending outpatient clinics in Karachi found that 34% had experienced physical violence and 73% of those who had were anxious or depressed (Fikree & Bhatti, 1999), and a recent Karachi study reported that 44% of 300 women in postnatal wards had experienced marital physical abuse (Fikree, Jafarey, Korejo, Afshan, & Durocher, 2006). But at the time of our study (2001–2004), there were no reliable figures for abuse among the overall population of women in Pakistan, and our study remains the only one to estimate rates of abuse in a representative national sample of women. When designing the study, we talked to many of the researchers who had carried out previous studies, especially about the problems they had encountered during the work and the solutions they had found to these problems.

In Pakistan, there are cultural norms about women's movements and interactions that can pose challenges for household surveys, irrespective of the topic. In some parts of the country, it is not acceptable for a woman to move outside the home other than under limited conditions and accompanied by a male family member. It is not acceptable for men, other than family members, to enter a household, and it is generally not acceptable for men to interview women. It is often not acceptable for female members of an interviewing team to travel in the same vehicle as the male members, so special transport arrangements are needed, as well as arrangements for secure accommodation for the female team members. In some conservative communities, elders and religious leaders will not allow women members of field teams to enter the community as they are considered to be acting inappropriately by undertaking this sort of work away from their homes. When the survey was being planned, some researchers indicated that they thought it would not be possible to carry out the survey in all districts because of the very restrictive attitudes about women in some districts and the considerable security concerns in some places, increasing the difficulties of travel and accommodation for women interviewers.

Survey Method

The study took place between 2001 and 2004 and comprised a design phase, reviewing previous work in Pakistan and elsewhere and consulting widely; a large-scale, nationally representative household survey to establish the frequency of violence and other forms of abuse against women and the factors increasing and decreasing the risk; community focus groups to discuss the findings separately with women and men and explore potential solutions; and a phase of sharing the findings with stakeholders to plan interventions to reduce the problem, based on evidence from the study. The CIET ethical review board, expanded for the occasion to include female members from Pakistan, gave approval for the household survey in September, 2002 and for the focus group work and key informant interviews in July, 2003.

Sample

A stratified cluster sample (last stage random) design was used to give representation of the four provinces and at the national level. Each district (97 at the time) contributed data, although not at a level sufficient to declare figures for individual districts. In each sample community, the survey team covered about 100 households, working together. The resulting sample of 23,430 eligible women older than 14 years lived in 20,034 households across the country.

We deliberately used as the sample a proportion (randomly selected in each district) of the sample sites previously visited in a different, less sensitive survey (Cockcroft et al., 2003). This meant the communities were already familiar with our field teams and could interpret the new survey as some sort of follow-up to the previous survey, rather than as something specifically about abuse against women, which may have led to community leaders refusing the team entry into the community at all. Not making public the topic of the survey also helped to minimize the risk of retribution against women in the community who participated in the survey as well as to reduce security risks for the women interviewers.

Survey Instruments, Interviewers, and Field Processes

We spent six months on the design and piloting of survey instruments and field processes, testing successively different methods to increase the rates of disclosure about violence and other forms of abuse, while taking precautions to protect both respondents and interviewers. The design involved wide consultations and a series of design focus groups. Pakistan is a culturally and socially diverse country, so we tested the instruments and procedures in different parts of the country to ensure they worked effectively in the different social and cultural conditions prevailing in different areas.

Increasing Disclosure

Questionnaire. The main questionnaire was completed in an interview with each eligible woman present in the household, excluding the most senior woman (the mother or mother-in-law) unless she was alone in the household. The questionnaire included questions about family norms and covered opinions about what constitutes abuse as well as about the experience of different forms of abuse, including physical violence, and reporting of this abuse. It also included questions about educational status, literacy, work activities, and income inside and outside the home, as factors potentially related to a woman's risk of experiencing different forms of abuse. We tested several possible options for ordering and wording of questions to make women feel more comfortable to disclose about abuse when they reached this point of the questionnaire. Among other things, it proved helpful to include, just before the questions about their own experience of forms of abuse, some questions about their sisters' experience of abuse. The questions about sisters also allowed us to collect information about violence against women leading to death, including so-called honor killings.

We also developed a second questionnaire, which we administered to the senior woman in each household, and to any male household members present. This questionnaire covered much less sensitive topics, including the household demographics and their norms and traditions. It included some questions about the acceptability of different practices related to restrictions and disciplining of women but did not include any direct questions about violence or other forms of abuse. We asked about these household characteristics and family beliefs because of their potential relationship to a woman's risk of experiencing violence.

Selection and Training of Interviewers. The women interviewers needed to be able quickly to establish a relationship with the women respondents so that these women felt able to disclose to them something as sensitive as having experienced physical violence or some other form of abuse. We mostly selected interviewers for this survey from among women who had worked with us previously and proved themselves to be efficient and conscientious. For this work, we selected women who were more than 20 years old (mostly 25 years and older) and who projected self-confidence as well as empathy. In the early piloting of the instruments and field processes we found that younger women, for example university students, although they could be very efficient interviewers generally, had a lower rate of disclosure of abuse than their older colleagues. We selected interviewers for each part of the country who came from that area, although not the sample communities, so they were familiar with the particular customs and norms of behavior, which vary quite markedly across Pakistan. The interviewers also dressed according to the norms of the different communities they visited, veiling their faces, for example, in some communities.

The training of the interviewers included, as usual, reviewing the contents of the instruments and practice interviewing in nonsample communities. For this survey, we noted the disclosure rates for the different interviewers during their field practice sessions. We continued the training and practice until all the interviewers were achieving similar levels of disclosure. We found that in the first field practice session, most of the interviewers had low rates of disclosure in their interviews. At this point, we added a women-only session in which we asked each interviewer to tell the rest of the group about a case of abuse of which she knew personally. The session took time and was sometimes emotional. The interviewers reported that it helped them to appreciate how hard it is to talk about such matters; in many cases, the abuse they described had happened either to themselves or to a family member. After this session, we asked the interviewers that in their interviews with the women respondents, just before asking them about their experience of violence and other forms of abuse, they should bring to mind the cases they themselves had described and tell the women, "I know how hard this is to talk about. I myself know of someone who has experienced abuse." We found that after this session in the classroom, the interviewers achieved markedly higher rates of disclosure of abuse, particularly for physical violence. Table 3.1 shows an example of the effect on disclosure rates. The interviewers reported that this simple procedure had a noticeable effect on the women they were interviewing. They themselves felt more comfortable asking the women about their experience of abuse, although they also felt more connected with the women and more affected by their painful stories.

Conduct and Privacy of Interviews. In the extended family setting still prevalent in many parts of Pakistan, it is difficult for a single interviewer to enter a household and interview a woman in private, particularly a more "junior" woman when a "senior" woman (such as the mother-in-law) is in the house. A request for privacy with the junior woman stimulates the curiosity and suspicion of the senior woman, who may either refuse the request for an interview or insist on being present. To allow women to be interviewed without being overheard, at least two women interviewers entered each household. One of them interviewed the senior woman (the mother or mother-in-law) using the less sensitive

Table 3.1 Effect of Women Discussing "A Case of Abuse They Knew About" and Bringing This to Mind When Interviewing Women About Their Experience of Violence and Other Forms of Abuse

	1st Day	2nd Day	3rd Day
Number of interviews	31	53	35
Refusals	1	0	0
Disclosure of violence and other forms of abuse			
Restrictions as a form of punishment	4	20	10
Emotional or verbal abuse	10	37	26
Harassment outside the home (verbal or physical)	6	13	17
Physical violence	1	19	15

NOTE: 1st day: Interviewers had not had the session about recalling a case of abuse they knew of and did not share anything about their own experience with the women they interviewed; 2nd day: Interviewers had attended a session about recalling a case of abuse they knew of and they mentioned about "knowing of a case" to the women before asking them about abuse; 3rd day: Interviewers had reviewed their experiences of the day before and discussed with each other the best way to mention to women about themselves knowing of cases of abuse.

questionnaire, while the other interviewed the eligible women, using the main questionnaire. If necessary, additional interviewers were called in to help interview the eligible women. If there was only one woman in a household, she responded to both the senior-woman questionnaire and the main questionnaire for eligible women.

The interviewer of the senior woman deliberately kept that interview in a public area of the household and conducted the interview in a loud voice, allowing other people to be present and listen in if interested. She continued the interview with some extra general questions provided for the purpose, even after the formal questionnaire was completed, until her colleague(s) had completed the interviews with the other women in the household. The interviewer(s) for the other women in the household took each woman aside—preferably into another room or another part of the courtyard—and conducted the interview quietly. If other women were waiting to be interviewed, the interviewer(s) did not allow them to listen in, but politely requested them to carry on with their tasks until their turn to be interviewed. Children over the age of 2 to 3 years were kept away from the interviews, recognizing they might repeat what they had heard while the woman was being interviewed.

At the beginning of the interview, the interviewers explained to the eligible women respondents that this was a survey about the experiences of women, that their responses would be treated as confidential, that their names were not recorded, that they could decline to be interviewed, that they could discontinue the interview at any point, and that they could decline to answer any question they were not comfortable with. They then sought their verbal consent to continue the interview. Of the 31,407 eligible women identified in the households (all those more than 14 years of age, irrespective of their marital status), some 23,430 (75%) were interviewed. Among those not interviewed, the usual reason was that the woman was not available in the household at the time (21%, 6,465). Only a few women declined to be interviewed (3%,

1,061), and even more rarely someone else in the household (usually the senior woman) declined to allow an eligible woman to be interviewed (1%, 451).

In most households, men were not present when the interviewers entered. If men were present, the interviewers explained to them that a male team member was outside the household and would like to interview them if they would step outside for this. They gave them a slip identifying which household they were from to ensure their data could later be matched to the correct household. When the men went outside, the male interviewers conducted their interviews, using the same questionnaire as that used for the senior women in the households. This technique both removed men from the household while the women were being interviewed and allowed us to collect male views about issues potentially related to the risk of violence against women.

Ensuring Safety of Women Respondents and Interviewers

Physical Safety of Women Respondents. Our arrangements to ensure privacy of the interviews (as described above) were intended not only to increase disclosure but also to ensure that the women who disclosed did not suffer for doing so. The fact of talking about these issues at all, whether or not they disclosed any violence or other forms of abuse, may be enough to get women in trouble with their families. Therefore, we advised the women respondents not to talk in any detail about what they had been asked and rather to mention some of the general questions if they were asked about the interview. The interviewers suggested to the women what questions they should mention if asked. The intention was to leave the impression that their questionnaire was similar to or the same as the less sensitive questionnaire administered to the senior women or the men in the households.

We cannot be certain how well these procedures protected all the women interviewed. However, we did have an opportunity to check this when we returned to each of the sample communities to undertake the focus group discussions. We undertook separate focus groups of eligible women (who had completed the main questionnaire), senior women (who had completed the other questionnaire), and men. At the time of the household survey, we had asked women if they would be willing to participate in later focus groups. In one community, of the 200 in the sample, we were not able to hold a focus group of eligible women because, as one of them explained to us, they were frightened to attend because husbands and mothers-in-law were already suspicious of them after the household survey. In general, though, women attending the focus groups did not report that they had experienced any difficulties after the survey, noting that other people did not know what they had spoken about in their interviews. Some had been questioned about the survey and had used the suggested responses to allay suspicions.

Physical Safety of Women Interviewers. Each field team included 12 female interviewers (working in six pairs) and three male members, as well as one female member responsible for quality control. The role of the male members was to interview any male household members present when the women interviewers entered the household, as well as to make contact with the community leaders on entering the community and get their permission to proceed with the interviews. They also had responsibility for ensuring the safety of the women team members. Each male team member accompanied a group of four women interviewers. He always knew which households the women were in and could check that all was well if they were delayed. The male team members were also responsible for safety of the whole team during travel and in the places where they stayed overnight. In particularly difficult places, the senior male provincial coordinators also accompanied the team to add further support and protection. In some areas it is dangerous to mention any nongovernmental organization (NGO) connection as conservative

elements perceive NGOs as subversive and even "evil," so the teams took with them documents making it clear they were conducting the survey on behalf of a government department.

The fieldwork was not without incident and some of the field teams had to deal with significant threats to their safety. They had practiced methods of dealing with various scenarios. The threats were mostly related to the general social and cultural environment in some communities, which reacted to the presence of a large group of female interviewers, rather than to suspicions about the topic of the survey. For example, in one community a religious scholar (*moulvi*) became incensed that women were walking about in the community and talking to community women, and he informed men in the community that if these women visited their houses they had the right to marry them forcibly. Mostly the women team members dealt with the threats themselves, but the male team members were always on hand in case they were needed.

Emotional Safety of Women Respondents and Interviewers. Talking about the experience of abuse is emotionally difficult for both the woman respondent and the woman interviewer. Among women who disclosed physical violence, only one-third had told anyone at all before the interview. The women interviewers were not trained nor in a position to offer counseling to women who disclosed physical violence or other forms of abuse. The training emphasized that the interviewers could not offer the women specific help and they should not raise any expectations of this. Respondents provided information of their experiences on the understanding that we would bring together their collective experiences and report them, in an attempt to help the women of Pakistan in the future. Many respondents specifically said they were willing to reveal their experiences in the hope that this might improve matters for other women in the future. Some said they felt relief by telling someone what had happened to them without fear of getting into trouble.

We gave careful consideration to the recommendation that researchers should give women survey participants details of sources of emotional support and other help (WHO, 2001). In the few places (mainly big cities) where there were services available, the interviewers offered the women respondents contact details for these services, having first checked that they could receive and keep the information safely. However, in most parts of Pakistan there is no such support available. An additional problem in Pakistan is the very low literacy level among women, limiting the usefulness of written material, which they would not be able to ask a male family member to read on their behalf.

The women interviewers heard many harrowing stories of respondents' experiences of violence and other forms of abuse during every day of their work. This is upsetting and emotionally draining. We provided for safe and private accommodation for the interviewers and, at the end of each day, the female quality control coordinator on the team facilitated a session to allow the women interviewers to share their experiences and emotions. This was also an opportunity to discuss how interviewers had dealt with different situations and to plan and prepare for the ongoing work. The teams worked together to cover each community and stayed together throughout the period of data collection, becoming close and supportive groups. In each region, a more senior female quality control associate regularly visited the teams to check progress. Part of her role was to check on how interviewers were coping with the emotional burden of the work and to provide additional support for individual interviewers experiencing any difficulties. None of the interviewers had to drop out because of not being able to cope with the emotional stresses of the work. Although they were upset about what they heard, many of the team members, female and male, said that their participation in the research had changed their lives and they felt proud to have been part of it. As one female interviewer said, "I learned that I should not keep silent about abuse and I should say

things are wrong if they are wrong. I try to defend my rights now."

Discussion

We believe we have been able to comply with the intention of all the guidelines of the WHO about ethical conduct of studies of violence against women (WHO, 2001), although in some instances we used methods different from those recommended in the guidelines.

We went to considerable lengths to protect both the women participants and the research teams. Our method of ensuring privacy of interviews in the Pakistani household context, with at least two interviewers entering each household, proved very effective. We did not limit the number of women interviewed per household to one, as suggested in the guidelines to prevent details of the interview from becoming known. We believe that sometimes it is important to try to find all women present as one might otherwise miss those most at risk, such as a separated or divorced woman living with her parents. In practice, we typically interviewed one or at most two women per household, mostly because others were not present at the time of the visit. We protected the privacy of the interview contents by advising women not to discuss the details, even with other women in the house, and by the implication that the content was the same as that of the much less sensitive questionnaire administered to the senior woman and any male household members who were present. We carefully trained our interviewers and they did not conduct or continue interviews when they could be overheard or when interrupted.

We arranged the fieldwork and logistics to protect the women interviewers as well as the women participants, including the role of the male team members. Despite our careful safety arrangements, the field teams did experience difficult situations, especially in the most conservative parts of the country. Nothing serious happened either to any of the interviewers, or to any of the interviewed women, as far as we could ascertain when we returned to the communities to conduct focus group discussions about the findings. But it is important not to underestimate the real risks of undertaking and participating in this sort of research.

The arrangements to protect the safety of the women participants and interviewers added to the costs of the work. We formed larger field teams to allow for two interviewers per household, added additional male members to the teams, and made special transport and accommodation arrangements for the teams.

In planning the study, we reviewed the existing evidence about how to minimize underreporting of violence in surveys (Ellsberg et al., 2001; Jewkes et al., 2000) and drew on our own experience. We designed the instrument to facilitate disclosure and piloted the instrument extensively in different parts of the country. We used only women interviewers, in any case usually a requirement in Pakistan when interviewing women on any topic, and selected and trained them carefully, testing the effects on disclosure rates as part of our piloting and then actual trainings. A key element was the empathy generated by interviewers recalling a case of abuse of which they themselves knew, and interviewers sharing this insight with the women at the point of the interview just before they asked about the actual experience of violence and other forms of abuse. This produced a marked increase in disclosure rates achieved during field practices as part of the training.

From the details provided by respondents regarding their abuse, we do not feel this procedure led to any false disclosure among women who had not been abused. Other authors agree that overreporting, or fabrication, of abuse is very rare in surveys (Ellsberg et al., 2001; Jewkes et al., 2000; Koss, 1993; Smith, 1994). We are aware, however, that any follow-up that does not include this step in the training will almost certainly underreport abuse, producing a misleading impression of a decrease in violence against women.

We believe our efforts were effective in increasing disclosure and minimizing underreporting. This conclusion is supported by the finding in our survey that only a third of the women disclosing physical abuse had told *anyone* about it before. Nevertheless, there will have been some abused women who did not feel able to disclose this in the interview, so the rates we found should be considered minimum estimates. The overall nonresponse rate among eligible women was 25%, but this was mainly because they were not present in the household when the interviewers entered; women only rarely declined to be interviewed (3%) or were not allowed to be interviewed (1%). Those women who were not interviewed may have had a different, and potentially higher, rate of abuse than those interviewed. Rates of violence and other forms of abuse reported from household surveys that do not include special arrangements to increase disclosure, such as those we employed, are likely to be serious underestimates. For example, if a repeat survey after an intervention is carried out without using the same arrangements to enhance disclosure used in the initial survey, it could lead to a spuriously large decline in estimated rates of abuse attributed to the intervention.

We made special arrangements to provide support for the field teams, especially the women interviewers. We believe these were largely successful; no women had to leave the work because of stress or emotional difficulties. What made it easier to provide support were the fieldwork arrangements that kept the teams working together in one place rather than scattered and working alone. Similarly, we made efforts to reduce any negative emotional consequences for women respondents recalling painful memories. Our interviewers were trained in what was to be done if a woman became upset during the interview, and they ended the interviews on a positive and empowering note (Parker & Ulrich, 1990). It was not possible to comply with the guideline about referring women to sources of support because these are largely absent in Pakistan. Setting up short-term support mechanisms in the context of a countrywide survey was not feasible, but as a result of the survey, improved mechanisms of support and reporting of violence against women are being developed.

We were strongly aware of our responsibility to ensure correct interpretation of our findings and their use in efforts to tackle the problem of abuse against women in Pakistan. Indeed, this was our only promise to the women who took part in the survey: that we would use the experiences they shared with us to try to help other women in the future. We would draw attention to the value—in ensuring use of findings to support interventions—of collecting information not only about the prevalence of violence against women but also about the factors that increase or decrease the risk. This allows an analysis of the possible benefits of actions aimed at decreasing the risk and allows planning for action to go beyond the laudable intention of "we must do something" to actual plans based on evidence of what might have the most impact (Andersson & Roche, 2006). We collected such information about potential risk factors and analyzed their actual relationships with the risk of violence and other forms of abuse. After taking account of the effects of other variables, we found that a woman was more likely to have experienced violence if she or her husband had no formal education, she was from a very poor household, she was married without her consent, the family had certain marriage practices such as polygamy and bride price, and if there was a family history of physical abuse. A woman who was in paid employment was actually slightly more likely to have experienced violence than a nonworking woman, and a woman who had experienced violence was more likely to believe that male violence against women could be justifiable. We used these findings, and others, to good effect in our presentations to different stakeholders. The details of the survey findings and our efforts to use the findings to promote action will be covered in separate papers.

The design and methods of this national survey produced, for the first time, a reliable estimate of the overall rate of violence and other forms of abuse experienced by women in Pakistan. Importantly,

we were also able to examine the factors that increased or decreased the risk of abuse in the overall population of women, and this formed the basis for the constructive discussions about the findings that followed.

References

Andersson, N., & Mhatre, S. (2003). Combating sexual violence in the south of Johannesburg. *South African Crime Quarterly, 3,* 5–9.

Andersson, N., & Roche, M. (2006). Gender and evidence-based planning: The CIET methods. *Development in Practice, 16,* 141–152.

Campbell, J. C. (2002). Health consequences of intimate partner violence. *Lancet, 359,* 1331–1336.

Cockcroft, A., Andersson, N., Omer, K., Ansari, N., Khan, A., & Chaudhry, U. U. (2003). *Social audit of governance and delivery of public services: Baseline survey 2002, national report.* Islamabad, Pakistan: National Reconstruction Bureau, CIET and CIDA. Available from http://www.ciet.org

Council for International Organizations of Medical Science. (1991). *International guidelines for ethical review of epidemiological studies.* Geneva: Author.

Ellsberg, M., & Heise, L. (2002). Bearing witness: Ethics in domestic violence research. *Lancet, 359,* 1599–1604.

Ellsberg, M., Heise, L., Pena, R., Agurto, S., & Winkvist, A. (2001). Researching domestic violence against women: Methodological and ethical considerations. *Studies in Family Planning, 32,* 1–16.

Ellsberg, M. C., Pena, R., Herrera, A., Liljestrand, J., & Winkvist, A. (1999). Wife abuse among women of childbearing age in Nicaragua. *American Journal of Public Health, 89,* 241–244.

Fanslow, J., & Robinson, E. (2004). Violence against women in New Zealand: Prevalence and health consequences. *New Zealand Medical Journal, 117*(1206), U1173.

Fikree, F. F., & Bhatti, L. I. (1999). Domestic violence and health of Pakistani women. *International Journal of Gynaecology and Obstetrics, 65,* 195–201.

Fikree, F. F., Jafarey, S. N., Korejo, R., Afshan, A., & Durocher, J. M. (2006). Intimate partner violence before and during pregnancy: Experiences of postpartum women in Karachi, Pakistan. *Journal of the Pakistan Medical Association, 56,* 252–257.

Garcia-Moreno, C., Jansen, H. A. F. M, Ellsberg, M., Heise, L., & Watts, C. H. (2006). Prevalence of intimate partner violence: Findings from the WHO Multi-Country Study on Women's Health and Domestic Violence. *Lancet, 368,* 1260–1269.

Heise, L. L., Raikes, A., Watts, C. H., & Zwi, A. B. (1994). Violence against women: A neglected public health issue in less developed countries. *Social Science and Medicine, 39,* 1165–1179.

Jewkes, R., Penn-Kekana, L., Levin, J., Ratsaka, M., & Schrieber, M. (2001). Prevalence of emotional, physical and sexual abuse of women in three South African provinces. *South African Medical Journal, 91,* 421–428.

Jewkes, R., Watts, C., Abrahams, N., Penn-Kekana, L., & Garcia-Moreno, C. (2000). Ethical and methodological issues in conducting research on gender-based violence in Southern Africa. *Reproductive Health Matters, 8,* 93–103.

Johnson, H. (1996). *Dangerous domains: Violence against women in Canada.* Toronto: Nelson.

Koss, M. P. (1993). Detecting the scope of rape: A review of prevalence research methods. *Journal of Interpersonal Violence, 8,* 198–222.

Krantz, G. (2002). Violence against women: A global public health issue. *Journal of Epidemiology and Community Health, 56,* 242–243.

Krug, E., Dahlberg, L. L., Mercy, J. A., Zwi, A., & Lozano, R. (2002). *World report on violence and health.* Geneva: World Health Organization.

Mhatre, S., Andersson, N., Ansari, N., & Omer, K. (2002). *Access to justice for women of Karachi: A pilot assessment.* Islamabad, Pakistan: CIET Canada. Available from http://www.ciet.org

Niaz, U. (2003). Violence against women in South Asian countries. *Archives of Women's Mental Health, 6,* 173–184.

Parker, B., & Ulrich, Y. (1990). A protocol of safety: Research on abuse of women. *Nursing Research, 39,* 248–250.

Piispa, M., & Heiskanen, M. (2005). Violence against women survey in Finland: Methodology and experiences. *Statistical Journal of the United Nations, ECE 22,* 255–263.

Posselt, H. (2005). Measuring violence against women in Australia. *Statistical Journal of the United Nations, ECE 22,* 239–253.

Rand, M. R., & Rennison, C. M. (2005). Bigger is not necessarily better: An analysis of violence against women estimates from the National Crime Victimization Survey and the National Violence Against Women Survey. *Journal of Quantitative Criminology, 21,* 267–290.

Schwartz, M. D. (2000). Methodological issues in the use of survey data for measuring and characterizing violence against women. *Violence Against Women, 6,* 815–838.

Smith, M. D. (1994). Enhancing the quality of survey data on violence against women: A feminist approach. *Gender & Society, 8,* 109–127.

Sorenson, S. B., Stein, J. A., Siegel, J. M., Golding J. M., & Burnham, M. A. (1987). The prevalence of adult sexual assault: The Los Angeles Epidemiologic Catchment Area Project. *American Journal of Epidemiology, 126,* 1154–1164.

Tjaden, P., & Thoennes, N. (2000). *Full report of the prevalence, incidence and consequences of violence against women: Findings from the National Violence Against Women Survey.* Washington, DC: National Institute of Justice and Centers for Disease Control and Prevention.

Walby, S., & Myhill, A. (2001). New survey methodologies in researching violence against women. *British Journal of Criminology, 41,* 502–522.

Watts, C., & Zimmerman, C. (2002). Violence against women: Global scope and magnitude. *Lancet, 359,* 1232–1237.

World Health Organization. (2001). *Putting women first: Ethical and safety recommendations for research on domestic violence against women.* Geneva: Author.

CHAPTER 4

Development of the Scale of Economic Abuse

Adrienne E. Adams, Cris M. Sullivan, Deborah Bybee, and Megan R. Greeson

Woman battering is a pervasive social problem perpetrated against millions of women in the United States each year (Tjaden & Thoennes, 2000). Battering involves a pattern of behavior, most often committed by men against women, that results in the perpetrator's gaining an advantage of power and control in the relationship (Dobash, Dobash, Wilson, & Daly, 1992; Johnson, 1995). Such behavior includes physical violence and the continued threat of such violence, but it also includes other forms of abuse—psychological (Arias & Pape, 1999; Follingstad, Rutledge, Berg, Hause, & Polek, 1990; Tolman, 1992), sexual (Bergen, 1996; Finkelhor & Yllo, 1985; Russell, 1990), and economic (Moe & Bell, 2004; Pence & Paymar, 1993; Raphael, 1996).

The consequences of battering on its victims can be quite severe. In addition to the physical injuries that women sustain as a result of physical assaults (Browne, 1993; Sutherland, Bybee, & Sullivan, 2002; Tjaden & Thoennes, 2000), ongoing experiences of physical abuse have deleterious effects on women's mental health. Researchers have consistently found high levels of depression, posttraumatic stress symptoms, suicidality, and substance abuse and dependence among women victimized by physically abusive partners (Cascardi, O'Leary, Lawrence, & Schlee, 1995; Golding, 1999; Khan, Welch, & Zillmer, 1993; McCauley et al., 1995; Vitanza, Vogel, & Marshall, 1995).

Evidence suggests that psychological forms of abuse may be equally as harmful, if not more so,

Adams, A. E., Sullivan, C. M., Bybee, D., & Greeson, M. R. (2008). Development of the Scale of Economic Abuse. *Violence Against Women, 14*, 563–588.

AUTHORS' NOTE: We would like to acknowledge the invaluable contributions of Dr. Rebecca Campbell, research assistants Tanya Anderson, Jillian Henry, Erin McIntosh, and Jessica Sanders, and the domestic abuse service providers who facilitated data collection. Most important, we wish to thank the women who volunteered to participate in this study, for it was their willingness to share their stories and experiences that made this project possible.

than physical forms of abuse. According to Follingstad and colleagues (1990), 72% of the abused women whom they interviewed attested that psychological abuse had a more severe impact on them than that wrought by the physical abuse. In another study, Orava, McLeod, and Sharpe (1996) found that when compared to nonabused women, abused women felt less personal power, were significantly more depressed, and had lower self-esteem. However, after controlling for the frequency of verbal abuse, most of the between-group differences were lost, suggesting that verbal abuse accounted for the differences between the two groups of women. Other studies examining the effects of psychological maltreatment have linked this form of abuse to an extensive range of behavioral and health outcomes, such as poor physical health, substance use, chronic disease, chronic mental illness, posttraumatic stress disorder, suicide ideation and attempts, depression, and low self-esteem (Aguilar & Nightingale, 1994; Arias & Pape, 1999; Cascardi et al., 1995; Coker, Smith, Bethea, King, & McKeown, 2000; Katz, Arias, & Beach, 2000; Khan et al., 1993; Marshall, 1996; Sackett & Saunders, 1999; Street & Arias, 2001; Vitanza et al., 1995).

In addition to experiencing physical violence and psychological abuse, approximately one third to one half of women in abusive relationships experience sexual abuse (Campbell, 1989; Hanneke, Shields, & McCall, 1986; Pagelow, 1992). This type of abuse includes physical sexual assaults as well as sexual exploitation and coercion (Bergen, 1996; Finkelhor & Yllo, 1985). The effects of sexual assault by an intimate partner include physical problems such as nausea, fatigue, bruising, and broken bones, as well as gynecological consequences such as infertility, bladder infections, and miscarriages (Adams, 1993; Bergen, 1996; Campbell & Alford, 1989). Women who are raped by their partners also suffer severe and long-term psychological consequences, such as anxiety, depression, and suicidal ideation (Frieze, 1983; Kilpatrick, Best, Saunders, & Vernon, 1988; Russell, 1990). This form of abuse

is particularly troubling given that it is characteristic of the most violent and dangerous abusive relationships (Browne, 1987; Campbell, 1989; Hanneke et al., 1986; Pagelow, 1992).

Although a great deal of research to date has examined the prevalence and consequences of physical, psychological, and sexual abuse, economic abuse has received far less attention from the scientific community. Economic abuse involves behaviors that control a woman's ability to acquire, use, and maintain economic resources, thus threatening her economic security and potential for self-sufficiency.

Preventing Women's Resource Acquisition

One significant way that abusive men interfere with a woman's ability to acquire resources is by preventing her from obtaining and maintaining employment. Research indicates that abusive men often forbid, discourage, and actively prevent their partners from working outside the home (Aguilar & Nightingale, 1994; Brewster, 2003; Curcio, 1997; Hudson & McIntosh, 1981; Riger, Ahrens, Blickenstaff, & Camacho, 1999; Sable, Libbus, & Huneke, 1999; Shepard & Pence, 1988; Tolman, 1989; Von De Linde, 2002; Walker, 1979). There is also evidence indicating that abusers actively interfere with their partners' ability to find employment. For example, Raphael (1996) described how abusive men sabotage their partners' efforts to find jobs by inflicting visible injuries, turning off the alarm clock, and refusing to provide child care to prevent their partners from attending job fairs and interviews.

In recent years, a growing body of research has documented abusive men's use of a variety of tactics to interfere with their partners' ability to sustain employment. For example, women interviewed by Riger, Ahrens, and Blickenstaff (2001) reported that their partners had interfered with their efforts to go to work, by sabotaging their cars, threatening and physically restraining them, failing to show up to care for their children, stealing their car keys and money, and refusing to give them a ride to work. These tactics as well as others, such as withholding medication, preventing sleep, cutting their hair, hiding their clothes, and inflicting injuries, have been reported elsewhere (Brandwein & Filiano, 2000; Brewster, 2003; Lloyd, 1997; Lloyd & Taluc, 1999; Moe & Bell, 2004; Raphael, 1996). Abusive men also interfere with their partners' ability to maintain employment by showing up at their partners' places of employment, harassing them with telephone calls throughout the work day, and harassing their coworkers (Lloyd, 1997; Lloyd & Taluc, 1999; Raphael, 1996; Riger et al., 2001). The impact of such work interference can be severe, including missed work days, loss of hours at work, and loss of a job (Sable et al., 1999; Shepard & Pence, 1988; Tolman & Wang, 2005).

In addition to demonstrating how abusive men prevent their partners from working, studies show that abusive men also interfere with their partners' efforts to take part in self-improvement activities aimed at increasing their marketability in the labor force and heightening their chance of obtaining a decent job. Interfering with educational pursuits is a common way that abusive men prevent self-improvement. In fact, researchers have consistently documented batterers' interference with their partners' ability to further their education, with the frequency of occurrence ranging from 23% (in one sample) to 62% (in another study; Anderson et al., 2003; Curcio, 1997; Riger et al., 1999; Shepard & Pence, 1988; Tolman, 1989).

In addition to revealing the interference that women experience as they attempt to obtain an education, job skills, and employment, evidence suggests that abusive men prevent women from acquiring income and assets by other means. For example, even if a woman is employed, her partner may demand that she hand over her paycheck, thus denying her from having her own money (Hofeller, 1982). Furthermore, abusive men may hinder a woman's acquiring money of her own by interfering with the receipt of other forms of support, such as child support, public assistance, disability payments, and education-based financial aid (Brewster, 2003; Moe & Bell, 2004; Ptacek, 1997). In addition to interfering with their partners' income, some abusive partners prevent women from acquiring assets by refusing to put their names on the deeds to their houses and on the titles of their cars and by not allowing them to have their own cars (Brewster, 2003).

Preventing Women's Resource Use

Another form of economic abuse involves preventing women from using resources that they already have. Specifically, abusive men exercise power by controlling how resources are distributed and by monitoring how they are used (Anderson et al., 2003; Brewster, 2003; Davies & Lyon, 1998; Dobash & Dobash, 1979; Hofeller, 1982; Martin, 1976).

Women in abusive relationships often report that their partners strictly limit their access to household resources. Some women are denied access to money even for necessities such as food, whereas others report that they are allotted a specific amount of money to be spent on household necessities and nothing more (Anderson et al., 2003; Coker et al., 2000; Davies & Lyon, 1998; Follingstad et al., 1990; Hofeller, 1982; Hudson & McIntosh, 1981; Pagelow, 1981; Pence & Paymar, 1993; Schechter & Gary, 1988; Tolman, 1989; Von De Linde, 2002; Walker, 1979). Women also report that, as opposed to their using money as necessary, their partners give them an allowance and make them ask for money when it is needed (Lloyd, 1997; Lloyd & Taluc, 1999; Pence & Paymar, 1993; Shepard & Campbell, 1992). Furthermore, studies show that abusive men hide jointly earned money, prevent their partners from having access to joint bank accounts, lie about shared assets, and withhold information about their finances (Brewster, 2003;

Coker et al., 2000; Pence & Paymar, 1993; Schechter & Gary, 1988; Von De Linde, 2002).

In addition to controlling how money is spent, abusive men dictate and monitor their partners' use of transportation. Women are prevented from using their cars and their shared transportation, whereas others have their access to transportation restricted (Ptacek, 1997; Rodenburg & Fantuzzo, 1993). One common way that abusive men restrict their partners' use of transportation is by taking the car keys or disabling the car (Martin, 1976; Rodenburg & Fantuzzo, 1993). All these tactics are instrumental in an abusive man's efforts to control his partner's ability to make use of her own or their shared economic resources.

Exploiting Women's Resources

In addition to dictating and monitoring how resources are used, some batterers intentionally deplete women's available resources, as a means of limiting their options. This can occur in a variety of ways, including stealing their partners' money, creating costs, and generating debt.

Anderson and colleagues (2003) reported on the frequency of stealing among a sample of 485 women who sought services from a domestic abuse advocacy program. They found that 38% of the women reported that their partners stole money from them. According to anecdotal reports from victim advocates, abusive men steal money from their partners through a variety of means. For example, an abusive man may take money from his partner's purse or wallet, steal her checkbook or ATM card and use it without permission, gamble with her money or their shared money, or demand that her money be put into a joint back account so that he can spend it freely (Anderson et al., 2003; Lloyd, 1997; Lloyd & Taluc, 1999; Pence & Paymar, 1993; Rodenburg & Fantuzzo, 1993; Schechter & Gary, 1988).

Women in abusive relationships also have a difficult time maintaining their economic resources when their partners engage in behaviors that generate costs. For example, research shows that abusive men steal, damage, and destroy their partners' possessions and household items (Brewster, 2003; Follingstad et al., 1990; Pearson, Thoennes, & Griswold, 1999; Ptacek, 1997; Rodenburg & Fantuzzo, 1993). They may also cause damage to their apartments, houses, and cars (Davies & Lyon, 1998; Rodenburg & Fantuzzo, 1993). Furthermore, women have reported that their partners have had their heat, electricity, and phone turned off (Anderson et al., 2003; Rodenburg & Fantuzzo, 1993). These tactics deplete women's economic resources in two ways: Not only do they lose the property they once had, but they also incur the costs to reinstate the utilities, replace the items, and repair the damage.

Finally, the exploitive control tactics employed by abusive men have been shown to interfere with a woman's ability to maintain economic resources by having debt generated in her name. Research suggests that some abusive men refuse to pay rent or make mortgage payments and refuse to pay other bills, thereby placing the responsibility and consequences on their partners (Brewster, 2003; Davies & Lyon, 1998; Ptacek, 1997). Another way that abusive men have been shown to generate debt for their partners is by obtaining credit cards in both partners' names and by using her credit card without her permission (Brewster, 2003). Thus, women in abusive relationships are at risk for accruing personal debt when shared resources are under her name or both names. In other words, abusive men take advantage of such a situation and use it as a means of threatening their partners' economic stability.

Effects of Experiencing Economic Abuse

Economic abuse can seriously impede women's economic, physical, and psychological health. One direct consequence of economic abuse is that the survivor becomes economically dependent on the abuser. Studies have consistently identified economic dependence as a critical obstacle for many women who are attempting to leave abusive partners (Aguirre, 1985; Gondolf & Fisher, 1988; Johnson, 1992; Okun, 1988; Strube & Barbour, 1983, 1984).

The lack of economic resources that economic abuse creates not only fosters economic dependence on an abuser but also threatens a woman's short-term and long-term economic health—and possibly her mental health. For women with limited economic resources, leaving an abusive relationship means having to face an uncertain economic future. Specifically, low-income women with abusive partners report a lack of resources needed for day-to-day survival, such as money, housing, child care, and transportation (Chalmers & Smith, 1984; Short et al., 2000). On top of that, many do not have the job skills and the wage-earning power to support themselves and their children (Labell, 1979). Women's options are further limited when their credit has been destroyed by an abusive partner, making it almost impossible to secure necessary resources such as housing (Correia & Rubin, 2001; Melbin, Sullivan, & Cain, 2003). Many women who do escape abusive relationships experience a decrease in their standards of living once they leave, ending up living in poverty, depending on government assistance, or becoming homeless (Barnett & LaViolette, 1993; Davis, 1999).

Economic abuse may also indirectly affect women's physical and psychological health. Studies have shown a strong relationship between the conditions of poverty and poor physical and psychological health (Brown & Moran, 1997; Lynch, Kaplan, & Shema, 1997; Stronks, Van de Mheen, Van den Bos, & Mackenbach, 1997). Low-income women who endure chronic sources of stress, such as substandard housing, inadequate food, and unstable income, have been shown to be at increased risk for depression, anxiety, chronic health problems, and poor general physical health (Dunn & Hayes, 2000; Hall, Williams, & Greenberg, 1985; McCallum, Arnold, & Bolland, 2002; McLeod & Kessler, 1990;

Stronks, Van de Mheen, & Mackenbach, 1998). Similarly, the health of women with an economically abusive partner may be compromised as they endure the stress associated with chronic economic deprivation and exploitation. This applies not only to women in economically abusive relationships but also to women who have left their abusive partners and are struggling to make ends meet on the few resources that they have available.

Current Study

Abusive men may employ a broad spectrum of economically abusive tactics in their attempts to maintain dominance and control over their partners, and these tactics have a detrimental impact on women's economic stability. The purpose of the present study was to develop a comprehensive measure that captures the economically abusive behaviors used by men who batter. A measure of economic abuse will enable researchers to examine the nature and extent of this form of abuse; the impact that it has on women's economic, physical, and mental health; and the implications that it has on women's ability to escape abusive partners. With a richer understanding of economic abuse, we can begin to develop interventions and tailor existing programming to the unique experiences and needs of women whose financial health has been compromised by an abusive partner.

Method

Initial Scale Construction

Items for the Scale of Economic Abuse (SEA) were initially derived from numerous sources, including the domestic violence literature and the knowledge and experience of domestic violence researchers, advocates, and survivors. Specifically, items were developed not only from a review of quantitative and qualitative studies that captured women's experiences with abusive partners but also from theoretical and anecdotal literature that described the control tactics used by abusive men. In addition, five measures of psychological abuse—the Psychological Maltreatment of Women Inventory (PMWI; Tolman, 1999), the Index of Spouse Abuse (Hudson & McIntosh, 1981), Index of Psychological Abuse (Sullivan, Parisian, & Davidson, 1991), Abuse Behavior Inventory (Shepard & Campbell, 1992), and the Measure of Wife Abuse (Rodenburg & Fantuzzo, 1993)—and the Interference With Work/School Scale (Riger et al., 2001) were examined for items that tapped economic abuse. Items were also generated with the assistance of three domestic violence advocates from a local domestic violence shelter program and two prominent domestic violence researchers. In addition, 12 survivors contributed to the development of the SEA items. Each woman completed an initial draft of the measure and suggested changes and additional items to be incorporated into the instrument.

This extensive process resulted in a measure consisting of 120 items that describe behaviors that control a woman's ability to acquire, use, and maintain economic resources. Women rated the frequency with which their partners had employed each of the economic abuse tactics according to a 5-point scale, ranging from 1 (*never*) to 5 (*quite often*). The scale also contains qualitative questions eliciting any additional forms of economic abuse that were experienced but not covered in the survey. Several experts, including survivors of intimate partner abuse, determined that the SEA had good face validity; that is, the SEA items appeared to capture economic abuse.

Measures

To help test the validity of the new measure, three additional instruments are contained in the interview. One is a widely used measure of psychological abuse, another a widely used measure of physical abuse, and one a measure of women's economic well-being.

PMWI. The short-version PMWI (Tolman, 1999) contains 14 items, and it was used to assess the degree of psychological abuse that women experienced in the last 6 months of their relationship. Women rated how frequently each of the 14 abusive acts occurred during the last 6 months of their relationship, on a scale ranging from 1 (*never*) to 5 (*very frequently*). Sample items include "My partner called me names" and "My partner told me my feelings were irrational or crazy." The PMWI has an internal consistency coefficient of .87.

Modified Conflict Tactics Scale. The Conflict Tactics Scale (CTS; Straus, 1979), as modified by Sullivan and colleagues (Sullivan, Tan, Basta, Rumptz, & Davidson, 1992), was used to assess the levels of violence that women experienced in the last 6 months of their relationships. The modified CTS is a 23-item measure that asks women to rate the frequency of each behavior during the last 6 months of their relationships, on a scale ranging from 1 (*never/none*) to 7 (*more than four times per week*). The types of physically abusive behaviors include "Pushed or shoved you" and "Choked or strangled you." This scale has demonstrated good internal consistency ($\alpha = .92$; Goodkind, Sullivan, & Bybee, 2004). In this sample, the reliability coefficient is .93.

Economic Hardship Index. Developed for this study, the Economic Hardship Index consists of 13 items designed to assess women's economic problems since the abusive relationship began. Examples of the yes–no items include "Have you had trouble buying food or other necessities for your family?" and "Have you had trouble with your credit rating?" The index has good internal consistency, with a Cronbach's alpha of .86. Participants were also asked to rate how much they thought that their partners had to do with their financial hardships (1 = *none/not at all*, 5 = *completely*).

Basic demographic data about participants were gathered within the interviews, including questions about race, age, education, employment status, number of children, income, and relationship status.

Procedure

To examine the psychometric properties of the new measure, face-to-face structured interviews were conducted with 103 women who were receiving residential and/or nonresidential services from one of five domestic abuse victim service agencies in a Midwestern state. Highly trained interviewers informed women of the study and invited them to participate. Women were assured that their decision to participate in the study would have no impact on their receipt of services from the agency. Given that the initial hours after leaving one's home and entering a shelter program can be an emotionally and physically exhausting time, shelter residents were not approached until they had been in shelter at least 24 hours.

The majority of interviews were conducted at the agencies in private rooms after informed consent was obtained. A few women opted to be interviewed at home. Interviews were tape-recorded to ensure coding accuracy, if permission was granted. Women were compensated $10 for participating. Interviews lasted 1 hour on average.

Results

Participants

Participants ranged in age from 18 years to 85, with an average age of 35 ($SD = 10.4$). Overall, 48% of the women were African American, 45% White, 5% Hispanic/Latina, and 1% Asian American. Furthermore, 88% of the women had completed high school and/or college. At the time of the interview, 63% of the women were unemployed; 21% had a full-time job; and 16%

were employed part-time. Over half the women (57%) reported an annual family income of less than $15,000, whereas 20% lived in a household earning between $15,000 and $30,000 and 23% reported more than $30,000 in family income per year.

The average woman in the sample had been involved with her abusive partner for 8 years and had two minor children. At the time that the abuse occurred, 81% of the women were living with their partners; 30% of whom were married. Demographics are reported in Table 4.1.

All the women had experienced psychological abuse, and 98% had suffered physical abuse during the last 6 months of their relationships. Similarly, 99% of the women had experienced economic abuse at some point during their relationships. The types of physical abuse most commonly experienced included pushing and shoving (82%) and grabbing (79%), whereas the most frequently reported forms of psychological abuse included yelling and screaming (99%) and name-calling (98%). Over half the women had been sexually assaulted (57%), and 65% had been strangled by their intimate partners.

Final Scale Construction

The goal in constructing the final SEA was to create an instrument that was brief, reflective of a broad range of economically abusive tactics, and widely applicable to respondents. Toward this end, several criteria were used to guide the scale construction process. As an initial criterion, the applicability of the items was considered; items that were not applicable to more than 25% of women in the sample were removed. In total, 37 items were removed because of inapplicability, including all items pertaining to school interference and items making reference to children. Once these items were removed, the expectation maximization method was used to provide estimates for the remaining missing data, to facilitate psychometric analysis with the full sample. Expectation maximization is a commonly used

Table 4.1 Demographics of the Sample (in Percentages)

Demographics	%
Age	
18–24	15
25–34	36
35–44	32
45–54	13
55 and over	4
Race	
African American/Black	48
Caucasian/White	45
Hispanic/Latina	5
Asian American	1
Other	1
Education	
Some high school	22
High school/GED	29
Some college	32
College graduate/trade school	17
Employment	
Unemployed	63
Employed part time	16
Employed full time	21
Income	
Under $5,000	25
$5,001–$15,000	32
$15,001–$30,000	20

Demographics	%
$30,001–$50,000	8
$50,001 and over	15
Children	
None	21
1	19
2–3	45
4 and over	14
Relationship status	
Married and living together	30
Ex-partner/divorced	5
Girlfriend/boyfriend and living together	50
Girlfriend/boyfriend but not living together	12
Other	3
Length of relationship	
Less than 1 year	13
13 months–5 years	39
61 months–10 years	22
121 months–15 years	12
Over 15 years	13

NOTE: $N = 103$.

method for estimating missing data (Schafer & Graham, 2002). In this sample, the expectation maximization method was used to estimate 4% of the values in the data matrix. Little's Missing Completely at Random (2002) test was nonsignificant ($p = 1.00$) indicating that the pattern of missing data was not significantly different from a random pattern and providing support for handling the missing values as "ignorable."

Once the missing values were estimated, the following criteria were used to reduce the pool of remaining items: item clarity, psychometric properties of items, and adequate coverage of the economic abuse dimensions. First, items were removed if they had been unclear or difficult for women to answer. For example, many women in the sample expressed difficulty responding to items that were not easily quantified according to frequency of occurrence, such as being prevented from getting a credit card or a vehicle of one's own. Second, item-total correlations and item means and standard deviations were taken into account in selecting items. For example, items with the highest item-total correlations were retained for further analysis, whereas items were removed if they had exceptionally low item-total correlations and/or were conceptually and empirically redundant with better performing items. A third criterion to reduce the scale items included the conceptual contribution of each item. Specifically, to ensure that the final scale represented a range of economically abusive tactics, the unique conceptual contribution of each remaining item was taken into account. Overall, this process resulted in the removal of an additional 54 items.

Principal components analysis (PCA) with oblique rotation was then used with the remaining 29 items to determine the underlying factor structure of the SEA. Oblique rotation was used because it was expected that any emerging factors would be correlated. Before performing the PCA, data suitability for factor analysis was assessed. Examination of the correlation matrix revealed the presence of many coefficients of .30 or higher. The Kaiser-Meyer-Oklin value was .87, exceeding the recommended value of .60 (Kaiser, 1974), and Bartlett's Test of Sphericity (1954) reached statistical significance, supporting the factorability of the correlation matrix.

The PCA began with a review of the originally proposed theoretical framework, which defined economic abuse as behaviors that control a woman's ability to acquire, use, and maintain economic resources. Through the data collection process, it became clear that the guiding theoretical framework appeared accurate, at least anecdotally. Women's experiences of economic abuse tended to involve control over their access to and use of resources, as well as economic exploitation that compromised resource maintenance. Thus, following Tabachnick and Fidell's recommendation (1996) that PCA be used to find a satisfactory solution with as few factors as possible that are consistent with the proposed theoretical framework, a three-factor solution was examined. Eleven items loaded highly onto the first factor; 11 items loaded highly onto the second factor; 4 items loaded highly onto the third factor; and 3 items loaded moderately onto two factors. The first factor accounted for 34.5% of the variance and included items that pertained to control over access to and use of resources. The second factor accounted for 10.8% of the variance and comprised items capturing economically exploitive tactics. The third factor accounted for 6.8% of the variance and comprised all the items pertaining to work interference.

For comparison purposes, a second PCA was performed but with two factors extracted. The two-factor solution revealed a clearer pattern, with most variables loading substantially onto only one component. Seventeen items loaded onto the first factor, which consisted of all the items involving actions that control access to and use of resources, and 11 items loaded onto the second factor, which included all of the economic exploitation items. One item, "Loan out your money or your shared money without your permission and/or knowledge," loaded moderately onto both factors. This item was dropped, and the analysis was rerun with the item excluded. In the end, the SEA consisted of 28 items containing two subscales: a 17-item Economic Control subscale, accounting for 34% of the variance, and an 11-item Economic Exploitation subscale, accounting for 11% of the variance (see Appendix for the final measure).

Reliability of the Scale

The internal consistency of the SEA was assessed by examining the Cronbach's alpha coefficient and item-total correlations of the total scale and each of the two subscales. The total SEA had a reliability coefficient of .93, with corrected item-total correlations ranging from .31 to .69. The

Economic Control and Economic Exploitation subscales also showed good internal consistency, with alpha coefficients of .91 and .89, respectively. The corrected item-total correlations of the Economic Control subscale ranged from .44 to .72, whereas the coefficients of the Economic Exploitation subscale ranged from .54 to .71.

To check the magnitude of cross-scale loadings, each item was correlated with the two subscales. As presented in Table 4.2, this analysis revealed that all the economic control items were more highly correlated with the Economic Control subscale than with the Economic Exploitation subscale, and all the economic exploitation items were more highly correlated with the Economic Exploitation subscale than with the Economic Control subscale. With the exception of two economic control items ("Do things to keep you from going to your job" and "Beat you up if you said you needed to go to work"), the economic control and economic exploitation items were more highly correlated with their own subscales than with the measures of physical or psychological abuse. Taken together, the factor analysis and correlational analyses strongly supported the existence of two distinct subscales.

Table 4.2 Item-Total and Item-Scale Correlations for Scale of Economic Abuse (SEA)

Economic Control	Control	Exploit	SEA	Physical	Psych
1. Steal the car keys or take the car so you couldn't go look for a job or go to a job interview.	.552**	.321**	.515**	.283**	.349**
2. Do things to keep you from going to your job.	.441**	.345**	.458**	.448**	.485**
3. Beat you up if you said you needed to go to work.	.453**	.285**	.435**	.546**	.243*
4. Threaten you to make you leave work.	.483**	.203*	.411**	.469**	.213*
5. Demand that you quit your job.	.541**	.219*	.559**	.369**	.350**
6. Do things to keep you from having money of your own.	.625**	.316**	.559**	.253**	.436**
7. Take your paycheck, financial aid check, tax refund check, disability payment, or other support payments from you.	.632**	.528**	.676**	.469**	.342**
8. Decide how you could spend money rather than letting you spend it how you saw fit.	.722**	.449**	.690**	.404**	.481**
9. Demand to know how money was spent.	.680**	.387**	.631**	.301**	.463**

(Continued)

(Continued)

Economic Control	Control	Exploit	SEA	Physical	Psych
10. Demand that you give him receipts and/or change when you spent money.	.612**	.272**	.525**	.314**	.372**
11. Keep you from having the money you needed to buy food, clothes, or other necessities.	.637**	.417**	.619**	.272**	.419**
12. Hide money so that you could not find it.	.605**	.317**	.546**	.316**	.289**
13. Keep you from having access to your bank accounts.	.569**	.338**	.535**	.382**	.241*
14. Keep financial information from you.	.603**	.236*	.501**	.167	.332**
15. Make important financial decisions without talking with you about it first.	.608**	.345**	.563**	.224*	.402**
16. Make you ask him for money.	.595**	.267**	.514**	.245*	.395**
17. Threaten you or beat you up for paying the bills or buying things that were needed.	.521**	.358**	.516**	.363**	.365**
Economic Exploitation					
1. Take money from your purse, wallet, or bank account without your permission and/or knowledge.	.438**	.633**	.594**	.518**	.411**
2. Force you to give him money or let him use your checkbook, ATM card, or credit card.	.508**	.641**	.648**	.431**	.295**
3. Steal your property.	.348**	.607**	.519**	.433**	.428**
4. Pay bills late or not pay bills that were in your name or in both of your names.	.469**	.637**	.618**	.318**	.429**
5. Build up debt under your name by doing things like use your credit card or run up the phone bill.	.246*	.577**	.435**	.388**	.215*
6. Refuse to get a job so you had to support your family alone.	.089	.537**	.309**	.246*	.104
7. Gamble with your money or your shared money.	.430**	.580**	.566**	.406**	.254**
8. Have you ask your family or friends for money but not let you pay them back.	.421**	.620**	.577**	.329**	.290**

Economic Control	Control	Exploit	SEA	Physical	Psych
9. Convince you to lend him money but not pay it back.	.269**	.650**	.483**	.268**	.265**
10. Pawn your property or your shared property.	.412**	.614**	.568**	.467**	.257**
11. Spend the money you needed for rent or other bills.	.346**	.713**	.565**	.336**	.261**

$*p < .05. **p < .01.$

Scale Validity

Correlation and regression analyses were used to examine the construct validity of the SEA. Table 4.3 depicts the correlations among the entire SEA; the two SEA subscales; the measures of physical abuse, psychological abuse, and economic hardship; and the demographic variables of age, race (dichotomously coded as 1 = White, 2 = non-White), and income. The correlation between the subscales was significant but of moderate strength ($r = .51$), indicating that although related, the subscales measure unique constructs. In addition, the SEA was not significantly correlated with age, race, or income. In fact, the correlations were all quite low. The lack of correlation between these demographic characteristics and the SEA suggests that the SEA shows no bias across these dimensions.

Table 4.3 Correlations Among Scale of Economic Abuse (SEA), Abuse, Economic Hardship, and Demographic Variables Demonstrating Scale Validity

	SEA	Control	Exploit	Physical	Psych	EHI	Age	Race	Income
SEA	1.000								
Control	.905**	1.000							
Exploit	.830**	.514**	1.000						
Physical	.608**	.524**	.540**	1.000					
Psych	.575**	.562**	.422**	.417**	1.000				
EHI	.523**	.403**	.527**	.194	.208*	1.000			
Age	−.156	−.110	−.169	−.085	−.054	−.188	1.000		
Race	−.158	−.085	−.177	.022	−.193	−.183	−.118	1.000	
Income	−.090	−.043	−.124	−.187	−.081	−.162	.374**	−.171	1.000

NOTE: $N = 103$. EHI = Economic Hardship Index.

$*p < .05. **p < .01.$

The SEA was positively correlated with the modified CTS ($r = .61$, $p < .01$) and the PMWI ($r = .58$, $p < .01$), indicating that higher levels of economic abuse are significantly related to higher levels of physical and psychological abuse. The correlation between the SEA subscales and the modified CTS and the PMWI were also positive and significant. Specifically, the Economic Control subscale was positively correlated with physical abuse ($r = .52$, $p < .01$) and psychological abuse ($r = .56$, $p < .01$), indicating that the more physical and psychological abuse that a woman experienced, the more that her partner controlled her access to and use of economic resources. Similarly, the positive correlation between the Economic Exploitation subscale of the SEA and the modified CTS ($r = .54$, $p < .01$) and the PMWI ($r = .42$, $p < .01$) suggests that the women who suffered higher levels of physical and psychological abuse were more economically exploited by their partners. Although the correlations between the measures of physical and psychological abuse and the SEA were all positive, the fact that they were of only moderate strength (ranging from .42 to .61) is evidence that economic abuse is a unique construct in need of a separate measure.

The construct validity of the SEA was further examined by assessing the relationship between the SEA and economic hardship. It was expected that higher economic abuse would be related to more economic problems. The Economic Hardship Index was derived from a pool of 24 items assessing the degree of economic difficulty experienced by survivors of abuse since their relationships with their abusers began. After reliability analysis, 11 of the 24 items were removed because of low item-total correlations. The resulting 13-item scale demonstrated good internal consistency, with an alpha coefficient of .86. As Table 4.4 illustrates, the women in the sample had experienced a range of economic problems since their relationships began. For example, the majority of the women struggled to find and maintain affordable housing. Specifically, 80% of

women indicated that they had had trouble finding an affordable place to live, whereas 86% had to stay with family or friends or in a shelter because they could not find a place of their own. Also, over half (52%) of the women had been evicted or had a house foreclosed. In addition to having housing problems, many of the women had trouble paying their bills and providing food and other necessities for their families. In fact, 53% of the women had gone as far as pawning or selling their property so that they could pay bills and provide food for their families, and 61% had had their telephone, electricity, and other utilities shut off.

Correlation analysis revealed a significant positive relationship between economic abuse and economic hardship ($r = .52$, $p < .01$). The Economic Control subscale of the SEA had a significant positive correlation with economic hardship ($r = .40$, $p < .01$), indicating that the women whose access to and use of resources are controlled by their abusive partners tend to experience a greater amount of financial hardship. The Economic Exploitation subscale was also significantly correlated with economic hardship ($r = .53$, $p < .01$), meaning that women whose economic resources are more seriously compromised as a result of their partners' actions tend to experience a higher degree of financial difficulty (see Table 4.3).

Hierarchical multiple regression was used to explore the relationship between economic problems and economic abuse. Specifically, three models were tested to examine the unique contribution of each SEA subscale, as well as the total SEA, to predict women's economic hardship, after controlling for the effects of women's demographic characteristics (age, race, and income) and levels of physical and psychological abuse.

Model 1 regressed the economic hardship scores onto the Economic Control subscale of the SEA. As shown in Table 4.5, independent variables were entered in four blocks. Controlling for the effects of the women's age, race, and income (Block 1), their levels of physical and

Table 4.4 Psychometric Properties and Item Frequencies for the Economic Hardship Index

Scale Item: Retained Items	M	SD	CITC	%
1. Have you had trouble finding an apartment or house you could afford?	.80	.41	.54	80
2. Have you had to stay with friends or family or in a shelter because you could not find a place to live?	.86	.34	.42	86
3. Have you had trouble getting a house, apartment, vehicle, or credit card because of your credit?	.83	.37	.46	84
4. Have you been evicted from a place you were renting or had your house foreclosed?	.51	.50	.57	52
5. Has your landlord ever threatened to evict you because you could not pay your rent?	.52	.50	.65	52
6. Have you had trouble buying food or other necessities for your family?	.73	.45	.54	73
7. Have you had to borrow money to pay rent or other bills because you did not have the money to pay them when they were due?	.80	.41	.49	80
8. Have you asked a community agency for help to pay your rent or other bills?	.75	.44	.55	75
9. Have you sold or pawned your property because you needed money for rent, bills, or other necessities?	.53	.50	.49	53
10. Have you been harassed by people/businesses you owe money to?	.70	.46	.51	70
11. Have you had trouble with your credit rating?	.81	.40	.49	81
12. Has your telephone, electricity, or other utilities ever been turned off?	.61	.49	.65	61
13. Has your credit rating made it difficult to get a phone?	.51	.50	.51	52

NOTE: 0 = *no*, 1 = *yes*; CITC = corrected item-total correlation.

a = .86, M = 9.0, SD = 3.6

psychological abuse (Block 2), and their degrees of economic exploitation in their relationships (Block 3), Model 1 tested whether economic control (Block 4) significantly predicted economic hardship.

This model accounted for 37% of the variance ($R^2 = .373$) in the economic hardship scores. The beta value associated with the economic exploitation variable was .503 ($p < .05$), indicating that women who scored one standard deviation

Table 4.5 Summary of Multiple Regression Predicting Economic Hardship (Model 1)

Predictors	Standardized b	t	R^2 Change
Block 1			
Age	−.062	−.69	.095
Race	−.139	−.136	
Income	−1.63	−1.51	
Block 2			
Physical abuse	−.203	−1.91	.034
Psychological abuse	−.118	−1.16	
Block 3			
Exploitation subscale	.503*	4.84*	.203*
Block 4			
Control subscale	.280**	2.52**	.042**
Total R^2	.373		
Total F	7.53*		

NOTE: Coefficients were from the final block, with all the variables in the model.

*$p < .001$. **$p < .05$.

higher on economic exploitation had, on average, scored a half standard deviation higher (.503) on economic hardship. The R^2 change attributed to the addition of the Economic Exploitation sub-scale was .203, significant at $p < .001$, indicating that exploitation accounted for an additional 20% of the variance in economic problems after the effects of age, race, and income and physical and psychological abuse had been removed.

For economic control, beta was .28, indicating that women who scored one standard deviation higher on economic control had, on average, scored about a quarter standard deviation (.28) higher on economic hardship. The R^2 change after the addition of the Economic Control sub-scale to the model was .042, significant at $p < .05$,

meaning that economic control accounted for 4% of the variance in economic hardship scores, after the effects of age, race, income, physical and psychological abuse, and economic exploitation were removed.

Model 2 reversed the entry order of the two SEA subscales, with economic exploitation being added last to examine the unique contribution of the Economic Exploitation subscale. In this model, after the effects of demographics, physical and psychological abuse, and economic control were taken into account, economic exploitation accounted for an additional 15.5% of the variance in economic hardship scores (R^2 change = .155, $p < .001$). Furthermore, examination of the beta coefficients associated with the Economic

Control subscale ($\beta = .280$) and the Economic Exploitation subscale ($\beta = .503$) revealed that economic exploitation made the strongest unique contribution to the prediction of economic difficulties.

In addition to examining the unique contribution of each SEA subscale to the prediction of economic hardship, a third model was tested to assess the predictive power of the total SEA. Variables for Model 3 were entered in three blocks: The demographic variables (age, race, and income) were entered as controls in the first block; physical and psychological abuse were entered as controls in the second block; and the SEA was entered in the third block. This model accounted for approximately 35% of the variance ($R^2 = .348$) in economic hardship scores. Beta was .674, indicating that women who scored one standard deviation higher on economic abuse scored, on average, .67 standard deviations higher on economic difficulties. The R^2 change attributed to the addition of the SEA was .219, significant at $p < .001$, meaning that economic abuse accounted for about 22% of the variance in economic hardship scores, after the effects of age, race, income, and physical and psychological abuse were removed.

Discussion

The findings of this study provide evidence for the reliability and validity of the SEA as an instrument to measure economic abuse as a distinct form of abuse. This scale is unique in that it is the first to tap a range of economically abusive tactics as a means of assessing the degree of economic abuse experienced in an abusive relationship. Whereas previous measures of abuse include a limited number of items tapping economic abuse or focus on one form of economic abuse, the SEA includes 28 items, 17 of which capture behaviors that control a woman's access to and use of resources and 11 that capture economically exploitive behaviors. These two dimensions, economic control and economic

exploitation, have been shown to be meaningfully distinct and useful for predicting the degree of economic hardship experienced by women with abusive partners. The SEA will be useful for gaining a complete picture of the ways in which economic abuse affects women's lives. Such information is needed to inform the development of interventions tailored to meet the unique needs of women affected by economic abuse.

This study also confirmed the need for a scale of economic abuse. Specifically, all the women interviewed had suffered psychological abuse; 98% had experienced physical abuse during the last 6 months of their relationships; and an astounding 99% of the women were subjected to some form of economic abuse at some point during their relationships. In other words, almost every woman had been involved with a partner who controlled her use of or access to economic resources and/or took advantage of her economically. These findings provide evidence that economic abuse is a distinct yet common form of harm experienced by women in abusive relationships. Furthermore, these findings empirically demonstrate that economic abuse is a significant component of the broad system of tactics used by abusive men to gain power and maintain control over their partners. Thus, additional research is warranted to examine the ways in which women experience economic abuse and the consequences that this form of abuse has on women's lives.

The findings of this study have important implications for practitioners who work with survivors of intimate partner abuse. This study provides evidence of a link between the abuse that women experience and the economic hardships that they face. Before participating in the interviews, many women had not made this connection between their financial difficulties and their partners' actions. Consequently, the interview process served as an awakening for many of the women. Their reactions to this realization ranged from sadness to outrage. Some shared feelings of self-blame, whereas others communicated a sense of relief in this new perspective. Most expressed frustration with the short-term implications and potential long-term consequences that they were to endure. They wanted answers; they wanted justice; they wanted something to be done.

This is where the work of specially trained practitioners is vital. Advocates play a central role in educating women about the system of abusive tactics used by batterers, as well as assisting women with their immediate financial needs. As shown, these issues are closely connected. Thus, it is important for practitioners to understand and attend to the various contextual factors contributing to women's financial difficulties. Educational and advocacy efforts should be focused at both the individual level and the community. At the individual level, advocates can help women understand the impact of the abuse on their financial standing and work to garner resources and restore their economic health. At the community level, practitioners can advocate in the community with and on behalf of women whose financial health has been compromised by abusive partners—for example, by intervening with employers, utility companies, landlords, community organizations, and financial institutions in an effort to improve how the system responds to women with economically abusive partners.

Findings need to be considered in light of the study's limitations. The majority of the women in the sample were either African American or White. They were primarily low-income women, and all were heterosexual and receiving services from a domestic abuse organization. As a result, the findings do not necessarily reflect the experiences of other groups of women. For example, it is possible that the nature and consequences of economic abuse differ for women from ethnic minority groups, middle- to high-income earners, women with disabilities, lesbian women, and informal help-seeking women. Additional studies of economic abuse involving more diverse samples of women are needed to understand the unique experiences of various groups of women and to assess the validity of the SEA.

The low-income status of the majority of women in this sample raises an additional concern. With more than three quarters of the women reporting a family income of under $20,000, one question involves whether the financial hardships reported on the Economic Hardship Index represent chronic financial problems stemming from insufficient income rather than economic abuse. However, the empirical findings of this study and the women's personal accounts strongly support the relationship between economic hardship and economic abuse. After responding to the economic hardship items, respondents were asked what they attributed their financial difficulties to: Only 5% of the women stated that their partners were not at all responsible for their financial difficulties, whereas 76% stated that their partners were very much or completely responsible for the economic hardships that they had faced. Correlation analyses showed that the level of economic abuse experienced was significantly correlated with the women's attribution of their economic struggles to their partners ($r = .296$, $p < .01$). In other words, women who experienced higher levels of economic abuse placed greater responsibility for their economic hardships on their abusers. However, because the study is based on cross-sectional data, a causal link between economic abuse and economic difficulties cannot be inferred. Longitudinal studies that examine the effects of economic abuse are needed.

In addition, the sample was limited in the number of women who had attended or attempted to attend school and in the number of women who had children in common with the abuser. The underrepresentation on these characteristics resulted in the exclusion of all items pertaining to school interference and tactics involving children. Thus, although the SEA captures a range of economically abusive tactics, it is missing these important types of economic abuse. This omission is potentially significant, given the frequency with which school interference and abuse tactics involving children are discussed in the literature (Anderson et al., 2003; Curcio, 1997; Moe & Bell, 2004; Ptacek, 1997; Raphael, 1996; Riger et al., 2001; Shepard & Pence, 1988; Tolman, 1989; Tolman & Raphael,

1997) and cited by practitioners and survivors. Accordingly, such tactics need to be taken into consideration in future studies examining economic abuse.

The most significant limitation of the study stems from an inconsistency in the time frames used as reference points for the respondents' reports of their experiences of abuse and economic difficulties. All the women reported their economic hardship and economic abuse from the time that their relationships began with their abusive partners. In comparison, the occurrence of physical and psychological abuse was reported for the last 6 months of their relationships. It is possible that there were differences in the physical and psychological abuse that women experienced earlier in the relationships—that is, before the 6-month time frame. Such differences may have changed the women's scores on the PMWI and CTS, thus affecting the relationship between these measures and economic abuse and economic hardship. Although this inconsistent time frame is not ideal, it was necessary given the nature of the economic abuse items. Specifically, many of the original economic abuse items capture events that occur with low regularity (e.g., signing a lease, buying a car); thus, the application of a 6-month time frame would not capture women's full experiences of economic abuse within their relationships. However, the significance of this limitation is minimized in the final scale, with the majority of items tapping events that would regularly occur. Future research could determine whether the use of a more specified time frame more effectively captures women's experiences of economic abuse as measured by the SEA.

Despite these limitations, this study represents an important step toward gaining a full understanding of the complexity of intimate partner abuse. Women not only experience physical, psychological, and sexual forms of abuse but are economically terrorized and controlled by their abusive partners. The nature and frequency of economic abuse deserves examination, as does the impact that this form of abuse has on women's short- and long-term well-being. Such information can be used to develop interventions and garner resources for use by women whose physical, emotional, and economic health has been compromised by an economically controlling and exploitive partner.

Appendix: Scale of Economic Abuse

Directions: I'm going to go through a list of things some men do to hurt their partner or ex-partner financially. Could you tell me, to the best of your recollection, how frequently your partner or ex-partner has done any of the following things since your relationship began?

1 = never, 2 = hardly ever, 3 = sometimes, 4 = often, 5 = quite often, 8 = not applicable, 9 = prefer not to answer

1. Steal the car keys or take the car so you couldn't go look for a job or go to a job interview.

2. Do things to keep you from going to your job.

3. Beat you up if you said you needed to go to work.

4. Threaten you to make you leave work.

5. Demand that you quit your job.

6. Make you ask him for money.

7. Take money from your purse, wallet, or bank account without your permission and/or knowledge.

8. Force you to give him money or let him use your checkbook, ATM card, or credit card.

9. Steal your property.

10. Do things to keep you from having money of your own.

11. Take your paycheck, financial aid check, tax refund check, disability payment, or other support payments from you.

12. Decide how you could spend money rather than letting you spend it how you saw fit.

13. Demand to know how money was spent.

14. Demand that you give him receipts and/or change when you spent money.

15. Keep you from having the money you needed to buy food, clothes, or other necessities.

16. Hide money so that you could not find it.

17. Gamble with your money or your shared money.

18. Have you ask your family or friends for money but not let you pay them back.

19. Convince you to lend him money but not pay it back.

20. Keep you from having access to your bank accounts.

21. Keep financial information from you.

22. Make important financial decisions without talking with you about it first.

23. Threaten you or beat you up for paying the bills or buying things that were needed.

24. Spend the money you needed for rent or other bills.

25. Pay bills late or not pay bills that were in your name or in both of your names.

26. Build up debt under your name by doing things like use your credit card or run up the phone bill.

27. Refuse to get a job so you had to support your family alone.

28. Pawn your property or your shared property.

References

Adams, C. (1993). I just raped my wife! What are you going to do about it, pastor? In E. Buchwald, P. Fletcher, & M. Roth (Eds.), *Transforming a rape culture* (pp. 57–86). Minneapolis, MN: Milkweed Editions.

Aguilar, R. J., & Nightingale, N. N. (1994). The impact of specific battering experiences on the self-esteem of abused women. *Journal of Family Violence, 9*, 35–45.

Aguirre, B. E. (1985). Why do they return? Abused wives in shelters. *Social Work, 30*, 350–354.

Anderson, M. A., Gillig, P. M., Sitaker, M., McCloskey, K., Malloy, K., & Grigsby, N. (2003). "Why doesn't she just leave?" A descriptive study of victim-reported impediments to her safety. *Journal of Family Violence, 18*, 151–155.

Arias, I., & Pape, K. T. (1999). Psychological abuse: Implications for adjustment and commitment to leave violent partners. *Violence and Victims, 14*, 55–67.

Barnett, O. W., & LaViolette, A. D. (1993). *It could happen to anyone: Why battered women stay.* Newbury Park, CA: Sage.

Bartlett, M. S. (1954). A note on the multiplying factors for various chi square approximations. *Journal of the Royal Statistical Society, 16*, 296–298.

Bergen, R. K. (1996). *Wife rape: Understanding the response of survivors and service providers.* Thousand Oaks, CA: Sage.

Brandwein, R. A., & Filiano, D. M. (2000). Toward real welfare reform: The voices of battered women. *Affilia, 15*, 224–243.

Brewster, M. P. (2003). Power and control dynamics in prestalking and stalking situations. *Journal of Family Violence, 18*, 207–217.

Brown, G. W., & Moran, P. M. (1997). Single mothers, poverty and depression. *Psychological Medicine, 27*, 21–33.

Browne, A. (1987). *When battered women kill.* New York: Free Press.

Browne, A. (1993). Violence against women by male partners: Prevalence, outcomes, and policy implications. *American Psychologist, 48*, 1077–1087.

Campbell, J. C. (1989). Women's responses to sexual abuse in intimate relationships. *Health Care for Women International, 10*, 335–346.

Campbell, J. C., & Alford, P. (1989). The dark consequences of marital rape. *American Journal of Nursing, 89*, 946–949.

Cascardi, M., O'Leary, K. D., Lawrence, E. E., & Schlee, K. A. (1995). Characteristics of women physically abused by their spouses and who seek treatment regarding marital conflict. *Journal of Consulting and Clinical Psychology, 63,* 616–623.

Chalmers, L., & Smith, P. (1984). Wife battering: Psychological, social, and physical isolation and counteracting strategies. *Review of Canadian Studies, 1,* 221–244.

Coker, A. L., Smith, P. H., Bethea, L., King, M. R., & McKeown, R. E. (2000). Physical health consequences of physical and psychological intimate partner violence. *Archives of Family Medicine, 9,* 451–457.

Correia, A., & Rubin, J. (2001). *Housing and battered women: A case study of domestic violence programs in Iowa.* Retrieved February 7, 2008, from http://new.vawnet.org/category/Main_Doc.php?docid=106

Curcio, W. (1997). *The Passaic County study of AFDC recipients in a welfare-to-work program: A preliminary analysis.* Ann Arbor: University of Michigan.

Davies, J., & Lyon, E. (1998). *Safety planning with battered women.* Thousand Oaks, CA: Sage.

Davis, M. F. (1999). The economics of abuse: How violence perpetuates women's poverty. In R. A. Brandwein (Ed.), *Battered women, children, and welfare reform: The ties that bind* (pp. 17–30). Thousand Oaks, CA: Sage.

Dobash, R. E., & Dobash, R. (1979). *Violence against wives: A case against the patriarchy.* New York: Free Press.

Dobash, R., Dobash, R. E., Wilson, M., & Daly, M. (1992). The myth of sexual symmetry in marital violence. *Social Problems, 39,* 71–91.

Dunn, J. R., & Hayes, M. V. (2000). Social inequality, population health, and housing: A study of two Vancouver neighborhoods. *Social Science and Medicine, 51,* 563–587.

Finkelhor, D., & Yllo, K. (1985). *License to rape: Sexual abuse of wives.* New York: Holt, Rinehart, & Winston.

Follingstad, D. R., Rutledge, L. L., Berg, B. J., Hause, E. S., & Polek, D. S. (1990). The role of emotional abuse in physically abusive relationships. *Journal of Family Violence, 5,* 107–120.

Frieze, I. (1983). Investigating the causes and consequences of marital rape. *Signs, 8,* 532–533.

Golding, J. M. (1999). Intimate partner violence as a risk factor for mental disorders: A meta-analysis. *Journal of Family Violence, 14,* 99–132.

Gondolf, E. W., & Fisher, E. R. (1988). *Battered women as survivors: An alternative to treating learned helplessness.* Lexington, MA: Lexington Books.

Goodkind, J. R., Sullivan, C. M., & Bybee, D. I. (2004). A contextual analysis of battered women's safety planning. *Violence Against Women, 10,* 514–533.

Hall, L. A., Williams, C. A., & Greenberg, R. S. (1985). Supports, stressors, and depressive symptoms in low-income mothers of young children. *American Journal of Public Health, 75,* 518–522.

Hanneke, C., Shields, N., & McCall, G. J. (1986). Assessing the prevalence of marital rape. *Journal of Interpersonal Violence, 1,* 350–362.

Hofeller, K. H. (1982). *Social, psychological, and situational factors in wife abuse.* Palo Alto, CA: R & E Research Associates.

Hudson, W. W., & McIntosh, S. R. (1981). The assessment of spouse abuse: Two quantifiable dimensions. *Journal of Marriage and the Family, 43,* 873–885.

Johnson, I. M. (1992). Economic, situational, and psychological correlates of the decision-making process of battered women. *Families in Society, 73,* 168–176.

Johnson, I. M. (1995). Community attitudes: A study of definitions and punishment of spouse abusers and child abusers. *Journal of Criminal Justice, 23,* 477–487.

Kaiser, H. F. (1974). An index of factorial simplicity. *Psychometrika, 39,* 31–36.

Katz, J., Arias, I., & Beach, R. H. (2000). Psychological abuse, self-esteem, and women's dating relationship outcomes: A comparison of the self-verification and self-enhancement perspectives. *Psychology of Women, 24,* 349–357.

Khan, F. I., Welch, T. L., & Zillmer, E. A. (1993). MMPI-2 profiles of battered women in transition. *Journal of Personality Assessment, 60,* 100–111.

Kilpatrick, D. G., Best, C. C., Saunders, B. E., & Vernon, L. J. (1988). Rape in marriage and in dating relationships: How bad is it for mental health? *Annals of the New York Academy of Sciences, 528,* 335–344.

Labell, L. S. (1979). Wife abuse: A sociological study of battered women and their mates. *Victimology, 4,* 258–267.

Little, R., & Rubin, D. (2002). *Statistical analysis with missing data* (2nd ed.). New York: Wiley.

Lloyd, S. (1997). The effects of domestic violence on women's employment. *Law and Policy, 19,* 139–167.

Lloyd, S., & Taluc, N. (1999). The effects of male violence on female employment. *Violence Against Women, 5,* 370–392.

Lynch, J. W., Kaplan, G. A., & Shema, S. J. (1997). Cumulative impact of sustained economic hardship on physical, cognitive, psychological, and social functioning. *New England Journal of Medicine, 337*, 1889–1895.

Marshall, L. L. (1996). Psychological abuse of women: Six distinct clusters. *Journal of Family Violence, 11*, 379–409.

Martin, D. (1976). *Battered wives.* San Francisco: Glide.

McCallum, D. M., Arnold, S. E., & Bolland, J. M. (2002). Low-income African-American women talk about stress. *Journal of Social Distress and the Homeless, 11*, 249–263.

McCauley, J., Kern, D. E., Kolodner, K., Dill, L., Schroeder, A. F., DeChant, H. K., et al. (1995). The "battering syndrome": Prevalence and clinical characteristics of domestic violence in primary care internal medicine practices. *Annals of Internal Medicine, 123*, 737–746.

McLeod, J. D., & Kessler, R. C. (1990). Socioeconomic status differences in vulnerability to undesirable life events. *Journal of Health and Social Behavior, 31*, 162–172.

Melbin, A., Sullivan, C. M., & Cain, D. (2003). Transitional supportive housing for women with abusive partners: Battered women's perspectives and recommendations. *Affilia, 18*, 445–460.

Moe, A. M., & Bell, M. P. (2004). Abject economics: The effects of battering and violence on women's work and employability. *Violence Against Women, 10*, 29–55.

Okun, L. (1988). Termination or resumption of cohabitation in women battering relationships: A statistical study. In G. T. Hotaling & D. Finkelhor (Eds.), *Coping with family violence: Research and policy perspectives* (pp. 107–119). Thousand Oaks, CA: Sage.

Orava, T. A., McLeod, P. J., & Sharpe, D. (1996). Perceptions of control, depressive symptomatology and self-esteem of women in transition from abusive relations. *Journal of Family Violence, 11*, 167–186.

Pagelow, M. D. (1981). *Woman-battering: Victims and their experiences.* Beverly Hills, CA: Sage.

Pagelow, M. D. (1992). Adult victims of domestic violence. *Journal of Interpersonal Violence, 7*, 87–120.

Pearson, J., Thoennes, N., & Griswold, E. A. (1999). Child support and domestic violence: The victims speak out. *Violence Against Women, 5*, 427–448.

Pence, E., & Paymar, M. (1993). *Education groups for men who batter.* New York: Springer.

Ptacek, J. (1997). The tactics and strategies of men who batter: Testimony from women seeking restraining orders. In A. P. Cardarelli (Ed.), *Violence between intimate partners: Patterns, causes, and effects* (pp. 104–123). Boston: Allyn & Bacon.

Raphael, J. (1996). *Prisoners of abuse: Domestic violence and welfare receipt.* Chicago: Taylor Institute.

Raphael, J., & Tolman, R. (1997). *Trapped by poverty, trapped by abuse.* Chicago: Taylor Institute and the University of Michigan.

Riger, S., Ahrens, C., & Blickenstaff, A. (2001). Measuring interference with employment and education reported by women with abusive partners: Preliminary data. In K. D. O'Leary & R. D. Maiuro (Eds.), *Psychological abuse in violent domestic relations* (pp. 119–133). New York: Springer.

Riger, S., Ahrens, C., Blickenstaff, A., & Camacho, J. (1999). *Obstacles to employment of women with abusive partners: A summary of select interview data* (Working Paper No. GCP-99-1). Chicago: University of Illinois at Chicago, Great Cities Institute.

Rodenburg, F. A., & Fantuzzo J. W. (1993). The measure of wife abuse: Steps toward the development of a comprehensive assessment technique. *Journal of Family Violence, 8*, 203–228.

Russell, D. E. H. (1990). *Rape in marriage.* New York: Macmillan.

Sable, M. R., Libbus, M. K., & Huneke, D. (1999). Domestic violence among AFDC recipients: Implications for welfare-to-work programs. *Affilia, 14*, 199–216.

Sackett, L. A., & Saunders, D. G. (1999). The impact of different forms of psychological abuse on battered women. *Violence and Victims, 14*, 105–117.

Schafer, J., & Graham, J. W. (2002). Missing data: Our view of the state of the art. *Psychological Methods, 7*, 147–177.

Schechter, S., & Gary, L. T. (1988). A framework for understanding and empowering battered women. In M. A. Straus (Ed.), *Abuse and victimization across the life span* (pp. 240–253). Baltimore: Johns Hopkins University Press.

Shepard, M. F., & Campbell, J. A. (1992). The Abusive Behavior Inventory: A measure of psychological and physical abuse. *Journal of Interpersonal Violence, 7*, 291–305.

Shepard, M., & Pence, E. (1988). The effect of battering on the employment status of women. *Affilia, 3,* 55–61.

Short, L. M., McMahon, P. M., Davis Chervin, D., Shelley, G. A., Lezin, N., Sloop, K. S., et al. (2000). Survivors' identification of protective factors and early warning signs for intimate partner violence. *Violence Against Women, 6,* 272–285.

Straus, M. A. (1979). Measuring intrafamily conflict and violence: The Conflict Tactics (CTS) Scale. *Journal of Marriage and the Family, 41,* 75–88.

Street, A. E., & Arias, I. (2001). Psychological abuse and posttraumatic stress disorder in battered women: Examining the roles of shame and guilt. *Violence and Victims, 16,* 65–78.

Stronks, K., Van de Mheen, H. D., & Mackenbach, J. P. (1998). A higher prevalence of health problems in low-income groups: Does it reflect relative deprivation? *Journal of Epidemiology and Community Health, 52,* 548–557.

Stronks, K., Van de Mheen, H., Van den Bos, J., & Mackenbach, J. P. (1997). The interrelationship between income, health and employment status. *International Journal of Epidemiology, 26,* 592–600.

Strube, M. J., & Barbour, L. S. (1983). The decision to leave an abusive relationship: Economic dependence and psychological commitment. *Journal of Marriage and the Family, 45,* 785–793.

Strube, M. J., & Barbour, L. S. (1984). Factors related to the decision to leave an abusive relationship. *Journal of Marriage and the Family, 46,* 837–844.

Sullivan, C. M., Parisian, J. A., & Davidson, W. (1991, August). *Index of Spouse Abuse: Development of a measure.* Paper presented at the annual meeting of the American Psychological Association, San Francisco.

Sullivan, C. M., Tan, C., Basta, J., Rumptz, M. H., & Davidson, W. S. (1992). An advocacy intervention program for women with abusive partners: Initial evaluation. *American Journal of Community Psychology, 20,* 309–332.

Sutherland, C. A., Bybee, D. I., & Sullivan, C. M. (2002). Beyond bruises and broken bones: The joint effects of stress and injuries on battered women's health. *American Journal of Community Psychology, 30,* 609–636.

Tabachnick, B. G., & Fidell, L. S. (1996). *Using multivariate statistics* (4th ed.). Boston: Allyn & Bacon.

Tjaden, P., & Thoennes, N. (2000). *Extent, nature, and consequences of intimate partner violence: Findings from the National Violence Against Women Survey.* Washington, DC: U.S. Department of Justice, National Institute of Justice.

Tolman, R. M. (1989). The development of a measure of psychological maltreatment of women by their male partners. *Violence and Victims, 4,* 159–177.

Tolman, R. M. (1992). Psychological abuse of women. In R. T. Ammerman & M. Hersen (Eds.), *Assessment of family violence: A clinical and legal sourcebook* (pp. 291–310). Oxford, UK: Wiley.

Tolman, R. M. (1999). The validation of the Psychological Maltreatment of Women Inventory. *Violence and Victims, 14,* 25–37.

Tolman, R. M., & Wang, H. (2005). Domestic violence and women's employment: Fixed effects models of three waves of women's employment study data. *American Journal of Community Psychology, 36,* 147–158.

Vitanza, S., Vogel, L. C. M., & Marshall, L. L. (1995). Distress and symptoms of posttraumatic stress disorder in abused women. *Violence and Victims, 10,* 23–34.

Von De Linde, K. (2002). *How are domestic violence programs meeting the economic needs of battered women in Iowa? An assessment and recommendations.* Harrisburg, PA: National Resource Center on Domestic Violence.

Walker, L. E. (1979). *The battered woman.* New York: Harper & Row.

PART II

Types of Violence Against Women

CHAPTER 5

The Extensive Sexual Violation and Sexual Abuse Histories of Incarcerated Women

Cathy McDaniels-Wilson and Joanne Belknap

A considerable amount of research links criminal offending and incarceration as one of the long-term effects of women's and girls' abuse victimizations (for a review, see Browne, Miller, & Maguin, 1999). Indeed, a distinguishing characteristic of incarcerated women and girls is their extraordinarily high rates of abuse victimization histories, often by a male relative or intimate partner (e.g., American Correctional Association, 1990; Arnold, 1990; Belknap & Holsinger, 2006; Belknap, Holsinger, & Dunn, 1997; Browne et al., 1999; Bunch, Foley, & Urbina, 1983; Carlen, 1983; Chesney-Lind & Rodriguez, 1983; Coker, Patel, Krishnaswami, Schmidt, & Richter, 1998; Comack, 1996; Cook, Smith, Tusher, & Raiford, 2005; Daly, 1992; Evans, Forwyth, & Gauthier, 2002; Fletcher, Rolison, & Moon, 1993; Fox & Sugar, 1990; Gaarder & Belknap, 2002; Gilfus, 1992; Girshick, 1999; Goodkind, Ng, & Sarri, 2006; Gray, Mays, & Stohr, 1995; Greenfeld & Snell, 1999; Harlow, 1999; James & Meyerding, 1977; Lake, 1993; Little Hoover Commission, 2004; Owen, 1998; Richie, 1996; Sable, Fieberg, Martin, & Kupper, 1999; Sargent, Marcus-Mendoza, & Chong, 1993; Sharp & Marcus-Mendoza, 2001; Shaw, 1992; Silbert & Pines, 1981; Singer, Bussey, Song, & Lunghofer, 1995; Snell & Morton, 1994). Not surprisingly, many incarcerated women and girls report that they believe their sexual victimization histories are related to their subsequent offending (e.g., Belknap & Holsinger, 2006; Belknap et al.,

McDaniels-Wilson, C., & Belknap, J. (2008). The extensive sexual violation and sexual abuse histories of incarcerated women. *Violence Against Women, 14,* 1090–1127.

AUTHORS' NOTE: The authors are very grateful to the women who participated in this study. They also thank Stacy Raye Kellogg, Emily Mills, Cameron Whitley, and Lisa Xiong for their assistance in data entry.

1997; Chesney-Lind & Rodriguez, 1983; Gaarder & Belknap, 2002; Gilfus, 1992; Maeve, 2000; Sargent et al., 1993; Van Dorn et al., 2005).

Since the late 1970s, feminist criminologists have increasingly referred to this link between victimization and trauma with subsequent offending as the "pathways" approach. Stated alternatively, the pathways approach identifies girls' and women's (and sometimes boys' and men's) victimization and trauma histories as risk factors for trajectories into offending behaviors. Applications of the pathways perspective have been largely qualitative, often using small samples, and identifying trauma and abuse victimizations as precursors of women's and girls' offending (e.g., Arnold, 1990; Chesney-Lind & Rodriguez, 1983; Fox & Sugar, 1990; Gaarder & Belknap, 2002; Gilfus, 1992).

Unfortunately, the numerous studies reporting the alarming rates of sexual abuse victimization and other trauma histories of incarcerated women and girls are limited in two important ways. First, the qualitative studies allowing more context and detail regarding the sexual abuses and abusers of delinquent girls and incarcerated women typically consist of small samples and are anecdotal in nature. Second, although the quantitative studies of offending girls' and women's sexual victimizations draw on larger samples, thus providing better estimates of the rates of sexual victimization, these designs rely on limited (usually one to three questions) and thus extremely vague abuse measures (many of which merge sexual and nonsexual abuses). Thus, the large quantitative studies are plagued by a serious lack of detail regarding the abuse, but the qualitative studies use exceedingly small samples.

The purpose of the current study on imprisoned women is to address the limitations of the existing small qualitative research typically using more detailed accounts of sexual victimizations *and* the large quantitative studies relying on vague definitions of the sexual victimizations. To our knowledge, this study provides the most detailed sexual abuse histories of any study on prisoners. In addition to the broad range of sexual victimization behaviors identified in the surveys, data on the victim-offender relationship (VOR), the offender's gender, and the age of the victim at the time of the violation or abuse were also collected.

Literature Review

Studies of the sexual abuse risks of women and girls are most typically conducted on community (local) or national samples, often employing some form of random sampling, using face-to-face interviews with approximately 250 to fewer than 1,000 women (e.g., Amodeo, Griffin, Fassier, Clay, & Ellis, 2006; Russell, 1984; Wyatt, Loeb, Solis, & Carmona; Wyatt, Newcomb, & Riderle, 1993). The national studies on women's and girls' sexual victimization rates, on the other hand, usually rely on self-report phone interviews with samples of 4,000 to 8,000 women (e.g., Kilpatrick & Saunders, 1997; National Center for Victims of Crime [NCVC] & Crime Victims Research and Treatment Center, 1992; Tjaden & Thoennes, 2000). In addition to the differences between national and community studies, sexual victimization studies vary in their measures of sexual abuses and violations. For example, all studies include penile-vaginal rapes as "rape," but Russell (1984) excluded oral and anal rapes from her measure of "rape" in a community study of women in San Francisco, and Wyatt and her colleagues (1993) included anal (and penile-vaginal) rapes but excluded oral rapes in their measure of "rape" in a community study of women in Los Angeles County. Most studies of sexual abuse, including childhood sexual abuse, rely on interviewing adult women (18 years old or older) at one point in time, asking them to distinguish abuses in childhood from those at adulthood. An exception is a national study of adolescents (Kilpatrick, 1996; Kilpatrick & Saunders, 1997).

Table 5.1 is a summary of studies of sexual abuse rates conducted on samples of nonincarcerated females. (For studies that included both females and males in their samples, only the findings on females are reported.) In some sense, it is difficult to compare the rates, given that the measures of sexual abuse (including rape) vary by study, but Table 5.1 provides a quick overview of the samples, measures, and reported rates.

Following are some patterns that emerge concerning the studies of sexual abuse of community (nonincarcerated) women: When phone interviews are used on national samples, about 15% of women report a lifetime prevalence of completed rapes (NCVC & Crime Victims Research and Treatment Center, 1992; Tjaden & Thoennes, 2000), but face-to-face interviews in community samples indicate a 24% lifetime prevalence rate reported by women (Russell, 1984). Few studies distinguished sexual abuses that occurred solely in adulthood, but a national study using phone interviews reported that one-tenth of adult women experienced a completed or attempted vaginal, oral, and/or anal rape at age 18 or older (Tjaden & Thoennes, 2000), whereas community samples using face-to-face

interviews reported far higher rates: 22% of Wyatt and colleagues' (1993) sample reported vaginal and or anal rapes as adults, and at least 38% of Russell's (1984) sample reported an attempted or completed penile-vaginal rape occurring after the age of 20. (Russell [1984] only presented these data as the women's "first" rapes or attempted rapes. Thus, if a woman reported rapes or attempted rapes before *and* after age 21, they were only recorded for the youngest age in her analysis.) Regarding sexual abuse rates found in studies on child sexual abuse (CSA) among nonincarcerated samples, again, the face-to-face community sample interviews resulted in far higher sexual abuse rates (e.g., Russell, 1984; Wyatt et al., 1993, Wyatt et al., 1999) than the phone interview national samples (e.g., NCVC & Crime Victims Research and Treatment Center, 1992; Tjaden & Thoennes, 2000; see Table 5.1). As expected, the broader the range of sexually violating behaviors in a measure, the higher the sexual abuse rate a study reported. Specifically, the more types of sexual violations that a measurement instrument included, the higher the rate of respondents who reported sexual abuse became.

Table 5.1 Results From Studies Assessing the Sexual Abuse Rates of Women and Girls in the General Population/Community

Study and Sample	Lifetime Prevalence		Childhood Prevalence		Adulthood Prevalence	
	Description	%	Description	%	Description	%
Community Samples	Attempted and/or completed penile-vaginal intercourse	44	Age at first attempted and/or completed penile-vaginal intercourse (in years)[a, b]		First attempted and/or completed penile-vaginal intercourse at age 21 years old or older[a, b]	38

(Continued)

(Continued)

Study and Sample	Lifetime Prevalence		Childhood Prevalence		Adulthood Prevalence	
	Description	%	Description	%	Description	%
Russell (1984): Face-to-face interviews with 930 women in San Francisco	Completed penile-vaginal intercourse	24	0 to 5	0		
	VOR for completed rapes		6 to 10	2		
			11 to 15	12		
	Husband/ ex-husband (if ever married)	12	16 to 20	29		
			VOR by age			
	Acquaintance	5	Incest with sexual contact[a, b, c]			
	Lover/ex-lover (prior consensual sex)	5	0 to 13	12		
			0 to 17	16		
	Date (no prior consensual sex)	3	Extrafamilial with petting or genital sex[b]			
	Friend of respondent	3	0 to 13	20		
	Stranger	3	0 to 17	31		
	Boyfriend (no prior consensual sex)	2	Incestuous and/or extrafamilial[a, b, c]			
	Authority figure	2	0 to 13	28		
	Friend of family	1	0 to 17	38		
	Other relative (not spouse)	1	Broad definition of incestuous and/or extrafamilial[a, b, c]			
			0 to 13	48		
			0 to 17	54		
Wyatt et al. (1993): Face-to-face interviews with 248 women in L.A. County			Any (from exposure to rape)	62	Vaginal and/or anal rapes	22
			Any sexual physical contact (from molesting to rape)	45		

Study and Sample	Lifetime Prevalence		Childhood Prevalence		Adulthood Prevalence	
	Description	%	Description	%	Description	%
Wyatt et al. (1999): Face-to-face interviews with 338 women in L.A. County			Sexual body contact prior to age 18	34		
Amodeo et al. (2006): Surveys/ interviews with 290 women raised in two-parent families in greater Boston			"Unwanted touching or interference with private parts (breasts, buttocks, or genitalia)" from 0 to 16 years old	28		
National samples (U.S.) National Victim Center (1992): Phone interviews with 4,008 women	Vaginal, anal, and/or oral rape (completed)	13	Vaginal, oral, and/or anal rape[a]		Vaginal, oral, and/or anal rape[a]	5
	Raped more than once[a]	5	Younger than age 12	3		
	VOR		Ages 12 to 17	4		
	Acquaintance	3				
	Stranger	3				
	Relative (not father or husband)	2				
	Husband	1				
	Father/ Stepfather	1				
	Boyfriend	1				
Kilpatrick & Saunders (1997) and Kilpatrick (1996): Phone interviews with 4,023 girls aged 12 to 17 year old			"Unwanted but actual sexual contact"			
			VOR	13		
			Friend	4		
			Stranger	3		
			Relative	3		
			Acquaintance (well known)	2		

(Continued)

(Continued)

Study and Sample	Lifetime Prevalence		Childhood Prevalence		Adulthood Prevalence	
	Description	%	Description	%	Description	%
Tjaden & Thoennes (2000): Phone interviews with 8,000 women	Completed or attempted vaginal, anal, and/or oral rape	18	Completed or attempted vaginal, oral, and/or anal rape[a]	9	Completed or attempted vaginal, oral and/or anal rape[a]	10.0
	Completed vaginal, anal, and/or oral rape	15	Younger than age 12	4	Female perpetrator	0.5
			Ages 12 to 17	5	VOR	
			VOR		Intimate partner	6
			Intimate partner	3	Acquaintance	2
			Relative (not spouse)	7	Stranger	2
			Acquaintance	8		
			Stranger	1		

Note: Studies are reported by whether the sample was a community or national one and by the year of publication. VOR = victim-offender relationship.

a. The authors computed these rates from these studies' reports of the age of the woman or girl at the time of her "first" rape out of the total percentage of women who reported rape (given that many of the rape victims were raped more than once in their lifetimes). For example, the National Victim Center reported that nearly one third of the 12.5% of women ever raped reported that their first rape occurred between the ages of 11 and 17 (.32 × 12.5% = 4%); also, the Tjaden and Thoennes (1998) National Violence Against Women Survey reported that more than one fifth of the 18% of women ever raped reported that their first rape occurred when they were younger than 12 (.22 × 18% = 4%).

b. Russell (1984) reported the age data by the number of women who reported their first rape or attempted rape at each age in subgroups of 0 to 5, 6 to 10, 11 to 15, 16 to 20, 21 to 25, and so on. Thus, if a woman reported rape at age 6 and another time at age 21, the age 21 assault would not be recorded, only the age at the first assault.

c. In Russell's (1984, p. 181) study, incest was "any kind of exploitive sexual contact or attempted sexual contact that occurred between relatives, no matter how distant the relationship, before the victim turned 18 years old." Extrafamilial child sexual abuse included attempted petting to rape for respondents' experiences occurring before the victim turned 14 years old and completed or attempted penile-vaginal rape for respondents' experiences occurring from ages 14 to 17 years old. Russell's (1984) "broad definition" of child sexual abuse includes noncontact experiences, such as exhibitionism and sexual advances not acted on, in addition to the other sexual abuses (contact and rape).

Table 5.2 is similar to Table 5.1, but it summarizes sexual abuse studies conducted on samples of female offenders usually selected from the population of women in prison. Two of the studies in Table 5.2 were large national studies, but most were from the state prison systems. Also similar to Table 5.1, the studies reported in Table 5.2 vary in how sexual abuse was measured. As expected, a comparison between the nonincarcerated (Table 5.1) and incarcerated (Table 5.2) samples of women and girls suggests higher rates of sexual abuse reported among women in the latter (prison) studies. However, given the vagueness of the measures and the variation across studies, even this is somewhat difficult to assess.

Table 5.2   Results From Studies Assessing the Sexual Abuse Histories of Incarcerated Women and Girls[3]

Study	Sample	Lifetime Prevalence		Childhood Prevalence		Adulthood Prevalence	
		Description	%	Description	%	Description	%
Local studies							
Lake (1993)	Self-reports of 83 women (47 interviewed, 36 surveyed) in Washington	"Forced sexual contact"					
		VOR					
		Family member	18				
		Stranger	30				
Sargent et al. (1993)	Interviews with 267 women incarcerated in Oklahoma	"Raped, sexually abused, or molested"	55	"Raped, sexually abused, or molested"	40	"Raped, sexually abused, or molested"	38
Bloom et al. (1994)	297 women incarcerated in California's three prisons			[general]	31	[general]	23
Johnston (1995)	Interviews with 100 mothers in California			[general]	31	[general]	34
Singer et al. (1995)	Interviews with 201 women in Cleveland, Ohio	[general]	81	[general]	48	[general]	68
Acoca (1998)	Interviews with 193 girls in San Diego, L.A., Alameda, and Marin counties, California			[general]	56		
				Molested/ fondled by anyone	18		
				VOR			
				Family friend/ neighbor	17		

(Continued)

(Continued)

Study	Sample	Lifetime Prevalence		Childhood Prevalence		Adulthood Prevalence	
		Description	%	Description	%	Description	%
				Acquaintance	17		
				Stepfather	4		
				Stranger	4		
				Raped or sodomized by anyone	40		
				VOR			
				Boyfriend	6		
				Stranger	6		
				Dating acquaintance	6		
				Family friend/ neighbor	6		
Browne et al. (1999)	Interviews with 150 women in Bedford Hills, New York	Raped or sexually attacked	33	[general]	59	Marital rape	35
				Any exposure	49		
				Sexual touching	51		
				Vaginal, oral, or anal penetration	41		
				VOR			
				Father or stepfather	27		
				Other male relative	42		
				Female relatives	2		
				Nonrelatives	56		
				Age at first sexual abuse			
				0–9 years	51		
				10–14 years	42		
				15–17 years	8		

Study	Sample	Lifetime Prevalence		Childhood Prevalence		Adulthood Prevalence	
		Description	%	Description	%	Description	%
Girshick (1999)	In-depth interviews with 40 women incarcerated in Black Mountain, North Carolina			0–17 years old		Rape	43
				"Touching"	13	VOR[b]	
				Completed or attempted rapes	23	Boyfriend	25
						Stranger	17
						Husband	12
						Acquaintance	2
						John	2
Mullings et al. (2000)	Face-to-face interviews with 500 incarcerated women in Texas			"Sexually abused, mistreated, or raped" while growing up	26		
Cook (2005)	403 women entering Georgia prison			By same-sex peer	14	Sexual abuse	27
				By peer 5-plus years older	43		
				During adolescence	27		
National samples							
Fox & Sugar (1990)	Interviews with 39 Aboriginal women incarcerated in Canada	Raped or sexually assaulted	54				
Shaw (1992)	Survey of 178 women incarcerated with federal sentences of 2 or more years in Canada	[general]	53				

(Continued)

(Continued)

Study	Sample	Lifetime Prevalence		Childhood Prevalence		Adulthood Prevalence	
		Description	%	Description	%	Description	%
Snell & Morton (1994)	Personal interviews with 2,823 incarcerated women in the U.S.	[general]	34	[general] before age 18	32	[general] after age 17	24
		Rape	24				
		Attempted rape	6				
		Other sexual abuse	4				
Harlow (1999)	Survey of 2,941 women in state prisons in the U.S.	[general]	39	[general] 0–17 years old	25		
		Attempted rape	4				
		Completed rape	33				
		VOR[b]	35				
		Knew abuser	16				
		Family	11				
		Parent/ guardian Other relative	8				
		Intimate	24				
		Spouse/ ex-spouse	14				
		Boyfriend	14				
		Friend/ acquaintance	10				
		Other	6				
		Stranger	4				

NOTE: VOR = victim-offender relationship.

a. Studies are reported by year of publication. When the studies had a vague or all-encompassing definition of sexual abuse, the table uses "[general]" in the prevalence description.

b. The authors computed the rates from these study reports by multiplying the type of sexual abuse by the percentage of all of that type of abuse committed by the named victim-offender relationship. For example, if a study reported that 40% of the sample had been raped and that a stranger committed 5% of the rapes, then the percentage of women in the sample experiencing rape by a stranger was computed to be 8%.

Method

Research Sites

All three of the women's prisons in Ohio were selected for participation in this study. The Ohio Reformatory for Women (ORW) in Marysville, Ohio, housing minimum-, medium-, and maximum-security prisoners, opened in 1916, is the oldest prison for adult women in Ohio, and is the reception site for all incoming offenders. The Franklin Pre-Release Center (FPRC) in Columbus, Ohio, opened in 1988, houses minimum- and medium-security women prisoners who serve the majority of their sentence at FPRC. The final site, the Northeast Pre-Release Center (NPRC), also opened in 1988, is a minimum-security women's prison in Cleveland, Ohio.

Measurement Instruments

For the purposes of the current study, *sexual violations* are sexual experiences that rarely "count" as offenses legally and that many individuals do not view as sexual abuse but that have been identified by some scholars as exploitative and troubling (e.g., Basile, 1999; Kelly, 1988; Russell, 1984). Examples include acquiescing to sex because of threats to end the relationship and acquiescing to sex because of verbal pressure. *Sexual abuses*, on the other hand, are sexual experiences that are usually both legally considered criminal and culturally considered wrong, such as rape and molestation. However, what "counts" as rape varies across jurisdictions, over time, and across studies on this topic. For example, some studies limit "rape" to penile-vaginal intercourse; others measure rape as penile-vaginal and anal intercourse; and still others include penile-vaginal, anal, and oral intercourse (e.g., see Tables 5.1 and 5.2).

In the current study, the first measure used for the women's sexual abuse history is the Sexual Experiences Survey (SES), which is a modified version of the Koss and Oros (1982) Sexual Experiences Survey. The original version consisted of 13 yes or no questions that addressed various degrees of sexual behaviors, with both male and female versions of the items (the females' version to self-report victimization experiences and the males' version to self-report perpetration behaviors). The SES designed for the current study consisted of 15 items ranging from "someone misinterpreting the level of sexual intimacy you desire," to more intrusive, violent, sexually aggressive or assaultive behaviors. Although the SES is useful for identifying a continuum of sexually violating and abusive behaviors, it does not account for the number of times that the respondent experienced a particular violation or abuse or the gender of the offenders. Thus, another adaptation of the original Koss and Oros SES in the current study was to ask participants who reported experiencing a violation (a) how many times they experienced the event (ranging from *1 time* to *6 or more* times) and (b) the gender of the abuser(s). (See Appendix A for the items in the modified SES designed for and used in the current study.)

Even with these changes to the Koss and Oros SES, we determined that an additional survey was necessary to document the VOR and the age of the victim at the time of the violation or abuse. Therefore, the first author developed the Sexual Abuse Checklist Survey (SACS) to document a more detailed account of the types of sexual violations and abuses (McDaniels-Wilson, 1995). The SACS specifically identified the following potential VORs: father, stepfather, grandfather, mother, stepmother, grandmother, uncle, aunt, brother, sister, male cousin, female cousin, male neighbor, female neighbor, male lover or boyfriend, female lover or girlfriend, male date, female date, husband, male counselor, female counselor, male minister or clergy, female minister or clergy, male teacher, female teacher, male stranger, and female stranger. For VORs not indicated on the list, the SACS provided three additional blank spaces for the women to write in the relationship and the types of abuses and their age(s) when abused by this person. Next to each potential abuser (including the blank ones for respondents to write in additional perpetrators), the following potential abuses were listed, for which the respondent could circle as many as applied: nudity, disrobing, genital exposure, being observed (i.e., showering, dressing, toileting), kissing, fondling, masturbation, finger penetration of vagina, finger penetration of anus, oral sex on the victim, oral sex on the abuser, penile penetration of vagina, and penile penetration of anus. (See Appendix B for the items in the SACS.) A comment section was included at the bottom of this survey for additional thoughts or reflections. Both the modified SES and the SACS were pilot tested.[1]

Despite the significant detail allowed by using the SACS, it is not without limitations. More specifically, although it allowed us to determine what ages the participant experienced sexual abuse by a specific perpetrator (e.g., father, stranger), if a participant circled more than one type of abuse (e.g., fondling and penile-vaginal penetration) *and* listed more than one age, we were unable to identify at which age a specific abuse by that particular abuser occurred. Also, given the abusers written in the blanks for "other" abusers not specified, we realize that future research should specifically ask about stepsiblings, friends, friends of the family, and ex-husbands. Similarly, the list of potential abuses should have included "attempted rape."

Finally, the first author developed a personal data sheet to collect demographic information from the participants. This included questions about their racial identity, age, number of children, and education.

Data Collection

The director of psychological services at each of the three prisons reviewed the proposal for the study, and each assisted by allocating staff from the records department or mental health unit.

Research packets were distributed to those prisoners who indicated an interest in participating. Each packet contained a consent form, a personal data sheet, a request for a more in-depth interview with the researcher, the SES, and the SACS.

Data were collected from April through October, 1996. The respondents were instructed not to report assaults experienced while in prison (as required by the prison officials as a condition of the study). Because of the nature of this material and the possibility of this information functioning as a trigger for repressed affect, participants were told to fill out a "kite," a request for mental health intervention, if needed. Clinical consultation and brief treatment were made available by two therapists. One was an expert in sexual abuse treatment under the supervision of a licensed clinical psychologist, and the other was a clinical psychologist. It should be noted that no prisoners requested this service.

The Sample

The prison officials restricted the study to allow about a third of the population for the sample. To this end, the Ohio Department of Corrections and Rehabilitation research staff conducted a computerized random sample, selecting 885 of all 2,903 women prisoners in the three Ohio women's prisons in June 1996. Of these 885 women sampled, 436 (49.3%) attempted to participate in this study, and out of these 436 women, 391 (89.7%) turned in usable sexual abuse surveys. (The completion rates did not vary across the three prison sites.)

It is important to address why half of the sampled women did not participate and why some who participated did not submit usable surveys. Regarding the lack of study participation, although we do not know the exact numbers, some of the sampled women were unable to take the survey because of being in mandatory lockdown, staying at the medical unit of the prison, or being AWOL at the time of data collection. There were occasions in which some participants began the survey, but because of the nature of the materials, reported that they could not complete it. Also, despite assurances by the research staff that their individual responses would not be communicated in any manner to officials, some declined to take the survey because they worried that the information might adversely affect their parole or discharge, an important limitation in this type of study. Regardless of the reason, we were sensitive to and accepting of the women unwilling or unable to take part in the study, whether it was their decision to decline to start or finish the study or whether it was because of circumstances such as participants in lockdown or at a prison medical facility at the time of data collection. The first author distributed and collected all of the surveys and remained in the prison room where the surveys were being completed until all surveys had been collected. This ensured that the prison staff had no access to the data and the research staff could answer any participants' questions about the study, survey, and consent form.

Demographic data were available for 380 of the 391 women who completed usable sexual abuse surveys (see Table 5.3). The women ranged in age from 18 to 69 years, with a mean age of 35.0 years. Thirty percent of the women were 18 to 29 years old ($n = 114$), 45% were 30 to 39 years old ($n = 168$), 20.5% were 40 to 49 years old ($n = 77$), and the remainder was 50 and older ($n = 16$). More than half of the women were African American (53.3%, $n = 201$), and 45% were White ($n = 168$); none were Latina or Asian/Asian American, 6 identified as "biracial," and 2 as American Indian. This is fairly representative of prisoner populations at these three women's institutions, which was 57% African American, 41% White, fewer than 2% (1.7%) Latina/ Hispanic, and the remaining few, Asian American, American Indian, and biracial.[2] Almost three-fifths of the women (58%, $n = 208$) had not graduated from high school; more than a quarter (28%, $n = 100$) had graduated from high school, and about 1 in 7 had attended some college (or

completed college; 15%, $n = 42$). Eighty-five percent of the women ($n = 317$) had children, with an average of 2.4 children per respondent. Fewer than half of the sample (45%, $n = 110$) had never married; one quarter (26%, $n = 63$) were married; and more than a quarter were divorced, separated, or widowed (29%, $n = 70$). About 70% reported being employed prior to incarceration, although some reported their employment as illegal activities (e.g., prostitution or drug selling).

Limitations of the Study

Despite the far more detailed surveys used in the current study of incarcerated women's self-reported sexual violation and abuse histories, there are still concerns with the study design and implementation. For example, we have no way of knowing whether the women who chose not to take the surveys or who were unable to do so were more or less likely to report sexual victimizations. We also have no means to verify the accuracy of the reports (e.g., Do the women remember correctly at what age(s) the event occurred? Did any respondents "make up" a sexual victimization for the survey?). It is reasonable to speculate that women who were unable to take the study because of being in lockdown or in the psychiatric or physical health wards may be more likely to have sexual abuse histories, particularly more severe sexual abuse histories, than women not in those parts of the prison because of previous research linking sexual abuse victimization with subsequent physical and mental health problems (e.g., Coker et al., 1998; Murphy et al., 1988; Neria, Bromet, Carlson, & Naz, 2005; Van Dorn et al., 2005).

In our efforts to not exaggerate the rates of sexual violations and abuses, we coded conservatively: SES and SACS items with no information were coded as "no" instead of "missing," unless it was the sex/gender of the offender or the number of times the person perpetrated the abuse. For example, if a woman

Table 5.3   Description of Sample[a] (*N* = 380)

	N	n	%
Age[b]	375		
18 to 29		114	30.4
30 to 39		168	44.8
40 to 49		77	20.5
50 to 59		14	3.7
60 to 70		2	0.5
Ethnicity	377		
White		168	44.6
African American		201	53.3
Latina		0	0.0
Biracial		6	1.6
Native American		2	0.5
Asian		0	0.0
Education (X = 10.9)	361		
11th grade or less		208	57.8
High school graduate		100	27.7
Partial college		53	14.7
Children (X = 2.39)	371		
No children		54	14.6
1 to 4		275	74.1
More than 5		42	11.3
Caretaker of dependent children	239		
Prisoner's spouse/partner		53	22.2
Prisoner's parent		101	42.3
Prisoner's other family		71	29.7
Government agency		14	5.9

	N	n	%
Marital status	243		
Married		63	25.9
Single/never married		110	45.3
Divorced/separated/widowed		70	28.8
Employment (prior to incarceration)	356		
Employed		247	69.4
Not employed		101	28.4
Student		8	2.2

a. Of the 391 women for whom we had self-reported sexual abuse data, there were 380 women for whom we had some demographic data. However, because of some missing demographic data, the numbers in the N column are less than 380. Percentages may not total 100.0% because of rounding.

b. The respondents' ages ranged from 18 to 69 years old, with an average age of 35.

circled "yes" under the item on the SES asking whether she had engaged in a sexual encounter with someone because it was useless to try to stop the person and made no marks in the remainder of the survey, we interpreted the results as the woman *not* having experienced the remaining violations. Thus, we believe that our findings are likely to underreport sexual violation and abuse rates.

Findings

Findings From the Modified Sexual Experiences Survey (SES)

Table 5.4 summarizes the findings reported in the modified version of Koss and Oros's (1982) SES. Seventy-two percent of the women reported some level of what we call *legal coercion*: sexual experiences that are not typically considered violations of the law and thus fit into the *sexual violations* definition discussed in the Method section. One-third (33.0%) of the women reported having sexual activity because the other person had threatened to end the relationship if they did not comply sexually. Approximately half the women reported each of the following *legal coercions*: experiencing oral, anal, or vaginal penetration (including by a foreign object) because of verbal pressure (44.5%) and experiencing kissing, petting, or fondling because of verbal pressure (47.1%); continued with an unwanted sexual activity because the other person was so aroused, it was useless to try to stop it (52.7%); "found out that someone had gotten you to engage in sexual activity with them by saying things they didn't really mean" (53.2%); and "had someone misinterpret the level of sexual intimacy you desired" (55.2%). Although the prevalence of such acts is of concern, we do not know whether the rates are consistent with those of nonincarcerated samples of women and girls.

Table 5.4 Levels Reported on the Modified Sexual Experiences Survey (SES) by Number of Times and Offender Gender (*N* = 391)

Type of Violation (N = 391)	Reported This Violation[a]		Times Violated[b]			Abuser Gender/Sex					
						Male(s)		Female(s)		Male(s) and Female(s)	
	%	n	Mean	Mode	N[c]	%	n	%	n	%	n
Legal coercion[d]	**71.6**	**280**									
Misinterpret level of sexual intimacy	55.2	216	4.1	6	213	99.1	211	20.7	44	19.7	42
Useless to try stop sex	52.7	207	3.9	6	201	99.9	199	13.9	28	12.9	26
Threaten to end relationship if no sex	33.0	129	4.1	6	124	96.0	119	16.1	20	12.1	15
Said things he/ she did not mean to have sex	53.2	208	4.3	6	205	98.5	202	16.6	34	15.1	31
Kiss, pet, fondle via verbal pressure	47.1	184	4.6	6	175	97.7	171	14.3	25	12.0	21
Penetration via verbal pressure	44.5	174	4.3	6	167	96.4	161	15.6	26	5.1	20
Illegal kiss, pet, fondle	55.8	218									
Use position of authority[e] to kiss/fondle	22.5	88	4.1	6	85	97.6	83	11.8	10	9.4	8
Threaten or use physical force to kiss/fondle	52.7	206	3.8	6	198	98.5	195	6.1	12	4.5	9
Illegal attempted penetration[f]	**43.5**	**170**									
Threaten or use physical force to attempt penetration	41.4	162	3.3	6	148	98.0	145	6.8	10	4.7	7

Type of Violation (N = 391)	Reported This Violation[a]		Times Violated[b]			Abuser Gender/Sex					
						Male(s)		Female(s)		Male(s) and Female(s)	
	%	n	Mean	Mode	N[c]	%	n	%	n	%	n
Use alcohol/drugs to attempt penetration	38.9	152	3.5	6	139	97.1	135	14.4	20	11.5	16
Illegal completed penetration[g]	**59.8**	**234**									
Use position of authority[e] to penetrate	18.4	72	3.9	6	68	98.5	67	1.0	4	4.4	3
Use alcohol/drugs to penetrate	38.6	151	4.5	6	141	98.6	139	12.8	18	11.3	16
Threaten or use physical force to penetrate	49.1	192	3.8	6	182	97.8	178	7.7	14	5.5	10
Identified an experience as *rape*[h]	**54.5**	**213**									
Rape	54.5	213	3.0	1	199	99.0	197	7.0	14	6.0	12
Gang rape	11.5	45	1.8	1	45	100.0	45	8.9	4	1.0	4
Complete penetration but not called *rape*[i]	**20.5**	**48**									

a. To avoid overreporting sexual violations, all missing data were recorded as zeroes regarding whether the respondents "reported this violation." All boldfaced violations include the total for women reporting one or more of the violations listed as subcategories.

b. These measures are for those women reporting how often they experienced this violation, on a scale of 1, 2, 3, 4, 5, or 6 or more times. Thus, the means and modes are based on a limit of 1 through 6 times. Also, some respondents reported experiencing the violation but did not circle the number of times so the n's, percentages, and means and modes were based on cases for which no data were missing for the number of times experiencing this violation.

c. The abuser's gender is based on those cases for which the specific abuse or violation was reported and whether the respondent reported the abuser's or abusers' gender. A respondent could be in the male abuser(s) or female abuser(s) column or in all three columns.

d. Legal coercion refers to behaviors that are not illegal (except when by an adult on a minor) used to obtain sexual intimacy.

e. Examples given of authority were boss, teacher, camp counselor, and supervisor.

f. Illegal attempts (that were uncompleted) to obtain oral sex, anal sex, vaginal intercourse, and/or penetration by objects other than the penis.

g. Illegal penetration via oral sex, anal sex, vaginal intercourse, and/or penetration by objects other than the penis.

h. Respondent reported an experience that they defined as rape or gang rape. Previous items did not use the word rape. All respondents who reported being raped also reported being gang raped.

i. Respondent reported experiencing completed penetration but reported "no" to the word rape. There were 48 cases out of 234 cases in which women reported completed penetration but reported "no" to the word rape (in this one case, missing data were not recorded as no's).

The next level of violation measured in our version of the SES we refer to as *illegal kissing, petting, and fondling*. The most common of these two measures was reported by about half of the sample (52.7%): someone threatened or used physical force (e.g., "twisting your arm, holding you down") to kiss, pet, or fondle the respondent. Slightly more than one-fifth (22.5%) of the sample reported a person using their position of authority (e.g., teacher, boss, camp counselor) to kiss, pet, or fondle them. Although this rate is relatively low compared to most of the other rates reported in this study, it is remarkable given that authorities are typically charged with protecting in some manner, yet these women were obviously vulnerable to such abuse. This is consistent with Kraska and Kappeler's (1995) finding that the most marginalized women in society (i.e., poorer, younger, and of color women) are those most susceptible to sexual violence perpetrated *by the police*. Notably, Kraska and Kappeler's study indicated that both female victims and female defendants encountered by the police were at risk. In sum, 56% of the sample reported experiencing one or both of these forms of illegal kissing, petting, and fondling (see Table 5.4).

The third level of sexual violation in our version of the SES we refer to as *illegal attempted penetration*. About two fifths of the sample reported each of these: someone used force or the threat of force to attempt to orally, anally, or vaginally penetrate the respondent (41.4%); or someone used alcohol and/or drugs to attempt to orally, anally, or vaginally penetrate the respondent (38.9%). A slightly larger portion (43.5%) of the sample reported one or both of these illegal attempted penetration violations with a significant overlap between them (i.e., if they experienced one form of illegal attempted penetration, they likely experienced the other). Three-fifths (59.8%) of the respondents reported at least one fourth-level violation: illegal completed penetration. The most frequently reported category of illegal completed penetration—in this case, by half of the sample

(49.1%)—was the threat of or use of force to orally, anally, or vaginally penetrate the respondent. Almost two-fifths (38.6%) of the sample reported that someone completed oral, anal, or vaginal penetration of them through the use of drugs and/or alcohol. Sexual abuse perpetrated by someone who used his authority (e.g., police, boss, teacher) was reported by almost one-fifth (18.4%) of the sample. Kraska and Kappeler's (1995) research on police-perpetrated sexual violence is relevant again in the interpretation of this finding (see Table 5.4).

Finally, consistent with other studies, we did not use the word *rape* in any of the survey items except the final two items on the SES, in which respondents were asked, "Have you ever been raped?" and "Have you ever been gang raped?" A number of findings are noteworthy. First, 11.5% of the sample reported having been "gang raped." More than half of the women (54.5%) reported having been "raped." (As expected, all of the women who reported that they were gang raped also reported that they were raped.) This is not only an astounding number of women reporting rape but a significant percent reporting gang rape victimization. Second, one-fifth (20.5%, *n* = 48) of the 234 women who reported a completed oral, anal, or penile penetration did not report "yes" to the word *rape* (or *gang rape*). This lack of identifying a rape victimization as "rape" is consistent with previous research indicating that many times when women are forced to have sex (particularly by someone they know), they report it as forced sex but not as "rape" (e.g., Russell, 1984; Schwartz & Leggett, 1999; Sudderth, 1998). This is typically explained by the belief that many people, including some victims, view "real rape" as when strangers jump out of alleys or from behind bushes and sexually assault (Estrich, 1987). Remarkably, in this study almost one-fifth of this sample reported being raped by persons in positions of authority, and more than one-fifth reported persons using their positions of authority to kiss, pet, or fondle them.

Table 5.4 also reports the number of times (with options ranging from *1 time* to *6 or more times*) that a particular violation was experienced by the respondents if they answered "yes" to experiencing the violation item. It is significant that the modal number of times reported for every violation except for "rape" and "gang rape" (both of which had a mode of 1) was *6 or more*. The lowest mean/average for the various violations was "gang rape" at 1.8 times and "rape" at 3.0 times. The average number of times reported for the remainder of the violations on the SES ranged from 3.3 to 4.6 times (see Table 5.4). These findings on the central tendency measures reaffirm what has been found in existing research regarding revictimization. For example, Gilfus's (1992) study of incarcerated women reported how their childhood victimizations put them at risk of not only becoming offenders (often living on the streets) but also their offending often led to subsequent victimizations, including rape and attempted murder. Even studies of nonincarcerated populations reported the high risk of sexual abuse revictimization for those sexually abused as children (e.g., Browne & Finkelhor, 1986; Murphy et al., 1988; Russell, 1984).

Finally, Table 5.4 reports the abuser's gender. Not surprisingly, for every sexual violation reported on the SES, from the least to the most extreme, the abusers are predominantly male (in 96% to 100% of the abuse categories). One respondent wrote on her survey how three of her female cousins sexually assaulted her when she was a child. Thus, although males were reported as being the perpetrators in more than nine-tenths of the violations, females could be perpetrators as well (in 1.0% to 20.7% of the violations). The violations for which females were most often listed as abusers were misinterpreting the level of sexual intimacy (20.7%); saying things they did not mean to have sex (16.6%); threatening to end the relationship if the woman did not comply (16.1%); using verbal pressure for penetration (15.6%); using alcohol and/or drugs to attempt penetration (14.4%) or to sexually penetrate (12.8%); using verbal pressure to kiss, pet, or fondle (14.3%); using a position of authority to kiss, pet, or fondle (11.8%); and the respondent claiming that it was useless to try to stop sex from occurring (13.9%). Thus, the violations most representative of female abusers were also the ones that tended to be under the legal coercion category.

The lowest rate of female perpetrators was for the abuser using her authority to sexually penetrate the respondent orally, anally, or vaginally (including with a foreign object); 1.0% of these violations involved female abusers. Females were reported as being the abusers in 6% to 9% of the following violations: (a) using threats of physical force or actual physical force to kiss, pet, or fondle (6.1%); (b) using threats of force or actual force in attempts to sexually penetrate (orally, anally, or vaginally; 6.8%); (c) "rape" (7.0%); (d) using threats of force or actual force to "successfully" sexually penetrate (orally, anally, or vaginally; 7.7%); and (e) "gang rape" (8.9%). The final column in Table 5.4 indicates that when a respondent reported a particular sexual violation by a female, she was also likely to have reported the same violation by a male. In conclusion, although these abuses were clearly gendered in their perpetration, the potential for sexual abuse perpetrated by females still poses a significant threat in these women's lives.

Findings From the SACS

Table 5.5 presents the findings from the SACS. In an effort to use as much data as possible from both the SES and SACS data, we included any cases in our sample in which women had completed at least one of the surveys (SES or SACS). Given that the SES was shorter and simpler than the SACS, it is not surprising that we had more completed SES's than SACS's. Given that we coded all blanks on either survey as "no," the rate of sexual violation or abuse was lower on the SACS than the SES. Again, we believe it is important to report the findings from both surveys separately and then to merge the findings (as we have done in Table 5.6).

Table 5.5 Sexual Violation, Abuse, and Abuser Gender Rates Reported on the Sexual Abuse Checklist Survey (SACS; $N = 391$)

Type of Violation[a]			Abuser Gender/Sex[b]					
			Male Abuser(s)		Female Abuser(s)		Male and Female Abusers	
	%	n	%	n	%	n	%	n
Level 1	**43.2**	**169**						
Nudity	30.7	120	28.9	113	6.1	24	4.6	18
Disrobing	24.0	94	22.8	89	4.6	18	3.6	14
Genital exposure	32.2	126	31.5	123	4.3	17	3.8	15
Observing undressing, bathing, etc.	26.9	105	25.3	99	5.1	20	4.1	16
Kissing	33.5	131	32.0	125	6.1	24	4.9	19
Level 2	**39.6**	**155**						
Fondling victim	38.6	151	36.8	144	6.4	25	5.1	20
Victim masturbate offender	22.0	86	19.9	80	4.1	16	3.3	13
Level 3	**36.3**	**142**						
Finger penetration of anus	19.2	75	18.4	72	2.3	9	1.5	6
Finger penetration of vagina	33.8	132	33.0	129	4.1	19	4.3	17
Level 4	**36.1**	**141**						
Oral sex on victim's genitals	28.4	111	26.9	105	5.6	22	4.1	16
Oral sex on abuser's genitals	29.7	116	28.6	112	4.6	18	3.6	14
Level 5	**45.0**	**176**						
Penis in anus	22.0	86	22.0	86	—	—	—	—
Penis in vagina	41.9	164	41.9	164	—	—	—	—
Reported either Level 4 and/or 5	**51.9**	**203**						
Reported any Level 3 to 5	**54.0**	**211**						
Reported any Level 2 to 5	**55.2**	**216**						
Reported any Level 1 to 5	**60.9**	**238**						

Type of Violation[a]			Abuser Gender/Sex[b]					
			Male Abuser(s)		Female Abuser(s)		Male and Female Abusers	
	%	n	%	n	%	n	%	n
No. of abusers of a specific VOR reported[d]								
None	39.1	153						
One	18.9	74						
Two	15.1	59						
Three	10.5	41						
Four-plus	16.4	64						

a. To avoid overreporting sexual violations, all unanswered items were recorded as "no." All boldfaced violations include the total for women reporting one or more of the violations listed beneath that level.

b. The percentages under abuser gender in this table refer to the percentage of the entire sample who reported a specific violation perpetrated by a male, female, or both male and female abusers. A respondent could be in each category (male, female, and both).

c. Eighteen women identified an abuser on the SACS (e.g., father) but did not identify which abuses/violations the individual perpetrated. So these 18 cases were added to the 220 cases that reported a Level 1 through 5 violation, although the abuses or violations may have been more severe than Level 1.

d. The categories of victim-offender relationship (VOR) included father, mother, boyfriend, girlfriend, male stranger, female stranger, and so on. Given that 60.9% of the women reported any level of SACS violation abuse, 39.1% of the women reported no VORs of any kind. (The overall rate of sexual abuse or violation is higher from the SES given that more respondents completed the SACS than the SES, and blanks were treated as no's on both surveys.) The number of abusers by victim-offender identified ranged from 0 to 13, but it is important to understand that this number is actually much higher because some women wrote more than one boyfriend, more than one brother, more than one husband, more than one stranger, yet this was coded as 1 for the VOR because on most surveys it was difficult to disentangle this. The modal number of abusers (by VOR) was 0, the mean was 1.7, and the median was 1.

As described in the Method section, this survey identified 33 potential abusers (e.g., father, stepfather, aunt, male stranger, female teacher) and a space for three other types of potential abusers not listed in the options, with a list of 13 abuses listed next to each abuser (e.g., fondling, oral sex on victim, oral sex on abuser, penis in anus, finger in vagina; see Appendix B).

Arguably, the items listed in Level 1 (nudity, disrobing, genital exposure, kissing, and observing dressing/undressing/showering) could be considered as not abusive, particularly by those who believe that feminist research exaggerates sexual victimization. And these charges would be most vulnerable if the person performing the behavior were not a stranger. Still, respondents circled the items under the instructions that they felt violated or abused in some way, and about two-fifths (43.2%) of the women reported at least one of the Level 1 violations. Between one quarter

Table 5.6 An Expanding Measure of the Most Extreme Sexual Abuses Combining the Modified SES and SACS Items (N = 391)[a]

Survey	Violation Item	%	n	%	n	%	n	%	n	%	n	%	n	%	n
SES	Reported yes to "Have you ever been raped?"	54.5	213												
SES	+ Reported oral, anal, and/or vaginal sex or other penetration via threat or force			60.6	237										
SACS	+ Reported penis in vagina or anus[b]					64.2	251								
SACS	+ Reported oral sex by victim on abuser's genitals							65.5	256						
SACS	+ Reported oral sex by abuser on victim's genitals									66.5	260				
SES	+ Reported oral, anal, or vaginal sex or other penetration via using a position of authority[c]											67.0	262		
SES	+ Reported oral, anal, or vaginal sex or other penetration via using drugs and/or alcohol													70.1	274

NOTE: SACS = Sexual Abuse Checklist Survey; SES = Sexual Experiences Survey. Plus signs (+) indicate that all of the figures for each type of sexual abuse in each row also include the other offenses listed above that row; thus, using more inclusive definitions of abuse increased the rate of occurrence. a. Most respondents answered both surveys, but some women either seemed to start answering one of the surveys and quit part way through or simply seemed to "skip" the second survey. This table uses various measures of what currently qualifies as the most extreme sexual assaults or abuses in most states. The numbers on the table represent the rate of the respondents who have been raped if the definition of rape is expanded to include the item next to the number in addition to the items before it. There is significant overlap: Many of the women who reported "yes" to the word rape also reported some of the following items, but the numbers/percentages only represent additional cases not covered in the numbers reported in the previous items. b. After adding "reported penis in vagina," the total increased to 250 and adding "penis in anus" increased it to 250. c. Authority included boss, teacher, camp counselor, and supervisor.

and one third of respondents reported specific violations classified under Level 1. In terms of the specific categories of Level 1 SACS violations, the rates reported from least to most frequent by the respondents were disrobing (24.0%), observing (un)dressing/showering (26.9%), nudity (30.7%), genital exposure (32.2%), and kissing (33.5%). The sense of violation experienced is perhaps best portrayed in what one woman wrote next to the item asking about sexual abuse by a father: "Just gawking at me while I'm in the bathroom or when I'm taking a bath, even while I'm sleeping."

Two-fifths (39.6%) of the women reported experiencing at least one Level 2 violation: being "fondled" or being coerced or forced into masturbating another person. Notably, almost all of these cases were when the women reported having been "fondled" (38.6%). More than one-fifth (22.0%) of the women reported being made to masturbate a perpetrator (see Table 5.5). Ninety-five percent ($n = 82$) of the women who reported the abuse of having to masturbate an abuser ($n = 86$) also reported being fondled by an abuser (not reported in the table). The Level 3 SACS violation categories included digital penetration of the victim's anus or vagina, and more than one-third (36.3%) of the sample reported at least one of these digital violations. Almost one-fifth (19.2%) reported finger penetration of the anus, and one-third (33.8%) reported finger penetration of the vagina (see Table 5.5). Eighty-seven percent ($n = 65$) of the women who reported digital penetration of the anus ($n = 75$) also reported being fondled by an abuser (not reported in the table). The Level 4 SACS violations reported in Table 5.5 constitute oral rapes, in which either the perpetrator has oral contact with the victim's genitals (28.4%) or the victim has oral contact with the abuser's genitals (29.7%). Slightly more than one-third of the women (36.1%) reported at least one of these oral sex abuses, and three-quarters (77.5%, $n = 86$) of the 111 women who reported oral sex on their own genitals also reported having to perform oral sex on another person's genitals (not reported in the table).

Notably, the single most reported sexual violation on the SACS survey was the one that most people would likely argue is the most serious violation: Two in five women (41.9%) reported experiencing penile-vaginal rape. More than one-fifth (22.0%) of the women reported the only other category in this most serious level (Level 5), penile-anal rape (see Table 5.5). It could certainly be argued that although it does not pose the threat of pregnancy, anal rape is more severe than penile-vaginal rape. Also, the word "rape" was never used on the SACS. The women were asked to circle the listed "forms of sexual abuse" or to write in others that were not on the survey. (See Appendix B for more details.)

Similar to the findings reported in Table 5.4, the findings in Table 5.5 indicate that the same women were experiencing numerous sexual abuses. Three-fifths (60.9%) of the women reported at least one type of abuse (or abuser) on the SACS instrument, and 52% reported at least one oral, penile, or vaginal rape. This is explained by the fact that many times, a perpetrator who abused the victim at the most serious levels often abused her at the less serious levels as well.

These findings also suggest further evidence of the risk of sexual abuse revictimization by subsequent abusers (referred to in Table 5.4). Thus, analysis of the SACS data included tabulating the number of abusers reported (see Table 5.5). It is important to recognize that some women wrote comments such as "three husbands," "three brothers," "two stepfathers," and "many strangers," on the SACS next to a given VOR. Given that it was difficult with the survey to determine these for all of the respondents, the abusers were coded as 1 per VOR; thus, these rates indicate "1" for a woman who was abused by three brothers (and reported no other abusers), or "2" if a woman reported one husband and two strangers as abusers. Two-fifths of the women reported no abusers, almost one-fifth reported 1 abuser, 15% reported 2 abusers, 10% reported 3 abusers, and 16% reported 4 to 13 abusers. One woman's written comment on the survey profoundly explains a reason for the revictimizations: "I just would like to say, once one person does it to you, it's almost becoming normal to allow others to do it. I learned how to zone out."

Finally, Table 5.5 also reports the abuser's gender. However, in this case, we present the findings in a different manner than in Table 5.4. Whereas Table 5.4 reported the gender of the abuser in those cases for which a particular violation was reported, Table 5.5 presents the abuser's gender in terms of the rate at which a particular violation was reported by anyone in the sample by that particular sex/gender or by both male(s) and female(s). Obviously, only a male could perpetrate penile penetration of the vagina or anus (and the SACS survey did not allow for penetration by foreign objects). For the non-penile-involved abuses, between 1.5% and 4.9% of the sample reported that they experienced one or more of these violations by both male and female abusers (not necessarily in the same incident). Two to 6.5% of the sample reported experiencing the nonpenile abuses by a female abuser (and they may or may not have experienced these same abuses by a male abuser). However, 18% to 37% of the sample reported experiencing the nonpenile abuses by a male abuser (and these may or may not have been perpetrated by a female abuser as well). As stated previously, penile-vaginal intercourse was the most commonly reported violation, a highly extreme violation only possible by men.

Findings Combining the SES and SACS Data to Examine Rape Rates

Given the "slippery slope" when trying to define *rape* or *sexual assault*, the purpose of Table 5.6 is to examine how the percentage of what is most typically legally codified as *rape* changes (increases) as the definition of what qualifies as *rape* or *sexual assault* broadens. However, as already noted in the findings from the SES data (Table 5.4) and the SACS data (Table 5.5), most of the women who reported sexual violations

reported a range of abuses, and in at least two-fifths of the cases (41.9%, $n = 164$), the women reported two or more abusers (see Table 5.5). Thus, as the definition is expanded, the number will not "jump" by as many who experienced the added violation but by the number experiencing the new violation, whose extreme sexual violation was not already captured in the prior, more restricted definition. Thus, Table 5.6 starts with the simplest and most traditional measure of rape (responding "yes" to the word *rape*), adding numerous other extreme violations, including oral and anal sexual abuse, and ending with oral, anal, or vaginal penetration achieved through alcohol and/or drugs. The eight items composing this measure qualify in most states as rape (or the most serious levels of sexual victimization).

As stated previously, if we measure *rape* only by the number of those who reported that they experienced "rape" (using the word), the rate was 54.4% in this sample. When we add cases that include the SES item of oral, anal, or vaginal penetration by a penis or a foreign object, the rate increases to 60.6% of the sample. After adding the SACS measure "penis in the vagina" or "penis in the anus," the rate rises to 64.2%. (Adding "penis in the anus" after "penis in the vagina" only increased the n by 1.) Adding the SACS "oral sex on the abuser" barely increased the rate to 65.5% (adding 5 cases), and adding the SACS "oral sex on the victim" barely increased the rate to 66.5% (adding 4 cases). Adding SES oral, anal, or vaginal penetration by an authority figure increased the rate by only two persons to 67.0%. The final item added to the most extreme measures of sexual abuse—the SES measure of oral, anal, or vaginal penetration through drugs and/or alcohol—increased the number by 12, and the percentage to 70.1%.

There are two major patterns in Table 5.6. First, given the significant overlap in sexual violations (the same abuser committing more than one abuse, such as anal and oral rape) and in abusers (26.9% of the sample having three or more sexual abusers), it is not surprising that expanding the definition often resulted in slight changes for some of the items. Second, all of the items in Table 5.6 reflect behaviors that constitute the legal definition of rape in most American states, and using a more inclusive definition increased the rape rate from 54.5% to 70.1% of the sample.

The VOR

Table 5.7 summarizes the VOR as reported through the SACS data. (The SES items did not ask about the VOR.) The single most frequently (25.6%) reported abuser was "male stranger." The next mostly commonly reported abusers were male lover or boyfriend (15.9%) and male date (15.9%), closely followed by husband (14.1%).[3] The next most frequently reported abusers, listed in order, were uncle (12.3%), brother (11.8%), male cousin (10.0%), stepfather (8.4%), male neighbor (8.4%), father (7.9%), female lover or girlfriend (5.1%), male in-law

(4.6%), grandfather (4.3%), and mother's male partner (4.3%). (The remaining VORs, such as male or female ministers, male or female counselors, and most female categories were reported by fewer than 1.5% of the sample.) When we controlled to only include the women who had ever been married, the rate of rape by husbands increased from 14.1% to 23.5%. When we combined male lover/boyfriend with male date, the rate was 24.3%. Thus, we concluded that although male strangers pose a significant threat, the rates are similarly high for male romantic partners. And when we combined father and stepfather, the rate was 15.3% (see Table 5.7). The VORs discussed thus far refer to "any level" abusers (meaning that they could have been reported by any or all of the five SACS levels). Examining the columns distinguished by the level of abuse in Table 5.7, the overall ranking of VORs are in a similar order as the "any level" abusers.

Table 5.7   SACS Level of Abuse for Fourteen Most Frequently Reported Abusers (*N* = 391)[a]

Abuser[b]	Any Level[c] %	n	Level 1[d] %	n	Level 2[e] %	n	Level 3[f] %	n	Level 4[g] %	n	Level 5[h] %	n
Male stranger	25.6	100	14.8	58	11.7	46	10.2	40	12.3	48	17.9	70
Male lover/ boyfriend	15.9	62	10.0	39	7.7	30	7.9	31	8.2	32	11.8	46
Male date	15.9	62	11.8	46	9.2	36	7.4	29	7.9	31	9.7	38
Husband	14.1	55	9.0	35	8.2	32	7.4	29	9.5	37	11.5	45
Uncle	12.3	48	6.9	27	7.7	30	5.9	23	4.6	18	4.6	18
Brother	11.8	46	6.1	24	5.6	22	4.3	17	3.6	14	6.6	26
Male cousin	10.0	39	7.7	30	6.6	26	5.1	20	2.6	10	4.6	18
Stepfather	8.4	33	5.9	23	5.4	21	3.8	15	2.8	11	4.9	19

(Continued)

(Continued)

Abuser[b]	Any Level[c]		Level 1[d]		Level 2[e]		Level 3[f]		Level 4[g]		Level 5[h]	
	%	n	%	n	%	n	%	n	%	n	%	n
Male neighbor	8.4	33	5.6	22	5.1	20	3.3	13	2.8	11	3.1	12
Father	7.9	31	5.4	21	5.6	22	4.1	16	3.1	12	4.1	16
Female lover	5.1	20	4.6	18	4.1	16	3.1	12	3.6	14	0.0	0
Male in-law	4.6	18	3.6	14	3.1	12	2.8	11	2.8	11	2.6	10
Grandfather	4.3	17	2.3	9	3.1	12	1.8	7	1.3	5	1.3	5
Mother's male partner	4.3	17	3.1	12	2.6	10	1.8	7	1.0	4	2.0	8
Husband (if ever married)[i]	23.5	31	13.6	18	12.9	17	9.8	13	14.4	19	18.2	24
Male date/ lover/ boyfriend[j]	24.3	95	25.5	98	25.1	98	14.8	58	15.9	62	19.7	77
Father or stepfather	15.3	60	10.2	40	5.9	23	7.7	30	5.4	21	10.2	40

a. In the entire sample of 391, all missing data were coded as "no" to avoid overreporting the level of sexual violations.

b. The abuser identity is listed in order of most to least frequently identified category of abuser for the 14 most frequently reported abusers. The following abuser relationships were reported by 1.0% to 1.5%: mother's male partner, father's male partner, male minister, aunt, stepmother, and female cousin. The following abuser relationships were reported by 0.0% and 0.8%: female minister, female in-law, female stranger, female date, mother's female partner, father's female partner, male counselor, female counselor, grandmother, mother, sister, female teacher, female neighbor, and male teacher.

c. This column is the percentage or rate of the 391 women in the sample for which there were reported any sexual abuses by an individual victim-offender relationship abuser, and the following columns report the percentage out of the 391 respondents who reported a particular violation.

d. Level 1 sexual violations were nudity, disrobing, genital exposure, observing someone undress, or kissing.

e. Level 2 sexual violations were fondling the victim or making the victim masturbate the abuser.

f. Level 3 sexual violations were abuser's finger penetrating the anus or vagina.

g. Level 4 sexual violations were cunnilingus or fellatio.

h. Level 5 sexual violations were penetrations of the vagina or anus by the penis.

i. This was calculated only for those 132 women who reported ever being married out of the 241 women for whom marital status was known. "Husband" above was for all women, whether ever married.

j. This was calculated combining if woman reported sexual abuse by male date or lover or boyfriend.

CSA Histories of the Incarcerated Women

Table 5.8 presents the incarcerated women's self-reported CSA victimization history calculated from the SACS data. (Victim age was not asked on the SES instrument.) In this study, half (50.1%) of the women reported some level of CSA before their 18th birthdays. Ten percent (10.2%) reported some level of CSA before they were 6 years old, and one-third (34.3%) by their 12th birthdays. Child sexual abusers were predominantly family members (7.9% reported familial CSA before age 6, 31.5% before age 12, and 40.2% before age 18). Significantly less common, yet still prevalent, were acquaintance child sexual abusers (e.g., dates, teachers, and neighbors). Six percent (6.1%) of the women reported an acquaintance sexually abusing them before age 6; 15.1% reported an acquaintance CSA before age 12; and a full quarter (25.1%) reported this before age 18 (see Table 5.8). Stranger child sexual abusers were reported by 2.6% of the women before they were 6 years old and 5.6% before they were 12 years old. Fifteen percent (14.6%) of the women reported a stranger had sexually abused them before they were 18 years old. Notably, ages 6 to 11 are the highest risk age group for CSA by a family member, but ages 12 to 17 are the highest risk age group for CSA by either an acquaintance or a stranger (see Table 5.8).

Table 5.8 Reports of Any Level of Child Sexual Abuse by Age and Abuser (From SACS) ($N = 391$)

Abuser's Relationship to Child Victim	0 to 5 Years Old		6 to 11 Years Old		0 to 11 Years Old		12 to 17 Years Old		0 to 17 Years Old	
	%	n	%	n	%	n	%	n	%	n
Any[a]	10.2	40	29.7	116	34.3	134	35.8	140	50.1	196
Familial[b]	7.9	31	27.6	108	31.5	123	19.9	78	40.2	157
Acquaintance'	6.1	24	9.7	38	15.1	59	18.4	72	25.1	98
Stranger	2.6	10	3.8	15	5.6	22	10.0	39	14.6	57
Specific[d]										
Male stranger	1.5	6	3.8	15	4.6	18	9.9	39	14.1	55
Brother	1.3	5	6.6	26	7.4	29	5.1	20	10.2	40
Uncle	1.3	5	5.3	21	6.4	25	4.6	18	10.2	40
Male cousin	2.0	8	5.1	20	6.4	25	3.3	13	9.2	36

(Continued)

(Continued)

Abuser's Relationship to Child Victim	0 to 5 Years Old		6 to 11 Years Old		0 to 11 Years Old		12 to 17 Years Old		0 to 17 Years Old	
	%	n	%	n	%	n	%	n	%	n
Male date	—	—	0.5	2	0.5	2	8.6	34	9.0	35
Stepfather	1.0	4	4.3	17	5.4	21	3.0	12	7.9	31
Father	2.8	11	3.0	12	4.6	18	4.6	18	7.7	30
Male neighbor	0.8	3	4.3	17	5.1	20	3.3	13	7.7	30
Male lover	—	—	—	—	—	—	4.8	19	4.9	19
Grandfather	1.5	6	2.3	9	3.3	13	1.5	6	3.8	15
Mother's male partner	0.3	1	2.0	8	2.3	9	2.0	8	3.8	15
Male in-law	—	—	0.8	3	0.8	3	2.8	11	3.3	13
Husband	—	—	—	—	—	—	2.5	10	2.6	10

a. These were calculated by gathering all of the data for which age information was available on child sexual abuse, including recoding of what was written in under "Other" on the survey. Other abusers not listed on the survey, although written in under "Other" and identified as abusing between the ages of 0 and 17 years old, included family friends, friends, babysitters, boyfriends of other family members, bosses, and other acquaintances.

b. Familial included father, stepfather, grandfather, cousin, brother, mother, sister, stepmother, grandmother aunt, in-laws, husband, sister, and uncle.

c. Acquaintance included minister, mother's or father's partner, counselor, neighbor, teacher, date, and a lover or boy/girlfriend.

d. Abusers are listed from most to least predominant. For some potential abusers, none was reported: father's female partner, female in-law, female counselor, sister, female neighbor, female teacher, and female date. Thus, these were omitted from the table, as were those that constituted 1.5% or fewer of the child and adolescent sexual abuse reports: father's male partner (1.5%, $n = 6$), aunt (1.3%, $n = 5$), female cousin (1.0%, $n = 4$), stepmother (1.0%, $n = 4$), female lover (0.8%, $n = 3$ [listed for the adolescent group only]), female stranger (0.5%, $n = 2$), male teacher (0.5%, $n = 2$), male minister (0.3%, $n = 1$), female minister (0.3%, $n = 1$), mother's female partner (0.3%, $n = 1$), mother (0.3%, $n = 1$), grandmother (0.3%, $n = 1$), and male counselor (0.3%, $n = 1$).

Table 5.8 also reports the specific VOR more generally than the family versus acquaintance versus stranger distinction. The VORs most likely to be reported as sexually abusing the women before the age of 6 were fathers (2.8%), male cousins (2.0%), male strangers (1.5%), brothers (1.3%), and uncles (1.3%). The VORs most likely to be reported as sexually abusing the women from age 6 through 11 years old were brothers (6.6%), uncles (5.3%), male cousins (5.1%), stepfathers (4.3%), male neighbors (4.3%), and male strangers (3.8%). The VORs most likely to be reported as sexually abusing the women aged 12 through 17 years old were male strangers (9.9%), male dates (8.6%), brothers (5.1%), male lovers (4.8%), uncles (4.6%), and fathers (4.6%). Notably, there were 10 women who reported sexual abuse by their husband when they were 12 to 17 years old (see Table 5.8).

Conclusion

The findings reported in this study document (a) an unexpectedly high level of sexual victimizations, including the most serious types of sexual abuses, self-reported by 391 incarcerated women; and (b) the need for detailed and comprehensive measures to more fully report on the extent and rates of sexual victimizations and violations (regardless of whether the group studied is incarcerated). Seventy percent of the incarcerated women reported sexual abuses that in most states would qualify as *rape* or the most serious *sexual assaults*. Furthermore, the women who reported sexual violations and abuses typically reported multiple sexual abuses and often multiple sexual abusers. Although two-fifths of the sample reported no sexual abusers, more than a quarter of the respondents (26.9%) reported having three or more sexual abusers.

The data contain some very disturbing findings. Among them are that 54.5% of the sample responded that they had been "raped," 11.5% reported "gang rape," 18.4% were sexually penetrated by an authority figure, 38.6% reported someone using alcohol or drugs to sexually penetrate them, 22.0% reported anal rape by a penis, 41.9% reported vaginal rape by a penis, 36.1% reported oral rape, and 50.1% reported child sexual violations or abuses. As expected, the sexual abusers were primarily male, yet it is important to note that sexual victimizations by females were also reported: For all types of sexual violation or abuse that did not involve a penis, 4.1% to 6.4% of the women reported the act perpetrated by a female abuser. The only abuse with lower frequency by female perpetrators was a female using a finger to penetrate the anus, which was reported by 2.3% of the sample.

Previously in this article (and summarized in Tables 5.1 and 5.2), we presented the frequencies reported in existing studies of sexual abuse in both community (nonincarcerated) samples of women and girls (see Table 5.1) and among incarcerated women and girls (see Table 5.2). As expected, the findings on self-reported sexual abuse from the current sample of 391 incarcerated women were more consistent with the existing studies of incarcerated samples than existing studies of community samples. Even in comparison to the existing studies on incarcerated women's self-reported sexual victimizations, however, the current study revealed far higher rates.[4]

This study provides a far more detailed account of incarcerated women's sexual abuse histories than previous researchers have documented. The findings reported herein lend support to the pathways perspective: Incarcerated women report significantly higher rates of sexual abuses and other sexual violations than reported by nonincarcerated samples of women and girls, indicating that sexual abuse is a significant risk factor for women's offending. Thus, future research must continue to address the trauma and victimization histories of offenders and, ideally, compare these histories to those of nonoffenders. Clearly, this suggests that policy makers should aspire to increase current efforts to identify and address children's sexual victimizations because of the importance of reducing the after effects of trauma and because such interventions, if done well, would likely reduce the probability of sexual victimizations being a trajectory into offending. Finally, programs focusing on recovery from sexual abuse continue to be needed for female offenders to reduce their probability of recidivism.

Appendix A: The Sexual Experiences Survey (SES)

This survey will ask you to answer questions about your sexual experiences. Thinking about material of this nature often raises issues for the individuals involved, so that you may find it necessary to speak to someone after you have participated in this study. If you need to discuss this questionnaire, please see the name and number listed on the cover sheet.

Remember, your participation is *voluntary*; you may stop at any time and for any reason.

A. **Questionnaire Definitions**. For the purpose of this study:
  - SEX PLAY means: kissing, fondling, or petting
  - SEX ACTS means: oral sex, anal sex, vaginal intercourse, or penetration by objects other than the penis

B. **Questionnaire Item Parts**. There are two parts to each questionnaire item:
  - Please answer each question by circling *yes* if you have had the experience or *no* if you have not had the experience. If yes, then answer both *a* and *b* for each item.

  Part A. Please answer Part A of each item by *circling the number of times* each event has happened in your life. The same forms of sexual abuse are repeated for each person.

  Part B. Answer Part B of each item by circling if the person who abused you was/were male(s), female(s), or male(s) and female(s).

  Part C. Questionnaire Items*

  1. Have you ever had someone misinterpret the level of sexual intimacy you desired? [misinterpret level of sexual intimacy]

  2. Have you ever been in a situation where someone became so sexually aroused that you felt it was useless to stop that person, even though you did not want to engage in sexual activity? [useless to try to stop sex]

  3. Have you ever engaged in sexual activity with someone even though you didn't want to because the person wanted to end your relationship? [threaten to end relationship if no sex]

  4. Have you ever found out that someone had gotten you to engage in sexual activity with him or her by saying things he or she didn't really mean? [said things didn't mean to have sex]

  5. Have you given in to SEX PLAY when you didn't want to because you were overwhelmed by someone's continual arguments and pressure? [kiss, pet, fondle via verbal pressure]

  6. Have you had SEX PLAY when you didn't want to because someone used his/her position of authority (boss, teacher, camp counselor, supervisor) to make you? [use position of authority to kiss/fondle]

  7. Have you had SEX PLAY when you didn't want to because someone threatened or used some degree of physical force (twisting your arm, holding you down, etc.) to make you? [threat/use physical force to kiss/fondle]

  8. Have you had someone ATTEMPT A SEX ACT when you didn't want to because someone threatened or used some degree of physical force (twisting your arm, holding you

down, etc.) but intercourse *did not* occur? [threat/use of physical force to attempt penetration]

9. Have you had someone ATTEMPT A SEX ACT when you didn't want to by giving you alcohol or drugs, but intercourse *did not* occur? [used alcohol drugs to attempt penetration]

10. Have you given in to a SEX ACT when you didn't want to because you were overwhelmed by someone's continual arguments and pressure? [penetration via verbal pressure]

11. Have you had a SEX ACT when you didn't want to because someone used his/her position of authority (boss, teacher, camp counselor, supervisor) to make you? [use position of authority to penetrate]

12. Have you had a SEX ACT when you didn't want to because someone gave you alcohol or drugs? [use alcohol drugs to penetrate]

13. Have you had a SEX ACT when you didn't want to because someone threatened or used some degree of physical force (twisting your arm, holding you down, etc.) to make you? [threat/use physical force to penetrate]

14. Have you ever been raped? [rape]

15. Have you ever been gang raped? [gang rape]

Under each item, Parts A and B read, as follows:

a. If yes, how many times have you had this experience? Please circle the number of times this experience has happened.

0   1   2   3   4   5   6+

b. If yes, please circle one of the following:

Abuser(s): Male(s) Female(s) Male(s) & Female(s)

NOTE: Asterisks (*) mean that the words in brackets are those used to identify the items in Table 5.4.

Appendix B: The Sexual Abuse Checklist Survey (SACS)

The purpose of this study is to identify the forms of sexual abuse that you may have experienced before you were incarcerated. Thinking about material of this nature often raises issues for the individuals involved, so that you may find it necessary to speak to someone after you have participated in this study. If you need to discuss this questionnaire, please see the name and number listed on the cover sheet.

Of the women who have had sexual abuse experiences, many report that they were abused by more than one person in the course of their lives.

Instructions: There are three columns for you to provide your age at the time of the abuse and information about the person(s) who may have abused you. IF you were not abused by any of the individuals listed, please do not circle anyone in Column A because circling that person means that she/he abused you.

Answer Column A first. Answer Columns B and C *only* if a person listed in Column A was circled.

- **Column A**: Column A identifies a list from 1 to 24 of individuals who may or may not be related to you. Which of the following people would you say sexually abused you? In Column A, please circle the person(s) who abused you.

- **Column B**: Only use Column B if the person listed in Column A was circled.

- **In Column B**, several forms of sexual abuse are given. Circle all of the forms of sexual abuse that you experienced from the person circled in Column A.

- **Column C**: In Column C, list your age at the time the abuse that you circled in Column B occurred.

---

*For the purposes of this survey, a partner is defined as someone with whom you were in a committed relationship.

SOURCE: Adapted from Koss and Oros (1982).

Column A	Column B	Column C
Abuser	Forms of sexual abuse	Age

- 1. Father: Nudity, disrobing, genital exposure, being observed (i.e., showering, dressing, toileting), kissing, fondling, masturbation, oral sex performed on you, oral sex performed on them, finger penetration of the anus, finger penetration of the vagina, penis penetration of the vagina, other

---

This survey continued with Column B and Column C staying the same but under abuser: 2. stepfather, 3. grandfather, 4. cousin (please specify male or female) M/F, 5. minister (please specify male or female) M/F, 6. mother's partner (please specify male or female) M/F, 7. father's partner (please specify male or female) M/F, 8. brother, 9. mother, 10. stepmother, 11. grandmother, 12. aunt, 13. in-law (please specify male or female) M/F, 14. stranger (please specify male or female) M/F, 15. counselor (please specify male or female) M/F, 16. husband, 17. sister, 18. uncle, 19. neighbor (please specify male or female) M/F, 20. teacher (please specify male or female) M/F, 21. date (please specify male or female) M/F, 22. intimate male partner (boyfriend/lover), 23 intimate female partner (girlfriend/lover), 24. Other (please specify) _____.

Notes

1. A total of 64 persons participated in the pilot study, including 25 students enrolled in a women's studies course at the Ohio State University (females = 24, and males = 1), 13 women in a halfway house for women recently released from prison, 5 members from a neighborhood mental health center who voluntarily sought counseling for issues pertaining to prior sexual abuse, 11 participants from a transitional housing program for mentally ill and homeless women, and 15 participants from a drug rehabilitation program for women. In this pilot study, 90% of the participants assessed the surveys as readable and easily understandable. Minor revisions and rewording were made after the pilot test. Tests of reliability were not conducted, but the Marlowe-Crowne Social Desirability Scale (Crowne & Marlowe, 1960) measuring socially desirable responding in self-report measures, was completed by most of the sample. It contained 33 true/false items that are desirable but rare or undesirable but common. Descriptive statistics for social desirability showed a mean of 16.4, with a standard deviation of 6.41. These findings indicate an acceptable level of respondents' self-reports that they were not trying to "please" the researchers.

2. These official data on the racial and ethnic identities of the populations in the three women's prisons were reported to the first author in a personal phone call on August 7, 2006 by Stephan W. Van Dine, Bureau of Research Chief of the Ohio Department of Rehabilitation and Corrections (ODRC). The statistics were from the ODRC data reported July 1, 1996 from the three sites. It is unfortunate that none of the 1.7% of the Latina prisoners completed surveys and that White prisoners were slightly overrepresented, and African American prisoners slightly underrepresented, in the study sample.

3. We were careful to make sure that a participant did not count a male lover or boyfriend and male date as 2 if it was the same person by closely examining those cases where women reported both. We did the same for female lover or girlfriend and female date.

4. As previously noted, most of the existing studies used vague measures of sexual abuse, such as "forced sexual contact" (Lake, 1993), "raped, sexually abused or molested" (Sargent et al., 1993), and "raped or sexually attacked" (Browne et al., 1999), and some did not actually provide the wording for the measure (listed as "general" in the figures; e.g., Bloom et al., 1994, Johnston, 1995; Singer, 1995). An exception to the current study

reporting higher sexual violations than existing studies of incarcerated women and girls was Acoca (1998), who stated that 56% of her sample of detained (delinquent) girls reported some level of CSA compared to 50% in our study.

References

Acoca, L. (1998). Outside/inside: The violation of American girls at home, on the streets, and in the juvenile justice system. *Crime and Delinquency, 44*, 561–589.

American Correctional Association. (1990). *The female offender: What does the future hold?* Arlington, VA: Kirby Lithographic.

Amodeo, M., Griffin, M. L., Fassier, I. R., Clay, C. M., & Ellis, M. A. (2006). Childhood sexual abuse among black women and white women from two-parent families. *Child Maltreatment, 11*, 237–246.

Arnold, R. A. (1990). Women of color: Processes of victimization and criminalization of black women. *Social Justice, 17*(3), 153–166.

Basile, K. C. (1999). Rape by acquiescence. *Violence Against Women, 5*, 1036–1058.

Belknap, J., & Holsinger, K. (2006). The gendered nature of risk factors for delinquency. *Feminist Criminology, 1*, 48–71.

Belknap, J., Holsinger, K., & Dunn, M. (1997). Understanding incarcerated girls: The results of a focus group study. *Prison Journal, 77*, 381–404.

Bloom, B., Chesney-Lind, M., & Owen, B. (1994). *Women in California prisons: Hidden victims of the war on drugs.* San Francisco: Center on Juvenile and Criminal Justice.

Browne, A., & Finkelhor, D. (1986). Impact of child sexual abuse: A review of the research. *Psychological Bulletin, 99*(3–4), 66–77.

Browne, A., Miller, B., & Maguin, E. (1999). Prevalence and severity of lifetime physical and sexual victimization among incarcerated women. *International Journal of Law and Psychiatry, 22*, 301–322.

Bunch, B. J., Foley, L. A., & Urbina, S. P. (1983). The psychology of violent female offenders: A sex-role perspective. *Prison Journal, 63*, 66–79.

Carlen, P. (1983). *Women's imprisonment: A study in social control.* London: Routledge Kegan Paul.

Chesney-Lind, M., & Rodriguez, N. (1983). Women under lock and key. *Prison Journal, 63*, 47–65.

Coker, A. L., Patel, N. J., Krishnaswami, S., Schmidt, W., & Richter, D. L. (1998). Childhood forced sex and cervical dysplasia among women prison inmates. *Violence Against Women, 4,* 595–608.

Comack, E. (1996). *Women in trouble.* Halifax, Canada: Fernwood.

Cook, S. L., Smith, S. G., Tusher, C. P., & Raiford, J. (2005). Self-reports of traumatic events in a random sample of incarcerated women. *Women & Criminal Justice, 16,* 107–126.

Crowne, D. P., & Marlowe, D. A. (1960). A new scale of social desirability independent of psychopathology. *Journal of Consulting Psychology, 24,* 349–354.

Daly, K. (1992). Women's pathways to felony court: Feminist theories of lawbreaking and problems of representation. *Review of Law and Women's Studies, 2*(1), 11–52.

Estrich, S. (1987). *Real rape.* Cambridge, MA: Harvard University Press.

Evans, R. D., Forwyth, C. J., & Gauthier, D. K. (2002). Gendered pathways into and experiences within crack cultures outside of the inner city. *Deviant Behavior, 23,* 483–510.

Fletcher, B. R., Rolison, G. L., & Moon, D. G. (1993). The woman prisoner. In B. R. Fletcher, L. D. Shaver, & D. G. Moon (Eds.), *Women prisoners: A forgotten population* (pp. 5–14). Westport, CT: Praeger.

Fox, L., & Sugar, F. (1990). *Survey of federally sentenced Aboriginal women in the community.* Ottawa: National Women's Association of Canada.

Gaarder, E., & Belknap, J. (2002). Tenuous borders: Girls transferred to adult court. *Criminology, 40,* 481–517.

Gilfus, M. E. (1992). From victims to survivors to offenders: Women's routes of entry and immersion into street crime. *Women & Criminal Justice, 4,* 63–89.

Girshick, L. B. (1999). *No safe haven: Stories of women in prison.* Boston: Northeastern University Press.

Goodkind, S., Ng, I., & Sarri, R. C. (2006). The impact of sexual abuse in the lives of young women involved or at risk of involvement with the juvenile justice system. *Violence Against Women, 12,* 456–477.

Gray, T., Mays, G. L., & Stohr, M. K. (1995). Inmate needs and programming in exclusively women's jails. *Prison Journal, 75,* 186–202.

Greenfeld, L. A., & Snell, T. L. (1999). *Women offenders.* Washington, DC: U.S. Department of Justice.

Harlow, C. W. (1999). *Prior abuse reported by inmates and probationers.* Washington, DC: U.S. Department of Justice, Bureau of Justice Statistics.

Kelly, L. (1988). *Surviving sexual violence.* Minneapolis: University of Minnesota Press.

Kilpatrick, D. G. (1996, November). *From the mouths of victims: What victimization surveys tell us about sexual assault and sex offenders.* Paper presented at the Association for the Treatment of Sexual Abusers Meeting, Chicago, IL.

Kilpatrick, D. G., & Saunders, B. E. (1997). The prevalence and consequences of child victimization. *National Institute of Justice Research Preview.* Retrieved from http://www.ncjrs.gov/pdffiles/fs000179.pdf

Koss, M. P., & Oros, C. J. (1982). Sexual Experiences Survey: A research instrument investigating sexual aggression and victimization. *Journal of Consulting and Clinical Psychology, 50,* 455–457.

Kraska, P. B., & Kappeler, V. E. (1995). To serve and pursue: Exploring police sexual violence against women. *Justice Quarterly, 12,* 85–112.

Lake, E. S. (1993). An exploration of the violent victim experiences of female offenders. *Violence and Victims, 8,* 41–51.

Little Hoover Commission, State of California. (2004). *Breaking the barriers for women on parole.* Retrieved from http://www.lhc.ca.gov/lhcdir/177/report177.pdf

Maeve, M. K. (2000). Speaking unavoidable truths: Understanding early childhood sexual and physical violence for women in prison. *Issues in Mental Health Nursing, 21,* 473–498.

James, J., & Meyerding, J. (1977). Early sexual experiences and prostitution. *American Journal of Psychiatry, 134,* 1381–1385.

Johnston, D. (1995). Jailed mothers. In K. Gabel & D. Johnston (Eds.), *Children of incarcerated parents* (pp. 41–55). New York: Lexington Books.

Murphy, S. M., Kilpatrick, D. G., Amick-McMullan, A. Veronene, L. J., Paduhvoich, J., Best, C. L., et al. (1988). Current psychological functioning of child sexual assault survivors. *Journal of Interpersonal Violence, 3,* 55–79.

National Center for Victims of Crime (NCVC), & Crime Victims Research and Treatment Center. (1992). *Rape in America: A report to the nation.* Arlington, VA: Authors.

Neria, Y., Bromet, E. J., Carlson, G. A., & Naz, B. (2005). Assaultive trauma and illness course in psychotic bipolar disorder: Findings from the Suffolk

County Mental Health Project. *Acta Psychiatrica Scandinavica, 111*, 380–383.

Owen, B. (1998). *In the mix: Struggle and survival in a women's prison.* Albany: State University of New York Press.

Richie, B. E. (1996). *Compelled to crime: The gender entrapment of battered black women.* New York: Routledge.

Russell, D. E. H. (1984). *Sexual exploitation.* Beverly Hills, CA: Sage.

Sable, M. R., Fieberg, J. R., Martin, S. L., & Kupper, L. L. (1999). Violence victimization experiences of pregnant prisoners. *American Journal of Orthopsychiatry, 69,* 392–397.

Sargent, E., Marcus-Mendoza, S., & Chong, H. Y. (1993). Abuse and the woman prisoner. In B. R. Fletcher, L. D. Shaver, & D. G. Moon (Eds.), *Women prisoners: A forgotten population* (pp. 55–64). Westport, CT: Praeger.

Schwartz, M. D., & Leggett, M. S. (1999). Bad dates or emotional trauma: The aftermath of campus sexual assault. *Violence Against Women, 2,* 148–162.

Sharp, S. F., & Marcus-Mendoza, S. T. (2001). It's a family affair: Incarcerated women and their families. *Women & Criminal Justice, 12,* 21–49.

Shaw, M. (1992). Issues of power and control: Women in prison and their defenders. *British Journal of Criminology, 32,* 438–452.

Silbert, M. H., & Pines, A. M. (1981). Sexual abuse as an antecedent to prostitution. *Child Abuse and Neglect, 5,* 407–411.

Singer, M. I., Bussey, J., Song, L. Y., & Lunghofer, L. (1995). The psychosocial issues of women serving time in jail. *Social Work, 40,* 103–113.

Snell, T. L., & Morton, D. C. (1994). *Women in prison: Survey of state prison inmates, 1991.* Washington, DC: U.S. Department of Justice.

Sudderth, L. K. (1998). "It'll come right back at me": The interactional context of discussing rape with others. *Violence Against Women, 4,*559–571.

Tjaden, P., & Thoennes, N. (2000). *Full report of the prevalence, incidence, and consequences of violence against women.* Washington, DC: U.S. Department of Justice.

Van Dorn, R. A., Mustillo, S., Elbogen, E. B., Dorsey, S., Swanson, J. W., & Swartz, M. S. (2005). The effects of early sexual abuse on adult risky sexual behaviors among persons with severe mental illness. *Child Abuse & Neglect, 29,* 1265–1279.

Wyatt, G. E., Loeb, T. B., Solis, B., & Carmona, J. V. (1999). The prevalence and circumstances of child sexual abuse: Changes across a decade. *Child Abuse & Neglect, 23,* 45–60.

Wyatt, G. E., Newcomb, M. D., & Riderle, M. H. (1993). *Sexual abuse and consensual sex.* Newbury Park, CA: Sage.

CHAPTER 6

Gendered War and Gendered Peace

Truth Commissions and Postconflict Gender Violence: Lessons From South Africa

Tristan Anne Borer

That war is profoundly gendered has long been recognized by feminist international relations scholars (Enloe, 2000; Jacobs, Jacobson, & Marchbank, 2000; Turshen & Twagiramariya, 1998). In World War I, 80% of war casualties were soldiers, which meant men. In World War II, only 50% of casualties were soldiers; by the Vietnam War, this number had fallen to 20%. By the 1990s, a full 90% of casualties were civilians, mainly women and children (Pettman, 1996). For those who survive, many are forcibly displaced, becoming refugees and internally displaced persons, 80% of whom are again women and children. Civil conflicts—the type which most often fuels calls for truth telling after transitions to democracy—have specific forms of violence, including state terror enacted by agents or by vigilante groups or paramilitaries with state complicity directed primarily against innocent civilians; much of this violence is again gender specific, with women being targeted through gender-based humiliation and torture. In general, most feminist scholars argue that sexual violence against women specifically is a constitutive aspect of war.[1] Although it is clear that war is gendered, less recognized are the ways in which the postwar period is equally gendered. What happens to women victims of war violence? What role does righting gender inequities play in postwar reconstruction? Although the gendered dimension of violent conflict has received much theoretical attention, what has not been adequately theorized is how truth-seeking exercises in the aftermath of conflict should

Borer, T. A. (2009). Gendered war and gendered peace: Truth commissions and post-conflict gender violence: Lessons from South Africa. *Violence Against Women, 15* , 1169–1193.

AUTHOR'S NOTE: The author thanks the anonymous reviewers for their helpful comments and suggestions for improving the manuscript. She also thanks John D. Nugent for his editing assistance.

respond to this fact. The difficulties of fore-grounding gender in truth telling are illustrated by examining the South African Truth and Reconciliation Commission (TRC). In this article, I argue that the TRC was not terribly successful at uncovering the truth about women's experiences, specifically of sexual violence, under apartheid. I offer several explanations for this, including the definition of human rights violations that governed the work of the commission, the primacy given to civil and political over economic and social rights violations, the adoption of a gender-neutral approach to truth gathering, and the criteria used for qualifying for amnesty. The article then explores some consequences of the failure to uncover the truth about sexual violence, including its impact on the government's reparations policy, and continued "peacetime" violence perpetrated against women in South Africa.

War Is Gendered. So Is Peace

Richard Rayner (1997) argued that military training involves socialization into an extreme kind of masculinity, in which a young soldier must prove he is a good soldier—that is, that he is neither a "girl" nor gay. This militarized masculinity, which results from breaking men down and reconstructing them as soldiers, Pettman (1996) argued, "regularly includes the vilification of women and consciously plays on young men's sexual insecurities and identities" (p. 93). Rayner (1997) argued that in this warrior culture militarism, masculinity and sexualized violence are connected: "There is a set of attitudes, including hypermasculinity, adversarial sexual beliefs, sexual promiscuity, acceptance of violence against women, hostility toward women, and sex-role stereotyping, that is correlated with rape and a proclivity for it" (p. 29). And while Rayner questions whether rape is a necessary corollary to the bottom line of an army's function—killing—others believe that sexual harassment and violence are not only inevitable but, indeed, a necessary part of the military. He quotes Reagan

administration Undersecretary of Defense for Policy Fred C. Iklé, for example, who argues that "military life may correctly foster the attitudes that tend toward rape, such as aggression and single-minded self-assertion" (Rayner, 1997, p. 29).

In light of Rayner's "warrior culture," it is not surprising that in all types of violent conflicts, women are targeted specifically as women by sexual violence. As a result, rape as a tool of war has become endemic. Diken and Lausten (2005) argued that rape can, in fact, be viewed as a prime strategy of asymmetric warfare, as soldiers attack civilian women rather than male combatants and have only the indirect aim of taking a territory. The Women's Rights Project of Human Rights Watch has detailed the variety of ways in which rape has been used as a war weapon and as a tool of political repression; it is clear that sexual violence is a worldwide and pan-cultural phenomenon (Human Rights Watch, 1995a, pp. 1–3).[2] Although it has become increasingly evident that women are vulnerable to rape by soldiers from the "other" side as a way of getting at "their" men, demonstrating the failure of their men as protectors, recent events have revealed that rape is not a tool reserved only for emasculating and humiliating the enemy. Women, it is now clear, face the prospect of being raped both by soldiers from their own countries and by peacekeepers; in both cases, women are being raped by soldiers who are supposedly their protectors.[3]

While overwhelmingly the case, women are not only victims in war. Despite widespread assumptions and popular images associating men with violence and war and women with peace, many women also join war efforts, in a variety of roles. They join voluntary state militaries and take up arms as combatants in liberation wars. What happens to these women—both victims/survivors and warriors—after war? Can truth telling bring gender relations to the fore as a concern for long-term sustainable peace? Pettman (1996, p. 126) argued that whatever women's participation in armed struggles, they are routinely pushed back into the private sphere when the fighting is over, their contributions erased. She is particularly interested in what happens to women and to gender relations after liberation movements have prevailed and the state has been captured, as was the case in many countries that subsequently instituted truth commissions, from El Salvador to South Africa. Repeatedly, she argues, after liberation women are relegated to roles of being protected and are made invisible in debates about how to build new, representative, and legitimate state institutions, including the military. Moreover, she notes a widespread pattern of regression in terms of women's claims and participation after the state is won, arguing that there is a near universal tendency for women to lose out in state consolidation politics. It appears to be difficult for women to translate their activism in wars and nationalist struggles into rights and effective participation when the fighting is done. Even in cases where large numbers of women bore arms, "'peace' seems to see enormous pressure on those women to return 'home,' to give up both jobs and political representation in favour of men" (Pettman, 1996, p. 137). Why might the trends prevail, and how might postwar truth telling prevent or ameliorate these problems? Pettman offers several hypotheses for why traditional gender roles are so often strongly reasserted, even within those states where women played important roles in antistate militaries and where gender interests were incorporated into revolutionary rhetoric.

One possible reason is that the transfer of state power is not always accompanied by effective control over territory and population. This was true during the cold war, when new governments almost immediately faced foreign-backed counterrevolutionary forces, such as South African-funded antistate forces in both Angola and Mozambique. More recently, power transfers in areas such as Afghanistan and Iraq support the notion that state capture and state consolidation are not necessarily synonymous. Faced with immediate legitimacy crises, Pettman argues, states tend to quickly prioritize state survival and defense, which often translates into intensified militarization. When this occurs, gender transformation policies are either postponed or abandoned altogether. Gender issues are also quickly set aside as well when the state immediately faces an economic crisis, such as reconstruction. When the state becomes the main source of rewards, competition for positions within it is fierce, with men being rewarded more handsomely than women. Moreover, it serves the state's interests to revert to traditional notions of "women's work," so women's labor is exploited cheaply. Third, new governments frequently need to absorb a large number of demobilized soldiers. And even though many women fought as soldiers, "soldier" comes to mean male, and "governments seek to 'disarm' soldier men as a potential threat to state power, and might reward them with 'returned' power over women, rather than risk further discontent through social policies that undermine men's roles and 'the' (patriarchal) family" (Pettman, 1996, p. 140). Underlying Pettman's three hypotheses of state consolidation, political economy, and male elite power interests is the reality that during wars, gender roles are often suspended; however, demobilization into a postwar context often means a return to prewar gender relations, a return to "normalcy."

In terms of sexual violence, similar dynamics appear to be at play. Because violence was considered a legitimate means for waging and ending conflict, men use violence against women in the aftermath of conflict to reestablish and retain control over family resources and over women's productive and reproductive rights. Across contexts, domestic violence incidents increase as women are revictimized by returning husbands and sons (Duggan & Abusharaf, 2006). Whatever the combination of reasons for a reversion to old gendered dynamics accompanied by continuing (and sometimes increased) violence against women, the implications for long-term sustainable peace are clear: failure to address gendered power relations both before and during conflicts means that they are unlikely to be addressed, much less transformed, in its aftermath (Pettman, 1996). It is precisely during this aftermath that the potential for truth telling to grapple with both the history and the future of gender power relations is at its highest.

Truth Telling and Gendered Peace

If women are specifically targeted with violence during war, will those responsible for such violence be held accountable at war's end? If not, what does this say about the government's commitment to the rule of law and human rights? Moreover, can truth-telling mechanisms help avert the problem of women's contributions to overthrowing authoritarian governments subsequently being erased? If not, then Pettman's (1996) statement that "even in postrevolutionary situations where women are declared legally equal, profound inattention to or defence of unequal gender relations ensures that national liberation will not mean women's liberation" (p. 140) is disturbing indeed in terms of prospects for lasting peace. Christine Bell and Catherine O'Rourke (2007), however, provide insight into just how difficult a postwar gendered focus might prove to be, pointing to the visible exclusion of women in all aspects of transitional justice processes, beginning with their near absence from the fora that decide which type of transitional justice mechanisms, if any, will be adopted. Because transitional justice mechanisms, including truth commissions, are generally products of peace negotiations, and because negotiation processes themselves are deeply gendered (with negotiators from both state and nonstate parties to the conflict as well as international negotiators being overwhelmingly men), conceptualizations of how accountability, justice, and human rights will be approached cannot help but be gendered.[4] Echoing Pettman's concerns, they conclude that "for women in transitions an emphasis on postconflict restoration without challenging uneven gender power relations can mean giving up the perverse equality gains of war and returning to the home

and perhaps other forms of abuse" (Bell & O'Rourke, 2007, p. 41). And indeed, this proved to be generally true in the South African case.

The South African TRC and Gendered Violence

In any truth commission, "the process of defining the terms of a commission's mandate, the 'truth' that it is aiming toward, is a high-stakes political terrain" (Nesiah, 2006, p. 6). In South Africa, the commissioners—seven of whom were women—had to determine how they would fulfill their given mandate, in terms of granting amnesties (deciding who the perpetrators were) and certifying those eligible for reparations (deciding who the victims were). The commissioners were guided by the Promotion of National Unity and Reconciliation Act of 1995, which stated that persons would be eligible for amnesty if they made "full disclosure of all the relevant facts relating to acts associated with a political objective" (Ch. 2, Sec. 3[1][b]). "Victims" were defined as those who had suffered physical or mental injury, emotional suffering, pecuniary loss, or a substantial impairment of human rights as a result of a gross violation of human rights (GVHR), along with (sometimes) their relatives and dependents (Ch. 1, Sec. 1[xix]). In determining whether a person had suffered a GVHR, the TRC again looked to the Act for guidance. Four things constituted gross violations of human rights: killing, abduction, torture, or severe ill-treatment (Ch. 1, Sec. 1[ix]), although severe ill-treatment was not clearly defined in the Act. While undoubtedly unintentional, these definitions (of victims, violations, and those eligible for amnesty) had profound implications for the TRC's ability to address both gendered violence of the past and gender justice in the future.

The Human Rights Violations Committee of the TRC collected more than 21,000 victim statements describing 37,672 human rights violations. An interesting gendered phenomenon emerged almost immediately during the period of statement giving: more African women—most middle aged or elderly—came to the Commission than any other category of people. Even more striking, however, was the fact that although most people who told the Commission about violations were women, they overwhelmingly testified about violations against men (South African Truth and Reconciliation Commission, 1998a, pp. 165–171). Women, it appeared, were unwilling to talk about their own experiences of human rights violations under apartheid. This held true especially in terms of reporting sexual violence that they had experienced. Indeed, of the over 21,000 testimonies given, only 140 explicitly mentioned rape (South African Truth and Reconciliation Commission, 1998b, p. 296), although given the prevalence of rape during wartime, the number was very likely much higher. In terms of the first charge in the TRC's mandate, "establishing as complete a picture as possible of the causes, nature and extent of the gross violations of human rights which were committed" (South African Truth and Reconciliation Commission, 1998a, p. 55), the TRC thus faced a rather large obstacle: the "truth" about women's experiences as women (as opposed to as wives and mothers) never fully emerged. Why did women refuse to discuss their own histories of apartheid-era violations, finding it more comfortable to tell the stories of their male relatives? At least two explanations are possible, both of which hold policy implications for future truth-telling exercises.

The first explanation is that the definition of GVHR that governed the work of the TRC—that is, that only killing, abduction, torture, or severe ill-treatment would count as a violation—affected women's testimonies. Fiona Ross (2003) argued that the Act's definitions of violence and violation were excessively narrow. With its focus on what are known as bodily integrity rights (South African Truth and Reconciliation Commission, 1998b, p. 64), other types of violence were not the focus of the Commission. Women, however, are more likely than men to

suffer from structural violence, which arises from social, economic, and political structures that increase the vulnerability of particular groups— for example, poor women who experience higher infant mortality rates due to limited access to health care systems (Peterson & Runyon, 1999). Indeed, socioeconomic vulnerability may well increase during violence with the economic burden of caring for and supporting the family being further shifted onto women who often find themselves as single heads of households due to high mortality and/or disappearance rates of men (Duggan & Abusharaf, 2006).

Heightened vulnerability was especially the case for women under the apartheid system, which was more than just a system of racism; it was also a highly developed system of economic segregation. The economic consequences of apartheid policies were profound indeed, and African women were the population group that suffered the most. The integrated systems of migrant labor, forced removals, inadequate or no education, neglect of traditional agriculture, and lack of basic health care combined to create a system of extreme poverty, with tremendously high unemployment rates, severely skewed income distributions, and tragic health differentials. Rural homeland areas were especially poverty-stricken, and this affected women more than men as men migrated to urban areas in search of employment, leaving women, children, elderly, and infirm behind. Beth Goldblatt and Sheila Meintjes (1998), in a submission on gender to the TRC, argued that the history of apartheid was not only one of racial domination. Less emphasized was "the way in which patriarchal power relations were integrated and used to bolster the power of the oppressors within indigenous communities" (p. 29). These power relations, while long predating apartheid, were exacerbated by it.[5]

Thus the primacy given to violations of civil and political rights by the Act creating the TRC had implications for how much truth the Commission would eventually be able to uncover. Feminist human rights scholars have long argued that the dichotomy between—and primacy given to—civil and political rights, which are seen as operating primarily in the public sphere of the state, and economic rights, which are seen as pertaining primarily to the private sphere, obscures and downplays the violations from which women most suffer (Charlesworth, 1995). To be clear: it is not that women do not suffer direct violence perpetrated by the state; they do. However, they are much more likely than men to suffer from violations of indirect or structural violence. It is precisely these social and economic rights which fell outside of the purview of the TRC. The consequences for women, Ross (2003) argued, were profound:

> Permitting the expression of pain of a particular kind, [the Commission] emphasised bodily violation at the expense of a broader understanding of apartheid and its consequences. Foregrounding certain forms of violence in the public record, it rendered some kinds of pain more visible while displacing other forms of experience and its expression. Its work points to the ease with which women's experiences are homogenised and the range of expressions to give voice to experience restricted. (p. 162)

The TRC was not unaware of the narrow interpretation of its mandate. It addressed, somewhat defensively, the issue of types of violations it investigated twice in its report: once, in a general overview of the difficulty of defining gross violations of human rights, and once specifically in relation to the gendered implications of this difficulty. In its general comment on interpreting the Act's definition of GVHR, the Commission reported:

> This definition limited the attention of the Commission to events which emanated from the conflicts of the past, rather than from the policies of apartheid. There had been an expectation that the Commission would

investigate many of the human rights violations which were caused, for example, by the denial of freedom of movement through the pass laws, by forced removals of people from their land, by the denial of franchise to citizens, by the treatment of farm workers and other labour disputes, and by discrimination in such areas as education and work opportunities. Many organizations lobbied the Commission to insist that these issues should form part of its investigations. Commission members, too, felt that these were important areas that could not be ignored. Nevertheless, they could not be interpreted as falling directly within the Commission's mandate. (South African Truth and Reconciliation Commission, 1998c, p. 12)

The Commission reiterated its stance that its hands were tied by its enabling Act, in its defense of not having adopted a wider interpretation of violations in terms of gender:

> The Commission's relative neglect of the effects of the "ordinary" workings of apartheid has a gender bias. . . . A large number of statistics can be produced to substantiate the fact that women were subject to more restrictions and suffered more in economic terms than did men during the apartheid years. The most direct measure of disadvantage is poverty, and there is a clear link between the distribution of poverty and apartheid policies. Black women, in particular, are disadvantaged, and black women living in former homeland areas remain the most disadvantaged of all. . . . To integrate gender fully, however, would have required the Commission to amend its understanding of its mandate and how it defined gross human rights violations. (South African Truth and Reconciliation Commission, 1998b, pp. 287–288)

Despite this defensiveness, however, the Commission honestly acknowledged its shortcomings in this area in its final report, noting that "the definition of gross violation of human rights adopted by the Commission resulted in a blindness to the types of abuse predominantly experienced by women" (South African Truth and Reconciliation Commission, 1998b, p. 316).

South African women did not tell their stories for a second reason: Women, in general, find it difficult to discuss their experiences of rape and other forms of sexual violence; this is true in private, if not more so in public. And indeed, as the statistic above of only 140 reported rapes testifies, women were reluctant to discuss this part of their personal history during apartheid; many refused outright to do so. There are undoubtedly many reasons why this was the case, some of which are generalizable across cultures, others of which are South Africa-specific. Some women chose not to testify out of a sense of shame, or fear of rejection by family members. Still others felt that bringing up old memories of sexual assault was too painful, certainly in terms of answering questions in a public forum about it. Some felt that they simply did not have the language to express what they had endured. Some women were aware that their rape was a symbolic act meant to humiliate men for not being able to protect them, and for that reason felt that testifying would only further humiliate men. Some women feared that they would no longer be marriageable, while others feared retaliation. Some were loath to make statements that their children might one day read (Ross, 2003).

Some reasons given for their silence were South Africa-specific. Especially in relation to having been raped by men in the liberation movement, some women did not want their testimony to be used to equate individual human rights violations by some ANC members with the systematic violations of apartheid (Goldblatt & Meintjes, 1998). Some women feared that recounting their rapes would be seen as selling out or outing their comrades. Others were afraid of jeopardizing their own careers, as noted by South African clinical psychologist Numfundo Walaza: "Another deterrent is that some of the

rapists hold high political positions today—so if you spoke out you would not only undermine the new government you fought for, but destroy your own possibilities of a future" (quoted in Krog, 1998, p. 240). Other, already-prominent women feared a future loss of status. Goldblatt and Meintjes (1998) quoted one woman who said, "Some of these women are now in high-powered positions—in government or as executives. How will it impact on them now in the positions that they hold, given the gender bias that people have about sexually abused women and the concept that women always ask for it anyway?" (p. 53). Walaza testified that these women's fears were not unfounded: "If you knew that a particular Minister had been raped—what would go through your mind when you saw her on television?" (quoted in Krog, 1998, pp. 239–240). In addition to some of the rape victims being public figures, another reason for not testifying was the fact that some of the rapists were also public figures. In a game of "he said/she said," women were undoubtedly aware of whose story was likely to be believed and were unwilling to be publicly discredited. Antjie Krog (1998) relates the story of Rita Mazibuko, who recounted to the Commission that she had been raped by members of the ANC in exile and had received aid from other ANC members, including Mathews Phosa and Jacob Zuma (South Africa's deputy president from June 1999 through June 2005). However, she reported to the Commission, she was warned by Phosa, who was by then a provincial premier in the new government, not to testify because he would be obliged to defend ANC members against her claim. Krog concluded that Mazibuko left the witness table a defeated woman, "as if she knows no one will stand up for her." Not even the truth commission: "The Truth Commission does not utter a single word in Mazibuko's defense. Not one of the commissioners, not one of the feminists agitating for women's rights, stands up and says: 'We respect the right of Rita Mazibuko to tell the truth as she sees it, just as we respect the right of Mathews Phosa to tell the truth as he sees it. But we expect him to do the same'" (Krog, 1998, p. 242). However, whereas Mazibuko opened herself to public criticism, ridicule, and charges of lying, Phosa didn't even bother to testify. In such an atmosphere, it was simply not in their interest for women to testify about sexual violence suffered at the hands of "allies."

For a variety of reasons, therefore, women were unwilling or unable to speak publicly about their experiences of sexual violence. Ross (2003) warned, however, against an overemphasis on the lack of testimony about sexual violence, and pointed out that women were not only unwilling to testify about their experiences as victims and survivors of this type of violence but also unwilling to testify about their experiences in other ways as well. She noted that little was revealed about women in roles other than victim. Moreover, because women's testimony was dominated by their accounting of what had happened to others, mostly their husbands and sons, the commission added little knowledge about women as activists and resisters. Women were also perpetrators, and very little is known about the circumstances surrounding their entry into these roles. Indeed, the one-dimensional focus on women solely as passive recipients of action translated into the unfortunate reference, by both the commission and the media, to women as secondary victims, as opposed to primary victims.[6]

Almost immediately after it began its public hearings in April, 1996, the TRC became aware that women were not testifying about their own experiences and tried to rectify the situation. In doing so, it tried to follow the advice given to it in a submission by Goldblatt and Meintjes, both South African feminist academics.[7] They argued that the hearing format already in place was not conducive to women testifying, in that the context of public hearings made it difficult for women to overcome the stigma attached to sexual violence. To rectify this, they made a series of recommendations regarding how women's testimony should be handled by both statement takers and in public hearings.[8] These included, among others, a provision that statements could be made confidentially, assuring that women need not testify publicly, allowing women deponents to request that their statements be taken by women, and that women be allowed to testify in closed hearings before only women commissioners. Another recommendation was for the Commission to organize a series of women's hearings, arranged in conjunction with women's organizations, attended by women commissioners only, and assisted by psychologists and social workers (Goldblatt & Meintjes, 1998). The TRC, for the most part, adopted these suggestions for making the Commission more gender sensitive and held three all-women public hearings in August and October of 1996 and July of 1997. In the course of these hearings, some women were willing to discuss their experiences as victims and activists under apartheid.[9] Through the several dozen women who testified, most of whom were political leaders or leaders in the activism movement, the TRC was able to ascertain that women did indeed suffer gross violations of human rights themselves including rape, other forms of sexual violence, physical and psychological abuse and torture in and out of detention, and even death. What the TRC did manage to uncover therefore confirms patterns of violence against women seen worldwide: South African women were subjected to rape and other sexual violence by parties from all sides of the political conflict, including the South African Defence Force and opposition groups including the African National Congress, the Inkatha Freedom Party (IFP), and the United Democratic Front (UDF) as well as by men in refugee centers. Despite service as soldiers on the battlefield and activists in civil society, women could not count on not being raped by their fellow liberationists.

In its final report, the Commission concluded that "women too suffered direct gross violations of human rights, many of which were gender specific in their exploitative and humiliating nature" (South African Truth and Reconciliation Commission, 1998c, p. 256). More specifically, it found that the state was responsible for the severe ill-treatment of women in custody; that women were abused in ways which specifically exploited their vulnerabilities as women; and that women in exile were also subjected to various forms of sexual abuse, including rape. It is worth noting, perhaps, that these findings on women, which amounted to little more than a few sentences, were the penultimate findings in a 62-page chapter devoted to findings and that no mention was made of women's suffering from socioeconomic violations under apartheid.

Despite its attempts to break out of the gender-neutral approach to truth gathering, the TRC was not terribly successful at doing so—at least not in a way that elicited a full understanding of the myriad ways in which women suffered under apartheid, in terms of civil/political and socioeconomic rights violations, in terms of sexual and nonsexual violence, and in terms of women in their full repertoire of roles, not simply as victims.[10] The TRC itself acknowledged this, noting that the pattern of women refusing to speak of themselves "persisted over the full period of the hearings" (South African Truth and Reconciliation Commission, 1998b, p. 283).

If one reason the TRC was unable to establish more truth about human rights violations under apartheid was because women were unwilling to tell their stories, men were also unwilling to come forward and tell the truth about their involvement in these abuses—specifically in terms of rape and other forms of sexual violence. And again, one reason for this relates to the legal mandate handed to the Commission by its enabling act, in this case the criteria for qualifying for amnesty. To qualify, the Act stated that the "act, omission or offence" for which an applicant was seeking amnesty had to be "associated with a political objective" (Promotion of National Unity and Reconciliation Act of 1995, Ch. 4, Sec. 18). Whether an objective was political or not was determined by a long set of criteria enumerated in the act, two of which were that it had to be proportional to the objective pursued and that it could not have been committed out of malice (Ch. 4, Sec. 20[3][f][ii]). The Commission determined that rape could be categorized as either

torture or severe ill-treatment and that a person could therefore be granted amnesty, if all criteria were met (B. Goldblatt, personal communication, June 4, 2007). The Amnesty Committee, however, never had the opportunity to wrestle with the questions of whether rape could ever be justified as being politically motivated, or could ever be committed without malice, or whether the means of rape could ever be deemed to be proportional to any ends, because no person applied for amnesty for the crime of rape or for any other sexual violations. The reasons for this are not clear, but one could surmise that several explanations were likely in play. One is that any potential amnesty applicants likely knew that proving the presence of the above criteria (political motivation, proportionality, absence of malice) would be extremely difficult.[11] Another is that raping women was simply not deemed a serious enough crime to warrant opening oneself up to public exposure. Finally, some potential applicants may have wagered on the fact that so few women would publicly testify about their rapes, and would likely not be willing to name names, for all of the reasons already noted.

That men did not apply for amnesty is unfortunate for several reasons, all of which have serious consequences for the human rights of women in the postapartheid and post-truth commission period. First, as Goldblatt and Meintjes (1998) noted, the process of examining the act of rape, even though very few perpetrators would have likely been granted amnesty for its perpetration in their opinion, would have allowed the Commission to highlight the deeply political function of rape during wartime.[12] That sexual violence is a tool of all conflicts, apartheid included, could have been confirmed by the TRC. As it is, however, the TRC's final report is almost silent on the issue. Although it does note that women were victims of sexual violence, no analysis is provided of how such violence functioned politically. Second, because no men applied for amnesty for rape, no one was held accountable for these crimes; if granted amnesty, which would likely have been rare, then amnesty would have served as a form of accountability, as the very fact of having been granted amnesty certified a person as a perpetrator. If denied amnesty, perpetrators would have at least been publicly unveiled as such, which one could argue was a form of accountability, more so than the silence that prevailed as a result of the absence of amnesty applications. The ability to apportion blame and hold perpetrators accountable is deemed a hallmark of a society based on the rule of law. The lack of accountability may well contribute to a climate of impunity—which is the antithesis of a human-rights-respecting culture based on respect for the rule of law. Third, applications for amnesty for rape and other forms of sexual violence would have helped to expose just how widespread the use of rape was during the period under TRC investigation. Only 140 women testified about rape before the commission; no men admitted to it. One could surmise from this that rape was not a serious problem for South African women; in doing so, one would be wrong. Rather, what existed in South Africa was a profound silence about women's violent experiences during apartheid—neither victims nor perpetrators were willing to reveal the truth about these experiences. What former TRC Commissioner Yasmin Sooka (2004) called a "conspiracy of silence" between victims and perpetrators (n. p.), Antjie Krog (1998) called a "bizarre collusion":

> Then again, few women have testified about rape, and fewer, if any, have named the rapists. So why would a rapist apply for amnesty at all? There seems to be a bizarre collusion between the rapist and the raped. Although rumors abound about rape, all these mutterings are trapped behind closed doors. Apparently high-profile women, among them Cabinet ministers, parliamentarians, and businesswomen, were raped and sexually abused under the previous dispensation—and not only by the regime, but by their own comrades in the townships and liberation camps, but no one will utter an audible word about it. (p. 239)

The South African case, then, offers a cautionary tale about the difficulties associated with the ability of truth-telling mechanisms to serve the cause of fostering a truly gendered human rights culture. Its overemphasis on bodily integrity rights at the expense of second-generation social and economic rights had the effect, Ross (2003) argues, of sanitizing apartheid and limiting the ability to recognize the duration of its effects. Indeed, although the TRC was able to uncover some part of the picture of women's experiences—revealing that women did, indeed, suffer gross violations of human rights under apartheid—this picture remained incomplete. What was not recorded by the Commission, and thus not open to the sort of analysis that the rest of the report invited, was the history of patriarchy that accompanied and supported the race-based discrimination of the apartheid system. This limitation has consequences for South African women in the postapartheid era, where patriarchy remains largely intact, despite the legal elimination of race-based discrimination. Although a full overview of the status of women in postapartheid South Africa is not possible here, it is clear that there continues to be widespread economic, social, and legal discrimination against women, along with high levels of violence, including sexual violence against them. In 2003, there were 52,425 officially reported rapes, a third of the estimated actual number. Forty percent of the victims were 18 years old or younger. At the moment, one might argue that rather than a culture of rights, there is a culture of sexual violence in South Africa. One study concluded that women in South Africa view violence and sexual coercion as a "normal" part of everyday life (Human Rights Watch, 2004, pp. 10–11).[13]

Lessons Learned? Policy Implications

In its final report, the TRC, in a section akin to a self-evaluation (although no such evaluation was mandated by its enabling act), listed several of the Commission's shortcomings (South

African Truth and Reconciliation Commission, 1998c, pp. 206–208). Its ability to uncover more truth about women's experiences or to hold perpetrators of gross violations of women's human rights accountable for their actions was not among them. The above analysis of the TRC's inability to provide more dignity to apartheid's women victims, to deliver a measure of gender justice in terms of at least apportioning blame for those responsible for gender-based crimes, and the reality of a postapartheid human rights culture in which women are still victimized because of their gender and still suffer as second-class citizens, indicate that a deeper evaluation was perhaps warranted. Although the TRC was not willing to offer some lessons learned for future truth-telling undertakings, some policy implications can nevertheless be derived from the South African experience.

One set of policy recommendations revolves around getting more truth, both from victims and perpetrators. In terms of getting more women to be forthcoming about their own experiences—as opposed to their experiences as women who lost sons, daughters, husbands, and fathers—the TRC did heed advice and hold women-only hearings. Other truth commissions have already adopted (and are likely to continue doing so) similar approaches to enabling gender-sensitive testimony to emerge, including allowing women to testify only before women commissioners, allowing them to testify in camera, and allowing them to remain anonymous. Other attempts to increase gender sensitivities could be added. Sooka (2004) suggested that at least half of all commissioners should be women and that databases, constructed to collect and analyze specific acts of violence to issue findings and recommendations, should be designed to allow for the specific collection of data appropriate to the experiences of women and girls and to allow for the disaggregation of data along gendered lines.[14] Although these policies may help elicit more information from women, they are not without controversy. Disagreement always arises when women are treated separately from men, and the

TRC was no exception. Although the TRC did adopt recommendations provided by them in terms of separate women's hearings, Beth Goldblatt and Sheila Meintjes (1999) were nevertheless unimpressed, accusing the TRC of failing to adopt a gendered analytical framework to guide its work, noting that women were treated separately in the final chapter of Volume 4 of the report, which only served to create "a ghettoised female subjectivity," in which women were relegated to a category of essentialized difference, at the same time as differences between women were homogenized.

Even if truth-telling mechanisms come to include more effective ways of getting women to discuss their own histories of violations, the second half of the equation—getting men to talk about their histories as perpetrators of these violations—remains unchanged. And if eliciting more truth from victims is difficult, doing so from perpetrators is undoubtedly even more so, if the TRC is an indication of the unwillingness of men to admit to rape as a tactic of conflict. Getting women to talk without simultaneously getting men to do the same does little more than maintain the culture of impunity, with little to no accountability, a situation hardly conducive to strengthening the rule of law. One recommendation is to hold the threat of prosecution over those who refused to testify and then to actually prosecute where evidence of wrongdoing exists. However, this recommendation is also not unproblematic. First, such a step would require other changes, such as reforms of national legal systems. Sooka (2004) argued that in most national legal systems, it is almost impossible to prosecute rape and crimes of sexual violence given the legal requirements, the evidentiary burden, and the culture and attitude of those who serve in the criminal justice systems. A second problem is that the recommendation presupposes the political will to prosecute violent sexual crimes. In South Africa there appears to be little will to carry out post-TRC prosecutions of any sort, let alone of rape and other forms of sexual violence (Amnesty International and Human

Rights Watch, 2003). Moreover, in South Africa, only a small fraction of rapes are reported to police, only about a third of those reported are prosecuted, and only about half of those prosecuted result in convictions (Human Rights Watch, 1995b, p. 90). It thus appears that both problems with the legal system and a lack of political will may indeed be unfortunate realities in the South African context. A third, and perhaps the most significant, problem is in gaining the cooperation of women in trials. If it is difficult for women to testify in the relatively friendly atmosphere of women-only hearings, it is significantly more difficult for them to do so in the hostile environment of a trial.[15] All in all, in terms of the ability of truth-telling mechanisms to elicit the full truth about gendered violations from either victims or perpetrators, there is little reason to express much optimism. Sadly, in this instance, some skepticism may be justified.

Other policy implications for future truth-telling exercises emerge from the South African experience. It is clear, for example, that the ability of a truth-telling mechanism to adopt a truly gendered approach is determined early on, embedded in the enabling legislation and the mandate handed to it.[16] Sooka (2004) noted, for example, that the South African TRC's enabling act made no reference to gender-based violations and did not mention women as a special target group. In contrast, the Sierra Leone TRC's enabling act stated that the Commission should pay special attention to the "subject of sexual abuses and to the experiences of children within armed conflict." In addition to the mandate itself, the way in which concepts are interpreted also affects the ability of truth-telling mechanisms to address gender issues. In South Africa, for example, the definition of gross violations of human rights did not specifically address gendered violence, specifically sexual violence. According to Sooka (2004), it was left to the "gender lobby," including women commissioners, to make the argument that torture and severe ill-treatment should be utilized to address sexual violence (p. 7). This had implications for the types of

reparations recommended by the TRC. Sexual violence in South Africa was only included as a subcategory in a long list of harms considered as torture or severe ill-treatment rather than being categorized as a separate violation. According to Goldblatt (2006), "sexual violence would have been more centrally placed on the national agenda had it been mentioned in the founding legislation of the TRC" (p. 80).[17] In contrast, in Sierra Leone, the TRC was mandated to record "violations and abuses of human rights and international humanitarian law related to armed conflict." Sooka (2004) argues that, when read together with the mandate to pay attention to sexual abuse, the TRC was able to apply a much wider, more comprehensive, definition of gross violations of human rights there, one which specifically included gender-based violations. As a result, Sooka notes that, unlike in South Africa, women and girls came out in large numbers to speak to the Sierra Leone commission.[18] In sum, if gender-based violence is to be taken seriously in truth telling, the enabling legislation for truth-telling mechanisms should include those forms of violence in definitions of concepts like victims and violations.

Gendered Peace? Reparations

If any lesson emerges from the South African case, it is that silence has consequences. It would be unfair to say that the TRC discovered no truth at all about gendered violence. Some truth did indeed emerge about gross violations of human rights suffered by women. However, three major elements were absent in the final work of the TRC. What did not emerge from the TRC's work, or in its final report, is an overarching picture of patriarchy resulting in the second-class citizenship of women. Nor did the reality that women suffered immeasurably more from violations of socioeconomic rights rather than civil and political ones. Finally, the TRC failed to apportion blame for those responsible for the violations suffered by women, leaving perpetrators unaccountable for their actions. Why are these absences consequential? Perhaps the most lasting impact a truth commission can have is the implementation of its recommendations. A truth commission cannot in and of itself bring about reforms needed to improve the status of women. It can, however, make recommendations to the state and to civil society groups regarding actions that could be taken, for example, to ensure accountability of perpetrators of such violence, or for improving the economic status of women, or for making it easier for women to escape violent relationships, or to receive medical treatment for HIV/AIDS. Of course, if recommendations do not exist, they can hardly be implemented. Perhaps the most serious consequence of the lack of a gendered lens was that the 45-page chapter on recommendations compiled by the TRC was silent on the issue of women. Despite a promising sentence in the chapter's introduction that states, "It is important to state explicitly that there is a need for sensitivity to the particular issues pertaining to women and children" (South African Truth and Reconciliation Commission, 1998c, p. 305), not one of the over 100 recommendations is explicitly aimed at improving the human rights of women.[19] The lack of a gendered lens resulted in another absence, notably the absence of a gendered reparations policy.

It would seem obvious that if women and a concern for gender are primarily absent in the input stage of designing transitional justice mechanisms,[20] the outputs of these mechanisms—such as reparations policies—will reflect this. And indeed, a comparative study conducted by International Center for Transitional Justice (ICTJ) on gender and reparations found that across contexts reparations programs have shared a number of features: they exclude women from policy design, they show a lack of deep knowledge of gender-based violence in defining violations to be repaired (although rape is generally included), the criteria used for defining beneficiaries tends to adversely affect women, the benefits given are not as women-friendly as could

be, and the implementation of reparations programs can hurt women (by requiring a bank account, for example—something many women do not have; Bell & O'Rourke, 2007). In addition, Duggan and Abusharaf (2006) detailed various obstacles impeding women's abilities to exercise their right to reparation, including a lack of legal autonomy (women are often not treated as equal citizens), legal pluralism (in many societies gender-based social and legal practices such as requiring a wife to obtain her husband's consent before approaching the legal system impede women's access to justice), and social and cultural attitudes and mores (the stigma attached to rape or social norms limiting women's ability to travel to collect reparations). Beyond this, gender biases can often be inadvertently reproduced or incorporated into a reparations policy whose designers believed was gender appropriate. Rubio-Marín (2006) noted, for example, that employment disability insurance schemes that are sometimes relied on to assess loss of income generation may be ill suited to assess the material destitution of women victims of sexual abuse who are abandoned by their partners, rendered unmarriageable, and then ostracized by their communities.

It is especially important, Duggan and Abusharaf (2006) argued, that reparations programs are designed with a commitment to repairing sexual violence. Not only is sexual violence perhaps the most egregious form of gender-based violence, its socioeconomic impact on women can undermine their chances for recovery and for reintegration into the family, the community, and the state. At the same time, judicial recourse through the courts is often unlikely for women victims of sexual violence, as laws for criminal and civil prosecution and redress of sexual crimes are often weak, discriminatory, or nonexistent, often most ill equipped to deal with complex crimes during times of transition. Transformation of norms and institutions is generally a slow process; reparations in the interim can not only lay the social and political groundwork for this transformation but also help temporarily offset some of the consequences of gendered violence (Duggan & Abusharaf, 2006). For all these reasons, then, it is important for governments to get their reparations programs right vis-à-vis women. Unfortunately, most evidence suggests that this has yet to be the norm.[21]

Not surprisingly, given the lack of attention paid to women in the TRC final report's chapter on recommendations, the chapter on reparations fails to mention women at all. This neglect, according to Goldblatt (2006), was not from a lack of effort on the part of civil society organizations, several of whom tried to make gender-sensitive suggestions throughout the TRC process.[22] In the end, however, the efforts of NGOs and activists amounted to little, with few of their suggested recommendations being adopted by the TRC. The result is that the reparations program recommended by the Commission, and the eventual program adopted by the government, remained in Goldblatt's (2006) words, "largely 'ungendered'" (p. 58). The gender neutrality of the reparations program was evident in the financial payout given to victims.[23] Although the TRC proposed a sum of approximately US$2,713 per victim per year for 6 years, with the amount varying according to location (urban or rural) and according to the number of dependents, the government agreed only to a one-time payment of US$3,750 (R30,000) to each victim with no variance for location or number of dependents. Both the TRC and the state were silent on the issue of harms suffered by women as a category. So, for example, women who lost breadwinners and thus faced a lifetime of impoverishment were given no more compensation than a person who suffered no material disadvantage at all (Goldblatt, 2006).[24]

However, while the reparations program may have been gender neutral in terms of input (i.e., the policy recommendations), it certainly was not so in terms of outcomes (i.e., its impact on women). To receive reparations, applicants had to have a bank account. Around the world, South Africa being no exception, many poor people do

not have such accounts. As women are the poorest members of society, this requirement disproportionately affected them. In several cases, women with no bank accounts had to sign the money over to their husband's accounts, where they undoubtedly had less control over it (Goldblatt, 2006). Moreover, until 1998, women married under customary law were considered minors for the purpose of some commercial transactions and thus lost control over their grants to their husbands in that way (Goldblatt, 2006). Another gendered implication of the program was that reparation was tied to truth telling; in other words, one could only be considered a victim—and thus eligible for reparations—if one came forward to tell one's story to the commission.[25] Many women victims of sexual violence undoubtedly felt unable to approach the TRC for reasons already noted. Women's resistance to being forthcoming about their own experiences meant they faced an excruciating choice: to risk estrangement from their families and social exclusion on one hand, and making themselves ineligible for reparations on the other (Anderlini, Conaway, & Kays, 2004). Rubio-Marín (2006) concluded that "forcing women to 'come out' as victims to qualify for reparations may have a largely inhibiting effect, especially for victims of sexual violence who hold back because of shame or fear" (p. 34). For this reason, Goldblatt (2006) recommended that future truth commissions delink the granting of reparations from truth telling.

Conclusion

The ICTJ concludes its report by stating that "many truth commissions have failed women—the crimes they have suffered are underreported, their voices are rendered inaudible, their depiction in commission reports is one-dimensional, and their needs and goals are deprioritized in recommendations for reparations, reform and prosecutions" (Nesiah, 2006, p. 41). This article, too, has provided a somewhat pessimistic overview of gender and truth telling in the South African context. Two final points are worth mentioning. First, it is of course not fair to blame the TRC for the realities that many South African women face daily: lives of poverty, violent relationships, and an overwhelming vulnerability to HIV/AIDS. The TRC was but one postapartheid institution, and societal changes—either positive or negative—are always multivariate. In addition, the TRC existed for a short period of time—less than half a decade. The work of undoing generations of patriarchal attitudes and their consequent effects on women will surely take much longer. Moreover, what happens after a truth commission has shut down is not the responsibility of that commission. Although a commission can lay the foundation for a culture based on human rights, it is the responsibility of the state, civil society, and individuals to build on the foundation. Still, the fact that the TRC did not employ a gender-sensitive approach to the past could not have helped South African women overcome the reality that Pettman (1996) noted: that women's lives rarely improve much, if at all, in all too many postconflict societies.

Second, whatever contributions the TRC and South Africa as a whole have made toward improving the lives of women, one thing remains clear: the legal provision of rights means little if they are not translated into a culture of rights. The TRC, throughout its work, highlighted the concept of human rights repeatedly over a period of time. Its commitment has been backed up by government policies. In terms of gender, South Africa has done rather well in the public sphere. By 1998, it ranked seventh in the world in governmental representation, with women constituting 25% of national-level representatives, and third in the world when ranked with other developing countries. The government also established a national Commission on Gender Equality. Furthermore, South Africa's active and independent Constitutional Court has handed down several judgments in support of women's rights, and parliament has passed several pieces of legislation prohibiting discrimination on the basis of race and gender. Such institutions and policies are clearly important; government actions send messages to its citizens about what is acceptable and what is valued. However, good institutions and processes are necessary but not sufficient underpinnings of a human rights culture. The question becomes how and whether the positive, human rights culture-promoting elements of the South African TRC and government are being translated into culture, in terms of attitudes, beliefs, and South Africans' shared understanding about being a people who embrace human rights. Although the TRC itself attempted to foster a human rights-respecting culture, it could not ensure that this culture would become firmly entrenched. As Sooka (2004) stated, "We do not suffer from a lack of law and policy but we suffer from a deficit of implementation" (p. 4). Formal commitments to gender equality must result in policies that mean real changes in women's lives. The possibility of these changes being wrought is immeasurably more difficult when one key institution devoted to raising awareness about the culture of human rights—such as a truth commission—turns a blind eye, no matter how unintentional, to the plight of women.

Funding

The author disclosed receipt of the following financial support for the research and/or authorship of this article: The United States Institute of Peace and the R. F. Johnson Fund at Connecticut College.

Notes

1. Feminist scholars are not alone in their analysis of the gendered dimension of war. In 2000, the UN Security Council unanimously passed Resolution 1325, which expresses "concern that civilians, particularly women and children, account for the vast majority of those adversely affected by armed conflict, including as refugees and internally displaced persons,

and increasingly are targeted by combatants and armed elements" (UN Security Council, 2000).

2. Although the ubiquity of rape during war has long been known, the issue received added scholarly attention with the revelation of the widespread use of rape in the various wars resulting in the breakup of the former Yugoslavia in the 1990s. Indeed, Diken and Lausten (2005) viewed rape as "a crucial signifier" in the Bosnian war (p. 114). The United Nations General Assembly concurred in GA Resolution 49/205 of 2005, which asserted that the "heinous practice [rape and abuse of women] constitutes a deliberate weapon of war in fulfilling the policy of ethnic cleansing carried out by Serbian forces in Bosnia and Herzegovina" (Diken & Lausen, 2005, p. 113). The breakup of Yugoslavia proved to be an illustrative, albeit tragic—one rough estimate is that between 20,000 and 50,000 Bosnian war rape survivors exist—case study for advancing an understanding of various aspects of war rape including how rape fosters nationalism, rape as a tool of ethnic cleansing, rape as a tool of community punishment, and the relationship between wartime rape and "peace" time domestic violence. The literature of wartime rape in Yugoslavia is vast; see, for example, Bracewell (2000), Diken and Lausten (2005), Jones (1994), Nikolic-Ristanovic (1996), Salzman (1998), and Stigelmayer (1994). Although there seems to be little disagreement that mass rape and war are correlated, less agreement exists on why this correlation exists. For an overview of various explanations for the root cause of rape during war, see Gottschall (2004).

3. In the first instance, recent scandals have highlighted both the scope and severity of sexual crimes against U.S. female soldiers by U.S. male soldiers. Over the past decade, for example, over 140 female cadets have reported rapes or assaults at the U.S. Air Force Academy in Colorado Springs. Moreover, since August 2002, at least 273 sexual assaults against U.S. female soldiers by their fellow soldiers have been reported in Afghanistan, Kuwait, and Iraq (National Public Radio, 2005). In terms of the second instance—which some might argue falls more in line with sexual exploitation than with rape and sexual assault—a March, 2005 UN report revealed that in 2004 UN peacekeeping soldiers were faced with 1,221 allegations of sexual exploitation and abuse of women under their protection in missions around the world, including Bosnia, Kosovo, Cambodia, Timor-Leste, West Africa, and the Democratic Republic of the Congo (DRC). This issue received widespread attention in early 2005 with the revelation that peacekeepers in DRC had sex with Congolese women and girls in exchange for food or small sums of money (Al-Hussein, 2005).

4. Given this gendered nature of peace negotiations, it should come as no surprise that other postconflict peacebuilding initiatives enshrined in peace agreements (besides transitional justice) are equally gendered. For example, attention is increasingly being drawn to the fact that the design of postconflict disarmament, demobilization, and reintegration (DDR) programs have paid insufficient attention to gender. Disarmament involves the collection and disposal of both heavy and light arms of ex-combatants on all sides of conflict; demobilization is a short-term process of downsizing or disbanding armed forces and reintegration is a complex long-term process in which ex-combatants are assisted in resettling in communities. Reintegration initiatives can vary and can include the provision of civilian clothing, cash payments, housing, land, job training, school fees, credit counseling, and psychological and health support (Dzinesa, 2007). Women combatants, of course, face special reintegration challenges, especially in terms of rape-related posttraumatic stress symptoms, access to land, and the legal ability to gain control over monetary resources and credit. Any DDR programs that do not take these special needs into account will necessarily have adverse effects on female ex-combatants. Such was the situation in Namibia, for example, where "bereft of gender-specific reintegration assistance, women former fighters, including single mothers encountered significant difficulties" (Dzinesa, 2007, p. 86). For this reason, the World Bank recommends the provision of female-friendly demobilization centers, equal assistance packages with male compatriots, and gender-focused health, medical, and developmental training (cited in Dzinesa, 2007, p. 75). Likewise, noting that DDR is not only a part of a broader postconflict reconstruction and development framework, but indeed—in the words of Kofi Annan—"the single most important factor determining the success of peace operations," a United Nations-sponsored conference on DDR and stability in Africa offered as one of its core recommendations that "reintegration programmes must be more gender-sensitive than in the past" (United Nations, 2005, pp. 2–5). In the case of South Africa, one can undoubtedly safely assume that

DDR initiatives inadequately met the needs of female ex-combatants as most scholars agree that DDR in general was "poorly planned, badly executed, and wholly inadequate in meeting the needs of ex-combatants," both men and women (Dzinesa, 2007, p. 81).

5. Goldblatt and Meintjes (1998) traced the consequences of these unequal power relations for African women in all spheres of life. For example, although intended to determine the movement of African men, the pass laws regulating migrant labor were even harsher in their effects on women. At the same time that women were left to care for children and the elderly, they were disadvantaged by custom in their access to land and to the labor market. As Marjorie Jobson, the Chairperson of the Board of the Khulumani Support Group—a victims' rights NGO—noted, "it was women who carried a significant proportion of the suffering caused by the uprooting and dumping of three million South Africans in inhospitable environments without adequate infrastructure" (Jobson, 2005).

6. The Promotion of National Unity and Reconciliation Act of 1995, the TRC's enabling legislation, defined victims not only as those who had directly suffered gross violations of human rights, but in certain circumstances as their relatives and dependents, as well. Hence when women testified about the harms suffered by their husbands and sons, they were deemed to be victims in the second sense noted in the legislation. As relatives of victims, the Commission and media took to referring to them as secondary victims, a term that does not appear anywhere in the Act or in the TRC's mandate. However, although the Act did not distinguish between primary and secondary victims, the Reparations and Rehabilitation Committee did make this distinction, defining secondary victims as relatives or dependents of primary victims who were only entitled to monetary reparations when the primary victim died (Goldblatt, 2006).

7. Their submission emerged from a workshop titled "Gender and the Truth and Reconciliation Commission," hosted by the Centre for Applied Legal Studies at the University of Witwatersrand in Johannesburg in March, 1996. Goldblatt and Meintjes were two of several women's activists lobbying the TRC, especially its women commissioners, to put gender issues on the agenda. Goldblatt (2006) stated that women had to "bargain" for gender issues and felt that they were "humored" (p. 56).

8. Before individuals gave testimony at public hearings, they first gave statements to statement takers. Individuals were then chosen from among the many statements given to present their stories publicly in hearings organized by the Human Rights Violations Committee, one of three Committees of the Commission (the other two being the Amnesty Committee and the Reparations and Rehabilitation Committee). About 10% of those who gave statements subsequently testified at these victims hearings. In total, 76 public hearings were held across the country between April, 1996 and June, 1997. For a detailed overview of the process of selecting testifiers as well as the rituals surrounding public hearings, see Ross (2003).

9. The TRC adopted other measures as well to encourage women to tell their own stories. By April 1997, the protocol preparing women deponents was modified to include a note which read: "IMPORTANT: Some women testify about violations of human rights that happened to family members or friends, but they have also suffered abuses. Don't forget to tell us what happened to you yourself if you were the victim of a gross human rights abuse" (Ross, 2003, p. 23).

10. Not all analysts take such a negative view of the TRC in terms of gender. Pumla Gobodo-Madikizela (2005), a former member of the TRC's Human Rights Violations Committee, has argued that the TRC was "progressive and gender-sensitive" in terms of its approach to women. Her claim is that women's unwillingness to testify about their own experiences was a deliberate strategy on the part of women to generate empathy for those who had suffered and that women were thereby taking on a special responsibility for the collective sense of national healing (pp. v–vii; see also World Bank, 2006).

11. Could any applicant have proved that her rape was motivated by politics? Although the answer will always remain unknown, and although Goldblatt and Meintjes (1998) predicted that the Commission would have had a difficult time separating political from personal motives, some evidence did surface before the TRC that hinted at the political nature of at least some rapes. Krog (1998) reported on a study about the use of rape in townships during the 1980s, the period of highest political violence. In one township, Sebokeng, a group of youth formed the South African Rapist Association (SARA), whose goal was to provide senior comrades with women to rape, as a way to keep them

busy. Had these youths applied for amnesty, the TRC would have had to establish whether the raping of nonpolitical women to keep the comrades busy could qualify as a political act.

12. That rape serves a political function during times of conflict is clear. However, it sometimes also serves an almost economic function, as was revealed in a chilling testimony before the TRC by a former ANC general, Andrew Masondo. The ANC made two separate submissions to the TRC, which were accompanied by testimonies. During one such submission, the ANC acknowledged the sexual abuse of women, which it euphemistically called "gender-specific offences." As explanation, Masondo revealed that women soldiers in the ANC army Umkhonto we Sizwe (MK) were viewed almost as economic commodities in MK camps in exile in Zambia, Angola, and Tanzania. He testified to the TRC that the ratio of female-to-male MK soldiers in these camps was roughly 22 to 1,000, and that the law of supply and demand simply took over (South African Truth and Reconciliation Commission, 1998b, p. 307; see also Graybill, 2001, pp. 263–264). The ANC submission omitted the names of perpetrators, none of whom subsequently applied for amnesty.

13. A particularly low point for women in South Africa was the rape trial of Jacob Zuma, the former Deputy President of South Africa, who was charged with raping a woman in December, 2005 and acquitted in May, 2006. Women's rights advocates were disheartened by the trial, where the judge allowed the accuser's sexual history to be brought up in cross-examination (which revealed, among other things, that she had been raped during exile while an antiapartheid activist). The trial, women's organizations assert, proved the continuing obstacles facing rape survivors in the postapartheid era.

14. These suggestions are consistent with those outlined in the International Center for Transitional Justice (ICTJ) report, *Truth Commissions and Gender: Principles, Policies, and Procedures*, highlighting the notion of "a technology of truth," which includes the organizing, classifying, and filtering of information. For example, those who take testimonies can be properly trained in a range of interview techniques and the breadth of human rights experiences to recognize cues to patterns of abuse, thereby cutting down on the underreporting of women's experiences. In addition, the statement-taking form can be structured so that victim testimony is not overdetermined by rigid categories of standardized legal boxes (Nesiah, 2006, pp. 8, 19–22).

15. Some feminist scholars have questioned the ability of a courtroom approach to deliver justice for gender-based violence, noting a disillusionment of survivors of sexual violence with adversarial processes. Bell and O'Rourke (2007) cited Mertus who contends that "adversarial legal forums subject witnesses to repeated attempts to undermine their credibility, prevent the complete expression of their individual accounts and reify their position as women victims lacking agency" (p. 33).

16. An even earlier necessary step, of course, although not the focus of this article, is the inclusion of women in all stages of the peace processes, including negotiations, so that women can influence the identification of reconstruction priorities. Many feminists, however, note that simply including women is not sufficient if no opportunities are provided for them to reshape end goals, where women are asked to operate along already set (gendered) assumptions about conflict, peace, and security. As Bell and O'Rourke (2007) noted, "The increased participation of women does not equate in any simple way with a feminist reshaping of either peace processes or transitional justice mechanisms" (p. 34).

17. She notes that one reason for a lack of gendered input into the enabling legislation is that women's organizations themselves showed little interest in the TRC at first. The commission was not seen as a priority for women activists, who focused their energies on more forward-looking tasks and on the immediate challenges facing women, giving the "backward-looking project" of transitional justice a lower priority (p. 53).

18. Bell and O'Rourke (2007) cite other advances in this regard, noting that "analysis of more general developments in the mandates of TCs indicates a positive trend, whereby the 'gender-neutral' stance of the early Latin American commissions of Argentina and Chile can be contrasted with the comprehensive understanding of harms demonstrated by the recent East Timor/Timor Leste commission" (p. 28). For a more in-depth overview of the Sierra Leone commission, as well as an overview of the gendered advances of the Peruvian commission, see World Bank (2006) and Nesiah (2006). Indeed, the World Bank (2006) credits the South African TRC's decision to hold gender hearings specifically for beginning slow but steady incremental improvement in attempts to secure accountability for gender-based violence through truth commissions. For a discussion of the gendered

approach of the Ghana National Reconciliation Commission (NCR), see Nesiah (2006).

19. Under a section titled "Prevention of Gross Human Rights Violations in the Future," the TRC does state that "the recognition and protection of socio-economic rights are crucial to the development and sustaining of a culture of respect for human rights" (South African Truth and Reconciliation Commission, 1998c, p. 308). However, this sentence is never fleshed out, nor are the economic rights of women in particular mentioned.

20. Christopher Colvin (2006) argued that an even earlier problem existed: Not only were women and gender absent from a discussion of reparations from the beginning but also was the entire issue of reparations itself neglected, both during the negotiations phase to end apartheid and the interim constitution and subsequent permanent constitution that these negotiations produced.

21. They do state, however, that incremental improvement has occurred. They note that progression toward a more gender-sensitive approach to justice can be tracked by comparing the processes of truth telling and reparation in the decade from 1993 (the El Salvador truth commission) to 2003 (the Peruvian truth commission). They conclude that "reparations for sexual violence may be moving away from being an afterthought by policymakers, often tacked onto State programs in the wake of political pressure and lobbying especially from external groups, to becoming a more fundamental issue which appears more centrally on the agenda of transitional governments" (Duggan & Abusharaf, 2006, p. 636).

22. Examples of these interventions include a request to parliament by the Center for the Study of Violence and Reconciliation (CSVR) that women be recognized in all symbolic reparations projects, the suggestion by a group of academics and NGOs to provide some mechanism for women to make statements (thus making them potentially eligible for reparations) after the official close of the commission in recognition of the difficulty some women feel in speaking about their experiences, and a series of additional recommendations by the CSVR. These included, among others, that research be conducted into gender biases inherent in quantifying reparations according to the approach used in civil damages claims.

23. In addition to recommending individual financial reparations, the TRC also made recommendations for symbolic reparations, community rehabilitation, and institutional reform.

24. An even more fundamental question besides whether women's harms were more egregious than those suffered by men is that of quantifying harm. Whether any amount of monetary compensation can ever suffice for human rights violations is a question much debated, with many maintaining that monetary measures can never remedy nonmonetary harms. Martha Minow, for example, argues that "no market measure exists for the value of living an ordinary life, without nightmares or survivor guilt" (quoted in Duggan & Abusharaf, 2006, p. 640). In relation to women and sexual violence, however, the question of quantifying harm is arguably even more complicated, when such intangible assets as purity and social standing have been taken and where in some cultures accepting money for sexual abuse makes matters worse (Duggan & Abusharaf, 2006).

25. In addition, one could be certified as a victim as a result of truth uncovered during an amnesty hearing. In either case, eligibility for reparations in South Africa was predicated on individual truth telling.

References

Al-Hussein, Z. R. Z. (2005). *A comprehensive strategy to eliminate future sexual exploitation and abuse in United Nations peacekeeping* (Report A/59/710). New York: United Nations.

Amnesty International and Human Rights Watch. (2003). *Truth and justice: Unfinished business in South Africa.* Retrieved July 24, 2009, from http://web.amnesty.org/library/Index/ENGAFR53001 2003

Anderlini, S. N., Conaway, C. P., & Kays, L. (2004). Transitional justice and reconciliation. In Women Waging Peace Network (Ed.), *Inclusive security, sustainable peace: A toolkit for advocacy and action* (pp. 1–15). Retrieved July 24, 2009, from http://www.womenwagingpeace.net/content/toolkit/chapters/Transitional_Justice.pdf

Bell, C., & O'Rourke, C. (2007). Does feminism need a theory of transitional justice? An introductory essay. *International Journal of Transitional Justice, 1*, 23–44.

Bracewell, W. (2000). Rape in Kosovo: Masculinity and Serbian nationalism. *Nations and Nationalism, 6*, 563–590.

Charlesworth, H. (1995). Human rights as men's rights. In J. Peters & A. Wolper (Eds.), *Women's* rights, human rights: International feminist perspectives (pp. 103–113). New York: Routledge.

Colvin, C. (2006). Overview of the reparations program in South Africa. In P. de Greiff (Ed.), The handbook of reparations (pp. 176–213). New York: Oxford University Press.

Diken, B., & Lausten, C. B. (2005). Becoming object: Rape as a weapon of war. Body & Society, 11, 111–128.

Duggan, C., & Abusharaf, A. M. (2006). Reparation of sexual violence in democratic transitions: The search for gender justice. In P. de Greiff (Ed.), The handbook of reparations (pp. 623–649). New York: Oxford University Press.

Dzinesa, G. A. (2007). Postconflict disarmament, demobilization, and reintegration of former combatants in Southern Africa. International Studies Perspectives, 8, 73–89.

Enloe, C. (2000). Maneuvers: The international politics of militarizing women's lives. Berkeley: University of California Press.

Gobodo-Madikizela, P. (2005). Women's contributions to South Africa's Truth and Reconciliation Commission. Washington, DC: Hunt Alternatives.

Goldblatt, B. (2006). Evaluating the gender content of reparations: Lessons from South Africa. In R. Rubio-Marín (Ed.), What happened to the women: Gender and reparations for human rights violations (pp. 48–91). New York: Social Science Research Council.

Goldblatt, B., & Meintjes, S. (1998). South African women demand the truth. In M. Turshen & C. Twagiramariya (Eds.), What women do in wartime: Gender and conflict in Africa (pp. 27–61). New York: Zed Books.

Goldblatt, B., & Meintjes, S. (1999, June). Women: One chapter in the history of South Africa? A critique of the Truth and Reconciliation Report. Paper presented at The TRC: Commissioning the Past conference.

Gottschall, J. (2004). Explaining wartime rape. Journal of Sex Research, 41, 129–136.

Graybill, L. (2001). Gender and post-conflict resolution in South Africa and Rwanda. Mind and Human Interaction, 12, 261–277.

Human Rights Watch. (1995a). The Human Rights Watch global report on women's human rights. New York: Author.

Human Rights Watch. (1995b). Violence against women in South Africa: The state response to domestic violence and rape. New York: Author.

Human Rights Watch. (2004). Deadly delay: South Africa's efforts to prevent HIV in survivors of sexual violence. New York: Author. Retrieved July 24, 2009, from http://www.hrw.org/reports/2004/southafrica0304/southafrica0304.pdf

Jacobs, S., Jacobson, R., & Marchbank, J. (Eds.). (2000). State of conflict: Gender, violence and resistance. New York: Zed Books.

Jobson, M. (2005). Women and the TRC: A perspective from Khulumani Support Group. Retrieved July 24, 2009, from http://www.khulumani.net/

Jones, A. (1994). Gender and ethnic conflict in ex-Yugoslavia. Ethnic and Racial Studies, 17, 115–134.

Krog, A. (1998). Country of my skull: Guilt, sorrow, and the limits of forgiveness in the new South Africa. New York: Random House.

National Public Radio. (2005, January 7). David Chu and Debby Tucker discuss the Pentagon's new sexual assault policies. All things considered. Washington, DC: Author.

Nesiah, V. (2006). Truth commissions and gender: Principles, policies, and procedures. New York: International Center for Transitional Justice.

Nikolic-Ristanovic, V. (1996). War and violence against women. In J. Turpin & L. A. Lorentzen (Eds.), The gendered new world order (pp. 195–210). New York: Routledge.

Peterson, V. S., & Runyon, A. S. (1999). Global gender issues (2nd ed.). Boulder, CO: Westview Press.

Pettman, J. J. (1996). Worlding women: A feminist international politics. New York: Routledge Press.

Rayner, R. (1997, June 22). The warrior besieged. New York Times Magazine, p. 55.

Ross, F. (2003). Bearing witness: Women and the Truth and Reconciliation Commission in South Africa. London: Pluto Press.

Rubio-Marín, R. (2006). The gender of reparations: Setting the agenda. In R. Rubio-Marín (Ed.), What happened to the women? Gender and reparations for human rights violations (pp. 20–47). New York: Social Science Research Council.

Salzman, T. A. (1998). Rape camps as a means of ethnic cleansing: Religious, cultural, and ethical responses to rape victims in the former Yugoslavia. Human Rights Quarterly, 20, 348–378.

Sooka, Y. (2004, September). Building peace through accountability: A comparative experience between South Africa and Sierra Leone. Paper presented at Peace Needs Women and Women Need Justice: A

Conference on Gender Justice in Post-Conflict Situations, New York. Retrieved from http://www .womenwarpeace.org/webfm_send/1506

South African Truth and Reconciliation Commission. (1998a). *Truth and Reconciliation Commission of South Africa report, Vol. 1.* Cape Town, South Africa: Juta Press.

South African Truth and Reconciliation Commission. (1998b). *Truth and Reconciliation Commission of South Africa report, Vol. 4.* Cape Town, South Africa: Juta Press.

South African Truth and Reconciliation Commission. (1998c). *Truth and Reconciliation Commission of South Africa report, Vol. 5.* Cape Town, South Africa: Juta Press.

Stiglemeyer, A. (1994). The rapes in Bosnia-Herzegovina. In A. Stiglemeyer (Ed.), *Mass rape: The war against women in Bosnia-Herzegovina*

(pp. 82–169). Lincoln: University of Nebraska Press.

Turshen, M., & Twagiramariya, C. (Eds.). (1998). *What women do in wartime: Gender and conflict in Africa.* New York: Zed Books.

United Nations. (2005). *Disarmament, demobilization, reintegration (DDR) and stability in Africa.* (Conference Report). Retrieved July 24, 2009, from http://www.un.org/africa/osaa/reports/ DDR%20Sierra%20Leone%20March%202006 .pdf

UN Security Council. (2000). *United Nations Security Council Resolution 1325 on Women, Peace and Security* (S/REs/1325). New York: United Nations. Retrieved July 25, 2009, from http://www .peacewomen.org/un/sc/1325.html

World Bank. (2006). *Gender, justice, and truth commissions.* Washington, DC: Author.

CHAPTER 7

Violence Against Women and Natural Disasters

Findings From Post-Tsunami Sri Lanka

Sarah Fisher

The tsunami that struck the coast lines of multiple South Asian countries on December 26, 2004 created a humanitarian disaster of vast proportions. In Sri Lanka, more than 30,000 people were killed and more than 860,000 displaced, across the North, South, and Eastern Provinces (UNOCHA, 2005, p. 62). Reports of rape and sexual abuse occurring in the first hours and days of the crisis soon emerged in the media. One told the story of a 17-year-old girl who was gang raped hours after being washed ashore (Senayake, 2005a). Another, of a young woman whose grandfather attempted to sexually assault her in a relief center (Senayake, 2005b).

Within the first week of the disaster, a group of Sri Lankan women's organizations, which went on to form the Coalition for Assisting Tsunami Affected Women (CATAW), set out to investigate reports of violence. They confirmed "incidents of rape, gang rape, molestation, and physical abuse of women and girls" and reported a "sense of insecurity and fear" and lack of security provision in camps (CATAW, 2005a, p. 18). Widespread media coverage of such incidents stopped after the initial aftermath. Yet the research presented in this article shows that post-disaster violence, and in particular, domestic violence, did not cease. It continued in camps and temporary shelters housing the displaced well beyond the initial weeks of the crisis.

This situation cannot be viewed outside of the overall high levels of violence against women that

Fisher, S. (2010). Violence against women and natural disasters: Findings from post-tsunami Sri Lanka. *Violence Against Women*, 16.

AUTHOR'S NOTE: This research was undertaken as part of a dissertation submitted to the University of Leeds, United Kingdom for an MA in international studies. The author is extremely grateful for a grant provided by the EU-funded Asia Link Project "Gender, Development, and Public Policy in the Asian Context" between the University of Leeds and the Asian Institute for Technology, Bangkok, Thailand. In particular, the author would like to thank all those who participated in the study, granting her their valuable knowledge and experiences.

have long prevailed in Sri Lanka (CENWOR, 2004; Hussein, 2000). Prevalence studies document the widespread incidence of domestic violence, rape, psychological abuse, incest, and sexual harassment (CENWOR, 2004; Wijayatilake & Gunaratne, 1999). As is the case internationally, domestic violence is the most endemic form, affecting an estimated 60% of Sri Lankan women (Wijayatilake & Gunaratne, 1999). Harmful societal attitudes toward women and violence against women are widespread and perpetuate abuse by accepting and justifying it, manifesting in prejudice and discrimination among the legal, police, and medical systems (CENWOR, 2004; Hussein, 2000; Wijayatilake & Gunaratne, 1999). As a result, the state does not afford women sufficient protection and men are commonly able to commit abuse with impunity (Wijayatilake & Gunaratne, 1999). Furthermore, cultural norms define violence against women as a "private issue" that cannot be discussed and one which is beyond the realm of the public sphere (Suriya Women's Development Centre, 2001; Wijayatilake & Gunaratne, 1999).

Widespread prevalence and acceptance of violence against women can be understood in relation to unequal gender relationships in both the family and society, which are recognized by feminist theory as the root causes of violence against women. Violence against women results from the subordinate status of women and serves to reinforce it, used as a means of control to maintain male power, privilege, and dominance (Bunch, 1990; Carillo, 1991). Worldwide, violence against women is the most pervasive abuse of human rights (Heise, Ellsberg, & Gottemoeller, 1999). By denying women their human rights, violence prevents women from participating in society and achieving their full potential, therefore presenting a major obstacle to development (Carillo, 1991; Heise et al., 1999). In this way, violence following natural disaster may present a barrier to more equitable post-disaster reconstruction and development.

Sri Lanka's long-standing precarious political and humanitarian state of affairs is also of relevance to national levels of violence against women and the incidence of post-disaster violence. In the two decades before the tsunami, Sri Lanka had been ravaged by a civil conflict with the Liberation Tigers of Tamil Eelam (LTTE), proclaiming to represent the Tamil minority living predominantly in the North and East, fighting the Sinhalese-dominated government for a separate Tamil state. During this time an estimated 800,000 people were displaced (UNHCR, 2004). Levels of violence against women are thought to have increased due to the conflict (Suriya Women's Development Centre, 2001; Wijayatilake & Gunaratne, 1999). Women had been subjected to rape, physical abuse, and sexual assault by various armed groups, and increased violence against women, including domestic violence, was observed in centers housing the displaced (CENWOR, 2004; UNHCR, 2004). The North and East of the country, most affected by the conflict, is also where the tsunami had the greatest impact. In these areas, the tsunami disaster compounded conflict-associated problems relating to internal displacement and humanitarian intervention.

Over the last decade, recognition of women's vulnerability to violence in conflict situations has increased. Yet this has not been equaled in natural disaster situations. Violence against women during natural disasters is an area that has received little attention by both disaster management and violence against women research and practice. The majority of research on the subject has been undertaken in North America. This may not be of most relevance to developing countries (Bradshaw, 2004), where the majority of natural disasters take place and the impacts are most far reaching.

This study seeks to address this gap by providing detailed examination of the incidence of violence against women in post-tsunami Sri Lanka. To explore some of the reasons for post-disaster violence, I begin with a brief introduction to the literature on gender, disasters, and violence against women. In the following section, the research methodology is outlined. I then present the study findings regarding the incidence of violence, factors contributing to violence, including issues related to gender-blind management of the crisis, and responses to post-tsunami violence. In the final section, implications for future disaster management are considered and recommendations made to reduce post-disaster violence.

Literature Review

Gender and Disaster

The gender and disaster literature suggests that disasters are experienced differently by men and women. This is because natural disasters result in a range of impacts that are gendered and tend to bring disproportionate suffering to women (Ariyabandu & Wickramasinghe, 2003; Enarson, 2000; Wiest, Mocellin, & Motsisi, 1994). Serving as a basis for examination of this situation, a gendered analysis of disaster highlights gendered roles, needs, and vulnerabilities to enable more effective and equitable response to emergencies (Bradshaw, 2004; Enarson & Morrow, 1997; UNIASC, 2006; Wiest et al., 1994).

Women's increased vulnerability to disasters is a manifestation of the social nature of natural disaster. Although a disaster begins with or is triggered by a natural event, its effect upon society is grounded in the social system in which it takes place (Blaikie, Cannon, Davis, & Wisner, 1994; Quarantelli, 1994). Disasters are therefore inherently social processes and as such they impact upon the individual differently. An individual's vulnerability is rooted in social relationships, determined by a number of factors, such as gender, ethnicity, class, age, and disability (Ariyabandu & Wickramasinghe, 2003; Blaikie et al., 1994).

Gender is a significant determinant of women's vulnerability, rooted in unequal power relationships between women and men and the social, political, and economic subordination of women (Wiest et al., 1994). Yet other social

factors that contribute to an individual's vulnerability mean that all women do not suffer to the same extent or in the same ways (Byrne & Baden, 1995). Widows, single or disabled women, women with low income, and those belonging to marginalized racial or cultural groups are particularly vulnerable (Enarson, 2000). Women's vulnerability is increased by traditional gender roles, including women's responsibility for care of children, the elderly, and the sick. These burdens become heavier following disaster. In addition, women have specific reproductive health needs and are vulnerable to gender-based violence (Ariyabandu & Wickramasinghe, 2003; Byrne & Baden, 1995; Eade & Williams, 1995; Enarson, 2000).

Due to the social basis of vulnerability, Quarantelli (1994) argues that there is a need for a far greater sociological approach to disasters in which key social aspects and behaviors, such as gender, receive more consideration. Disaster theorists have criticized traditional disaster research for "ignoring in most cases references to gender" (Wiest et al., 1994, p. 2). The neglect of gender as an aspect of disaster vulnerability has implications for humanitarian assistance. It can result in programs that do not meet women's needs and risk increasing gendered inequalities. For example, interventions that fail to consult with women or distribute a disproportionate amount of relief to men exacerbate women's lack of voice and access to resources (Byrne & Baden, 1995; Enarson & Morrow, 1997). Known as "gender mainstreaming," the consideration of gender issues throughout all aspects of policy and programming (UNECOSOC, 1997) is a recommended strategy for ensuring a gender perspective in disaster management (UNIASC, 2006).

Violence Against Women and Disaster

Research on violence against women during disaster situations and humanitarian emergencies has focused primarily on conflict as opposed to natural disaster situations. Although data specifically related to its incidence during natural disaster situations are limited, there is evidence to suggest that levels of domestic and sexual violence against women increase following natural disasters.

Studies of multiple disasters in the developed world, mostly the United States and Canada, reveal strong indicators of increased domestic violence in disaster-affected communities (Dobson, 1994; Enarson, 1999, 1999b; Enarson & Fordham, 2001; Enarson & Morrow, 1997; Fothergill, 1999; Morrow, 1997). Following the Red River floods in the United States in 1997, local violence intervention centers recorded considerable increases in crisis calls and requests for protection orders while experiencing a reduction of resources (Enarson & Fordham, 2001; Fothergill, 1999). Enarson's (1999a) study of domestic violence programs in the United States and Canada also found that those most severely hit by disaster faced increased service demand, from both new and existing users, yet fewer resources. Increases in domestic violence were also documented following Hurricane Andrew in the United States (Enarson, 1999b; Enarson & Morrow, 1997; Morrow, 1997), an earthquake in California (Wilson, Phillips, & Neal, 1998), and a flood in Australia (Dobson, 1994).

Although detailed research on the phenomenon from the developing world is scarce, violence against women during natural disaster situations has been observed in countries of the South. Increased domestic and sexual violence was noted following Hurricane Mitch in Nicaragua and Honduras (Delaney & Shrader, 2000; Solorzano & Montoya, 2000). Incidents of sexual violence were reported in the aftermath of a cyclone in Bangladesh (Kafi, 1992 as cited in Ariyabandu & Wickramasinghe, 2003) and increased domestic violence following a volcanic eruption in the Philippines (Delica, 1998).

Many factors may account for the increased likelihood of violence following disaster. Disaster-affected communities endure considerable loss, stress, and trauma. Disruption to the everyday life of households, including family responsibilities for income generation and household tasks, can cause changes in traditional gender roles (Byrne & Baden, 1995; Morrow, 1997). Economic hardships and frustrations and struggles to replace housing, jobs, and possessions bring increased tensions and stress to relationships, sometimes leading to conflict and domestic violence (Enarson, 1999a, 1999b). Social dislocation and the resultant loss of traditional community support and protection mechanisms exacerbate women's vulnerability to violence (Ariyabandu & Wickramasinghe, 2003; Byrne & Baden, 1995; Wiest et al., 1994).

Gendered differences have been observed in the ways that men and women cope with the impacts of disasters. Whereas women are more likely to express grief and seek support from other women, men are more likely to repress emotional suffering and express anger and frustration destructively through aggression, violence, and alcoholism (Delaney & Shrader, 2000; Miller, Turner, & Kimball, 1981; Wiest et al., 1994). Overcrowded temporary accommodation centers leave women and children vulnerable to sexual violence (Delaney & Shrader, 2000; Wiest et al., 1994). Women can be attacked when using facilities or carrying out tasks such as water collection. Poorly designed humanitarian interventions can increase this risk (Dugan, Fowler, & Bolton, 2000; UNIASC, 2005). In addition, economic hardship leaves women susceptible to sexual exploitation and prostitution, sometimes by men in positions of authority such as the police, the military, and humanitarian workers (UNIASC, 2005; Wiest et al., 1994). It is therefore recommended that gender-based violence prevention and response, as well as other gender issues, are mainstreamed throughout humanitarian interventions (for detailed guidance developed by the UNIASC, see UNIASC, 2005).

Method

This research is part of a wider qualitative study examining violence against women in post-tsunami

Sri Lanka and responses by international humanitarian organizations with specific programs to address this violence. The latter topic will be addressed in a future publication. This article focuses on aspects of the study concerned with the prevalence of violence, whether levels of violence increased following the disaster, reasons for postdisaster violence, and responses by humanitarian actors. The research was designed to increase sociological understanding of the incidence of violence against women during natural disasters, to inform disaster management practice, and reduce violence in future disaster situations.

Qualitative data were collected over a period of 3 months, beginning approximately 5 months after the tsunami. Purposive sampling was used to select a range of informants, most working on tsunami-related gender-based violence initiatives. A total of 60 semistructured interviews were conducted with staff members of Sri Lankan women's, community and nongovernmental organizations (25), international nongovernmental organizations and UN agencies (31), and governmental representatives (4).

Interviews were conducted in English given participants' high levels of English proficiency. They were recorded and transcribed verbatim, except in a few instances when, due to the sensitivity of the subject matter, detailed notes were made. The semistructured format of interviews permitted information and opinions on a wide range of relevant issues to be gathered and expressed freely. For analysis, data were coded and grouped into emergent issues and themes. Select secondary sources complement this research, such as documents provided by humanitarian agencies and news reports. Although media accounts can be unreliable, those included were verified by primary informants or checked for consistency with other findings.

This methodology was chosen for a number of reasons. There was a lack of formal reports and investigation of incidents of violence and it would not have been ethical to interview tsunami-affected women about personal exposure to violence. Nor would this have been productive

due to the personal and culturally sensitive nature of the issue. The most appropriate and reliable method was therefore to interview individuals involved in responding to violence. This chosen approach had the limitation that it was not possible to collect quantitative data to compare violence prevalence before and after the disaster.

Further material was obtained through monitoring activities conducted by the author in accommodation centers and participation in interagency meetings. This work was undertaken on behalf of the Women's Division of the Disaster Relief Monitoring Unit of the Sri Lankan Human Rights Commission. It permitted observations in displaced settings and conversations with disaster-affected women and men, including camp managers. Commission staff provided translation for these discussions. In private, women-only circumstances, enquiries were made about the occurrence of violence. Although responses could not be taken at face value, some women reported incidents of violence or expressed safety concerns.

Given the limited time period in which the research was conducted, the findings reflect the circumstances for the first 7 months following the tsunami only. Sources remain anonymous due to the sensitivity of the subject matter and the political situation in Sri Lanka.

Findings

Violence in the Immediate Tsunami Aftermath

From the very onset of the tsunami, girls and women in affected areas were subjected to rape and other forms of physical and sexual abuse. Some incidents during the initial turmoil of the disaster were reported in the press. These reports included the rape of a young woman by her "rescuer" after being saved from the waves (Senayake, 2005a) and the gang rape of two women on a beach they visited to view the destruction

(CATAW, 2005b). Lack of security and chaotic conditions in camps that were forming created further environments in which girls and women were vulnerable to violence. Reports of this nature included sexual abuses and molestation of minors (Senayake, 2005b). Although incidents of rape, assault, and molestation were investigated and confirmed by the CATAW (2005a), informal and media reports were rarely matched with police reports.

Although women were perhaps most vulnerable to sexual violence in the first few chaotic weeks of the disaster, violence, and particularly, domestic violence, continued beyond this period. Reports from other countries show that post-tsunami violence against women was not only confined to Sri Lanka. Incidents of rape, sexual harassment, and domestic abuse were reported in tsunami-affected areas of Indonesia, India, and Thailand (APWLD, 2005a, 2005b).

Domestic Violence After the Disaster Emergency Phase

Following the initial aftermath of the disaster, domestic violence was considered by more than 4 out of 5 respondents to be the most prevalent and sustained form of post-disaster violence against women. In all provinces affected by the tsunami, disaster-related domestic abuse was reported as widespread. Respondents acknowledged that violence was probably more visible due to communal living conditions and, in addition, it was not possible to know whether violence in specific relationships predated the tsunami. Yet over two-thirds of respondents felt certain that relationships had become more violent and many others that it may have. One quantitative indication of this was provided by a women's group in the East. The group had received over double the number of referrals for domestic violence support services during the period following the tsunami than during an equivalent period before (personal communication, 2005).

There is one regional difference that should be noted. In Jaffna, Northern Province, informants were less likely to feel that domestic abuse had increased, although the circumstances related to the disaster were acknowledged to have made the likelihood of violence greater. There is a possible explanation for this. Although the impact of the tsunami was considerable in Jaffna, its effect was of less significance than that of the civil war of the last 20 years. The war had a greater impact in Jaffna, meaning that this area had already experienced a humanitarian emergency and mass internal displacement more significantly than others. This brought familiarity with living in temporary accommodation centers, in which high levels of violence were already reported (UNHCR, 2004).

Interviewees were able to recount specific, and sometimes numerous, incidents of domestic violence in temporary shelters. Husbands blaming their partners for failing to save their children from the waves was a common context for abuse. Male violence was used as a means of control and dominance during arguments over financial matters. Reported incidents in accommodation centers included a man severing his wife's leg with a shovel and another stripping his wife naked in public and attacking her with a broken bottle. Some incidents were fatal. A woman reportedly died after being set on fire by her husband following a dispute over his expenditure of the family's compensation money on alcohol. Other reported cases led to suicide or attempted suicide.

Respondents felt that domestic violence was fuelled by a combination of factors. These included psychological trauma, stresses and pressures associated with loss of homes and livelihoods, and poor conditions and lack of privacy in accommodation centers. In addition, male alcohol consumption was believed to have increased and, in turn, contributed to increased violence. These findings mirror the situation following Hurricane Andrew, where domestic abuse service providers felt disaster-induced frustrations and uncertainty had increased domestic conflict and violence (Enarson & Morrow, 1997). Yet although issues such as trauma and male alcohol consumption may "trigger" violence in disaster situations, they must not be confused with the underlying causes of violence against women, grounded in gender inequality. For this reason, it is useful to use Deraniyagala's identification of such factors as "isolated" or "immediate" causes, distinct from the true, root causes (Deraniyagala, 1992 as cited in Wijayatilake & Gunaratne, 1999).

Other Forms of Violence After the Disaster Emergency Phase

Incidents of rape, sexual abuse, harassment, and molestation continued in accommodation centers, beyond the disaster's emergency phase. Respondents were aware of reported cases, yet due to fear of stigmatization and the likelihood of victims knowing the perpetrators, violence remained predominantly hidden. As a relief worker explained, "People don't want to talk about it but it is happening" (personal communication, 2005).

Sexual assaults took place in poorly lit toilets (Oxfam International, 2005). In one camp it was reported that male residents purposely triggered a power cut at night and molested women while they were sleeping. Women were also at risk of attack when journeying to their damaged homes or venturing out to fulfill everyday needs. In one incident reported, a woman with learning difficulties was raped after becoming lost when she left the camp to fetch necessities. A further incident of abuse of a woman with a learning disability was reported, highlighting the increased risk for disabled women observed in other disaster situations (Fothergill, 1999).

Economic marginalization and lack of access to resources left women reliant on men and vulnerable to manipulation and sexual exploitation. Instances were reported of men offering impoverished tsunami-affected women money or goods for sex, or engaging in relationships under a false pretense that marriage would follow. Following Hurricane Mitch in Nicaragua and Honduras, Delaney and Shrader (2000) also found coerced prostitution to be a problem in some rural areas, particularly among adolescent girls.

Soon after the tsunami there was an increase in marriages of young women and girls. Men quickly sought to replace lost wives, sometimes marrying girls as young as 13. This situation was worsened by how a greater number of women died due to the tsunami than men (Oxfam International, 2005). Some marriages were arranged by girls' parents to lessen their own financial burdens. New marriages left the men's children vulnerable to abuse, some abandoned by fathers with new wives. "Tsunami marriages" were also reported in other countries: for example, in India, where they were fueled by government assistance to couples who had supposedly planned marriages before the tsunami (APWLD, 2005a) and in Aceh, Indonesia, where forced marriages of young women ensured protection and supplies (APWLD, 2005b). In addition, child abuse and incest were concerns. Girls who had lost their mothers were especially vulnerable to abuse by family members, not only fathers but also uncles and brothers. In the North and East, several respondents reported LTTE recruitment of child soldiers (male and female) taking place in camps.

Abuse occurred at the hands of men in positions of power and authority, a finding consistent with other disasters (Wiest et al., 1994). Incidents of rape, physical abuse, sexual harassment, and exploitation were reported to have been committed by police and the paramilitary Special Task Force (STF) positioned in camps to provide security. In addition, from one camp came reports of sexual harassment by humanitarian workers while women were bathing. In these situations women were particularly powerless to defend themselves or seek reprisal.

Reasons for Post-Disaster Violence

A number of factors associated with the social upheaval wrought by the tsunami and management of the disaster contributed to women's increased vulnerability to violence.

Men frequently vented their anger, frustration, stress, and depression through domestic violence and alcohol consumption. This finding reflects those from other tsunami-affected countries and other disasters (APWLD, 2005a, 2005b; Delaney & Shrader, 2000; Miller et al., 1981). Following Hurricane Mitch in Nicaragua and Honduras, increased violence and alcohol consumption were identified as male coping strategies and indicators of poor psychosocial well-being (Delaney & Shrader, 2000). In Sri Lanka, levels of male alcohol consumption were of concern prior to the tsunami, yet alcoholism was reported to have increased and to be rife among tsunami-affected men. This was believed to have exacerbated violence. Women were also forced by their partners to give up excess food donations by selling them to raise funds for alcohol (WCDM, 2005). It should be reiterated, however, that alcohol consumption per se does not cause violence. Although it appears to have been an aggravating factor, it is not possible to determine the extent to which alcohol contributed to violent behavior relative to other, perhaps less visible factors, such as stress or depression.

Lack of privacy and crowded living conditions created a situation conducive to sexual assault and harassment. In addition to women's vulnerability to attack by males living in the same camp, lack of privacy and personal space increased the likelihood of women experiencing abuse by their partners. Due to the close proximity of children and neighbors, women were uncomfortable with sexual intimacy. This was sometimes met with violent responses from men asserting what they felt to be their sexual "rights" over their partners. Tensions between couples and violence, associated with male sexual demands and women's concerns about cramped conditions and possible pregnancy, have also been documented in a disaster-affected community in the Philippines (Delica, 1998). In one camp, concerns were expressed that reduced sexual relationships between partners may have increased the likelihood of sexual abuse of children. To protect children, the management committee left lights on in the shelters at night. Yet women felt this compounded their own difficulties in meeting their husband's sexual demands.

Gender-blind programs and policies of governmental and nongovernmental agencies heightened women's vulnerability to violence. An example of this was the government's tsunami compensation scheme, which paid cash relief to the male head of household. Women's economic marginalization and dependence on men worsened, increasing their vulnerability to violence. Furthermore, men purchased alcohol with compensation money and spending cash relief was a significant source of conflict and violence between couples. Similarly, following Hurricane Andrew, women preferred checks to be issued in their own name, to prevent their partners misusing the money for personal means (Enarson & Morrow, 1997).

Inadequate consideration was paid to women's protection needs in the planning of facilities, such as toilet and bathing areas in camps. Five months after the tsunami, in most of the accommodation sites visited, men's and women's hygiene facilities were separate, covered, and at a suitable distance from the camp. Some had lighting. Yet facilities varied significantly. Even at this time, some bathing facilities did not provide sufficient privacy.

Low participation of women in planning and decision making at the local, district, and state levels was a considerable barrier to gender-sensitive disaster response and resulted in insufficient attention to post-disaster violence. Reflecting women's general political marginalization, locally, women's involvement in camp management committees was limited. Although overall membership varied by camp, women's representation was unequal to men's. In Muslim areas, women were completely excluded from the camp management process, a situation also reported from Aceh in Indonesia (APWLD, 2005b). The role of camp manager and other public leadership roles were predominantly assumed by males, as observed in other disasters (Delaney & Shrader, 2000). Due to this situation and the general low regard for women's welfare, issues adversely affecting women, such as alcohol consumption, were frequently ignored. Women, who through involvement in decision making and other male domains were deemed to be overstepping their roles as women, sometimes met open hostility. A female camp committee member was reportedly forced to flee her local area after being threatened by the male committee leader, due to her role on the committee.

In addition, the inadequate response to post-tsunami violence and predisaster factors restricting the effective management of violence were responsible for increasing women's vulnerability to violence. These issues are addressed briefly below.

Responses to Post-Tsunami Violence

Following the reports of violence that emerged in the media during the immediate crisis, Sri Lankan women's organizations quickly sought to draw attention to safety concerns and spur remedial action. After the Coalition for Assisting Tsunami Affected Women (CATAW) had investigated and confirmed incidents of abuse, it issued a press release highlighting the failure of the relief process to address women's safety and well-being (CATAW, 2005a). In both the initial and the later stages of the disaster, women's groups were extremely active in responding to violence, as well as the wider neglect of gender issues, through a variety of approaches. These included advocacy, research and monitoring, service provision, campaigning and raising awareness, and efforts to increase women's participation in the relief and reconstruction process (Fisher, 2009).

A future article will examine organizational responses by international agencies that undertook specific programs to address post-tsunami violence, often in collaboration with Sri Lankan

women's organizations. Here it should be noted that the overall response to post-disaster violence was inadequate. Awareness among humanitarian actors of the potential for violence was low, and the majority failed to take sufficient measures within their work to prevent abuse. Procedures for monitoring, recording, and responding to reports were lacking.

The Sri Lankan government was slow and reluctant to acknowledge and respond to the issue, exacerbated by the lack of official reporting of incidents to the police. In the 2nd week of the crisis, the activism of Sri Lankan women's organizations provided a catalyst for some measures to improve security. In the South, the police were positioned in camps. In the North and East, it was the STF, a paramilitary arm of the police usually deployed for counter-insurgency operations (CATAW, 2005b). Unfortunately, however, these personnel had received no training or instructions on violence and protection. They saw their role primarily as maintaining discipline in camps, and many failed to intervene in cases of abuse. When incidents were reported to the police, it was common for officers to refuse to "interfere," reflecting the deeply entrenched perception in Sri Lanka of domestic violence as a "family" or "private" matter (Wijayatilake & Gunaratne, 1999). On some occasions the perpetrator was "advised" or "warned," but more commonly police were sympathetic toward abusers. These are known to be common responses from Sri Lankan police (UNCHR, 2004).

Furthermore, there were the reported incidents of abuse committed by police and STF officers. In the North and East, the situation with security provision was particularly sensitive because the STF had been present in the area for many years due to the conflict. With brutal militarization over the years, women had come to fear them. It must be noted, however, that feelings toward the presence of police and military officers in camps did vary across communities and districts. Despite allegations of misconduct and abuse, in some camps the presence of police or security forces was welcome.

Practice of health workers was also problematic. Medical staff mostly attended to women's physical injuries. More holistic care, encompassing sexual and reproductive health needs and violence, was lacking. In known cases of abuse, responses were often inappropriate or insensitive. One such incident involved the sexual abuse of a tsunami-affected girl by her school principal. Behavior of police and hospital staff made the girl feel responsible for the abuse and confidentiality was breached. Misconduct and poor practice by police officers, health professionals, and other officials reflected negative social attitudes and beliefs related to violence against women and toward women in general. These problems associated with the overall poor management of violence against women in Sri Lanka restricted effective response in the disaster context.

Conclusions

The findings of this article suggest that increased levels of violence against women can be experienced in disaster-affected communities for a considerable amount of time after the onset of the crisis. Disaster-related incidents of violence took place in Sri Lanka well beyond the tsunami's immediate aftermath. In the chaos of the first hours and days of the crisis, the likelihood of rape and other forms of sexual violence were perhaps at their highest. At this time, opportunistic perpetrators of sexual violence took advantage of the turmoil, seizing occasions where girls and women were extremely vulnerable to abuse. These circumstances and types of incidents may have lessened to some extent following the emergency phase. Yet sexual violence, harassment, and particularly domestic violence continued during post-tsunami rehabilitation and reconstruction.

Many factors can contribute to post-disaster violence against women, some of which in the context of the tsunami are consistent with other disasters. Stress and other psychological impacts of disaster, and the male tendency to vent emotional suffering through violence and alcoholism, are perhaps the most significant. These triggers must not be confused with the true underlying causes of gender-based violence related to patriarchy and male privilege. Both during disaster and at other times, male perpetrators use violence as a means to assert power and control over women. Violence in disaster situations, therefore, must not be viewed as distinct from the violence in society perpetrated against women at "normal" times. Although violence increased in Sri Lanka as a result of the "triggers" associated with the devastation and chaos of the crisis, levels of violence were already high (CENWOR, 2004). Post-disaster violence was a manifestation of women's preexisting vulnerability to violence, which is exacerbated at times of disaster.

This study has highlighted the potential for gender-blind humanitarian interventions to heighten women's vulnerability to violence, and in the final section the policy implications for future disaster management are considered. For disaster programs to be responsive to those in most need, they must engage with social inequalities and the unequal access to power and resources contributing to disaster vulnerability. Interventions that fail to do so risk further marginalizing the most vulnerable (Byrne & Baden, 1995; Eade & Williams, 1995). Action steps are recommended to both prevent and respond to the immediate causes of post-disaster violence and to address the underlying causes of violence against women.

Reducing Violence Against Women During Disaster: Policy Considerations

The failure to address women's protection needs following the tsunami crisis must be understood within the context of the overall neglect of gender issues within responses to the disaster. Increased vulnerability of Sri Lankan girls and women to violence was one of many impacts of the tsunami that could have been lessened by more gender-sensitive disaster management.

Addressing post-disaster violence necessitates a wider, gendered approach to disaster management, taking into consideration the diversity of women's disaster needs.

As women are known to experience increased vulnerability to social impacts of disaster (Ariyabandu & Wickramasinghe, 2003; Enarson, 2000; Wiest et al., 1994), it is critical that national governments and humanitarian agencies recognize gender-sensitive emergency planning and response as a key priority. Gender must be a focus of disaster management policy and program development, and practice must be monitored to identify gender bias. To assist this process, there are minimum standards and guidance for humanitarian response (see Sphere Project, 2004) and guidelines specifically informing gendered analysis (see UNIASC, 2006). On a practical level, full adherence to guidelines is not readily achieved, particularly given the nature of emergency situations. In the long term, organizations need to work toward implementation of a gender mainstreaming strategy (UNIASC, 2005). This will ensure routine consideration to gender throughout all stages of disaster prevention and management, with the ultimate aim of embedding gender equity within organizational culture. In the shorter term, initial steps should be taken to implement key gender-friendly practice points.

Collection of sex- and age-disaggregated data, and other vulnerability indicators, should be prioritized to identify needs and vulnerabilities of disadvantaged groups. Baseline data should include numbers of single women and female-headed households, pregnant and lactating women, and persons with disabilities (UNIASC, 2006). Nongovernmental organizations working in disaster-prone areas can assist emergency planning by assembling local population profiles (Enarson & Fordham, 2001).

Women should be registered in their own name, with assistance money and relief items distributed to them directly. Needs assessments should inform allocation to prevent unmet needs and excesses that may be misappropriated by men. Involvement of female staff and beneficiaries, and supervision and monitoring of distribution, are additional recommendations (Sphere Project, 2004; UNIASC, 2005). These measures should increase women's access to resources and economic independence, thereby reducing vulnerability to violence and sexual exploitation. With these aims and to support women's long-term disaster recovery, programs to strengthen women's livelihoods should be a focus. In particular, programs should target young, unmarried women, who may be at most risk of exploitation or early marriage.

Full and equal participation of women should be ensured throughout all stages of disaster management planning, decision making, and practice (Sphere Project, 2004; UNIASC, 2006). Increased partnerships and consultation with grassroots women's groups and other community-based organizations can facilitate this. This is one of many reasons why there should be greater collaboration with local women's organizations, including provision of assistance and resources to them. Their understanding of local needs and culture can enable greater reach of vulnerable groups and their work can hold many benefits for disaster-affected women. In addition, supporting work of this kind can offer opportunities to address long-term vulnerability to violence and promote women's advancement. For in the case of Sri Lanka, women's groups were found to have integrated women's strategic needs into disaster response, addressing the inequalities underlying violence and other gendered disaster impacts (Fisher, 2009).

For disaster management to effectively protect women from post-disaster violence, further actions to specifically address this threat are required. To inform this effort, humanitarian and governmental agencies should use the guidelines developed by the UNIASC (2005). This resource provides comprehensive guidance on various activities that should be undertaken to prevent, monitor, and respond to abuse, during emergency planning, the earlier stages of disaster, and recovery and rehabilitation. Yet the first challenge is to promote far greater awareness among humanitarian actors of women's vulnerability to post-disaster violence and of the potential for interventions to heighten this vulnerability. Ensuring that interventions do not have adverse gendered outcomes must be recognized as part of the obligation that humanitarian agencies have to "do no harm."

In the immediate emergency phase, procedures for violence monitoring, reporting, and response must be put in place. These should include referral mechanisms for holistic care provision, including services to meet the medical, psychological, and social support needs of victims, as well as to provide legal redress (UNIASC, 2005). Documentation of incidents by humanitarian agencies and women's groups could provide an evidence base to strengthen advocacy initiatives for increased protection measures. Once temporary accommodation centers are established, they should be provided with security. Reporting, monitoring, and response mechanisms must be clearly communicated with clear links and lines of responsibility to humanitarian staff and security providers. Reporting and disciplinary procedures for rights violations by those in positions of authority are also required. Training to sensitize all humanitarian staff, security personnel, and other key service providers on gender, violence prevention, and response should be prioritized.

Women's protection needs should be a key concern when designing accommodation centers. Attention should be paid to reducing all opportunities for sexual violence, for example, when women are using sanitation facilities, collecting firewood, or being allocated food aid (Dugan et al., 2000). Camp design must consider the layout and spacing of facilities, consult women on these issues, and provide lighting and sufficient cover to ensure privacy (Dugan et al., 2000; Sphere Project, 2004; UNIASC, 2005).

Resources to support women affected by violence should be channeled through experienced local providers of these services, such as women's groups. This would allow these organizations that have the greatest capacity to respond appropriately to such a culturally sensitive issue to reach more women. Equally, effective service provision is necessary from governmental agencies, particularly the legal and health sectors, given how poor practice by police and health workers has been shown to inhibit the management of violence. Capacity building, including training initiatives, should be undertaken to increase multisectoral commitment and ability to manage violence in times of disaster and otherwise. This work should address the harmful social attitudes dominant among service providers and society at large, which could also be a focus of campaigning and awareness-raising in disaster-affected communities.

With the view to designing interventions that reduce the tendency for post-disaster violence, a priority for the research agenda should be the identification of alternative, nondestructive ways to help men channel disaster-related frustrations. There is also a potential for health promotion programs with men to reduce alcohol consumption and for psychosocial initiatives to address stress and trauma. The actions that have been proposed in this article are necessary steps toward post-disaster violence prevention and response becoming an integral part of disaster management. In this way, women and girls affected by disaster can be granted the protection and service provision to address post-disaster violence that they need.

Declaration of Conflicting Interests

The author declared no potential conflicts of interest with respect to the authorship and/or publication of this article.

Funding

The author disclosed receipt of the following financial support for the research and/or authorship of this article: This study was supported by a grant provided by the EU-funded Asia Link Project, "Gender, Development and Public Policy in the Asian Context," between the University of Leeds, United Kingdom, and the Asian Institute for Technology, Bangkok, Thailand.

References

Ariyabandu, M., & Wickramasinghe, M. (2003). *Gender dimensions in disaster management—A guide for South Asia.* Colombo, Sri Lanka: ITDG South Asia.

Asia Pacific Forum on Women, Law and Development. (2005b). *Women's human rights concerns in tsunami affected countries.* Chiang Mai, Thailand: Author. Retrieved June 11, 2005, from http://www.apwld.org/tsunami_humanrights.htm

Asia Pacific Forum on Women, Law and Development. (2005a). *Why are women more vulnerable during disasters? Violations of women's human rights in the tsunami aftermath.* Chiang Mai, Thailand: Author. Retrieved April 10, 2006, from http://www.apwld.org/pdf/tsunami_report _Oct2005 .pdf

Blaikie, P. M., Cannon, T., Davis, I., & Wisner, B. (1994). *At risk: Natural hazards, people's vulnerability and disasters.* London: Routledge.

Bradshaw, S. (2004). *Socio-economic impacts of natural disasters: A gender analysis.* Manual prepared for the Economic Commission for Latin America and the Caribbean, Women and Development Unit, United Nations, Santiago, Chile. Available from http://www.eclac.cl

Bunch, C. (1990). Women's rights as human rights: Towards a re-vision of human rights. *Human Rights Quarterly, 12,* 486–498.

Byrne, B., & Baden, S. (1995). *Gender, emergencies and humanitarian assistance* (Bridge Report No. 33). Brighton, UK: Institute of Development Studies. Retrieved September 1, 2005, from http://www .bridge.ids.ac.uk

Carillo, R. (1991). Violence against women: An obstacle to development. In Center for Women's Global Leadership (Compiler), *Gender violence: A development and human rights issue* (pp. 17–37). New York: Center for Women's Global Leadership.

Centre for Women's Research. (2004). *Study on sexual and gender-based violence in selected locations in Sri Lanka* (Report commissioned by UNHCR Sri Lanka). Colombo, Sri Lanka: Author.

Coalition for Assisting Tsunami Affected Women. (2005a, January 1). Women's groups appeal for an inclusive framework for disaster response. *Options, 3*(6), 18–19.

Coalition for Assisting Tsunami Affected Women. (2005b, January 15). Gender specific issues relating to post-tsunami displacement. *Options, 3*(6), 19–22.

Delaney, P. L., & Shrader, E. (2000). *Gender and post-disaster reconstruction: The case of Hurricane Mitch in Honduras and Nicaragua.* Washington, DC: World Bank. Available from http://www .gdnonline.org

Delica, Z. G. (1998). Balancing vulnerability and capacity: Women and children in the Philippines. In E. Enarson & B. H. Morrow (Eds.), *The gendered terrain of disaster: Through women's eyes* (pp. 225–231). Westport, CT: Praeger.

Dobson, N. (1994). From under the mud-pack: Women and the Charleville floods. *Australian Journal of Emergency Management, 9*(2), 11–13.

Dugan, J., Fowler, C. J., & Bolton, P. A. (2000). Assessing the opportunity for sexual violence against women and children in refugee camps. *Journal of Humanitarian Assistance.* Retrieved February 7, 2005, from http://www.jha.ac/ articles/a060.htm

Eade, D., & Williams, S. (1995). *The Oxfam handbook of development and relief* (Vols. 1–3). Oxford, UK: Oxfam.

Enarson, E. (1999a). Violence against women in disasters: A study of domestic violence programs in the United States and Canada. *Violence Against Women, 5,* 742–768.

Enarson, E. (1999b). Women and housing issues in two U.S. disasters: Hurricane Andrew and the Red River Valley Flood. *International Journal of Mass Emergencies and Disasters, 17,* 39–63.

Enarson, E. (2000, May). *Gender issues in natural disasters: Talking points and research needs.* Paper prepared for the International Labour Organisation InFocus Programme on Crisis Response and Reconstruction Workshop, Geneva, Switzerland. Retrieved February 8, 2005, from http://www .gdnonline.org/resources/ilo-talking.doc

Enarson, E., & Fordham, M. (2001). Lines that divide, ties that bind: Race, class, and gender in women's flood recovery in the US and UK. *Australian Journal of Emergency Management, 15*(4), 43–52.

Enarson, E., & Morrow, B. H. (1997). A gendered perspective: The voices of women. In W. G. Peacock, B. H. Morrow, & H. Gladwin (Eds.), *Hurricane Andrew: Ethnicity, gender and the sociology of disasters* (pp. 116–140). London: Routledge.

Fisher, S. (2009). Sri Lankan women's organisations responding to post-tsunami violence. In E. Enarson & P. G. D. Chakrabarti (Eds.), *Women, gender and disaster: Global issues and initiatives* (pp. 233–249). Delhi, India: Sage.

Fothergill, A. (1999). An exploratory study of woman battering in the Grand Forks flood disaster: Implications for community responses and policies. *International Journal of Mass Emergencies and Disasters, 17,* 79–98.

Heise, L., Ellsberg, M., & Gottemoeller, M. (1999). *Ending violence against women* (Population Reports, Series L, No. 11). Baltimore, MD: Johns Hopkins University School of Public Health, Population Information Program.

Hussein, A. (2000). *Sometimes there is no blood: Domestic violence and rape in rural Sri Lanka.* Colombo, Sri Lanka: International Centre for Ethnic Studies.

Miller, J. A. M., Turner, J. G., & Kimball, E. (1981). Big Thompson flood victims: One year later. *Family Relations, 30,* 111–116.

Morrow, B. H. (1997). Stretching the bonds: The families of Andrew. In W. G. Peacock, B. H. Morrow, & H. Gladwin (Eds.), *Hurricane Andrew: Ethnicity, gender and the sociology of disasters* (pp. 141–170). London: Routledge.

Oxfam International. (2005, March). *The tsunami's impact on women* (Briefing note). Oxford, UK: Author. Available from http://www.oxfam.org.uk

Quarantelli, E. L. (1994). *Draft of a sociological disaster research agenda for the future: Theoretical, methodological and empirical issues* (Preliminary Paper No. 228). Newark, DE: University of Delaware Disaster Research Center.

Senayake, S. (2005a, January 7). *Tsunami survivor's life scarred by rape.* Retrieved February 5, 2005, from http://cnews.canoe.ca/CNEWS/World/Tsunami/2005/01/07/826059-ap.html

Senayake, S. (2005b, January 1). *Officials probe child rape in Sri Lanka.* Retrieved February 5, 2005, from http://www.lankalibrary.com/news/rape.htm

Solorzano, I., & Montoya, O. (2000). Men against marital violence: A Nicaraguan campaign. *ID21 Insights, 35.* Retrieved February 4, 2005, from http://www.id21.org/insights/insights35/insights-iss35-art05.html

Sphere Project. (2004). *The Sphere Project humanitarian charter and minimum standards in disaster response.* Geneva, Switzerland: Author. Available from http://www.sphereproject.org

Suriya Women's Development Centre. (2001). A call to strengthen activities to stop wartime violence against women. *Pravada, 7*(4), 31–32.

United Nations Economic and Social Council. (1997, September 18). *Report on the Economic and Social Council for 1997 (A/52/3).* New York: Author. Retrieved February 22, 2008, from http://www.un.org/documents/

United Nations High Commissioner for Refugees. (2004). *UNHCR helps Sri Lanka deal with sexual & gender-based violence* (Focus on Protection Newsletter No. 5). Colombo, Sri Lanka: Author.

United Nations Inter-Agency Standing Committee. (2005). *Guidelines for gender-based violence interventions in humanitarian settings.* Geneva, Switzerland: Author. Retrieved June 21, 2010, from http://www.womenwarpeace.org/webfm_send/347

United Nations Inter-Agency Standing Committee. (2006). *Women, girls, boys and men: Different needs—Equal opportunities: Gender handbook in humanitarian action.* Geneva, Switzerland: Author. Retrieved June 21, 2010, from http://www.sheltercentre.org/sites/default/files/IASC%20Gender%20Handbook%20Final.pdf

United Nations Office for the Coordination of Humanitarian Affairs. (2005). *Indian Ocean earthquake—Tsunami 2005 flash appeal.* Geneva, Switzerland: Author. Retrieved January 28, 2005, from http://www.un.org/News/dh/infocus/Tsunami/tsunamiflashappeal.pdf

Wiest, R. E., Mocellin, J. S. P., & Motsisi, D. T. (1994). *The needs of women in disasters and emergencies.* Report prepared for the United Nations Development Programme, Disaster Management Training Programme, and the Office of the

United Nations Disaster Relief Coordinator, University of Manitoba, Disaster Research Institute, Winnipeg, Canada.

Wijayatilake, K., & Gunaratne, C. (1999). *Monitoring progress on the elimination of discrimination against and the achievement of equality for women: Sri Lanka report on domestic violence.* Colombo, Sri Lanka: Centre for Women's Research.

Wilson, J., Phillips, B. D., & Neal, D. M. (1998). Domestic violence after disaster. In E. Enarson & B. H. Morrow (Eds.), *The gendered terrain of disaster: Through women's eyes* (pp. 225–231). Westport, CT: Praeger.

Women's Coalition for Disaster Management. (2005). *Gender watch* (No. 1–6). Batticaloa, Sri Lanka: Author.

CHAPTER 8

Understanding Human Trafficking in the United States

T. K. Logan, Robert Walker, and Gretchen Hunt

Samirah and Enung were recruited from their home in Indonesia by a wealthy family to work in America. Both women signed a contract stating they would be paid US$100–US$200 a month to work in a home taking care of a family. But, when they arrived their passports and travel documents were confiscated and they were made to work close to 21 hr a day, to sleep on small mats in the kitchen of the large home, and were given very little to eat. They were threatened, physically assaulted, and rarely allowed out of the house. They were also subjected to what can only be called torture for such transgressions as stealing food because they were often hungry. For example, throughout their time with the family they were forced to run up and down stairs until exhausted, beaten with broom handles and rolling pins, cut with knives, and forced to stand while being scalded with boiling hot water. And for all this, they were not directly paid although some money was sent back to their families in their home country. Even though the two women, both aged close to 50 years, had been in America for 5 years working for this family, they only knew a few English words. Further, on at least one occasion a witness saw Samirah crawling up the basement stairs bleeding from the forehead and Samirah and Enung both told the witness that Samirah had been beaten by the home owner. On another occasion a landscaper at the home was confronted by Enung, who was raggedly dressed and very hungry, pleading with him for his doughnuts. Even so, it wasn't until one of the women ran away to get help that their situation was discovered by authorities (Eltman, 2007; Vitello, 2007; Warner, 2007).

This account of human trafficking is one of many that are becoming more frequently reported in the media in the United States. There

Logan, T. K., Walker, R., & Hunt, G. (2009). Understanding human trafficking in the United States. *Trauma, Violence, & Abuse, 10,* 3–30.

are similarities across the reported cases which often include little or no pay for menial and difficult work, debt bondage, confiscated documents such as passports, undocumented immigrant status, long and grueling work hours, as well as threats of harm, physical assault, and emotional abuse. Each of these elements represents an antithesis of fundamental human dignity and basic citizen and human rights; however, there seems to be less governmental and policy concern about human trafficking than there is about international terrorism or the legality of immigration. Although there is increasing media and policy attention to this issue, it is still a crime that receives relatively little public outrage—almost rising to the level of national denial—as if slavery, which is the essence of human trafficking, could not possibly exist in this democracy. However, the evidence contradicts this impression. Human trafficking does exist in the United States.

This article will address what is known about human trafficking in the United States by examining several studies done with experts or people who have worked on human trafficking cases in the United States, human trafficking victim interviews, media reports, and other documents including books, reports, and papers that provide knowledge about human trafficking in the United States. This article has five main goals: (a) to define what human trafficking is and is not; (b) to describe factors identified as contributing to vulnerability to being trafficked and keeping a person entrapped in the situation; (c) to examine how the crime of human trafficking differs from other kinds of crimes in the United States; (d) to explore how human trafficking victims are identified; and (e) to provide recommendations to better address human trafficking in the United States.

Human trafficking, at its most basic level, is defined by the Trafficking Victims Protection Act of 2000 as (a) the recruitment, harboring, transporting, supplying, or obtaining a person for labor or services through the use of force, fraud, or coercion for the purpose of involuntary servitude

or slavery; or (b) sex trafficking in which a commercial sex act is induced by force, fraud, or coercion, or in which the person induced to perform sex acts is under 18 years of age. The key elements of the Trafficking Victims Protection Act (TVPA) indicate it is illegal to use force, fraud, or coercion to exploit a person for profit or for personal services. The use of coercion can be direct and physically violent, or it can be through psychological means. Although most news accounts of human trafficking focus on the violence endured by the victims of human trafficking, the powerful effects of psychological coercion play a key role in entrapment and continued enslavement (Kim, 2007; Logan, 2007).

Labor exploitation can include forced labor and debt bondage, whereas sexual exploitation includes compulsory sex acts within the commercial sex industry. Although often termed "sex trafficking," sexual exploitation in private homes by individuals who often demand sex and work (in the home or even outside of the home) is categorized by the law as labor exploitation. Also, although not an explicit component of the U.S. law, internationally the consent of the victim to circumstances characterized by human trafficking is not relevant when threats, coercion, or the use of force have been used to exploit someone.[1]

One misconception about *human trafficking* (perhaps related to the term itself) is that people must be transported to meet the definitional threshold of the human trafficking law. However, the current legislation does not require that a person be physically transported across locations in order for the crime to meet the definition of human trafficking (U.S. Department of State, 2007). Another confusing aspect of *human trafficking* (again probably related to the term itself) is that individuals are always brought into the country, legally or illegally, as part of the trafficking situation. First, it must be recognized that people can be trafficked within their own country. Second, human trafficking is different from human smuggling (The Human Smuggling and Trafficking Center, 2005). Human smuggling is typically done with the consent of the smuggled individual who intends to enter the U.S. by any means. Usually, with human smuggling the relationship between the transporter and the smuggled individual ends once the target destination is reached. In human trafficking, the transportation of an individual may be just the first phase of the crime; the transportation is but a means to the end of obtaining labor. In fact, the better organized human trafficking operations include both components, and will actually use the fee charged for transporting the individual into the United States as a form of debt bondage to entrap people into the trafficking situation. Thus, although human smuggling and human trafficking are conceptualized as legally separate concepts, they often overlap.

Human trafficking is not a new phenomenon. In fact, it is closely related to slavery in various forms throughout history. For example, in imperial Rome, 30% to 40% of the population was made up of slaves trafficked in from Thrace, Gaul, Britain, and Germany (Collingridge, 2006). During this time, wars were often fought merely to procure more slave labor (Cahill, 1995; Goldsworthy, 2006; Rawson, 1993). Furthermore, America is no stranger to slavery. There is a rich history of slavery in America beginning in 1619 with both White and African slaves being imported to Virginia (Davis, 2006; Jordan & Walsh, 2007) and culminating in a law to abolish importation of African slaves (1807), a civil war because of slavery (1860–1865), and laws that finally intended the abolition of slavery itself (1863). However, just as it took numerous laws and even several constitutional amendments and Supreme Court decisions to eradicate race-based slavery, other more insidious forms of slavery developed and have flourished even in recent times. For example, Douglas Blackmon (2008) detailed how, for decades after the official abolition of American slavery, thousands of African Americans were sold or forced into labor to pay debts that were incurred due to trumped-up charges through the criminal justice system. This form of slavery very much resembles the stories of human trafficking today. These slaves were cheap labor for the land owners; they labored without, or for minimal, compensation, were repeatedly bought and sold, and were forced through physical assault and bondage to work.

Similar to the Blackmon analysis of slavery before and after the official abolition, Bales (2000) argues that the old slavery system was one in which, although slaves were treated harshly, slaves were expensive, thought of as valuable property, and there was a strong incentive to keep slaves alive and relatively healthy to ensure the slaveholder's investment. However, in today's slavery context, Bales argued that slaves have very low value, they are cheap, and are only worth what they bring in terms of immediate profit to the owners rather than being valuable themselves as property and that they are essentially a disposable commodity. It is suggested that this kind of exploitation is particularly attractive to small and large organized crime rings, and there is speculation that human trafficking is the third largest profitable trafficking activity after drug and gun trafficking (Hyland, 2001).

Trafficking in humans is profitable for several reasons. First, traffickers gain from fees charged to the trafficked victim as well as from the profits from the victims' labor. Traffickers maximize their profits by keeping their costs low. Costs are minimized by not paying victims or by paying them very little, housing victims in unsanitary and crowded living conditions, and making the victims work for many hours (Neville & Martinez, 2004). Also, victims can be used over and over again and basically become disposable when their use is no longer producing value. As an example of this is illustrated in Bales' (1999) work:

> On more than ten occasions I woke early in the morning to find the corpse of a young girl floating in the water by the barge. Nobody bothered to bury the girls. They just threw their bodies in the river to be eaten by the fish. (p. 4)

In another report (Family Violence Prevention Fund, 2005), one victim was quoted as saying,

I was sick so many times. And when you're sick, you know what they tell you? They go, "You can die if you want to." They tell you that straight up. They just let you stay there and be sick and suffer. (p. 19)

In addition, the lack of identification, prosecution, and sentencing of perpetrators for trafficking in humans make this kind of crime particularly profitable and low risk for the trafficker. In other words, until recently there has been limited prosecution or attention paid to this particular crime, and penalties for those engaged in human trafficking were trivial (Bales, 2000, 2005; Hyland, 2001). Also, murder investigations are less pursuable when the victims are unknown, lack identity, lack concerned relatives, and lack even witnesses to their lives, let alone the crimes that lead to their deaths.

Although human trafficking is receiving increased attention in the United States, estimates and details about human trafficking in this country remain elusive. Even globally the estimates of bodies used as slaves are unknown. A recent Trafficking in Persons Report (U.S. Department of State, 2007) indicated the following:

The International Labor Organization . . . estimates there are 12.3 million people in forced labor, bonded labor, forced child labor, and sexual servitude at any given time; other estimates range from 4 million to 27 million. . . . Annually, according to U.S. Government-sponsored research completed in 2006, approximately 800,000 people are trafficked across national borders, which does not include millions trafficked within their own countries. (p. 8)

These numbers are general estimates, which means the true scope and nature of human trafficking, both globally and in the United States, remains unknown. There are several problems that contribute to the difficulty of accurately estimating the nature and scope of human trafficking.

It is difficult to estimate the true number of victims because some estimates are based on the number of immigrants (documented and estimates of undocumented immigrants) who enter the United States each year. It is also difficult to estimate how many people are smuggled into the United States due to the nature of the crime. In addition, documented and undocumented immigrants can be trafficked after they have entered the United States. Also, official estimates may underrepresent the true nature of the problem because it is very difficult to know how many marginalized U.S. citizens are trafficked.

Further, many victims are forced to commit criminal acts themselves (e.g., prostitution involvement), are involved in illegal activities such as drug use or using false documents, or are undocumented and afraid to come forward because of their status in the United States. Their own criminal activities or legal status makes it difficult, if not impossible to bring their situations to light. The victims of human trafficking are part of a covert society that is hidden to anyone except those who use trafficked persons. The victims are walled off from society and from their family and they are not on the books for tax or other employment records. In the strict legal sense, they do not exist and since their activities are often illegal, they dare not become visible. Bales (1999) quoted a researcher in Brazil as saying that once a person's documents are confiscated, "the worker is dead as a citizen, and born as a slave" (p. 128).

There are also problems with identification by the U.S. law enforcement personnel who are typically trained to focus on perpetrators of crimes. When the trafficked person is involved in illegal activities such as prostitution or is an undocumented immigrant (being undocumented is actually not a crime, but it is a deportable offense), it may be difficult to define them as victims rather than just as criminals. Thus, law enforcement officials often do not look past the criminal activity to see whether it is part of a larger problem such as human trafficking, leaving some victims of human trafficking identified only as criminals.

In essence then, both the victims and the traffickers collude to keep the crime hidden and law enforcement do not always look past the obvious criminal activity to see the more complex crime of human trafficking making identification and estimates of the nature and scope very difficult. On the other hand, some critics suggest the estimates that are reported are blown out of proportion due to the faulty assumptions on which the estimates are based (Markon, 2007). Clearly more research is needed to better determine the extent and scope of human trafficking in the United States. Whether or not you believe the estimates are too large or too small it is difficult to ignore the fact that, based on media reports alone, this crime is happening in the United States. This article provides a snapshot of human trafficking in the United States.

Methods

Review of Studies

In gathering research studies made available in 2007 or earlier on the prevalence and scope of human trafficking, three main criteria had to be met: (a) The study or report focused on an assessment of social service, health, or legal needs of victims and/or it focused on the scope and extent of human trafficking in the United States; (b) The report included a systematic research method such as a telephone or mail survey of professionals, case studies, or interviews with victims to obtain information; and (c) The report focused on multiple sectors of forced labor rather than just one sector. The main goal of this search was to obtain empirical data rather than policy papers or essays about the problem.

To obtain reports on human trafficking that met the empirically focused criteria several activities were initiated. First, key organizations active in addressing human trafficking were contacted to obtain reports on assessing needs for

services among human trafficking victims. In addition, an Internet search was conducted using multiple search terms to identify reports on human trafficking in the United States. A library search with a variety of databases was used with multiple search terms (e.g., *human trafficking; human trafficking and needs assessment; modern-day slavery*). A national human trafficking LISTSERV was contacted to inquire about other reports. Lastly, the reference section for each report that was obtained was examined for other report citations.

Using all of these methods and criteria yielded very few reports or studies. Four state-specific reports and five reports using information gathered from across the nation were included. Below are the basic methodological descriptions for each of the nine studies that were used for this article, starting with the four state-focused reports and then describing the five nationally focused reports.

- Florida State University Center for the Advancement of Human Rights released their report in 2003. This report primarily compiled information and recommendations from a working group of experts from around the state. However, they also used four in-depth case studies of trafficking cases that were prosecuted in Florida. These case studies were developed through court documents, published media sources, and from interviews with victims and law enforcement officials associated with the various cases.

- Dr. Cache Seitz Steinberg released a report in 2004 on human trafficking in Houston. This report compiled information from a mail survey of 70 service provider, law enforcement, legal services, and government agency representatives (with a 32% response rate). Fifteen (21%) of those agencies reported serving a victim of human trafficking within the past 2 years. This report also included information from an interview with 1 victim of human trafficking, interviews with 11 community experts, and a review of statistics on human trafficking cases from the U.S. Attorney's Office Southern District of Texas.

• Dr. T. K. Logan released a report in 2007 on human trafficking in Kentucky. This report compiled information from telephone surveys with 140 service provider, law enforcement, and other legal service provider representatives (with an 86% response rate). Almost half (46%) reported experience with a case of human trafficking in Kentucky.

• The California Alliance to Combat Trafficking and Slavery Task Force (CACTSTF) released a report of human trafficking in California in 2007. This report used multiple data sources including an online or mail survey of a 101 service provider and legal services representatives (with an overall response rate of less than 10%). Over half (59%) reported experience with cases of human trafficking. This study also included in-depth interviews with 13 service providers in 3 rural areas of the state.

• Dr. Heather Clawson and colleagues released a report in 2003 using data collected through telephone interviews from 98 service providers (with a 62% response rate) from across the nation who reported experience working with human trafficking victims. This study also used information from focus groups with service providers and trafficking victims.

• The Free the Slaves organization along with the Human Rights Center at the University of California released a report in 2004 which used telephone surveys with 49 service providers who have worked with human trafficking victims or were experts in human trafficking from across the nation (no response rate reported). This study also used information from 131 forced labor incidents reported in the media and 8 case studies of forced labor from a variety of regions across the United States.

• The Family Violence Prevention Fund released a report in 2005 using information from interviews with 21 survivors of human trafficking from across the nation.

• Dr. Heather Clawson and colleagues released a report in 2006 using information collected from phone surveys of 121 law enforcement representatives (with a 58% response rate) from cities across the nation with known human trafficking activities. The sample was divided by victim-witness coordinators (n 7), line officers (n 30), and state and local investigators (n 84). The majority (68%) reported experience working with human trafficking cases. This study also included in-depth telephone interviews with seven supervisors or managers representing federal, law enforcement, and other key agencies, legal case reviews, as well as an analysis of discussion forums with three antitrafficking task forces.

• D. Wilson and colleagues published a paper is 2006 from the results of a mail survey of 83 law enforcement agency directors (with a 51% response rate) from across the nation regarding their experiences and knowledge of human trafficking. Almost a quarter (23%) of the respondents reported involvement in a human trafficking crime investigation within the last 3 years and 17% had made an arrest related to the crime of human trafficking during this time period.

Other documents were also consulted to provide a more comprehensive picture of human trafficking. These other documents include media reports, papers, reports, and several books on the topic. For example, Batstone (2007) and Skinner (2008) wrote books using journalist interview techniques with victims of human trafficking and people who work with slaves from around the world including the United States. Bales (1999, 2005, 2007) has done some extensive case study research on human trafficking across the world and has used international research on human trafficking to draw conclusions about the nature and scope of human trafficking.

Results

Human Trafficking Victims in the United States: Where Are They?

Table 8.1 shows the various sectors of human trafficking in the United States based on information from people who have worked cases, from actual cases, or from the media reports of forced labor. The major types of trafficking sectors mentioned in these reports include the following: sex work (prostitution, commercial sex, 23%–66%), other sex work–related activities (exotic dancing, pornography, entertainment, 3%–30%), domestic labor (7%–45%), personal service (domestic or sexual servitude, servile marriage, 1%–37%), factory labor/sweatshop (5%–33%), restaurant labor (9%–33%), and agricultural or other labor (10%–46%). Other mentioned sectors included begging/trinket selling and the food industry.

The reports underscore some gaps in the current state of knowledge on human trafficking. First, the category termed *personal service* or *servile marriage* is relatively large and is mentioned in 6 of 8 studies (one study did not discuss labor sectors), although, in the Logan (2007) study, when all of the respondents (those with and without direct experience of human trafficking) were asked about what sectors trafficking was likely to emerge, very few mentioned this category. Therefore, although this category is clearly observed by those working with human trafficking victims, it does seem to be overlooked by general service providers. However, it does seem to meet the legal definition under the U.S. law. Specifically, human trafficking is defined as "the recruitment, harboring, transportation, provision or obtaining of a person for labor or *services* [italics added] through the use of force, fraud, or coercion." This is where there is a common link between domestic violence and human trafficking, or where the line between the two can become blurred. For example, see the cases below as reported by respondents who had experience

with human trafficking cases in the Logan (2007) report.

One victim, who was smuggled into U.S., was sold to an immigrant man by the people who loaned her money to come into the U.S. This man basically used her as a sexual slave.

A woman was in the U.S. legally with a temporary visa. She was working for a man and ended up getting involved in a romantic relationship with him. She was working 18 hour days and he was not paying her. He wouldn't let her leave the house except for work. He was also using sexual and domestic violence as a way to keep her intimidated. (p. 45)

A second problem is that the categories where human are trafficked in the United States are incomplete and based on limited research. For example, some cases that have surfaced in the media but were not mentioned in the reports include hotel workers, nail salon workers, landscape and gardening laborers, casino servers, an African children's choir, (e.g., Batstone, 2007), and Chinese acrobats (U.S. Department of Justice, 2007). Furthermore, it is possible that there are other sectors where persons are trafficked, but who have not yet been identified for a variety of reasons. For example, a recent *New York Times* article (Urbina, 2007) described the magazine crew industry (the magazine subscription peddlers who go door to door in neighborhoods across America) which included many elements that seemed to meet the threshold of the federal human trafficking legislation, although few if any cases from this industry have been prosecuted under this legislation. Specifically, this article described how both teenagers looking to leave home and travel as well as homeless teenagers were recruited to work on a magazine crew. However, once they started the job, some were forced to work 10 to 14 hr a day, 6 days a week peddling subscriptions door to door. The article goes on to describe the work conditions such as how in some cases the lowest

Table 8.1 Human Trafficking Victims in the United States: Where Are They?[a]

Type of Trafficking	CACTSTF (2007) N = 58	Clawson, Small, Go, and Myles (2003) N = 98	Clawson, Dutch, and Cummings (2006) N = 82	Florida State University (2003) N = 4	Family Violence Prevention Fund (2004) N = 21	Free the Slaves (2004) N = 131	Logan (2007) N = 64	Seitz Steinberg (2004) N = 15
Sex work (specific mention of prostitution or sex work)	46%	66%	60%	X	X	46.4%	23.2%	40%
Sex laboring (nonprostitution sectors of sex industry such as stripping)	—	—	28%	—	—	—	—	12%
Pornography	—	27%	—	—	—	—	—	—
Entertainment (Sex tourism/entertainment)	—	30%	8%	—	—	3.1%	—	—
Personal service (domestic or sexual servitude with one person; servile marriage)	—	37%	10%	—	X	0.8%	23.2%	28%
Domestic labor	31%	45%	31%	X	X	27.2%	7.3%	33%
Agricultural or other labor (general, construction, coal mining)	11%	46%	25%	X	—	10.4%	14.5%	12%
Factory/sweatshop labor	5%	19%	—	—	X	4.8%	—	33%
Restaurant/bar labor	—	25%	—	—	X	—	8.7%	33%
Begging/trinket selling	—	4%	—	—	—	—	—	6%
Food service industry	—	5%	—	—	—	3.8%	—	—
Unspecified	7%	—	33%	—	—	—	23.2%	—

NOTE: *N* = Number of participants; *X* = mentioned in the report, but percentages were not provided.

a. Those included are respondents who worked with victims, cases mentioned, or actual cases. One report did not discuss labor sectors.

seller of the day was required to sleep on the floor and that some days they had less than US$10 a day for food. Further, the workers were not directly paid, but were told their pay was going to be kept on the books and that all of their living expenses were being deducted from their pay. Also, some of the workers who were interviewed described how they had seen others severely beaten by managers for missing their sales quota or for talking about wanting to quit the crew in front of others. In another case, some of the men on the crew were forced to fight each other if they missed their sales quota. Several individuals interviewed for this article also talked about how they were afraid to walk away from the job. This example is just one area that trafficking like conditions exist, yet remains hidden in plain sight.

The third issue to note is there has been a focus on sex trafficking for a number of years (Hynes & Raymond, 2002; Raymond et al., 2002; Raymond & Hughes, 2001) and some reports on human trafficking suggest it is the largest category of human trafficking and other studies find other types of labor are larger sectors (Webber & Shirk, 2005). The 2008 Trafficking in Persons report suggested that when trafficking estimates include both those trafficked within a country's boarders and across the country's borders, labor trafficking may be larger than sex trafficking (U.S. Department of State, 2008). There is some controversy in the literature about the extent of sex trafficking versus labor trafficking. Some argue that there has been a narrower focus on identification and prosecution of sex trafficking as well as more resources in recent years, which may have resulted in the failure to find victims of other kinds of trafficking (Srikantiah, 2007; Webber & Shirk, 2005). Richard (1999) suggested from a review of several cases of forced labor that non-sex-related forms of trafficking have been in operation longer than trafficking involving the sex industry. However, there are other issues that must be considered when trying to interpret the estimates of what labor sector individuals are likely to be trafficked into.

Although it may be true that more prosecutions have focused on sex-related cases of human trafficking due to greater attention and resources, the intense focus may also be due to more practical reasons. First, sex work requires individuals to interact with the public thus making them more visible than a group of individuals forced to work and live in a closed factory. Even if the larger public doesn't realize that human trafficking is taking place, they may realize and dislike the fact that prostitution is occurring in their neighborhood, which prompts them to make complaints to law enforcement. Second, sex work is in a way more public than, say, domestic service and thus it is easier for law enforcement to investigate and charge—especially because the women selling sex are considered engaging in illegal activities. Third, there has been a lot more media attention focused on sex work in general, and specifically young women being trafficked into sex work. In summary, what this means is that it is not clear whether or not human trafficking is more likely to occur within the sex work–related or the non-sex work-related areas of forced labor, and more research is needed to properly document forms of human trafficking in the United States and worldwide (Webber & Shirk, 2005).

Fourth, it is critical to understand that even independent of being in the sex trade, women and girls (and sometimes men and boys) are vulnerable to sexual exploitation through forced sexual acts. In other words, there are cases of women in domestic labor, personal service, restaurant, hotel, agricultural, and other segments of the work force where women have been sexually assaulted as part of the trafficking experiences (Batstone, 2007; Richard, 1999). For example, one of the respondents in the Logan (2007) report described a domestic servitude case where the victim was exploited for labor inside and outside of the home as well as sexually exploited, "A young girl was raped and beaten by a man; she lived with the man and his wife and was used for domestic chores inside their home and forced to work cleaning in a hotel as well" (p. 46).

What Makes People Vulnerable to Being Enslaved?

Across all the reports, it is apparent that extreme poverty remains the single most important factor in becoming a target of human trafficking. Poverty among immigrants is an especially prevalent theme. More specifically, though it is true that some U.S. citizens are trafficked in America, the majority—at least based on the best information we have to date—are immigrants (Bales, 1999, 2005; Clawson, Small, & Myles, 2003; Logan, 2007). In fact, out of the nine reports included for analysis, all nine linked human trafficking with immigrants, and several of them specifically associated human trafficking with undocumented immigrants. For example, one report indicated 75% of the agency representatives they spoke with reported the victims they worked with were undocumented immigrants (Clawson et al., 2003).

The poverty that the immigrants experience in their countries of origin threatens even basic survival, thus making them vulnerable to any promises of livelihood. However, Bales (2005) argued that it is more complex than poverty alone, in part, because not all impoverished people become trafficking victims. First, he argues that vulnerability to trafficking must be viewed within a local cultural context. Second, he argues that vulnerability to trafficking is increased due to a mix of poverty (indexed by population density, infant mortality rate, the number of children younger than 14, and level of the country's food production), level of civil unrest and violence, cultural acceptance of trafficking, and corruption in local governments (Bales, 2005). Bales especially focuses on the importance of local government corruption in areas where human trafficking flourishes. He argues that corruption in the local governments facilitates not only recruitment of people into human trafficking but also accounts for the lack of punishment or accountability of the traffickers. In other words, human trafficking is a low-risk, high-profit endeavor in those areas where local governments permit or even protect traffickers.

People typically are trafficked in three main ways (Bales, 1999): (a) born into slavery; (b) kidnapped, sold, or physically forced; or (c) tricked. In some countries, families may be indentured servants because they were born into it. Families may have been slaves or in debt bondage literally for generations (Skinner, 2008). In some circumstances, children and even adults are actually kidnapped or physically forced into slavery. And in some countries children are sold into slavery by parents or other caregivers. Respondents in the Logan (2007) report emphasized the selling of children into trafficking situations because of the economic situations of the families, "They live in desperate economic conditions and the victim's family sells them for money or they sell themselves to make money and pay off a debt" (p. 26). Another respondent described the situation as follows:

> A trafficker will go to a family and deceive them about what will happen if they take a family member, like a child, to the U.S. They will be told the child will receive an education or that they'll be able to send money back home or that they will have a better future, etc. When the person gets over here they cut off contact so the person is essentially stuck in the situation. (p. 26)

Not only does the family often gain financially from sending their children with the trafficker, but in some cases they may feel this is an opportunity for their children to have a better life than they would have at home (Bales, 1999, 2005).

Being kidnapped, forced, or sold into trafficking has been noted in the media more frequently in other countries. However, the U.S. media has also reported cases of kidnapping and force into trafficking. For example, a September, 2007 report by CBS highlighted a case of an American high school girl who was kidnapped by a friend's father and forced into the sex industry (Kennedy,

2007). This report also suggests that runaways are vulnerable to being lured or even sold into trafficking situations as well.

A third route to slavery is being tricked. Even in the face of grueling poverty and destitution there can be hope (Vollman, 2007). It is this hope that can make a person vulnerable. Hope plays into vulnerability in two ways—hope for a better life and a willingness to take what would seem to others to be extreme risks. Logan (2007) found that the majority of survey respondents (96%) believed that poverty was an important vulnerability factor, but responses also reflect some of the complexity that Bales described as noted in the following quotes:

They want to come to America for a better life. Then people use their dreams against them and put them into trafficking.

They are desperate and willing to accept a dangerous opportunity. They just want to better their life so they take chances.

They simply wanted to make a better life for themselves and their families and are willing to work really hard to do so. This work ethic made them easy prey.

Young Americans who are in desperate situations are looking for ways out and can get manipulated into trafficking situations. (p. 24)

Victims often believe they are taking legitimate jobs such waitressing, childcare, domestic work, or landscaping, but find out when they arrive that they were tricked. Some victims even are induced to sign bogus contracts making the whole experience seem even more legitimate, and sometimes psychologically binding them even more to the trafficker. A large part of being misled has to do with characteristics of traffickers in terms of what they promise people and that people often trust what traffickers say for a variety of reasons (probably including the willingness to take risks for a better life). The following quotes from Logan (2007) exemplified these contexts:

People are defrauded by traffickers; they are offered a job and then the situation changes when they get to the U.S. They are then put in a position that they feel they can not get out of like being sexually assaulted or involved in illegal activities. This sometimes happens through fraud in mail order bride situations.

Sometimes people respond to some sort of ad to work in the U.S. or they are approached by individuals known to family. For example, they are deceived in their home country by trusted people and are either smuggled in or arrive with a visa of some sort. When they get here their situation changes.

They are approached by people in their community who become their friends and who invite them to come along to the U.S. [but who misled them into trafficking situations]. (p. 25)

Logan's (2007) respondents also mentioned two other factors that increase vulnerability to human trafficking: personal characteristics and isolation. Personal characteristics, such as lack of education or lack of knowledge about legal rights or how to get help, as well as cultural factors that facilitate trafficking conditions or even acceptance of human trafficking as part of the culture, were mentioned by half of the respondents in the Logan report. Also, being female and/or being young, healthy, and strong were mentioned in several of the reports as vulnerability factors. Several reports indicated the majority of victims the service representatives worked with were female (73%–90%); however, those same representatives also had worked with male victims (10%–45%; Clawson et al., 2003; Clawson, Dutch, & Cummings, 2006; Logan, 2007; Seitz Steinberg, 2004). Also between one-third and one-half of the representatives mentioned working with children or young adult victims of human trafficking (Clawson et al., 2003, 2006; Logan, 2007; Seitz Steinberg, 2004). Several participants from the

Logan report mentioned either being substance users or making poor choices increased vulnerability to being trafficked.

Isolation was also mentioned as a vulnerability factor (Logan, 2007). This factor may play a role in vulnerability in being recruited into human trafficking and continuing entrapment. In other words, immigrants may be isolated from their family due to separation or estrangement, not speaking the language of the country they are in, having substantial cultural differences that separate them from the community, or being an immigrant or undocumented immigrant (thus were isolated due to their legal status), all work to isolate individuals leaving them vulnerable to a variety of negative situations.

In summary, many people who are poor yet hopeful for a better life are sometimes misled into thinking they are going to work under certain conditions or for a certain amount of pay that does not become the reality. Many of the traffickers are well connected through large or small organized crime rings that include capacity for handling recruitment, transportation, and forced labor work as well as being able to obtain the cooperation of local governments (Bales, 1999, 2005). When immigrants are trafficked, legally or illegally, they are basically denied official status in the United States. If they have passports or visas, these articles are typically confiscated on arrival by the traffickers. Legal

visas are allowed to expire and thus, the trafficked person becomes an undocumented worker and may be vulnerable to being deported by Immigration and Customs Enforcement (ICE; Clawson et al., 2003; Logan, 2007). The lack of legal status and lack of papers to even clarify identity play a large role in entrapment.

What Keeps People Entrapped?

Four main themes about what keeps people entrapped emerged from across the reports: (a) fear, (b) lack of knowledge about alternatives, (c) isolation, and (d) physical and psychological confinement (see Table 8.2). Fear was the biggest factor mentioned in keeping people entrapped. Of course, fear of physical and sexual violence is not ungrounded given that violence can be both explicit and implicit. Threats to harm family members can also induce fear. But there other fears victims have as well, including fear of deportation, fear of being jailed or having other legal problems (e.g., losing their children, prosecution for criminal activity), and fear of law enforcement or the U.S. government. As mentioned above, in many countries government officials, including police, are corrupt and sometimes in collusion with the traffickers. This makes the idea of going to the U.S. police appear to be a risky venture for many victims.

Table 8.2   What Keeps People Entrapped?[a]

	CACTSTF (2007)	Clawson, Small, Go, and Myles (2003)	Clawson, Dutch, and Cummings (2006)	Logan (2007)
	N = 68	*N* = 98	*N* = 121	*N* = 140
Fear				
Fear of retaliation	91%	87%	46%	70%
Fear of deportation	97%	82%	66%	34.3%

	CACTSTF (2007)	Clawson, Small, Go, and Myles (2003)	Clawson, Dutch, and Cummings (2006)	Logan (2007)
	N = 68	*N* = 98	*N* = 121	*N* = 140
Fear of jail/legal problems	—	—	33%	21.4%
Lack of trust in the system/fear of law enforcement	90%	70%	48%	8.6%
General fear	—	31%	—	—
Lack of knowledge about alternatives				
Lack of knowledge about available services/ law enforcement role	88%	83%	31%	46.4%
Lack of knowledge about victim rights	85%	52%	14%	—
Not able to identify self as a victim	—	24%	—	9.3%
Don't have any other options	—	—	—	15%
Isolation				
Lack of social support/ isolation	77%	78%	—	—
No transportation	—	9%	—	—
Language issues	85%	57%	15%	19.3%
Culturally inappropriate services	—	13%	—	—
Physical confinement				
Held in captivity	68%	16%	—	21.4%
Shame				
Feelings of shame	—	42%	10%	20%

NOTE: See note to Table 8.1.

a. Reports included in this table gave proportions of respondents who indicated the issue. Reports not included in this table may have mentioned the issue but did not provide percentages.

A second set of reasons given for what keeps people entrapped was lack of knowledge about alternative options. Specifically, victims may not know about services available to help them, or that they do not believe they have any options other than to stay in the situation. Further, victims often don't know their rights or that what is happening to them is a crime. This lack of information can be worsened by poor language skills that reduce the ability to learn about rights even if they are exposed to any sources of news or information. They also do not know the institutions to turn to for help. Without this basic recognition there would be no impetus for seeking help.

The next most frequently noted set of responses for what keeps people entrapped was isolation. Not only is isolation a vulnerability factor but it is a tactic used by traffickers to control victims. Isolation from the public is accomplished by limiting contact with outsiders and monitoring any potential contact to ensure it is superficial in nature. Victims are also isolated from family members and other member of their ethnic and religious community. Also, individuals may be isolated through the lack of transportation and language/cultural barriers. By isolating victims, the controller is essentially reducing resistance attempts and increasing the dependence of the victim on the trafficker.

Also, physical and psychological confinement keeps victims entrapped in the situation. For example, one respondent in the Logan (2007) study talked about a case of a woman who "came to the U.S. as a bride, but when they got here he kept her chained in a hotel room and used her as a sexual slave" (p. 45). Although physical confinement is an important factor in keeping victims entrapped, most of the stories that have surfaced do not include that kind of physical confinement. The psychological confinement or coercion is a powerful tool in control and entrapment (Kim, 2007). Psychological confinement can be created through control of the victims' money and control of their passports, visas, or other identifying documents. Psychological confinement can also

be created through debt bondage. The use of debt bondage may include the use of bogus contracts, the lack of transparency for how much of the debt diminishing, and exorbitant charges and interest rates making the debt close to impossible to pay off. Another strategy of psychological confinement is the use of drugs or alcohol addiction to keep people entrapped (Logan, 2008; Raphael & Ashley, 2008; Raymond et al., 2002; Zimmerman, 2003; Zimmerman et al., 2006).

Another strategy of psychological confinement is related to psychological degradation and abuse. Threats about shaming victims by exposing their circumstances to their family or to the public (e.g., their cultural group) may be especially powerful in binding the victim to the situation. For example, one respondent in the Logan (2007) study reported a case where a "women was raped by acquaintance; he used cultural and religious shame tactics and basically blackmailed her into becoming domestic servant and sexual slave" (p. 45). Another study (Raymond et al., 2002) of trafficked women quoted a victim as saying, "They just broke me down, shattered my will and hopes. I was humiliated" (p. 196).

One recent case of human trafficking provides a good illustration of the tactics used to control victims. In July 2007, a news report was released about criminal charges of human trafficking pending against China Star Acrobats, a Las Vegas company that had a team that traveled and performed at schools across the United States (Packer, Curtis, McCabe, 2007; U.S. Department of Justice, 2007). Investigators found nine individuals, including five minors who were classified as victims of human trafficking. The victims alleged they were not being paid the salary they were promised, their passports and work visas were withheld from them, and they were fearful that their families in China, or they themselves, would be harmed if they attempted to leave. They also alleged their every movement was watched and controlled; they were forced to sleep in crowded bedrooms in a house located in a Las Vegas suburb; received rationed meals of limited quantity; got very little sleep; and when not performing acrobatics, were forced to do chores such as cleaning homes, yard work, or renovating homes. One news story interviewed a neighbor who said he believed they had plenty of chances to escape and that, although they didn't appear to be happy, they weren't asking for someone to help them either. However, that same neighbor admitted they spoke little English. This case highlights the powerful effect of psychological entrapment—even when they seemingly had the opportunity to escape, they did not. Not until one woman, who served as an interpreter for the group, took a risk and contacted law enforcement did the situation come to light.

It is important to note that, counter to many of the media reports of human trafficking cases, physical violence is only one of many tactics that are used. As indicated in the China Star Acrobat case described earlier, the victims were primarily controlled through psychological means rather than through chains or constant violence. It is much more efficient for the controllers to subordinate people psychologically rather than having to keep them continually chained up or continually using physical violence. Psychological means of entrapping people gains the trafficker the ultimate compliance; even if given a chance to escape, the victim is unlikely to take the risk.

Adaptations to Slavery

When individuals are presented with an aversive situation the instinctive and hardwired response is to somehow change the situation (Gilbert, 2000). In human trafficking situations, the instincts of flight or fight must be stifled because they are impossible. Gilbert suggests this kind of entrapment is most harmful to health and mental health. However, there are other ways to potentially change the situation to make the circumstances less threatening or aversive. This negotiational stance may lead to human trafficking victims asking for more money, for better living circumstances, or trying to gain favor through other means with the trafficker (Batstone, 2007; Florida State University, 2003). Sometimes asking for changes to the situation are successful, as in one case described in the Florida State University report. The women in this case, who were trafficked into commercial sex labor, asked for and received access to Spanish television, radio stations, and magazines. Also, the women on at least one occasion demanded to be taken out to a dance club, and the traffickers complied although the women were closely monitored. These small negotiations may have made the situation more tolerable for the women. On the other hand, trying to directly change the situation may involve increased risks. For example, one woman from the case described above protested when the traffickers insisted she speed up her sex acts with clients so she could service more of them. In response, they locked her in a closet for 15 days, only allowing her out to use the bathroom. In other instances, if the women refused to service a client they were beaten and/or raped by their captors.

As noted above, one of the most frequently noted components of the human trafficking experiences is the high level of fear victims feel in the situation (Bales, 1999; Logan, 2007). As noted above, fear plays a central role in keeping people entrapped in the situation, and it is certainly central to the control tactics. Similar to the kinds of fears that have been documented for prisoners of war and kidnap or torture victims, victims of human trafficking experience multiple sustained fears. The fears victims experience may include fear of intentionally inflicted pain; fear of deformity or permanent injury due to physical assault, neglect, or inadequate medical treatment; fear of violence against loved ones; or the fear of the inability to satisfy the demands of the trafficker as well as the fear that achieving critical goals are or will be blocked (e.g., sending money to starving family members; Farber, Harlow, & West, 1957; Gilbert, 2000; Lazarus, 1999). The fear is complex, in that it can be a composite of all these specifics rather than a fear of one event. Fear can impose serious constraints on thinking and decision making and likely plays a significant role in why people do not escape when they seemly have opportunity (Loewenstein, Weber, Hsee, & Welch, 2001; Logan, Walker, Jordan, & Leukefeld, 2006).

Once behavioral submission is adopted, cognitive changes often occur as part of the process. For example, cognitions may become narrowed, distracted, or numbed (Clawson, Dutch, & Williamson, 2008). Narrowed cognitions can occur when individuals are focusing all of their energy on survival and/or threat vigilance (Gross, 1998a, 1998b). A different way to cognitively accommodate threatening or aversive environments is through distraction, such as fantasizing or shifting attention away from the threat (Gross, 1998a, 1998b). Still another mechanism is to cognitively reappraise the situation as one that is more easily accepted—a rationalizing process. Gross (1998a) defined reappraisal as an act that "involves cognitively transforming the situation so as to alter its emotional impact" (p. 284). Gross (1998b) found that reappraisal was associated with less negative emotion. This process may include an individual reappraising an aversive situation as not as bad as it could be, minimizing the harm, justification for the situation, social comparisons to others who are worse off, or acceptance of the situation. This process could also include believing that they are performing their duty to their family, their contractual obligation or duty to their word, or even their destiny, as in the case of some young girls in Thailand who believe that although they were forced into prostitution, they must remain as a part of their karma or religious duty (Batstone, 2007).

Mental defeat may also result from the circumstances. Mental defeat (Ehlers, Maercker, & Boos, 2000) is defined as "the perceived loss of all autonomy, a state of giving up in one's mind all efforts to retain one's identity as a human being with a will of one's own" (p. 45). Ehlers et al. (2000) found that mental defeat was also associated with total subordination, such as feeling merely an object to the other,

loss of self-identity, prepared to do whatever the other asked, and not caring if one lives or dies. The feeling of mental defeat was associated with more chronic posttraumatic stress disorder (PTSD) and depression symptoms. It is also important to note that mental defeat was independent of exposure severity and perceived threat to life. These authors speculated that other aspects of traumatic situations, such as intentional harm by others, humiliating acts, frequency of uncontrollable maltreatment, and/or prolonged sleep deprivation, may influence the probability of experiencing mental defeat. They also speculate that people who experienced mental defeat were those who interpreted the experience as revealing something negative about themselves (e.g., that they were inferior, not worthy, or unable to cope). Some of these negative emotions have been mentioned in studies with victims of human trafficking (Clawson et al., 2008; Zimmerman, 2003; Zimmerman et al., 2006), but more research is clearly needed on how people survive this situation.

In summary, it is generally recognized that congruence between emotions and behaviors is desirable, and when they are found to be inconsistent, cognitive strategies generally try to lull them back into balance. The stresses of the trafficking situation is almost guaranteed to create dissonance between thoughts, feelings, and behavior that can greatly reduce flexible coping and rational decisions that could be expected of people in free conditions. Further, negative emotions and certain adaptation strategies may have significant consequences for health, mental health, and recovery.

What or How Is This Crime Different From Other Crimes?

Two of the reports specifically asked respondents to describe how human trafficking was different from other crimes (Clawson et al., 2003; Logan, 2007). Both surveys asked this particular question in an open-ended format. There were seven main themes that emerged from this question: (a) more difficult to identify, (b) prejudice toward the victims, (c) greater needs, (d) fewer resources and services, (e) greater fear and safety concerns, (f) more limited access to justice, and (g) complex criminal cases.

More difficult to identify. The first issue that was mentioned repeatedly in the Logan (2007) report was the difficulty in identifying victims. Victims may be more difficult to identify for several reasons discussed earlier, including the covert nature of the human trafficking activity, language and cultural barriers, lack of victim knowledge about their rights, isolation, and fear.

Prejudice toward victims. Respondents in the Logan (2007) study also cited prejudice against immigrants in general, and toward human trafficking victims in particular, as being a bigger problem with this crime compared to other crimes. The prejudice is primarily communicated through the media. For example, there is some backlash regarding immigration in the United States. One respondent said (Logan, 2007), "They are not just victimized by the trafficker; the society/community doesn't see them and can't help them," (p. 52) and, "The media gives the message that if you're an immigrant you are probably illegal, you're useless, you have no rights, you just have to face the consequences of what happens to you" (p. 33). Another said, "Our society is judgmental towards immigrants" (p. 52). Another respondent summed up this theme, "Public backlash against immigrants is a huge issue because the public mentality is that they are making the human trafficking stories up to get a visa" (p. 52). This theme was also mentioned in the Clawson et al. (2003) report.

Greater needs. Another major theme mentioned in both the Logan and the Clawson et al. (2003) report was that human trafficking victims have greater needs because they basically walk away from their situation with nothing except for the clothes on their back. Thus, they have no way to feed themselves, nowhere to live, and no transportation. They are isolated leaving them with nobody to turn to except service agencies. They often have language and cultural barriers increasing their needs. They have suffered extreme emotional and physical pain that requires appropriate services to relieve suffering as much as possible (Zimmerman et al., 2008). Basically their whole life has been eviscerated and they need to somehow rebuild their life. The extensive needs of victims were mentioned in several reports as outlined in Table 8.3.

Fewer resources and services. Despite the fact that victims of human trafficking have greater needs, there are fewer resources and services for this group than victims of any other crime. Table 8.4 lists the organizational barriers to serving victims mentioned in five of the reports. The lack of adequate resources, funding, and staffing needed to serve human trafficking victims was frequently mentioned as a barrier to serving victims. In addition, because many service agencies do not understand human trafficking crimes as well as other crimes, services for human trafficking victims are harder to obtain. One respondent from the Logan (2007) report summarized this issue, "There needs to be more education, agencies tend to be reactionary. They don't act until there it is a problem for them" (p. 53). Thus, more training, knowledge, and policies and procedures are needed to effectively serve victims of human trafficking. And the complexity of the cases as well as the overwhelming needs of victims require the service agencies to coordinate with other agencies which can sometimes be difficult. A number of other issues were mentioned as organizational barriers to serving victims, such as safety concerns or being able to adequately protect victims, and potentially staff; victim's legal status may pose a barrier to providing services and, in general, educating other services and the larger society about human trafficking.

Table 8.3   Victim Needs[a]

Victim Needs	Clawson, Small, Go, and Myles (2003) N = 98	Clawson, Dutch, and Cummings (2006) N = 121	Logan (2007) N = 64	Seitz Steinberg (2004) N = 15
Basic living needs (food, housing, clothing, transportation, access to public benefits)	—	—	76.7%	—
Housing	98%	65%	69%	40%
Food	95%	26%	20%	—
Transportation	96%	—	5%	33%
Clothing	—	18%	11%	—
Protection/safety	90%	11%	18.8%	—
Victim compensation/money	76%	—	25%	—
Financial needs				
Job training	86%	12%	—	—
Employment	90%	3%	17.2%	33%
Education	89%	6%	—	40%
Child care	65%	9%	—	—
Life skills	88%	10%	—	—
Help to get back home	—	6%	9.4%	—
Medical care				
Medical	98%	39%	—	40%
Dental	80%	12%	—	—
Mental health	95%	23%	40.6%	—
Crisis intervention	88%	3%	—	33%
Self-help groups/group counseling	58%	27%	—	—
Substance abuse treatment	52%	6%	—	—
Access to services/justice				
Interpreter	86%	15%	32.8%	—
Legal	97%	26%	79.7%	—

Victim Needs	Clawson, Small, Go, and Myles (2003)	Clawson, Dutch, and Cummings (2006)	Logan (2007)	Seitz Steinberg (2004)
	N = 98	N = 121	N = 64	N = 15
Court orientation	85%	—	—	—
Advocacy	97%	26%	—	—
Services				
Outreach	96%	9%	—	—
Info/referrals	95%	6%	31.3%	33%
Service coordination/case management	91%	24%	—	33%

Note: See note to Table 8.1.

a. Reports included in this table gave proportions of respondents who indicated the issue. Reports not included in this table may have mentioned the issue but did not provide percentages.

Table 8.4   Organizational Barriers to Serving Victims[a]

Organizational Barriers	CACTSTF (2007)	Clawson, Small, Go, and Myles (2003)	Clawson, Dutch, and Cummings (2006)	Logan (2007)	Seitz Steinberg (2004)
	N = 69	N = 98	N = 121	N = 64	N = 63
Lack of adequate resources	57%	78%	38%	42.2%	41%
Lack of adequate funding	62%	72%	—	—	51%
Lack of adequate staff	—	—	—	—	44%
Lack of adequate training	59%	65%	37%	—	34%
Lack of knowledge of victim rights	—	25%	—	—	—
Lack of policies and procedures	—	5%	10%	—	—

(Continued)

(Continued)

Organizational Barriers	CACTSTF (2007) N = 69	Clawson, Small, Go, and Myles (2003) N = 98	Clawson, Dutch, and Cummings (2006) N = 121	Logan (2007) N = 64	Seitz Steinberg (2004) N = 63
Ineffective coordination with federal agencies	—	44%	13%	—	—
Ineffective coordination with local agencies/ awareness and education of services for other service providers	—	39%	8%	42.2%	—
Difficulty working with victim service agencies/law enforcement	—	—	18%	25%	—
Lack of formal rules and regulations/TVPA does not help	—	18%	5%	—	—
Language issues	65%	39%	28%	39.1%	22%
Lack of cultural knowledge	—	—	—	—	8%
Safety concerns	49%	38%	—	—	13%
Victim legal status	48%	17%	—	—	—
Feeling of no support and isolation	—	7%	—	—	—
Victim distrust/victim outreach	—	—	45%	—	—
Difficulty identifying victims	—	—	—	—	38%
Awareness and education of the general public				32.8%	

NOTE: TVPA = Trafficking Victims Protection Act; *N* = Number of participants. Figures from the second column through the last column are percentages of items listed in the first column.

a. Reports included in this table gave proportions of respondents who indicated the issue. Reports not included in this table may have mentioned the issue but did not provide percentages.

Greater fear and safety concerns. This theme has been mentioned repeatedly throughout the various reports. These victims fear for themselves, in part because they may be facing multiple perpetrators and even a large organized crime ring. These victims may also fear for the safety of their families in countries where it is hard to extend protections from the United States and where governments may not be interested in cooperating for a variety of reasons.

More limited access to justice. Another major theme was that human trafficking victims have more limited access to justice because of their undocumented status. Because the victims have a more limited understanding of the U.S. legal system and their legal rights, and because human trafficking often overlaps with other criminal activity, victims may instead appear as criminals themselves.

Complex criminal cases. Almost a quarter of respondents from the Logan report indicated that human trafficking cases are very complex and the protections are limited, thus making it a very difficult crime to prosecute and to help victims. More specifically, as provided by Logan (2007), "Human trafficking can operate on a much bigger and more complex scale" and requires "a lot of cooperation between agencies (e.g., Immigration and Customs Enforcement, FBI, social service agencies, lawyers)" (p. 52). It was also mentioned that because many service agencies do not understand human trafficking crimes as well as other crimes, legal services for human trafficking victims are harder to obtain. Other factors that further complicate the issue are "Human trafficking is organized and controlled by a group for money," "There are often multiple perpetrators involved," and "There are often multiple victims involved." Other legal complications include, "Human trafficking cases have [more complex and time consuming] government paperwork issues," "may require dealing with multiple countries," "Human trafficking is a hard crime to prove," and all these

factors increase "the level of legal services needed" (p. 45). These themes were also mentioned in the Clawson et al. (2003) report. Related to this theme Wilson et al. (2006) found that the crime is so complex it is difficult for legal agencies to coordinate or to decide who should lead the investigations potentially causing diffusion of responsibility (e.g., federal, state, or local officials). Also, the boundary around terming someone a *defendant,* a *witness,* or a *victim* may be very difficult to identify, thus compounding decisions about what stance to take with prosecutors, police, and even defense attorneys.

How Do Human Trafficking Victims Become Identified?

As mentioned above, identifying human trafficking victims is challenging. Three of the reports discussed ways that victims of human trafficking have been discovered. One way victims of human trafficking are identified is through law enforcement, either because they are trained to identify the situation or the situation is identified during the course of an ongoing investigation of other crimes (Clawson et al., 2006; Logan, 2007). Human trafficking victims are also sometimes identified through neighbors, customers, coworkers, or other community members (Clawson et al., 2006; Free the Slaves, 2004; Logan, 2007). This is one reason it is critical that awareness of human trafficking is raised not just among service providers but for every citizen in the United States.

Victims have also been identified because they sought social, medical, or employment dispute services and were subsequently identified as human trafficking victims (Free the Slaves, 2004; Logan, 2007). Although it is rare that victims self-identify as *human trafficking victims,* there are "red flags" that can indicate a possible trafficking situation (Florida State University, 2003).

Red flags or indicators that may suggest further inquiry into the situation to determine whether or not it might be a human trafficking case can be divided into three categories: (a) situational indicators, (b) story indicators, and (c) demeanor. Several of the reports mention situational indicators such as the individual living circumstances (Clawson et al., 2006; Logan, 2007). For example, lack of English-speaking persons in an establishment, frequent movement of individuals through an establishment, many people living together in a private residence, or people living where they work were all mentioned as possible cues for further investigation of the situation.

Listening to an individual's story was also mentioned as important in distinguishing between a bad work situation and one of being trafficked. One report provides a very comprehensive list of possible questions to ask while interviewing someone about his or her situation, to help determine whether or not it is characterized by trafficking (Florida State University, 2003). Although the list is too long to reproduce here, there are several major themes or categories mentioned across several of the reports (Clawson et al., 2006; Florida State University, 2003; Free the Slaves, 2004; Logan, 2007). For example, asking about how someone got to the United States or to the area in which they are currently residing, asking about their migration or immigration status, and who had/has control of their travel arrangements and documents. Also asking questions about their employment situation is central to determining the nature of the situation. This would include questions about their freedom to leave their current employment, what happens if they make a mistake at work, whether they owe their employer money, whether they were misled regarding their current work situation, about how much and how they are paid for their work, what their work hours and conditions are like, whether they are moved around a lot for their job, and whether they are forced to have sex as part of their job.

In addition, assessing safety, threats, and physical deprivation and abuse is important. Asking about whether they or their family have been threatened; whether they have been deprived of,

or are required to ask permission for, food, water, sleep, medical care, or other life necessities; and whether they have been physically harmed. Asking about social isolation such as restricted movement or communications is also important (e.g., are they free to contact friends or family? Are they free to communicate with those outside of the work situation? Can they buy food and clothing on their own? Are they free to have an intimate relationship? Are they free to bring friends to their home?). The Campaign to Rescue and Restore Victims of Human Trafficking has a screening tool for victims of human trafficking which includes many of the same themes mentioned above (U.S. Department of Health and Services, 2008).

Finally, an individual's demeanor during the interview may provide some information about his or her situation as well. For example, if someone seems very nervous or fearful, or if someone answers questions evasively, these may be indicators of a situation that needs further investigation. Also, seeing a person who is never left alone or does not seem to be able to speak for him or herself may be an indication of a trafficking situation (Clawson et al., 2006; Family Violence Prevention Fund, 2005; Logan, 2007).

Recommendations for Future Research and Services

There were four main themes in recommendations (see Table 8.5), including more resources and enhanced approaches for (a) training, education, and protocols; (b) services and outreach; (c) legal protections; and (d) research. These four are not presented in order of importance as all are critical.

Training, education, and protocols. It is clear that public awareness of human trafficking is very important. The lack of awareness includes victims themselves, health and human service providers, and law enforcement as well as the general public. Human trafficking is a crime that

Table 8.5 Recommendations

Recommendations	CACTSTF (2003)	Clawson, Small, Go, and Myles (2003)	Clawson, Dutch, and Cummings (2006)	Florida State University (2003)	Family Violence Prevention Fund (2005)	Free the Slaves (2004)	Logan (2007)	Seitz Steinberg (2004)	Wilson, Walsh, and Kleuber (2006)
Training, education, and protocols (9)	×	×	×	×	×	×	×	×	×
Training of law enforcement	×	×	×	×	×	×		×	×
Training of service providers	×	×	—	×	×	—	×	×	—
Education of the general public	×	—	—	×	×	—	×	×	—
Develop protocols for service providers/law enforcement	×	×	×	×	×	—	×	×	×
Better coordination/collaboration	×	×	×	×	×	×	×	×	×
Outreach and services (8)	×	×	×	×	×	×	×	×	
Better outreach and identification	×	×	—	×	×	×	×	×	—
Change negative media depictions of immigrants	—	—	—	—	—	—	×	—	—
More funding to address human trafficking	×	—	—	×	×	—	×	—	—
Fund more services	×	×	—	×	×	×	×	—	—

(Continued)

(Continued)

Recommendations	CACTSTF (2003)	Clawson, Small, Go, and Myles (2003)	Clawson, Dutch, and Cummings (2006)	Florida State University (2003)	Family Violence Prevention Fund (2005)	Free the Slaves (2004)	Logan (2007)	Seitz Steinberg (2004)	Wilson, Walsh, and Kleuber (2006)
More housing	×	×	—	×	×	—	—	—	—
Resource manual/referral list	—	×	—	—	—	—	—	×	—
Develop experts database	—	×	—	—	—	—	—	—	—
Legal protections (5)	×	×	—	×	—	×	×	—	—
Increase access to legal protections	×	×	—	×	—	—	×	—	—
Ensure better protections for workers	×	—	—	×	—	×	—	—	—
Change legislation to better protect immigrants and/or human trafficking victims	×	—	—	—	—	×	×	—	—
Improve victim's understanding of the criminal justice process	—	×	—	—	—	—	—	—	—
Research (5)	×	×	—	×	×	—	×	—	—
More research/data	×	×	—	×	—	—	×	—	—
Talk to victims to better understand	—	—	—	—	×	—	×	—	—

NOTE: × = was mentioned in the report.

affects individuals, groups of individuals, and the communities in which the crime is occurring. However, neighbors, customers, and citizens may be the ones needed to respond to victims, given the hidden and clandestine nature of the crime, and this may be more effective than placing the entire burden for identifying victims on the police and service agencies. Public awareness campaigns on the rights of victims of trafficking, the laws protecting victims and criminalizing the conduct of traffickers, and services available must be broadcast widely in a variety of languages. Public awareness campaigns should also target members of the community (e.g., neighbors) who may spot a possible trafficking situation.

It is also clear that training does have a meaningful impact on raising the awareness of service providers who may encounter victims of trafficking (Logan, 2007). Training should be conducted on the specific needs of trafficking survivors as opposed to other crime victims; the legal process and protections for trafficking victims; methods and means of force, fraud, and coercion as experienced by victims; the profiles of traffickers; strategies for public awareness and outreach; cultural competency; working with interpreters; and successful strategies for collaboration. In particular, a better understanding of the legal protections available to human trafficking victims is critical to increasing victim access to legal protections and to justice.

Further, there is a need to coordinate training across service agencies. Cross trainings, interagency meetings, and identifying a point of contact within each relevant agency can facilitate interagency collaboration (Clawson et al., 2003). Also, establishing interagency protocols to clearly define agency and organization roles to reduce duplication of efforts and to increase opportunities for sharing information may be important. Further efforts and funding should be allocated to building collaborations and strengthening trust among agencies for the most effective delivery of services to trafficking victims as well as effective prosecutions.

Services and outreach. More resources for human trafficking victims are needed for agencies already serving victims of trafficking as well as those that may come into contact with possible victims to address the multiple and pressing needs of the victims to recover from these traumatic experiences. Resources, at a minimum, should include the following: temporary and safe shelter as well as longer term housing, physical and mental health care, public benefits, legal assistance, drug and alcohol counseling, job training or assistance in obtaining employment, basic English language training, and assistance should the victim chose to relocate or return to home country. Resources should also be provided to facilitate language access at every point of service access for victims. In addition, resources are needed to translate information and agency documents into a variety of languages as well as for bilingual/bicultural staff for outreach to specific communities. Furthermore, several reports recommended developing resource manuals, referral lists, or a database of experts to facilitate services for human trafficking victims.

The various studies highlighted victims in certain sectors of labor and sex work, but there needs to be more effort to identify victims who may be present in other labor sectors that are even more hidden from public view, including factory and agricultural work. At the same time, there may be labor sectors that are more visible to the public but where victims remain unidentified such as restaurant workers. Thus, outreach services need to expand into less overtly criminal areas to identify trafficked persons. In addition, there is a need to better identify U.S. citizens who fall prey to traffickers.

Results of the Logan (2007) report strongly suggested that the media may have a great influence on human trafficking victims in several ways. Not only are the police depicted negatively in the media, but the backlash against immigrants that is repeatedly shown on news and television may have very negative repercussions for help seeking. It seems that dual messages are being given to immigrants as well as to U.S.

citizens. On one hand, there may be media messages that help is out there for human trafficking victims, and on the other hand, they are bombarded with negative messages about immigrants in America. These dual messages need to be addressed and media campaigns targeting human trafficking victims must be developed within the current sociopolitical context portrayed in local and national news as well as through radio and other media entertainment outlets. Further, the stereotypes of human trafficking in general that are depicted in the media need to be addressed as part of awareness and education about human trafficking for every citizen in the United States. Human trafficking situations are often not what is stereotypically shown on television, and unless these stereotypes are broken down, victims will remain unidentified, revictimized, and silenced.

Also, outreach and services must be sensitive to individual victim needs and goals which may be challenging. A recent report examined reasons human trafficking victims declined or did not use services; although this research was not done in the United States, the themes that emerged may be important for those working with human trafficking victims in the United States to consider (Brunovskis & Surtees, 2007). One of the greatest challenges identified in the report was the communication between the service organization and the victim. Not only were language barriers an issue in terms of victims understanding the full scope of services being offered but often the timing of when services were offered was problematic. In other words, victims were often told about services at the time of identification, which can sometimes be a crisis point, which is generally not a good point for decision making. None of the victims they identified said they had received written materials about the services that were being offered. Also, there was an issue with trust and fear. For example, victims were sometimes afraid to believe that they could accept help without owing something back to the agency as the offer sometimes may seem similar to the trafficking process. Other victims were too fearful of their trafficker to use services. Another

issue that came up was that sometimes victims were embarrassed, afraid using services would stigmatize them, afraid using services would embarrass their families, or did not want to be labeled as *victims*. The third main issue that was discovered in this report was that victims sometimes did not feel comfortable with the rules and requirements contingent on services which discouraged them from taking advantage of what services had to offer. The other reason is they were not able to take advantage of services due to the hours the services were in operation or due to child care or transportation issues.

Legal protections. Victims, defined so under the U.S. law, have the right not to be held in detention facilities or charged with crimes underlying the trafficking offense and have a right to additional protection and services if they are willing to cooperate with the criminal investigation and prosecution of the trafficker. However, there is a need for clarification of the stance of the U.S. justice system toward victims of trafficking. Victims may be treated (a) as defendants in the commission of state and/or federal crimes; (b) as witnesses who must be detained due to lack of legal immigration status and risk of flight; (c) as victims who need protective services; or, to the confusion of all, (d) as all of the above. Recognition of trafficking victims' essential human rights would advance the nature of legal responses to this crime. Not only are the available legal protections complex and time consuming to pursue, but also the victims often have no money to pay for attorneys and may lack citizenship or clear immigration status. And even if funds were available, there is limited understanding among attorneys about the crime of human trafficking and a shortage of availability among those who are willing and able to take on these cases.

Furthermore, the time it takes to gain protections and for cases to be prosecuted is very long, and victims get frustrated, especially if their basic living needs and other needs are not being addressed. Victims may also feel they are being revictimized in the process, which can also lead to frustration and lack of cooperation over time. In addition, those who advocate for victims need a better understanding of the legal protections for victims so that they can better educate and advocate for the victims they are helping. Several of the reports emphasized that better cooperation and coordination with law enforcement and other legal agencies would be helpful in addressing victim needs as well as victim protections and justice. Stronger legislation to protect victims and to ensure better protections for workers was also mentioned in several reports. Furthermore, strengthening the current laws to better protect human trafficking victims is critical.

More specifically, the benefits provided by the U.S. government to human trafficking victims are conditioned on the willingness and ability of the victim to report the crime to law enforcement and the subsequent agreement of law enforcement to investigate the violation as a human trafficking offense. However, though prosecution is definitely an end goal, restoration of the human rights of all victims should be the primary goal, and is broader than simply prosecution of the trafficker. Thus, basic human rights and protections should be available to all victims of trafficking, whether or not they are able to cooperate in investigation. Some international experts suggest that states incorporate more of a human rights focus by ensuring that victims of human trafficking are provided benefits during a period of reflection (e.g., 3 months) before they decide whether or not to prosecute. The U.N. Recommended Principles and Guidelines on Human Rights and Human Trafficking (Anti-slavery, 2002) also specified that protection and care should not depend on the victim's cooperation:

> States shall ensure that trafficked persons are protected from further exploitation and harm and have access to adequate physical and psychological care. Such protection and care shall not be made conditional on the capacity or willingness of the trafficked person to cooperate in legal proceedings. (p. 3)

However, according to the U.S. law, only those under 18 years of age are deemed to be vulnerable enough to not need to testify or cooperate in the criminal investigation or prosecution.

Also, guidance is needed to better address the kind of legal interventions that are most helpful and restorative to victims. Although the State Department Report (U.S. Department of State, 2006) did include short mention of best practices, such as the goal of using planned versus blind raids to plan for the needs of victims, and the need to interview victims apart from the traffickers, these have not been issued in a more formal protocol, nor have they been made a prerequisite for receiving federal anti-trafficking funding. This has resulted in situations where law enforcement conducts a raid without adequate planning for victims, and in the worst situation, where victims are jailed and put in removal proceedings without having meaningful access to services or interviews by social service providers. In essence, the U.S. laws treat trafficking victims less from a preservation of human rights perspective than from a victim/witness perspective. If the victim agrees to be a witness or to aid in investigation, then they enjoy certain protections not unlike what the government can do under a witness protection plan in prosecuting organized crime. If the victim does not agree to aid investigation, he or she may be denied services and jailed or deported, thereby denying some of the most basic human rights of safety and protection. The U. S. should follow the lead of international law, which emphasizes the "primacy of human rights" by strongly indicating that the victims should be at the center of all efforts "to prevent and combat trafficking and to protect, assist and provide redress to victims" (Anti-slavery, 2002, p. 3).

Research. Ongoing research is needed to enhance understanding of the best ways to identify, serve, protect, and support victims of trafficking as they are seeking justice. Establishing a routine data system to track these cases and information about these cases may be important (CACTSTF, 2007). This may include surveying other parties who may come into contact with a trafficking case, including law enforcement, prosecutors, child protective service workers, labor and employment agencies, as well as the individuals themselves who have been trafficked. Research is also needed to capture the geographic clustering of victims in the United States, to better inform outreach and education strategies. Research should also focus on the particular dynamics of U.S. citizen victims of human trafficking. The research findings must be reported beyond the peer-reviewed journal. Data and findings must be presented in public reports that are shared with the media and with policy makers to bring findings closer to action potential.

Research on human trafficking in the United States is difficult for a variety of reasons as summarized in the following statement (Brennan, 2005):

> The first challenge is the diversity of trafficking contexts: Trafficked persons come from a variety of source countries, end up scattered throughout sites in the United States, and are forced into different forms of labour and servitude. They speak different languages, have different socioeconomic backgrounds, varying education and work histories, as well as differences in age, sex, and race/ethnicity. They also have different experiences entering and exiting their trafficked experiences, including experiences of transit. The length of time they were held in servitude varies from weeks to years, and while some experience psychological coercion others also undergo physical brutality. (p. 38)

Thus, future research will also need to address the challenges inherent in research on human trafficking to be successful. Finally, it is critical that researchers collaborate with service and law enforcement agencies and vice versa.

Conclusions

The analysis of nine reports examining human trafficking in the United States strongly suggests that human trafficking does exist in the United States across a variety of labor sectors and is extremely beneficial or profitable for traffickers. The reports have also documented a number of vulnerability factors and factors that keep people entrapped in the situation. However, there is much we do not know about human trafficking including the scope and breadth of the crime. Clearly more research is needed to better understand the scope, extent, and characteristics of human trafficking. But above all, there is a need for rethinking the stance of the U.S. justice system with regard to how victims of human trafficking are to be viewed and treated. A recognition of the severity of human rights violations that surround trafficking should make it pointedly clear to the justice system that first and foremost, victims are in need of protections as crime victims, especially during the period when they are contemplating whether or not prosecution is possible. All other justice concerns should be secondary to this first condition.

This is not to say that current U.S. policies and laws are wholly inadequate in aiding victims. However, using a human rights lens may facilitate the goal of ensuring that victims of human trafficking are restored, whether or not prosecution of their traffickers occurs. Such restoration may well deter further trafficking because victims, once freed or rescued, may not endure the same vulnerabilities and conditions (e.g., poverty, abuse) that led them to become ensnared in a trafficking situation in the first place. However, there is much more to be done to guarantee that laws designed to assist trafficked persons address their fundamental human rights and do not create a dichotomy between "good" (cooperative) and "bad" (noncooperative) victims when the human rights violations are the same in both contexts. Doing so will guarantee that we are truly able to reach and assist more individuals harmed by human trafficking. In addition, addressing those profiting from human trafficking with appropriate and swift legal repercussions is critical.

At the same time, identification and services for victims must be a high priority. Not only is awareness and training important but more resources for service agencies are critical. Human trafficking cases are complex and time consuming, and although services clearly have an important role in helping victims of this crime, their budgets are often stretched to the limit in serving the clients and cases they already have. Furthermore, these cases are so complex that the coordination between services, cross training, and openness to partnering with other agencies must be incorporated into the response to the needs of these victims. Clearly, communities need lead organizers to take initiative and to invite the participating agencies to the table, but agencies must also be willing to be at the table and, if not initially invited, they must be willing to initiate their involvement.

Fundamentally, human trafficking is a deprivation of the most basic entitlements and human rights, and this absence of entitlements and rights limits the ability to achieve a meaningful life. In the case of an undocumented immigrant human trafficking victim, the individual is deprived of not only citizenship but also deprived of a life with choices such as being able to quit his or her job and whether or not to marry, to have children, to worship, to go to the store, or to socialize. These individuals are also deprived of the recognition of his or her labor as legitimate and worthy of adequate reward such as fair pay. More drastically, individuals in these situations are often deprived of basic living needs such as adequate food, access to health care, and safety. Rights are not equally applied to every individual in the United States or across the world; however, basic human rights are considered fundamental to a civilized society. Human trafficking victims cease to be individual agents and instead become pawns for the benefit of others. Bales (2000) summarized human trafficking, "It is not just

stealing someone's labor, it is the theft of an entire life" (p. 7).

Critical Findings Summary

- Human trafficking, at its most basic level, is defined by the Trafficking Victims Protection Act of 2000 as (a) the recruitment, harboring, transporting, supplying, or obtaining a person for labor or services through the use of force, fraud, or coercion for the purpose of involuntary servitude or slavery; or (b) sex trafficking in which a commercial sex act is induced by force, fraud, or coercion, or in which the person induced to perform sex acts is under 18 years of age.

- A review of nine reports on human trafficking in the United States suggests that human trafficking does exist in the United States.

- Human trafficking in the United States cuts across a variety of labor sectors including commercial sex work, domestic, personal service, factory, restaurant, farm, and agricultural labor. However, there may be other labor sectors that have not been identified, which calls for more investigation or research.

- Factors that affect vulnerability to trafficking include poverty, immigrant status, hope for a better life, being female, being young, and being isolated.

- Factors that influence continued entrapment include fear, lack of knowledge about alternatives, isolation, and physical and psychological confinement.

- Adaptations to human trafficking involve behavioral and cognitive strategies, and both the circumstances and the coping strategies used for survival may affect short-term as well as long-term health and mental health conditions.

- There were several themes identified as distinguishing human trafficking from other crimes including the following: (a) It is more difficult to identify, (b) prejudice toward the victims, (c) victims have greater needs, (d) fewer resources and services to address this crime, (e) greater fear and safety concerns for victims and their families, (f) more limited access to justice for victims, and (g) human trafficking are very complex criminal cases.

- Identifying human trafficking victims is challenging. Some victims were identified during the course of a criminal investigation. Other victims sought social, medical, or employment dispute services and were subsequently identified as human trafficking victims. Although it is rare that victims self-identify as human trafficking victims, there are red flags that can indicate a possible trafficking situation. These red flags include looking at a person's situation and listening to their story. The Campaign to Rescue and Restore Victims of Human Trafficking has a screening tool to use with victims of human trafficking.

Implications of the Review Summary

- Fundamentally, human trafficking is a deprivation of the most basic entitlements and human rights, and this absence of entitlements and rights limits the ability to achieve a meaningful life.

- In the case of an undocumented immigrant human trafficking victim, the individual is deprived of not only citizenship, but also deprived of a life with choices such as being able to quit his or her job, and whether or not to marry, to have children, to worship, or go to the store, or to socialize. These individuals are also deprived of the recognition of his or her labor as legitimate and worthy of adequate reward such as fair pay. More drastically, individuals in these situations are often deprived of basic living needs such as adequate food, access to heath care, and safety.

- Rights are not equally applied to every individual in the United States or across the world; however, basic human rights are considered fundamental to a civilized society. Human trafficking victims cease to be individual agents and instead become pawns for the benefit of others. Bales (2000) summarized human trafficking, "It is not just stealing someone's labor, it is the theft of an entire life" (p. 7).

- Human trafficking is a crime that affects individuals, groups of individuals, and the communities in which the crime is occurring. Thus, awareness for every citizen in the United States is important.

- Human trafficking is a hidden crime and most victims choose to not self-identify. It is critical that service providers and law enforcement be aware of red flags and to screen potential cases to determine whether it might be a case of trafficking.

- Given the substantial needs of victims, ongoing awareness and training of service providers and protocols for coordinating within and across agencies is recommended.

- To effectively address the level of outreach to better identify victims of human trafficking and to serve their vast needs more resources for services is critical. Resources, at a minimum, should include language access services, temporary and safe shelter as well as longer term housing, physical and mental health care, public benefits, legal assistance, drug and alcohol counseling, job training or assistance in obtaining employment, basic English language training, and assistance should the victim chose to relocate or return to home country.

- There is a need for better clarification of the U.S. justice system toward victims of trafficking to ensure their safety and other needs are central rather than conditional.

- Ongoing research on human trafficking in the United States is challenging but necessary to further our understanding of the dynamics of human trafficking, how to better reach out to victims, and how to help victims with recovery and restoration of rights.

Note

1. Article 3 of the United Nations Protocol to Prevent, Suppress and Punish Trafficking in Persons, especially Women and Children (Protocol) provides the definition of trafficking in persons:

> (a) "Trafficking in persons" shall mean the recruitment, transportation, transfer, harboring or receipt of persons, by means of the threat or use of force or other forms of coercion, of abduction, of fraud, of deception, of the abuse of power or of a position of vulnerability or of the giving or receiving of payments or benefits to achieve the consent of a person having control over another person, for the purpose of exploitation. Exploitation shall include, at a minimum, the exploitation of the prostitution of others or other forms of sexual exploitation, forced labor or services, slavery or practices similar to slavery, servitude or the removal of organs; (b) The consent of a victim of trafficking in persons to the intended exploitation set forth in subparagraph (a) of this article shall be irrelevant where any of the means set forth in subparagraph (a) has been used.

References

Anti-slavery International. (2002). *Recommended principles and guidelines on human rights and human trafficking report of the United Nations.* London: Author. Retrieved October 22, 2008, from http://www.antislavery.org.au/pdf/UN_RecHRHT.pdf

Bales, K. (1999). *Disposable people: New slavery in the global economy.* Berkeley and Los Angeles: University of California Press.

Bales, K. (2000). Expendable people: Slavery in the age of globalization. *Journal of International Affairs, 53,* 461–484.

Bales, K. (2005). *Understanding global slavery: A reader.* Berkeley: University of California Press.

Bales, K. (2007). *Ending slavery: How we free today's slaves.* Berkeley: University of California Press.

Batstone, D. (2007). *Not for sale: The return of the global slave trade—and how we can fight it.* New York: HarperCollins.

Blackmon, D. A. (2008). *Slavery by another name: The re-enslavement of black Americans from the civil war to world war II.* Garden City, NY: Doubleday.

Brennan, D. (2005). Methodological challenges in research with trafficked persons: Tales from the field. In F. Laczko & E. Gozdziak (Eds.), *Data and research on human trafficking: A global survey* (Vol. 43, pp. 35–54). Geneva: International Organization for Migration.

Brunovskis, A., & Surtees, R. (2007). *Leaving the past behind: When victims of trafficking decline assistance* (Fafo Report 2007: 40). Retrieved July 23, 2008, from http://www.fafo.no/pub/rapp/20040/20040.pdf

Cahill, T. (1995). *How the Irish saved civilization.* Garden City, NY: Doubleday.

California Alliance to Combat Trafficking and Slavery Task Force (CACTSTF). (2007). *Human trafficking in California: Final report.* Retrieved July 18, 2008, from http:// safestate.org/documents/HT_Final_Report_ADA.pdf

Clawson, H., Dutch, N., & Cummings, M. (2006). *Law enforcement response to human trafficking and the implications for victims: Current practices and lessons learned* (Grant No. 2004-WG-BX-0088). Washington, DC: U.S. Department of Justice. Retrieved July 18, 2008, from http://www.ncjrs.gov/pdffiles1/nij/grants/216547.pdf

Clawson, H., Dutch, N., & Williamson, E. (2008). *National symposium on the health needs of human trafficking victims: Background brief.* Washington, DC: U.S. Department of health and Human Services, Office of the Assistant Secretary for Planning and Evaluation.

Clawson, H., Small, K., Go, E., & Myles, B. (2003). *Needs assessment for service providers and trafficking victims* (Doc. No. 202469). Fairfax, VA: National Criminal Justice Reference Service. Retrieved July 2, 2007, from http://www.ncjrs.gov/pdffiles1/nij/grants/202469.pdf

Collingridge, V. (2006). *Boudicca: The life and legends of Britain's warrior queen.* Woodstock, NY: Overlook Press.

Davis, D. (2006). *Inhuman bondage: The rise and fall of slavery in the new world.* New York: Oxford University Press.

Ehlers, A., Maercker, A., & Boos, A. (2000). Posttraumatic stress disorder following political imprisonment: The role of mental defeat, alienation, and perceived permanent change. *Journal of Abnormal Psychology, 109*(1), 45–55.

Eltman, F. (December 17, 2007). Long Island couple found guilty in "slavery" case. *The New York Sun Times.* Retrieved November 4, 2008, from http://www.humantrafficking.org/uploads/publications/florida_responds2human_trafficking_fsu.pdf

Family Violence Prevention Fund & World Childhood Foundation. (2005). *Turning pain into power: Trafficking survivors' perspectives on early intervention strategies.* San Francisco: Author. Retrieved July 18, 2008, from http://endabuse.org/programs/immigrant/files/PaintoPower.pdf

Farber, I., Harlow, H., & West, L. (1957). Brainwashing, conditioning, and DDD (debility, dependency, and dread). *Sociometry, 20,* 271–285.

Florida State University. (2003). *Florida responds to human trafficking.* Tallahassee: Author (Center for the Advancement of Human Rights). Retrieved July 2, 2007, from www.cahr.fsu.edu/the%20report.pdf

Free the Slaves & Human Rights Center (University of California). (2004). *Hidden slaves: Forced labor in the United States.* Retrieved July 18, 2008, from http://safestate.org/documents/HT_Final_Report_ADA.pdf

Gilbert, P. (2000). Varieties of submissive behavior as forms of social defense: Their evolution and role in depression. In L. Sloman & P. Gilbert (Eds.), *Subordination and defeat: An evolutionary approach to mood disorders and their treatment* (pp. 3–45). Mahwah, NJ: Lawrence Erlbaum.

Goldsworthy, A. (2006). *Caesar: Life of a colossus.* New Haven, CT: Yale University Press.

Gross, J. (1998a). Antecedent- and response-focused emotion regulation: Divergent consequences for experience, expression, and physiology. *Journal of Personality and Social Psychology, 74,* 224–237.

Gross, J. (1998b). The emerging field of emotion regulation: An integrative review. *Review of General Psychology, 2,* 271–237.

Hyland, K. (2001). Protecting human victims of trafficking: An American framework. *Berkeley Women's Law Journal, 16,* 29–71.

Hynes, H., & Raymond, J. (2002). Put in harm's way: The neglected health consequences of sex trafficking in the United States. In J. Silliman & A. Bhattacharjee (Eds.), *Policing the national body: Sex, race, and criminalization.* Boston: South End.

Jordan, D., & Walsh, M. (2007). *White cargo: The forgotten history of Britain's white slaves in America.* New York: New York University Press.

Kennedy, K. (2007, September 12). The realities of human trafficking. *CBS news.* Retrieved January 21, 2008, from www.cbsnews.com/stories/2007/09/11/earlyshow/printable3250963.shtml

Kim, K. (2007). Psychological coercion in the context of modern-day involuntary labor: Revisiting U.S. v Kozminski and understanding human trafficking. *University of Toledo Law Review, 38,* 941–972.

Lazarus, R. (1999). *Stress and emotion: A new synthesis.* New York: Springer.

Loewenstein, G., Weber, E., Hsee, C., & Welch, N. (2001). Risk as feelings. *Psychological Bulletin, 127,* 267–286.

Logan, T. (2007). *Human trafficking in Kentucky.* Lexington: University of Kentucky. Retrieved July 18, 2008, from http://cdar.uky.edu/VAW/docs/Human%20Trafficking%20in%20Kentucky.pdf

Logan, T. (2008, September 22–23). *The multiple roles of substance abuse in human trafficking.* Presentation to the National Symposium on the Health Needs of Human Trafficking Victims, Health and Human Services, Washington, DC.

Logan, T., Walker, R., Jordan, C., & Leukefeld, C. (2006). *Women and victimization: Contributing factors, interventions, and implications.* Washington, DC: American Psychological Association.

Markon, J. (2007, September 23). Human trafficking evokes outrage, little evidence. *Washington Post.* Retrieved October 25, 2007, from http://www.washingtonpost.com/wp-dyn/content/article/2007/09/22/AR200709 2201401_pf.html

Neville, S., & Martinez, S. (2004). The law of human trafficking: What legal aid providers should know. *Clearinghouse Review Journal of Poverty Law and Policy, 37,* 551–566.

Packer, A., Curtis, L., & McCabe, F. (2007, July 4). China Star Acrobats: Trio face slavery charges. *Las Vegas Review-Journal,* Retrieved December 28, 2007, from www.lvrj.com/news/8317652.html

Raphael, J., & Ashley, J. (2008). *Domestic sex trafficking of Chicago women and girls.* Chicago: DePaul University College of Law and Illinois Criminal

Justice Information Authority. Retrieved September 24, 2008, from http://www.icjia.state.il.us/public/pdf/ResearchReports/Sex%20Trafficking%20Report%20May%202008.pdf

Rawson, E. (1993). The expansion of Rome. In J. Boardman, J. Griffin, & O. Murray (Eds.), *The Roman world* (pp. 39–59). New York: Oxford University Press.

Raymond, J., D'Cunha, J., Dzuhayatin, S., Hynes, H., Rodriguez, Z., & Santos, A. (2002). *A comparative study of women trafficked in the migration process: Patterns, profiles, and health consequences of sexual exploitation in five countries (Indonesia, the Philippines, Thailand, Venezuela, and the United States).* Belgium: Coalition Against Trafficking in Women. Retrieved July 18, 2008, from http://action.web.ca/home/catw/attach/CATW%20Comparative%20Study%202002.pdf

Raymond, J., & Hughes, D. (2001). *Sex trafficking of women in the united states* (NIJ Publication No. 98-WT-VX-0032). New York: Coalition Against Trafficking in Women. Retrieved July 2, 2007, from www.uri.edu/artsci/wms/hughes/sex_traff_us.pdf

Richard, A. (1999). *International trafficking in women to the United States: A contemporary manifestation of slavery and organized crime*—An intelligence monograph. Washington, DC: Center for the Study of Intelligence. Retrieved July 18, 2008, from https://www.cia.gov/ library/center-for-the-study-of-intelligence/csi-publications/books-and-monographs/trafficking.pdf

Seitz Steinberg, C. (2004). *Needs assessment human trafficking in Houston.* Houston, TX: University of Houston, Office of Community Projects Graduate School of Social Work. Unpublished report.

Skinner, E. B. (2008). *A crime so monstrous: Face-to-face with modern-day slavery.* New York: Free Press.

Srikantiah, J. (2007). Perfect victims and real survivors: The iconic victim in domestic human trafficking law. *Boston University Law Review, 87,* 157–211.

The Human Smuggling and Trafficking Center. (2005). *Fact sheet: Distinctions between human smuggling and human trafficking.* Retrieved September 15, 2007, from http://www.state.gov/documents/organization/49875.pdf

Urbina, I. (2007, February 21). For youths, a grim tour on magazine crews. *New York Times.* Retrieved October 8, 2007, from www.nytimes.com/2007/02/21/us/21magcrew.html?nTop%2FReference%2FTimes%20Topics%2FSubjects%2FL%2FLabor

U.S. Department of Health and Human Services, Administration of Children & Families. (2008). *Screening tool for victims of human trafficking.* Retrieved September 4, 2008, from http://www.acf.hhs.gov/ trafficking/campaign_kits/tool_kit_social/screen_questions.html

U.S. Department of Justice. (2007, July 3). *Three arrested for involuntary servitude.* Federal Bureau of Investigation press release. Retrieved July 10, 2007, from http:// lasvegas.fbi.gov/pressrel/2007/servitude070307.htm

U.S. Department of State. (2006, June). *Trafficking in persons report.* Retrieved June 30, 2008, from http://www.state.gov/documents/organization/66086.pdf

U.S. Department of State. (2007, June). *Trafficking in persons report.* Retrieved February 5, 2007, from http:// www.state.gov/g/tip/rls/tiprpt/2007

U.S. Department of State. (2008, June). *Trafficking in persons report.* Retrieved September 16, 2008, from http:// www.state.gov/g/tip/rls/tiprpt/2008

Victims of Trafficking and Violence Protection Act of 2000, Pub. L. No. 106-386 (2000, October 28). Retrieved June 30, 2008, from http://www.state.gov/documents/organization/10492.pdf

Vitello, P. (2007, December 3). From stand in Long Island slavery case, a snapshot of a hidden U.S. problem. *New York Times.* Retrieved January 21, 2008, from http://www.nytimes.com/2007/12/03/nyregion/03slavery.html

Vollman, W. (2007). *Poor people.* New York: Harper Perennial.

Warner, C. (2007, May 29). Millionaire Long Island couple charged with slave labor. *Associated Content.* Retrieved February 8, 2008, from http://www.associatedcontent.com/article/256920/millionaire_long_island_couple_charged.html?page=2

Webber, A., & Shirk, D. (2005). Hidden victims: Evaluating protections for undocumented victims of human trafficking. *Immigration Policy in Focus, 4,* 1–27.

Wilson, D., Walsh, W., & Kleuber, S. (2006). Trafficking in human beings: Training and services among US law enforcement agencies. *Police Practice and Research, 7,* 149–160.

Zimmerman, C. (2003). *The health risks and consequences of trafficking in women and adolescents: Findings from a European study.* London: London School of Hygiene & Tropical

Medicine. Retrieved September 16, 2008, from http://www.lshtm.ac.uk/hpu/docs/trafficking final.pdf

Zimmerman, C., Hossain, M., Yun, K., Gajdadziev, V., Guzun, N., Tchomarova, M., et al. (2008). The health of trafficked women: A survey of women entering posttrafficking services in Europe. *American Journal of Public Health, 98*(1), 55–59.

Zimmerman, C., Hossain, M., Yun, K., Roche, B., Morison, L., & Watts, C. (2006). Stolen smiles: A summary report on the physical and psychological health consequences of women and adolescents trafficked in Europe. London: London School of Hygiene & Tropical Medicine. Retrieved September 16, 2008, from http://www.lshtm .ac.uk/hpu/docs/StolenSmiles.pdf

CHAPTER 9

"You Just Give Them What They Want and Pray They Don't Kill You"

Street-Level Sex Workers' Reports of Victimization, Personal Resources, and Coping Strategies

Rochelle L. Dalla, Yan Xia, and Heather Kennedy

National and international organizations (e.g., American Medical Association, World Health Organization) are attracting widespread attention to the public health concern of violence against women (Watts & Zimmerman, 2002). Recognition that female victimization represents transgressions against human rights and constitutes a serious risk for physical and emotional problems has fueled the attention (Watts & Zimmerman, 2002). One of the eight most prevalent forms of global violence against women, as identified by Watts and Zimmerman (2002), is violence against prostituted women.

Street-level prostitutes are particularly vulnerable to physical and sexual victimization (Miller, 1993, 1995; Williamson & Folaron, 2001). Of significance, the sheer scope and magnitude of violence against street workers has increased dramatically in the past decade, paralleling the street culture crack epidemic (Inciardi, Lockwood, & Pottieger, 1993). Still, "physical and sexual violence towards prostitutes has seldom been the focus of public or academic interest" (Watts & Zimmerman, 2002, p. 1238). The marginalized status of prostituted women, some argue (Overall, 1992; Pheterson, 1990), largely accounts for the limited academic interest in or concern for their physical and emotional well-being. Using qualitative and quantitative strategies, this investigation was designed to (a) document the extent of violence against street-level prostituted

Dalla, R. L., Xia, Y., & Kennedy, H. (2003). "You just give them what they want and pray they don't kill you": Street-level sex workers' reports of victimization, personal resources, and coping strategies. *Violence Against Women, 9,* 1367–1394.

women, including perceptions of and responses to that violence, and (b) explore relationships between factors associated with stress theory among this vulnerable population. Programmatic intervention to mitigate health risks associated with victimization is useless without rich, well-documented data guiding such efforts.

Literature Review

Inherently, victimization implies an interpersonal power differential in which one party dominates another (Hagan, 1989). MacMillan (2001) noted that violent victimization includes interactions in which individuals are unable to prevent or protect themselves from attack. Thus, "victimization has implications for one's sense of agency, self-efficacy, and perceptions of others in the social world" (p. 11). Victimization may have profound psychological consequences (Farley & Barkan, 1998; Menard, 2001; Norris, Kaniasty, & Thompson, 1997) and significantly alter long-term developmental trajectories (MacMillan, 2001).

Not all individuals are equally at risk for victimization. Compared to men, women in intimate heterosexual relationships are significantly more likely to experience physical and sexual assault (Watts & Zimmerman, 2002), and exposure to and involvement in environments characterized by crime and deviance increase risk of victimization (Sampson & Lauritsen, 1994). The sex industry, as one such environmental context, breeds violence and victimization. Street-level prostitution presents significant personal risk (Maher, 1996; Miller, 1993; Williamson & Cluse-Tolar, 2002), particularly when drug use is involved (Williamson & Folaron, 2001). Still, "societal attitudes concerning prostitutes continue to be that they are unrapeable, do not suffer physical attack, deserve violence inflicted upon them, or that no harm is done when [they] are hurt or killed" (Williamson & Folaron, 2001, p. 464).

Despite recent attention to prostituted women's experiences with violence, studies to date have been either qualitative *or* quantitative, thus limiting the amount and type of information obtained; have been largely atheoretical in nature; have failed to examine lifespan victimization (i.e., childhood and adulthood victimization); and have neglected personal (e.g., social support) and psychological (e.g., sense of agency) factors that may mitigate negative consequences of victimization. To address gaps in previous research, this study was theoretically grounded, qualitative and quantitative data were collected, and lifespan victimization was explored. A brief review of relevant literature is presented below.

Childhood Victimization

A majority of individuals working in the sex industry have experienced childhood abuse (Dalla, 2001; McClanahan, McClelland, Abram, & Teplin, 1999; Simons & Whitbeck, 1991). Physical and sexual abuse have been identified as precursors to involvement in violent and nonviolent crime, including prostitution (Hagan & McCarthy, 1997), although the percentage of prostituted women who experienced childhood sexual abuse varies considerably from 10% to 50% (Russell, 1988), to 60% (Silbert & Pines, 1983), to more than 70% (Bagley & Young, 1987). Some (Nandon, Koverola, & Schludermann, 1998; Seng, 1989; Simons & Whitbeck, 1991) believe the link between childhood sexual abuse and later prostitution is indirect, mediated by runaway behavior.

Research indicates that childhood victimization may have profound short- and long-term consequences for mental health. Childhood victims of physical and sexual abuse have increased prevalence of anxiety, depression, and symptoms of posttraumatic stress disorder (PTSD) (McLeer, Deblinger, Atkins, Foa, & Ralphe, 1988; Menard, 2001; White, Halpin, Strom, & Santilli, 1988). And teenagers in correctional and mental health institutions tend to report high rates of childhood physical abuse (Cavaiola & Schiff, 1988; Lewis, Shanok, & Balla, 1979). Long-term consequences of childhood abuse are also well documented. Abused children show higher rates of psychological distress in adulthood (Chu & Dill, 1990; Kessler & Magee, 1994). Antisocial behavior, including drug and alcohol abuse (Bagley, Bolitho, & Bertrand, 1997; Bagley & Ramsey, 1986; Conte & Schuerman, 1987), and symptoms of emotional distress (i.e., depression, poor self-esteem, sexual dysfunction) have been identified among adult survivors of childhood sexual abuse (Burnam et al., 1988). Arboleda-Flores and Wade (1999) further reported that childhood physical abuse doubled the odds of having a major depressive episode in adulthood. Given the broad body of literature documenting lifecourse implications of childhood experiences of victimization, it was deemed critical to explore lifelong exposure to violence in the present investigation.

Victimization of Prostituted Women

Church, Henderson, Barnoar, and Hart (2001) reported that outdoor versus indoor prostitution was associated with higher levels of violence perpetrated by clients than were the effects of the city, drug use, and duration of or age that the women began prostitution. Others have focused on the extent and severity of violence experienced by street workers. Miller (1993) found a significant proportion of participants had experienced sexual assault (93%), forced or coerced sex with self-identified police officers (44%), rape (75%), and robbery (56%). Physical assault with and without weapons (i.e., being beat up, stabbed, or slashed) was also commonly reported. Williamson and Folaron (2001) reported findings of exposure to and intensity of violence experienced by street workers similar to those of Miller and others (Silbert & Pines, 1982).

Farley and Barkan (1998) examined violence experienced by prostituted women across the life span in relation to experiences of PTSD. PTSD was related to childhood physical abuse and to the occurrence of rape in adult prostitution.

The more types of violence reported (e.g., childhood sexual assault, adult rape and physical assault), the greater the severity of PTSD symptoms. A significant association also emerged between the number of types of lifetime violence experiences and severity of PTSD numbing and hyperarousal symptoms.

Understanding lifespan exposure to violence clearly provides new avenues from which to explore vulnerability and risk associated with victimization. Of importance, the crack cocaine epidemic of the previous decade significantly heightened the danger associated with street-level prostitution (Faugier & Sargeant, 1997).

Drug Culture

Drug addiction has been widely examined in relation to female prostitution. Crack cocaine specifically, and its use by street-level sex workers, has received much academic attention. Potterat, Rothenberg, Muth, Darrow, and Phillips-Plummer (1998) examined the sequence and timing of prostitution entry and drug use among prostitution-involved women and a comparable control group. Drug use was more common among the prostitution-involved women and preceded sexual activity in both groups. Moreover, the majority of prostitution-involved women (66%) reported drug use prior to prostitution involvement. In contrast, Dalla (2000) found an equal number of participants reporting drug addiction following prostitution entry as preceding entry. Her work supports that of Graham and Wish (1994), who examined female drug use in relation to deviant behavior and found that drug use did not always precede prostitution work. Drug use, they contended, may evolve as a coping strategy among women already involved in prostitution.

Regardless of entry motivation, the entire culture of street-level prostitution has been dramatically altered due to the inundation of crack cocaine (Inciardi et al., 1993). Many (Barry, 1995; Fullilove, Lown, & Fullilove, 1992; Sterk &

Elifson, 1990) have described a newly emerging form of prostitution, namely, the direct exchange of sex for crack. The street presence of crack cocaine is directly and indirectly related to the diminishing price of sexual services and the increased danger and vulnerability associated with street-level prostitution (Faugier & Sargeant, 1997; Inciardi et al., 1993). Addiction-motivated street workers are increasingly willing to provide cheaper and more degrading sexual services in exchange for the drug (Dalla, 2002; Maher, 1996). Still, this is not an entirely new phenomenon. Heroin "bag brides" engaged in similar behavior (Goldstein, 1979); the difference rests in the sheer magnitude with which the behavior has expanded among female crack addicts (Feucht, 1993; Inciardi, 1995). According to Maher (1996) and others (Jones et al., 1998), not only have the tricks become cheaper and the violence more pronounced, but street workers are also increasingly viewed as carriers of HIV and as morally contaminated.

Theoretical Orientation

To provide unique data on the victimization of prostituted women, including reactions to such, stress theory formed the foundation of this investigation. According to stress theory (Lazarus, 1966; Lazarus & Folkman, 1984; Lazarus & Launier, 1978), individuals presented with a potentially stressful event react first by making a primary cognitive appraisal of the event as irrelevant, benign/positive, or stressful (Lazarus & Folkman, 1984). Secondary cognitive appraisal occurs as one evaluates internal (e.g., locus of control, impulse control) and external (e.g., social support) resources and one's options for managing the event. Events are perceived as stressful based on unique perceptions of the events as exceeding or taxing one's coping resources (Lazarus & Launier, 1978).

Although coping strategies are tactics used to minimize stress, they need not be conscious or effective; denial and drug use (i.e., escapism) are

considered coping responses (Matheny, Aycock, Pugh, Curlette, & Cannella, 1986). In this investigation, a survey of life events comprised potentially stress-inducing circumstances. Internal resources were operationalized with three surveys: emotional well-being (i.e., depression), locus of control, and impulse control. Social support was examined as an indicator of perceived external resources, and five coping strategies were evaluated.

Based on prior research and the theoretical model, six hypotheses were formulated:

Hypothesis 1: Active coping strategies (e.g., seeking assistance) will be positively associated with emotional and practical support.

Hypothesis 2: Passive (e.g., internalizing) or potentially harm-inducing (e.g., escapism) coping strategies will be positively associated with depression and negatively associated with emotional and practical support.

Hypothesis 3: External locus of control will be positively associated with depression and negatively associated with emotional and practical support.

Hypothesis 4: Number of life events will be positively associated with external locus of control.

Hypothesis 5: Low impulse control will be negatively related to talking coping strategies and positively related to escapism and an external locus of control.

Hypothesis 6: Coping responses will be determined first based on internal resources (e.g., impulse control) and second on perceived external resources (i.e., social support).

Method

Participants

The final sample consisted of 43 women. Inclusion required that participants be female, involved or formerly involved in streetwalking prostitution, and 18 years of age or older. When interviewed, participants averaged 33.3 years of age; most identified themselves as White ($n = 20$) or Black ($n = 18$). The majority lived in shelters ($n = 16$), and most ($n = 40$) were no longer actively involved in prostitution, although length of time since the last prostitution incident varied considerably, as did tenure in the sex industry (range = 6 months to 44 years; see Table 9.1).

Table 9.1 Demographic Data

Variable	Total Sample (N = 43)
Age	
Mean	33.3
Mode	37.0
Range	19–56
Race/ethnicity (*n*)	
Black	18
White	20
Native American	5
Marital status (*n*)	
Never married	22
Married	10
Divorced/separated	11
Residence (*n*)	
Shelter	16
Friends	3
Prison	14
Partner or husband	6
Alone or with children	4
Education	
Mean	9.3
Range	7th grade–2 years of college
GED (*n*)	14

(Continued)

(Continued)

Variable	Total Sample (N = 43)
Children	
Mothers (n)	38
Number of children (total)[a]	105
Mean	2.4
Range	1–7
Children's residence (n)	
Mother	10
Father	19
Grandparent or aunt	21
On own	14
Foster care	22
Adopted	8
Other[b]	11
Prostitution	
Age at entry	
Mean	19.4
Mode	18
Range	11–31
Time in sex industry[c]	
Mean	11.5 years
Range	6 months–44 years
Onset of drug abuse[d] (n)	41
Preprostitution	16
Concurrent with prostitution	8
Postprostitution	17

NOTE: GED = General Equivalency Diploma.

a. Does not include number of pregnancies; numerous participants reported abortions.

b. Includes individuals living with extended kin, in mental health facilities, and incarcerated.

c. Multiple modes exist; includes streetwalking as well as other forms of prostitution (e.g., sugar daddy involvement).

d. Drugs of choice included crack, amphetamines, alcohol, and heroin.

Procedures

Most participants (*n* = 26) were located through an intervention program designed to assist prostituted women in leaving the streets. The program offered weekly group meetings and one-on-one counseling. Of the program clientele, 90% were voluntary participants; 10% attended as a probation requirement. Due to the voluntary nature of the program, group attendees were transitional, and involvement was sporadic at best. With support from the program director and the approval of program attendees, the principal investigator (PI) attended weekly group meetings for 17 months. Each week, the PI explained her presence in the group, including the purpose and goals of the investigation. Interviews were scheduled with interested individuals. Two additional recruitment strategies were used to obtain a diversified sample of prostituted women not involved in an intervention program.

To accomplish this, 14 participants were recruited while incarcerated in a women's prison in an adjacent state. Approval from the prison warden was obtained to conduct personal, private, tape-recorded interviews with women meeting participation requirements. Finally, 3 participants were located through word of mouth. None of the 3 had participated in counseling or any intervention program.

All data were collected by the PI in two North American midwestern cities. After signing an informed consent form, participants were given the choice of individually completing the surveys or having the PI read each question and all response choices. Surveys were completed in an average of 35 minutes. Participants then engaged in an in-depth, tape-recorded interview with the PI focusing on violence experienced during childhood, on the streets (e.g., by clients, strangers, pimps), and with intimates. Audiotaped data were transcribed verbatim by trained research assistants. Based on prison policy, incarcerated participants could not receive compensation; all other participants received $20.00 for their time.

Instruments

Life Events

To assess life events or stressors, a revised version of the Family Inventory of Life Events and Changes (Olson et al., 1982) was used, consisting of 26 items (e.g., divorce, victim of violence, was jailed or had trouble with the law). Participants indicated if the event had occurred within the previous year; responses were then summed so that higher scores indicated more occurrences of potentially stressful life events (M = 13.3, range = 4 to 21).

Depression

To assess emotional well-being, an internal resource, a seven-item depression inventory assessing feelings over the previous 2 months, was used. Items included, for instance, "I have had little energy and not felt like doing anything" and "I have felt depressed." Response choices ranged from 1 (*rarely*) to 4 (*most of the time*). Two items were reverse coded so that higher scores indicated greater feelings of depression (M = 2.5, range = 1.3 to 4.0, SD = 0.74). The instrument demonstrated high reliability (.83) using Cronbach's test.

Locus of Control

Locus of control, another internal resource, refers to the extent to which individuals see themselves as in control of and responsible for events in their lives. Locus of control was assessed using a seven-item instrument that included statements such as "I have little control over the things that happen to me" and "I often feel helpless in dealing with problems in life." Respondents answered each statement using a Likert-type response scale ranging from 1 (*not true*) to 4 (*always true*). Two items were reverse coded so that higher scores indicated greater external locus of control (scale M = 1.6, range = 1.0 to 3.3, SD = 0.49). The survey evidenced high reliability (Cronbach's alpha = .65).

Impulse Control

Impulse control, the third internal resource measured, refers to the ability to delay gratification; those lacking impulse control tend to act on the spur of the moment without thought for future consequences. Impulse control was measured using a 20-item instrument that asked participants to respond on a 5-point Likert-type scale, ranging from 5 (*strongly agree*) to 1 (*strongly disagree*), to statements such as "I often act on the spur of the moment without stopping to think" and "I like to test myself every now and then by doing something a little risky." Several statements were reverse coded so that higher scores indicated limited impulse control. The scale mean was 3.0 (SD = 1.0), and the scale demonstrated high reliability (.70) based on Cronbach's alpha.

Social Support

Social support, an external resource, may buffer potentially negative or stressful experiences. To assess network composition and type of support received, the Norbeck Social Support Questionnaire (Norbeck, Lindsey, & Carrieri, 1981, 1982) was administered. Respondents were asked to list up to 10 "significant" people in their lives. Respondents answered each question for each individual included in their network list using a 5-point Likert-type response scale; response choices ranged from 1 (*not at all*) to 5 (*a great deal*). Emotional support was assessed with four questions such as "How much does this person make you feel liked or loved?" The subscale mean was 2.9 (SD = 1.4) with an internal reliability of .95. Practical support, the giving of symbolic or material aid, was assessed by asking two questions such as "If you need to borrow some money, a ride to the doctor, or some other form

of immediate help, how much could this person help you?" This scale demonstrated a mean of 2.6 (SD = 1.3) and an alpha coefficient of .93.

Coping

The Coping Resources Inventory–Form D (Hammer & Marting, 1987) was used to identify participants' strategies for managing stress. This 26-item instrument was designed to measure five types of coping: social (e.g., talking to someone), escapism (e.g., eating, using drugs), externalizing (e.g., hitting someone or something), internalizing (e.g., keep feelings to self)/ and active (e.g., do something about the situation). Participants responded to statements indicating the extent to which they would employ each of the five strategies; response choices ranged from 1 (*would not do*) to 4 (*would always do*). Total subscale scores were computed for each strategy. Using Cronbach's alpha, the reliability coefficient for each subscale was as follows: Social = .77, Escapism = .72, Internalize = .71, Externalize = .77, and Active = .78.

Data Analyses

Interview Data

Thematic analysis (Aronson, 1994; Taylor & Bogdan, 1984) was used for analyzing all text-based data. The process begins with a thorough reading of all transcribed data and the listing of patterns of experiences. Patterns are then classified into meaningful categories. The classified data are then expounded on by adding all information from the transcribed interviews that relates to those patterns or themes. Themes are defined as units derived from patterns (Taylor & Bogdan, 1984). The next step involves combining and cataloging related patterns into subthemes. The process requires researcher interpretation based on rigorous identification and compilation of related ideas, thoughts, and experiences into meaningful concepts when examined together. All data were coded by the PI and a graduate-level research assistant. When coding discrepancies arose, original transcripts were reexamined until coding agreement could be reached.

Survey Data

Survey data were analyzed using standard statistics (i.e., correlation, *t*-test, and hierarchical regression techniques). Statistical significance was evaluated using standard parametric and nonparametric tests, as appropriate.

Results

Qualitative Analyses: Interview Data

Childhood Sexual Abuse

In all, 32 participants (74%) reported experiencing childhood sexual abuse. Sexual molestation, in and of itself, does not necessarily result in damaging long-term consequences. When attempting to understand the potential repercussions of sexual abuse, Sauzier, Salt, and Calhoun (1990) reported that certain factors appear most salient, including the perpetrator's relationship with the victim, how long the abuse continued, age when the abuse began, the severity of abuse (e.g., fondling versus penetration), and whether someone intervened on behalf of the victim. The potential for long-term psychosocial damage is greater when the perpetrator is a trusted adult (e.g., nuclear family member), the abuse is sustained over a long period of time, and the acts involve penetration (Finkelhor, 1987).

Sexual perpetrators, in the order most commonly implicated by the participants, included biological fathers, stepfathers, family friends, brothers, and uncles. Other perpetrators, including grandfathers, adopted and foster fathers and brothers, neighbors, and mothers' boyfriends, were also mentioned. One woman was sexually molested by her biological mother and another by an older sister. And 8 participants (25%) had been victimized by more than one individual; 5 participants reported that, in addition to themselves, their siblings were also victims of sexual abuse. Although several participants were unable to report how long the molestation continued, others were quite cognizant of this information. Sexual victimization, among those who were able to provide the information, ranged from 2 years or less (*n* = 5) to 3 to 5 years (*n* = 4), to 6 to 8 years (*n* = 4), to 10 or more years (*n* = 6). Molestation began for 8 women (25%) during infancy or toddlerhood (age 3 or earlier). And 3 participants were impregnated by their abusers: one at age 11 by an older brother, another at age 13 by her biological father, and the third at age 14 while in foster care (by another foster child).

Childhood Physical and/or Emotional Abuse

Of the participants, 6 reported being victims of physical abuse during childhood by parents or parental figures; 9 reported witnessing severe and sustained domestic violence. Shan, for instance, was physically abused as a child and reported frequently witnessing her father beating her mother. She explained that although her mother was physically present, she was emotionally absent. She stated, "My mother, she just fed us. . . . She was just there." Others described similar experiences. Landis was raised in a home where domestic violence was commonplace. She was often beaten by both her mother and an older brother. About her brother she stated, "He was very violent toward me . . . . I got pregnant, and he was still beating me; my mom allowed it. It was like she didn't even care." Simply stated, the physical presence of an adult caregiver accounted for little if those caregivers failed to "act" as parental figures. Finally, verbal degradation and emotional abuse characterized relationships between several participants and their parental figures. To illustrate, Randi's older sister was accidentally killed 2 weeks prior to Randi's birth.

Randi explained how, when angry, her mother would degrade and ridicule her by saying, "I wish you were the one who died and your sister lived!" Randi's experience provides but one example of the cruelty inherent in many of the verbal assaults endured by participants during childhood. Participants often reported being told they were "no good for anything" or that they were worthless and "would never amount to anything."

Violence on the Streets

Street prostitution is a form of self-destruction. As explained by one participant, "There were times when the only way out of a situation was by the grace of God." Another reported, "Once you hit the streets, there's no guarantee you'll come back." Most participants ($n = 31$) relayed incidents of severe abuse suffered at the hands of their partners, clients, and/or pimps. Many reported having been beaten with objects, threatened with weapons, and abandoned in remote regions. Rape was commonly reported (3 had been gang raped, and 4 had been raped on multiple occasions). One participant's teeth had been knocked out by her boyfriend; she had also been raped at knifepoint by a trick. When asked to explain how she returned to the streets after being raped, she explained, "I just looked at it as not getting paid." Her response likely indicates a coping mechanism that apparently allowed her to return to the dangerous street environment without paralyzing fear and perhaps also with some level of personal dignity intact. When asked to describe her feelings of being beaten with a tire iron and left for dead, Sam responded, "I didn't care. I didn't think about it. I got 150 stitches and was back on the streets that same day." Another explained her attitude toward the potential for personal harm by saying "You just give them what they want and pray they don't kill you." Participants rarely reported crimes of victimization to authorities. One explained, "Society and law enforcement consider a prostitute getting raped or beat as something she deserves. It goes along with the lifestyle. There's nothing that you can do."

Self-Protection

During the interviews, participants were asked to describe steps they took to protect themselves from potential harm. Participants reported using the following strategies: relying on intuition in determining the "safety" of a client, meeting clients in designated areas, refusing to travel more than a few blocks with them, and making exchanges in visible areas (e.g., near street lights). One participant explicitly noted that she would not date "White men driving red trucks"; the word on the streets, she explained, was that they were "dangerous." And 3 participants reported jumping from moving vehicles after sensing danger; although most participants refused to get into clients' cars, the potential for violence was too great. Others reported always carrying weapons; as Alissa explained, "I carried a knife, and I let it be known." Physical safety, however, was never guaranteed. One woman remarked, "Every time I got in a car I knew my life was in danger; I didn't care." Moreover, despite the potential for harm, several participants ($n = 8$) reported thriving on the "excitement" of the streets, the lights, the sounds, and as one woman remarked, "It was a high just getting home alive some nights." It is possible that these women had become so emotionally numb that life-threatening situations were necessary in order to feel any sensation at all.

Yet even those women who reported feeling attraction to the glamour and the excitement of the streets also admitted that the streets held a much darker side. Tara, for instance, reported liking it when she worked the streets and then stated, "[But] I wouldn't encourage nobody to do it. It's dangerous. It's not a life to have." Similarly, Sam explained, "I was addicted to the prostitution too, to the excitement, not just the drugs . . . . I just loved it out there." After reflection, however, she described a recent experience:

We had a class and they played tapes, and we had to write down how we felt while we were listening to the songs. And they played

"Roxanne, you don't have to put on that red dress tonight," and a vision came to me. I was walking down the street at 3 or 4 in the morning, and it was drizzling and one car was going by every half hour, just lonely as could be. And it made me realize how lonely that life really was, that it wasn't anything exciting. It was lonely. It was very lonely.

In sum, participants reported extensive experience with street violence. Several indicated surprise that they were still alive. Moreover, despite the danger inherent in street work, several participants were drawn to the danger, the excitement, and the "glamour" of street prostitution; surviving life-threatening encounters created an emotional high for some of the participants.

Violence From Partners and Pimps

Not only were participants exposed to violence on the streets, they also experienced violence in their intimate relationships. In fact, despite being subjected to multiple forms of bodily injury by clients (tricks/johns), intimate partners were the source of the majority and most severe forms of abuse reported by the participants. Many were hospitalized on numerous occasions for injuries received from beatings by their partners. One received a broken eardrum. Another was shot at by her ex-husband; the bullet missed her but hit her 4-year-old daughter. Another described being beaten with a shoe for not telling her partner she was pregnant. Still another stated that her boyfriend "brought me home a disease once and then beat me for it." And Cammie, who was only 19, described how her boyfriend beat her unconscious and then drove her around a graveyard describing how he was going to bury her alive. She reported constantly having "choke marks on my neck or bruises on my face" and continued by stating, "What is really sad is that I expected that; I didn't think there was anything better for me." Several described being beaten on a weekly basis. Few sought help.

Pimp-controlled prostitution continues to exist (Williamson & Cluse-Tolar, 2002). Of participants, 17 reported having worked for a pimp, 5 women had children with men described as their pimps, and 2 reported relationships with their pimps lasting more than 10 years. Pimps were typically described as having several women working for them simultaneously, a situation described as a "stable." In this type of situation, the pimp has sexual access to all women working for him, and physical violence is frequently used to maintain power and control. Involvement with a pimp was described as beginning in one of two ways. In the first instance, a woman already involved in the sex industry may develop an ongoing relationship with a man who then begins pimping her for drug money or other desirable commodities. Eventually, she begins assisting him in finding other women to join the group (the stable), but she is generally considered the "main" woman. In this study, Tara and Monika were stable members. When asked how they felt about being one of many, each responded, "It meant less work for me."

The second process by which someone begins working for a pimp involves young females, usually runaways, who are befriended by (typically) much older men who provide them with shelter and clothing. Only later do they discover they are indebted and expected to return the favors. About the man who became her pimp when she was 14, one participant reported, "I thought he was just being a friend and helping out; I thought 'Well, cool.'" Of interest, when asked whether they had worked for a pimp, 3 participants simply responded, "The rock [crack] was my pimp." Their lives, in other words, were completely controlled by their addictions.

Participants were adamant in distinguishing relationships between men who were "partners" from those who were "pimps," although the differences were subtle. Both partners and pimps were characterized as prone to physical violence and abuse, both fathered children of the women, both were aware of the women's prostitution and drug-related activities, and often both partners and pimps introduced the women to the streets. The primary differences were described as the following: (a) Pimps typically "required" that the women make a specific amount of money; (b) the women gave all their earnings to their pimps who, in turn, provided shelter and clothing; and (c) the pimps often had several women working for them at once with whom they were also sexually involved. Women with partners not considered pimps reported personally determining the amount of money they made, controlling (at least to some degree) how it was spent, and a belief that their partners did not engage in sexual relations with others.

Of the participants, 10 indicated that although their partners were neither tricks nor pimps, their partners were aware of their prostitution activity. When asked to describe how a marriage or a similar relationship works when prostitution is involved, Mandy explained, "They're dysfunctional . . . . They [the men] are usually using [drugs], and so they want you to go out prostituting so they can have dope." This was confirmed by several women ($n = 8$) who reported being introduced to sex work by their partners, who encouraged or forced continued prostitution to support personal drug habits. Several participants indicated that their partners would babysit their children while they worked the streets; partners benefited in that the women would return with drugs or enough money to buy drugs.

Quantitative Analyses: Survey Data

Independent samples t tests were conducted to compare participants located through WellSpring ($n = 26$) with those located while incarcerated ($n = 14$) or through word of mouth ($n = 3$). Comparisons were made on all survey indices and the following demographic variables: age, education, number of children, and age when prostituting began. Only one significant difference emerged. Participants located through the WellSpring program were slightly less educated

(M = 8.5 years, $SD = 5.1$) ($F = 5.32, p < .05$) than those who were incarcerated or contacted through word of mouth (M = 10.5 years, $SD = 3.4$). All participants were then grouped together for the remaining statistical analyses.

Hypothesis 1: Active coping strategies (e.g., seeking assistance from someone else, taking action) will be positively associated with emotional and practical support. Hypothesis 1 was partially supported (see Table 9.2).

Emotional support was positively associated with two types of coping strategies: seeking social assistance ($r = .30, p < .05$) and taking action ($r = .32, p < .05$). Practical support was significantly related to taking action ($r = .32, p < .05$) and emotional support ($r = .95, p < .01$).

Hypothesis 2: Passive or potentially harm-inducing coping strategies (e.g., escapism, keeping feelings inside) will be positively associated with depression and negatively associated with emotional and practical support.

Partial support was also found for Hypothesis 2. Using escapism and internalization as coping strategies was not significantly related to depression (see Table 9.2). However, as predicted, escapism was significantly and negatively associated with seeking assistance from others ($r = -.53, p < .01$) and taking action ($r = -.35, p < .05$). Furthermore, escapism was positively associated with internalizing coping behaviors ($r = .52, p < .01$). Finally, although not predicted, taking action as a coping strategy was positively associated with seeking assistance from others ($r = .58, p < .01$).

Hypothesis 3: External locus of control will be positively associated with depression and negatively associated with emotional and practical support.

Hypothesis 3 was supported. Results indicate that external locus of control was significantly and negatively associated with emotional support ($r = -.31, p < .05$) and practical support ($r = -.30, p < .05$) and positively associated with depression (S = .59, p < .01).

Table 9.2 Correlational Analyses: Significance of Associations

	1	2	3	4	5	6	7	8	9	10	11
1. Escapism	–										
2. Talk to someone	–.53**	–									
3. Internalize	.52**	–.09	–								
4. Externalize	.14	–.04	.01	–							
5. Take action	–.35*	.58**	.15	–.20	–						
6. Emotional support	–.10	.30*	–.09	.08	.32*	–					
7. Practical support	–.06	.29	–.09	.08	.32*	.95**	–				
8. Depression	.13	–.10	–.07	.23	–.29	–.20	–.19	–			
9. Life events	.35*	–.41**	.33*	.13	–.21	.05	.11	–.04	–		
10. Locus of control	.26	–.21	–.01	.16	–.23	–.31*	–.30*	.59**	–.15	–	
11. Impulse control	.22	–.37*	–.33*	.17	–.49**	.01	.02	.23	–.07	.34*	–

*$p < .05$. **$p < .01$.

Hypothesis 4: Number of life events will be positively associated with external locus of control.

Hypothesis 4 was not supported. However, number of life events was significantly associated with *type* of coping behavior. Specifically, the greater the number of life events reported, the more likely it is that individuals reported using escapism ($r = .35$, $p < .05$) and internalizing behavior ($r = .33$, $p < .05$), and the less likely respondents were to seek assistance from others ($r = −.41$, $p < .01$).

The most commonly reported types of life events included increases in arguments or fights with parents ($n = 7$), close friend or family member died ($n = 6$), close friend or family member seriously hurt or injured ($n = 5$), became involved in counseling or therapy ($n = 5$), and decrease in amount of alcohol or drugs using ($n = 4$).

Hypothesis 5: Lower impulse control will be negatively related to talking to someone as a coping strategy and positively related to escapism and having an external locus of control.

As indicated in Table 9.2, partial support was found for the fifth hypothesis, impulse control was significantly and negatively related to talking to someone ($r = −.37$, $p < .05$) and positively related to external locus of control ($r = .34$, $p < .05$). Significant associations between impulse control and escapism were not evident. However, two unexpected findings emerged: Impulse control was negatively associated with internalizing ($r = −.33$, $p < .05$) and with taking action ($r = −.49$, $p < .01$).

Regression Analyses

Separate hierarchical multiple regression analyses assessed the effect of internal resources (Block 1) and external resources (Block 2) on each of the five coping strategies. Hypothesis 6 was partially supported. Table 9.3 shows the univariate statistics, R^2 changes from Models 1 and 2, and standardized regression weights from Model 2.

Table 9.3   Summary Statistics and Results From Regression Models

Copying Strategy	Internal or External Resource	R^2 Change		Standardized Regression Weights From Model 2
		Model 1	Model 2	
Active		.26**	.10*	
	Depression			−.14
	Locus of control			.12
	Impulse control			−.49**
	Practical support			.33*
Social		.14	.09*	
	Depression			.08
	Locus of control			−.02
	Impulse control			−.38*
	Emotional support			.31*

Copying Strategy	Internal or External Resource	R² Change		Standardized Regression Weights From Model 2
		Model 1	Model 2	
Internalizing		.12		
	Depression			−.06
	Locus of control			.15
	Impulse control			−.36*
	Emotional support			−
	Practical support			−
Externalizing		.06		
	Depression			.19
	Locus of control			.01
	Impulse control			.12
	Emotional support			−
	Practical support			−
Escapism		.09		
	Depression			−.06
	Locus of control			.24
	Impulse control			.15
	Emotional support			−
	Practical support			−

NOTE: *$p < .05$. **$p < .01$.

For active coping strategies (i.e., doing something about the problem), Model 1 with all three internal resource variables had an $R^2 = .26$, adjusted $R^2 = .20$, F(3, 39) change = 4.49, $p < .01$, with impulse control having a negative significant regression weight, indicating impulse control was negatively associated with using active coping strategies. Model 2, with external resource variables added, had an R^2 change = .10, F(3,39) change = 5.95, $p < .05$, with practical support and impulse control having significant regression weights. Emotional support was excluded from Model 2, indicating that given all other variables, emotional support did not contribute significantly to variations in choosing active coping strategies.

For social coping strategies (e.g., talking to someone), Model 1 with internal resource variables (Block 1) had an $R^2 = .14$, adjusted $R^2 = .11$, F(l, 41) change = 6.38, p = .01. Impulse control had a negative significant regression weight, indicating that impulse control was negatively associated with social coping strategies but not the two other internal resources (i.e., depression, locus of control). Model 2 retained all three internal resource variables and emotional support when external resource variables (Block 2) were added in the analysis, with an R^2 change = .09, F(3,39) change = 5.95, $p < .05$. Emotional support had a positive significant regression weight, and impulse control had a negative significant regression weight, indicating that higher levels of social coping was significantly related to less impulse control and more perceived emotional support. Simply stated, after controlling internal resources, perceived emotional support was a significant predictor of using social coping strategies.

Hierarchical regression models for escapism, internalizing, and externalizing did not exhibit significant R^2 change and F values. External resource variables were excluded from the models for these coping strategies. For escapism, R^2 change = .09, F(3, 39) change = 1.28, $p > .05$. For internalizing, R^2 change = .12, F(3,39) change = 1.80, $p > .05$. For externalizing, R^2 change = .06, F(3,39) change = 0.89, $p > .05$. Internal and external resources were not found to be significantly associated with escapism, internalizing, or externalizing except for impulse control, which had a negative significant regression weight in the model for internalizing coping strategies.

Discussion

Certain populations, including women and individuals residing in deviant or crime-infested contexts, are particularly vulnerable to the threat of psychological and physical harm. This investigation sought to examine victimization across the life span and from a theoretical frame of reference among street-level sex workers, specifically. The uniqueness of this investigation lies not in the phenomenon under examination (i.e., victimization); exposure to violence among street workers has been well documented. However, this investigation provides multiple types of data (qualitative interviews and self-report survey indices) and a manner for conceptualizing that information (through stress theory) for enhanced programmatic planning and intervention purposes.

Simply stated, victimization may exert profound impacts on an individual's sense of security and agency and may significantly diminish optimal well-being. According to stress theory, assessment of threat or harm is an individual-specific phenomenon based largely on primary (cognitive registration of the event) and secondary (evaluation of internal and external resources) appraisals for determining responses (i.e., coping strategies). The manner in which one copes with or responds to potentially threatening circumstances may or may not be effective and may or may not present additional challenges to well-being. For instance, drug use is commonly reported among street-level prostituted women and serves as a form of escapism, but for many, chemical addiction furthers the necessity of remaining on the streets to support the addiction. Such information is valuable for assisting street workers in responding more effectively to their dangerous environmental contexts and social service agencies in providing optimal intervention.

Results from intensive interviews revealed lifelong patterns of abuse and victimization. Participants overwhelmingly reported experiencing sexual, physical, and/or verbal abuse and witnessing various forms of domestic violence during their formative years. Unfortunately, victimization continued into their adult lives. Not surprisingly, violence on the streets from pimps, strangers, and clients was a commonly reported phenomenon and largely supports findings from previous investigations (Maher, 1996; Raphael & Shapiro, 2002) documenting the vulnerability of women engaged in street-level prostitution to various forms of victimization. Unexpectedly, however, participants reported experiencing greater and more severe violence from intimate partners than from clients or strangers. Significantly, although participants clearly distinguished partners from pimps, the behaviors of both were described as frighteningly similar. Williamson and Cluse-Tolar (2002) drew parallels between pimp-controlled prostituted women and women experiencing domestic violence by intimates. Both types of relationships are ultimately based on power and control, and more importantly, both types of relationships provide the women with certain "needs," which may include a sense of love and belonging (Williamson & Cluse-Tolar, 2002). When a prostituted woman's primary source of support is her partner or pimp, who benefits greatly from her prostitution activities, the challenges for leaving prostitution rise exponentially. Women who have experienced an entire life of victimization are most at risk for remaining with abusive men and least likely to expect otherwise.

These data have strong implications for intervention. Violence perpetrated by strangers likely has different consequences than prolonged violence from intimates; domestic violence intervention services must address the multiple sources of violence experienced across the life span by women attempting to leave the streets. In addition, finding safe housing is a priority for effectively assisting female sex workers; it cannot be assumed that having a place of residence (i.e., not homeless or living on the streets) means living within an environment free of assaultive behaviors. Correlational analyses provide additional data significant for providing effective, comprehensive intervention. First, assisting prostituting women in forming healthy social support systems (e.g., with mentors, sponsors, prostitution survivors) is critical. Turning to others for assistance, emotional and physical, was strongly related to more positive coping strategies (e.g., taking action) and negatively related to health-compromising coping behaviors (i.e., escapism). Moreover, emotional and practical support were negatively associated with external locus of control, indicating that lack of supportive relations (or inability to access those resources) is related to a lower sense of agency or competence in affecting one's environment.

Of concern also is the strong correlation between use of escapism and internalization as coping strategies; both challenge the development

and maintenance of healthy support network relationships and likely feed off one another to create a cycle of self-compromising behaviors, when seeking assistance could offer more positive outcomes to stress-inducing circumstances.

Interesting also was that number of life events was negatively associated with seeking assistance from others. Lacking causal data, it is equally likely that individuals experiencing numerous stress events within a relatively brief amount of time (one year) overwhelm support network members, thus creating a sense that one cannot turn to others as additional events occur. On the other hand, it could be argued that lacking rich emotional and practical support systems, individuals are more likely to take greater risks or rely on themselves out of necessity, thus resulting in more stressful life events. Regardless, correlational analyses reveal the need, both directly and indirectly, for intervention and prevention programs to provide educational and practical guidance in establishing, accessing, and maintaining strong (and health-promoting) networks of support.

Despite the valuable findings presented here, future work using path analyses to test (rather than simply explore) the theoretical model (i.e., stress theory) among this vulnerable population is warranted. Such data will reveal particular points for intervention and preventive efforts. More specifically, it may be revealed that present theoretical models do not adequately capture the phenomenon of interest when applied to particularly vulnerable populations. New theoretical models, with preventive goals, may be warranted. Finally, limitations of the present investigation must be acknowledged. First, each participant was interviewed at one point only. Thus, process data (i.e., examining change through time) are impossible. Second, participants reported experiences throughout the life course; childhood events were described retrospectively. Despite the clarity with which childhood phenomena and exposure to victimization were reported, memories of the formative years are nonetheless filtered and interpreted through an adult lens. Third, despite an attempt to obtain a diversified sample of prostituted women (i.e., through an intervention program, word of mouth, and prison), the data reflect a nonrandom participant group.

Finally, a recent investigation of prostitution in the Chicago metropolitan area (Raphael & Shapiro, 2002) reveals significant violence perpetrated against prostituting women *generally* (not only street workers). Violence against vulnerable female populations is not open for debate as it cannot be denied. The task of academicians is to conduct rigorous research that enables service providers and policy advocates to apply attendant data to real-life phenomena as a means of enhancing overall well-being for *all* at-risk female populations.

References

Arboleda-Flores, J., & Wade, T. (1999, August). *Childhood and adult victimization as risk factors for major depression.* Paper presented at the annual meeting of the American Psychological Association, Washington, DC.

Aronson, J. (1994). A pragmatic view of thematic analysis. *Qualitative Report, 2*(1), 1–3.

Bagley, C., Bolitho, F., & Bertrand, L. (1997). Sexual assault in school, mental health, and suicidal behaviors in adolescent women in Canada. *Adolescence, 32,* 341–366.

Bagley, C., & Ramsey, R. (1986). Sexual abuse in childhood: Psychosocial outcomes and implications for social work practice. *Journal of Social Work and Human Sexuality, 4,* 33–47.

Bagley, C., & Young, L. (1987). Juvenile prostitution and child sexual abuse: A controlled study. *Canadian Journal of Community Mental Health, 6,* 5–26.

Barry, K. (1995). *The prostitution of sexuality: The global exploitation of women.* New York: New York University Press.

Burnam, A., Stein, J., Golding, J., Siegel, J., Sorenson, S., Forsythe, A., et al. (1988). Sexual assault and mental disorders in a community population. *Journal of Consulting and Clinical Psychology, 56,* 843–850.

Cavaiola, A., & Schiff, M. (1988). Behavioral sequelae of physical and/or sexual abuse in adolescents. *Child Abuse & Neglect, 12,* 181–188.

Chu, J., & Dill, D. (1990). Dissociative symptoms in relation to childhood physical and sexual abuse. *American Journal of Psychiatry, 147,* 887–892.

Church, S., Henderson, M., Barnoar, M., & Hart, G. (2001). Violence by clients towards female prostitutes in different work settings. *British Medical Journal, 322,* 524–527.

Conte, J. R., & Schuerman, J. R. (1987). Factors associated with an increased impact of child sexual abuse. *Child Abuse & Neglect, 11,* 201–211.

Dalla, R. L. (2000). Exposing the "pretty woman" myth: A qualitative investigation of the lives of female streetwalkers. *Journal of Sex Research, 37,* 344–353.

Dalla, R. L. (2001). Et tu Bruté: A qualitative analysis of streetwalking prostitutes' interpersonal support networks. *Journal of Family Issues, 22,* 1066–1085.

Dalla, R. L. (2002). Night moves: A qualitative investigation of street-level sex work. *Psychology of Women Quarterly, 26,* 63–73.

Farley, M., & Barkan, H. (1998). Prostitution, violence, and posttraumatic stress disorder. *Women & Health, 27,* 37–49.

Faugier, J., & Sargeant, M. (1997). Boyfriends, "pimps" and clients. In G. Scambler & A. Scambler (Eds.), *Rethinking prostitution: Purchasing sex in the 1990s* (pp. 121–136). New York: Routledge.

Feucht, T. E. (1993). Prostitutes on crack cocaine: Addiction, utility, and marketplace economics. *Deviant Behavior, 14,* 91–108.

Finkelhor, D. (1987). The trauma of child sexual abuse: Two models. *Journal of Interpersonal Violence, 2,* 348–366.

Fullilove, M., Lown, A., & Fullilove, R. (1992). Crack 'hos and skeezers: Traumatic experiences of women crack users. *Journal of Sex Research, 29,* 275–287.

Goldstein, P. J. (1979). *Prostitution and drugs.* Lexington, MA: Lexington Books.

Graham, N., & Wish, E. D. (1994). Drug use among female arrestees: Onset, patterns, and relationships to prostitution. *Journal of Drug Issues, 24,* 315–329.

Hagan, J. (1989). *Structural criminology.* New Brunswick, NJ: Rutgers University Press.

Hagan, J., & McCarthy, B. (1997). *Mean streets: Youth crime and homelessness.* New York: Cambridge University Press.

Hammer, A. L., & Marting, M. S. (1987). *Coping Resources Inventory-Form D.* Palo Alto, CA: Consulting Psychologists Press.

Inciardi, J. (1995). Crack, crack house sex, and HIV risk. *Archives of Sexual Behavior, 24,* 249–269.

Inciardi, J. A., Lockwood, D., & Pottieger, A. E. (1993). *Women and crack cocaine.* New York: Macmillan.

Jones, D., Irwin, K., Inciardi, J., Bowser, B., Schilling, R., Word, C, et al. (1998). The high-risk sexual practices of crack-smoking sex workers recruited from the streets of three American cities. *Sexually Transmitted Diseases, 3,* 187–193.

Kessler, R., & Magee, W. (1994). Childhood family violence and adult recurrent depression. *Journal of Health and Sociological Behavior, 35,* 13–27.

Lazarus, R. (1966). *Psychological stress and the coping process.* New York: McGraw-Hill.

Lazarus, R., & Folkman, S. (1984). *Stress, appraisal, and coping.* New York: Springer.

Lazarus, R., & Launier, R. (1978). Stress-related transactions between person and environment. In L. A. Pervin & M. Lewis (Eds.), *Perspectives in interactional psychology* (pp. 287–327). New York: Plenum.

Lewis, D., Shanok, S., & Balla, D. (1979). Perinatal difficulties, head and face trauma, and child abuse in the medical histories of seriously delinquent children. *American Journal of Psychiatry, 136,* 419–423.

MacMillan, R. (2001). Violence and the life course: The consequences of victimization for personal and social development. *Annual Review of Sociology, 27,* 1–22.

Maher, L. (1996). Hidden in the light: Occupational norms among crack-using street-level sex workers. *Journal of Drug Issues, 26,* 143–173.

Matheny, K. B., Aycock, K. B., Pugh, J. L., Curlette, W. L., & Cannella, K.A.S. (1986). Stress coping: A qualitative and quantitative synthesis and implications for treatment. *The Counseling Psychologist, 14,* 499–549.

McClanahan, S. R, McClelland, G. M., Abram, K. M., & Teplin, L. A. (1999). Pathways into prostitution among female jail detainees and their implications for mental health service. *Psychiatric Services, 50,* 1606–1613.

McLeer, S., Deblinger, E., Atkins, M., Foa, E., & Ralphe, D. (1988). Post-traumatic stress disorder in sexually abused children. *Journal of the American Academy of Child and Adolescent Psychiatry, 27,* 650–654.

Menard, S. (2001). Short and long term consequences of criminal victimization. In S. Menard, D. Huizinga, & D. Elliott (Eds.), *Violent behavior in the life course* (pp. 110–126). Thousand Oaks, CA: Sage.

Miller, J. (1993). "Your life is on the line every night you're on the streets": Victimization and resistance among street prostitutes. *Humanity & Society, 17,* 422–445.

Miller, J. (1995). Gender and power on the streets: Street prostitution in the era of crack cocaine. *Journal of Contemporary Ethnography, 23,* 427–452.

Nandon, S. M., Koverola, C., & Schludermann, E. H. (1998). Antecedents to prostitution: Childhood victimization. *Journal of Interpersonal Violence, 13,* 206–221.

Norbeck, J. S., Lindsey, A. M., & Carrieri, V L. (1981). The development of an instrument to measure social support. *Nursing Research, 30,* 264–269.

Norbeck, J. S., Lindsey, A. M., & Carrieri, V. L. (1982). Further development of the Norbeck Social Support Questionnaire: Normative data and validity testing. *Nursing Research, 32,* 4–9.

Norris, F., Kaniasty, K., & Thompson, M. (1997). The psychological consequences of crime: Findings from a longitudinal population-based study. In R. Davis, A. Lurigio, & W. Skogan (Eds.), *Victims of crime* (2nd ed., pp. 146–166). Thousand Oaks, CA: Sage.

Olson, D. H., McCubbin, H. I., Barnes, H., Larsen, A., Muxen, M., & Wilson, L. (1982). *Family inventories: Inventories used in a national survey of families across the life cycle.* Unpublished manuscript, University of Minnesota, St. Paul.

Overall, C. (1992). What's wrong with prostitution? Evaluating sex work. *Signs, 17,* 705–724.

Pheterson, G. (1990). The category "prostitute" in scientific inquiry. *Journal of Sex Research, 27,* 397–407.

Potterat, J. J., Rothenberg, R. B., Muth, S. Q., Darrow, W. W., & Phillips-Plummer, L. (1998). Pathways to prostitution: The chronology of sexual and drug milestones. *Journal of Sex Research, 35,* 333–340.

Raphael, J., & Shapiro, D. (2002). *Sisters speak out: The lives and needs of prostituted women in Chicago.* Chicago: Center for Impact Research.

Russell, D. E. H. (1988). The incidence and prevalence of intrafamilial and extrafamilial sexual abuse on female children. In L. E. A. Walker (Ed.), *Handbook on sexual abuse of children* (pp. 19–36). New York: Springer.

Sampson, R., & Lauritsen, J. (1994). Violence victimization and offending: Individual-, situational-, and community-level risk factors. In A. Reiss & J. Roth (Eds.), *Understanding and preventing violence* (Vol. 3, pp. 1–114). Washington, DC: National Academy Press.

Sauzier, M., Salt, P., & Calhoun, R. (1990). The effects of child sexual abuse. In B. Gomes-Schwartz, J. M. Horowitz, & A. P. Cardarelli (Eds.), *Child sexual abuse: The initial effects* (pp. 75–108). Newbury Park, CA: Sage.

Seng, M. J. (1989). Child sexual abuse and adolescent prostitution: A comparative analysis. *Adolescence, 24,* 665–675.

Silbert, M. H., & Pines, A. M. (1982). Victimization of street prostitutes. *Victimology: An International Journal, 7,* 122–133.

Silbert, M. H., & Pines, A. M. (1983). Early sexual exploitation as an influence in prostitution. *Social Work, 28,* 285–289.

Simons, R. R., & Whitbeck, L. B. (1991). Sexual abuse as a precursor to prostitution and victimization among adolescent and adult homeless women. *Journal of Family Issues, 12,* 361–379.

Sterk, C., & Elifson, K. (1990). Drug-related violence and street prostitution. In M. De La Rosa, E. Lambert, & B. Gropper (Eds.), *Drugs and violence: Causes, correlations, and consequences* (pp. 208–221). Rockville, MD: National Institute on Drug Abuse.

Taylor, S. J., & Bogdan, R. (1984). *Introduction to qualitative research methods: The search for meaning.* New York: John Wiley

Watts, C., & Zimmerman, C. (2002). Violence against women: Global scope and magnitude. *Lancet, 359,* 1232–1244.

White, S., Halpin, B., Strom, G., & Santilli, G. (1988). Behavioral comparisons of young sexually abused, neglected, and nonreferred children. *Journal of Clinical Child Psychology, 17,* 53–61.

Williamson, C., & Cluse-Tolar, T. (2002). Pimp-controlled prostitution: Still an integral part of street life. *Violence Against Women, 8,* 1074–1092.

Williamson, C., & Folaron, G. (2001). Violence, risk, and survival strategies of street prostitution. *Western Journal of Nursing Research, 23,* 463–475.

CHAPTER 10

Attitudes Toward Wife Beating

A Cross-Country Study in Asia

Manju Rani and Sekhar Bonu

ntimate partner violence (IPV) against women violates the basic human rights of women (Burton, Duvvury, & Varia, 2000). The high prevalence of IPV directed toward women documented in both developing and developed countries (Heise, Ellsberg, & Gottemoeller, 1999) appropriately qualifies it as a "hidden and unacknowledged epidemic" (Coeling & Harnan, 1997). Recent research highlights that such abuse has intergenerational (Jewkes, Jonathan, & Penn-Kekana, 2002; Martin et al., 1999; Rao & Bloch, 1993) and socioeconomic (Morrison & Biehl, 1999) impacts as well as effects on fetal and infant mortality (Jejeebhoy,1998a) and on health burdens of affected women (Heise, Pitanguy, & Germain, 1994; World Health Organization, 1999a). The Forty-Ninth World Health Assembly Resolution declared the prevention of violence, including gender-based violence, as a public

health priority (World Health Organization, 1999b).

Wife beating—one of the specific aspects of IPV—is frequently viewed as physical chastisement: the husband's right to "correct" an erring wife (Jejeebhoy, 1998b; Straus, 1976). Wife-beating prevalence is believed to be widespread across Asia despite substantial intercountry differences in economic development and in the female literacy and labor force participation rates. For example, estimates of ever experiencing IPV by women in Bangladesh varied from 35% to 42% (Bates, Schuler, Islam, & Islam, 2004). Almost 11% and 19% of ever-married women in India and Bangladesh, respectively, in South Asia reported wife beating in the past 12 months (International Institute for Population Sciences & ORC Macro, 2000; Schuler, Syed, Riley, & Shireen, 1996). Similar estimates of wife beating

Rani, M., & Bonu, S. (2009). Attitudes toward wife beating: A cross-country study in Asia. *Journal of Interpersonal Violence, 24,* 1371–1397.

in the past 12 months (11%) were observed in Cambodia, one of the poorest countries in East Asia (National Institute of Statistics, Directorate General for Health [Cambodia], & ORC Macro, 2001). Wife beating is also perceived to be widespread in West and Central Asia. A study in Turkey found that almost 58% of women reported having an experience of violence (Ilkkaracan, 1998). In Egypt, one third of women reported being beaten ever since marriage (El-Zanaty, Hussein, Shawky, Way, & Kishor, 1996).

Comprehending the underlying attitudes toward wife beating may be indispensable to understand dynamics of wife beating and to design effective interventions. Quantification of attitudes toward wife beating may also help us to understand the actual prevalence, as respondents may feel less hesitant in reporting how they feel about different issues on wife beating than in reporting personal experience of IPV. However, empirical evidence is limited on the extent of acceptance of wife beating and the factors that predict those attitudes in Asia.

Although the literature on IPV suggests that violence is directed toward the woman in most of the instances, the differentials in attitudes toward wife beating by sex are not well documented. Do women, as victims of violence, disapprove of it and men as perpetrators of violence strongly support it? Most of the evidence on attitudes toward domestic violence is either based on responses of only women (Haj-Yahia, 1998, 2002; Kim & Mmatshilo, 2002) or only men (Fikree, Razzak, & Durocher, 2005; Martin et al., 1999). Few studies that include responses from both men and women suggest that either both genders share similar attitudes toward wife beating (Heise et al., 1999) or that in some settings, women may even justify wife beating more than men (Rani, Bonu, & Diop-Sidibé, 2004). More empirical evidence in Asia is needed about differentials in the underlying attitudes and their determinants among men and women to inform programmatic interventions.

What factors influence attitudes toward wife beating? Will the current socioeconomic changes associated with economic growth, urbanization, and increasing female literacy and labor force participation change the attitudes toward wife beating and, in turn, the practice of wife beating, on their own? Studies that examined determinants of wife beating documented higher socioeconomic status and higher female literacy rates being associated with lower reporting of experience of wife beating (Bates et al., 2004; El-Zanaty et al., 1996; Heise et al., 1999; Koenig, Ahmed, Hossain, & Mozumder, 2003; Schuler et al., 1996). However, these reported differences in the actual experience of wife beating by socioeconomic status and female education may just be artefacts of reporting bias because of potential differentials in social stigma attached with wife beating in different socioeconomic population groups. Examining these differentials in attitudes toward wife beating may provide a better picture. In addition, comparative studies of countries at different socioeconomic stages may provide insights into the potential role of socioeconomic development over time in changing the norms toward wife beating. However, there are few comparative studies on determinants of acceptance of wife beating in Asia, and more empirical evidence is needed in this area.

Life cycle and familial factors have also been documented to be important predictors of experience of wife beating, with decreasing risk of violence with increasing age of husband or wife and with having a living son (Schuler et al., 1996). Many studies that examined the relationship between indicators of wife beating and women's autonomy noted mixed results. Domination of major household decisions by women was associated with higher risk of wife beating in the Philippines (Hindin & Adair, 2002). Similarly, participation of women in credit and saving groups in Bangladesh and having personal earnings that contribute more than nominally to marital household led to increased experience of IPV (Bates et al., 2004; Koenig et al., 2003; Rahman, 1999). Although associations of these factors (life cycle and familial factors, women's autonomy) have been examined with actual experience of wife beating, it would be interesting to examine how these factors shape attitudes toward wife beating. If, indeed, higher female autonomy leads to favorable change in attitudes toward wife beating, declines in actual practice may be expected in the long term, though short-term increases in practice may be observed, especially if a corresponding change in attitudes among men does not take place or is slow to happen.

This study uses data from the demographic and health surveys conducted in seven Asian countries—three in South Asia (Bangladesh, India, and Nepal), one in East Asia (Cambodia), and three in Central and West Asia (Armenia, Kazakhstan, and Turkey)—to provide comparative empirical evidence for the following:

1. Quantitative estimates of acceptance for wife beating for transgression of specified gender norms in selected Asian countries at different stages of socioeconomic development;

2. Differences in the levels and predictors of attitudes between women and men toward acceptance of wife beating: Four (Armenia, Kazakhstan, Nepal, and Turkey) out of seven countries included in this study have comparable data available for both men and women, allowing us to assess the gender differentials in the extent of acceptance and in the predictors for acceptance of wife beating. We hypothesize that the effect of the enabling factors on reducing the acceptance of wife beating will be higher among women than among men, at least in the short run, as men may not easily give up their traditional privileges.

3. Predictors of acceptance of wife beating across countries with different socioeconomic and cultural settings: We use a conceptual framework based on social learning theory (Bandura, 1977) and ecological model (Heise et al., 1999) to examine the predictors of acceptance of wife beating. The conceptual framework has been explained in detail elsewhere (Rani et al., 2004). Based on this conceptual framework and literature review, predictor variables were selected that may influence attitudes toward gender norms and wife beating by producing a conflict between reality and myth of male superiority (e.g., increasing female education and economic empowerment of women bringing them on par with men), by exposure to more egalitarian social networks and authority structures other than kinship-based ones (e.g., attending school, working outside the home, urbanization), and by exposure to nonconformist ideas (e.g., through education).

The comparative analysis will help to examine whether the association with a particular enabling factor will be context specific.

Study Setting

Table 10.1 presents the sociodemographic characteristics of the countries included in the study. Although all the three South Asian countries and Cambodia represent the low-income and predominantly rural countries, Turkey represents a middle-income country, and Armenia and Kazakhstan represent the transitional economies. In addition, although South Asian countries and Cambodia report high levels of female illiteracy, Armenia, Kazakhstan, and Turkey fare relatively well on this indicator (see Table 10.1). In addition, the custom of dowry is most prevalent in South Asian countries. The main religion varied from Islam in Turkey and Bangladesh, to Christianity in Armenia, to Hinduism in India and Nepal, to Buddhism in Cambodia. The political environment and visibility given to domestic violence also varies greatly across these countries. Turkey and India had specific legal provisions

Table 10.1   Selected Socioeconomic, Demographic, and Legal Characteristics of the Countries Included in the Study

Country	Gross National Income per Capita (US$)–2002[a]	% Rural	% Female Labor Force Activity Rates (Age 15–64)	Female Illiteracy Rate % (15 and older)	Dominant Religion	Laws Dealing Specifically With Domestic Violence[b]
Armenia	800	33	48	2	Christianity (99%)	No
Kazakhstan	1,520	44	45	3	Islam (56%)	No
Turkey	2,510	34	37	23	Islam (93%)	Yes
Bangladesh	380	74	46	69	Islam (86%)	Yes
India	470	72	30	54	Hindu (81%)	Yes
Nepal	230	88	38	75	Hindu (85%)	No
Cambodia	300	83	53	42	Buddhism (96%)	Yes

SOURCE: Rest of the data were calculated by the authors from the household survey data used in this study. a. The World Bank (2002) provided GNP data. b. Literature review.

pertaining to domestic violence before these surveys were conducted, although domestic violence laws were brought into effect in Cambodia and Bangladesh in 2005 and 2006, respectively. In Kazakhstan, the president declared the fight against domestic violence to be a national priority in 1998, though there are no explicit laws against domestic violence, as is the case in Armenia and Nepal. There are shelters for women—though mainly for destitute and abandoned women and perhaps not specifically for battered women—in almost all of these countries run by either nongovernmental organizations or government. However, these facilities are very limited, are badly maintained, and generally carry stigma.

Data and Method

The data for the study came from Demographic and Health Surveys (DHS) implemented between 1998 and 2001 by the respective country's national institutions and Macro International Inc., with financial support by the U.S. Agency for International Development. DHS's are nationally representative, cross-sectional, household sample surveys with large sample sizes, typically between 5,000 and 15,000 households (with the exception of India, where the total sample size is about 80,000 households). The sampling design in most cases typically involves selecting a nationally representative probability sample of women aged

15 to 49 and men aged 15 to 59 years based on multistage cluster sampling, using strata for rural and urban areas, and different regions of the countries (Macro International Inc., 1996). However, no survey of men was conducted in India and in Cambodia, although data on attitudes toward wife beating were collected only from men in Bangladesh. The survey instruments—household, women's, and men's questionnaires—are comparable across different countries, yielding intercountry comparable data.

To assess women's and men's degree of acceptance of wife beating, the respondents were asked, "Sometimes a husband is annoyed or angered by things which his wife does. In your opinion, is a husband justified in hitting or beating his wife in the following situations?" The following five scenarios were presented to the respondents for their opinions in most of the countries: if the wife burns food, if she argues with her husband, if she goes out without informing her husband, if she neglects her children, and if she refuses to have sexual relations with her husband. Slightly different situations were given in India and Turkey to reflect the local culture and norms. For example, in India, these included "when the wife's parents don't give adequate dowry," "[she] shows disrespect to in-laws," and "[he] suspects her of being unfaithful"; and in Turkey, it included "talking to other men" and "spending needlessly." The scenario on "refusing sexual relations" was not presented in Bangladesh and India. The exact wording of the questions asked in each country is presented later. In each situation, the respondent was asked to reply either *yes*, *no*, or *don't know* if he or she did not have any opinion.

Although women's surveys included both married and nonmarried respondents in Armenia, Cambodia, Kazakhstan, and Turkey, only ever-married respondents were sampled in India and Nepal. For men's surveys, both married and nonmarried respondents were included in Armenia and Kazakhstan, only ever-married

men in Nepal, and only currently married men in Bangladesh and Turkey.

Weighted percentages were calculated for both women and men who justified wife beating in each specific situation or justified wife beating in at least one of the situations presented to examine the overall extent of acceptance. Bivariate analyses were conducted to explore the unadjusted relationship between different sociodemographic characteristics and justification of wife beating for any reason.

A multivariate logistic regression was estimated separately for men and women in each country to assess the independent association of different explanatory variables with acceptance of wife beating. A binary outcome variable was created for acceptance of wife beating, coded as 0 if the respondent did not agree with any of situations when a husband was justified in beating the wife or did not have any opinion on the issue and coded as 1 if the respondent agreed with at least one situation when the husband was justified in beating the wife.

The explanatory variables in multivariate logistic regression models included individual-level demographic characteristics (age, sex composition of the living children, marital status, and duration of marriage) and socioeconomic characteristics (number of years of schooling, employment status, and contribution toward total household expenditure). The household characteristics included household wealth and religion. Because of a lack of data on the traditional measures of income—expenditure or consumption—an index of household wealth based on principal components analysis of household assets was constructed to measure the socioeconomic status of the household following the method used by Filmer and Pritchett (1998). The only community-level explanatory variable included in the analysis was urban or rural residence. Table 10.2 gives the definition, specification, and distribution of the sample by selected explanatory variables used in the multivariate logistic models.

In Armenia, Kazakhstan, Turkey, and Nepal—where data were available for both men and

Table 10.2 Sample Distribution by Selected Socioeconomic and Demographic Characteristics

	Armenia		Kazakhstan		Turkey		Nepal		Bangladesh	India	Cambodia
	Female	Male	Female	Male	Female	Male	Female	Male	Male	Female	Female
Year of Survey	2001	2001	1999	1999	1998	1998	2000	2000	2000	1998–99	2000
Sample size	6,430	1,719	4,800	1,440	8,565	1,966	8,726	2,261	2,556	89,199	3,741
Urban (%)	61.3	59.6	55.6	54.9	66.5	68.3	9.6	10	19.9	28.1	17.5
Education (%)											
None	0.0	0.2	0.0	0.0	16.7	6.6	72.0	37.7	34.9	53.4	28.2
Primary	0.4	0.3	0.6	45.9	53.0	46.6	14.8	29.7	30.6	16.9	54.6
Secondary	80.1	77.6	79.3	40.3	23.5	33.9	12.0	27.1	23.1	15.4	16.8
Higher	18.7	21.9	20.1	13.8	6.8	12.9	1.2	5.6	11.5	14.2	0.4
Age (%)											
15–19	18.1	15.3	16.5	15.7	20.1	0.0	10.8	3.1	0.9	9.2	23.6
20–29	27.6	23.8	28.3	24.8	34.5	23.1	38.1	28.1	19.4	38.3	26.7
30–39	26.8	25.7	30.2	27.8	26.6	36.3	29.7	29.5	35.6	31.6	28.4
40–49	27.5	27.8	25.1	19.9	18.9	29.2	21.4	22.3	28.4	21.0	21.3
50–59	NA	7.3	NA	11.8	0.0	11.4	NA	17.1	15.6	NA	NA

	Armenia		Kazakhstan		Turkey		Nepal		Bangladesh	India	Cambodia
	Female	Male	Female	Male	Female	Male	Female	Male	Male	Female	Female
Year of Survey	2001	2001	1999	1999	1998	1998	2000	2000	2000	1998–99	2000
Marital status											
Currently married	64.1	67.6	62.9	64.8	69.0	100.0	95.6	97.2	100.0	93.8	59.1
Widowed/divorced	7.1	1.6	11.8	5.1	3.2	NA	4.4	2.8	NA	6.2	9.1
Marital duration											
0–9 years	22.1	22.7	26.3	22.2	28.7	39.3	38.9	32.9	36.0	38.0	22.9
10–19 years	34.3	32.5	36.1	32.2	22.5	30.2	42.2	40.2	43.7	33.0	29.7
20–29 years	13.2	12.4	11.3	8.5	17.5	24.0	12.1	10.5	10.7	23.0	12.6
30-plus years	1.7	1.6	1.0	7.1	3.6	6.6	6.8	16.5	9.7	5.9	3.0
Never married	28.8	30.8	25.3	30.1	27.8	NA	NA	NA	NA	NA	31.8
Sex composition of living children											
Daughter only	11.4	10.4	17.5	14.0	12.2	16.6	14.5	NA	15.1	14.0	10.8
Only sons	17.5	15.4	19.7	14.7	15.3	20.5	18.3	NA	19.3	19.9	12.3

(Continued)

(Continued)

	Armenia		Kazakhstan		Turkey		Nepal		Bangladesh	India	Cambodia
	Female	Male	Female	Male	Female	Male	Female	Male	Male	Female	Female
Year of Survey	2001	2001	1999	1999	1998	1998	2000	2000	2000	1998–99	2000
Has a son and daughter	38.1	38.4	34.2	36.1	37.3	53.4	55.1	NA	55.7	54.1	40.6
No children	33.0	35.8	28.6	35.2	29.2	9.5	12.1	NA	9.9	12.1	36.3
Employment											
Not working	88.0	44.2	53.4	NA	60.8	8.3	23.9	2.2	NA	60.9	18.3
Non-cash employment	10.2	15.2	5.0	NA	15.4	3.8	59.8	41.8	NA	12.9	13.3
Cash-paying employment	1.8	40.6	41.4	NA	23.8	87.9	16.3	56.0	NA	26.2	68.4
Contribution to HH expenditure											
< 50%	95.2	80.5	74.3	NA	91	NA	98.1	63.6	NA	88.6	70.6
50%	3.0	7.8	9.6	NA	5.0	NA	1.0	9.3	NA	4.8	5.6
> 50%	1.9	11.7	16.2	NA	4.0	NA	0.9	27.1	NA	6.6	23.8

NOTE: NA = not available; HH = household.

women—a model using pooled data from both male and female respondents was also fitted to test the significance of gender differences in acceptance of wife beating as well to test the significance of interaction between gender and socioeconomic characteristics such as urban residence, wealth, education, and employment status. However, the results from the pooled models are not shown for the sake of brevity, as the findings from these models just corroborate the finding from the models fitted separately for men and women.

Results

Justification of Wife Beating in Different Circumstances

The proportion of women justifying wife beating for at least one of the reasons ranged from 29% in Nepal to 57% in India. The acceptance of wife beating among men varied from 26% in Kazakhstan to 56% in Turkey (see Table 10.3).

Both men and women were least likely to approve of wife beating for reasons related to food preparation and her refusal to have sexual relations (see Table 10.3). In India, almost 33% of women justified wife beating if the husband suspects his wife of infidelity, and in Turkey, 22% of women and 36% of men justified wife beating if the wife talks to other men.

With few exceptions, neglecting children was the most common reason agreed to by both women and men as a justification for wife beating, followed by arguing back with the husband and going out without informing the husband.

Predictors of Acceptance of Wife Beating

Table 10.4 presents the bivariate relationship between different demographic, household, and socioeconomic characteristics of respondents and the probability of accepting wife beating.

Urban residence, household wealth, and education levels emerged as the three most consistent negative predictors of wife beating across almost all the countries with few exceptions. However, some of the associations seen in bivariate analysis may be confounded by other variables. For example, the relationship seen with urban residence may be caused by household wealth or education if wealthier and more educated populations are disproportionately distributed in urban areas. Similarly, the relationship with employment status or contribution to household expenditures may also be confounded by the household wealth and education.

Results From Multivariate Analysis

Socioeconomic Predictors

Though in the bivariate analysis, urban respondents were less likely to justify wife beating (except Nepalese women, where the association was in the opposite direction and was not significant; see Table 10.4), the relationship remains significant only among women in Armenia in the multivariate analysis (see Table 10.5).

Higher household wealth was associated with lower acceptance among both men and women in three of the richest countries (Armenia, Kazakhstan, and Turkey) and in Bangladesh, with odds of acceptance of wife beating decreasing in each subsequent richer quintile (monotonic relationship). However, the association was not statistically significant in two of the poorest countries: Cambodia and Nepal. In India, the women in the richest quintile were less likely to justify wife beating than in the poorest quintile, however, women in the second-poorest and middle quintile were more likely to justify wife beating than those in the poorest quintile.

Association with religion was inconsistent across different countries. In Armenia and Turkey, where Christianity and Islam, respectively, are the main religions, the women belonging to minority "other" religions were more likely to justify wife

Table 10.3 Percentage of Men and Women Who Justified Wife Beating for Transgression of Different Gender Norms

Questions Included	Armenia		Kazakhstan		Turkey		Nepal		Bangladesh	India	Cambodia
	Female	Male	Female	Male	Female	Male	Female	Male	Male	Female	Female
Burns food[a]	4.9	5.8	4.3	NA	6.8	4.5	5.0	3.4	8.6	24.6	10.8
Neglects children[b]	27.1	27.4	26.1	22.1	24.5	23.0	25.2	27.0	23.3	40.0	25.7
Goes out without telling husband	19.9	24.1	11.2	9.7	NA	NA	12.2	16.0	24.6	36.6	23.8
Argues with husband	14.3	27.4	11.3	10.5	34.0	36.1	8.7	17.0	24.3	NA	16.9
Refuses to have sex with him	6.5	9.0	5.9	3.9	15.9	14.8	3.1	8.5	NA	NA	8.8
Talks with other men	NA	NA	NA	NA	22.4	36.2	NA	NA	NA	NA	NA
Spends needlessly	NA	NA	NA	NA	21.8	17.2	NA	NA	NA	NA	NA
Suspected of being unfaithful	NA	NA	NA	NA	NA	NA	NA	NA	NA	32.8	NA
Shows disrespect for her in-laws	NA	NA	NA	NA	NA	NA	NA	NA	NA	33.9	NA

Questions Included	Armenia		Kazakhstan		Turkey		Nepal		Bangladesh	India	Cambodia
	Female	Male	Female	Male	Female	Male	Female	Male	Male	Female	Female
Her natal family does not give expected money, jewels, or other items	NA	NA	NA	NA	NA	NA	NA	NA	NA	6.8	NA
Agrees with at least one reason											
Total	32.3	41.9	30.1	27.1	48.7	56.0	28.8	34.1	36.6	56.3	35.0
Only among currently married	35.0	40.6	32.3	25.5	49.3	56.0	28.7	34.1	36.6	56.8	39.6

NOTE: NA = not available.

a. The exact question asked varied slightly across countries: If the wife does not cook food properly (India), fails to provide food on time (Bangladesh), and food is late or not well prepared (Cambodia).

b. In India, the exact question was "neglects the house or children."

Table 10.4 Percentage of Respondents Who Justified Wife Beating by Selected Socioeconomic and Demographic Characteristics

	Armenia		Kazakhstan		Turkey		Nepal		Bangladesh	India	Cambodia
	Female	Male	Female	Male	Female	Male	Female	Male	Male	Female	Female
Residence											
Rural	48.8**	52.2***	40.9**	33.5**	64.7**	72.4***	28.3	35.0**	39.1***	60.0**	36.9***
Urban	22.0	34.9	21.5	21.9	38.0	48.3	33.2	25.5	26.4	47.4	25.8
Wealth											
Poorest	55.4***	57.1***	52.6***	42.1***	72.6***	82.5***	28.7	42.2***	45.3***	61.6**	37.3***
Second	43.8	55.9	39.9	33.6	66.6	70.7	29.7	32.4	39.9	62.6	40.0
Third	29.5	36.8	34.8	33.7	51.8	62.2	29.5	42.5	38.2	64.5	36.1
Fourth	23.8	35.1	21.6	16.8	38.8	53.0	26.8	31.0	34.9	56.6	37.7
Richest	14.4	27.5	13.8	16.9	16.5	25.6	29.1	23.0	31.2	38.2	25.4
Religion											
Catholic	32.0***	41.7*	15.6***	12.9***	NA	NA	NA	NA	33.4	65.5**	NA
Hindu	NA	NA	NA	NA	NA	NA	28.3***	34.5	NA	56.9	NA
Muslim	NA	NA	40.1	36.9	45.8	56.6***	43.1	37.7	37.2	57	NA
Buddhist	NA	NA	NA	NA	NA	NA	NA	NA	NA	NA	34.9
Other	53.4	56.8	20.3	19.5	60.2	3.3	26.3	29.8	28.6	43.4	37.6
Education											
None	37.2***	44.4**	NA		68.3***	77.7***	28.4	40.1***	47.0***	62.0**	37.7***
Primary			38.9**	31.9**	55.9	71.2	30.6	37.9	40.1	59.0	36.5
Secondary			27.6	25.8	24.2	46.9	29.5	27.1	27.9	54.0	24.8
Higher	11.3	33.0	17.4	15.0	4.2	14.1	19.4	7.0	13.2	37.3	21.9

	Armenia		Kazakhstan		Turkey		Nepal		Bangladesh	India	Cambodia
	Female	Male	Female	Male	Female	Male	Female	Male	Male	Female	Female
Age group											
15–19	33.5*	44.6**	32.4	26.3	49.8***	62.7**	32.1**	46.3**	48.1	61.6**	25.6***
20–29	31.4	44.2	30.0	30.0	44.2	54.1	30.4	39.2	39.9	56.8	34.2
30–39	34.4	46.0	30.8	26.0	46.1	52.0	27.7	32.4	38.2	56.7	39.4
40–49	30.4	36.0	27.8	26.9	50.3	57.9	25.7	30.7	34.2	54.6	39.4
50–59	NA	36.7	NA	25.3	NA	64.6	NA	30.7	32.6	NA	NA
Marital status											
Never married	27.7**	44.4	27.7***	29.9	41.3**	NA	NA	NA	NA	NA	24.5**
Currently married	35.0	40.6	32.3	25.5	49.3	56.0	28.7	34.1	36.6	56.8	39.6
Separated/divorced	26.8	50.6	23.2	32.4	46.1	NA	30.0	33.7	NA	55.6	39.1
Marital duration											
5–9 years	34.4***	43.5	33.3	43.5	47.2***	56.0**	30.2*	36.7	36.9	55.5***	37.0***
10–19 years	35.3	40.5	30.0	40.5	47.0	52.1	28.8	32.3	38.0	57.4	40.5
20–29 years	29.9	35.4	28.0	35.4	52.7	57.1	26.5	37.4	34.9	56.7	39.6
30-plus years	42.0	49.5	33.5	49.5	61.0	70.0	25.0	37.1	31.2	60.9	48.3
Sex composition of living children											
No children	27.8***	39.5	28.4***	22.7	42.6***	48.5***	31.0	NA	35.5	56.0	26.1***
At least one son	31.4	41.0	26.6	22.6	41.2	52.0	28.3	NA	36.6	55.5	39.9

(Continued)

(Continued)

	Armenia		Kazakhstan		Turkey		Nepal		Bangladesh	India	Cambodia
	Female	Male	Female	Male	Female	Male	Female	Male	Male	Female	Female
At least one daughter	32.1	41.6	25.6	28.4	43.2	61.0	28.9	NA	37.2	54.9	38.4
Both son and daughter	36.7	43.3	35.8	29.5	54.5	49.7	28.4	NA	34.2	57.9	40.2
Employment status											
Not working	29.0**	39.4***	34.3***	NA	45.6	59.0**	32.2**	18.4	NA	51.6**	37.8
Not paid	58.2	59.6	35.8	NA	67.5	74.8	27.2	37.6	NA	68.3	41.3
Paid	47.9	38.0	23.9	NA	37.2	54.9	29.3	32.0	NA	62.9	21.6
Contribution to HH expenditure											
None or < 50%	33.2***	44.1**	32.7***	NA	48.6***	NA	28.7	36.7**	NA	56.2	34.9
50%	18.2	26.2	27.9	NA	29.9	NA	32.1	30.6	NA	62.6	40.1
51%–plus	12.4	37.2	19.3	NA	32.4	NA	36.0	29.2	NA	59.5	34.0
Sex of head of household											
Male	33.3**	46.5*	23.8***	21.3*	47.8***	49.1	28.8	32.1	31.6	56.9***	36.4**
Female	29.5	40.7	32.7	28.7	37.9	56.2	28.7	34.1	36.6	54.7	30.7

NOTE: NA = not available; HH = household. The significance levels are given for different category within a column (i.e., among female or males) and not across columns (i.e., not between rural female and rural male). In Armenia, because of very small number of respondents in "none" and "primary" education category, the two groups are combined with "secondary" education, in Kazakhstan, the none and primary categories have been combined.

*p < .1. **p < .05. ***p < .01.

Table 10.5 Adjusted Odds Ratio From Multivariate Logistic Regression Assessing the Association Between Selected Characteristics and Acceptance of Wife Beating

	Armenia		Kazakhstan		Turkey		Nepal		Bangladesh	India	Cambodia
	Female	Male	Female	Male	Female	Male	Female	Male	Male	Female	Female
Urban (rural)	0.65***	1.06	0.97	1.27	0.88	0.88	1.37	1.20	0.87	0.98	0.80
Wealth (poorest)											
Second	0.74**	0.99	0.69**	0.73	0.88	0.58**	1.09	0.67**	1.08	1.08**	1.08
Third	0.56***	0.50**	0.60**	0.90	0.59***	0.51**	1.02	1.08	1.05	1.21***	0.94
Fourth	0.50***	0.48**	0.40***	0.34***	0.41***	0.40***	0.87	0.73	0.69**	0.99	1.03
Richest	0.31***	0.34***	0.26***	0.47**	0.19***	0.20***	0.91	0.65	0.57**	0.60***	0.81
Religion											
Catholic	1.00	1.00	1.00	1.00	NA	NA	NA	NA	0.90	1.75**	NA
Hindu	NA	NA	NA	NA	NA	NA	NA	1.00	NA	1.00	NA
Buddhist	NA	NA	NA	NA	NA	NA	NA	NA	NA	NA	1.00
Muslim	NA	NA	2.53***	3.20***	1.00	a	1.84**	0.93	1.00	1.08	NA
Other	1.65**	1.39	1.16	1.85**	1.40**	a	0.98	0.71	0.75	0.78**	1.10
Education (none)											
Primary	E	E	E	E	0.74***	0.99	1.11	0.78	0.79**	0.99	1.05
Secondary	E	E	E	0.89	0.29***	0.47**	0.97	0.46	0.55***	0.93	0.81
Higher	0.34***	0.85	0.57***	0.41**	0.07***	0.14***	0.56**	0.12**	0.27***	0.60***	a

(Continued)

(Continued)

	Armenia		Kazakhstan		Turkey		Nepal		Bangladesh	India	Cambodia
	Female	Male	Female	Male	Female	Male	Female	Male	Male	Female	Female
Age group (15–19)											
20–29	0.82	0.93	0.75	1.39	0.67***	2.49**	0.91	0.80	0.64	0.86***	1.03
30–39	0.69**	0.90	0.77	1.48	0.58***	1.52	0.75**	0.47**	0.59	0.76***	1.08
40–49	0.68**	0.63	0.75	2.14	0.56***	1.08	0.65**	0.36**	0.51	0.60***	0.98
50–59	NA	0.68	NA	1.62	NA	0.63	NA	0.34**	0.49	NA	NA
Marital status (currently married)											
Separated/ divorced	0.82	1.51	0.83	1.52	1.22	NA	1.17	0.95	NA	0.86**	1.06
Never married	0.94	1.67	0.56**	1.20	1.40	NA	NA	NA	NA	—	0.69
Marital duration (< 10 years)											
10–19 years	1.17	1.11	0.98	0.73	1.03	1.03	1.07	1.10	1.00	1.09**	1.06
20–29 years	0.95	1.11	0.95	0.54	1.20	1.24	1.00	1.51	0.97	1.24***	1.05
30-plus years	1.24	1.81	1.25	0.78	1.31	1.64	1.04	1.15	0.79	1.53***	1.67

	Armenia		Kazakhstan		Turkey		Nepal		Bangladesh	India	Cambodia
	Female	Male	Female	Male	Female	Male	Female	Male	Male	Female	Female
Sex composition of living children (none)											
At least one son	0.89	1.06	0.88	1.01	0.99	0.96	1.09	NA	1.08	0.98	0.94
At least one daughter	0.92	0.96	1.07	1.05	1.17	1.16	1.15	NA	1.19	1.03	0.94
Both son and daughter	0.71	0.73	1.17	1.00	1.21	0.76	1.09	NA	1.27	0.95	0.82
Employment status (not working)											
Not paid	1.70***	1.77**	1.18	NA	1.25**	1.37	0.86	2.40**	NA	1.63***	1.91**
Paid	1.64**	1.29	0.97	NA	1.07	1.00	0.91	2.09	NA	1.49***	2.48***
Contribution to HH expenditure (none/< 50%)											
50%	0.79	0.52**	1.17	NA	0.88	NA	1.17	0.92	NA	1.00	1.15
51% plus	0.53**	0.90	0.79	NA	0.75	NA	1.41	0.83	NA	0.85**	0.82
Head of household (male)	1.05	0.83	1.00	1.42	1.22	1.50	1.00	0.93	1.13	1.04	1.34**

NOTE: NA = not available or not applicable; HH = household; E = included in the reference group due to small sample size.

a. Very small number of respondents in the comparison category—hence combined with main category (e.g., too few respondents in Cambodia for higher education were grouped with "secondary education").

**p < .05. ***p < .01.

beating. No significant relationship was observed with religion in Bangladesh and Cambodia. In Kazakhstan and Nepal, Muslim respondents (only women in Nepal) were more likely to justify wife beating than Christian and Hindu respondents, respectively, the reverse was true in India, where no significant differences were seen between Hindu and Muslim women, but Christian women were more likely to justify wife beating compared to Hindu women (see Table 10.5).

Education was the second most consistent negative predictor of acceptance of wife beating after household wealth except in Cambodia—the country with the lowest female literacy rates—and among men in Armenia. A monotonic relationship was seen with decreasing odds of acceptance with each increasing level of education in Turkey and Bangladesh. However, in Armenia (women only), Kazakhstan, Nepal, and India, the negative effect of education was significant only at higher education level.

Demographic Predictors

A monotonic negative association was observed in all countries (except for women in Cambodia and men in Turkey) between acceptance of wife beating and age, though the relationship was statistically significant only in Armenia (women only), India, Nepal (both men and women) and Turkey (women only), with older respondents less likely to justify wife beating (see Table 10.5). In countries where both never- and ever- married respondents were sampled (Armenia and Kazakhstan, plus women in Turkey and Cambodia), never-married women were significantly less likely to justify wife beating than currently married women in Kazakhstan and Cambodia, though no significant differences were observed among men in Armenia and Kazakhstan. No significant differences were seen between divorced or separated respondents compared to currently married respondents, except in India, where divorced/separated women were less likely to justify wife beating compared to currently married respondents.

No significant relationship was seen between duration of marriage and acceptance of wife beating among men in any of the five countries. Among women, the association was significant only in India, with acceptance of wife beating increasing with the duration of marriage. The reverse relationship of wife-beating acceptance with age and duration of marriage in India suggests that women who get married early were more likely to justify wife beating than women who married later. Because in many cultures women must bear sons to maintain their status in the family, it was anticipated that women with sons or with both sons and daughters might be less likely to justify wife beating. However, in our study, no significant association was seen in any of the countries among either men or women between wife-beating acceptance and sex composition of living children. Having a male head of household significantly increased the odds of acceptance of wife beating among women in Cambodia. No relationship between wife-beating acceptance and sex of head of the household was seen among women in the other four countries and among men in any of the countries at the 95% level.

Employment and Financial Independence

Acceptance of wife beating was higher among men and women who were working in non-cash-paid jobs than respondents who were not working except in Nepalese women, although the relationship was not statistically significant in some cases (for Kazakhstan women and Turkey men). Women employed in cash-paid jobs were either as likely to justify wife beating as nonemployed women (Kazakhstan, Turkey, and Nepal) or were more likely to justify wife beating (Armenia, India, and Cambodia). No significant differences were seen among men working for pay and men not working among the three countries for which these data were available.

The financial independence of the women, as measured by contribution to total household expenditures, had a significant negative association with acceptance of wife beating only in Armenia and India, though the odds ratio was less than 1 in four other countries also. For men, the relevant data were available only in Armenia and in Nepal. In both the countries, men who contributed half or more than half of the total household expenditure were less likely to justify wife beating, but the differences were not statistically significant.

Gender Difference in Acceptance of Wife Beating

The gender differences in acceptance of wife beating were analyzed in the four countries (Armenia, Kazakhstan, Nepal, and Turkey) for which data were available for both men and women. Men were significantly more likely to justify wife beating in Armenia, Nepal, and Turkey. In Kazakhstan, although women were more likely to justify wife beating (34.0% women versus 28.8% men), the differences were not

statistically significant at the 95% level. The gender differences were also not significant for any of the norms examined individually in Kazakhstan (see Table 10.6).

The gender differences remain significant in Armenia, Nepal, and Turkey even in the multivariate pooled analysis with both men and women's data combined together (data not shown). For different reasons, the patterns of acceptance of wife beating were similar across men and women (see Table 10.2), with the lowest proportion of both men and women justifying wife beating for food-related reasons and the highest proportion of both men and women justifying wife beating for neglecting children. However, though both men and women were most likely to justify wife beating for neglecting children, the gender differences were not significant for transgressing this norm in any of the four countries. On the other hand, men were significantly more likely to justify wife beating than women for reasons such as arguing with husband, going out without telling her husband, talking to other

Table 10.6 Difference in Acceptance of Wife Beating for Transgressing Different Gender Norms Between Men and Women in Percentage Points

Male-Female Differences	Armenia	Kazakhstan	Turkey	Nepal
She burns the food	0.9	NA	−2.3**	−1.6
Neglects children	0.3	−4.0	−1.5	1.8
Goes out without telling husband	4.2**	−1.5	NA	3.8**
Argues with husband	13.1***	−0.8	2.1**	8.3***
Refuses to have sex with him	2.5**	−2.0	−1.1	5.4***
Talks with other men	NA	NA	13.8***	NA
Spends needlessly	NA	NA	−4.6***	NA
Justifies violence for at least one reason	9.6***	−3.0	7.3**	3.3**

NOTE: NA = not available.

**p < .05. ***p < .01.

men, and refusing to have sex (except in Turkey; see Table 10.6).

Differential Effect of Predictors Among Men and Women

Table 10.5 shows the separate analyses for men and women. In addition, pooled models including both male and female respondents were fitted in all the four countries with interaction terms to test the statistical significance of difference of effect of a predictor variable between men and women (data not shown). In general, with few exceptions, most of the socioeconomic predictors that have negative association with acceptance of wife beating have either negative association only among women or have a stronger negative association among women compared to men. For example, urban residence was associated with lower odds of acceptance of wife beating only among women with no significant association among men in Armenia. Similarly, the negative association with education was much stronger and significant only among women in Armenia, though the opposite was the case in Nepal. The effect of household wealth did not vary by gender, although in Kazakhstan the women from the richest quintile were significantly less likely to justify wife beating than men from the same quintile as compared to the poorest quintile.

The gender differentials in association of age with acceptance of wife beating were mainly seen in Nepal and Turkey. Although the negative relationship was only significant among women in Turkey, the association was in the opposite direction, though not significant for men. In Nepal, although significant negative association with age was observed in both men and women, the association was significantly stronger among men. Although never-married women were less likely to justify wife beating compared to currently married women in both Armenia and Kazakhstan, the relationship was in the opposite direction among men (though not statistically significant). Although no significant gender differential were observed for contribution to household expenditure in either Armenia or Nepal for which these data were available, significant gender differentials were observed in Nepal with respect to employment status. Whereas working women either for kind or cash were less likely to justify wife beating, the opposite was observed for men, with a significant interaction term in the pooled model (data not shown).

Discussion

The study shows that wife beating is accepted for transgression of gender norms by at least 30% of both men and women in all the countries investigated in this study. Among women, the highest rates were observed in India (57%), followed by Turkey (49%)—both countries having comprehensive laws dealing specifically with domestic violence but widely different female illiteracy rates (54% in India compared to 23% in Turkey). On the other hand, acceptance of wife beating in Nepal (29%), with very high female illiteracy rates, was comparable to those observed in Armenia (35%) and Kazakhstan (32.3%), which have very low female illiteracy rates. An intriguing difference was seen between India (57%) and Nepal (29%)—both with similar female illiteracy rates, religions, and highly patriarchal societies. Even though some of the differences between Nepal and India may be because of additional questions asked on dowry and being unfaithful in India, a significantly higher proportion of women in India justified wife beating than in Nepal even for three comparative scenarios presented (e.g., for food-related reasons—24% in India versus 5% in Nepal). In general, the level of acceptance of wife beating in Asia was lower than that observed in certain sub-Saharan African countries where at least 50% of women or men justified wife beating in the seven countries examined (Rani et al., 2004).

However, the aggregate comparative estimates of the study presented above need to be seen in light of the few limitations of the study. First, the aggregate estimates are based on both ever-married and currently married respondents in Armenia, Cambodia, and Kazakhstan but only for ever-married respondents in India, Nepal, and Turkey. In addition, slightly different questions were included in some of the countries to reflect the local situations. Although five situations were given for assessing justification of violence in a majority of the surveys, only four questions were asked in the Bangladesh and Kazakhstan men's survey, and six questions were asked in India's survey, making the variable on "justifies violence for at least one reason" not strictly comparable across countries.

Many studies noted an inverse relationship of reported experience of wife beating with household wealth and education. Our study also suggests that urban residence, household wealth, and education were associated with lower acceptance, yet the relationship was not always statistically significant, especially in the poorest countries (e.g., Cambodia and Nepal). The association with urban residence was mediated largely through household wealth and education. However, in Armenia, urban residence was associated with a lower acceptance of wife beating even after controlling for the effect of household wealth and education. The relationship between household wealth and acceptance of wife beating was not significant in the two poorest countries in the study, Cambodia and Nepal, and was only significant at the level of the richest quintile in the fourth poorest country, India. More important, the association with education was either not seen (in Cambodia) or seen only at the level of higher education (i.e., no significant inverse association with primary or secondary education) in the majority of these countries, with few exceptions (Turkey and Bangladesh). Although this study, along with another earlier study, emphasizes the importance of investing in education (of both men and women), which is also justified in its own right for several other reasons, one should not become too optimistic about changing the norms regarding wife beating by just relying on improvement in female education. With the very low completion rates of secondary education and higher education among women currently in those developing countries included in this study and constraints to rapid progress in improving the proportion of women with higher education, it might take a few decades to bring any perceptible change in attitudes toward gender norms and wife beating through increase in higher education, unless proactive action is taken in a comprehensive manner. The comparative scenario with countries at different stages of female education well illustrates this point. Both Armenia and Kazakhstan—which have very high rates of secondary-level education among women—have similar levels of wife-beating acceptance as Cambodia and Nepal, which, conversely, have very low rates of secondary-level education. The differences in education effects across countries and the small effect of primary education within countries may be caused by differences in the types of education provided—adaptive or transformative, and how it is used—to challenge gender bias or to perpetuate traditional gender norms. These are some subjects for further research that will provide evidence for effective policy and programs to eliminate the practice of wife beating.

Consistent with the findings of another study (Sen, 1999), the results of this study show that employment or financial independence of women alone may not change the attitude toward wife beating. Women working in non-cash-paying or cash-paying jobs were either more likely or equally as likely to justify wife beating than non-working women in all the study countries, after controlling for the effect of education and household wealth. To explain these contradictory results, one needs to further examine the social context, circumstances, and motivations for women's participation in the labor force. If women experience the same patriarchal social structures at the workplace and similar gender inequities, the notion of male superiority may be further reinforced rather than being challenged. No significant association was seen between acceptance of wife beating and 50% contribution toward household expenditures among women. However, women who contributed more than 50% of total household expenditures were less likely to justify wife beating in Armenia and India, with differences not statistically significant in the rest of the countries. However, the effect of this predictor variable at population level in reducing the overall acceptance rates will not be substantial at least in the short run because of the very small percentage of women in this category in both India (6.6%) and Armenia (1.9%; see Table 10.2).

Are the norms related to gender roles and wife beating declining over time? The use of cross-sectional data does not allow us to tease out the difference in cohort effect (the change in the attitudes over time in the same age group cohorts) and the age effect (the change in the attitudes with age in the same cohort). Assuming no age effect, the lack of any significant relationship in four of the seven countries suggests no change in attitudes during a span of 30 to 45 years with younger cohorts (15 to 19 years old) as likely to justify wife beating as the older cohorts (40 to 49 years among women and 50 to 59 years among men) after controlling for other socioeconomic characteristics. The negative relationship seen with age in three South Asian countries either suggests a declining acceptance of wife beating with age or increasing acceptance of wife beating over time. One conclusion that can be drawn from the data, however, is the effective intergenerational transmission of norms among both men and women. We expected to find lower acceptance among the younger cohorts, at least in the bivariate analysis, as they grew up in more urbanized environments with better economies and higher educational achievements. The negative relationship with the increasing age and acceptance of wife beating further corroborates the limited effect that current education and economic growth are having on changing norms regarding gender roles and wife beating.

The comparative levels of acceptance of wife beating and gender differentials provide some insight into the current situation of society as it moves toward being more gender egalitarian. Africa, with higher overall rates of acceptance than in Asia, has significantly more women who are accepting of wife beating than men (Rani et al., 2004), but the reverse holds true in Asian countries in this study. This leads us to speculate that as societies move in the direction of being more gender egalitarian, at one extreme would be situations when women would be holding onto gender norms more tightly and accepting wife beating more than men because of deep social learning that remained untouched by early inroads of modernism.

In the next phase, the changes will be more pronounced in women than in men because a substantial proportion of men will not easily give up their traditional sex-stereotyped roles (Jewkes et al., 2002; Straus, 1976). The higher resistance to change among men was exemplified to some extent in Armenia, where urban residence and higher education had a significant negative association only among women, but no such effect was seen among men. At this stage, the actual prevalence of wife beating may be higher because men may resort to further violence when their dominance is being challenged. This is also exemplified in higher reporting of wife beating as the women in the Philippines increase their decision-making role (Hindin & Adair, 2002) and as membership in credit and saving associations lead to higher personal earnings in Bangladesh (Bates et al., 2004; Rahman, 1999). Hence, reducing the prevalence of wife beating requires male liberation as well as women's liberation from the binding cultural stereotypic norms (Straus, 1976) so that both men and women realize the unjustness and irrationality of these norms, leading to overall decline in the prevalence of wife beating. The situation in these study countries reveals that there is a long way to go before the final stage is achieved.

The widespread acceptance of the gender roles and justification of use of violence to enforce them may also become a major hurdle in success of other reproductive health programs (i.e., family planning programs), care seeking for sexually transmitted diseases or voluntary testing and counseling, and condom use for prevention of HIV/AIDS if the women do not confront men because of the threat of domestic violence, as a large proportion of women in these societies considered "arguing with husband" and "refusing sex" as valid reasons for wife beating. Many studies have already documented the link between underuse of different reproductive health services and the experience of domestic violence (Diop-Sidibé, Campbell, & Becker, 2006; Maman, Campbell, Sweat, & Gielen, 2000; Martin et al., 1999). This indicates that to increase their effectiveness, reproductive health programs must also address the social norms that increase women's vulnerability to violence.

Many of the social norms, including that for wife beating, evolve over generations and have been internalized by both men and women without their ever questioning it, unless confronted by new nonconforming situations that lead to the questioning and challenging of those norms. To eliminate the practice of wife beating, these societies first need to fundamentally change the underlying attitudes toward wife beating through direct, proactive efforts.

References

Bandura, A. (1977). *Social learning theory.* Englewood Cliffs, NJ: Prentice Hall.

Bates, L. M., Schuler, S. R., Islam, F., & Islam, M. K. (2004). Socio-economic factors and processes associated with domestic violence in rural Bangladesh. *International Family Planning Perspectives, 30*(4), 190–199.

Burton, B., Duvvury, N., & Varia, N. (2000). *Justice, change, and human rights: International research and responses to domestic violence* (Synthesis paper). Washington, DC: International Center for Research on Women and the Center for Development and Population Activities. Retrieved from http://www.icrw.org/docs/domesticviolencesynthesis.pdf

Coeling, H. V., & Harnan, G. (1997). Learning to ask about domestic violence. *Women's Health Issues, 7*(4), 263–267.

Diop-Sidibé, N., Campbell, J. C., & Becker, S. (2006). Domestic violence against women in Egypt—Wife beating and health outcomes. *Social Science and Medicine, 62,* 1260–1277.

El-Zanaty, F., Hussein, E. M., Shawky, G. A., Way, A. A., & Kishor, S. (1996). *Egypt Demographic and Health Survey 1995.* Calverton, MD: National Population Council (Egypt) and Macro International Inc.

Fikree, F. F., Razzak, J. A., & Durocher, J. (2005). Attitudes of Pakistan men to domestic violence: A study from Karachi, Pakistan. *International Journal on Men's Health and Gender, 2*(1), 49–58.

Filmer, D., & Pritchett, L. (1998). *Estimating wealth effects without expenditure date—Or tears: An application to educational enrollments in States of India* (World Bank Policy Research Working Paper No. 1994). Washington, DC: Development Economics Research Group, World Bank.

Haj-Yahia, M. M. (1998). Beliefs about wife-beating among Palestinian women. *Violence Against Women, 4*(5), 533–558.

Haj-Yahia, M. M. (2002). Beliefs of Jordanian women about wife-beating. *Psychology of Women Quarterly, 26,* 282–291.

Heise, L., Ellsberg, M., & Gottemoeller, M. (1999). *Ending violence against women* (Population Reports, Series L, No. 11). Baltimore, MD: Johns Hopkins University School of Public Health, Population Information Program.

Heise, L., Pitanguy, J., & Germain, A. (1994). *Violence against women: The hidden health burden.* Washington, DC: World Bank.

Hindin, M. J., & Adair, L. S. (2002). Who's at risk? Factors associated with intimate partner violence in the Philippines. *Social Science and Medicine, 55,* 1385–1399.

Ilkkaracan, P. (1998, November). Exploring the context of women's sexuality in eastern Turkey. *Reproductive Health Matters, 6*(12), 66–75.

International Institute for Population Sciences (IIPS) & ORC Macro. (2000). *National Family Health Survey (NFHS-2), 1998–99: India.* Mumbai, India: Author.

Jejeebhoy, S. J. (1998a). Association between wife-beating and fetal and infant death: Impressions from a survey in rural India. *Studies in Family Planning, 29,* 300–308.

Jejeebhoy, S. J. (1998b). Wife-beating in rural India: A husband's right? Evidence from survey data. *Economic and Political Weekly (India), 33,* 855–862.

Jewkes, R., Jonathan, L., & Penn-Kekana, L. (2002). Risk factors for domestic violence: Findings from a South African cross-sectional study. *Social Science and Medicine, 55*, 1603–1617.

Kim, J., & Mmatshilo, M. (2002). Women enjoy punishment: Attitudes and experiences of gender-based violence among PHC nurses in rural South Africa. *Social Science and Medicine, 54*, 1243–1254.

Koenig, M. A., Ahmed, S., Hossain, M. B., & Mozumder, A. B. M. K. A. (2003). Individual and community-level determinants of domestic violence in rural Bangladesh. *Demography, 40*(2), 269–288.

Macro International Inc. (1996). *Sampling manual* (DHS-III Basic Documentation No. 6). Calverton, MD: Author.

Maman, S., Campbell, J., Sweat, M. D., & Gielen, A. C. (2000). The intersection of HIV and violence: Directions for future research and interventions. *Social Science and Medicine, 50*, 459–478.

Martin, S. L., Kilgallen, B., Tsui, A. O., Maitra, K., Singh, K. K., & Kupper, S. L. (1999). Sexual behaviors and reproductive health outcomes: Associations with wife abuse in India. *Journal of the American Medical Association, 282*, 1967–1972.

Morrison, A., & Biehl, M. L. (1999). *Too close to home: Domestic violence in the Americas* (Inter-American Development Bank). Washington, DC: Johns Hopkins University Press.

National Institute of Statistics, Directorate General for Health (Cambodia), & ORC Macro. (2001). *Cambodia Demographic and Health Survey 2000.* Phnom Penh, Cambodia: Author.

Rahman, A. (1999). Micro-credit initiatives for equitable and sustainable development: Who pays? *World Development, 27*, 67–82.

Rani, M., Bonu, S., & Diop-Sidibé, N. (2004). An empirical investigation of attitudes towards wife-beating among men and women in seven sub-Saharan African countries. *African Journal of Reproductive Health, 8*(3), 116–136.

Rao, V., & Bloch, F. (1993). *Wife-beating, its causes and its implications for nutrition allocations to children: An economic and anthropological case study of a rural South India community.* Washington, DC: Policy Research Department, Poverty and Human Resources Division, World Bank.

Schuler, S. R., Syed, M. H., Riley, A. P., & Shireen, A. (1996). Credit programs, patriarchy and men's violence against women in rural Bangladesh. *Social Science and Medicine, 43*, 1729–1742.

Sen, P. (1999). Enhancing women's choices in responding to domestic violence in Calcutta: A comparison of employment and education. *European Journal of Development Research* (U.K.), *11*(2), 65–86.

Straus, M. A. (1976). Sexual inequality, cultural norms and wife-beating. In E. C. Viano (Ed.), *Victims and society.* Washington, DC: Visage Press.

World Health Organization. (1999a). *Violence against women, a priority health issue.* (WHO/FRH/WHD/97.8). Geneva: Author.

World Health Organization. (1999b). Putting women's safety first: Ethical and safety recommendations for research on domestic violence against women. Geneva: Author.

CHAPTER 11

Intersections of Immigration and Domestic Violence

Voices of Battered Immigrant Women

Edna Erez, Madelaine Adelman, and Carol Gregory

O ver the past 30 years, feminist academics and practitioners have revealed the extent and variety of gender violence, ranging from street-level sexual harassment (Stanko, 1985) to woman battering (Dobash & Dobash, 1979). According to Chesney-Lind (2006), "naming of the types and dimensions of female victimization had a significant impact on public policy, and it is arguably the most tangible accomplishment of both feminist criminology and grassroots feminists concerned about gender, crime, and justice" (p. 7). Indeed, feminist criminological research was part of the battered woman's movement's hard-won efforts to criminalize domestic violence (Adelman & Morgan, 2006). Feminist criminologists, their cross-disciplinary associates, and others also have been part of the growing critique of the limits or unintended effects of the criminalization of domestic violence (Britton, 2000; Chesney-Lind, 2006; Coker, 2001; Snider, 1998). Together, scholars and activists have identified harms induced by the criminal justice system not only on battered women, and poor battered women of color in particular, but also on men who batter, and in particular poor men of color who batter (Merry, 2000).

Noting the interconnection between racist violence, violence against women, and the institutionalization of the battered woman's movement within U.S. social service and criminal justice systems, feminist criminologists and others have called for antiracist, multicultural feminist analyses of gender violence and other forms of crime (Burgess-Proctor, 2006; Potter, 2006; see Baca Zinn & Thornton Dill, 1996, and Crenshaw,

Erez, E., Adelman, M., & Gregory, C. (2009). Intersections of immigration and domestic violence: Voices of battered immigrant women. *Feminist Criminology, 4,* 32–56.

AUTHORS' NOTE: This research was conducted with the support of Grant #98-WT-VX-0030 from the National Institute of Justice. Views expressed in this article are those of the authors and not of the funding agency.

1991, for foundational elaborations on intersectionality). Much of this analysis has looked at immigrant status as part of one's racial location in the social hierarchy (e.g., Crenshaw, 1991; Scales-Trent, 1999). Here, we build on the history of feminist criminology with an integrated feminist analysis of immigration and domestic violence. Rather than consider immigration as a variable or static category within race, we consider immigration as part of the multiple grounds of identity shaping the domestic violence experience. It is part of the interactive dynamic processes that, along with race, gender, sexual orientation, and class, inform women's experiences of and responses to domestic violence. We do so by analyzing one-on-one interviews with immigrant battered women from a variety of countries, revealing common experiences among immigrants in an effort to highlight *immigrant* as a separate and multiplicative aspect of identity, violence, and oppression.

We situate our study within the literature on gender, immigration, and domestic violence, noting the scholarly focus on discrete groups of immigrants (e.g., by ethnicity or national origin) rather than the commonalities experienced by various immigrant groups. We then outline our research methods and sample, followed by an analysis of the data that focus on commonalities across immigrant battered women's experiences. Specifically, we suggest that although significant investment has been made by federal and state governments, and local community-based organizations, to improve the criminal justice system response to immigrant battered women in terms of legal reform, law enforcement training, and increased services, immigrant battered women continue to face considerable structural barriers to safety. These barriers exist prior to immigration (e.g., social pressure to marry) and as a result of immigration (e.g., economic disadvantage that has gendered consequences). In turn, immigration law and women's perceptions of law enforcement inform their attitudes toward reporting intimate partner violence. We conclude with a discussion of our research findings and

their implications for theory and practice, expressing concern with the level of awareness of existing legal options for battered immigrant women and the growing anti-immigrant trend across the United States to devolve enforcement of federal immigration law to local authorities.

Feminist Theory of Intersectionality

Feminist discourse on intersectionality has developed over the past two decades. Although there are some differences in interpretation and application, intersectionality theory considers the ways that hierarchies of power exist along multiple socially defined categories such as race, class, and gender. These categories mutually construct each other via structural inequalities and social interaction, creating a matrix of intersecting hierarchies that is not merely additive but multiplicative in terms of unearned privilege, domination, and oppression (Baca Zinn & Thornton Dill, 1996; Collins, 1991/2000; Crenshaw, 1991; Higginbotham, 1997; Steinbugler, Press, & Johnson Dias, 2006). In this way, both opportunities (including social and material benefit) and oppressions may be simultaneously created by intersecting forms of domination (Baca Zinn & Thornton Dill, 1996; Steinbugler et al., 2006). Thus, for instance, "a gay Black man may experience privilege vis-à-vis his maleness but be marginalized for his race and sexuality" (p. 808). Angela Harris (1990), along with other critical race feminism legal scholars, refers to this notion of intersecting, indivisible identities as "multiple consciousness." Theories of intersectionality have inspired scholars across many disciplines to notice how various forms of privilege and oppression operate simultaneously as well as to reveal those forms of social identities that go unnoticed.

Writings on intersectionality use country of origin as an example of how racial and ethnic identities result in domination or oppression. Crenshaw (1991) specifically refers to immigrant status as an example of how race affects violent victimization in the United States. In this article, we show how the experiences of legal and undocumented immigrants are different from those of U.S. citizens and yet similar to one another, regardless of country of origin. Notwithstanding the racialized politics associated with immigration in the United States, and recognizing the racism that many immigrants face, our effort here is to build on the substantial literature on intersectionality to reveal the intersection of immigration and domestic violence. We do so to highlight the salience of immigration for battered women in terms of how immigration affects the level and types of intimate partner violence women experience and shapes marital dynamics and women's help-seeking opportunities. We also examine how immigration and the policing of immigration may compromise women's safety. Thus, although we attend to the racialized category of immigration and the racist anti-immigrant sentiment aimed at immigrants, analytically, we have separated immigrant status from race/ethnicity as a category of intersectionality.

Immigration

Twenty-first century migration across international borders is a significant global phenomenon (Sassen, 1998). Motivated by a combination of push and pull factors such as impoverishment and economic opportunities, political instability and the opening of previously closed borders, and the loss or gain of family ties, large numbers of people enter key receiving countries such as the United States each year. The United States is considered "a nation of immigrants." Nevertheless, who is allowed to legally immigrate has varied over time. U.S. immigration and naturalization laws have shaped the resulting immigrant pool in terms of gender, race or nationality, sexual orientation, and marital status. These social identities have been central to U.S. immigration law, ranging from the exclusion of Chinese prostitutes

in the 1870s to the men-only Bracero Program instituted in 1942 (Calavita, 1992). Subsequent changes in immigration policy, including an amnesty initiative in the mid-1980s, led to heterosexual family reunification and an increase in the numbers of women and children who migrated to the United States. Such gendered, racialized, and sexualized patterns reflect how immigration and naturalization law serves to police the purported moral as well as political boundaries of the nation (Gardner, 2005). These immigration laws affect why, when, how, and with whom women immigrate and their experiences of domestic violence subsequent to arrival in the United States.

One factor among many that motivates emigration from Southern toward Northern tier states is immigration policies that focus on family reunification. Other factors include the intensification of economic globalization under neo-liberal policies and relative ease of movement between political borders. Together, these factors are responsible for women making up an ever-increasing proportion of immigrants to the United States. Indeed, by the turn of the century, "close to 60 percent of immigrants from Mexico, China, the Philippines and Vietnam were female"; a similar percentage of female immigrants were between ages 15 and 44, significantly younger than their native-born counterparts (Zhou, 2002, p. 26). This young age cohort requires of female immigrants a long-term commitment to domestic and workplace labor in their new country of residence. In addition to their unpaid domestic and paid workplace labor, female immigrants also frequently contribute financially to the economy of their countries of origin via remittances home. In areas other than age and labor, however, female immigrants, as a whole, are a diverse group: migrating alone or with children and family; undocumented and/or dependent on male kin who sponsor their immigration. Some women arrive as highly skilled workers and successfully secure well-paid jobs. Other women, regardless of their skill sets, become among the lowest paid in the U.S. workforce. Still, female immigrants share the gendered effects of their border crossing.

As research on the gendered nature of immigration has emerged in terms of changing patterns over time of migration, identity formation and transformation, education, fertility, health care, and employment (Gabaccia, 1992; Hondagneu-Sotelo, 2003; Pessar, 1999; Strum & Tarantolo, 2002), so too has insight into the so-called domestic lives of immigrants. Ethnographers, for example, have analyzed how the meaning of marriage, along with women's and men's expectations of intimate relationships, may change as a result of migration patterns, access to education, and women's economic opportunities (Hirsch, 2003). These studies of immigrant domestic life help trace continuities and disruptions of the construction of gender across the migration process. For our purposes, one of the most critical links lies between the transformation of gender across the migration process and domestic violence.

Immigration and Domestic Violence

Violence against women is one of the most common victimizations experienced by immigrants (Davis & Erez, 1998; see also Erez, 2000, 2002; Raj & Silverman, 2002). Working together, battered immigrant women, activists, and scholars have documented how immigration intensifies domestic violence and creates vulnerabilities that impair immigrant women's management of domestic violence, preventing them from successfully challenging men's violence, from securing decreases in rates or types of men's violence, or from leaving their intimate partners. According to domestic violence scholars, "immigrant women arrive with disadvantages in social status and basic human capital resources relative to immigrant men" (Bui & Morash, 1999, p. 774) or cannot participate as actively in networks as male counterparts do (Abraham, 2000). As a result, barriers to safety

for immigrant women include a lack of resources for battered women, social isolation or lack of local natal kin, economic instability, and perceptions that disclosure of battering to outsiders sullies community status. Criminal justice agencies that lack translation services and/or knowledge of immigration law, lack of trust in law enforcement and/or government authorities, and immigration law that dictates legal and sometimes economic dependency on the batterer, who may be undocumented or lacking legal immigrant status, also pose significant barriers (Bui, 2004; Dasgupta, 2000; Wachholz & Miedema, 2000).[1]

U.S. immigration law endangers battered immigrant women by giving near total control over the women's legal status to the sponsoring spouses, replicating the doctrine of coverture, under which "a wife could not make a contract with her husband or with others" (Calvo, 1997, p. 381). Coverture, in effect, identifies the married couple as a single legal entity, within which the husband has control over the property and body of the wife and their children. Similarly, women who immigrate as wives of U.S. citizens, legal permanent residents, diplomats, students, or workers are legally dependent on others to sponsor, pursue, and complete their visa petitions. This legal dependency intensifies gendered inequality, creates new ways for men to abuse and control their intimate partners, and entraps battered women (Erez, 2002; Salcido & Adelman, 2004). As part of the Violence Against Women Act (VAWA), legal reforms have been instituted to relieve some of the legal and economic dependencies imposed on battered immigrant women. These reforms include self-petition, which lets an abused spouse apply for a green card on his or her own; cancellation of removal, which lets an abused spouse who has already been subjected to removal proceedings request to remain in the United States; the U-visa, which lets a victim of crime (including domestic violence) who has been helpful to its investigation or prosecution apply for a nonimmigrant visa and work permit; and access to public benefits such as food stamps

(Orloff, 2002; see also Wood, 2004). Obstacles to these well-intentioned legal reforms for immigrant battered women remain, in particular due to the complex nature of legal qualifications, including who is eligible to apply for which form of legal relief, and meeting the threshold required to demonstrate having been subjected to battery or extreme cruelty. The rise in anti-immigrant public sentiment has resulted both in the exclusion of some immigrants from access to education and medical care and in increased local law enforcement of federal immigration law. When coupled with post-9/11 delays in processing visa applications, the consequences of anti-immigrant sentiment further complicate the implementation of legal reforms for immigrant battered women.

Knowledge of immigrants' experiences with domestic violence is largely culled from case studies of discrete communities. Due in large part to the depth of social and cultural capital required to conduct sensitive research with members of marginalized immigrant communities, researchers tend to focus on small, local samples of battered women from specific immigrant communities (but see Menjivar & Salcido, 2002). Thus, we have insightful contributions based on the experiences of domestic violence by immigrant women to the United States from, for example, Bosnia (Muftic & Bouffard, 2008), Cambodia (Bhuyan, Mell, Senturia, Sullivan, & Shiu-Thornton, 2005), Mexico (Salcido & Adelman, 2004), Russia (Crandall, Senturia, Sullivan, & Shiu-Thornton, 2005), South Asia (Abraham, 2000), and Vietnam (Bui & Morash, 1999). These studies generate critical albeit partial knowledge with regard to immigration and domestic violence. In addition, until now, much of the holistic knowledge on immigrant battered women has been (rightly) directed toward services and policy-based interventions.

In this study, we take a different approach. We offer a detailed analysis situated within a theoretical framework of intersectionality, using *immigrant* as a positioned identity within the social structure as well as within interactions.

This approach highlights the commonalities experienced by battered immigrant women, regardless of their ethnic or national group membership or countries of origin. Aware of the specific and unique contextual elements affecting domestic violence in each immigrant group, and the heterogeneity of domestic violence experiences that immigrant women from different cultures or ethnic groups endure, in focusing on the commonalities experienced rather than the unique elements of violence against immigrant women, we expect to highlight the theoretical value of the findings as well as draw public policy implications.

Research Methods

As previously noted, extant case studies of immigrant battered women typically consist of small, local samples derived from within one discrete community group. Our goal was to create a relatively large sample of diverse participants to be interviewed about their experiences with immigration and domestic violence. Diversity of participants in this study is based on each participant's language, ethnicity, nationality, cultural groupings, and country of origin. The sampling frame originated in states with large numbers of recent immigrants, with diverse immigrant communities, and with communities residing in both urban and rural areas: California, New York, Florida, Texas, Michigan, Wisconsin, and Iowa were selected as research sites.

Major immigration legal assistance organizations in these states helped to identify relevant social service agencies that provide direct services to immigrants. The directors of the social service agencies were contacted by phone about possible participation. In addition, members of social service agencies from other parts of the country who attended various regional and national meetings related to training or discussions about battered immigrant women and other issues concerning domestic violence and immigration were also approached for possible participation. Representatives from several agencies in New Jersey, Ohio, and Washington who expressed interest in participation were added to the list of participating agencies. Altogether, 17 agencies participated in the study, conducting interviews.

The interviews also addressed contacts with the criminal justice system, which some immigrant women may be unwilling to discuss with strangers. In light of the sensitive nature of the interview content and common reluctance among immigrant battered women to disclose detailed accounts of victimization and criminal justice experiences to outsiders, each participating agency instructed its bilingual social service provider to initiate contact with battered immigrant women with whom the provider had previously established rapport and a helping relationship of trust. As with much feminist research, one considers the positionality of the research subject in devising the methodology and conducting the research. The providers' relationship with the immigrant women was an integral component of the data collection phase because the providers were not only familiar with interviewees' strengths, concerns, and needs but also shared their language and, commonly, their culture. Therefore, the provider asked each woman if she was willing to be interviewed, explained the purpose of the research project, and, once the woman gave her consent, conducted the interview.

We recognize that where a power differential existed between the social service agency staff and the helpseeking interviewees, it may have compromised the validity of those data pertaining directly to access to or quality of social services. However, as noted below, many of the social service agents were battered immigrant women turned advocates, where the power differential was minimal. Furthermore, given the logistical barriers (e.g., training and sending interviewers to agencies in multiple states) and skill-based challenges (e.g., language competency) involved in collecting sensitive data from such a diverse sample, on balance we determined

that access to a range of immigrant battered women, secured in large part due to the relationship of trust they had established with the agency staff and the linguistic comfort afforded to participants, overrode this limited, albeit important, methodological concern.

The bilingual social service providers who conducted the interviews ($n = 20$), were employees or volunteers who either had training in social services or, in some cases, were themselves survivors of domestic violence who had become battered women advocates. Each was given sets of questionnaires and instructions concerning the interviews (e.g., ethical standards such as confidentiality and interview techniques such as probing questions). The questionnaires, originally written in English, were sent ahead of time to the agencies so that the interviewers could become familiar with their content and be prepared, if necessary, to conduct simultaneous translations.[2] The social service providers/interviewers most often conducted interviews in the immigrant women's native language (i.e., in about two thirds of the cases).

The interviewees ($n = 137$) were immigrant women who sought help related to their immigration and/or domestic violence problems. As such, they are not necessarily representative of all battered immigrant women but represent a subsample of this population: those who have overcome barriers to reveal abuse or seek help, and those whose battering came to the attention of social services, often due to the gravity of their victimization. Furthermore, they are not representative of the subgroup of immigrant women seeking help, as they have been recruited through requests for interviews by agencies that agreed to participate in the study. There were several organizations that for practical or resource reasons did not elect to participate ($n = 8$). Some could not afford the time to conduct lengthy interviews; others were not successful in identifying battered immigrant women who were willing to participate. The sample, therefore, is not a random representation of the universe of battered immigrant women in the United States. The value of the data reported in this study, however, lies in providing accounts of the dynamics of the interaction between domestic violence and immigration from a diverse sample of women who vary by language, ethnicity, nationality, and country of origin.

Most interviews were conducted in the first (non-English) language of the interviewees, as reported by the interviewers.[3] English also was used in some interviews in part or throughout the interview, if the woman being interviewed was well versed and expressed comfort in speaking English. The interviews lasted between 45 minutes and 2½ hours and included closed and open-ended questions about the women's demographic characteristics, circumstances of their arrival in this country, experiences with abuse and violence in their home countries and in the United States, and their attempts to seek criminal justice and/or social services to ameliorate their situations.

Interviewees were offered a modest stipend ($20) for their time, regardless of whether they completed the interview. Interviews were completed most commonly in one session, but a few were completed during a second session. Any requests to skip a certain question because an interviewee was uncomfortable about describing issues she considered private were honored. Despite an extensive list of interview questions, most women responded to our questions in great detail. Translation problems invalidated some of the responses or resulted in partial responses.[4] For these reasons, the results for a small number of items in the interview schedule present only the range of responses rather than a quantified version of the responses.

Quantitative data were calibrated and the open-ended questions transcripts were analyzed through coding techniques described by Glaser (1992). As we read each response, we searched for and identified patterns and variations in participants' experiences and we reached a set of conceptual categories or propositions. The analysis was conducted by applying the logic of analytic induction, which entails the search for "negative cases" and progressively refining empirically based conditional statements (Katz, 1983). When negative cases were encountered, we revised our propositions until the data were saturated, making the patterns identified and the propositions offered consistent throughout the data. Once no new conceptual categories could be added, or propositions had to be reformulated, it was assumed that saturation had been reached.

Research Sample Profile

Female immigrants to the United States in the final research sample ($n = 137$) came from 35 countries.[5] They self-identified with a variety of religions: Christian (58%, of which 36% identified as Catholic),[6] Muslim (22%), Hindu (5%), and Jewish (1%). The age of the women ranged from 19 to 56 years, with a mean age of 32.5 and median age of 31.

In terms of marital status, approximately the same percentage of women were married in their home countries (45%) or were never married (i.e., single and/or living apart from an intimate partner) before coming to the United States (43%). The rest of the sample were either divorced (4%), separated (2%), or living with someone (2%) in their home countries prior to immigrating to the United States. At some point after immigrating to the United States, most single women got involved with an intimate partner. The percentage of "never married" decreased from 43% to 6% and those living with someone increased from 2% to 18%. Although the percentage of women in the sample who were married during the interview was the same as those who were married in their home countries prior to the move to the United States (45%), the percentage of women who stated their marital status was "divorced" at the time of the interview increased from 4% to 18%, and the percentage of women who were separated from their spouses rose from 2% to 23% of the sample.

The range of years the women have lived in the United States was from 1 to 30 years, with a

Table 11.1 English Proficiency

English Language Literacy	Fluent	Some Ability	No Ability	Total
Reading	27%	46%	27%	100%
Writing	25%	37%	38%	100%
Speaking	26%	48%	25%	99%

mean of 8.7 years and a median of 6. The length of time they lived with the abuser was between 1 and 30 years, with a mean of 7.6 and median of 6 years.

In terms of family size, the overwhelming majority of interviewees had children (86%). The mean number of children was 2.4, and the median was 2. The educational level of the interviewees ranged from 5 to 16 years of education, with a mean of 11.6 and a median of 11 years of education (where 12 refers to high school graduate), excluding one woman who stated she had no education at all.

A quarter (25%) of the women in this sample had no ability to speak English, whereas 48% had some ability and another 26% were fluent English speakers. Thus, the use of interviewers skilled in the participants' native language was imperative. Only 27% were fluent readers of the English language, whereas 25% were fluent writers. The vast majority of women sampled had only some or no ability to read (46% some ability; 27% no ability) or write (37% some ability; 38% no ability) in English. The English proficiency of the sample as reported by interviewees is detailed in Table 11.1.

Immigration status varied among interviewees and between interviewees and their intimate partners at the time of the interview (see Table 11.2). Immigration status was divided into the following categories: U.S.-born citizens, naturalized citizens, lawful permanent residents (LPRs), VAWA self-petition, work visa, undocumented,

and temporary visa. Consistent with the definition of immigrant, none of the women in this sample were U.S.-born citizens, whereas 11% of partners were natural-born citizens. Two categories described the largest percentage of female participants: LPR and undocumented. Thirty-four percent of participants were LPRs whereas 36% of their partners were LPRs, and 24% of participants were undocumented immigrants whereas only 15% of partners were undocumented. Naturalized citizens were 19% of our sample of women and 34% of partners. Nine percent of participants and 4% of partners had temporary visas, 9% were VAWA self-petitions, and 5% had work visas. No partners in this study had work visas or were VAWA self-petitions. In general, male partners occupied a citizenship status with greater rights and privileges than did the female victims in this study.

More than half of the women (58%) were employed at the time of the interview. Most often, employment involved unskilled work, and domestic labor was the most common type of work reported (15%) by those employed. Almost half of the women (42%) had no gainful employment. More than three quarters of the husbands or partners (78%) were employed, most often in menial, service, unskilled, or skilled labor. About one quarter of both men (27%) and women (26%) sent money remittances to family in their home countries. More than one third of the women (39%) either used or planned to use public benefits.

Table 11.2 Immigration Status

Immigration Status	Female Immigrants	Intimate Partners
U.S.-born citizen	—	11%
Naturalized citizen	19%	34%
Lawful permanent resident (LPR)	34%	32%
		4% amnesty LPR[a]
VAWA self-petition	9%	—
Work visa	5%	0%
Undocumented	24%	15%
Temporary visa[b]	9%	4%
Total	100%	100%

NOTE: VAWA = Violence Against Women Act. a. Previously undocumented, but secured LPR as part of 1986 Immigration Reform and Control Act. b. Temporary visas included tourist, student, and work visas.

Women reported being subjected to a lengthy period of abuse, ranging from 6 months to 25 years, with a mean of 5.5 years and median of 4 years of mistreatment, which included physical, mental, and sexual abuse, as well as verbal assaults. Women were also subjected to threats of being reported to Immigration and Naturalization Services (INS, now referred to as Immigration and Customs Enforcement [ICE]), being deported, or having their children taken away. The abuse also included tactics of isolating the woman to perpetuate her dependency on the abuser (e.g., she was not allowed to go to English classes, to go to school, to have employment, to be in touch with friends or family members, etc.).

Getting Married

All the women in the study had been married at one time. These marriages may have originated outside or inside the United States.

Regardless of its place of origin, women indicated a lack of choice or a feeling that their resistance to the marriage was ignored. One third of the women in our study experienced arranged marriages,[7] typically through parents or relatives, often meeting the spouse days or weeks before the marriage. Women reported futile resistance to such arrangements. One woman explained, "I refused to marry him. . . . Nobody heard my refusal." Another echoed this sense of entrapment:

Yes, in five days, between knowing/hearing about him and setting the date of the wedding, we were married. I had not seen him before the wedding day. My father told me that he has drinking problems but God willing he will change after marriage. I did not want to marry him, but I had no choice.

Two thirds self-selected their spouses, having met in the country of origin through family, friends, work, or another connection such as shared neighborhood or religion. Those who met their spouses in the United States did so through immigrant community resource organizations. The impetus to marry was generally instigated by forces from without, primarily from family and peers, and even by those who married for love. Women who married for love highlighted the salient effect of familial and communal pressure to marry. Of the women who stated that they chose to marry their mates (two thirds of the sample), more than one quarter (27%) felt pressured to get married. Pressure to marry derived from financial instability, being too young to effectively resist, or, in a few cases, pregnancy. One woman who was married at age 15 explained, "We had no opinion or choice. Whatever our parents would say, we had to do." Others who were perceived of as too old also felt pressure to marry:

> I was the oldest girl in my family, and my younger sister already received a proposal, and my family felt that I was holding the marriage up since no one who had seen me in the past had wanted to marry me. There were 15 other men who had seen me and rejected me, so there was a lot of pressure to marry.

Women also stated how they wed to escape ongoing abuse they were suffering at home.

> I was abused by [my] father physically. The day I left the house, and was proposed to by [my soon-to-be] husband, my father beat me so badly I accepted the marriage proposal, in attempt to get out of the violence I was living in at home.

In this way, for the young as well as those perceived to be too old to remain unmarried, marriage was an escape route from economic instability, surveillance and constant pressures by peers and family, victimization, or unplanned pregnancy. However, in the long term, marriage became yet another site of entrapment for newly immigrant women.

Becoming an Immigrant Battered Woman

Women reported various reasons for coming to the United States. One third (34%) followed their spouses, and one eighth (13%) married U.S. citizens, most of whom ($n = 10$) were military men.[8] About one fifth (16%) came for family reunification. A substantial proportion of the women immigrated for economic reasons: 29% came to improve their economic status and 12% to work. Another significant proportion fled violence in the home country (18%) or political repression (10%).

In the United States,[9] most of the women (87%) reported that the gendered division of labor was clear-cut; women focused on being a wife and mother and were solely responsible for housework and child care. In a minority of cases (17%), women were responsible for grocery or child-related shopping. Most often, they did not have access to a car or did not have a driver's license (60%). Men were responsible for gainful employment and money transactions related to the family, and only in a minority of cases (13%), the women stated that their men helped with work around the house.

According to female interviewees, the abuse resulted in severe mental and physical harm, including depression, withdrawal, numbness, and anxiety. About one third of the women (34%) required hospitalization to treat the injuries that resulted from the battering. Almost half of the women (46%) reported being battered while they were pregnant, with the abuser often trying to hit, kick, or otherwise interfere with the pregnancy. This abuse took place in all parts of the house, in particular in the bedroom or kitchen. Contrary to popular myths concerning domestic violence, it also occurred in public areas such as medical clinics, cars, and various social service offices, in front of family, children, neighbors, and other community members. Members of the husband's family often participated in the abuse.[10] Victimization in the presence of others is indicative of a perception that the abuse is justified or that it will garner no consequence to the perpetrator. The former suggests that the offender's actions are condoned by friends, family, and the community. The latter raises questions about institutional responses to publicly displayed abuse and how the immigrant status of the victim affects the perceptions and reactions of medical and social service workers.

Immigrant women have an added risk of victimization due to relocation. For women who immigrated with a spouse or partner, the move seemed to have an adverse effect on men's level of violence and control tactics. Following their arrival to the United States, for half of these women, the level of violence increased, and almost one quarter (22%) stated that the violence began after arrival: "It has gotten worse. Now he takes out all the frustration on me." For one fifth (20%) of the women, the level of violence stayed the same, for 6% it decreased, and for 2% it stopped. The escalation of abuse was particularly difficult for immigrant women who had left their natal families behind: "I don't have family here, so he tells me that I don't have another choice but to stay with him." Another woman argued that "if he were in Syria, he would take into consideration my parents and would not act abusively as in U.S." Lacking natal family and an extended kin network led to a high rate of social isolation and a deep sense of vulnerability for immigrant women.

Immigration affected husbands and wives differently. For example, some women reported that immigration removed what they understood as constraints against domestic violence, which were rooted in their home countries. "If I want to compare it to Iraq and the U.S., of course the move has affected us. In Iraq we have family, parents, relatives. Here there is drinking and open society, especially for men." Women explained that men acquired new interests, such as alcohol, drugs, gambling, and women, which often accompanied the abusive behaviors of the spouse.

In addition to marital arguments to which men who batter often respond with abuse (e.g., jealousy, infidelity, drinking, money issues, child discipline, or education issues), there also were distinct issues created by the move to the United States that caused tension in the marriage and exacerbated the abuse. For example, many of the women reported that remittances they or their husbands made (i.e., sending money to family members in country of origin) often precipitated arguments or fights. Other issues included the husband's inability to provide for the family in the new country or his insistence that the wife, although now in the United States, continue to be a "traditional woman and never ask him about anything" or that she remain "a very traditional Latina wife, waiting on him hand and foot and never raising my voice on him." Women often explained the reasons for their battering as "my being a bad wife and mother" or "I needed to do what he told me to do, when he told me to do it."

According to women who took advantage of economic opportunities opened for them in the new country, this change provoked their spouses and led to abuse: "In the U.S. he suffered jealousy attacks and saw me prosper—he did not like that."

Economic Challenges

Economic challenges are not unique to immigrant families, but finding suitable employment or any job at all presents major difficulties for most immigrant families. The difficulty of securing employment that matches one's skills is a significant source of conflict between husbands and wives (e.g., being an engineer but working at a gas station). One woman attributed domestic violence to her husband's unemployment and resultant idleness: "He did not work, stayed home, which made him crazy." Another suggested that unemployment, per se, was not the problem. Rather,

the dissatisfaction, failure, disappointment, not being able to meet one's economic expectations in life switches the burden on the wife. She becomes the reason of his failures. She is blamed all the time. She consistently tries to please him; it doesn't work. She gets all the frustration and all kinds of abuses.

At the same time, battered immigrant women also are deprived of supportive community, extended family, or a social network that could help them during such difficulties.

If a spouse did not have work in home country, family or relatives would extend him money and help him. Here in U.S., there are many bills to pay; there is no one to give you a hand. One gets embarrassed.

On the other hand, for women working outside the home, their absence is often seen by men as a threat to the gender hierarchy. Women reported that although they worked outside the home, they controlled little to none of the money they earned and were subject to abuse and domination by their husbands.

It was really good in the beginning, and then he lost his first job and things started getting really bad. It has not been very happy at work, and that is why he would take things out on me. We used to be happy. He would always keep the money and occasionally would demand a lot of sex, but then after a few years, he really started beating me up . . . [in particular] when I had to file his immigration papers.

Immigrant Status

Some women reported that the increase in emotional, sexual, and physical abuse coincided with immigration-specific activities such as entering the country, filing immigration papers, or accessing social welfare systems. The majority of women who came with their spouses reported

that the transition and move to the United States altered the dynamics of the relationship: "He has had more power to manipulate in the U.S. because I am illegal and depended on him and I didn't have any rights here". An immigrant woman's dependency on her male partner elevates his position of dominance over her. At the same time, legal dependency represents a macrostructural vulnerability that systematically marginalizes immigrant women by limiting their access to goods and resources, such as work, social services, protection under the law, and so on. Although law is not intentionally gender biased, one that creates a status-marriage dependency, such as immigration law, makes immigrant women more vulnerable to the domestic violence power dynamic (Erez, 2000; Menjivar & Salcido, 2002).

Husbands became increasingly abusive, and the physical and emotional battering became more conspicuous and severe. One woman explained that "the relationship had gotten bad in Mexico and continued the same in the U.S. The abuse changed from verbal to physical." Another woman agreed that the violence worsened after immigration: "I believe when I came to the U.S. my husband treated me more like a kid. I do not have control over my life." Still another woman explained how "he has become more abusive. He knows the system; I don't. He speaks English; I don't. I don't have family support or someone living with me, so he can lie about me." Even one woman who had divorced her husband still was being threatened by him with regard to her immigration status: "He's going to call INS, because I lied that I was single instead of divorced. [From California] he stalks me, contacts me at home, at work in Michigan."

The overwhelming majority of women (75%) described how men used immigrant status to force them into compliance. "He used my immigration status against me. He would tell me that without him, I was nothing in this country." Men threatened women in a number of ways with regard to immigration including that they would call ICE officials and report their immigration status (40%); get them deported (15%); withdraw their petition to immigrate or otherwise interfere with the naturalization process (10%); take away the children or deny their custodial rights (5%); and, more generally, use immigration status to humiliate or degrade them (5%). One undocumented woman succinctly stated, "He makes threats to report me to the INS if I don't do what he wants."

Women also illustrated the connection between immigration and domestic violence being particularly painful for mothers. "He would tell me I did not have any rights in this country. He threatened to take our children— and he finally did!" In another instance, a woman was forced to trade custody of her children for an adjustment of her immigration status. In addition, mothers feared that their children would be deprived of opportunities for a brighter future that, in the minds of the women, the United States can provide. One woman was concerned about "employment for my older children and their immigration status. [My] son wants to be a U.S. citizen, to attend school and work here." Women did not want to jeopardize their children's immigration status and thought that divorce or leaving the United States would have negative consequences for their children.

Many battered immigrant women who do not have lawful permanent residency believe that divorce means losing their right to work or stay in this country. "If ever I challenge him to stay here, he will divorce me; I will lose my green card and will not be able to financially survive." This translates to jeopardizing her ability to sustain herself financially. Although the VAWA (1994) and its subsequent reauthorization (2000) Public Law 103-322, Violence Crime Control and Law Enforcement Act of 1994 Public Law 106-386, Victims of Trafficking and Violence Protection Act of 2000 provided battered immigrant women a self-petition option, most immigrant women are not aware of it. A husband uses the woman's lack of knowledge, dependency, and immigration status as a weapon to threaten and demand compliance. A man can easily manipulate his control over the relationship and the family because of an immigrant woman's actual or perceived legal dependency: "What prevents me from leaving is the immigration status. I need my green card." Abusers commonly convinced immigrant women that they have no rights (or that they are not entitled to any rights in this country) or that the abusers have the power to cancel their status at any time. Some threatened to withdraw the petitions already filed on the women's behalf or to tell ICE officials that the women married for the sole purpose of legal residency. Most of the women reported enduring abuse for long periods of time because of their desire to remain in the United States, in hopes that their husbands would change their immigration status to legal.

Culture and Community

The majority of the women (65%) reported abuse-tolerant perspectives in their home countries where, they explained, domestic violence is not considered a crime. On one end of the abuse tolerant-intolerant continuum, a woman stated that "my national community doesn't believe that domestic violence exists." Another woman described another position along the continuum: "In Armenian culture, it is okay for a husband to hit his wife, and she should accept it. In America, it is considered a crime." Other women also drew a sharp contrast between their home countries, where domestic violence is a normal part of the marriage, and the United States: "There's a difference because here it's a crime. In Nicaragua if the couple makes up, then it's okay." Overall, women reported being raised in households where fathers and husbands were considered authoritarian decision makers with the right to wield violence as needed to secure women's compliance and that their communities expected them to reproduce such marital arrangements.

The man is the center of authority. He is the supreme decision maker. He is the breadwinner; without him, in general, it is very hard to survive financially, especially if you are unskilled or uneducated.

I was raised in a Hindu household . . . to be obedient and considerate of your elders.

Tradition [says] that you stay with the person you married no matter what he does. Women stay home, to be housewife and put up with domestic violence. Here divorce is acceptable more so domestic violence not accepted.

Women in Latin America and Mexico are supposed to suffer a lot with their husbands.

We have to listen to men more than the American women. We have to stay home most of the time when we get married. We have to be more responsible for children and husbands.

These general comments were reinforced by more individualized lessons:

My mother and father told me to go back and be a better wife. Otherwise I would be shaming them.

My mother told me to bear it, since it was my decision to marry him.

At first they were sad, told me to be patient. God will solve it.

Family members warned that divorce would negatively affect their children's welfare or chances for a good marriage or would decrease their younger sisters' prospects to marry. They used fear of shame, gossip, and guilt to convince their daughters to stay with their abusive husbands. In addition, some women also expressed fears, based on their respective husbands' threats, that leaving would lead to serious injury or even death. Despite their fear and familial admonitions to "put up with domestic violence" and "listen to men," the majority (85%) of women made one or more attempts to leave the abusers. Many of the women tried from 1 to 15 times to extricate themselves from the violence. Some women stated that they attempted to leave hundreds of times.

Reporting Abuse

Women reflected on the expectation that "everything stays in family. Sometimes we don't even tell our families, only after many years of problems." According to their immigrant communities, marital strife was to be kept private and should not be disclosed:

A man can do anything; he is the head of the family, and a woman should always sacrifice to make things work. The expectations for men and women are different. Our culture does not welcome outside intervention. We don't involve outsiders in family issues. We do not consider domestic violence as a crime; police do not get involved. We don't go to shelters. Legal system does not get involved.

They don't like [public intervention], because they want to have the liberty of committing family violence at will.

In this town, it will label the woman. It will make it harder on the woman. [Public intervention is] not a good idea.

In the face of abuse-tolerant and privacy-affirmative perspectives, more than half (54%) of the women stated that they did not report the abuse because of their culture or religion. Nearly half the women did end up dealing with the criminal justice system as a result of the abuse (46%); however, in one-third of these cases (35%), it was because someone other than the victim called the police (neighbor, family member, friend, or hospital staff).

Given the public pressure to keep domestic violence private, women struggled to maintain their social identity and status within their immigrant communities as they struggled to obtain safety for their children and themselves. "I will be ostracized and then where will I go?" Women reflected on distinctions between "home" and "here" attitudes toward criminal justice and other public interventions into domestic violence: "Here the police will help you. In El Salvador, they won't." Unaccustomed to involving outsiders or reporting domestic violence to the police at home ("I'm from Haiti; there is no such law to protect women against domestic violence"), women discussed the tension here in immigrant communities about disclosing abuse to family members and law enforcement.

Female interviewees "became aware of domestic violence in this country, because we know that many people can help us with our problem," including law enforcement, who "are very responsive here and very helpful." Immigrant women "now . . . think [domestic violence] is a crime here," and "Americans treat it like a crime, because that's what it is." Moreover, "here in U.S., a woman demands her rights. The Arab woman does not have a say in Arab countries." As a whole, women identified that "in the U.S. there is more support and protection for the victims, more services" and that "a woman in U.S. has her say, can make her own decisions. The government helps her to have the kids. In our country, no welfare benefits." One woman was impressed that "the clergy here in U.S. encourage you to report [domestic violence] to authorities."

Overall, women felt empowered by having at least the option to mobilize the justice system for help. It provided them a "big relief," or they found it "positive" or "helpful." In some cases, individual women's growing awareness was matched by communal acceptance of domestic violence as a behavior that deserves intervention, in particular when abuse resulted in serious injury. Women distinguished between those who shared ethnic or national identities in the home country and those in the United States.

The Armenians from Armenia think police intervention is bad but Armenians in the U.S. generally do not think police intervention is a bad thing.

In Mexico, they do not interfere until the woman is sent to the hospital; in the U.S. they interfere at an early stage, before there is need to send women to hospital.

Women also distinguished between known cases of domestic violence and those that remain hidden from sight, due to either literally or figuratively closed doors:

It depends. When cases are really bad, like publicly seen abuse, the community 100% supports. When cases happen behind closed doors, the community is hesitant.

It depends from case to case. If you or your family has a social standing.

However, they were well aware that their communities, or segments thereof, did not view favorably intervention by outsiders, in particular law enforcement.

The community is accepting the outside intervention, except the religious leaders. Still even if the spouse is very abusive, they do not give religious divorce to victims. The batterer immediately remarries while the victim is helpless. Also, the community is not very supportive to a divorced woman.

In light of these mixed messages, "it makes you hesitate. Even if you know it is the right thing to do, you postpone the outside intervention."

Some immigrant women had negative experiences (either in the home country or here) with the justice system. Ambiguous messages about and ambivalent attitudes toward law enforcement when coupled with a persistent lack of material resources made many battered women reluctant to seek such intervention. These immigrant community views affected women's responses to the abuse, prolonged their marriages, or prevented them from seeking outside help. Still, individual women prevailed with assistance from immigrant community organizations to secure a semblance of physical security, social standing, and legal stability: "My children and the family unit is what keeps me in the relationship. However, he has promised to stop hitting me. I used to fear deportation, not anymore—I filed my own papers. I also wanted to protect my children."

Conclusion

Battered women in general face a number of interrelated and intricate barriers that complicate their pursuit of safety. Women struggle with, among other factors, embarrassment and shame about disclosing abuse and seeking help from social service or criminal justice agencies; emotional connection to and economic dependency on batterers; reluctance to break up families; and fear of myriad forms of violence, control, and retaliation by abusers and their communities. Although heterosexual men who batter are found in all social groups and at all economic levels, regardless of ethnicity, religion, national origin, cultural affiliation, or immigration status (Volpp, 2001), we have demonstrated that men who batter immigrant women, the majority of whom are immigrants themselves, have access to unique forms of domination and control, some of which are facilitated or even sanctioned by federal immigration law.

In our analysis of 137 battered women who had immigrated to the United States from 35 countries across the globe, we found that the general difficulties that battered women face coexist with challenges they experience as immigrants. Battered immigrant women face a range of legal, economic, and social challenges to safety. Legal challenges include lack of familiarity with or access to social service or criminal justice systems that possess limited immigrant-related cultural and linguistic competencies; legal dependency on batterers; and lack of legal

knowledge. In terms of economic barriers, immigrant battered women report that their communities' economic marginalization combined with the continued responsibility for sending remittances home figures large in batterers' justification for abuse. The social implications of battering are no less central to immigrant battered women than legal and economic barriers. Internal to the community, individual women are limited by a deep fear of losing social status in and the support of their immigrant communities—often the only communities they know—and a fear of various forms of violence, control, and retaliation by the husband and his family, often the only kin they have in the new country. Among other social complications external to the community, immigrant battered women face racist anti-immigrant public sentiment that exacerbates their desire to keep violence private in order to transmit an untarnished and positive image of immigrant community. These patterns persist, despite any differences among the sample.

The interaction of domestic violence and immigration informs not only the level and type of abuse men perpetrate but also individual and community-based responses to the abuse. We found that, over time, immigration shaped the meaning that battered women gave to the controlling behaviors and violence perpetrated against them by their intimate partners. For the most part, women distinguished between attitudes and practices related to domestic violence "here" and "there." That is, they labeled their home countries as abuse tolerant and their adopted country as abuse intolerant. Moreover, despite existing antiracist critiques of the institutionalization of the criminalization of domestic violence, and mixed messages from their own communities as to the appropriateness of reporting domestic violence to the authorities, immigrant battered women seemed to appreciate that domestic violence was considered a crime in the United States and perceived that law enforcement officers were willing to assist as they sought safety for themselves and their children.

However, although at least some immigrant battered women feel empowered to mobilize the criminal justice system, few seem to be familiar with new policies promulgated to protect battered immigrant woman, such as the VAWA self-petition option. And even for those who obtain relevant information and meet legal criteria, pursuit of such remedies may be limited by lack of access to legal assistance or fear of turning to legal authorities, including the criminal justice system. Undocumented immigrants, as well as those in the midst of applying for legal status, or even legal immigrants may avoid engagement with the criminal justice system, in particular if they are part of a "mixed-status" immigrant family or in order to prevent law enforcement from entering an immigrant-majority neighborhood.

The commonalities among immigrants from across such a wide range of countries of origin raise two additional concerns related to immigrant battered women and the criminal justice system. First, over the past decade, the criminalization of immigrants has escalated in the United States, where immigrants are perceived of as criminals in the making who make "real" Americans vulnerable to uninsured drivers, lower wages, unemployment, and property crimes as well as drug, gang, and trafficking-related violent crime. It is "immigrant" on "American" visible forms of crime that populate public discourse. Rarely mentioned is the less visible crime of intimate partner violence. When referenced, intimate partner violence among immigrants is either naturalized (i.e., that's just the way they are) or culturalized (i.e., that's how they treat their women). Naturalization and culturalization of immigrant domestic violence blame intimate partner violence on membership within the group, minimize the effect of intimate partner violence on its victims, and dismiss victims' claims for justice. Moreover, it erases intimate partner violence among so-called "assimilated" and/or native-born members of U.S. society. As such, although we acknowledge that meanings and patterns of domestic violence vary across cultures, we write against the tendency to stereotype

domestic violence as an inherent part of "other" cultures (Razack, 1998; Volpp, 1996, 2001). Such views reinforce the notion that gender-based violence does not warrant state intervention because it is part of the "way of life" (Ferraro, 1989), is the "mentality," or is "part of the culture" (Adelman, Erez, & Shalhoub-Kevorkian, 2003) of certain religious, ethnic, or national groups. This perception also precludes examinations of how structural inequalities and systemic responses (e.g., criminal justice system) may sometimes diminish the material conditions and safety options for individual immigrant women and their families. Dismissing domestic violence as an immigrant or cultural problem also precludes serious considerations of how to ameliorate commonly experienced structural inequalities or how to work with battered immigrant women to identify helpful systemic responses.

Second, in the post-9/11 era, the trend in cities, counties, and states is to enter "287(g) agreements" with the federal government to enforce immigration law as proxies for ICE (Versanyi, 2008). This means that local law enforcement officers, those charged with protecting battered women, are now responsible for enforcing the civil matters of federal immigration law as well. Undocumented immigrants, as well as legal immigrants who face criminal charges, are at risk for deportation, with or without their children. As a result, immigrants, in general, and immigrant women, in particular, regardless of legal status, may go further underground with their need for domestic violence services, thereby rejecting the investment made into the criminal justice system for victims of domestic violence. Further complicating immigrant battered women's pursuit of safety is the recent move by local governments to bar undocumented immigrants from education and social services. These developments make ambiguous which government agencies, including the criminal justice system and members of law enforcement, immigrants and their families have the right to approach—and whom to trust. Individual immigrant women, who commonly shoulder the responsibility for their children's welfare, face the structurally produced hardship of choosing between their safety and a stable, brighter future for their children. Designing social and legal policies that do not further entrap battered immigrant women will continue to challenge feminist criminologists.

Notes

1. Collaborative efforts among battered immigrant women, activists, and researchers also have resulted in the identification of strategies productively used by immigrant women. For examples of barriers and safety strategies, see online materials available at www.immigrantwomennetwork.org, produced by the National Network to End Violence Against Immigrant Women. Many of these issues shaped the legislation addressing the plight of battered immigrant women in the Violence Against Women Act of 1994 and its subsequent revisions.

2. Due to confidentiality requirements, it was not possible to conduct quality control of the translation. However, agencies did not report translation of the questions as a problem.

3. Primary languages included Arabic, Armenian, Bengali, Farsi, French, Haitian, Hindi, Japanese, Malaysian, Portuguese, Russian, Spanish, and Turkish.

4. Most questions invalidated due to translation pertained to criminal justice procedural issues associated with the events described during the interviews.

5. These countries are Armenia, Bahrain, Bangladesh, Brazil, Colombia, Costa Rica, Egypt, El Salvador, former Yugoslavia, Albania, Germany, Great Britain, Guatemala, Guyana, Haiti, Honduras, India, Iran, Iraq, Israel, Palestine, Japan, Latvia, Lebanon, Mexico, Morocco, New Zealand, Nicaragua, Peru, Syria, Trinidad, Turkey, Venezuela, Vietnam (South), and Yemen.

6. Christians described themselves as Adventist, Armenian Apostolic, Assyrian Christian, Baptist, Jehovah's Witness, Lutheran, Mormon, Pentecostal, Protestant, or Roman Catholic.

7. This applied to the marriages they reported, whether in their countries of origin or in the United States.

8. The circumstances and experiences of these "military brides" are described in Erez and Bach (2003).

9. This clear-cut division of labor was also the case in the home country. We focus on the U.S. responses to examine whether division of labor changed as a result of immigration to the United States.

10. Those who have family members in the United States can immigrate due to family unification laws. Thus, men who immigrate have family members in the United States whereas women who follow their husbands leave their own families behind.

References

Abraham, M. (2000). *Speaking the unspeakable: Marital violence among South Asian immigrants in the United States.* New Brunswick, NJ: Rutgers University Press.

Adelman, M., Erez, E., & Shalhoub-Kevorkian, N. (2003). Policing violence against women in a multicultural society: Gender, minority status and the politics of exclusion. *Police and Society, 7,* 103–131.

Adelman, M., & Morgan, P. (2006). Law enforcement versus battered women. *Afflia: Journal of Women and Social Work, 21*(1), 28–45.

Baca Zinn, M., & Thornton Dill, B. (1996). Theorizing difference from multiracial feminism. *Feminist Studies, 22*(2), 321–331.

Bhuyan, R., Mell, M., Senturia, K., Sullivan, M., & Shiu-Thornton, S. (2005). "Women must endure according to their karma": Cambodian immigrant women talk about domestic violence. *Journal of Interpersonal Violence, 20*(8), 902–921.

Britton, D. M. (2000). Feminism in criminology: Engendering the outlaw. *Annals of the American Academy of Political and Social Science, 571*(1), 57–76.

Bui, H. (2004). *In the adopted land: Abused immigrant women and the criminal justice system.* Westport, CT: Praeger.

Bui, H., & Morash, M. (1999). Domestic violence in the Vietnamese community: An exploratory study. *Violence Against Women, 5,* 769–795.

Burgess-Proctor, A. (2006). Intersections of race, class, gender and crime: Future directions for feminist criminology. *Feminist Criminology, 1*(1), 27–47.

Calavita, K. (1992). *Inside the state: The Bracero Program, immigration and the INS.* New York: Routledge.

Calvo, J. (1997). Spouse-based immigration law: The legacy of coverture. In A. Wing (Ed.), *Critical race feminism: A reader* (pp. 380–386). New York: New York University Press.

Chesney-Lind, M. (2006). Patriarchy, crime and justice: Feminist criminology in an age of backlash. *Feminist Criminology, 1*(1), 6–26.

Coker, D. (2001). Crime control and feminist law reform in domestic violence law: A critical review. *Buffalo Criminal Law Review, 4*(2), 801–860.

Collins, P. H. (2000). *Black feminist thought: Knowledge, consciousness and the politics of empowerment.* New York: Routledge. (Original work published 1991)

Crandall, M., Senturia, K., Sullivan, M., & Shiu-Thornton, S. (2005). "No way out": Russian-speaking women's experiences with domestic violence. *Journal of Interpersonal Violence, 20*(8), 941–958.

Crenshaw, K. (1991). Mapping the margins: Intersectionality, identity politics and violence against women. *Stanford Law Review, 41*, 1241–1298.

Dasgupta, S. (2000). Charting the course: An overview of domestic violence in the South Asian community in the United States. *Journal of Social Distress and the Homeless, 9*(3), 173–185.

Davis, R. C., & Erez, E. (1998). *Immigrant population as victims: Toward a multicultural criminal justice system* [Research in brief]. Washington, DC: National Institute of Justice.

Dobash, R. E., & Dobash, R. (1979). *Violence against wives: A case against the patriarchy.* New York: Free Press.

Erez, E. (2000). Immigration, culture conflict and domestic violence/woman battering. *Crime Prevention and Community Safety: An International Journal, 2*, 27–36.

Erez, E. (2002). Migration/immigration, domestic violence and the justice system. *International Journal of Comparative and Applied Criminal Justice, 26*(2), 277–299.

Erez, E., & Bach, S. (2003). Immigration, domestic violence and the military: The case of "military brides." *Violence Against Women, 9*(9), 1093–1117.

Ferraro, K. J. (1989). Policing woman battering. *Social Problems, 36*(1), 61–74.

Gabaccia, D. (Ed.). (1992). *Seeking common ground: Multidisciplinary studies of immigrant women in the U.S.* Westport, CT: Greenwood Press.

Gardner, M. (2005). *The qualities of a citizen: Women, immigration and citizenship, 1870–1965.* Princeton, NJ: Princeton University Press.

Glaser, B. G. (1992). *Basics of grounded theory analysis.* Mill Valley, CA: Sociology Press.

Harris, A. (1990). Race and essentialism in feminist legal theory. *Stanford Law Review, 42*, 581–616.

Higginbotham, E. (1997). Introduction. In E. Higginbotham & M. Romero (Eds.), *Women and work: Exploring race, ethnicity, and class* (xv–xxxii). Thousand Oaks, CA: Sage.

Hirsch, J. S. (2003). *A courtship after marriage: Sexuality and love in Mexican transnational families.* Berkeley: University of California Press.

Hondagneu-Sotelo, P. (Ed.). (2003). *Gender and U.S. immigration: Contemporary trends.* Berkeley: University of California Press.

Katz, J. (1983). A theory of qualitative methodology. In R. Emerson (Ed.), *Contemporary field research* (pp. 127–148). Boston: Little, Brown.

Menjivar, C., & Salcido, O. (2002). Immigrant women and domestic violence: Common experiences in different countries. *Gender & Society, 6*(6), 898–920.

Merry, S. (2000). *Colonizing Hawai'i: The cultural power of law.* Princeton, NJ: Princeton University Press.

Muftic, L. R., & Bouffard, L. A. (2008). Bosnian women and intimate partner violence: Differences in experiences and attitudes for refugee and nonrefugee women. *Feminist Criminology, 3*, 173–190.

Orloff, L. (2002). Women immigrants and domestic violence. In P. Strum & D. Tarantolo (Eds.), *Women immigrants in the United States* (pp. 49–57). Washington, DC: Woodrow Wilson International Center for Scholars and the Migration Policy Institute.

Pessar, P. (1999). Engendering migration studies: The case of new immigrants in the United States. *American Behavioral Sciences, 42*, 577–600.

Potter, H. (2006). An argument for Black feminist criminology: Understanding African American women's experiences of intimate partner violence using an integrated approach. *Feminist Criminology, 1*(2), 106–124.

Raj, A., & Silverman, J. (2002). Violence against immigrant women: The roles of culture, context, and legal immigrant status on intimate partner violence. *Violence Against Women, 8*, 367–398.

Razack, S. (1998). *Looking white people in the eye: Gender, race, and culture in courtrooms and classrooms.* Toronto, ON: University of Toronto Press.

Salcido, O., & Adelman, M. (2004). "He has me tied with the blessed and damned papers": Undocumented immigrant battered women in Phoenix, Arizona. *Human Organization, 63*(2), 162–173.

Sassen, S. (1998). *Globalization and its discontents.* New York: New Press.

Scales-Trent, J. (1999). African women in France: Immigration, family and work. *Brooklyn Journal of International Law, 24,* 705–737.

Snider, L. (1998). Toward safer societies: Punishment, masculinities and violence against women. *British Journal of Criminology, 38*(1), 1–39.

Stanko, E. (1985). *Intimate intrusions.* New York: HarperCollins.

Steinbugler, A. C., Press, J. E., & Johnson Dias, J. (2006). Gender, race and affirmative action operationalizing intersectionality in survey research. *Gender & Society, 20*(6), 805–825.

Strum, P., & Tarantolo, D. (Eds.). (2002). *Women immigrants in the United States.* Washington, DC: Woodrow Wilson International Center for Scholars and the Migration Policy Institute.

Versanyi, M. (2008, April 20). Should cops be la migra? *Los Angeles Times.* Retrieved April 22, 2008, from www.latimes.com

Volpp, L. (1996). Talking "culture": Gender, race, nation, and the politics of multiculturalism. *Columbia Law Review, 96*(6), 1573–1617.

Volpp, L. (2001). Feminism versus multiculturalism. *Columbia Law Review, 101*(5), 1181–1218.

Wachholz, S., & Miedema, B. (2000). Risk, fear, harm: Immigrant women's perceptions of the "policing" solution to women abuse. *Crime, Law and Social Change, 34*(3), 301–317.

Wood, S. (2004). VAWA's unfinished business: The immigrant women who fall through the cracks. *Duke Journal of Gender, Law & Policy, 11,* 141–155.

Zhou, M. (2002). Contemporary female immigration to the United States: A demographic profile. In P. Strum & D. Tarantolo (Eds.), *Women immigrants in the United States* (pp. 23–34). Washington, DC: Woodrow Wilson International Center for Scholars and the Migration Policy Institute.

CHAPTER 12

Invisible or Pathologized?

Racial Statistics and Violence Against Women of Color

Kathleen J. Ferraro

Within sociology and the larger public, people know that statistics can be used to support just about any position (Best, 2001). The creation of statistical data and its manipulation is a human process. It may be employed to perpetuate racial stratification or to critique it. In *Thicker Than Blood*, Tukufu Zuberi (2001) presents a concise and eloquent argument about the uses and misuses of racial statistics, particularly for sociologists. Chronicling the history of racial statistics in eugenics and their contribution to essentialist notions of race, Zuberi nevertheless argues for the race conscious use of statistics in the struggle for racial justice. The Statement of the American Sociological Association on *The Importance of Collecting Data and Doing Social Scientific Research on Race* (American Sociological Association, 2003) takes the position that the collection of data on race is essential for understanding and addressing social inequalities. The paradox that racial statistics simultaneously reify race as an objective fact yet remain as indispensable tools for illustrating the ongoing effects of racism creates a demand for the deracialization of racial statistics. Zuberi argues that this process cannot be separated from the deracialization of society (2001: 106). We cannot eradicate racism by rejecting the use of racial statistics, but we can perpetuate racism by abstracting statistics from their historical and social context and by treating race as a coherent, homogeneous, causal variable.

The challenge to deracialize statistics has not often been met by social scientists. According to Martin and Yeung (2003), professional sociologists have given increased attention to "the conceptual category of race" since the 1930s. By examining a sample of articles published in the *American Sociological Review* since its inception, Martin and Yeung demonstrate that although there is superficial recognition of the importance of race to all social phenomena, the majority of

Ferraro, K. (2008). Invisible or pathologized? Racial statistics and violence against women of color. *Critical Sociology*, *34*, 193–211.

AUTHOR'S NOTE: The author would like to thank Akil Kokayi Kolfani, David Fasenfest, and the anonymous reviewers for their helpful suggestions on earlier drafts.

analyses between 1982 and 1999 simply include race as a control variable in regression analyses (2003: 533–4). This statistical approach to race contributes to confusion about causal effects versus causal theories described by Zuberi (2001: 94–7 and 123–33). That is, including race in a statistical model may provide important information about associations, but cannot be treated as an examination of a causal theory about any phenomenon. Without careful contextualization of data, these analyses can obscure the social processes of domination and lead to spurious conclusions about race as a cause. This confusion has been particularly apparent in conservative, racial realist interpretations of research on race and crime, poverty, and education (Brown et al., 2003). I am using the term "racial realist" as explained by Michael K. Brown et al. in *Whitewashing Race* (2003). Although racial realists span the political spectrum, Brown et al. describe three claims that distinguish their views on race. First, all racial realists view racism as a "thing of the past" that is perpetuated by efforts to document and ameliorate racism. Second, whatever inequalities persist are viewed as a consequence of the failure of people of color rather than ongoing discrimination and institutional racism. Finally, they share the view that the "civil rights establishment" has betrayed people of color for their own political advantage. In sum, the racial realist position holds that color-blind policies are the best prescription for ending racial differences and that differences in resources, status, and life chances are a consequence of individual lassitude and immorality (Brown et al., 2003: 6–8). For example, racial realists describe the horrific rates of incarceration of African American; Latina/o; and American Indian men, women, and youth as evidence of individual behavioral deficiencies and cultural pathologies in communities of color (cf. McWhorter, 2000; Thernstrom and Thernstrom, 1997). Extracting arrest and incarceration data from systematic analyses of accumulated layers of disadvantage, what Brown et al. term "disaccumulation" (2003: 23), these scholars reinforce a view of race as a cause of criminal behavior rather than a social construction reflecting white privilege and policies of exclusion and marginalization that continue into the twenty-first century.

How can sociologists devoted to racial justice use statistics in a manner that enlarges understanding rather than reinforces racial stratification? Zuberi argues that we can contribute to the deracialization of statistics and society by developing "social statistics in a way that keeps the human being and human effort evident" (2001: 106). Statistical data help to demonstrate the harmful impacts of racism and are necessary to deconstruct racial realist arguments. But without linkages to human complexities, historical legacies, and structured disaccumulation, it is too easy to employ racial statistics to illustrate personal and cultural pathologies rather than structural, accumulated disadvantages.

Statistical Data on Violence Against Women

I would like to focus on one arena of social data, violence against women, which has benefited from increased inquiry over the past thirty years. There are several national-level general surveys, including the National Family Violence Surveys, the National Violence Against Women Survey, the National Crime Surveys, and the National Survey of Families and Households, that have produced data on incidence, prevalence, and victim/perpetrator characteristics of various forms of violence. The Bureau of Justice Statistics also collects data on homicide, including intimate partner homicide. In addition, there have been thousands of focused studies on all aspects of violence against women. The body of scholarship on this topic is voluminous and has contributed to a vast shift in public understanding of the nature and extent of violence against women as well as improved resources and legislation.

Yet this scholarship has not come to terms adequately with the meanings of race and the intersections of race, class, and gender for the experiences of violent victimization or developing appropriate responses (Sokoloff and Dupont, 2005). Kimberle Crenshaw's *Mapping the Margins: Intersectionality, Identity Politics, and Violence Against Women of Color* (1991) first articulated the silences and exclusions of the anti-violence against women movement that was based on an assumption of the homogeneity of women's encounters with violent victimization. As a consequence of this and other scholarly and political critiques, serious efforts emerged in the 1990s to develop intersectional analyses of violence against women, including the emergence of INCITE! Women of Color Against Violence and their annual conferences, The Color of Violence (see Sudbury, 2005; and the INCITE! web page). National and state coalitions against domestic violence have women of color caucuses and committees. The Institute on Domestic Violence in the African American Community at the University of Minnesota is dedicated to providing research and technical assistance to communities. Several books provide rich, qualitative data about the experiences of African American, American Indian, Latina, and Asian/Pacific Islander women with intimate partner violence (Abraham, 2000; Bui, 2004; Dasgupta, 2007; McGillivray and Comaskey, 1999; Raphael, 2000; Richie, 1996; Ross, 1998; Smith, 2005a; Websdale, 2001; West, 1999). But *statistics* on the race of victims and perpetrators are still routinely presented in the abstract, disconnected from human beings and social context. Racial statistics on victimization have the potential to draw attention and resources to neglected populations of victims and their unique circumstances. They simultaneously have the potential to reify race, obscure other dimensions of identity and simplify the extraordinarily complex "matrix of oppression" (Collins, 2000) faced by victims of intimate partner violence. As with data on crime perpetration, conservative politicians and racial realists may employ these data to reinforce their individualistic interpretations

of behavior that emphasize the pathology of families of color.

Survey Data on Intimate Partner Violence

The National Violence Against Women Survey (NVAWS), jointly sponsored by the National Institute of Justice and the Centers for Disease Control and Prevention, is based on telephone interviews with a nationally representative sample of 8,000 women and 8,000 men conducted in 1995 and 1996 (Tjaden and Thoennes, 2000a, 2000b). Researchers collected data on a range of interpersonal victimizations over the lifetime and in the 12 months preceding the interviews. Among other variables, data on race and ethnicity were collected and highlighted in the final reports. This survey is the foundation for many of the reports on rates of intimate partner violence in training materials, advocacy, and scholarly work since its publication in 2000. On the issue of race/ethnicity, the survey found similar rates of violent victimization overall for white, African American, and "Hispanic" women and men; higher rates for American Indian people; and lower rates for Asian/Pacific Islanders (Tjaden and Thoennes, 2000a: 21–2). For intimate partner violence, however, African Americans, American Indians/Alaska Natives, and mixed race women and men had higher rates of all three forms of victimization (rape, physical assault, and stalking), with the exception that African American women had lower rates of stalking (Tjaden and Thoennes, 2000b: 25–6). Asian/Pacific Islander women and men had significantly *lower* rates than each of the other groups. These findings suggest that African American, American Indian, and mixed race women and men are not at a greater risk of violent victimization in general than are white women and men but are at greater risk of intimate partner violence.

Since Hispanic is coded as an ethnicity rather than race, separate analyses are provided on rates of victimization for Hispanics. For overall victimization and intimate partner victimization, Hispanic women indicated few differences in physical assault or stalking (2000a: 27; 2000b: 23). However, Hispanic women "were significantly more likely than non-Hispanic women to report that they were raped by a current or former intimate partner at some time in their lifetime" (2000a: 27). On the other hand, in terms of all rapes, Hispanic women "were significantly less likely to report they had ever been raped than women who identified themselves as non-Hispanic" (2000b: 23). The finding of higher rates of intimate partner victimization among African American, American Indian, and mixed raced people of both sexes is consonant with earlier data produced by the National Crime Victimization Surveys and the National Family Violence Surveys (Straus and Gelles, 1989), as well as with qualitative and ethnographic research in specific communities.

The NVAWS is unusual in its inclusion of data on American Indian and Asian/Pacific Islander women, as the bulk of research and scholarship treats "race" as a black/white or white/"other" phenomenon. In part, this reflects the low percentage of the overall US population that is American Indian (1.5% including mixed-raced American Indians in 2000), as well as the separate criminal justice system that governs misdemeanor offenses on reservations. The NVAWS indicates that American Indian/Alaska Native women and men report higher rates of victimization and Asian/Pacific Islander women and men report lower rates of victimization than other racial groups (Tjaden and Thoennes, 2000a: 25–6; 2000b: 23). The authors' discussion of these findings focuses on the "willingness to report" by women of different racial groups, suggesting that differences may not reflect true rates of victimization, but rather women's willingness to report their experiences to researchers. This is a factor in all survey research, particularly research on sensitive topics. Experts on violence against Asian/Pacific Islander women have discussed the cultural barriers to reporting domestic

violence and suggest survey and official data grossly underestimate the extent of intimate partner violence against this group of women (Asian and Pacific Islander Institute on Domestic Violence, 2002; Dabby, 2002; Dasgupta, 2002). There is no evidence or cultural analysis suggesting that American Indian women are *more* likely than women of other racial groups to reveal domestic violence to researchers or official agents. Given that "willingness to report" affects all victimization research, there is no reason to assume that the higher rates of victimization against American Indian women are merely the artifact of this methodological problem.

The authors also note that the finding of higher rates of victimization of American Indian women and men "is consistent with previous research that shows American Indian couples are significantly more violent than their white counterparts" (Tjaden and Thoennes, 2000a: 26). This wording subtly shifts meaning from reporting of violent victimization to depicting American Indian couples as more violent than whites. It is interesting that the wording focuses on American Indians and whites, since it is actually Asian/Pacific Islanders who report the lowest rates of intimate partner violence. Why not report that the findings are consistent with previous research demonstrating that white couples are significantly more violent than their Asian/Pacific Islander counterparts? The authors note that there may be significant differences among tribal groups, but they have no data to help identify these differences. They also mention that "demographic, social, and environmental factors" (2000a: 26) or "cultural attitudes, community services, and income" (2000a: 56) should be examined to understand the differences in rates of victimization between various racial and ethnic groups. At several points in both reports, Tjaden and Thoennes suggest that differences "may be explained by demographic, social, and environmental factors" (2000a: 26). With a nod to these other sources of influence, the possibility that race *is* the explanatory factor remains open.

There are substantive reasons to question the comparability of data collected from different racial and ethnic groups. The survey was administered by telephone between November, 1995 and May, 1996. Estimates of the proportion of households in tribal communities that had basic telephone service in those years range from 39 to 53 percent (Economic Development Administration, 1999; US Department of Commerce, 1999). Thus, at least half of American Indian households living on reservations were excluded from participation. There was no effort to incorporate cultural sensitivity to Native, African American, Asian/Pacific Islander, or Hispanic communities in the administration of the questionnaire, although a Spanish language version was employed where relevant. It is not clear that questions meant the same thing to people answering from these diverse cultural locations. Because American Indians/Alaska Natives made up less than one percent of the US population in 1995–96, only 88 women of the 8,000 interviewed identified themselves as American Indian/Alaska Native. The authors do not report the tribal affiliations of these women or attempt to unravel the cultural variations among tribes (see Snipp, 1989). The validity of conclusions about "significant differences" between groups based on these small samples with unknown hidden biases is questionable.

A recent report from the US Bureau of Justice Statistics (BJS), *American Indians and Crime,* by Steven W. Perry (2004), provides the most detailed data on the violent victimization of American Indians/Alaska Natives. Drawing on data from the National Crime Victimization Surveys (NCVS) from 1992 to 2001, Perry indicates that American Indians have the highest level of violent victimization of all races, a per capita rate twice that of the US resident population (2004: iv). Although American Indian males, like males of all races, are more likely than females to be victims of violence, American Indian women are much more likely to be victims than women from other racial groups. According to Perry,

> The rate of violent crime victimization among American Indian females (86 per 1,000) was 2 1/2 times the rate for all females. The victimization rate among American Indian females was much higher than that found among black females (46 per 1,000 aged 12 or older), about 2 1/2 times higher than that among white females (34), and 5 times that of Asian (17) females. (2004: 7)

This report is the only BJS report on violence that calls readers' attention to the high levels of violent offending by *whites* by highlighting this data in the introduction (Perry, 2004: v). Overall, about 60 percent of American Indian victims of violence described the offender as white, which is about the same percentage of all victims of violence combined (2004: v). But for white and black victims, a member of their own race perpetrates most violence; that is, most violent victimization of whites and blacks is *intraracial.* In contrast, most violent victimization of American Indians is *interracial* and is most often perpetrated by whites. Although this statistic is not highlighted as a major finding, whites perpetrated an astounding 78 percent, nearly four out of five, rapes and sexual assaults of American Indian women (Perry, 2004: 9). This rate of interracial rape is significantly distinct from all other research on rape that demonstrates it is overwhelmingly an intraracial crime (LaFree, 1989; Greenfeld, 1997).

The report does highlight findings on the role of alcohol in violent victimization, both in the foreword by Lawrence A. Greenfeld and in the tabular and bulleted "highlights" at the beginning of the 50-page report. The report does not indicate the race of the offender using alcohol and/or drugs, but does state that "Overall, American Indian victims reported alcohol use by 62 percent of the offenders, compared to 42 percent for all races" (2004: 10). Readers are left with the impression that victimization of American Indians is often linked to alcohol without clarifying the race of the user. There is, thus, potential for reading this report as evidence of American Indian alcoholism as a primary contributor to victimization despite lack of clear data supporting this victim-blaming stereotype.

The NVAWS and the NCVS produce different results about the rates of victimization and the differences between races, with NCVS finding greater differences between black and white women. There are, however, consistent results from both sources. First, males are much more likely to be victims of violence than females, but females are much more likely to be victims of *intimate partner* violence than males. Second, all non-lethal forms of interpersonal violence have *decreased* over the past decade among all racial groups, although not *significantly* so for American Indians and Asian Americans. Third, American Indians are at least twice as likely as all other racial groups to be victimized by interpersonal violence and are most likely to be victimized by a person outside of their racial group. Finally, African American, American Indian, and mixed race people are more likely to be victimized by an intimate partner than are white or Asian/Pacific Islander people.

Homicide data are widely viewed as the most valid victimization data since definitional and self-report issues are not as relevant for homicides. Even these data may be skewed by organizational decisions about how to classify homicides (Websdale, 1999). Beyond issues of reliability, the gravity of intimate homicides demands attention to all factors that may contribute to variations on the rate of this crime. The data on homicide indicate that African Americans and American Indians are more likely to be killed by an intimate partner than are whites or Asian/Pacific Islanders. Overall, blacks were six times more likely than whites to be murdered in 2002, and the intimate partner homicide rate was higher for black girlfriends than any other group (Fox and Zawitz, 2004). The intimate partner homicide rate is higher for black women than white women, but there has been a much more rapid decline in the intimate partner homicide rate for all black people than for whites. The greatest decline in intimate partner homicide has been in deaths of black men. On the other hand, the intimate partner homicide rate for white women has remained fairly steady while it has declined for all other groups over the past decade.

The Social Interpretation of Statistical Survey Data

How do scholars, activists, and the general public receive these racial statistics? How are they linked to the human being *and* to human effort? And what do they mean to the people whose lives they describe and in terms of any possible generalizations we can infer? I would like to address these questions as a modest effort at humanizing and deracializing the data on violence against women.

Data indicating that African American and American Indian women are more likely to be victims of interpersonal violence are routinely cited in academic and activist literature. On the one hand, both activists and scholars have critiqued the invisibility of women of color in the anti-violence movement and research (Richie, 2000; Smith, 2004, 2005b). They have argued that it is imperative that the broad category "women" be reconsidered to encompass race, ethnicity, nation, sexuality, and class. The goals and policies for ending violence against women have been based on the assumption that the needs of middle class white women would be an adequate framework for the development of efforts aimed at all. Women of color *do not have* identical experiences to women belonging to the dominant racial category in the US, white women, regardless of their social class and geographic location. It is necessary to develop information on violent victimization that is specific to each group of women, rather than assume homogeneity. This much is obvious. Women who first broke the silence about violence against women of color were harshly criticized for reinforcing negative images and diverting attention from racism (Williams, 1991). It took courage and support from others to continue to write and speak about this violence, particularly when people in the white-dominated anti-violence movement often insisted that violence against women "cuts across all classes and races." While this is, of course, true, it does not mean that class and race do not matter in the experience of rape, incest, sexual assault, battering, stalking, and homicide. The use of statistical data to demonstrate that African American and American Indian women experienced even higher rates of victimization than white and Asian American women helped to highlight the need to recognize the ways in which race matters in violence against women.

At the same time, these data also can reinforce racial realist notions about the pathologies of African American and American Indian communities. In my ride-alongs with police officers to domestic violence calls in Phoenix, Arizona in the 1980s, I heard several officers make explicit comments about "the way these people are," in reference to black and Latino households (Ferraro, 1989a). The idea that intimate partner violence occurs primarily among low-income, inner-city people of color was precisely the idea that statements about "cutting across class and race" were meant to counter (Bograd, 2005). Statistical statements such as those contained in government reports and repeated on web-sites and educational materials around the country that state that African American women have rates of abuse 35 percent higher than other groups *may* be used to endorse notions that black families are more pathological than others. When American Indian women are described as having rates twice or two and a half times as great as other women, particularly when these data are presented in a context emphasizing high rates of alcohol use by perpetrators, again it *may* contribute to racist stereotypes about the pathologies inherent in American Indian communities. This is true despite the other statistics indicating that *white* people are the most common perpetrators of violence against American Indians and that more American Indian people abstain from drinking alcohol than do whites or Hispanics

(Beauvais, 1998). Recent research indicates that both popular stereotypes and prior research reports have exaggerated rates of alcohol dependence among American Indians and failed to appreciate the cultural distinctiveness among diverse tribes (Spicer et al., 2003).

The complicated relationships between social and economic marginality, alcohol and drug abuse, and intimate partner violence are not well understood and have been the site of contentious disagreements (Gelles and Loseke, 1993). There is a correlation between drug and alcohol abuse and the perpetration of intimate partner violence as well as other crimes (Durose et al., 2005; Fals-Stewart, 2003; Zubretsy and Digirolamo, 1996). However, there is little evidence regarding the causal nature of that relationship. Obviously many people abuse drugs and alcohol without also abusing their intimate partner. In severe and lethal cases of intimate partner violence, there are high rates of alcohol and drug abuse by perpetrators and victims (Ferraro, 2006; Websdale, 1999). This *correlation,* however, is best viewed as one aspect of a constellation of factors that increase risk for severe levels of intimate partner violence rather than as a cause.

The data cannot dictate how people will perceive and use them. Indeed, we do not know how most of the social audience makes sense of these data. The selection of language and the focus of analyses encourage a reading of the findings that de-emphasizes white violence. No reports are titled "Violent Crime and Whites," reflecting the now common recognition of the invisibility of whiteness as a racial category, particularly in the discussion of social problems. As Zuberi (2001) argues, the presentation of the data on race and victimization tends to depict race as at least a potential causal variable. When authors suggest that the correlations between race and victimization may be explained by other factors, they imply that they may not, that peoples race may be the cause of their victimization. And as Zuberi makes clear, suggesting that race is the cause of a social outcome, such as violent victimization, is illogical and unhelpful (2001: 123–34). What helps us understand social experiences is linking statistical data with history, social relations, and human meaning. It seems particularly dangerous to cite racial statistics without either identifying the meanings and contexts they describe or embedding them in history. For some women who experience violence, such as American Indian members of specific nations, there is no written record of their experiences to provide non-Indians a context for the abstract data. Andrea Smith (2003, 2004) argues that even intersectional analyses of violence against women have failed to take into account the histories of colonization and genocide against American Indians, and the ongoing economic, social and environmental violence that shapes interpersonal violence against Native peoples (see also Chen, 2006).

The Criminal Processing System and Intimate Partner Violence

One of the important ways that race matters to the experience of intimate partner violence is the relationship of different racial groups to the criminal processing system (Walker et al., 2000). From the beginning of the anti-violence against women movement people have voiced concerns about a criminal justice focus in terms of the implications for all marginalized groups (Ferraro, 1996). The relationship of battered women of color to the police is complicated. On the one hand, there has been a laissez-faire attitude toward crimes between low-income people of color that left battered women unprotected. Particularly when other resources for protection are absent, such as a working vehicle and money for travel and other housing, the protection of police is important. At the same time, women of color are reluctant to drag police into their affairs and to subject their partners to police intervention (Bui, 2004; Richie, 1996). Like all women, women of color may have ongoing love for their partners, as well as complicated dependencies involving money, transportation, childcare and extended friend and family relationships. These relational webs are threatened when men are arrested and incarcerated. African American men are already vulnerable to intense policing and, in some areas, to police brutality. Women of all races who call the police, especially in densely populated, low-income areas where behavior is highly public, may be viewed as traitors and snitches and face hostility from their communities (Websdale, 2001: 166). Calling in outside authorities may also generate involvement of Child Protective Services who may view domestic violence as an indication of an unsafe environment for children (Ferraro and Moe, 2003).

In the mid-1980s, a number of factors coalesced to change police policies regarding domestic violence (Ferraro, 1989b, 1996). Mandatory arrest policies were adopted by many large metropolitan police departments and eventually became statutory requirements in many states (Crime Control Institute, 1986). These policies mandate arrest for all domestic violence incidents when probable cause exists. Since the development of mandatory arrest for domestic violence policies, it has become more common for women to be arrested, and this trend is common knowledge among people in the community (Miller, 2005). Women are deterred from calling the police for fear of their own arrest. For undocumented immigrant women, there is a fear of deportation, despite recent legal protections provided by the Violence Against Women Act. Another new problem is the "one strike" policies in public and even privately rented housing that evicts tenants when crimes are committed at their residence, even if they are the victims (Renzetti, 2001). Finally, a common tactic of abusers of all races is to threaten retaliation against the woman and those she loves if she involves the police.

An analysis by Wells and DeLeon-Granados (2002) uses racial statistics to demonstrate the racial and gender impact of the criminal justice response to domestic violence. Examining data from all counties in California for 1987 to 2000, they found that black males were much more likely to be arrested for domestic violence than were Hispanic males, who were much more likely to be arrested than white males. Data is not provided on American Indians or Asian/Pacific Islanders. Between 1987 and 2000, the increase in rates of arrest per 100,000 adults was 17 percent for black males, 22 percent for white males, and 47 percent for Hispanic males. The rate of increase for females was much more dramatic, since the base number was almost zero in 1987. For black women, the percentage change was 378 percent; for white women, 405 percent; and for Hispanic women, 569 percent. The rates of incarceration are even more astounding. For men, the percentage increase was: 90 percent for blacks, 153 percent for whites, and 145 percent for Hispanics. For women, it was: 1,025 percent for blacks, 1,706 percent for whites, and 2,557 percent for Hispanics (Wells and DeLeon-Granados, 2002: 35–6). The initial low rates of arrest and incarceration of women make the extraordinary percentage increases less dramatic than they appear. However, the data do indicate that the "get tough" policy has resulted in many more people being arrested and incarcerated, and that women of all races face a significantly increased risk of arrest and incarceration for domestic violence.

Some might view this increase as a good thing. It demonstrates that domestic violence is a crime that will not be tolerated, and it isolates violent abusers from their victims, at least for a short period. However, Wells and DeLeon-Granados report that criminal justice intervention has relatively little impact on one specific form of victimization, intimate partner homicide (2002: 17). "Our findings imply that the net effect of arrests, convictions, and incarceration [for domestic violence] is not to reduce female victimization, but to ensnare more women in the criminal justice system net" (2002: 21). As women become more aware of the consequences of calling the police for help, fewer women, especially low-income women of color, will access this avenue of help.

The Lived Experience of Violence

How do these statistical data play out in the lived experiences of women? The story of Angel, a woman I interviewed as part of a study of the relationship between women's victimization and offending, exemplifies the complex relationships between racially based disaccumulation, interpersonal violence, and the criminal justice response to intimate partner violence. Angel is an African American woman serving time for writing bad checks.[1] She has seven children and had been in two long-term relationships. Both of Angel's parents had been heroin addicts, and she spent most of her childhood in her father's home. Her father ran a prostitution ring and sold drugs, and she describes the household as extremely violent and chaotic. When she was nine, one of her favorite uncles was shot to death in front of her. The offender was never apprehended or punished. "It was a black on black crime on the south side of Chicago—who cared, you know?" Her father died of an overdose when Angel was 16, and she set up her own household. She knew what she did *not* want in her life and focused on education. Angel completed two and a half years of college on scholarship before becoming pregnant with her first child, dropping out of college and getting married. Her husband was extremely abusive, both mentally and physically, and after seven years and three more children, she left him on the east coast and moved to Arizona. He tracked her down and convinced her to resume the relationship, but he quickly became violent again and she fled with her children. Angel gave up a job she loved to move to another city, and this led to her financial problems and eventually to writing bad checks and bank fraud:

I moved from there and came out here and started selling computer software and was doing very well, but I had an abusive husband. I was trying to get away and I was terrified of him and I left my job here in

Tucson and I moved to Phoenix and took a better job and then the job—that company—went out of business within two months, so here I was with all of the responsibilities with the children and giving up my other good job and had nothing, and quickly the rent rolls around and the, everything, and so one thing led to another and here I sit.

Angel felt that her check writing was linked to her negative childhood experiences. She did not blame her crimes on the intimate partner abuse she suffered, but did feel that she would not have had the problems that led her to jail without her husband's abuse. When asked if she had ever tried to call the police for help with his violence, she explained:

No, I never called the police in Tucson. I didn't have relatives here at the time. And what the Tucson Police Department had been doing is taking both people in. And so I was terrified to call the police because I didn't know what would happen to the children. I had nobody to take them, so if I had called the police on him they would've taken us both to jail. They would've taken my children to CPS and then foster care, and it would've turned into a nightmare.

Angel did not frame her terror about calling the police in terms of racism or concerns about images of black men. Rather, she felt certain she would be arrested as part of the pattern of dual arrests for domestic violence in the city and that her children would become ensnared in the child protective bureaucracy. She viewed her time in jail as "somewhat of a vacation" because she had been able to read and work on the novel she was writing by hand. Her mother (now clean and sober) had come out to Arizona to care for the children, and if she received prison time, Angel had outlines for two other books. The intimate partner violence she endured had undermined her career goals and financial stability, contributed to her dependence on bad checks to make ends

meet, and led to separation from her children. She nevertheless focused on using her time constructively. She concluded our interview by telling me, "You have to try to find the goodness in all the bad things that happen to us in life and there's plenty if you look." Angel's energy, love and optimism, despite the bad things that had happened to her, are invisible in statistical data describing her race and victimization. Her terror of the criminal justice and welfare systems, as well as her violent ex-husband, are also invisible to those who insist that getting tough on domestic violence is the most appropriate approach to empowering women.

Controlling for Class

When the socioeconomic status of victims is taken into consideration, differences in rates of victimization between racial groups diminish or disappear. For example, Benson and Fox (2002) conducted a detailed analysis of the National Survey of Families and Households (NSFH) and found that race and ethnic disparities in rates of intimate partner violence were greatly reduced or eliminated by examining the effects of neighborhood context (2002: 126). Their analysis of employment instability, subjective economic distress, and number of debts placed women in highly disadvantaged communities at greater risk of intimate partner victimization. According to Benson and Fox:

Our analyses show that when controls for community context are in place, the association between race/ethnicity and violence weakens or disappears. That is, the effect of race and ethnicity on intimate violence is in large part a function of the greater likelihood of Black and Hispanic couples to reside in neighborhoods with concentrated economic disadvantage. (2002: 126)

Similarly, Centerwall (1984) found that a six-fold difference between blacks and whites in rates of intraracial domestic homicide in Atlanta and New Orleans disappeared when socioeconomic status was considered.

The importance of economic disadvantage in explaining higher rates of intimate partner violence against women of color is not synonymous with Wilson's argument that class has supplanted race as the major cause of inequality in the USA (Wilson, 1978). Rather, racial statistics can demonstrate that residential segregation, wealth disparities, and racially based limits on opportunities for occupational success and advancement persist. The disaccumulation of people of color is related to violent interpersonal victimization. Race matters because it continues to influence people's access to housing, wealth, and good jobs, and these resources influence the chances of becoming violent toward and being violently victimized by family members. Race also influences the access to fast and skilled medical care that may mean the difference between life and death (Websdale, 1999: 7).

Like many studies relying on national survey data, Benson and Fox do not analyze rates of violence among American Indians because this data is not included in the NSFH. Data on economic and social distress in American Indian communities, however, suggest that they are among the most disadvantaged neighborhoods in the USA. In terms of deracializing statistics, it would be helpful to contextualize information on high rates of victimization with information on the ways that American Indian communities, especially on reservations, have been systematically disadvantaged. There is tremendous variation in living conditions among American Indian communities, from the small Mashantucket Pequot nation in Connecticut that operates one of the most successful casinos in the nation to the Lakota nation in Pine Ridge, South Dakota where approximately 63 percent of the population lives below poverty level (US Census Bureau, 2004). On some reservations, the unemployment rate is 85–90 percent and housing conditions are crowded and substandard. In 1990, 20 percent of households on reservations lacked complete

plumbing facilities, compared with 1 percent of US households overall. On the Navajo and Hopi reservations, about one-half of households lacked complete plumbing (US Census Bureau, 1995: 3). Some traditionalists prefer not to have running water or electricity in their homes, but other people would like the conveniences most people in the US take for granted. The significance of these "neighborhood characteristics" is different for American Indian people than for all other groups in the US, as many tribes consider their homelands part of their identities and have no desire to move. As Roberta Blackgoat, a leader of resistance to the forced relocation of Navajos from Big Mountain, Arizona said, "Our way has no word for relocation" (Cockburn, 1997). It is not housing discrimination that limits their residential choices on reservations but centuries of government policies that have contributed to disaccumulation within communities.[2]

The American Indian women I have met who have been victims of intimate partner violence have had much more difficulty escaping abusers than women from other racial groups (Ferraro, 2006). Reticence to leave their homes on the reservation makes moving away from abusers an unattractive option. For many of the tribes in the Southwest, land and homes are held in women's names and inheritance is matrilineal. While this is a source of power, it is also a more compelling reason to stay put rather than flee an abusive partner. Large parts of the reservations are rural with undeveloped roads and few telephones. Tribal police cover huge amounts of territory, so it may take hours for a woman to find a working phone, contact an officer, and have someone arrive to protect her. Extended clan relationships may mean there are more relatives to help protect a woman and her children and provide resources; they may also mean that the abusive partners relatives will shield him from arrest or prosecution. Serious assaults and rapes are under the jurisdiction of the FBI. All of the issues of fear and mistrust of police that exist in other communities of color are multiplied by the historical relationship between many tribal members and the FBI. For these and many other reasons, American Indian women face unique barriers to escaping violence.

Crystal is an American Indian woman who was charged with first-degree murder in the stabbing death of her husband.[3] Her parents were traditional and spoke only their Native language, and English was Crystal's second language. Although her family did not have much income, they had wealth in the traditional sense: land, animals, a strong family, and respect in the community. Crystal did not finish high school and had no interest in further education. She married a man from another tribe and had five children. They lived in government housing in a small community on a large, rural reservation. The abuse she suffered was physically severe and emotionally devastating. She had teeth knocked out, permanent bumps on her head, a large indentation on her forearm, was losing the sight in one eye, and had trouble remembering and concentrating. Her husband's rages had been random and sporadic, but his emotional abuse was constant. He monitored her movements and accused her of having sex with her relatives and any man in the vicinity, and only referred to her as "bitch" or "whore." "It seemed like that was my name." She was beaten with a lead pipe, a rubber hose, pots and pans, "anything he could get his hands on," kicked with steel-toed boots, burnt with cigarettes, raped, pulled by her hair, slammed into walls, punched, slapped, and pinned to the floor. She was also badly beaten while pregnant. Crystal did not work and relied on her husband for all her income. Members of his family knew about the abuse but refused to intervene. Crystal's parents lived in a remote area and she did not want them to know what was going on. Her husband would not let her visit them and neither Crystal nor her parents had a telephone in their homes. On the day of her husband's death, he had repeatedly told Crystal, "You're gonna get it when we get home, bitch." Like most times when he became violent, she did not know what she did wrong or how to calm him down. They were driving around with two of

the children in the car, trying to locate people who owed him money. After listening to his threats for several hours, Crystal grabbed the children and jumped out of the car. She tried for hours to get help from relatives and the police and was finally able to get a ride from her sister-in-law. When they returned to her apartment to pick up milk and diapers for the baby, her husband suddenly appeared at the side of their car. He reached through a partially open window, grabbed Crystal by the hair and began to slam her head against the inside of the car while yelling threats about what she was "going to get at home." She picked up a knife she had brought along and blindly stabbed out with it. It struck her husband and he died before he could be taken to the hospital. Crystal was sentenced to probation in a treatment facility for American Indian women suffering from domestic violence and alcohol problems.[4]

Like Angel, Crystal did not trace her problems to racism. Her focus was on her family and the confusion and despair she experienced due to her husband's violence and eventual death. The context of the violence she endured and inflicted reflects both the historical legacies of colonialism and the contemporary disaccumulation on many reservations, as many Native activists have argued (Chen, 2006; Smith, 2005a). She wanted to stay on the reservation, but there were few options there for her to support herself and children apart from her husband. The lack of police protection left her alone and vulnerable. The closest battered women's shelter was 200 miles from her home and she had no way to get there. Traditional methods for resolving interpersonal conflicts had been undermined by 150 years of intervention by the US government that imposed a tribal council and legislation reflecting western European legal practices. The community that would have worked to heal the problems in her marriage in the 1700s was not available to her in the 1990s.[5]

Like racial statistics, women's stories can also be viewed as evidence of individual deficiencies and cultural pathologies. They cannot stand alone, without the context provided by historical, social and statistical data describing the ways their individual problems are related to structured disaccumulation. Statistical analyses of existing survey data to explore possible connections between structural disadvantage and intimate partner violence illustrate the potential for racial statistics to contribute to racial justice. Yet even data that illustrate structural disadvantage do not provide historical and community context (Hamby, 2005). Without knowledge of the specific and varied ways that racial and ethnic groups have been targets of discrimination, abuse, and genocide, current disadvantages can be taken as evidence of cultural deficiencies. The Moynihan Report (1965) and Dinesh D'Souza's (1995) *The End of Racism* are examples of how data on rates of poverty can be used to support racist causal theories. Moynihan's influential contention that the "tangle of family pathology" rooted in slavery was the principle source of black poverty was in clear contradiction to historical and contemporary knowledge of the ways black families negotiate racist discrimination (Gutman, 1976). Since individualistic and moralistic interpretations of social problems are so widespread in the mainstream media, even racially conscious statistical analyses must be carefully linked to historical and contemporary information on social policies that have produced and maintain racial stratification. Statistical data must also be supplemented with the complex stories of people's lives to avoid simplifying social problems like intimate partner violence and reifying abstract categories like race.

Methodological Issues in Deracializing Statistics

It is the rich narrative data collected by ethnographers and qualitative interviews that provide the human face to the racial statistics. Rates of victimization begin to make violence against women of color visible, but do not reveal the lived realities of racism and the accumulated disadvantages and frustrations of women who are abused by their intimate partners. The disproportionate representation of African American and American Indian women among victims of intimate partner violence must be understood within the context of the histories of slavery, colonization, genocide and racism, contemporary structural disadvantages, and the complicated entanglements of each woman's life. Although there are similarities in all women's experiences of intimate partner violence, this context informs the experiences of African American and American Indian women in a manner distinct from women of other racial and ethnic groups. Scholarship and policies that ignore these distinctions may only contribute to the obstacles confronting women of color.

At the same time, narrative data may also be skewed in ways that reinforce stereotypes and highlight deficiencies over strengths. All women's stories of abuse by intimate partners contain elements of pathology and when we focus on individuals, it is easy to lose sight of the larger context of social inequality and injustice. Qualitative data depend on the selection biases of researcher and researched. Only those willing and available to tell their stories become part of the documentary fabric describing the lives of any group. How researchers hear those stories may be different than how they are felt by the people who share them. The pathos of these stories may overwhelm the sociological imagination and our ability to understand the political in the personal. My argument for contextualizing racial statistics with qualitative and historical descriptions raises many methodological and epistemological questions. How can we use racial statistics to illuminate the ongoing disparities between racial and ethnic groups without contributing to the racial realist belief that cultural pathologies are at the root of social problems? Can qualitative data ground abstract statistical categories without obscuring the historical and political contexts that shape people's lives? Can sociological data ever capture the complexity of people's experiences? These challenges cannot be resolved through more sophisticated methodological techniques. The deracialization of data, both quantitative and qualitative, depends upon an ongoing commitment to the deracialization of society.

Notes

1. Angel selected this pseudonym.
2. This is not to suggest that there is no housing discrimination against American Indian people who choose to live off reservation.
3. I do not identify Crystal's tribal affiliation in order to minimize the possibility of identification.
4. Crystal's problems are described in greater detail in Ferraro (2006).
5. Efforts to create indigenous alternatives to criminal justice processing, such as the Navajo Peacemaking Courts, have been highly problematic. See Smith (2005c).

References

Abraham, M. (2000) *Speaking the Unspeakable: Marital Violence Among South Asian Immigrants in the United States.* Rutgers University Press: New Brunswick.

American Sociological Association (2003) *The Importance of Collecting Data and Doing Social Scientific Research on Race.* American Sociological Association: Washington, DC.

Asian and Pacific Islander Institute on Domestic Violence (2002) *Socio-Cultural Contexts: Research Series.* Fact Sheet. Asian and Pacific Islander Institute on Domestic Violence: San Francisco.

Beauvais, F. (1998) American Indians and Alcohol. *Alcohol Health and Research World* 22(A): 253–60.

Benson, M. L. and Fox, G. L. (2002) *Economic Distress, Community Context and Intimate Violence: An Application and Extension of Social Disorganization Theory, Final Report.* US Department of Justice: Washington, DC. URL (consulted 12 January 2005): http://www.ncjrs.org/pdffiles1/nij/grants/193434.pdf

Best, J. (2001) *Damned Lies and Statistics: Untangling Numbers from the Media, Politicians, and Activists.* University of California: Berkeley.

Bograd, M. (2005) Strengthening Domestic Violence Theories: Intersections of Race, Class, Sexual Orientation, and Gender. N.J. Sokoloff (Ed.) *Domestic Violence at the Margins,* pp. 25–38. Rutgers University Press: New Brunswick.

Brown, M. K., Carnoy, M., Currie, E., Duster, T, Oppenheimer, D. B., Shultz, M. M. and Wellmann, D. (2003) *Whitewashing Race: The Myth of a Color-Blind Society.* University of California Press: Berkeley.

Bui, H. N. (2004) *In the Adopted Land: Abused Immigrant Women and the Criminal Justice System.* Praeger: Westport.

Centerwall, B. S. (1984) Race, Socioeconomic Status, and Domestic Homicide, Atlanta, 1971–2. *American Journal of Public Health* 74(8): 813–5.

Chen, M. (2006) Rising Violence against Native Women Has Colonial Roots. *The New Standard* 7 November 2006. URL (consulted 21 November 2006): http://newstandardnews.net/content/?actions=show_item&itemid=3853

Cockburn, A. (1997) Big Mountain Land-Grab: Theft of Indian Lands Exposes Sham of Indian Sovereignty Under US Laws. *Los Angeles Times, Orange County Edition* 27 April 1997, Commentary section. URL (consulted 24 January 2005): http://www.worldfreeinternet.net/news/nws32.htm

Collins, P. H. (2000) *Black Feminist Thought: Knowledge, Consciousness, and the Politics of Empowerment,* 2nd Edition. Routledge: New York.

Crenshaw, K. (1991) Mapping the Margins: Intersectionality, Identity Politics, and Violence against Women of Color. *Stanford Law Review* 43(6): 1241–99.

Crime Control Institute (1986) Police Domestic Violence Policy Change. *Response* 9:16.

Dabby, F. C. (2002) *Violence Against Women: A Lifetime Spiral, a Tightly Coiled Spring. Domestic Violence in Asian & Pacific Islander Communities: Proceedings of the National Summit 2002,* pp. 5–9. Asian and Pacific Islander Institute on Domestic Violence: San Francisco.

Dasgupta, S. D. (2002) *Homicide, Gender, and Culture. Domestic Violence in Asian & Pacific Islander Communities: Proceedings of the National Summit 2002,* pp. 47–51. Asian and Pacific Islander Institute on Domestic Violence: San Francisco.

Dasgupta, S. D. (2007) *Body Evidence.* Rutgers University Press: New Brunswick.

D'Souza, D. (1995) *The End of Racism: Principles for a Multiracial Society.* The Free Press: New York.

Durose, M. R., Harlow, C. W., Langan, P. A., Motivans, M., Rantala, R. and Smith, E. L. (2005) *Family Violence Statistics.* Bureau of Justice Statistics: Washington, DC.

Economic Development Administration (1999) *Assessment of Technology Infrastructures in Native Communities.* US Department of Commerce: Washington, DC.

Fals-Stewart, W. (2003) The Occurrence of Partner Physical Aggression on Days of Alcohol Consumption: A Longitudinal Diary Study. *Journal of Consulting and Clinical Psychology* 71(1): 41–52.

Ferraro, K. J. (1989a) Policing Woman Battering. *Social Problems* 36(1): 61–74.

Ferraro, K. J. (1989b) The Legal Response to Battering in the US. M. Hanmer, J. Radford and E. Stanko (Eds.) *Women, Policing and Male Violence: International Perspectives,* pp. 155–84. Routledge: London.

Ferraro, K. J. (1996) The Dance of Dependency: A Genealogy of Domestic Violence Discourse. *Hypatia* 11(4): 77–91.

Ferraro, K. J. (2006) *Neither Angels nor Demons: Women, Crime, and Victimization.* Northeastern University Press: Boston.

Ferraro, K. J. and Moe, A. M. (2003) Mothering, Crime, and Incarceration. *Journal of Contemporary Ethnography* 32(1): 9–40.

Fox, J. A. and Zawitz, A. W. (2004) *Homicide Trends in the United States.* US Department of Justice: Washington, DC. URL (consulted 22 January 2005): http://www.ojp.usdoj/gov/bjs/homicide/homtrnd.htm

Gelles, R. J. and Loseke, D. R. (1993) *Current Controversies on Family Violence.* Sage: Newbury Park.

Greenfeld, L. A. (1997) *Sex Offenses and Offenders: An Analysis of Data on Rape and Sexual Assault,* February 1997, NCJ-163392. Bureau of Justice Statistics: Washington, DC.

Gutman, H. (1976) *The Black Family in Slavery and Freedom, 1750–1925.* Pantheon: New York.

Hamby, S. L. (2005) The Importance of Community in a Feminist Analysis of Domestic Violence among Native Americans. N.J. Sokoloff (Ed.) *Domestic Violence at the Margins,* pp. 174–93. Rutgers University Press: New Brunswick.

INCITE! *Women of Color against Violence.* URL (consulted 23 October 2006): http://www.incitenational.org

LaFree, G. (1989) *Rape and Criminal Justice: The Social Construction of Sexual Assault.* Wadsworth: Belmont.

McGillivray, A. and Comaskey, B. (1999) *Black Eyes All of the Time: Intimate Violence, Aboriginal Women, and the Justice System.* University of Toronto Press: Toronto.

McWhorter, J. H. (2000) *Losing the Race: Self-Sabotage in Black America.* Free Press: New York.

Martin, J. L. and Yeung, K. T. (2003) The Use of the Conceptual Category of Race in American Sociology, 1937–99. *Sociological Forum* 18(4): 521–35.

Miller, S. L. (2005) *Victims as Offenders: The Paradox of Women's Violence in Relationships.* Rutgers University Press: New Brunswick.

Moynihan, D. P. (1965) *The Negro Family: The Case for National Action.* US Department of Labor: Washington, DC.

Pern, S. W. (2004) *American Indians and Crime.* US Department of Justice: Washington, DC.

Raphael, J. (2000) *Saving Bernice.* Northeastern University Press: Boston.

Renzetti, C. (2001) One Strike and You're Out. *Violence Against Women* 27(6): 685–98.

Richie, B. E. (1996) *Compelled to Crime: The Gender Entrapment of Battered Black Women.* Routledge: New York.

Richie, B. E. (2000) A Black Feminist Reflection on the Antiviolence Movement. *Signs: Journal of Women in Culture and Society* 25(4): 1133–7.

Ross, L. (1998) *Inventing the Savage: The Social Construction of Native American Criminality.* University of Texas Press: Austin.

Smith, A. (2003) Not an Indian Tradition: The Sexual Colonization of Native Peoples. *Hypatia* 18(2): 70–85.

Smith, A. (2004) Beyond the Politics of Inclusion: Violence Against Women of Color and Human Rights. *Meridians* 4(2): 120–5.

Smith, A. (2005a) *Conquest: Sexual Violence and American Indian Genocide.* South End Press: Boston.

Smith, A. (2005b) Looking to the Future: Domestic Violence, Women of Color, the State, and Social Change. N.J. Sokoloff (Ed.) *Domestic Violence at the Margins,* pp. 416–34. Rutgers University Press: New Brunswick.

Smith, A. (2005c) Book Review: Restorative Justice and Family Violence. *Violence Against Women* 11(5): 724–30.

Snipp, M. (1989) *American Indians: The First of This Land.* Russell Sage: New York.

Sokoloff, N. J. and Dupont, I. (2005) Domestic Violence: Examining the Intersections of Race, Class and Gender. An Introduction. N. J. Sokoloff (Ed.) *Domestic Violence at the Margins,* pp. 1–13. Rutgers University Press: New Brunswick.

Spicer, P., Beals, J., Croy, C., Mitchell, C., Novins, D. K., Moore, L. and Manson, S. M. (2003) The Prevalence of DSM-III-R Alcohol Dependence in Two American Indian Populations. *Alcoholism: Clinical and Experimental Research* 27(11): 1785–97.

Straus, M. A. and Gelles, R. J. (1989) *Physical Violence in American Families.* Transaction: New Brunswick.

Sudbury, J. (2005) INCITE! Critical Resistance Statement With an Introduction by Julia Sudbury. N. J. Sokoloff (Ed.) *Domestic Violence at the Margins,* pp. 102–14. Rutgers University Press: New Brunswick.

Thernstrom, S. and Thernstrom, A. (1997) *America in Black and White: One Nation, Indivisible.* Simon and Schuster: New York.

Tjaden, P. and Thoennes, N. (2000a) *Extent, Nature, and Consequences of Intimate Partner Violence: Findings From the National Violence Against Women Survey.* US Department of Justice: Washington, DC.

Tjaden, P. and Thoennes, N. (2000b) *Full Report of the Prevalence, Incidence, and Consequences of Violence Against Women: Findings From the National Violence Against Women Survey.* US Department of Justice: Washington, DC.

US Census Bureau (1995) *Housing of American Indians on Reservations.* US Department of Commerce: Washington, DC.

US Census Bureau (2004) *State and County Quick Facts.* URL (consulted 23 January 2005): http://quickfacts.census.gov/qfd/states/46000.html

US Department of Commerce (1999) *Falling Through the Net: Defining the Digital Divide.* National Telecommunications and Information Administration: Washington, DC.

Walker, S., Spohn, C. and DeLone, M. (2000) *The Color of Justice.* Wadsworth/Thomson Learning: Belmont.

Websdale, N. (1999) *Understanding Domestic Homicide.* Northeastern University Press: Boston.

Websdale, N. (2001) *Policing the Poor: From Slave Plantation to Public Housing.* Northeastern University Press: Boston.

Wells, W. and DeLeon-Granados, W. (2002) *Analysis of Unexamined Issues in the Intimate Partner Homicide Decline: Race, Quality of Victim Services, Offender Accountability, and System Accountability, Final Report.* US Department of Justice: Washington, DC. URL (consulted 13 January 2005): http://www.ncjrs.org/pdffiles1/nij/grants/196666.pdf

West, T. C. (1999) *Wounds of the Spirit: Black Women, Violence, and Resistance Ethics.* New York University Press: New York.

Williams, P. J. (1991) *The Alchemy of Race and Rights.* Harvard University Press: Cambridge, MA.

Wilson, W. J. (1978) *The Declining Significance of Race: Blacks and Changing American Institutions.* University of Chicago Press: Chicago.

Zuberi, T. (2001) *Thicker Than Blood: How Racial Statistics Lie.* University of Minnesota Press: Minneapolis.

Zubretsky, T. M. and Digirolamo, K. M. (1996) The False Connection Between Adult Domestic Violence and Alcohol. In A. R. Roberts (Ed.) *Helping Battered Women,* pp. 222–8. Oxford University Press: New York.

CHAPTER 13

When Crises Collide

How Intimate Partner Violence and Poverty Intersect to Shape Women's Mental Health and Coping

Lisa A. Goodman, Katya Fels Smyth, Angela M. Borges, and Rachel Singer

Being poor means "going through life knowing that there is no safety net to catch you should you fuck up and fall. There is no trust fund, no parents with cash on hand to cover a month's rent; the way the stress of being poor or working class can rip apart a family or destroy its members often means there's no family to call, period" (Tea, 2004, p. XII).

Nearly one quarter of the women in this country have been physically or sexually assaulted by an intimate partner (Tjaden & Thoennes, 2000). A disproportionate number of these women also struggle with poverty (Vest, Catlin, Chen, & Brownson, 2002). Until recently, the connection between domestic violence and poverty has been underresearched, poorly understood, and ignored by most policy makers and direct service providers (Eby, 2004; Lown, Schmidt, & Wiley, 2006; Sutherland, Sullivan, & Bybee, 2001). Typically, researchers have considered income or class a variable to be controlled for; domestic violence service providers have not emphasized long-term economic viability, just as social service providers have not made domestic violence a central concern (Farmer & Tiefenthaler, 2003; Lott & Bullock, 2007; Tiefenthaler, Farmer, & Sambira, 2005), and mental health practitioners have not shaped interventions in ways that account for survivors' poverty (Goodman & Epstein, 2008). As a result, domestic violence policies and practices rarely suit the needs of those in greatest need of help.

This knowledge, policy, and practice gap is a legacy of the domestic violence movement's origins. Early domestic violence activists purposely highlighted the classlessness of domestic violence to portray it as a problem affecting all women. In doing so, they hoped to bring larger scale public attention to the problem, while at the same time framing it primarily as a problem of gender oppression (Meier, 1997; Schechter, 1982). Indeed, for many years, it was considered heresy

Goodman, L. A., Smyth, K. F., Borges, A. M., & Singer, R. (2009). When crises collide: How intimate partner violence and poverty intersect to shape women's mental health and coping. *Trauma, Violence, & Abuse, 10*, 306–329.

to note any connections among race, class, and domestic violence (Kanuha, 1996; Richie, 2000). This strategy served the movement well. It heightened public awareness of violence against women and sparked the development of intimate partner violence (IPV) interventions in the criminal justice system, health care system, religious institutions, and the employment sector among other places (Goodman & Epstein, 2008; Richie, 2005).

In the last decade, however, a rapidly growing body of evidence has begun to challenge this classless framing, instead demonstrating incontrovertibly that poverty plays an enormous role in the occurrence and perpetuation of domestic violence (Humphreys, 2007; Raphael, 2003) as well as its effects. Still, the early framing echoes in a social services system response that ignores the particular needs and circumstances of low-income women, thereby compounding their risk and intensifying abuse's consequences (Purvin, 2007). The development of a more comprehensive set of tools for aiding and supporting survivors of partner violence requires greater understanding of what it means to live at the highly vulnerable intersection of poverty and partner violence and the profound costs this location has for women's mental health. This article highlights the complex relationship between poverty, IPV, and mental health. We describe how IPV and poverty co-occur at a high rate, magnify each other's effects, and, in each other's presence, constrain coping options. The first section describes how poverty can both contribute to and result from partner violence. The second section describes three consequences of both IPV and poverty (stress, powerlessness, and social isolation) that help explain the ways that partner violence and poverty intersect and reinforce each other to shape survivors' lived experiences, and we highlight some of the resultant consequences for mental health. Our discussion points to difficulties that are missed when women contending with both poverty and IPV are viewed primarily as poor (and being battered) or as battered (and also poor). The third section

introduces the term "survival-focused coping" to describe women's methods of coping with partner violence in the context of poverty. The concept of survival-focused coping recognizes the constant negotiations and adjustments that low-income survivors make to exert control in the face of dramatically limited and high-stake choices. For a summary of sections 1 to 3, see Table 13.1. The final section suggests implications for practice and research, with a particular focus on mental health.

The Co-occurrence of Poverty and IPV

A variety of terms have been used to describe those living in poverty in America, including *low socioeconomic status (low SES), poor, low-income,* and *disadvantaged* (Baker, 1996). The lack of consensus on terminology is matched by disagreement about how to define poverty. Some definitions are based on the level of income, no matter the source; others are based on extent of use of public assistance. Most definitions focus solely on financial resources at a particular moment in time without regard to the situation's persistence and most ignore the complex interactions among class, race, ethnicity, gender, sexual orientation, religion, and geographic location that inform the lived experience of poverty and the diversity of people who live in poverty (Smith, 2005). Although acknowledging the limitations of a conceptualization of poverty that fails to take into account race and other factors, for the purposes of this article we use the terms poor and low-income (interchangeably) to describe people living close to or below the poverty line as defined by the U.S. Census.[1] We recognize that this subsumes many diverse groups and hope it will enable us to lay the theoretical groundwork for more refined work in the future.

In 2003, 12.3% of the U.S. population, or 36.5 million Americans, were living below the poverty line (U.S. Census Bureau, 2006). The majority are women and their children, and more than half (55%) are ethnic minorities (Miranda & Green, 1999; Proctor & Dalaker, 2003). Compared with 11% of white women, 25% of African American women and 23% of Latinas are poor (U.S. Census Bureau, 2006).

Given the large number of poor women in this country, a critical research finding of recent years is that household income level is one of the most, if not *the* most, significant correlates of partner violence (Cunradi, Caetano, & Schafer, 2002; Vest et al., 2002). The lower the income, the more likely there will be violence (Bachman & Saltzman, 1995; Greenfeld et al., 1998; Vest et al., 2002). Among 19,000 women in a pooled multistate sample, those with incomes below US$25,000 were almost twice as likely to experience abuse as those with higher incomes (Vest et al., 2002). In addition, studies consistently find that the *majority* of homeless women have been physically assaulted by intimate partners (Browne & Bassuk, 1997; Goodman, 1991); that lifetime rates of physical IPV for women reliant on temporary assistance for needy families (TANF, more popularly known as "welfare") range from 30% to 74%, depending on the way that IPV is measured (Barusch, Taylor, & Derr, 1999; Colten, Cosenza, & Allard, 1996; Lloyd & Taluc, 1999; Tolman & Rosen, 2001); and that women living in subsidized housing projects are at elevated risk, with 19% reporting IPV in the last year, according to one study (DeKeseredy, Alvi, Schwartz, & Perry, 1999). At this point, the evidence is impossible to ignore.

A number of prospective studies demonstrate that past exposure to violence predisposes women to unemployment and poverty and that poverty further increases women's risk for subsequent victimization. Although these studies have suggested a range of potential explanations for this strong association, a few come up repeatedly across studies. The remainder of this section discusses some of these explanations, highlighting first the ways in which poverty contributes to IPV and then the ways that IPV contributes to or helps maintain poverty.

As important as untangling this relationship is, the sequencing is largely artificial, as poverty and IPV are inextricably tied together in a downward spiral, as discussed in subsequent sections.

Poverty's Contribution to IPV

Although numerous cross-sectional studies have documented the correlation between poverty and IPV, only a few longitudinal studies have been done to track the unfolding of this damaging association. Those few that do exist demonstrate clearly that partner violence often follows from poverty. For example, one prospective study that followed 265 women leaving a domestic violence shelter found that participants who reported the lowest level of financial resources or income 2 years later were more likely to be re-abused during the course of those 2 years compared to those with more resources (Bybee & Sullivan, 2002; Sullivan, 1997; Sullivan, Basta, Tan, & Davidson, 1992). Similarly, a national survey found that even controlling for violence at baseline, women's employment instability and financial strain increased the subsequent likelihood of re-abuse (Benson & Fox, 2004).

These findings are not surprising. It is perhaps self-evident that because women from impoverished communities lack the resources of middle- or upper-class women, they are more likely to rely on the practical and financial support of an abusive partner and therefore face more material hurdles in leaving an abusive or potentially abusive relationship (Costello, Chung, & Carson, 2005; Goodman & Epstein, 2008). Other factors associated with poverty that may entrap women in abusive relationships include language barriers in trying to engage with the social services or legal systems, fear of racism, and immigration problems that may prevent women from seeking outside sources of support (Humphreys, 2007).

However, the risks poor women face are also socially and politically created. For example, prior to 1996, many women who left abusive relationships depended on the welfare system for economic support during and after that process (Purvin, 2007). With the advent of welfare reform in 1996, however, a new federal policy was established that removed any legal entitlement to financial aid on the basis of need and imposed a 5-year lifetime limit on welfare benefits. This new policy heightened low-income women's risk dramatically by forcing them into a situation where they had to find employment quickly or face absolute destitution and homelessness (Lindhorst & Padgett, 2005; Purvin, 2007). One longitudinal ethnographic study involving repeated interviews with women in Cleveland, Ohio, as they reached this limit illuminates the dilemmas it created (Scott, London, & Myers, 2002). Facing the time limit and trying to find and keep a job while also caring for their children, some women were able to avoid homelessness and sustain employment only by relying on their (abusive) partners for child care, transportation, and assistance with household labor. Those who could not obtain employment (or whose controlling partners sabotaged their efforts to stay employed) were forced to rely still more heavily on emotionally and physically abusive partners for instrumental help or direct financial assistance. For these women, as for most victims, their partners were more than abusers; they were significant social, emotional, and material supporters. These women's choice to remain with their abusers represented a complex calculation in the face of bad and worse options (Goodman & Epstein, 2008).

IPV as a Contributor to Poverty

Research also demonstrates that IPV decreases a woman's likelihood of escaping poverty. Several longitudinal studies, for example, illustrate IPV's role in disrupting women's ability to obtain and maintain employment. Based on more than 1,000 women in Illinois, one study found that IPV at Time 1 was associated with decreased employment stability 2 years later, even after controlling for other relevant factors (Staggs,

Long, Mason, Krishnan, & Riger, 2007). Another study of low-income homeless and housed women found that IPV survivors were one third as likely as low-income nonvictims to maintain employment for at least 30 hours per week for 6 months following their report of abuse, and they were only one-fifth as likely to work full time during that period (Browne, Salomon, & Bassuk, 1999).

A number of qualitative studies have revealed the dynamics underlying these findings. Abusive men may directly sabotage their partners' ability to do their jobs (e.g., by destroying work, educational materials, the family car, or clothing), harass women at their work places, refuse to provide transportation or child care, or inflict visible bruises the night before a critical job interview (Bybee & Sullivan, 2005; Moe & Bell, 2004; Raphael, 2000). In this way, abuse can be a direct cause of unemployment for all women. Poor women, if they have jobs, may not have the leverage with their employers to explain the problem or seek help; they may be in nonprofessional jobs where they can be easily replaced, so employers have little incentive beyond caring and goodwill to hold a job for a woman who cannot reliably make it to work on time (Raphael, 2000).

Even in the absence of such direct interference, abused women may struggle with psychological and emotional issues such as depression, anxiety, posttraumatic stress disorder (PTSD), and drug or alcohol dependence that then become impediments to employment (Browne et al., 1999; Tolman & Rosen, 2001). Finding a job and securing reliable, affordable child care can be challenging for any woman, and a woman with little education and work experience often has access only to jobs that are highly stressful and inflexible. At least one qualitative study found that for many of the participants who were simultaneously contending with the psychological difficulties wrought by abuse and the threat of continuing violence, the added obligations and maneuvering necessary for obtaining and maintaining a job proved impossible (Moe & Bell, 2004).

Not only does IPV impede women's efforts to obtain employment, it may also contribute to poverty by pushing them into housing instability or outright homelessness (Tolman & Rosen, 2001). One study based on a nationally representative sample of California women found that those who reported IPV in the last year had almost four times the odds of reporting housing instability, including difficulty in paying rent, mortgage, or utility bills, frequent moves, overcrowded living conditions, or doubling up with family or friends, compared to women without IPV histories (Pavao, Alvarez, Baumrind, Induni, & Kimerling, 2007). Although this study was cross-sectional and could not determine which came first, other research shows that between 22% and 57% of homeless women identify partner abuse as the immediate cause of their homelessness (Bassuk et al., 1997; Institute for Children & Poverty, 2002; Levin, McKean, & Raphael, 2004; Wilder Research Center, 2004). Many women are also evicted from their homes, or are denied access to housing, based on the crimes their abusive partners have committed against them (Lapidus, 2003; Renzetti, 2001).[2]

This high rate of co-occurrence has potentially profound implications because it suggests that the historical understanding that poverty and IPV operate as independent variables is fallacious and that service and system responses that do not recognize that they are, in fact, highly correlated are not addressing a common presentation of IPV: IPV in the context of poverty.

The next section discusses how persistent poverty and IPV, which are commonly perceived as distinct and highly differentiated in cause and consequence even if their occurrence is correlated, may nevertheless be subjectively experienced in strikingly similar ways. Separately and together, poverty and IPV create both the external reality and the internal experience of stress, powerlessness, and social isolation.

We begin with a clarification: Most of the literature examining the correlations between IPV and poverty fails to differentiate between short-term, episodic poverty that is at odds with a

woman's life history and with the circumstances of those in her social support network versus chronic poverty that is a situation shared by those in her social network. Nevertheless, the discussion that follows is concerned primarily with women whose poverty is persistent rather than those who become poor upon fleeing their batterers. Much of the literature on IPV and poverty also fails to distinguish between types and severity levels of IPV; therefore, consistent with the Centers for Disease Control and Prevention, we define the term broadly to encompass physical and sexual violence, threats of violence, and psychological and emotional abuse that occurs in the context of prior violence (Saltzman, Fanslow, McMahon, & Shelley, 1999).

Three Effects of Poverty and IPV: Stress, Powerlessness, and Social Isolation

Although few studies have addressed the psychological impact of poverty and IPV in combination, anecdotal evidence and indirect empirical investigation suggest that when poverty and IPV occur together, their negative effects—including stress, powerlessness, and social isolation—magnify each other. When still other aspects of women's identities (e.g., race, immigration status, or sexual orientation) are marginalized, the experience may be still more harmful.

Stress and Powerlessness

The current article defines *stressors* as chronic conditions or acute events that present challenges to well-being and *stress* as the experience produced by attempting to manage or alter those stressors without the capacity or resources (personal, relational, and material) to do so effectively. When stress becomes sufficiently intense and/or sustained, it induces both real and perceived powerlessness (Levine & Ursin, 1991).

Powerlessness has a variety of definitions, ranging from the experience of being manipulated by another individual with more authority or control, as in the case of IPV (Livingston, Hequembourg, Testa, & VanZile-Tamsen, 2007), to the more general experience of lacking control of a situation, an important context, or significant aspects of one's life, as is often the case for impoverished women (Hägglund & Ahlstrom, 2007).

Women in abusive relationships experience the ongoing stressor of coercive control—established via means such as psychological and economic abuse—punctuated by acute stressors in the form of episodes of physical violence that serve to maintain that control (Bybee & Sullivan, 2005; Dutton & Goodman, 2005; Raphael, 2000). As discussed in the coping section, below, women typically use a wide range of strategies to manage the stress of domestic violence, none of which may ultimately succeed in stopping it (Bowker, 1983; Gondolf & Fisher, 1988; Goodman, Dutton, Weinfurt, & Cook, 2003). Earlier conceptualizations of battered women's responses suggested that these dynamics ultimately create a sense of learned helplessness in women—a psychological state in which women "learn" to be helpless and generalize that learning to other parts of their lives (see, e.g., Walker, 1979, 1984). Subsequent understandings, however, suggest that women are stymied in their efforts to stay safe not primarily because of psychological obstacles such as learned helplessness but because of inadequate social services (Gondolf & Fisher, 1988; Goodman & Epstein, 2008) and the absence of viable alternatives to their current situations. Battered women do not learn to be helpless; instead, they experience and internalize the reality of powerlessness despite their active attempts to protect themselves and their loved ones (Goodman et al., 2003).

Less commonly recognized, though also demonstrated by the research literature, is that the experience of poverty is also composed of a series of chronic and acute stressors that must be managed, regardless of whether they can be eliminated,

and that the result may likewise be the external reality and the internal experience of powerlessness. Empirical research has consistently and robustly shown that lower income individuals are more likely to experience acute and chronic stressors (including traumatic experiences) than are higher income individuals (House et al., 1994; Mickelson & Kubzansky, 2003; Turner, 1995), and that those stressors are associated with subsequent stress and mental health difficulties, such as symptoms of anxiety and depression (Dunn & Hayes, 2000; McLeod & Kessler, 1990). Indeed, prospective research indicates that poverty nearly doubles rates of depression among women (e.g., Bassuk, Buckner, Perloff, & Bassuk, 1998) and that the highest rates of PTSD can be found among women with the lowest incomes (Bachman & Saltzman, 1995; Vest et al., 2002; Vogel & Marshall, 2001).

Numerous dimensions of daily living that others take for granted are sources of worry, stress, and even trauma for very low-income women. Many, if not most, poor women wake up every morning to substandard and overcrowded living conditions, lack of transportation, unpaid bills, insufficient resources with which to parent their children, dangerous streets, hunger or food insecurity, and a social services system that often thwarts their efforts to help themselves (Burnham, 2002; Evans & English, 2002; Green, 2000; Moane, 2003; Siefert, Heflin, Corcoran, & Williams, 2001). They have a general sense that securing the basics for safety and survival is uncertain, and they devote a significant portion of their cognitive, financial, and social resources to navigating daily life, where the fallout of negative decisions or mistakes can be catastrophic: missing a bus may mean losing a job; failing to have the right paperwork collected may mean losing public benefits; and being at an under-the-table job instead of at home with the children when a child welfare department representative visits may mean the loss of child custody (Goodman & Epstein, 2008; Riger, Raja, & Camacho, 2002). Moreover, the submission to state intrusion required to obtain the cash and other forms of subsistence necessary to survive often means being insulted, dismissed, shamed, or worse by those in public offices (Bullock, 1995; Laughon, 2007; Lott, 2002).

If these daily stressors were not enough, impoverished communities populated by large numbers of unemployed, underemployed, or sporadically employed people living close together are often subject to high rates of community violence and other types of crime (Bailsman & Goe, 2004; Greif, 2005; Patterson, 1991; Rattner, 1990). Residents may not feel free to help each other or take action to "take back" their communities from gangs or violence, as doing so could be dangerous for them, and they know that the police will be unhelpful at best (Alvi, Schwartz, DeKeseredy, & Maume, 2001; Holzman, Hyatt, & Dempster, 2001; Raphael, 2001). Mothers in poor communities have to worry about their own and their children's safety as they walk to school or visit a friend (Halpern, 1999; Lipsey & Wilson, 1993). Often, families stay cooped up in crowded apartments rather than face the dangers of life outside their doors (Brodsky & Marx, 2001). For mothers parenting their children in such communities, the very behaviors necessary for keeping their families safe from harm (staying inside and relatively isolated) may not be optimal for maintaining emotional and physical well-being. Furthermore, low-income women are more likely than their higher income counterparts to have histories of childhood sexual and physical abuse, the mental health consequences of which may be ongoing (Bassuk, Dawson, & Huntington, 2006; Browne & Bassuk, 1997).

In the face of ongoing and acute stressors, and with limited financial and social resources at their disposal, many poor women, such as IPV survivors, use adaptive and persistent strategies to mitigate the stressors they face, including under-the-table jobs, creative budgeting, and presenting whatever and only those elements of themselves and their situations that are likely to lead to benefits, support, assistance, or forgiveness (Edin & Lein, 1997). However, even women's

best attempts often fail in the face of rigid bureaucracies, unresponsive landlords, lack of transportation or child care, or employers who will not or cannot demonstrate flexibility (Belle & Doucet, 2003; Dodson, 1998). Tellingly, a participant in one study defined poverty as "having no options" (Wasylishyn & Johnson, 1998).

When poverty and IPV intersect, the experience of having no options and the subsequent sense of powerlessness is likely to be especially intense. Take the experience of Helen, an African American mother of four who is dealing with both poverty and partner violence. Her story comes from an ethnographic study exploring the impact of IPV on low-income families in three cities (Purvin, 2007).

Helen received an expedited Section 8 certificate to enable her to move away from her current residence, a public housing development where her abuser could easily find her on his release from prison. Despite an incredibly tight housing market, she was able to locate an apartment fairly quickly. However, even with her combined income from employment and social security for a disabled child, Helen was unable to put together the up-front money (first and last month's rent plus security deposit). She tried unsuccessfully to get financial assistance from the welfare department, the housing authority, other community agencies, and every single one of the more than 30 advocacy programs for abused women in the area. The welfare department could only offer assistance if she was actually homeless and the domestic violence programs could only offer her counseling and assistance with a restraining order. As of the study's end, Helen was unable to locate assistance and would quite possibly lose her housing certificate, thereby remaining exposed and potentially vulnerable to someone who had attacked her with a machete (Purvin, 2007, p. 202).

Helen did her best to keep herself and her children safe and was brave enough to seek outside help. In fact, after jumping through the requisite hoops, she managed to secure a housing subsidy and find an apartment. However, the systems designed to support poor women (e.g., welfare and public housing) did not provide sufficient resources to actually get her into the new apartment, and when she turned to the systems established to respond to IPV, they were equally ill equipped to help her with her housing difficulties.

Repeated failed attempts to significantly and lastingly change a situation or adopt a different outlook produce in women—poor or battered or both—the (correct) belief that many stressors simply cannot be overcome (Banyard, 1995; Fine, 1983–1984) in concert with the knowledge that basic safety or survival may depend on overcoming them. This is the core of powerlessness. Poor battered women are seemingly surrounded by systems and services that purport to assist them, further heightening women's sense of impotence. It is, therefore, not surprising that powerlessness, in turn, is associated with a range of familiar mental health concerns, particularly depression (Campbell, 1989). Indeed, depression has been described as a "disorder of power" (Drake, Price, & Drake, 1996, p. 30). At least one study has demonstrated explicitly the association between perceptions of powerlessness and depression among IPV survivors over time (Campbell, Sullivan, & Davidson, 1995), and powerlessness—or lack of control—has been shown to mediate the relationship between poverty and depressive symptoms (Dunn & Hayes, 2000; Mirowsky & Ross, 1986). What is less clear is *how* the powerlessness induced by poverty interacts with that produced by IPV to influence psychological vulnerability to specific mental health disorders and just how the combination shapes women's perceptions of themselves, the world, or the future.

Social Isolation

Women experiencing either IPV or poverty are disadvantaged not only in their increased risk for experiencing chronic and acute stressors and subsequent feelings of powerlessness but also in the resources they have to cope with these conditions (Brown & Harris, 1978; Kessler, 1979; McLeod & Kessler, 1990). Social support is a recognized resource for coping with stress and powerlessness (Thoits, 1986); its import is only heightened in the absence of material and financial resources. Social support can be defined as the availability of instrumental and emotional assistance through interpersonal relationships. Emotional assistance means having people available to inspire, encourage, advise, or listen; instrumental assistance means having people available who can offer material or practical aid (Kocot & Goodman, 2003).

Social support can be provided by informal networks, including family, neighbors, and friends, or through formal networks, including community agencies or systems. Social support may serve to alter the perception of a stressor, perhaps mitigating its appraisal as a threat, or it can serve as "coping assistance" (Thoits, 1986), bolstering a woman's capacity to address her problems or helping to shift the situation itself. According to the support mobilization model, for example, individuals facing an acute life event draw from the emotional and tangible resources of their informal social networks to enhance their capacity to deal with a problem (Eckenrode & Wethington, 1990; Mickelson & Kubzansky, 2003). As we explore below, both IPV and poverty dramatically compromise the creation and utility of social supports.

IPV survivors in shelters, in the community, and in the criminal justice system report insufficient or inadequate informal and formal social support (Barnett, Martinez, & Keyson, 1996; Levendosky et al., 2004). Research further demonstrates that the less support survivors have, the more likely they are to experience ongoing abuse over time, perhaps because they do not have access to the emotional and practical assistance necessary to bolster their efforts to stay safe (Goodman et al., 2005). Some women are purposely isolated by their batterers, who demand that they rupture their contacts with members of their informal social networks; others have "used up" available support and have nowhere else to turn; and many have friends and family who do not understand, are not sympathetic to what they are going through, or are essentially overwhelmed or paralyzed by the fact of the abuse (Kocot & Goodman, 2003; Liang, Glenn, & Goodman, 2005). In addition, many are not willing or able to turn to the formal support system, including the advocacy, mental health, or justice system (Goodman et al., 2003; Lempert, 1996). Women offer a number of explanations for this, including worry about stigmatization, practical obstacles, the absence of sufficient cultural competence or diverse staff in many domestic violence agencies, the one-size-fits-all responses available in the criminal justice and other systems, and the values conflict between what providers can offer and what domestic violence survivors want (Goodman & Epstein, 2008; Laughon, 2007).

It is important to note, however, that research on social support and domestic violence has not explored how SES might influence the provision of informal or formal social support to survivors, nor do most studies of the relationship between IPV and social support control for SES. Indeed, it is possible that part of the relationship reported between social isolation and IPV may be an artifact of participants' SES (Levendosky et al., 2004); as discussed below, social networks function fundamentally differently in economically stretched communities.

Most of the literature on the function of social support networks for individuals under stress has focused on the middle-class experience, where all members of the network are unlikely to be synchronously experiencing significant stress (Mickelson & Kubzansky, 2003). Because the social context of social support for middle-class individuals is qualitatively different from that for lower income individuals, the social support available for the latter group is often quite different. In fact, despite the commonly held assumption, originally supported by anecdotal and qualitative studies (e.g., de Anda, 1984; Stack, 1974), that low-income

individuals are more likely to have an extended support network than are those with higher incomes, recent empirical research demonstrates that poverty actually decreases the availability of emotional and instrumental social supports, even among ethnic minority groups who place a strong value on community (House, Landis, & Umberson, 1988; Krause & Borawski-Clark, 1995; Mickelson & Kubzansky, 2003; Roschelle, 1997; Turner & Marino, 1994). Although poor women are more likely to need network members for material as well as social resources, their networks as a whole are less able to consistently provide such support (Edin & Lein, 1997). In one recent study based on a national probability sample of adults, for example, lower income levels were associated with both lower levels of emotional support and higher levels of negative interactions (though not with social contact or frequency of problem disclosure). This held true across racial/ethnic groupings (Mickelson & Kubzansky, 2003).

A number of explanations have been offered for the differences in social network functioning among poor versus nonpoor populations: First, although people with low incomes may have extended networks, the tensile strength of those networks is weaker because the commodities that pass between people in any social network—whether trust, financial assistance, or time—are not in adequate supply to maintain the health of the network. Thus, the costs associated with network involvement may actually outweigh the benefits (Belle, 1983). As suggested by a number of qualitative accounts, when network members themselves are equally economically stressed and in dire need of resources, they can become conduits of stress rather than conduits of assistance and support (Belle & Doucet, 2003; Eckenrode & Gore, 1981; Edin & Lein, 1997; Stack, 1974). As described earlier, whereas middle-class individuals typically must cope with only one or two significant stressors at a time, poor women often face multiple acute and chronic life events at once (Brown & Harris, 1978; House et al., 1994; Turner, 1995). Women know that asking for help from friends and family to deal with so many difficulties might prove overwhelming to anyone, let alone to individuals with limited resources of their own; sometimes it simply does not make sense to ask (Goodman, Glenn, Bohlig, Banyard, & Borges, 2009; Mickelson & Kubzansky, 2003).

In addition, most middle- and upper-class women have access to an extended network of people through educational and professional networks and other contexts that are simply taken for granted as sources of information, advice, or support. These networks are not necessarily close friends or relatives but are nonetheless potentially helpful when it is time to search for a new job, relocate to a new area, or find the best child care options. Researchers define "linking social capital" as the "networks of trusting relationships between people who are interacting across explicit, formal, or institutionalized power or authority gradients in society" (Szreter & Woolcock, 2004, p. 6). For example, a middle-class woman in search of legal advice may know a neighbor or a friend of a friend who is a lawyer, or she may be able to ask a colleague in her profession or an alumnus of her college to help her find one. A poor woman with the same need is unlikely to have access to these kinds of seemingly incidental, but profoundly important, sources of information, referrals, and guidance. Put differently, middle-class women are likely to have in their social networks people who can also bridge (or provide directly) professional supports of a type that women who are poor must go outside their networks to access. It is important to reiterate that we are by no means suggesting that poor women are worse than anyone else at forming social networks; instead, we want to underscore the diminished utility of social networks when most of the network members are themselves struggling and have few bridges between personal and professional resources. A lack of linking social capital, versus more generic social networks, is itself an enormous obstacle to

employment and other forms of well-being for members of poor communities (Szreter & Woolcock, 2003).

Finally, supports such as mental health services that are available to higher income groups are often inaccessible to lower income women. The federal Department of Health and Human Services reported in 2001 that despite the overwhelming challenges they face, women living in poverty have insufficient access to adequate mental health care or other social services (U.S. Department of Health and Human Services, 2001). They cannot afford to pay market rates for mental health treatment and are unlikely to have insurance benefits associated with their jobs that provide for mental health care (Belle & Doucet, 2003; Rosen, Tolman, & Wamer, 2004). When they can find a way to obtain free or subsidized care or counseling, services may be inaccessible for a range of reasons including inadequate child care, inability to get time off from work for appointments, transportation difficulties, fear of stigma, problematic provider attitudes, negative past experiences, and gaps between what they need and what services can offer (Foster, 2007; Goodman & Smyth, in press; Lazear, Pires, Isaacs, Chaulk, & Huang, 2008). These obstacles are particularly acute for low-income women of color (Laughon, 2007; The Commonwealth Fund, 2006).

Both IPV and poverty can, therefore, trigger the experience of extreme social isolation, where a woman feels that she cannot reach out to people who might be able to help her and that those she can reach out to will not or cannot help her. A number of studies have demonstrated the role of social isolation as a risk factor for depression among low-income women (Belle, 1983; Coiro, 2001) and for symptoms of anxiety, depression, and PTSD among IPV survivors (Campbell et al., 1995; Coker, Watkins, Smith, & Brandt, 2003). As with powerlessness, however, little research consideration has been given to how the isolation produced by poverty interacts with the isolation produced by IPV, either to increase women's vulnerability to specific mental health disorders or to shape their perceptions and coping responses.

The Reciprocally Reinforcing Effects of Stress, Powerlessness, and Social Isolation in the Context of Both Poverty and IPV

Given the paucity of research on the intersecting effects of poverty and IPV on women's well-being, just how the impact of one condition interacts with the impact of the other remains virtually unstudied. It is possible that the effects of each condition are additive, with the stress, powerlessness, and isolation of poverty magnifying the stress, powerlessness, and isolation of IPV. It is also possible that the effects of the two conditions compound each other, such that one exponentially increases the damaging consequences of the other. Although the question of magnitude may be important, it is perhaps more critical that we understand the extent to which the two sets of experiences may create something different from the sum of their parts for women who must live with both as they attempt to manage their situations and emotional well-being.

To use an analogy, compared to a victim of a single assault, a survivor of multiple traumatic events or a sustained period of trauma exposure not only experiences more severe PTSD but may also develop a narrative about the world in which safety is fleeting and there are few opportunities to exert control (Herman, 1992). Similarly, a woman living with both extended poverty and partner abuse instead of just one or the other may experience more than simply added stress, powerlessness, and isolation. Because she has so few internal or external references to experiences of safety, predictability, and control, an impoverished survivor of IPV may develop a narrative about her world in which the absence of these basic conditions is the norm and the alternative seems almost unachievable. Indeed, the danger, unpredictability, and lack of control that lie at the heart of traumas such as domestic violence fit almost seamlessly with those same basic themes running through the rest of an extremely poor woman's life, creating a bidirectional downward spiral.

Although there is little research on the subjective experience of living with the stress, powerlessness, and isolation of poverty and IPV, one qualitative account of the experience of low-income, African American IPV survivors described an overwhelming sense of "tiredness" (Laughon, 2007). This is an important framing that requires further consideration. For example, how might this kind of exhaustion be currently misinterpreted by providers unfamiliar with the lived experience of low-income victims of partner abuse, and how might this misinterpretation—possibly as laziness, lack of motivation, or biological defect—misinform the providers' response?

With regard to quantitative research on how poverty and IPV combine to create psychological distress in particular, few large-scale studies have conducted direct comparisons of the mental health of lower and higher income IPV survivors. One notable exception is the National Violence Against Women Study, a population-based random-digit dial survey of residents in all 50 states and the District of Columbia, which explored risk and protective factors for PTSD symptoms among IPV survivors (Coker, Weston, Creson, Justice, & Blakeney, 2005). Among the 369 female victims of partner abuse in the study sample, lower SES (that is, lower income and absence of private health insurance) was one of the chief factors associated with higher risk of moderate to severe PTSD symptoms. Furthermore, although not directly focused on IPV survivors, other research demonstrates that the chronic stressors associated with poverty increase psychological vulnerability to depression following an acute negative life event (Elliott, 2000). In contrast, however, a second large-scale study of the potential contribution of SES to psychological distress—this time, depression—among IPV survivors failed to demonstrate such a contribution (von Eye & Bogat, 2006). In this latter study of

206 pregnant women, when IPV was considered, neither income nor social welfare (food stamps and Medicaid) predicted the development or level of depression over time. These studies were based on different types of samples, conceptualizations of IPV, and outcomes of interest, and are therefore difficult to compare directly. Perhaps one reason that the second study did not demonstrate a relationship between SES and depression is that most of its participants were of fairly low income and so there was much less variability in the sample. Clearly, more research is needed to disentangle and flesh out this complex set of findings.

In short, because both IPV and poverty result in stress, powerlessness, and social isolation, poor women in battering relationships are doubly jeopardized. Building on theory and a small group of directly and indirectly relevant research studies, we hypothesize that the effects of each experience have an impact on women's well-being that, although separate in origin, may be melded in lived experience and mental health outcomes, possibly even creating a special vulnerability to each other. If supported by future research, this is essential knowledge for anyone who works with battered women, not only because of the impact of poverty and IPV on women's internal landscape but because, as we discuss below, stress, powerlessness, and social isolation can also significantly constrain women's coping strategies.

Coping in the Context of Poverty and IPV

As we have seen, IPV and poverty create parallel effects, potentially magnifying the impact of each and potentially creating reinforcing vulnerabilities. Further compounding the damaging nature of this pairing is that the coping tactics needed to achieve greater safety and stability in one domain may be undermined by the realities of the other domain. In other words, the experience of living with IPV in the context of poverty not only

creates challenges; the options available for remedying the situation are limited.

Without simple physical safety, handling the overwhelming nature of poverty (which itself, as noted earlier, reduces physical safety) becomes all the more challenging, and without material resources, women have few tools to keep themselves safer in the face of an abusive partner. In the context of IPV, for example, a woman living in poverty may make the correct assessment that searching for a job could trigger her abusive partner's controlling or violent behavior and is, therefore, unsafe. Conversely, in the context of poverty, an IPV survivor may make the correct assessment that her social network cannot provide support: Friends or family do not have money to spare for her to leave town or have her glasses fixed; there is too little social capital in the community that could hold her husband accountable; there is no couch in a friend's house for her and her children to sleep on. Those strategies are, therefore, foreclosed to her.

Coping has been defined as a person's pattern of responses to stressful situations such as threats to safety or well-being (Lazarus & Folkman, 1984). A commonly accepted conceptual distinction made in the coping literature is that between problem-focused coping, used to solve or manage specific external problems or threats, and emotion-focused or avoidant coping, used to deal with the emotions associated with the problem. An individual's choice between them is usually tied to her self-perceived ability to control a given harmful event (Folkman, 1984). If change is not perceived as possible, the model holds, she is likely to choose emotion-focused coping over problem-focused coping (Roth & Cohen, 1986). The former path produces the short-term benefit of reduced stress and anxiety but does not solve the problem. The latter may produce increased distress in the short term but, the model suggests, allows for the eventual resolution, or at least shifting, of the situation. It is, therefore, thought to be desirable to increase individuals' perceptions of choice (Drake et al., 1996). Indeed, previous research has shown that emotion-focused coping is associated with poorer mental health, compared to more problem-focused strategies (Fondacaro & Moos, 1989; Rayburn et al., 2005).

We contend, however, that the framing of coping as either problem-focused or emotion-focused is insufficient to explain women's navigation of the stress, powerlessness, and social isolation bred by IPV in the context of persistent poverty and minimizes the increased danger that can come from a woman taking steps to change her situation without adequate safety precautions in place. At the intersection of poverty and partner violence, the multiplicity of present or looming crises transforms coping into a series of juggling acts, where survival requires the constant shifting of attention from crisis to crisis.

Such shifting puts a woman's survival tactics at odds with how formal support systems are arranged, where there is an expectation that a rather static prioritization of problems can be arrived at consensually by the woman and her advocates or service providers. Generally, the brutality and acute nature of IPV episodes generates a systemic response that assumes that the violence is the primary problem. However, research suggests that many very low-income women do not see domestic violence as their primary problem (Pearson, Griswold, & Thoennes, 2001; Purvin, 2007). This is a reflection of the complexity and fragility of poor women's survival, not their denial of the abuse. Indeed, one study of low-income IPV victims (meaning they all recognized IPV as a challenge) found that when asked about the most stressful or upsetting event that they had to cope with in the last month, over half of the sample reported something other than IPV, such as homelessness; problems with their children, family, or friends; lack of coordination among services; or substance abuse-related problems (Eby, 2004).

When a woman finds a way to deal with a problem in one domain, either of her own volition or at the urging of an advocate, her efforts may simply create another equally difficult problem in the other, producing a series of impossible binds (Goodman & Epstein, 2008). Although the

need to make trade-offs is a core part of the human condition, the stakes involved in the choices that low-income women have to make may be particularly high. Does a woman take the job that will enable her to leave the welfare rolls but require that her young children be left unsupervised with her abusive partner? Does she lend money to a family member in trouble, thereby losing the nest egg she was saving for first month's rent on a new apartment away from her abuser? Does she take the job that does not provide health insurance, knowing that she may well need it next time her partner hurts her?

Attempting to "take control" of IPV or "solve the problem" or "stop taking it" through problem-focused coping may be an ineffective strategy that might actually damage emotional and physical well-being for low-income women who have restricted resources and relatively diminished social power (Fine, 1982). For these women, efforts at problem-focused coping often fail in the face of an overtaxed, under-resourced human service system and overwhelmed social networks producing a sense of futility and despair. Indeed, Fine (1982) has hypothesized that problem-focused coping may decrease mental health in a context of social powerlessness. Supporting this idea, one study of very low-income IPV survivors found that problem-focused coping was positively correlated with depression and PTSD for women who had little social support, though not for women with greater levels of social support (Kocot & Goodman, 2003).

We suggest women are, in fact, utilizing a third type of coping, which we call "survival-focused coping" (others have offered somewhat similar concepts, including Gondolf & Fisher, 1988; Hamby & Grey-Little, 2007; Lempert, 1996). Survival-focused coping is distinct from either emotion or problem-focused coping. Instead, it is aimed at surviving in the short term, meeting basic needs, and keeping oneself and one's loved ones as safe as possible. Sometimes, it is about creating breathing room in hopes that something dramatic will change. (Given that the lives of people who are poor are so inconsistent and punctuated by sudden crises as well as very occasional, fleeting opportunities, this is not inherently irrational.) It is composed of constant negotiations, small steps, and trade-offs to minimize the harm of specific situations and people, while protecting things that are too valuable to risk—perhaps children, a family member, or a sense of one's self as not a failure as a girlfriend or wife. We call these constant negotiations acts of "microcontrol." The use of microcontrol within the context of survival-focused coping is an attempt to make small, fine-tuned adjustments, while keeping a constant eye open for opportunities that could lead to bigger changes on one hand or signals of a dramatic new threat on the other. The long-term impact of current decisions and choices is perhaps less a priority than it would be for a woman with more resources, as a woman using survival-focused coping knows she needs to focus on survival in the here and now. The future is too unpredictable and outside her control. Although a woman using survival-focused coping may appear passive to those not in her circumstances, this view may well reflect attitudes that attribute poverty to personal failings rather than to socioeconomic structures and systems that thwart women at every turn (American Psychological Association [APA], 2000; Bullock, 1995).

Take the example of Aida, a Latina mother of four, whose story is described in the ethnographic study noted earlier (Purvin, 2007). At the time of the interview, Aida and her children were living in public housing, a system designed to address the needs of low-income women but not victims of partner abuse. Although Aida did not define herself as a victim of domestic violence, she expressed concern about her husband Marcos's controlling and threatening behavior:

> Public housing leaseholders are held liable for all problems in their residences. Repeated disturbances, particularly those involving the police, can lead to eviction proceedings. Because becoming homeless with her children was not a consequence she wanted to risk, Aida chose to remain silent about Marcos's behavior. In addition to not disclosing her fears about Marcos to anyone other than the ethnographer, Aida attempted to placate him in his jealous rages rather than risk a fight escalating to the point where neighbors would hear and call the police. (p. 201)

Aida may feel she can survive—physically and psychologically—another beating but be less sure she can survive an eviction, though she takes whatever actions she can to avoid the beatings. Indeed, the very fact that she confided in the ethnographer could reflect an effort to probe for new avenues of support and assistance in addressing the violence. Aida is not in denial, nor is she blindly allowing the violence to continue. She is engaging in acts of microcontrol to survive her situation. Yet, she may indeed feel powerless because she, and perhaps those around her, do not even recognize the small adjustments and decisions she makes every day. Given the research (noted above) linking perceptions of powerlessness to depression, we hypothesize that if women in Aida's situation were supported in framing acts of microcontrol as robust manifestations of coping in the face of multiple constraints, they might be less likely to experience depression and more likely to build on these small acts.

Implications for Practice and Research

Despite the enormous success of the domestic violence movement in bringing policy, research, and systemic interventions to bear on the plight of IPV survivors, too little has been done to illuminate the lived experience of very low-income battered women or to target their specific short- and long-term needs for emotional well-being, safety, and material security. This section explores avenues for expansion in each of the two key areas: domestic violence advocacy and mental health intervention with survivors. Also, see Table 13.2 for a summary of implications. Needless to say, these are two responses that touch only a portion of the women described throughout this article and certainly are not the only arenas in need of expansion. They are, however, the systems most tightly linked to the issues raised in this article. As important as it is that interventions designed for domestic violence survivors meet the needs of low-income women, it is just as imperative that the systems designed for low-income women also respond to impoverished survivors. Although it is beyond the scope of this article to discuss avenues for improving the latter systems, we refer readers to emerging literature on trauma-informed systems of care for low-income communities (Cocozza et al., 2005; Markoff, Finkelstein, Kammerer, Kreiner, & Post, 2005).

Domestic Violence Advocacy and Support

Advocacy has emerged as the preferred method for engaging with survivors and communities on the subject of partner violence. Although advocacy for survivors may take a variety of forms, its goals appear to span a continuum, ranging from expanding access to services for survivors and their children on one end (considered "case-level" advocacy) to system change on the other end (considered "cause-level" advocacy; Lens & Gibelman, 2000). At either end of the continuum, advocates traditionally work within a range of systems, including the criminal justice, social services, shelter, and health care systems, among others (Goodman & Epstein, 2008).

Over the last two decades of the domestic violence movement, case-level advocacy has become increasingly specialized, targeting specific problems—for example, housing, criminal prosecution, or child welfare issues. Davies, Lyon, and Monti-Catania (1998) have characterized this approach as "service-defined." That is, it begins with a service: An advocate offers a client a limited menu of options for assistance based primarily on the availability of the service or on the mission of the organization. This model of advocacy addresses narrowly circumscribed problems rather than supporting women's own needs and goals as well as the context surrounding any one specific issue (Goodman et al., 2009). Although targeted advocacy may work well for those survivors who require support only in very specific domains, it may work much less effectively for impoverished survivors whose difficulties cross domains and interact with each other in complex ways. For them, this kind of service fragmentation results not only in conflicting choices, mixed messages, and impossible binds, but it also produces the experience in women of being nothing more than the sum of their discrete problems (Smyth, Goodman, & Glenn, 2006).

Over the last few years, a number of authors have developed alternative models of advocacy. For example, Davies and her colleagues (1998) have proposed an approach, called *woman-defined advocacy,* which starts from the client's perspective on her needs and goals, rather than from a menu of service options. Advocates then work creatively within and outside of traditional systems to help women move forward with their lives in ways that are consistent with these needs and goals.

Relationship-centered advocacy represents an expansion of the woman-defined approach.[3] As with woman-defined advocacy, relationship-centered advocacy starts with women's narrative about their own wishes and objectives. In addition, it emphasizes the need to provide emotional and instrumental support in a highly integrated way and in the context of an ongoing relationship, viewing the advocacy relationship as central to women's abilities to name their needs and goals and work toward addressing them (Goodman et al., 2009).

Expanding still further, the *full frame approach* goes beyond one-on-one advocacy to identify ways that programs and organizations can help combat poor women's social isolation through the explicit building of social capital and linking relationships among programs and among community members (Smyth et al., 2006).

All three of these models—woman-defined advocacy, relationship-centered advocacy, and the full frame approach—call upon advocates to reach across silos and systems, crossing organizational cultures to respond to the survivor and her needs as she frames them. Survivors themselves do not see their issues as distinct, necessarily, and may be enormously relieved to feel that the people with whom they are working are collaborating to provide integrated support.

In addition to developing more integrative and survivor-centered approaches, it is critical for advocates to develop specific strategies to address the immediate financial situations of some low-income survivors. Only recently have advocates begun to pursue such strategies. In some states, for example, advocates have convinced their state governments to devise flexible, one-time cash assistance programs for survivors in transition (Economic Stability Working Group, 2002). In other states, advocates have persuaded private employers and other private funders to establish policies supporting the provision of "bridge funds," short-term loans, pay advances, and vacation time payouts for survivors in crisis (www.safeatworkcoalition.org, 2006). Advocates in a growing number of states are also working with victims and employers to ensure prompt compliance with court-ordered wage garnishment to meet child support obligations for survivors (Economic Stability Working Group, 2002). These are a few simple examples of a broad range of strategies that could be developed to support advocates' work with low-income survivors (see Goodman & Epstein, 2008 for a fuller discussion of potential strategies).

However, of course, targeting efforts to help women increase their income are, in and of themselves, insufficient to respond to the financial needs of low-income survivors. At a broader level, efforts to develop longer term opportunities for battered women's economic advancement cannot succeed unless they are part of a large-scale movement to address women's poverty (Goodman & Epstein, 2008). Coalitions working toward improvements in poverty, housing, education, rights for the disabled, welfare, and labor rights are key allies. As one example, anti-domestic violence advocates are now collaborating with antipoverty activists to implement "living wage" legislation. Because women are disproportionately represented in low-wage jobs, raising the minimum rate of pay would enable more survivors to leave abusive partners on whom they are financially dependent (Sklar, Mykyta, & Wefald, 2001). Of course, different policy packages will be appropriate for different subgroups of low-income women, as prevailing economic conditions vary widely. What works to provide economic stability to a survivor in rural New Hampshire may not be effective for a woman in New York City. The key is recognition that both case-level responses that address the particular needs of individual women and cause-level advocacy that targets policies and systems are needed to meet the immediate and longer term needs of low-income survivors.

Mental Health Practice

Notwithstanding the critical efforts of multicultural, liberation, and feminist psychology to bring attention to social oppression as a critical obstacle to emotional well-being (Smith, 2008; Sue & Lamb, 2002), mental health practitioners lack theoretical and practical frameworks that enable them to respond effectively to the needs of low-income women (Lott, 2002; Smith, 2005). This is as true for IPV survivors as it is for other populations (Green & Sanchez-Hucles, 1997; Grigsby & Hartman, 1997).

As noted in an earlier section, only a small portion of low-income survivors find their way to mental health practitioners. When they do, they may well encounter interventions that are short term, symptom focused, and relatively inattentive to contextual factors such as clients' immediate (and potentially urgent) material needs, not to mention the potentially ongoing threat of violence (Smyth et al., 2006). By failing to include a central focus on the material conditions that perpetuate domestic violence and shape its psychological consequences and coping strategies, current mental health models fail to address the full range of survivors' needs (see Goodman & Epstein, 2008 for a fuller discussion of mental health provider responses to domestic violence survivors).

We suggest first that within the context of a therapeutic relationship, mental health practitioners consider adopting (and evaluating) the survivor-focused coping framework described earlier. This framework acknowledges both the gravity and the constraints of survivors' situations and helps them identify areas of strength and power. By helping women name and expand upon small acts of microcontrol, practitioners may help survivors battle the experience of helplessness, identify supports and strategies for change, and build upon existing individual, social, and institutional resources (Goodman & Epstein, 2008).

It is unlikely, however, that this kind of framing alone will be sufficient to improve the emotional (much less material) well-being of low-income survivors. A woman living with poverty and violence needs more than just a new outlook and new coping tools; she needs real options. Although it is not solely the responsibility of the mental health provider to find her client new housing or get her car fixed, it is the provider's responsibility to forge meaningful connections with people who can provide such help. Just as domestic violence advocacy work requires meaningful collaboration across traditional silos, so, too, does effective mental health intervention with low-income survivors require the development of partnerships between mental health practitioners and other service providers. Although there are many systemic, cultural, and practical barriers to such collaboration, surmounting the barriers must not be left to the client. Mental health practitioners need to work to overcome these obstacles to work effectively with women struggling with the dual impact of poverty and partner violence.

Finally, to integrate contextual factors such as poverty and abuse into current mental health intervention models, mental health service providers need systematic and ongoing training about the nature of poverty and the highly imperfect systems upon which very low-income people must rely. This training should include attention to the intersection of poverty and a variety of other phenomena, including partner violence. Equipped with in-depth knowledge of poverty and domestic violence, providers will be in a better position to appreciate and build on the variety of coping strategies women already adopt to deal with the stress, powerlessness, and social isolation of both conditions.

Research

Although this article synthesizes disparate domains of scholarship to describe the impact of domestic violence and poverty, respectively, few studies have investigated directly the experience of women caught in the nexus of the two. Future research should explore more deeply how the effects of poverty and the effects of partner violence, especially stress, powerlessness, and isolation, combine as a potentially inseparable set of lived experiences and how these experiences, in turn, come to shape women's options and perspectives about themselves and the world. Researchers also need to understand better which factors may serve to protect some impoverished survivors (Vogel & Marshall, 2001).

This research should build on the knowledge that study results depend on the subgroup under investigation; it may well be that the intersection of poverty and IPV looks and feels quite different for homeless compared to housed poor women, or for Latina women compared to white women. Indeed, researchers need to be mindful of the distinct experiences of a variety of subpopulations of impoverished survivors, including immigrants, ethnic minorities, single mothers, women with disabilities and other chronic health conditions, minimum wage workers, women receiving public assistance, the homeless, migrant workers, and older women (APA, 2000). These populations are usually left out of general population studies as they often do not have access to phones and are without stable residences (Wenzel, Tucker, Hambarsoomian, & Elliott, 2006).

At the same time, researchers need to investigate further the extent to which the concepts of survival-focused coping and microcontrol are meaningful heuristics for understanding women's coping strategies and whether these concepts can be used effectively as the bases for innovative forms of support for impoverished battered women. Ultimately, new forms of practice may emerge as these phenomena come to be understood more deeply.

Even as researchers continue to explore women's experiences, we also need to pursue research on emerging and promising approaches to supporting women. We need, for example, to understand the effectiveness and limits of interventions such as woman-defined advocacy, relationship-centered advocacy, and the full frame approach, or mental health interventions that use the concept of survivor-focused coping. These kinds of evaluation will require a broad range of methods, including participatory action research, case studies, grounded theory methodologies, and quantitative approaches.

Finally, it is critical to note that the kinds of research that will produce a deeper understanding of women's experiences and how to support them must involve collaboration: Only through ongoing engagement with people who have experienced or worked directly with the phenomena of interest can researchers be sure that they are framing meaningful questions, capturing relevant information without creating harm, and producing knowledge that can be useful to the providers and participants they aim to support.

Table 13.1 Narrative Table: Major Findings of Review

- Given the large number of poor women in this country, a critical research finding of recent years is that household income level is one of the most, if not *the* most, significant correlates of intimate partner violence (IPV).
- Although few studies have addressed the psychological impact of poverty and IPV in combination, anecdotal evidence and indirect empirical investigation suggest that when poverty and IPV occur together, their negative effects—including stress, powerlessness, and social isolation—magnify each other.
- Women experiencing either IPV or poverty are disadvantaged not only in their increased risk for experiencing chronic and acute stressors and subsequent feelings of powerlessness but also in the resources they have to cope with these conditions. For example, although they are more likely to need network members for material as well as social resources, their networks are less able to consistently provide such support.
- Because both IPV and poverty result in stress, powerlessness, and social isolation, poor women in abusive relationships are doubly jeopardized. It appears that the effects of each experience have an impact on women's well-being, that although they are separate in origin, they are melded in lived experience and mental health outcomes, possibly even creating a special vulnerability to each other. As a result, women experiencing both IPV and poverty are at high risk for depression, posttraumatic stress disorder, and other forms of emotional distress.
- Current conceptualizations of coping strategies as either problem-focused or emotion-focused are insufficient to explain women's navigation of the stress, powerlessness, and social isolation bred by IPV in the context of persistent poverty. At this intersection, the multiplicity of present

or looming crises transforms coping into a series of juggling acts; survival requires the constant shifting of attention from crisis to crisis. The long-term impact of current decisions and choices is perhaps less a priority than it would be for a woman with more resources.

- Given these realities, we propose a third distinct type of coping, which we call "survival-focused coping." Survival-focused coping is aimed at surviving in the short term, meeting basic needs, and keeping oneself and one's loved ones as safe as possible. It is composed of constant negotiations, small steps, and trade-offs (what we call acts of "microcontrol") to minimize the harm of specific situations and people, while protecting things that are too valuable to risk—perhaps children, a family member, or a sense of one's self as not a failure as a girlfriend or wife. Although a woman using survival-focused coping may appear passive to those not in her circumstances, this view may well reflect attitudes that attribute poverty to personal failings rather than to socioeconomic structures and systems that thwart women at every turn.

Table 13.2   Narrative Table: Implications for Practice, Policy, and Research

- Despite the enormous success of the domestic violence movement in bringing policy, research, and systemic interventions to bear on the plight of IPV survivors, too little has been done to illuminate the lived experience of very low-income battered women or to target their specific short- and long-term needs for emotional well-being, safety, and material security.
- Domestic violence advocacy has become increasingly specialized, targeting specific problems—for example, housing, criminal prosecution, or child welfare issues. This model of advocacy addresses narrowly circumscribed problems rather than supporting women's own needs and goals as well as the context surrounding any one specific issue. This approach does not work well for impoverished survivors whose difficulties cross domains and interact with each other in complex ways.
- Over the last few years, several alternatives have been proposed. These models (a) start from the client's perspective on her needs and goals, rather than from a menu of service options; (b) emphasize the need to provide emotional and instrumental support in a highly integrated way and in the context of an ongoing relationship; (c) work to build social capital and link relationships among programs and among community members; and (d) call upon advocates to reach across silos and systems, crossing organizational cultures to meet women's needs. These models need to be recognized, further developed, and evaluated.
- Advocates also need to expand their use of specific strategies to address the immediate financial situations of low-income survivors as well as their longer term economic needs. These efforts cannot succeed unless they are part of a large-scale movement to address women's poverty. Coalitions working toward improvements in poverty, housing, education, rights for the disabled, welfare, and labor rights are key allies.
- Mental health practitioners should move beyond short-term, symptom-focused interventions to consider adopting (and evaluating) a survivor-focused coping framework that both acknowledges the gravity and constraints of survivors' situations and helps them identify areas of strength and power. By helping women name and expand upon small acts of microcontrol,

(Continued)

(Continued)

practitioners may help survivors battle the experience of helplessness, identify supports and strategies for change, and build upon existing individual, social, and institutional resources.

- A woman living with poverty and violence needs more than just a new outlook and new coping tools; she also needs real options. Just as domestic violence advocacy work requires meaningful collaboration across traditional silos, so, too, does effective mental health intervention with low-income survivors require the development of real and enduring partnerships between mental health practitioners and other service providers.
- Research needs to explore the distinct experiences of a variety of subpopulations of low-income IPV survivors, including immigrants, ethnic minorities, single parents, people with disabilities and other chronic health conditions, minimum wage workers, families receiving public assistance, the homeless, migrant workers, and older people. These populations are often left out of general population studies as they often do not have access to phones and are without stable residences.
- Researchers must collaborate more closely with domestic violence advocates, mental health and social service providers, and survivors themselves. Only through ongoing engagement with people who have experienced or worked directly with the phenomena of interest can researchers be sure that they are framing meaningful questions and producing knowledge that can be useful to the providers and participants they aim to support.

Conclusion

It is clear that much needs to be done to develop research, practice, and policy that addresses the intertwined external realities and internal experiences of victimization and poverty in integrated ways. This is largely uncharted terrain, and change is likely to be difficult, obstacle ridden, and incremental. Nevertheless, it is critical that advocates, mental health providers, and researchers work to understand better the insidious intersection of IPV and persistent poverty; to craft more humane and effective responses; and to develop support structures and policies that will enable frontline providers to support those IPV survivors in greatest need.

Notes

1. The U.S. Census measures poverty by taking into account the family size and the number of children living in a given household, with the threshold of US$10,488 for a single adult and US$13,896 for a single parent and child (Weighted average poverty thresholds for families of specified sized: 1959 to 2006. Retrieved January 9, 2008, from www.census.gov/ps).

2. The Violence Against Women Act of 2005 limited some landlords' ability to engage in such revictimization of battered women, but the law's protections apply only to public and some government-subsidized housing. Women in private homes or apartments typically remain unprotected unless local laws provide otherwise.

3. "Relationship-centered advocacy" represents a name change from the former "feminist relational advocacy." This change was made to reflect better the core ingredient of the model.

References

Alvi, S., Schwartz, M. D., DeKeseredy, W. S., & Maume, M. O. (2001). Women's fear of crime in Canadian public housing. *Violence Against Women. Special Issue: Violence Against Women in Public Housing, 7,* 638–661.

American Psychological Association. (2000, August 6). *Resolution on poverty and economic status.* Retrieved March 3, 2008, from http://www.apa .org/pi/urban/povres.html

Bachman, R., & Saltzman, L. (1995). *Violence against women: Estimates from the redesigned national crime victimization survey, special report.* Washington, DC: Department of Justice, Bureau of Justice Statistics.

Baker, N. L. (1996). Class as a construct in a "classless" society. In M. Hill & E. D. Rothblum (Eds.), *Classism and feminist therapy: Counting costs* (pp. 13–24). New York: Harrington Park.

Banyard, V. L. (1995). "Taking another route": Daily survival narratives from mothers who are homeless. *American Journal of Community Psychology, 23,* 871–891.

Barnett, O. A., Martinez, T. E., & Keyson, M. (1996). The relationship between violence, social support, and self-blame in battered women, *Journal of Interpersonal Violence, 11,* 221–233.

Barusch, A., Taylor, M. J., & Derr, M. (1999). *Understanding families with multiple barriers to self-sufficiency.* Salt Lake City: Social Research Institute, University of Utah.

Bassuk, E. L, Buckner, J. C, Perloff, J. N., & Bassuk, S. S. (1998). Prevalence of mental health and substance use disorders among homeless and low-income housed mothers. *American Journal of Psychiatry, 155,* 1561–1564.

Bassuk, E. L., Buckner, J. C., Weinreb, L. F., Browne, A., Bassuk, S. S., Dawson, R., et al. (1997). Homelessness in female-headed families: Childhood and adult risk and protective factors. *American Journal of Public Health,* 87, 241–248.

Bassuk, E., Dawson, R., & Huntington, N. (2006). Intimate partner violence in extremely poor women: Longitudinal patterns and risk. *Journal of Family Violence, 21,* 387–399.

Bausman, K. W., & Goe, W. R. (2004). An examination of the link between employment volatility and the spatial distribution of property crime rates. *American Journal of Economics and Sociology, 63,* 665–696.

Belle, D. (1983). The impact of poverty on social networks and supports. *Marriage and Family Review, 5,* 89–103.

Belle, D., & Doucet, J. (2003). Poverty, inequality, and discrimination as sources of depression among US women. *Psychology of Women Quarterly, 27,* 101–113.

Benson, M. L., & Fox, G. L. (2004). *Economic distress, community context, and intimate violence: An application and extension of social disorganization theory.* Washington, DC: National Institute of Justice.

Bowker, L. H. (1983). *Beating wife-beating.* Lexington, MA: DC Heath and Company.

Brodsky, A. E., & Marx, C. M. (2001). Layers of identity: Multiple psychological senses of community within a community setting. *Journal of Community Psychology, 29,* 161–178.

Brown, G. W., & Harris, T. (1978). Social origins of depression: A reply. *Psychological Medicine, 8,* 577–588.

Browne, A., & Bassuk, S. S. (1997). Intimate violence in the lives of homeless and poor house women: Prevalence and patterns in an ethnically diverse sample. *American Journal of Orthopsychiatry, 67,* 261–278.

Browne, A., Salomon, A., & Bassuk, S. S. (1999). The impact of recent partner violence on poor women's capacity to maintain work. *Violence Against Women, 5,* 393–426.

Bullock, H. E. (1995). Class acts: Middle-class responses to the poor. In B. Lott & D. Maluso (Eds.), *The social psychology of interpersonal discrimination* (pp. 118–159). New York: Guilford.

Burnham, L. (2002). Welfare reform, family hardship, and women of color. In R. Albelda & A. Withorn (Eds.), *Lost ground: Welfare reform, poverty, and beyond.* Cambridge, MA: South End Press.

Bybee, D. L, & Sullivan, C. M. (2002). The process through which a strengths-based intervention resulted in positive change for battered women over time. *American Journal of Community Psychology, 30,* 103–132.

Bybee, D. L., & Sullivan, C. M. (2005). Predicting revictimization of battered women 3 years after exiting a shelter program. *American Journal of Community Psychology. Special Issue: Theoretical and Methodological Innovations in Research on Intimate Partner Violence, 36,* 85–96.

Campbell, J. C. (1989). A test of two explanatory models of women's responses to battering. *Nursing Research, 38,* 18–24.

Campbell, R., Sullivan, C. M., & Davidson, W. S. (1995). Women who use domestic violence shelters: Changes in depression over time. *Psychology of Women Quarterly, 19,* 237–255.

Cocozza, J. J., Jackson, E. W., Hennigan, K., Morrisey, J. P., Reed, B. C, Fallot, R., et al. (2005). Outcomes for women with co-occurring disorders and trauma: Program level effects. *Journal of Substance Abuse Treatment, 28,*109–119.

Coiro, M. J. (2001). Depressive symptoms among women receiving welfare. *Women and Health, 32,* 1–23.

Coker, A. L., Watkins, K. W., Smith, P. H., & Brandt, H. M. (2003). Social support reduces the impact of partner violence on health: Application of structural equation models. *Preventive Medicine: An International Journal Devoted to Practice and Theory, 3,* 259–267.

Coker, A. L., Weston, R., Creson, D. L., Justice, B., & Blakeney, P. (2005). PTSD symptoms among men and women survivors of intimate partner violence: The role of risk and protective factors. *Violence and Victims, 20,* 625–643.

Colten, M. E., Cosenza, C., & Allard, M. A. (1996). *Domestic violence among Massachusetts AFDC recipients: Preliminary results.* Boston: Center for Survey Research, University of Massachusetts.

Costello, M., Chung, D., & Carson, E. (2005). Exploring pathways out of poverty: Making connections between domestic violence and employment practices. *Australian Journal of Social Issues, 40,* 253–267.

Cunradi, C., Caetano, R., & Schafer, J. (2002). Socioeconomic predictors of intimate partner violence among White, Black, and Hispanic couples in the United States. *Journal of Family Violence, 17,* 377–389.

de Anda, D. (1984). Informal support networks of Hispanic mothers: A comparison across age groups. *Journal of Social Service Research, 7*(3), 89–105.

Davies, J., Lyon, E., & Monti-Catania, D. (1998). *Safety planning with battered women: Complex lives/difficult choices.* Thousand Oaks, CA: Sage.

DeKeseredy, W. S., Alvi, S., Schwartz, M., & Perry, B. (1999). Violence against and the harassment of women in Canadian public housing: An exploratory study. *Canadian Review of Sociology and Anthropology, 36,* 499–516.

Dodson, L. (1998). *Don't call us out of name: Untold lives of women and girls in poor America.* Boston: Beacon.

Drake, R. E., Price, J. L., & Drake, R. E. (1996). Helping depressed clients discover personal power. *Perspectives in Psychiatric Care, 32,* 30–35.

Dunn, J. R., & Hayes, M. V. (2000). Social inequality, population health and housing in two Vancouver neighbourhoods. *Social Science and Medicine, 51,* 563–587.

Dutton, M. A., & Goodman, L. A. (2005). Coercive control in intimate partner violence: Towards a new conceptualization. *Sex Roles, 52,* 743–757.

Eby, K. (2004). Exploring the stressors of low-income women with abusive partners: Understanding their needs and developing effective community responses. *Journal of Family Violence, 19,* 221–232.

Eckenrode, J., & Gore, S. (1981). Stressful events and social support: The significance of context. In B. Gottlieb (Ed.), *Social networks and social support.* Beverly Hills, CA: Sage.

Eckenrode, J., & Wethington, E. (1990). The process and outcome of mobilizing social support. In S. Duck & R. C. Silver (Eds.), *Personal relationships and social support* (pp. 83–103). London: Sage.

Economic Stability Working Group of the Transition Subcommittee of the Governor's Commission on Domestic Violence. (2002). *Voices of survival: Vie economic impacts of domestic violence, a blueprint for action.* Boston: Commonwealth of Massachusetts.

Edin, K., & Lein, L. (1997). *Making ends meet: How single mothers survive welfare and low-wage work.* New York: Russell Sage.

Elliott, M. (2000). The stress process in neighborhood context. *Health & Place, 6,* 287–299.

Evans, G. W., & English, K. (2002). The environment of poverty: Multiple stressor exposure, psychophysiological stress, and socioemotional adjustment. *Child Development, 73,* 1238–1248.

Farmer, A., & Tiefenthaler, J. (2003). Explaining the recent decline in domestic violence. *Contemporary Economic Policy, 21,* 158–172.

Fine, M. (1983–1984). Coping with rape: Critical perspectives on consciousness. *Imagination, Cognition and Personality, 3,*249–267.

Fine, M. (1982). When nonvictims derogate: Powerlessness in the helping professions. *Personality and Social Psychology Bulletin, 8,* 637–643.

Folkman, S. (1984). Personal control and stress and coping processes: A theoretical analysis, *Journal of Personality and Social Psychology, 46,* 839–852.

Fondacaro, M. R., & Moos, R. H. (1989). Life stressors and coping: A longitudinal analysis among depressed and non-depressed adults, *Journal of Community Psychology, 17,* 330–340.

Foster, R. P. (2007). Treating depression in vulnerable women: A feasibility study of clinical outcomes in community service settings. *American Journal of Orthopsychiatry, 77,* 443–453.

Gondolf, E. W., & Fisher, E. R. (1988). *Battered women as survivors: An alternative to treating learned helplessness.* Lexington, MA: Lexington Books.

Goodman, L. A. (1991). The prevalence of abuse in the lives of homeless and housed poor mothers: A comparison study. *American Journal of Orthopsychiatry, 61,* 489–500.

Goodman, L., & Epstein, D. (2008). *Listening to battered women: A survivor-centered approach to advocacy, mental health, and justice.* Washington, DC: American Psychological Association.

Goodman, L. A., Glenn, C., Bohlig, A., Banyard, V., & Borges, A. (2009). Feminist relational advocacy: Processes and outcomes from the perspective of low-income women with depression. *The Counseling Psychologist,* 848–876.

Goodman, L. A., & Smyth, K. F. (in press). Social justice for marginalized women: Multicultural and feminist roots of the full frame approach to social services. In M. Constantine (Ed.), *Social justice and empowerment initiatives in psychology and education.*

Goodman, L. A., Dutton, M. A., Weinfurt, K. & Cook, S. (2003). The Intimate Partner Violence Strategies Index: Development and application. *Violence Against Women, 9*(2), 163–186.

Goodman, L. A., Dutton, M. A., Vankos, N. & Weinfurt, W. (2005). Women's resources and use of strategies as risk and protective factors for re-abuse over time. *Violence Against Women, 77*(3), 311–336.

Green, B., & Sanchez-Hucles, J. (1997). Diversity: Advancing an inclusive feminist psychology. In J. Worell & N. G. Johnson (Eds.), *Shaping the future of feminist psychology: Education, research and practice* (pp. 173–203). Washington, DC: American Psychological Association.

Greenfeld, L., Rand, M., Craven, D., Klaus, P., Perkins, C., Ringel, C., et al. (1998). *Violence by intimates: Bureau of justice statistics fact book* (NCJ 767237). Washington, DC: U.S. Department of Justice.

Greif, G. L. (2005). Group work with urban African-American parents in their neighborhood schools. In G. L. Greif & P. H. Ephross (Eds.), *Group work with populations at risk* (2nd ed., pp. 349–360). New York: Oxford University Press.

Grigsby, N., & Hartman, B. R. (1997). The barriers model: An integrated strategy for intervention with battered women. *Psychotherapy: Theory, Research, Practice, Training, 34,* 485–497.

Hägglund, D., & Ahlstrom, G. (2007). The meaning of women's experience of living with long-term urinary incontinence is powerlessness. *Journal of Clinical Nursing, 16,* 1946–1954.

Halpern, R. (1999). After-school programs for low-income children: Promise and challenges. *Future of Children, 9,* 81–95.

Hamby, S., & Grey-Little, B. (2007). Can battered women cope? A critical analysis of research on women's responses to violence. In K. A. Kendall-Tackett & S. M. Giacomoni (Eds.), *Intimate partner violence* (pp. 28/1–28/15). Kingston, NJ: Civic Research Institute.

Herman, J. L. (1992). *Trauma and recovery.* New York: Basic Books.

Holzman, H. R., Hyatt, R. A., & Dempster, J. M. (2001). Patterns of aggravated assault in public housing: Mapping the nexus of offense, place, gender, and race. *Violence Against Women. Special Issue: Violence Against Women in Public Housing, 7,* 662–684.

Homes for the Homeless: The Institute for Children & Poverty. (2002, April 9). *Hidden migration of families to homeless shelters may be a strategy to keep their kids out of foster care.* Retrieved March 3, 2008, from http://www.homesforthehomeless .com/index.asp?CID=1&PID=36&NID=48

House, J. S., Landis, K. R., & Umberson, D. (1988). Social relationships and health. *Science, 247,* 540–545.

House, J. S., Lepkowski, J. M., Kinney, A. M., Mero, R. P., Kessler, R. C., & Herzog, A. R. (1994). The social stratification of aging and health. *Journal of Health and Social Behavior, 35,* 213–234.

Humphreys, C. (2007). A health inequalities perspective on violence against women. *Health & Social Care in the Community, 75,* 120–127.

Kanuha, V. (1996). Domestic violence, racism, and the battered women's movement in the United States. In J. L. Edleson & Z. C. Eisikovits (Eds.), *Future interventions with battered women and their families. SAGE series on violence against women* (Vol. 3, pp. 34–50). Thousand Oaks, CA: Sage.

Kessler, R. C. (1979). Stress, social status, and psychological distress. *Journal of Health and Social Behavior, 20,* 259–272.

Kocot, T., & Goodman, L. A. (2003). The roles of coping and social support in battered women's mental health. *Violence Against Women, 9,* 1–24.

Krause, N., & Borawski-Clark, E. (1995). Social class differences in social support among older adults. *The Gerontologist, 35,* 498–508.

Lapidus, L. M. (2003). Gaining access: An assessment of community responsiveness to the needs of Haitian immigrant women who are survivors of intimate partner violence. *Violence Against Women, 11,* 269–289.

Laughon, K. (2007). Abused African American women's processes of staying healthy. *Western Journal of Nursing Research, 29,* 365–384.

Lazarus, R. S., & Folkman, S. (1984). *Stress, appraisal, and coping.* New York: Springer.

Lazear, K. J., Pires, S. A., Isaacs, M. R., Chaulk, P., & Huang, L. (2008). Depression among low-income women of color: Qualitative findings from cross-cultural focus groups. *Journal of Immigrant and Minority Health, 10*(2), 127–133.

Lempert, L. B. (1996). Women's strategies for survival: Developing agency in abusive relationships. *Journal of Family Violence, 11,* 269–289.

Lens, V., & Gibelman, M. (2000). Advocacy be not forsaken! Retrospective lessons from welfare reform. *Families in Society, 81,* 611–620.

Levendosky, A., Bogat, G. A., Theran, S. A., Trotter, J. S., von Eye, A., & Davidson, W. S. (2004). The social networks of women experiencing domestic violence. *American Journal of Community Psychology, 34,* 95–109.

Levin, R., McKean, L., & Raphael, J. (2004, January). *Pathways to and from homelessness: Women and children in Chicago shelters.* Center for Impact Research. Retrieved November 20, 2006, from http://www.impactre-search.org/publications

Levine, S., & Ursin, H. (1991). What is stress? In M. R. Brown, C. Rivier & G. Koob (Eds.), *Stress: Neurobiology and endocrinology* (pp. 1–21). New York: Marcel Dekker.

Liang, B., Glenn, C., & Goodman, L. A. (2005). Feminist ethics in advocacy relationships: A relational vs. rule-bound approach. *The Community Psychologist, 38,* 26–28.

Lindhorst, T., & Padgett, J. D. (2005). Disjunctures for women and frontline workers: Implementation of the family violence option. *Social Service Review, 79,* 406–429.

Lipsey, M. W., & Wilson, D. B. (1993). The efficacy of psychological, educational, and behavioural treatment: Confirmation from meta-analysis. *American Psychologist, 48,* 1181–1209.

Livingston, J. A., Hequembourg, A., Testa, M., & VanZile-Tamsen, C. (2007). Unique aspects of adolescent sexual victimization experiences. *Psychology of Women Quarterly, 31,* 331–343.

Lloyd, S., & Taluc, N. (1999). The effects of male violence on female employment. *Violence Against Women, 5,* 370–392.

Lott, B. (2002). Cognitive and behavioral distancing from the poor. *American Psychologist, 57,* 100–110.

Lott, B., & Bullock, H. (2007). *Psychology and economic injustice: Personal, professional, and political intersections.* Washington, DC: American Psychological Association.

Lown, A., Schmidt, L., & Wiley, J. (2006). Interpersonal violence among women seeking welfare: Unraveling lives. *American Journal of Public Health, 96,* 1409–1415.

Markoff, L. S., Finkelstein, N., Kammerer, N., Kreiner, P., & Post, C. A. (2005). Implementing a model of change in integrating services for women with substance abuse and mental health disorders and histories of trauma. *Journal of Behavioral Health Services and Research, 32,* 227–240.

McLeod, J. D., & Kessler, R. C. (1990). Socioeconomic status differences in vulnerability to undesirable life events. *Journal of Health and Social Behavior, 31,* 162–172.

Meier, J. (1997). Domestic violence, character, and social change in the welfare reform debate. *Law and Policy, 19,* 205–265.

Mickelson, K. D., & Kubzansky, L. D. (2003). Social distribution of social support: The mediating role of life events. *American Journal of Community Psychology, 32,* 265–281.

Miranda, J., & Green, B. (1999). The need for mental health services research focusing on poor young women. *Journal of Mental Health Policy and Economics, 2,* 73–80.

Mirowsky, J., & Ross, C. E. (1986). Social patterns of distress. *Annual Review of Sociology, 12,* 23–45.

Moane, G. (2003). Bridging the personal and the political: Practices for a liberation psychology. *American Journal of Community Psychology, 31,* 91–101.

Moe, A. M., & Bell, M. (2004). Abject economics: The effects of battering and violence on women's work and employ ability. *Violence Against Women, 10,* 29–55.

Owen, G., Heineman, J., Shelton, E., & Gerrard, M. D. (2004, July). *Key facts from the survey of Minnesotans without permanent housing.* Wilder

Research Center Homeless in Minnesota. Retrieved December 15, 2007, from http://www.wilder.org/reportsummary.0.html?tx_ttnews%5Btt_news%5D=536

Patterson, E. B. (1991). Poverty, income inequality, and crime rates. *Criminology, 29,* 755–776.

Pavao, J. M., Alvarez, J., Baumrind, N., Induni, M., & Kimerling, R. (2007). Intimate partner violence and housing instability. *American Journal of Preventive Medicine, 32,* 143–146.

Pearson, J., Griswold, E. A., & Thoennes, N. (2001). Balancing safety and self-sufficiency: Lessons on serving victims of domestic violence for child support and public assistance agencies. *Violence Against Women, 7,* 176–192.

Proctor, B., & Dalaker, J. (2003). *Poverty in the United States: 2002 (Current population reports, Series P60-222).* Washington, DC: U.S. Government Printing Office. Retrieved March 4, 2008, from http://www.census.gov/hhes/www/poverty.html

Purvin, D. (2007). At the crossroads and in the crosshairs: Social welfare policy and low-income women's vulnerability to domestic violence. *Social Problems, 54,* 188–210.

Raphael, J. (2000). *Saving Bernice: Battered women, welfare, and poverty.* Boston: Northeastern University Press.

Raphael, J. (2001). Domestic violence as a welfare-to-work barrier: Research and theoretical issues. In C. M. Renzetti, J. L. Edleson, & R. K. Bergen (Eds.), *Sourcebook on violence against women* (pp. 443–456). Thousand Oaks, CA: Sage.

Raphael, J. (2003). Battering through the lens of class. *Journal of Gender, Social Policy & the Law, 11,* 367–368.

Rattner, A. (1990). Social indicators and crime rate forecasting. *Social Indicators Research, 22,* 83–95.

Rayburn, N. R., Wenzel, S. L., Elliott, M. N., Hambarsoomian, K., Marshall, G. N., & Tucker, J. S. (2005). Trauma, depression, coping, and mental health service seeking among impoverished women. *Journal of Consulting and Clinical Psychology, 73,* 667–677.

Renzetti, C. M. (2001). "One strike and you're out": Implications of a federal crime control policy for battered women. *Violence Against Women. Special Issue: Violence Against Women in Public Housing, 7,* 685–698.

Richie, B. E. (2000). A Black feminist reflection of the anti-violence movement. *Signs, 4,* 1133–1137.

Richie, B. E. (2005). Foreword. In N. J. Sokoloff & C. Pratt (Eds.), *Domestic violence at the margins: Readings on race, class, gender, and culture* (pp. xv–xiv). New Brunswick, NJ: Rutgers University Press.

Riger, S., Raja, S., & Camacho, J. (2002). The radiating impact of intimate partner violence. *Journal of Interpersonal Violence, 17,* 184–205.

Roschelle, A. R. (1997). *No more kin: Exploring race, class, and gender in family networks. Understanding families* (Vol. 8). Thousand Oaks, CA: Sage.

Rosen, D., Tolman, R. M., & Warner, L. A. (2004). Low-income women's use of substance abuse and mental health services. *Journal of Health Care for the Poor and Underserved, 15,* 206–219.

Roth, S., & Cohen, L. J. (1986). Approach, avoidance, and coping with stress. *American Psychologist, 41,* 813–819.

Saltzman, L. E., Fanslow, J. L., McMahon, P. M., & Shelley, G. A. (1999). *Intimate partner violence surveillance: Uniform definitions and recommended data elements, version 1.0.* Atlanta, GA: Centers for Disease Control and Prevention, National Center for Injury Prevention and Control.

Schechter, S. (1982). *Women and male violence: The visions and struggles of the battered women's movement.* Boston: South End.

Scott, E. K., London, A. S., & Myers, N. A. (2002). Dangerous dependencies: The intersection of welfare reform and domestic violence. *Gender & Society, 16,* 878–897.

Siefert, K., Heflin, C. M., Corcoran, M. E., & Williams, D. R. (2001). Food insufficiency and the physical and mental health of low-income women. *Women & Health Special Issue: Welfare, Work, and Well-being: Part I, 32,* 159–177.

Sklar, H., Mykyta, L., & Wefald, S. (2001). *Raise the floor: Wages and policies that work for all of us.* New York: Ms. Foundation for Women.

Smith, L. (2005). Psychotherapy, classism, and the poor: Conspicuous by their absence. *American Psychologist, 60,* 687–696.

Smith, L. (2008). Positioning classism with counseling psychology's social justice agenda. *The Counseling Psychologist, 36,* 895–924.

Smyth, K., Goodman, L. A., & Glenn, C. (2006). The full-frame approach: A new response to marginalized women left behind by specialized services. *American Journal of Orthopsychiatry, 76,* 489–502.

Stack, C. (1974). *All our kin: Strategies for survival in a black community.* New York: Harper & Row.

Staggs, S. L., Long, S. M., Mason, G. E., Krishnan, S., & Riger, S. (2007). Intimate partner violence, social support, and employment in the post-welfare reform era. *Journal of Interpersonal Violence, 22,* 345–367.

Sue, S., & Lamb, A. G. (2002). Cultural and demographic diversity. In J. C. Norcross (Ed.), *Psychotherapy relationships that work: Therapist contributions and responsiveness to patients* (pp. 401–422). New York: Oxford University Press.

Sullivan, C. M. (1997). Societal collusion and culpability in intimate male violence: The impact of community response toward women with abusive partners. In A. P. Cardarelli (Ed.), *Violence among intimate partners: Patterns, causes, and effects* (pp. 154–164). Needham Heights, MA: Allyn & Bacon.

Sullivan, C. M., Basta, J., Tan, C., & Davidson, W. S. (1992). After the crisis: A needs assessment of women leaving a domestic violence shelter. *Violence and Victims, 7,* 267–275.

Sutherland, C., Sullivan, C., & Bybee, D. (2001). Effects of intimate partner violence versus poverty on women's health. *Violence Against Women, 7,* 1122–1143.

Szreter, S., & Woolcock, M. (2004). Health by association? Social capital, social theory and the political economy of public health. *International Journal of Epidemiology,* 650–667.

Tea, M. (Ed.). (2004). *Without a net: The female experience of growing up working class.* Seattle, WA: Seal Press Seattle.

The Commonwealth Fund. (2006). *Closing the divide: How medical homes promote equity in health care: Results from the Commonwealth Fund 2006 Health Care Quality Survey.* Retrieved March 25, 2008, from http://www.commonwealthfund.org/publications/publications_show.htm?doc_id=506814

Thoits, P. A. (1986). Social support as coping assistance. *Journal of Consulting and Clinical Psychology, 54,* 416–423.

Tiefenthaler, J., Farmer, A., & Sambira, A. (2005). Services and intimate partner violence in the United States: A county-level analysis. *Journal of Marriage and Family, 67,* 565–578.

Tjaden, P., & Thoennes, N. (2000). *Full report of the prevalence, incidence, and consequences of violence against women.* Washington, DC: US. Department of Justice.

Tolman, R. M., & Rosen, D. (2001). Domestic violence in the lives of women receiving welfare. *Violence Against Women, 7,* 141–158.

Turner, J. B. (1995). Economic context and the health effects of unemployment *Journal of Health and Social Behavior, 36,* 213–229.

Turner, R. J., & Marino, F. (1994). Social support and social structure: A descriptive epidemiology. *Journal of Health and Social Behavior, 35,* 193–212.

U.S. Census Bureau. (2006). *Poverty status of people by family relationship, race, and Hispanic origin: 1959 to 2006 (Internet release).* Retrieved December 25, 2007, from http://www.census.gov/

U.S. Department of Health and Human Services. (2001). *Youth violence: A report of the surgeon general.* Rockville, MD: US. Department of Health and Human Services. Retrieved January 2, 2008, from http://www.mentalhealth.org/youthviolence/surgeongeneral/SG_Site/home.asp

Vest, J., Catlin, T., Chen, J., & Brownson, R. (2002). Multi-state analysis of factors associated with intimate partner violence. *American Journal of Preventive Medicine, 22,* 156–164.

Vogel, L. C., & Marshal, L. L. (2001). PTSD symptoms and partner abuse: Low-income women at risk. *Journal of Traumatic Stress, 14,* 569–584.

von Eye, A., & Bogat, G. A. (2006). Mental health in women experiencing intimate partner violence as the efficiency goal of social welfare functions. *International Journal of Social Welfare, 75,* 531–540.

Walker, L. E. (1979). *The battered woman.* New York: Harper & Row.

Walker, L. E. (1984). *The battered woman syndrome.* New York: Springer.

Wasylishyn, C., & Johnson, J. L. (1998). Living in a housing cooperative for low-income women: Issues of identity, environment and control. *Social Science & Medicine, 47,* 973–981.

Wenzel, S. L., Tucker, J. S., Hambarsoomian, K., & Elliott, M. N. (2006). Toward a more comprehensive understanding of violence against impoverished women. *Journal of Interpersonal Violence, 21,* 820–839.

CHAPTER 14

Adult Domestic Violence in Cases of International Parental Child Abduction

Sudha Shetty and Jeffrey L. Edleson

Public concern for children exposed to domestic violence has grown substantially in the past decade as a result of a growing number of research studies revealing (a) that children exposed to domestic violence may experience subsequent negative developmental outcomes (Edleson, 1999a; Fantuzzo & Mohr, 1999; Margolin, 1998; Onyskiw, 2003; Rossman, 2001) and (b) that almost half of the families in which adult domestic violence occurs also show evidence of child maltreatment (Appel & Holden, 1998; Edleson, 1999b; McGuigan & Pratt, 2001; O'Leary, Slep, & O'Leary, 2000). Accompanying the explosion in published literature on children exposed to domestic violence has been a variety of new public policy (Dunford-Jackson, 2004) and programmatic efforts (see http://www.thegreenbook.info).

It is not just the public but also battered mothers who are concerned for their children. Children frequently play a major role in battered mothers' decision making about staying or leaving an abusive partner. Studies in the United States (Humphreys, 1995a, 1995b; Levendosky, Lynch, & Graham-Bermann, 2000; Short et al., 2000) and Canada (N. Z. Hilton, 1992) have repeatedly shown that battered mothers express deep concern for their children's safety. This concern may lead mothers to stay with an abusive partner out of fear of greater harm if they leave. It may also lead them to flee with their children for safety. In fact, the majority of residents of

Shetty, S., & Edleson, J. L. (2005). Adult domestic violence in cases of international parental child abduction. *Violence Against Women, 11,* 115–138.

AUTHORS' NOTE: The authors wish to acknowledge the many law students and staff serving on the Hague Convention Project at Seattle University Law School, particularly Regina Ahn from University of Notre Dame Law School and Tracy Sarich, Haywood Burns Fellow, Seattle University School of Law.

battered women's shelters are often children brought with their battered mothers who are fleeing an abusive partner (Minnesota Department of Public Safety, 2004).

In an increasingly interconnected world, one group of battered women overlooked and in dire need of our attention in the next decade is mothers who flee with their children for safety across international borders. It is not surprising that in their search for safety, mothers flee across national boundaries. What is surprising is the web of international treaties and domestic legislation and programs in the United States that may work against securing safety for battered mothers and their children who have fled from abusive partners.

In this article, we discuss the Hague Convention on the Civil Aspects of International Child Abduction (hereinafter the Convention) and how it affects battered mothers and their children seeking safety in the United States. We first discuss the Convention and its relevant articles. We then examine the extent to which adult domestic violence appears to be present in cases of parental child abduction. Next, we examine cases in which battered mothers have contested the forced return of their children to an abusive partner in the child's country of habitual residence by using specific defenses allowed under the Convention. And finally, we focus on several steps needed in research, training, and legislation that may increase the likelihood of safe outcomes for battered mothers and their children engaged in court proceedings involving international child abduction.

We should note that it is not just mothers who may abduct their children across borders. Some men who batter use the courts to extend their harassment of a battered partner through lengthy custody fights (Jaffe, Lemon, & Poisson, 2003). Threats of abductions and actual abductions of their children across international borders are sometimes part of this extended postseparation harassment. But for the battered mother who is left behind in the United States, there are several sources of support, as will be noted below. It is

the abducting mother, who is battered and fleeing across international borders for her safety and that of her children, for whom there is little or no assistance and whose motives are often doubted. It is the situation of these women and their children that is the focus of this article.

The Hague Convention and U.S. Responses to It

The Convention on the Civil Aspects of International Child Abduction was completed at The Hague in October, 1980 and put into effect in the United States through passage of the International Child Abduction Remedies Act passed by Congress in July, 1988 (see http://www.hcch.net/e/conventions/menu28e.html for full text of the Convention and http://travel.state.gov/icara.html for the full text of the International Child Abduction Remedies Act). To date, approximately 67 countries are parties to the Convention (U.S. Department of State, 2003).

The Convention establishes international law for handling cases in which children are abducted from one country to another. States party to the Convention are expected to help quickly return abducted children to their habitual residence, where other issues, such as custody, can be resolved by local jurisdictions (W. M. Hilton, 1997). The Convention contains certain exceptions that permit the best interests of the child to override the mandatory return of a child from one country to another, and these will be discussed at greater length later in this article.

There are likely several thousand cases of international child abduction both into and out of the United States each year. According to one newspaper report, U.S. courts handled 2,688 Hague cases (approximately 400 annually) between 1995 and 2002 (Cambanis, 2002). The actual number of abduction cases is far higher than those seen by the courts. For example, the U.S. Department of State's Office of Children's Issues has been contacted since the late 1970s in 16,000 cases of child abduction both into and out of the United States (see http://travel.state.gov/famly/abduction.html). The Office of Children's Issues handles the outgoing cases, or abductions of children out of the United States to foreign countries. The U.S. Department of State (2003) recently reported to Congress that in 2003, there were 904 international abduction cases filed by U.S.-based parents and opened for intervention. The highest numbers of children with open outgoing cases of abduction were thought to be in Mexico (154), Germany (41), Jordan (34), Japan (33), Egypt (33), Canada (29), and India (28).

The National Center for Missing and Exploited Children (NCMEC) is the U.S. nongovernmental agency officially charged with assisting left-behind parents with incoming cases (i.e., parents in foreign countries seeking the return of their children abducted into the United States). The NCMEC reported that in 2002, there were 445 applications for assistance from parents in other countries seeking to have their children returned to them from parents who had abducted them to the United States (NCMEC, 2002). This is an increase from 241 cases in 1998 (Subcommittee on International Child Abduction, 1999). These applications for return under the Convention came primarily from left-behind parents in Europe and Eurasia (169), Mexico (129), and Central and South America (69). It is likely that there are many more international abduction cases that are never formally reported to either the U.S. Department of State or the NCMEC. For example, the NCMEC assists in cases entering the federal courts, but some parents bypass the federal courts and go directly to state courts for assistance.

Interviews with staff of the U.S. Department of State and the NCMEC indicate that current efforts related to the Convention focus on exclusively assisting left-behind parents to locate and seek the return of their children from abducting or taking parents. This is a reflection of the belief as embodied in the Convention and much of the social science literature, public policy, and current intervention efforts that child abduction

has grave negative implications for a child's development and that a prompt return of the child to their country of habitual residence is almost always in the best interests of the child's well-being (Weiner, 2000).

The U.S. Department of State, through its Office of Children's Issues (http://travel.state.gov/abduct.html), works with left-behind parents in the United States to provide them with information and to assist them by providing liaison activities with U.S. and other foreign authorities, working to ensure that the Convention is being applied as intended in this country and others, and coordinating between government agencies. The NCMEC provides, with the American Bar Association, a network of pro bono attorneys to assist left-behind parents from other countries as well as support attorneys and judicial officers through training efforts and provide extensive information on international child abduction through its Web site (http://www.ncmec.org).

Rethinking the Hague Convention in Cases of Domestic Violence

What if the abducting parent is a battered mother who is fleeing with her children to safety in another country? In her detailed review of the Convention, Weiner (2000) laid out a new perspective on international child abduction. She argued that the Convention was drafted with a stereotypical male abductor in mind, who takes children from their primary caregiver, their mothers. This has led to a focus on solely assisting the left-behind parents in their efforts to have their children returned. Weiner has argued that the international community has been slow to recognize that some abducting parents are battered women fleeing for their own and their children's safety. In fact, a recent interview with a staff member in the Abduction Unit of the Office of Children's Issues at the U.S. Department of State indicated that fleeing battered mothers who are fearful for their safety and that of their children are expected to use local battered women's services and locate their own attorneys. This staff member also indicated that adult-to-adult domestic violence is not seen as a common issue among these families and that when it is raised, it is often viewed as an unsubstantiated allegation (G. DeBoer, U.S. Department of State, personal communication, May 20, 2004).

The views expressed above leave battered mothers, such as Karin Von Krenner, unprotected in U.S. courts. Von Krenner and her young son escaped brutal domestic violence in Cyprus and fled home to the United States after years of being held against her will. Shortly thereafter, she was declared an international fugitive and hunted down. Armed federal marshals forcibly removed her 8-year-old son, Kristopher, from her home. When she desperately tried to retain a lawyer in Boise, Idaho, she was met with blank stares and resistance. No one had heard of the Hague Convention, and no one knew where to learn more about it. One attorney told her she had no case and that she was wasting her time (K. Von Krenner, personal communications, May 23, 2004; August 12, 2004). In her case, as in so many others, Von Krenner and her son had no access to adequate representation in U.S. courts.

The little research available on families where parental child abductions have occurred suggests that Karin Von Krenner's situation is not unique. Adult domestic violence is, in fact, a significant issue in parental abductions and supports Weiner's rethinking of how we intervene in these cases. Approximately one third of all published and unpublished Convention cases we have identified using online legal databases include a reference to some type of family violence, and 70% of these include details of adult domestic violence (http://www.law.seattleu.edu/accesstojustice/hague). Weiner (2003) also points out that seven of nine Convention cases that reached an appeals court in the last half of 2000 involved an abducting mother who claimed she was a victim of domestic violence.

Some of the earliest literature on parental abduction also mentions domestic violence in a prominent way. For example, Agopian (1981) devotes an entire chapter to a review of the early research on domestic violence but then ironically mentions little about such violence in the results of his survey of 91 child abduction cases in Los Angeles. He does note that examining the relationship between the custodial parent and the offender can help trace the complex flow of events leading to the crime. The child theft may be a continuation of an established climate of conflict between the custodial parent and offender (pp. 86–87).

The case Agopian then uses to illustrate this concept is one in which the father abducts the children and then calls and threatens "if you don't stop the divorce, you won't ever see the kids again" (p. 87).

One of the largest studies of abducted children, the second National Incidence Studies of Missing, Abducted, Runaway and Thrownaway Children, was conducted with a random sample of 16,111 adult caregivers in the United States during 1999 (Sedlak, Finkelhor, Hammer, & Schultz, 2002). In their subanalyses of family-only abductions, Hammer, Finkelhor, and Sedlak (2002) estimated that nationally/ there were approximately 56,500 abductions reported to authorities by family caregivers and that 57% of the abductors were the child's father, the child's stepfather, or the mother's boyfriend, with a quarter (25%) of the abductors being the child's mother. Unfortunately, it does not appear that the reasons, for example, domestic violence by one parent against another, were clearly recorded in this study of abductions.

Greif and Hegar's (1993) book on parental kidnapping is much more direct about the presence of family violence in cases of parental abduction. Their survey of 368 parents and three grandparents in 45 states and 6 countries is one of the largest and most frequently cited in the literature (the return rate on this survey was only 15% to 27%, depending on how the rate is computed). Greif and Hegar constructed five types of parental child abductions, three of which appear to include abductors or left-behind parents who were violent toward their partners. Overall, the majority (54%) of all the marriages in which abductions occurred involved parent-to-parent domestic violence, and 30% of the left-behind parents either admitted to being violent toward other family members or had been accused of it (Greif & Hegar, 1993).

Sagatun-Edwards and her colleagues (Johnston, Sagatun-Edwards, Bloomquist, & Girdner, 2000) report a study of 634 abduction cases in two California counties. Although these were primarily domestic abductions (only 7.5% were abductions out of the United States), they found that "mothers who abducted were more likely to take the children when they or the children were victims of abuse, and fathers who abducted were more likely to take the children when they were the abusers" (pp. 2–3). They also found that "mothers were more likely to have the children placed with them at the conclusion of the case, regardless of their role in the abduction" (pp. 2–4).

A more recent study reported by Chiancone, Girdner, and Hoff (2001) surveyed the responses of 93 left-behind parents of children abducted out of the United States. Only one table and one paragraph in their lengthy report are devoted to family violence issues. Here, they note that 84 of the 93 left-behind parents reported the abductor had threatened their lives or those of other family members prior to the abduction. Sixty percent of left-behind parents reporting threats said their lives had been threatened, 21% reported their children's lives threatened, and 42% reported the abductor also threatened the lives of others. Their results would suggest that many of the child abductors were abusive toward the left-behind parents, some of their children, and others.

The results of the Greif and Hegar (1993), Johnston et al. (2000), and Chiancone et al. (2001) studies appear somewhat contradictory when trying to understand who are likely victims and perpetrators of violence among abducting and left-behind parents. Chiancone et al. found that most of the abductors were reported to have used violent threats against those left behind. Greif and Hegar, on the other hand,

studied a group that included many violent left-behind parents whose children were abducted. Johnston et al. (2000) found differing motives among mothers and fathers who abducted their children, with mothers fleeing for safety from abusive partners and fathers likely using the abduction as part of their abuse toward the left-behind parent.

Unfortunately, we have little data in these studies of cases involving abduction of children into the United States. For example, in the study by Greif and Hegar (1993; Hegar & Greif, 1991), only abductions originating in the United States were studied. One might hypothesize that those abducting their children out of the United States may be seeking to avoid the reach of the U.S. criminal justice system, whereas those coming into the United States may be seeking criminal justice protections and social services not offered in the countries from where they fled. However, this remains a hypothesis until a more careful study of parents abducting their children into the United States is completed.

One place in which a glimpse of the factors involved in cases of abduction into the United States may be observed is through a careful examination of international child abduction cases before U.S. courts. The following sections describe in detail a selected group of such cases and the degree of success battered mothers have had in contesting the forced return of their children to the country in which the mother's abuser lives.

Hague Convention Defenses for Battered Mothers

The published literature on implementing the Convention suggests that court decisions should not be focused on child custody but rather on a determination of whether a child can be safely returned to his or her habitual residence, where local courts may consider custody and visitation issues (W. M. Hilton, 1997). In practice, drawing the line between custody decisions and decisions to return the child to a country of habitual residence seems to be much more difficult. Judges are being asked to decide what is in the best interests of the child, which is not so different from the issues raised in custody and visitation determinations in local family courts.

Cases involving petitions under the Convention reveal several defenses that battered mothers have used when they find themselves sued by a left-behind parent. Almost two thirds of family violence-related Convention cases we located appeared to raise claims that children would face a grave risk if they returned to their country of habitual residence. Many other cases raised issues of habitual residence, consent of the left-behind parent for the abducting parent to remove the children, and the child's age that permitted them to have a say in where they were to live, among others.

Below, we focus primarily on a grave risk defense and its applicability in Convention cases. We focus on grave risk because we see this defense as perhaps the most important, but also the least recognized, among a number of strategies battered mothers have used to defend themselves and their children. After considering this defense in detail, we will also review several other defenses mentioned above that battered mothers have used to defend against the forcible return of their children to abusive partners in other countries.

Grave Risk (Article 13[B])

Article 13(b) of the Convention provides an exception to the return of a child to his or her habitual residence if "there is a grave risk that his or her return would expose the child to physical or psychological harm or otherwise place the child in an intolerable situation" (the Convention, 1980, Article 13[b]). There is a great deal of controversy in the published literature on the degree to which Article 13(b) can and should be applied in Convention cases. W. M. Hilton's (1997) review of the use of the grave risk defense

reveals that court decisions and official interpretations of the Convention usually limit the application of this defense to cases in which there is internal strife in the country of habitual residence or where the courts of the country of habitual residence cannot or will not protect the child and his or her family. He argues that grave risk was not intended to be applied to the behavior of individual parents, stating "that a particular party might cause the child to be in peril is not sufficient" grounds for claiming grave risk (p. 143). This line of thinking is carried into current training curricula for judges and lawyers that equate violence against women with a custody issue and insist that it should be settled in the child's country of habitual residence (Hoff, 1997).

The use of a grave risk defense is also often criticized for other reasons. For example, Skoler (1998) has written a scathing critique of the use of Article 13(b) and concludes that "the Article 13b phrase, 'psychological harm,' has been interpreted so broadly and so liberally, as to frequently render the Hague Abduction Convention increasingly ineffective, undermined by its own language" (p. 560).

Cases Involving Grave Risk

Despite the above cautions, the grave risk defense has been raised in broader terms and upheld in a series of U.S. court cases. In fact, the courts seem to be struggling with what constitutes grave risk in a series of rulings. For example, in *Nunez-Escudero v. Tice Menley* (1995), the mother, her parents, and a psychologist provided testimony about severe physical abuse of the mother by the father, who was suing for return of his infant son to Mexico. The mother also stated a fear for her child's safety if returned to the father in Mexico. The district court held that a grave risk to the child did exist, but the circuit court held that the claim was too vague and sent the case back to the lower court stating that the mother must present more convincing evidence of grave risk to the child. In *Rodriguez v. Rodriguez* (1999), child abuse and domestic violence exposure were both offered as part of a grave risk defense. The daughter in the case testified that she had observed her brother and her mother being beaten and was afraid of also being beaten. The court stated that if the other parent removes or retains the child to safeguard it against further victimization, and the abusive parent then petitions for the child's return under the Convention, the court may deny the petition. Such action would protect the child from being returned to an "intolerable situation" and subjected to a grave risk of psychological harm (p. 462).

Although domestic violence was part of the testimony, the court ruling concerning grave risk focused on the danger of future child physical abuse to the Rodriguez children. Finally, in *Blondin v. Dubois* (1998), the court heard testimony by the mother that the father had beaten her severely, including times when she was holding one of their children. The child had received blows when in her mother's arms, and the father had at other times threatened to kill the child and the mother. The mother testified that the father beat her during a later pregnancy and subsequently threatened both her life and that of their children. In one of the only published rulings accepting child exposure to domestic violence as grave risk under the Convention, the district court ruled that grave risk existed as a result of beatings of the mother in the children's presence and direct abuse to the older child. A circuit court upheld this aspect of the lower court's ruling stating, "We emphasize, however, that we do not disturb or modify the district court's finding that returning [the children to the father's] custody (either expressly or *de facto)* would expose them to a 'grave risk' of harm, within the meaning of Article 13(b)" *(Blondin v. Dubois [II],* 1999, p. 250). In two subsequent appeals, courts upheld these lower court rulings.

The courts have considered not just the physical danger to a child when deciding on grave risk. In one case, *Steffen v. Severina* (1997), proof was given to the court that the child had attached and

bonded with the abducting parent—the child's mother—and the child's removal from the mother would force the child to be detached and unbonded, thus, the court ruled, constituting a grave risk of harm under the Convention.

Emerging Research on Risk and Domestic Violence Exposure

As stated earlier, these court rulings reveal judges who are struggling to define the degree to which physical and psychological harm to the children at the hands of the left-behind parent represents grave risk and intolerable situations under the Convention's Article 13(b). Judges do not appear to use a child's exposure to adult domestic violence as a sole or even primary reason for finding grave risk, despite growing social science evidence to the contrary.

Two areas of social science research clearly point to the potential for risk and harm to a child from exposure to adult domestic violence. First, exposed children may themselves be at greater risk of physical harm. A number of research reviews of the co-occurrence of documented child maltreatment in families where adult domestic violence is also occurring have found a 41% median co-occurrence of child maltreatment and adult domestic violence in families (Appel & Holden, 1998), with the majority of studies finding a co-occurrence of 30% to 60%, depending on the samples studied (Edleson, 1999b).

Second, almost 100 published studies report associations between exposure to domestic violence and current child problems or later adult problems. A number of authors have produced partial reviews of this growing body of literature and its limitations (Edleson, 1999a; Fantuzzo & Mohr, 1999; Margolin, 1998; Rossman, 2001). Overall, existing studies reveal that on average, children exposed to adult domestic violence exhibit more difficulties than those not so exposed. For example, several studies have reported that children exposed to domestic violence exhibit more aggressive and antisocial behaviors (often called externalized behaviors) as well as fearful and inhibited behaviors (internalized behaviors) when compared to nonexposed children (Fantuzzo et al., 1991; Hughes, 1988; Hughes, Parkinson, & Vargo, 1989). Exposed children also showed lower social competence than did other children (Adamson & Thompson, 1998; Fantuzzo et al., 1991) and were found to show higher average anxiety, depression, trauma symptoms, and temperament problems than children who were not exposed to violence at home (Hughes, 1988; Maker, Kemmelmeier, & Peterson, 1998; Sternberg et al., 1993).

Emerging Public Policy on Domestic Violence Exposure

Notwithstanding the above social science evidence, it appears that possibly only one published court opinion has thus far suggested that exposure to adult domestic violence in and of itself poses a grave risk or intolerable situation to a child under the Convention (*Blondin v. DuBois*, 1998). Of course, this may raise more of an issue of judicial knowledge and training than of fact. The same outcomes have long been observed in domestic family courts, where some judges have ruled that although an abusive man severely beats the mother, if he does not directly attack the children, his behavior is likely to have little impact on the children.

The emerging social science research and changing judicial attitudes have led to major changes in U.S. public policy regarding the appropriate response to children in cases where domestic violence exists. Led by the National Council of Juvenile and Family Court Judges, there are many changes under way in how the courts and social services respond to children exposed to domestic violence (Edleson, 2004; National Council of Juvenile and Family Court Judges, 1999). Perhaps most relevant is the passage of rebuttable presumption laws in 23 U.S. states (Dunford-Jackson, 2004). For example,

Wisconsin is one of the most recent states to pass such a law that stipulates that it "is detrimental to the child and contrary to the child's best interest for that parent [who committed domestic violence] to have either sole or joint legal custody of the child" [Wis. Stat. §767.24(2)(d)(1) (2004)].

Certainly, our society's definitions of child maltreatment and what constitutes the best interest of a child have been constantly changing during the past half century (Kalichman, 1999). Global definitions have also been changing through the establishment of international treaties, such as the U.N. Convention on the Rights of the Child, and to the extent that at least five European countries have even defined spanking as a form of illegal child maltreatment. With new knowledge about the impact that exposure to domestic violence has on children, our laws have been in a state of change, as have court decisions about the welfare of children. It is likely that similar changes will occur in both thinking and court decisions about domestic violence vis-à-vis grave risk to children under the Convention.

Establishing Domestic Violence Exposure as Grave Risk

The ICARA, the implementing legislation of the Convention, requires clear and convincing evidence of the level of risk to a specific child. The social science literature points to several factors to consider when establishing grave risk. First, the level of violence in the family must be established. Current research suggests that the level of domestic violence is known to vary greatly across families (Straus & Gelles, 1990). Second, it is very likely that children's exposure to violence at home and what meaning they attach to it will vary greatly (Peled, 1998). Third, the child's own ability or lack of ability to cope with the violent environment may also affect the level of harm to the child. Harm that children experience may be moderated by a number of factors, including how a child interprets or copes with the violence (Hughes, Graham-Bermann, &

Gruber, 2001). Fourth, children are likely to have varying risk and protective factors present in their lives (Hughes et al., 2001; Masten & Coatsworth, 1998). Protective factors may include a battered mother, siblings, or other adults who offer protection to the child as well the level of legal and social service protections likely available to the child and his or her battered mother in their country of habitual residence. Risk factors that co-occur with domestic violence might include parental substance abuse, presence of weapons in the home, both maternal and male caregiver mental health issues, and other neglect. These and other factors may combine with domestic violence in some families to create greater or lesser risk to the child.

Finally, as stated earlier, the risk of harm resulting from exposure may also vary from child to child. Two additional pieces of information are important to examine when thinking about harm or risk of harm: (a) the degree to which a child is involved in violent events and (b) the documented level of child maltreatment and emotional harm. Children's immediate responses to violent situations may create increased risk for their own well-being. Children's responses to domestic violence have been shown to vary from their becoming actively involved in the conflict, to distracting themselves and their parents, or to distancing themselves (Margolin, 1998). This, combined with the fact that a large number of studies document the co-occurrence of child maltreatment and greater levels of childhood problems in families where adult domestic violence is also present, reveals the possibility of increased risk for children in these homes.

All of these factors are important elements to consider when assessing the level of exposure a child experiences and the possible impact of such exposure. It is clear from the few published Convention cases that have considered child exposure that most judges will expect more detailed assessments of harm to the child resulting from exposure to domestic violence.

Given the fact that public policies and court rulings regarding children's exposure to domestic violence have changed only recently in the United States, it is also likely that courts in other countries will not yet consider this a risk to the child, raising the prospect of potential increased risks to children on return to their country of habitual residence. In fact, U.S. case law suggests that an analysis of whether the country of habitual residence has court proceedings and social services capable of protecting the child may be appropriate in certain cases.

Other Common Defenses in Convention Cases

Trends in research, policy, and case law in the United States increase the likelihood that battered mothers will raise Article 13(b) defenses involving grave risk or an intolerable situation in a child's country of habitual residence. Yet these defenses are not the only ones that battered mothers have raised in Convention hearings. Others focus on violations of human rights, definitions of habitual residence, a child's level of maturity, and acquiescence by the left-behind parent. Each of these will be discussed briefly.

Violation of Human Rights (Article 20)

Article 20 of the Convention states the following: "The return of the child under the provisions of Article 12 may be refused if this would not be permitted by the fundamental principles of the requested State relating to the protection of human rights and fundamental freedoms" (the Convention, 1980, Article 20). This Article has been raised in several Convention cases involving abductions into the United States from Germany, Sweden, Italy, and Argentina. In each case, the violation of human rights appears to be tied closely to the issue of grave risk to the child or the return of the child representing an intolerable situation under Article 13(b) of the Convention. The courts appear to have roundly dismissed claims of human rights violations as unfounded in every instance (*Danaipour v. McLarey*, 2002; *Fabri v. Pritikin-Fabri*, 2001; *Mendez Lynch v. Mendez Lynch*, 2002; *Steffen v. Severina*, 1997).

Beaumont and McEleavy (1999) conclude that Article 20 has "nearly faded without a trace" (p. 172). This may be because Article 20 is so often paired with claims of grave risk or intolerable situations. Evidence supporting claims under Article 13(b) have been taken more seriously than human rights claims. Human rights claims may also be viewed as redundant of grave risk claims. The growing movement to consider violence against women and children a global human rights issue promises to raise the future prospects of this defense for battered mothers and their children.

Habitual Residence (Article 3a and Article 14)

In Convention cases, the left-behind parent must first establish that there was a wrongful removal before the case moves forward. Specifically, Article 3a refers to a parent's right of custody in the location where the child is "habitually resident immediately before the removal" (the Convention, 1980, Article 3a) but never goes on to define how habitual residence is established. In Article 14 of the Convention, judicial authorities are instructed to consider the removal of the child within the context of "the State of habitual residence of the child" (the Convention, 1980, Article 14).

This language in the Convention has resulted in a number of battered mothers contesting the left-behind parent's claim that their child's habitual residence is the country from which the children were abducted. Generally, battered mothers counter that the United States should be considered the child's habitual residence instead of the country from which they fled.

The courts have produced mixed rulings on this issue, with some interpreting habitual residence broadly to recognize the child's acclimatization

(which is usually a fact-intensive inquiry regarding school enrollment, friends, social patterns, sports clubs, etc.), the intent of both parties regarding permanent residence, and physical geography. For example, in *Feder v. Evans (II)* (1995), the court stated,

> We believe that a child's habitual residence is the place where he or she has been physically present for an amount of time sufficient for acclimatization and which has a "degree of settled purpose" from the child's perspective. We further believe that a determination of whether any particular place satisfies this standard must focus on the child and consists of an analysis of the child's circumstances in that place and the parents' present, shared intentions regarding their child's presence there. (p. 224)

In a case involving domestic violence and often cited in other opinions (*Ponath v. Ponath*, 1993), the court ruled that "coerced residence is not habitual residence within the meaning of the Convention" (p. 398). This concept is clearly illustrated in *Tsarbopoulos v. Tsarbopoulos (II)* (2001) when the court ruled to deny a left-behind father's request for return of his children to Greece. The mother had fled to the state of Washington, testified that she had been a victim of physical and emotional abuse at the hands of her husband, and said that it was never her intent to make Greece her permanent home. The family had long lived in the United States and only in recent years moved to Greece. The judge agreed that the parents did not share the desire to change their habitual residence from the United States to Greece and pointedly stated that the mother's so-called consent to do so must be examined carefully in the context of the father's use of violence. The judge ruled that the children's habitual residence was Washington and that there was no wrongful removal (i.e., the Convention did not apply in this case). It is interesting in this case that the judge highlighted the issue of consent within the context of domestic violence and relied on the fact that the mother had not acclimatized to Greece as evidence of her intent not to establish habitual residence for her children.

Parental Consent or Acquiescence (Article 13a) and 1 Year Elapsed (Article 12)

Even if habitual residence in the country of removal is established, there are other defenses available. Under Article 13a of the Convention, a child's return to his or her place of habitual residence is not required if the person caring for the child at the time of abduction "had consented to or subsequently acquiesced in the removal or retention" (the Convention, 1980, Article 13a). Somewhat related to this is Article 12 of the Hague Convention, which mandates the return of children "where a child has been wrongfully removed or retained . . . and, at the date of the commencement of the proceedings . . . a period of less than one year has elapsed from the date of the wrongful removal or retention" (the Convention, 1980, Article 12). Article 12 also indicates that even if a year has passed, a child should be returned to his or her place of habitual residence "unless it is demonstrated that the child is now settled in its new environment" (the Convention, 1980, Article 12).

These two issues of acquiescence and a 1-year time period were intertwined in a recent case where the mother, on her arrival in Iowa, filed for a no contact order against and later alleged attacks by the left-behind father who was residing in France. Unfortunately, the specific attacks to which she testified were not documented in the no contact order, and there was never a formal hearing regarding that order to further verify these attacks. The court ruled that even though a year had passed before the Convention case was filed, the left-behind father had attempted reconciliation during this period and that these efforts neither represented acquiescence by him nor did his attempts to reconcile disqualify his claims

under the Convention because more than a year had elapsed. The court found that the children's habitual residence should be considered France, not the United States, and ordered them returned (*Antunez-Fernandez v. Conners-Fernandez,* 2003).

A case on which we worked but that is unpublished and sealed involved a battered mother and her two children—one child only days old—who were thrown out of the house by the father. He shipped all of her and the children's belongings to her and wrote to the children regularly after she fled to the United States with her children. The judge in the case ruled that the children could remain in the United States because there was grave risk to them of further abuse if they were returned and that the father had acquiesced to the children's departure by sending all of their belongings and writing regularly.

A number of battered mothers have also successfully hidden themselves and their children for more than a year and then claimed that more than a year has passed, thus allowing the children to stay with them in the United States under Article 12. This does not appear to have been a successful strategy. The fact that the abducting parent has hidden for more than a year may be used by the court to disallow this defense and start the clock over (*Lops v. Lops,* 1998).

Child Maturity (Article 13)

An unnumbered section of Article 13 of the Convention also states that a child's return to his or her place of habitual residence is not required if "the child objects to being returned and has attained an age and degree of maturity at which it is appropriate to take account of its views" (the Convention, 1980, Article 13). In several cases, the court, when deciding on a child's return, has considered the opinions of 8-year-olds and 9-year-olds. In *Mendez Lynch v. Mendez Lynch* (2002), the court ruled that a 9-year-old should be repatriated to his place of habitual residence despite his expressed wish not to do so. In *Blondin v. Dubois (III)* (2000), however, the court ruled that an 8-year-old was mature enough to express her opinions about where she wished to live, and the court appears to have taken her testimony on this and her exposure to domestic violence under serious consideration when deciding not to force her return to France. On appeal, a higher court affirmed in *Blondin v. Dubois (IV)* the importance of the child's wish not to return in its decision to allow the child to remain in the United States. The court ruled that in the instant case, we conclude that the District Court properly considered Marie-Eline's views as part of its "grave risk" analysis under Article 13(b), and that it did not clearly err in finding that Marie-Eline was old and mature enough for her views to be considered in this context *(Blondin v. Dubois [IV],* 2001, p. 166).

Conclusion

As the weight of the emerging social science evidence and U.S. public policy change brings about expanded definitions of a child's best interest, it is likely that rulings in Hague Convention cases may change as well. Exposure to adult domestic violence may pose a grave risk and intolerable situation to many children growing up in homes where such violence is being perpetrated. There is little logic to arguments that suggest internal strife in a country qualifies as a grave risk to a child but adult-to-adult domestic violence exposure does not. To use a play on the Convention's own words, this seems like an intolerable situation.

Underlying some of these arguments against the broader use of Article 13(b) and other defenses appears to be an attitude that suggests the adult victim should have stayed in the child's country of habitual residence and litigated the issue there. As Weiner (2003) has so clearly pointed out, we used to ask in a victim-blaming way, "Why does she stay with her abuser?" but in Convention cases, this is turned around on the adult victim, and we ask, "Why didn't she stay?" to litigate with her abusive partner. Convention cases highlight, as Weiner (2003) suggests, that women flee for their safety because of the inadequate protections available in other countries and that forcing battered women's children to return to their country of habitual residence may expose them to further violence and also force their mothers to return to the abusive partner at least temporarily while custody and divorce litigation takes place.

There are a number of steps that need to be taken to better address the safety needs of battered mothers fleeing with their children to the United States. First, there is a major gap in the social science research literature on parental child abductions. We have little systematic information on the parents who abduct their children into the United States from other countries and almost no understanding of their motives. A systematic study of this group of parents is sorely needed.

Second, specialized training focused on abduction cases involving domestic violence and technical assistance for judicial officers and attorneys are needed. Development of an addendum to current curricula (Hoff, 1997) is very important. This addendum would address domestic violence, its relationship to grave risk, and how this defense can be raised in Convention cases. In the meantime, recognizing that developing and disseminating new training materials will take time, we have created a depository of information essential for attorneys and advocates representing battered mothers facing Convention proceedings. As part of this effort, the Access to Justice Institute at Seattle University School of Law has developed a Web site focused exclusively on Hague Convention cases involving domestic violence. The aim of the Web site (http://www .law.seattleu.edu/accesstojustice/hague) is to provide educational information for advocates and attorneys who are representing battered mothers who have abducted their children into the United States and whose children are now facing extradition orders under the Convention in U.S. courts. The site is divided into three broad categories: (a) summaries of Convention cases involving family violence that have been identified using online legal databases, (b) a list of contact information of attorneys who have represented battered mothers in U.S. courts, and (c) secondary resources, such as academic articles, online journals, and links pertaining to the Convention and domestic violence issues.

Finally, although it would be difficult to amend the Hague Convention on the Civil Aspects of International Child Abduction, a special commission could be convened by the Hague Conference on Private International Law to clarify the proper use of the Convention in cases of adult domestic violence. More immediately, Congress can and should amend the U.S. implementing legislation embodied in the 1988 International Child Abduction Remedies Act to include exposure to adult domestic violence as a valid form of grave risk and to broaden definitions of *habitual residence* to include ones in which a child's well-being is secured. This step will not amend the original treaty but is perhaps more expedient in that it would broaden the definitions of terms such *as grave risk* and *habitual residence* for U.S. courts. Similar efforts should be made in other countries that are parties to the Convention.

Battered mothers who flee to the United States across an international border for the safety of their children and themselves deserve the same protections we provide other battered mothers and their children who cross city or state lines. We should work to change the interpretation of the international treaty at both the international and domestic levels and change the U.S. implementing legislation. Federal judges hearing these cases have an obligation to be knowledgeable of the Convention and the risks that mothers and children face both here and abroad. Battered mothers and their children deserve access to attorneys and advocates who can effectively represent them in these complex cases. And public and private funders must see the safe resolution of these cases not just as an international issue but as one that is critically relevant to the families in their own communities.

Mothers who abduct their children and flee to find a safe haven are not perpetrators, as the Hague Convention implies, but are victims of their partner's violence. They are also victims of an international treaty, written with good intentions, but, when implemented, has unintended negative consequences for their safety and that of their children.

References

Adamson, J. L., & Thompson, R. A. (1998). Coping with interparental verbal conflict by children exposed to spouse abuse and children from nonviolent homes. *Journal of Family Violence, 13,* 213–232.

Agopian, M. W. (1981). *Parental child-stealing.* Lexington, MA: Lexington Books.

Appel, A. E., & Holden, G. W. (1998). The co-occurrence of spouse and physical child abuse: A review and appraisal. *Journal of Family Psychology, 12,* 578–599.

Antunez-Fernandez v. Connors-Fernandez, 259 F Supp. 2d 800 (N.D. Iowa 2003).

Beaumont, P R., & McEleavy, P E. (1999). *The Hague Convention on International Child Abduction.* New York: Oxford University Press.

Blondin v. Dubois, 19 E Supp. 2d 123 (S.D.N.Y. 1998).

Blondin v. Dubois (II), 189 F 3d 240 (2nd Cir. 1999).

Blondin v. Dubois (III), 78 F Supp. 2d 283,286 (S.D.N.Y. 2000).

Blondin v. Dubois (IV), 238 F. 3d 153 (2nd Cir. 2001).

Cambanis, T. (2002, April 16). Advocates say children put at risk. *Boston Globe,* p. B1. Retrieved July 22, 2004, from http://www.boston.com

Chiancone, J., Girdner, L., & Hoff, P. (2001). *Issues in resolving cases of international child abduction by parents.* Washington, DC: Office of Juvenile Justice and Delinquency Prevention, U.S. Department of Justice.

Convention on the Civil Aspects of International Child Abduction. (1980). Netherlands: The Hague.

Danaipour v. McLarey, 183 F Supp. 2d 311 (D. Mass. 2002).

Dunford-Jackson, B. L. (2004). The role of family courts in domestic violence: The U.S. experience. In P. G. Jaffe, L. L. Baker, & A. J. Cunningham (Eds.), *Protecting children from domestic violence: Strategies for community intervention* (pp. 188–199). New York: Guilford.

Edleson, J. L. (1999a). Children's witnessing of adult domestic violence, *Journal of Interpersonal Violence, 14,* 839–870.

Edleson, J. L. (1999b). The overlap between child maltreatment and woman battering. *Violence Against Women, 5,* 134–154.

Edleson, J. L. (2004). Should childhood exposure to adult domestic violence be defined as child maltreatment under the law? In P. G. Jaffe, L. L. Baker, & A. J. Cunningham (Eds.), *Protecting children from domestic violence: Strategies for community intervention* (pp. 8–29). New York: Guilford Press.

Fabri v. Pritikin-Fabri, WL 800076 (N.D. Illinois 2001).

Fantuzzo, J. W., DePaola, L. M., Lambert, L., Martino, T., Anderson, G., & Sutton, S. (1991). Effects of interparental violence on the psychological adjustment and competencies of young children, *Journal of Consulting and Clinical Psychology, 59,*258–265.

Fantuzzo, J. W., & Mohr, W. K. (1999). Prevalence and effects of child exposure to domestic violence. *The Future of Children, 9,* 21–32.

Feder v. Evans-Feder (II), 63 F. 3d 217 (3d Cir. 1995).

Greif, G. L., & Hegar, R. L. (1993). *When parents kidnap: The families behind the headlines.* New York: Free Press.

Hammer, H., Finkelhor, D., & Sedlak, A. J. (2002). *Children abducted by family members: National estimates and characteristics.* Washington, DC: Office of Juvenile Justice and Delinquency Prevention, U.S. Department of Justice.

Hegar, R. L., & Greif, G. L. (1991). Parental kidnapping across international borders. *International Social Work, 34,* 353–363.

Hilton, N. Z. (1992). Battered women's concerns about their children witnessing wife assault, *Journal of Interpersonal Violence, 7,* 77–86.

Hilton, W. M. (1997). Limitations on Article 13(b) of the Convention on the Civil Aspects of International Child Abduction. *American Journal of Family Law, 11,* 139–144.

Hoff, P. M. (1997). *The Hague Convention on the Civil Aspects of International Child Abduction: A curriculum for American judges and lawyers.* Washington, DC: American Bar Association.

Hughes, H. M. (1988). Psychological and behavioral correlates of family violence in child witness and victims. *American Journal of Orthopsychiatry, 58,* 77–90.

Hughes, H. M., Graham-Bermann, S. A., & Gruber, G. (2001). Resilience in children exposed to domestic violence. In S. A. Graham-Bermann & J. L. Edleson (Eds.), *Domestic violence in the lives of children: The future of research, intervention, and social policy* (pp. 67–90). Washington, DC: American Psychological Association.

Hughes, H. M., Parkinson, D., & Vargo, M. (1989). Witnessing spouse abuse and experiencing physical abuse: A "double whammy"? *Journal of Family Violence, 4,* 197–209.

Humphreys, J. C. (1995a). Dependent-care by battered women: Protecting their children. *Health Care for Women International, 16,* 9–20.

Humphreys, J. C. (1995b). The work of worrying: Battered women and their children. *Scholarly Inquiry for Nursing Practice: An International Journal, 9,* 127–145.

International Child Abduction Remedies Act of 1988, 42 U.S.C.A. § 11603 *et seq.* (West 1998).

Jaffe, P. G., Lemon, N., & Poisson, S. (2003). *Child custody and domestic violence: A call for safety and accountability.* Thousand Oaks, CA: Sage.

Johnston, J. R., Sagatun-Edwards, I., Blomquist, M. E., & Girdner, L. K. (2000). *Prevention of family abduction through early identification of risk factors.* Washington, DC: Office of Juvenile Justice and Delinquency Prevention, U.S. Department of Justice.

Kalichman, S. C. (1999). *Mandated reporting of suspected child abuse* (2nd ed.). Washington, DC: American Psychological Association.

Levendosky, A. A., Lynch, S. M., & Graham-Bermann, S. A. (2000). Mothers' perceptions of the impact of woman battering on their parenting. *Violence Against Women, 6,* 247–271.

Lops v. Lops, 140 F. 3d 927 (11th Cir. 1998).

Maker, A. H., Kemmelmeier, M., & Peterson, C. (1998). Long-term psychological consequences in women of witnessing parental physical conflict and experiencing abuse in childhood. *Journal of Interpersonal Violence, 13,* 574–589.

Margolin, G. (1998). Effects of witnessing violence on children. In P. K. Trickett & C. J. Schellenbach (Eds.), *Violence against children in the family and the community* (pp. 57–101). Washington, DC: American Psychological Association.

Masten, A. S., & Coatsworth, D. (1998). The development of competence in favorable and unfavorable environments. *American Psychologist, 53,* 205–220.

McGuigan, W. M., & Pratt, C. C. (2001). The predictive influence of domestic violence on three types of child maltreatment. *Child Abuse and Neglect, 25,* 869–883.

Mendez Lynch v. Mendez Lynch, 220 F. Supp. 2d 1347 (M.D.Fla. 2002).

Minnesota Department of Public Safety. (2004). *Interagency task force on domestic violence and sexual assault prevention report to the legislature.* St. Paul: Author.

National Center for Missing and Exploited Children. (2002). *NCMEC Annual Report 2002.* Alexandria, VA: Author.

National Council of Juvenile and Family Court Judges. (1999). *Effective intervention in domestic violence and child maltreatment: Guidelines for policy and practice.* Reno, NV: Author.

Nunez-Escudero v. Tice Menley, 58 F. 3d 374 (8th Cir. 1995).

O'Leary, K. D., Slep, A. M. S., & O'Leary, S. G. (2000). Co-occurrence of partner and parent aggression: Research and treatment implications. *Behavior Therapy, 31,* 631–648.

Onyskiw, J. E. (2003). Domestic violence and children's adjustment: A review of research. *Journal of Emotional Abuse, 3,* 11–45.

Peled, E. (1998). The experience of living with violence for preadolescent witnesses of woman abuse. *Youth and Society, 29,* 395–430.

Ponath v. Ponath, 829 F. Supp. 363 (D.Utah, 1993).

Rodriguez v. Rodriguez, 33 F. Supp. 2d 456 (D.Md. 1999).

Rossman, B. B. R. (2001). Long-term effects of exposure to adult domestic violence. In S. A. Graham-Bermann & J. L. Edleson (Eds.), *Domestic violence in the lives of children: The future of research, intervention, and social policy* (pp. 35–66). Washington, DC: American Psychological Association.

Sedlak, A. J., Finkelhor, D., Hammer, H., & Schultz, D. J. (2002). *National estimates of missing children: An overview.* Washington, DC: Office of Juvenile Justice and Delinquency Prevention, U.S. Department of Justice.

Short, L. M., McMahon, P. M., Chervin, D. D., Shelley, G. A., Lezin, N., Sloop, K. S., et al. (2000). Survivors' identification of protective factors and early warning signs for intimate partner violence. *Violence Against Women, 6,* 272–285.

Skoler, G. (1998). A psychological critique of international child custody and abduction law. *Family Law Quarterly, 32,* 557–602.

Steffen v. Severina, 966 F. Supp. 922 (D.Ariz, 1997).

Sternberg, K. J., Lamb, M. E., Greenbaum, C., Cicchetti, D., Dawud, S., Cortes, R. M., et al. (1993). Effects of domestic violence on children's behavior problems and depression. *Developmental Psychology, 29,* 44–52.

Straus, M. A., & Gelles, R. J. (1990). *Physical violence in American families.* New Brunswick, NJ: Transaction Publishers.

Subcommittee on International Child Abduction of the Federal Agency Task Force on Missing and Exploited Children and the Policy Group on International Parental Kidnapping. (1999). *A report to the attorney general on international parental kidnapping.* Washington, DC: U.S. Department of Justice. Retrieved July 22, 2004, from http://www.ncjrs.org/html/ojjdp/ojjdp_report_ip_kidnapping/RptParentalKidnap.pdf

Tsarbopoulos v. Tsarbopoulos (II), 176 F Supp. 2d 104 (E.D. Wash. 2001).

U.S. Department of State. (2003). *Report to Congress on international child abductions in response to the statement of managers accompanying F-103 Omnibus Appropriations Bill PL. 108-7.* Retrieved July 22, 2004, from http://travel.state.gov/family/abdution_hague_05.html

Weiner, M. H. (2000). International child abduction and the escape from domestic violence. *Fordham Law Review, 69,* 593.

Weiner, M. H. (2003). The potential and challenges of transnational litigation for feminists concerned about domestic violence here and abroad. *American University Journal of Gender, Social Policy, and the Law, 11,* 749–800.

Wisconsin Statute §767.24(2)(d)(1) (2004).

CHAPTER 15

Domestic Violence Between Same-Gender Partners

Recent Findings and Future Research

Joan C. McClennen

A lthough empirical studies on domestic violence between opposite-gender partners has steadily increased since the 1970s, similar research on same-gender partners remained virtually nonexistent until 20 years later (Renzetti, 1992). Relying on empirical data, policies and programs are lacking in their ability to provide protection and services for same-gender individuals experiencing domestic violence, thus creating further social injustices for this oppressed population. Empirical data are needed to provide evidence of these injustices and to dismiss existing myths about this social problem. This article reports many of the recent findings about domestic violence between lesbian and gay male partners as well as recommendations for future research using various methodological approaches.

Recent Findings

Domestic violence is more recently referred to as *intimate partner violence* (IPV), as this new terminology differentiates this type of family violence from others (children and the elderly) while being inclusive of any intimate relationship regardless of the couples' marital status, age, or gender (Centers for Disease Control and Prevention [CDC], 2002). In America's homophobic society, researching IPV between lesbian and gay male partners is, at best, challenging as, in their efforts to preclude oppressive forces from gaining information that could be used to further persecute them, these individuals have created a conspiracy of silence about the existence of IPV within their homes. This silence results in many of these individuals

McClennen, J. C. (2005). Domestic violence between same-gender partners: Recent findings and future research. *Journal of Interpersonal Violence, 20,* 149–154.

being double closeted—entombed in their same-gender identity and in their personal pain of abuse.

Findings from existing research reveal many similarities between same-gender and opposite-gender IPV. The prevalence rate of approximately 25% to 35% of all partners experiencing IPV is comparable (Gunther & Jennings, 1999); thus, of the 19 million same-gender couples (Island & Letellier, 1991), about 5.7 million report being either a victim or perpetrator of IPV. Also similar are the types of violence reported, including sexual, physical, financial, and emotional abuse (Merrill & Wolfe, 2000; Renzetti, 1992). Common is the spiral of violence—the violence increasing in frequency and severity over time (Tully, 1999). Despite the similarities, IPV between lesbian and gay male partners differs in its theoretical underpinnings and is fraught with myths.

Although applicable to opposite-gender partners, the patriarchal theory, with its cultural endowment of domination by men over women, cannot explain the existence of same-gender partner abuse; however, four theoretical approaches are proposed as underlying this phenomenon. Originally, Island and Letellier (1991) attributed partner abuse to perpetrators' personality disorders. Renzetti (1996) asserted the feminist theory, with its emphasis on sociopolitical oppression of at-risk populations, underlies same-gender IPV. Integrating the former two theories, Merrill (1996) proposed the social-psychological theory, attributing IPV between same-gender partners to oppression, learned behaviors, and individual choices. Although agreeing with the social-psychological theory as underlying gay male IPV, McClennen (1999) proposed that, when referring to lesbian IPV, the patriarchal social-psychological theory is more apposite, as the addition of the feminist term emphasizes the sexism and gender socialization experienced by all women regardless of their gender orientation. These theoretical approaches provide guidelines for future research and intervention with persons addressing same-gender IPV.

The theory of IPV between same-gender partners being primarily mutual battering is dismissed by a majority of research as a myth (McClennen, Summers, & Vaughan, 2002). Mutual battering is considering victims' actions of self-defense against their perpetrators' attacks as synonymous with voluntary acts of engaging in physical fights. In demystifying mutual battering, perpetrators are differentiated from their victims by their intent and by their emotional reactions following the violence (Morrow, 1994). Perpetrators intentionally instigate coercive acts, blaming their victims for their actions and feeling exhilarated after the incidents, whereas victims often blame themselves and feel emotionally distraught. The continued belief in the existence of mutual battering has contributed to victims being rebuffed by helping professionals, who cannot believe that IPV could occur between individuals of the same gender.

Being rebuffed by professionals, same-gender victims' help-seeking behaviors, as supported by recent research, are directed principally toward their friends (McClennen, Summers, & Vaughan, 2002). Formal sources (attorneys and shelters) are seldom sought, and therapeutic sources (psychologists and social workers) are perceived as lacking in helpfulness. The inability to receive helpful, responsive professional services and protection contributes to victims' maintaining long-term relationships with their perpetrators, as they remain silent about their abuse.

Provision of appropriate interventions is determined by the causes, or correlates, of problems. Just as between opposite-gender partners, the principal correlate attributed to the existence of same-gender partner abuse is power imbalance (Renzetti, 1992). Determining the composition of this imbalance is more challenging than with opposite-gender abuse where, historically, men have been imbued with power over women, and a differential in size results in women more often being harmed by the abuse. For lesbian partners, the correlate of power imbalance has been attributed to the combined factors of perpetrators' lack of communication and social skills, perpetrators' experiencing intergenerational transmission of violence and exhibiting substance abuse and faked illnesses, victims' internalized homophobia, and couples' status differentials (McClennen, Summers, & Daley, 2002). For gay male partners, the factors contributing to power imbalance remain anomalies.

After power imbalance, the major correlates of lesbian IPV are dependency and jealousy (McClennen, Summers, & Daley, 2002). As to gay male IPV, following power imbalance, the major correlates are dependency, jealousy, and substance abuse, followed closely by possessiveness and independence (McClennen. Summers, & Vaughan, 2002). Most likely, further studies would provide evidence of perpetrators' lack of communication and social skills as well as intergenerational transmission of violence and HIV as contributing to gay male IPV.

A plethora of data is needed as to the theoretical underpinnings, myths, and correlates of same-gender partner abuse. Knowledge of the existence, realities, and correlates of IPV between same-gender partners can assist professionals in providing protective services, assessing clients' relationships, providing helpful intervention services, and conducting further research into this multifaceted social problem.

Future Research

Within the next 10 years, the most important thing professionals and laypersons need in order to learn about same-gender IPV is increased empirically based data about a plethora of issues, including the dynamics, help-seeking behaviors, correlates, and interventions. Especially dearth in its existence is research about children living within same-gender-headed households where the adults are experiencing IPV. These data need to be manifested by increased education, advocacy, policies, programs, and effective assessment and treatment strategies.

Same-gender persons are in need of education and advocacy, as many are unaware of the existence, let alone the magnitude, of lesbian and gay male IPV. Factual information is intended to reduce the stigma of same-gender persons who are experiencing partner abuse and to empower victims and perpetrators seeking professional assistance. Advocating with same-gender persons, professionals can assist in grassroots and social planning strategies toward ameliorating this social problem.

Social workers, psychologists, medical personnel, law enforcement, clergy, educators, and any other professionals working with same-gender persons need education to assist in changing policies, establishing programs, and providing appropriate intervention strategies to serve this population. Approximately 21 states have laws making sodomy a criminal offense, thus forcing same-gender victims into confessing a criminal offense as a prerequisite to receiving help in a domestic dispute; seven states exclude same-gender persons from the protection afforded opposite-gender partners (Smith & Dale, 1999). Policies and laws are needed to provide same-gender persons the same rights and protection afforded opposite-gender partners.

Culturally sensitive programs and services are needed for intervention with same-gender persons experiencing IPV. Counselors need to use assessment tools designed uniquely for same-gender partners. Evaluation is needed to ensure the effectiveness and efficiency of established programs and services.

Methodological Innovations

Research studies within the same-gender community require improved methodological approaches. Sample sizes are usually small, using nonprobability techniques. Research using large sample sizes and probability techniques would greatly enhance the validity of findings and their generalizability. Numerous national surveys have been conducted on the prevalence of IPV. Additional funding is needed to conduct nationwide surveys and research focusing exclusively on same-gender IPV.

Participatory qualitative research has been found effective in uniting the researcher and the population being researched into a collaborative effort while conducting studies. This type of research has provided a wealth of information about IPV between same-gender partners. Rather than being researched, individuals experiencing the problem become an integral part of the study, from designing the data collection instruments to validating the findings and conclusions.

With computerization evolved a plethora of innovative methods to collect data. Researchers are using chat lines, Websites, Web cams (electronic interviews), and e-mails (Hash & Cramer, 2003). Along these same lines are toll-free telephone lines with a guarantee of anonymity. Technology will continue to provide new strategies for studying IPV between same-gender partners.

References

Centers for Disease Control and Prevention. (2002). *Intimate partner violence fact sheet.* Retrieved September 27, 2002, from cdc.gov/ncipc/factsheets/ipvfacts.htm

Gunther, J., & Jennings, M. A. (1999). Sociocultural and institutional violence and their impact on same-gender partner abuse. In J. C. McClennen & J. Gunther (Eds.), *A professional guide to understanding gay and lesbian domestic violence: Understanding practice interventions* (pp. 29–34). Lewiston, NY: Edwin Mellen Press.

Hash, K. M., & Cramer, E. P. (2003). Empowering gay and lesbian caregivers and uncovering their unique experiences through the use of qualitative methods. In W. Meezan & J. I. Martin (Eds.), *Research methods with gay, lesbian, bisexual, and transgender populations* (pp. 47–64). Binghamton, NY: Harrington Park Press.

Island, D., & Letellier, P. (1991). *Men who beat the men who love them: Battered gay men and domestic violence.* Binghamton, NY: Haworth.

McClennen. J. C. (1999). Prevailing theories regarding same-gender partner abuse: Proposing the feminist social-psychological model. In J. C. McClennen & J. Gunther (Eds.), *A professional's guide to understanding gay and lesbian domestic violence: Understanding practice interventions* (pp. 3–12). Lewiston, NY: Edwin Mellen Press.

McClennen, J. C, Summers, B., & Daley, J. G. (2002). Lesbian partner abuse scale. *Research on Social Work Practice, 12*(2), 277–292.

McClennen, J. C., Summers, B., & Vaughan, C. (2002). Gay men's domestic violence: Dynamics, help-seeking behaviors, and correlates. *Journal of Gay and Lesbian Social Services, 14*(1), 23–49.

Merrill, G. S. (1996). Ruling the exceptions: Same-sex battering and domestic violence theory. In C. M. Renzetti & C. H. Miley (Eds.), *Violence in gay and lesbian domestic partnerships* (pp. 9–22). Binghamton, NY: Harrington Park Press.

Merrill, G. S., & Wolfe, V. A. (2000). Battered gay men: An exploration of abuse, help seeking, and why they stay. *Journal of Homosexuality, 39*(2), 1–30.

Morrow, J. (1994, April). Identifying and treating battered lesbians. *San Francisco Medicine, 17,* 20–21.

Renzetti, C. M. (1992). *Violent betrayal: Partner abuse in lesbian relationships.* Newbury Park, CA: Sage.

Renzetti, C. M. (1996). The poverty of services for battered lesbians. In C. M. Renzetti & C. H. Miley (Eds.), *Violence in gay and lesbian domestic partnerships* (pp. 61–68). Binghamton, NY: Harrington Park Press.

Smith, R., & Dale, O. (1999). The evolution of social policy in gay/lesbian/bisexual domestic violence. In J. C. McClennen & J. Gunther (Eds.), *A professional's guide to understanding gay and lesbian domestic violence: Understanding practice interventions* (pp. 257–276). Lewiston, NY: Edwin Mellen Press.

Tully, C. T. (1999). Hate crimes, domestic violence, and the lesbian and gay community. In J. C. McClennen & J. Gunther (Eds.), *A professional's guide to understanding gay and lesbian domestic violence: Understanding practice interventions* (pp. 13–28). Lewiston, NY: Edwin Mellen Press.

PART III

Prevention and Direct Intervention

CHAPTER 16

Sexual Assault Support Services and Community Systems

Understanding Critical Issues and Needs in the LGBTQ Community

Jeffrey L. Todahl, Deanna Linville,
Amy Bustin, Jenna Wheeler, and Jeff Gau

Listen to me and take seriously the situation that I am in.

Research participant

Sexual violence, including sexual degradation, forcible and nonforcible rape, and all versions of nonconsensual sexual contact, directed at children and adults (Logan, Cole, & Shannon, 2007) occurs at high rates in the United States. According to the National Institute of Justice, 17.6% of U.S. women have experienced completed or attempted rape (Tjaden & Thoennes, 2000). Regional data are largely consistent with national data. For example, of the 1.3 million adult women living in Oregon, about 230,000 (or 18%) have been raped at least once in their lifetime (Kilpatrick & Ruggiero, 2003). Moreover, rape tends to occur early in victims' lives. According to the National Violence Against Women Survey, 54% of rapes of women occur before age 18 (22% before age 12). For men, 75% of rapes occur before age 18 and 48% before age 12 (Tjaden & Thoennes, 2000). Both males and females are raped, though the majority of rape victims are female, while the vast majority of perpetrators of rape are male (Catalano, 2004;

Todahl, J. L., Linville, D., Bustin, A., Wheeler, J., & Gau, J. (2009). Sexual assault support services and community systems: Understanding critical issues and needs in the LGBTQ community. *Violence Against Women, 15,* 952–976.

Kilpatrick, 2002). These rates likely underestimate actual rates of sexual violence, as many male and female victims do not report sexual assault. Broad definitions of sexual violence—those that include sexual degradation and nonphysically forced sexual coercion—are associated with significantly higher incidence and prevalence rates. Furthermore, nonphysically forced sexual coercion experiences are sometimes perceived by victims and perpetrators as normal, thereby further contributing to lower reported rates of sexual violence (Basile, 2002).

Although researchers have now extensively studied several facets of sexual violence, data collection instruments usually assume heterosexuality among participants and rarely assess for sexual orientation (Balsam, Rothblum, & Beauchaine, 2005). Consequently, very little is known about sexual violence victimization rates for individuals who identify as lesbian, gay, bisexual, transgender, and/or queer (LGBTQ; see Table 16.1 for a description of terms).[1] Similarly, rates of sexual violence among same-sex couples have received very little research attention.[2] The evidence that does exist is impaired by several methodological limitations, including varying definitions of sexual violence and sexual orientation, a small number of sexual assault items, lack of adequate probabilistic samples, and no data specific to transgendered persons (Kilpatrick & Ruggiero, 2004). A nonprobabilistic survey by Balsam et al. (2005) comparing lesbian, gay, bisexual, and heterosexual siblings found that bisexual and gay men reported rates of childhood sexual violence that were much higher than heterosexual men, though comparable to women of all sexual orientations. Difference by sexual orientation seemed to remain steady in adulthood:

> Although less than 2% of heterosexual men reported being raped in adulthood, more than 1 in 10 gay and bisexual men reported this experience. More than twice as many lesbian and bisexual women (15.5% and 16.9%, respectively) reported an experience

of rape in adulthood than heterosexual women (7.5%). (p. 484)

Although other researchers have drawn similar conclusions, the comparative rates of sexual violence between straight and LGB populations remain uncertain and comparative rates for transgendered populations are unknown (Duncan, 1990; Heidt, Marx, & Gold, 2005; Hickson et al., 1994; Tjaden, Thoennes, & Allison, 1999).

Relative to heterosexual sexual assault victims, a rapidly growing body of primarily nonempirical literature argues that social conditions create significantly unique experiences for LGBTQ sexual assault victims (Bieschke, Perez, & DeBord, 2007; Renzetti, 2001). These unique factors, rooted in discrimination, marginalization, and social oppression faced by LGBTQ persons overall, translate into poor access to services for LGBTQ sexual assault victims, disproportionate reduction in safety, and generally poor response to assault disclosure in the health, social service, and criminal justice sectors (Girshick, 2002).

Numerous socially derived perceptions of LGBTQ persons converge to reduce availability and access to services and contribute to discriminatory, accusatory, and insulting responses when services are sought and received. Poor service availability, for instance, is associated with gender and heterosexist assumptions (e.g., perceptions that males are not sexually assaulted and that same-sex sexuality is deviant and, consequently, that LGBTQ persons are less deserving of services). In an analysis of more than 20 national, statewide, and local studies of antigay violence, 52% to 87% of respondents were subjected to verbal harassment, 21% to 27% were pelted by objects, and 13% to 18% were stalked or chased (Berrill, 1990). Research suggests that harassment and violence directed at transgendered persons by the general public may occur at even higher rates (Kenagy, 2005; Lombardi, 2001). Given these findings, LGBTQ persons live

Table 16.1 Description of LGBTQ Terms

Term	Description
Lesbian	Women whose primary emotional, erotic, and relational preferences are same-sex (homophilic) and for whom some aspect of their self-labeling acknowledges these same-sex attachments (Bieschke et al., 2007)
Gay men	Men whose primary emotional, erotic, and relational preferences are same-sex (homophilic) and for whom some aspect of the self-labeling acknowledges these same-sex attachments (Bieschke et al., 2007)
Bisexual	Individuals whose emotional, erotic, and relational preferences are toward both same-sex and other-sex individuals, either serially or simultaneously, and for whom some aspect of their self-labeling acknowledges the same-sex attachments (Bieschke et al., 2007)
Transgender	Individuals who are gender-variant or gender-"transgressive," that is, express their gender in ways not considered socially "appropriate" based on their (perceived) biological sex; also referred to as "gender-bending/blending." Transgender is a broad term that applies to people who live all or substantial portions of their lives expressing an innate sense of gender other than their birth sex (Human Rights Campaign, n.d.).
Queer	Queer is regarded as a derogatory term by some, though by others it is used as a unifying term for people who are lesbian, gay, bisexual, and/or transgender—or another nonheterosexual gender identity or sexuality.

NOTE: LGBTQ = lesbian, gay, bisexual, transgender, and queer. Designation as lesbian, gay, or bisexual refers to the sex(es) of one's (actual or imagined) intimate partner choices, not gender expression. Conversely, designation as transgender (or any of its variants) refers to gender expression, not the sex of one's (actual or imagined) partner choices. And self-labeling may change over time.

in an inherently dangerous environment and reasonably assume that they may be targeted, mistreated, and blamed—even by service providers, law enforcement, and health care professionals. Because of these negative perceptions of same-sex relationships, LGBTQ persons may endure internalized discrimination or may be reluctant to seek services in an effort to manage negative stereotypes.

An LGBTQ survivor legitimately may fear that his or her sexual orientation or gender identity may become the focus of attention—or even the perceived cause of the assault—rather than the assault itself and his or her needs and recovery (Renzetti, 1998). LGBTQ survivors also report being outed as a result of the sexual assault and are exposed to associated risks to their housing, employment, and faith community, as well as a negative response from family and acquaintances (Cruz, 2003; Mendez, 1996; Merrill & Wolfe, 2000). According to several reports, very few agencies reach out to sexually assaulted members of the LGBTQ community (Barret & Logan, 2002). Indeed, given that U.S. society generally does not accept same-sex partnerships (Vaid, 1995), there is very little motivation to create

LGBTQ-sensitive services for LGBTQ survivors of sexual assault (Ristock, 2001).

Although proponents have persuasively argued that LGBTQ survivors of sexual violence endure unique obstacles related to social attitudes and system responses, research that delineates the nuances of these obstacles, drawn directly from LGBTQ persons' perspectives, is needed. A qualitative study that investigated the dynamics of abusive lesbian relationships generated several questions for further research, including "What is the impact of homophobia, heterosexism, racism, and other forms of oppression on abuse? What are the similarities and differences between gay male partner violence, lesbian partner violence, and transgender partner violence?" (Ristock, 2003, p. 339). Research addressing LGBTQ intimate partner violence and, for the purposes of this study, sexual violence in particular (a) can generate a more complete understanding of the relationship between community attitudes toward LGBTQ persons and associated community responses to LGBTQ sexual assault victims, and this increased understanding (b) can inform training and community attitudes, leading to improvements in service delivery and general community responses.[3] The central premise of this study is that understanding and preventing sexual violence of LGBTQ persons must be grounded in information from members of the LGBTQ community. For the purposes of this study, *community* is defined as a formal or informal network of individuals that exists because of members' sense of common identity, certain similar collective experiences relative to society at large, and a "unity of will" (Tonnies, 1887). With regard to the LGBTQ community, it should be recognized that not all persons who identify as LGBTQ or combinations thereof identify with, perceive, or feel a personal affiliation with the LGBTQ community and that tremendous diversity exists within the LGBTQ community (National Resource Center on Domestic Violence [NRCDV], 2007). Bieschke et al. (2007) stated that "within LGBT communities there are multifaceted dimensions of

individual differences and diversity, multiple layers of identity, and multiple layers of oppression" (p. 403).

The purpose of this exploratory, concurrent triangulation, mixed methods study (Creswell, 2003) was to develop a more complete understanding of the issues and challenges facing LGBTQ survivors of sexual violence. The study collected quantitative descriptive data using an online and paper and pencil survey that included a mixture of Likert-type scale, dichotomous, and short answer questions, as well as qualitative focus group data. By using a mixed method approach, the researchers were able to corroborate findings by collecting Likert-type scale beliefs and attitudes and exploring variables in greater detail via open-ended focus group interviews. This study was organized around the following three aims: (a) to understand the LGBTQ community's knowledge, attitudes, and behavior in regard to sexual violence; (b) to understand the current ways in which sexual violence is discussed and handled in the LGBTQ community; and (c) to understand the most important steps toward sexual violence prevention in our community.

Method

This study occurred in the context of a project titled "Engaging Change" (EC), a community engagement project developed and coordinated by a sexual assault survivors' service organization located in a midsized city in the Pacific Northwest. EC is funded by federal Rape Prevention Education Grant Programs via the Oregon Attorney General's Sexual Assault Task Force. It is one of several statewide prevention projects in Oregon, though the only of its kind designed to enhance community awareness and change systems so as to prevent LGBTQ sexual violence. EC's vision is to support and enhance community involvement and engagement in sexual violence prevention in the LGBTQ community, to decrease sexual violence occurring in LGBTQ communities, and to instill LGBTQ-sensitive policies and procedures in key community systems. This study comprised one of EC's strategies, which was to engage the LGBTQ community in order to better understand sexual violence from the perspective of members of the LGBTQ community and to use this information to shape training, services, and prevention programs.

Participants

This study included two data collection methods: (a) an Internet-based and paper and pencil survey (see Table 16.2) and (b) focus group interviews. Survey participants were recruited via nonprobability convenience and snowball techniques, including a local LISTSERV comprising largely sexual and domestic violence social service

activists and providers, sexual violence agency bulletin boards, and two local organizations providing services and outreach to the LGBTQ community. The survey announcement afforded participation by individuals who self-identify as heterosexual or LGBTQ (i.e., "You have been selected to participate because you have very good familiarity with the LGBTQ community in our area"). Survey participants had the option of completing the survey online or with paper and pencil. Both versions of the survey were identical. Among all completed surveys, 83 were completed online and 43 were completed in writing. Focus group participants were recruited with purposive strategies, including an invitation to participate at the end of the survey and via nomination by EC Advisory Coalition members. Given that survey responses were anonymous, the extent to which participants completed the survey only, the focus group

Table 16.2 Sample Demographic Characteristics

	n	%
Sex		
Female	83	63.8
Male	40	30.8
Transgender/other	6	4.6
Did not respond	1	0.8
Sexual Orientation		
Gay	30	23.0
Lesbian	26	20.0
Bisexual	24	18.5
Heterosexual	24	18.5
Other/multiple categories	25	19.2
Did not respond	1	0.8

(Continued)

(Continued)

	n	%
Race		
Minority status	31	23.8
White	99	76.2
Did not respond	0	0.0
Survivor of sexual assault		
Yes	70	53.8
No	50	38.5
Did not respond	9	7.7

interview only, or both the survey and the focus group interview is unknown.

Survey and focus group data were analyzed separately, although data collected during a pilot of the survey ($n = 23$) shaped the focus group questions.[4] For example, many pilot survey respondents reported that they were not aware of LGBTQ-friendly services for survivors of sexual violence in the local area. This survey finding led to the qualitative focus group question, "What are the main LGBTQ-friendly services and resources that are currently available for someone who has been sexually assaulted?" Likewise, the survey items were constructed based on two prestudy focus group conversations with EC Advisory Coalition members. Although qualitative and quantitative strategies were used to develop the survey and the focus group questions in this study, the qualitative and quantitative data collected were analyzed separately. Information collected by both methods was very consistent. These consistencies are highlighted in the results section.

The Survey

The survey ($n = 130$), developed for the purposes of this study and in collaboration with EC's Advisory Coalition, includes 11 dichotomous items, 16 Likert-type scale items, and 7 open-ended questions. Following human subjects approval, the survey was advertised and posted for 6 weeks. For the purposes of the survey, sexual assault was defined as "any touch or act that is sexual in content and is used for the gratification of the perpetrator by force, threat of force, trickery, coercion, bribery, or between two people where an imbalance exists in age, size, power, development, or knowledge. Sexual assault includes child sexual abuse, rape, incest, ritual abuse, sexual harassment and stalking."

Analytic Strategy

Frequency distributions for each of the outcome measures will be summarized for the entire sample and within three contrasts of interest: females versus males/transgendered persons, survivors of sexual assault versus those never sexually assaulted, and LGBTQ versus heterosexual orientation. Given the dichotomous and discrete ordinal nature of the outcome measures (i.e., 5-point Likert-type scale ranging from *disagree strongly* to *agree strongly*), a logistic regression analysis (Hosmer & Lemeshow, 2000) and corresponding odds ratios with 95% confidence intervals (CIs) will be used to examine relationships between outcome measures and the contrasts. Although a *t* test is fairly robust to violations of statistical assumptions, this is true mainly when there is a large sample size and an equal *n* in each group (Myers & Well, 2001; Pagano, 1995), a situation not present in the current study. In addition, some have argued (e.g., Velleman & Wilkinson, 1993) that ordinal levels are too limited to treat as an interval scale and examining mean differences between ordinal measures is not the best way to analyze the data.

Results

Sample Characteristics

Table 16.2 shows that most of the 130 survey participants in the study are White (76%), are female (64%), and report having been sexually assaulted (54%). Reports of sexual orientation are relatively evenly split among gay, lesbian, bisexual, heterosexual, and the "other/multiple" category. The average age of the sample is 36.0 (*SD* = 13.9) years old, with the youngest participant 15 years old and the oldest 71 years old. Based on the definition of *sexual violence* used in this study, 70 (58.3%) respondents reported being sexually assaulted at some point in their lives, 50 (41.6%) have not been sexually assaulted, and 10 (7.6%) did not respond.

General Findings

The majority of participants in this study believed that sexual violence is a problem in society (94% agreed or strongly agreed), that sexual violence is a problem within the LGBTQ community (72% agreed or strongly agreed), and that sexual violence prevention tailored to the LGBTQ community is needed (86.7% agreed or strongly agreed). At the same time, many did not regard themselves as familiar with existing efforts to prevent sexual violence in the LGBTQ community, and many (41.5%) believed or strongly

believed that open dialogue specific to sexual violence in the LGBTQ community is not occurring in the local region. An even higher percentage of participants (60.3%) disagreed or strongly disagreed that the overall local community is currently well equipped to handle incidents of sexual assault that occur in the LGBTQ community. And when asked if law enforcement is well equipped, 68.7% of participants disagreed or strongly disagreed.

Distribution of Items

The most skewed items in the distribution are "Would you recommend sexual assault support services (SASS) to someone you cared about?" (–4.02) and "Sexual violence is a problem in our society" (–2.81). These are items with the smallest variance and least likely to discriminate among groups. The least skewed items are "I think that most people in the local LGBTQ community have healthy sexual encounters" (–0.02) and "I think that alcohol is often used within the LGBTQ community to intentionally lower another person's sexual boundaries" (–0.21).

Logistic Regression Models

Twelve of the logistic regression contrasts are significant at $p \leq .05$. Although 57 models were run, no specific adjustments to the *p* values were made. Because of the exploratory nature of the study, all statistically significant results will be interpreted. However, *p* values are provided (see Table 16.3) for the reader so adjustments can be made.

The most statistically significant contrast category was the female versus male and transgender comparisons. Females were 2.8 times more likely to have used SASS services or known someone who has ($p = .013$, 95% CI = 1.2 to 6.3) compared to their male/transgendered counterparts. In addition, compared to their male/transgendered counterparts, females were 3.1 times more likely to be aware of LGBTQ-friendly

Table 16.3   Logistic Regression Output for Contrasts

	Odds Ratio	SE	95% CI	p
Have you used SASS services or know someone who has?				
Female vs. males/transgender	2.8*	0.4	1.2 to 6.3	.013
Survivors sexual assault vs. no sexual assault	1.1	0.4	0.5 to 2.3	.887
LGBTQ vs. heterosexual orientation	0.5	0.5	0.2 to 1.3	.146
Would you recommend SASS to someone you care about?				
Female vs. males/transgender	1.0	0.9	0.2 to 6.0	.961
Survivors sexual assault vs. no sexual assault	0.4	1.1	0.0 to 3.6	.400
LGBTQ vs. heterosexual orientation	1.1	1.1	0.1 to 10.1	.950
I am aware of services that work with survivors of sexual violence that are not LGBTQ friendly.				
Female vs. males/transgender	3.1*	0.5	1.1 to 8.9	.036
Survivors sexual assault vs. no sexual assault	1.6	0.5	0.6 to 4.1	.336
LGBTQ vs. heterosexual orientation	1.4	0.6	0.4 to 4.5	.578
Sexual violence is a problem in our society.				
Female vs. males/transgender	2.1*	0.3	1.1 to 3.7	.017
Survivors sexual assault vs. no sexual assault	1.7	0.3	0.9 to 3.1	.077
LGBTQ vs. heterosexual orientation	0.3*	0.7	0.1 to 0.9	.010
Sexual violence is a problem for members of the Eugene-Springfield LQBTQ community.				
Female vs. males/transgender	1.6*	0.2	1.1 to 2.4	.031
Survivors sexual assault vs. no sexual assault	1.8*	0.2	1.2 to 2.8	.009
LGBTQ vs. heterosexual orientation	0.7	0.3	0.4 to 1.3	.270
Sexual violence prevention that is sensitive to the unique needs of the LGBTQ community is needed in the Eugene-Springfield area.				
Female vs. males/transgender	1.3	0.2	0.8 to 2.0	.229

	Odds Ratio	SE	95% CI	p
Survivors sexual assault vs. no sexual assault	1.3	0.2	0.8 to 2.1	.234
LGBTQ vs. heterosexual orientation	0.4*	0.5	0.1 to 0.9	.041
I am interested in working for sexual violence prevention.				
Female vs. males/transgender	1.4*	0.1	1.1 to 1.9	.026
Survivors sexual assault vs. no sexual assault	1.2	0.1	0.9 to 1.6	.327
LGBTQ vs. heterosexual orientation	0.5*	0.2	0.3 to 0.9	.009
I think that our community members are interested in sexual violence prevention.				
Female vs. males/transgender	1.3	0.2	0.9 to 2.1	.170
Survivors sexual assault vs. no sexual assault	1.3	0.2	0.8 to 1.9	.276
LGBTQ vs. heterosexual orientation	0.6	0.3	0.3 to 1.0	.054
I am familiar with existing efforts to prevent sexual violence in the LGBTQ community.				
Female vs. males/transgender	1.1	0.2	0.8 to 1.5	.747
Survivors sexual assault vs. no sexual assault	1.0	0.2	0.7 to 1.4	.996
LGBTQ vs. heterosexual orientation	0.9	0.2	0.6 to 1.3	.546
Open dialogue around sexual violence in the LGBTQ community is happening in the Eugene-Springfield area.				
Female vs. males/transgender	0.8	0.2	0.6 to 1.2	.287
Survivors sexual assault vs. no sexual assault	0.9	0.2	0.6 to 1.4	.734
LGBTQ vs. heterosexual orientation	0.5*	0.3	0.3 to 0.9	.011
Our community is currently well equipped to handle incidents of sexual assault that occur in the LGBTQ community.				
Female vs. males/transgender	1.1	0.2	0.7 to 1.6	.822
Survivors sexual assault vs. no sexual assault	0.9	0.2	0.6 to 1.4	.687
LGBTQ vs. heterosexual orientation	1.0	0.3	0.6 to 1.7	.977

(Continued)

(Continued)

	Odds Ratio	SE	95% CI	p
Law enforcement is currently well equipped to handle incidents of sexual assault that occur in the LGBTQ community.				
Female vs. males/transgender	0.8	0.2	0.6 to 1.2	.384
Survivors sexual assault vs. no sexual assault	0.8	0.2	0.6 to 1.2	.363
LGBTQ vs. heterosexual orientation	1.0	0.2	0.6 to 1.5	.883
ER medical staff are currently well equipped to handle incidents of sexual assault that occur in the LGBTQ community.				
Female vs. males/transgender	0.6*	0.2	0.4 to 0.9	.008
Survivors sexual assault vs. no sexual assault	0.8	0.2	0.5 to 1.1	.146
LGBTQ vs. heterosexual orientation	0.8	0.2	0.5 to 1.2	.227
I am confident that in sexual situations, I know how to ask for consent.				
Female vs. males/transgender	0.6*	0.2	0.4 to 0.9	.036
Survivors sexual assault vs. no sexual assault	0.8	0.2	0.6 to 1.3	.400
LGBTQ vs. heterosexual orientation	0.8	0.3	0.5 to 1.4	.480
I think that most people in the local LGBTQ community have healthy sexual encounters.				
Female vs. males/transgender	0.9	0.2	0.6 to 1.3	.434
Survivors sexual assault vs. no sexual assault	0.9	0.2	0.6 to 1.3	.549
LGBTQ vs. heterosexual orientation	0.7	0.2	0.4 to 1.1	.105
I obtain verbal consent with every sexual encounter.				
Female vs. males/transgender	0.9	0.2	0.7 to 1.2	.529
Survivors sexual assault vs. no sexual assault	0.8	0.2	0.6 to 1.1	.209
LGBTQ vs. heterosexual orientation	0.9	0.2	0.6 to 1.3	.478
I think alcohol influences a person's ability to give consent in sexual situations.				
Female vs. males/transgender	1.2	0.2	0.7 to 1.8	.505
Survivors sexual assault vs. no sexual assault	1.4	0.2	0.9 to 2.2	.153
LGBTQ vs. heterosexual orientation	1.0	0.3	0.6 to 1.7	.989

	Odds Ratio	SE	95% CI	p
I think that alcohol is often used within the LGBTQ community to intentionally lower another person's sexual boundaries.				
Female vs. males/transgender	1.1	0.2	0.8 to 1.5	.682
Survivors sexual assault vs. no sexual assault	1.2	0.2	0.9 to 1.8	.252
LGBTQ vs. heterosexual orientation	1.3	0.2	0.8 to 2.0	.237

NOTE: SE = standard error; CI = confidence interval; SASS = sexual assault support services; LGBTQ = lesbian, gay, bisexual, transgender, and queer. The first category of each contrast is coded with the value of 1 and the second category the value 0.

*p < .05.

services for survivors of sexual violence ($p = .036$, 95% CI = 1.1 to 8.9), 2.1 times more likely to see sexual violence as a problem in our society ($p = .017$, 95% CI = 1.1 to 3.7), 1.6 times more likely to see sexual violence as a problem in the local community ($p = .031$, 95% CI = 1.1 to 2.4), 1.4 times more likely to be interested in working for sexual violence prevention ($p = .026$, 95% CI = 1.1 to 1.9), 0.6 times *less* likely to feel that local ER staff are well equipped to handle incidents of sexual violence in the LGBTQ community ($p = .008$, 95% CI = .04 to .09), and .06 times *less* likely to feel confident asking for consent in a sexual situation ($p = .036$, 95% CI = 0.4 to 0.9).

The sexual orientation comparison of LGBTQ versus heterosexual shows four statistically significant differences. Compared to their heterosexual counterparts, LGBTQ participants are 0.3 times *less* likely to see sexual violence as a problem in our society ($p = .010$, 95% CI = 0.1 to 0.9), 0.4 times *less* likely to see a need for sexual violence prevention sensitive to the local LGBTQ community ($p = .041$, 95% CI = 0.1 to 0.9), 0.5 times *less* likely to be working for sexual violence prevention ($p = .009$, 95% CI = 0.3 to 0.9), and 0.5 times *less* likely to feel that an open dialogue around sexual violence is occurring in the local area ($p = .001$, 95% CI = 0.3 to 0.9).

Comparing survivors of sexual assault to those never sexually assaulted reveals one statistically significant difference. Compared to their never sexually assaulted counterparts, sexual assault survivors are 1.8 times more likely to see sexual violence as a problem in the local community ($p = .009$, 95% CI = 1.2 to 2.8).

Focus Group Interviews

Following human subjects approval, four semistructured focus groups, each 2 hours in length, were completed in a 3-week period and included a total of 14 participants. Focus group participants ranged in age from 19 to 76 years (mean age = 41 years). Six participants identified as male, eight as female, and two as transgendered. Five focus group participants identified as lesbian, three as bisexual, six as gay, and four as queer. Thirteen identified as White, one as Native American, and one as Latino (one participant selected two race identity categories). Each focus group interview included eight questions that centered around LGBTQ needs, service availability, and prevention specific to sexual violence in the local community: For example, (a) what are the main LGBTQ-friendly services and resources that are currently available for someone that has been sexually assaulted? And where are the main barriers/gaps in services for the LGBTQ community? (b) What are the attitudes about sexual violence in the LGBTQ community—both from the point of view of those in the LGBTQ community and those outside the LGBTQ community? (c) What do you think is the best way to do sexual violence prevention work in the LGBTQ community? In other words, if you were in charge, how would you design a sexual violence prevention plan?

Qualitative Data Analysis

The researchers used a grounded theory method of analysis for the focus group data. As suggested by Strauss and Corbin (1990), data analysis began with open coding where sections of words, sentences, and phrases were examined for specific phenomena. These segments were coded and the phenomena were conceptually labeled and developed into initial categories. The language of focus group participants often guided the development of codes and categories. The categories were further divided into subcategories. Axial coding that involved making new connections between categories and subcategories followed open coding.

As the categories were compared, questions were asked about how each category related to the others in order to denote the nature of the relationships between them. These questions aided in organizing the data by determining the causal conditions that gave rise to or maintained the category (phenomenon), the context in which the phenomenon was embedded, the intervening conditions (general environment) that influenced the phenomenon and facilitated or constrained the strategies adopted to manage the phenomenon, and the consequences of the phenomenon. Verifying the relationships between the categories and their subcategories was achieved by gathering supportive evidence of those relationships in the data. The goal was to craft a comprehensive understanding of the

phenomenon that is both grounded in the data through direct and indirect collection of multiple perspectives or voices and consistently examined by the researchers for personal biases (Merlis & Linville, 2004).

As suggested in selective coding (Strauss & Corbin, 1998), a storyline was then created to identify the core category and central phenomenon of "low community awareness and support for sexual violence in the LGBTQ community." The core category was then systematically related to other categories through the grounded theory paradigm to produce an overall analytic version of the story. The story was then laid out in graphic form to show a theoretical model of the central phenomenon (Figure 16.1). Saturation occurred at this stage because the analysis did not produce any new codes or categories and all of the data were accounted for in the core categories of the theoretical model.

Each category was assigned a color, and then the researcher highlighted statements made by the participants with the appropriate color that matched the statement to the category. To foster trustworthiness of the findings, the qualitative analysts cross-coded each transcript, and feedback was elicited from other researchers to check for any inherent biases. Additionally, to foster dependability of the study findings, an audit trail was created that provided a step-by-step process of data collection and analysis (Anfara, Brown, & Mangione, 2002). Finally, to ensure transferability of the findings, the researchers strove to provide thick descriptions of the study phenomenon and used a criterion-based sampling strategy (Anfara et al., 2002).

Focus Group Results

Focus group participants identified the central phenomenon as "low community awareness and support for sexual violence in the LGBTQ community." In fact, many participants described their sense that because it did not seem like the larger community even recognized the LGBTQ community, they certainly did not acknowledge

Figure 16.1 Theoretical Model of Understanding Critical Needs and Issues Around Sexual Assault in the LGBTQ Community

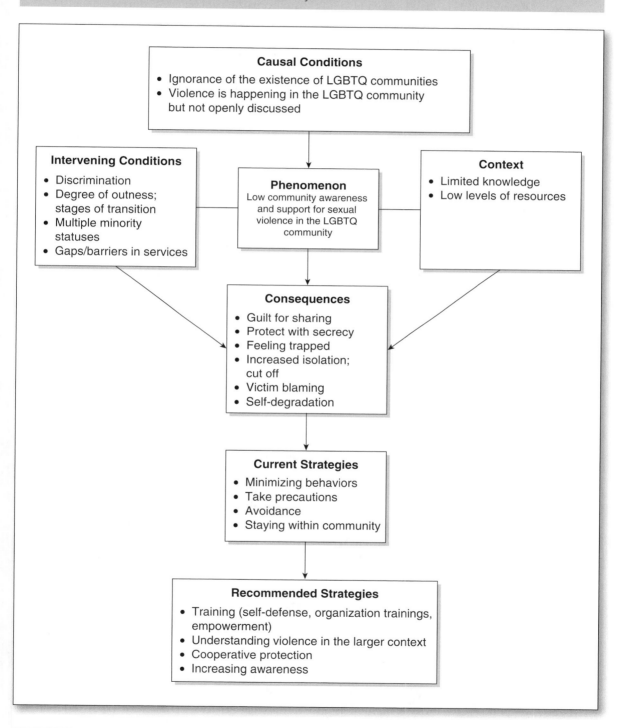

NOTE: LGBTQ = lesbian, gay, bisexual, transgender, and queer.

or provide help for sexual violence within the LGBTQ community. The central phenomenon of low general community awareness about LGBTQ sexual violence and low support for LGBTQ sexual assault survivors reported in the focus group interviews was also reported by survey respondents. Among the seven open-ended survey questions, participants overwhelmingly and primarily attributed lack of community awareness about sexual violence overall, and bias and misunderstanding toward the LGBTQ community specifically, as key factors for improved intervention and prevention. In that regard, participants' open-ended survey responses were remarkably similar to the ideas and opinions offered by focus group participants. In the sections that follow and in Figure 16.1, the causal conditions, context, and intervening conditions that influence this phenomenon are described and illustrated. Consequences of the phenomenon and the current and recommended strategies will also be described. Furthermore, complementary survey and focus group responses will be illustrated throughout this section. Survey responses portrayed in this section were selected based on the following criteria: (a) The comment appears to reflect the sentiment of many study participants, (b) the comment is consistent with the findings generated by the focus group interviews, and (c) the comment illuminates key qualitative findings in a clear and vivid manner.

Causal conditions. Two types of causal conditions emerged from the data that gave rise to the central phenomenon. These causal conditions were (a) societal ignorance of the existence of LGBTQ communities and (b) limited open discussion of the sexual violence occurring within the LGBTQ community. The majority of focus group participants talked about how society in general ignores LGBTQ persons, making the education and awareness of sexual violence within the LGBTQ community even less likely. One participant talked about how the media are unlikely to increase awareness of sexual violence within the LGBTQ community

when "you don't see very many commercials to begin with that pertain to gay issues, anyway." Another participant stated, "From my perspective, most people I run across are very ignorant; they seem to think that we [queer people] don't exist."

Nine focus group participants talked about how sexual violence definitely exists within the LGBTQ community, but there is very limited within-community open discussion about it. One participant stated, "I don't in general feel that I am around queer situations where there is a lot of discussion of sexual assault." Another participant supported this position: "I have never really heard of anyone talking about sexual violence, even though I have known of people who were sexually assaulted within the [LGBTQ] community." Given that focus group participants generally felt that society ignores LGBTQ people and that sexual violence within the LGBTQ community is not discussed, it makes sense that participants also felt that there is low awareness and support for sexual violence within the LGBTQ community.

These findings were also reported by survey respondents. One individual stated, "I think there isn't as much talk about what sex and sexual violence looks like for LGBTQ folks, so people have a hard time understanding how and if they've been assaulted." Another survey respondent commented, "This community rarely talks about LGBTQ domestic violence, let alone sexual assault. It is too much a taboo subject for the community—but needs to be addressed." And another said, "Gay men need to talk about it. Domestic sexual violence and rape are a reality. Rape of heterosexual/gay/bi men by heterosexual men is fairly unaddressed."

Context of the phenomenon. Particular contextual markers—or the patterns of conditions that contribute to low community awareness and support for sexual violence intervention and prevention in the LGBTQ community—were described by focus group participants. These contextual markers included (a) limited knowledge about LGBTQ people and sexual violence in the general community and (b) limited resources.

The majority of focus group participants talked about poor understanding in the general community with regard to LGBTQ people and sexual violence. Within this contextual marker, three subcategories emerged: (a) unhelpful myths about LGBTQ people, (b) a need for a definition of sexual violence, and (c) the dismissal of sexual violence as a problem in the LGBTQ community. Some of the unhelpful myths in the general community reported by focus group participants were that "old lesbians are not sexual," "gay men are promiscuous," "men can't be raped," "rape can only happen between a man and a woman," and "transgender people are predatory." Several focus group participants described that they believe they have needed to justify why gender violence affects LGBTQ people. Survey respondents also described harmful myths:

Many people don't want to hear about the "gay lifestyle," let alone try to help prevent sexual assault. Many haters don't want to hear about the sex life aspect of gay people; they would either like to believe we are asexual or pedophiles [sic].

Another myth centered on assumptions about gender-based violence: "People don't believe the survivors because they believe sexual violence only happens between men and women."

One third of focus group participants discussed the need for a clear definition of sexual violence. One participant even declared that she did not ever correlate sex and violence as she felt that violence could never be sexual. She stated, "Even if it is violence against sexual organs, it is not sexual." Another participant said that the lack of clarity can lead to different interpretations of behavior based on the sexual orientation of the people involved in the behavior:

A woman might go to a bar and they might have a guy slap them on the butt and the woman would be like, "Hey, what are you doing?" and the guy would say, "I am gay so it is not sexual and therefore okay."

The need for a clear definition of *sexual violence* was also mentioned by many survey respondents; for example, one participant said, "There needs to be a clear understanding of sexual violence. There should be little ambiguity."

Finally, several focus group participants remarked that the larger community's dismissal that sexual violence even exists within the LGBTQ community contributed to the poor understanding of sexual violence in the LGBTQ community. This point was also raised by survey respondents, several of whom believed that lack of acknowledgment of sexual violence within the LGBTQ community also occurs among members of the LGBTQ community: "People need to start talking about this issue. I think queer communities haven't even begun a dialogue about sexual assault that occurs within queer couples. This needs to begin and be acknowledged before any activism even starts." Another stated, "There needs to be greater awareness within the LGBTQ community that sometimes perpetrators of sexual violence are within our community."

Many of the focus group participants mentioned that resources are hard to find and that they found certain individuals to be more helpful than organizations. For instance, one participant said, "If I have a problem, the resources I go to are not going to be organizations for the most part. So, it is more of a community of individuals that I would go to for help." Additionally, focus group participants expressed concern that agencies and organizations often do not advertise their level of openness to LGBTQ people. These ideas were also very widely described by survey respondents, and many associated lack of resources with oppression. For example, one participant said, "One reason is the homophobia in our society; it influences everyone. Not as many services are available which are safe and welcoming." And "if you believe you will not be supported you will not likely seek help."

Intervening conditions. In addition to context, several "intervening conditions" influenced "low community awareness and support for sexual violence in the LGBTQ community." As described by Strauss and Corbin (1990), intervening conditions are the factors that facilitate or constrain the strategies taken within the specific context and can serve as mediating factors. Four intervening conditions were described by focus group participants: (a) discrimination, (b) multiple minority statuses, (c) gaps/barriers to services, and (d) degree of outness/stage of transition.

The majority of focus group participants thought that discrimination against LGBTQ people affected the general community's ability to effectively serve LGBTQ people around issues of sexual violence. Focus group participants discussed the different faces of discrimination (e.g., health care system, legal rights), as illustrated by the following quotes:

> There is no show of respect for transgender people by doctors, nurses, clinic personnel, counselors.

> I think that one thing that is true for all of us is that we are not just dealing with what someone who is part of the mainstream society is dealing with, this straightforward event that occurred. We are dealing with a whole layer of who we are that is considered a perversion. This neutralizes it for some people, and they might say, "Well, you are a lesbian anyway, big deal." And then you don't know if you will be further victimized by society who is supposed to be part of the solution for you.

Survey respondents also discussed the impact of discrimination at length. For instance, one participant said, "There is way too much stigma associated with sexual assault, particularly same-sex sexual assault." And "basic medical forms are set up for hetero relationships. That in and of itself is not LGBTQ positive." Another survey respondent stated:

People in the LGBTQ community are discriminated against and may still carry huge amounts of shame, and are subjected to (disproportionately) more shame, which makes it even harder to speak out. When people are afraid to be treated differently, they have a harder time disclosing rape or any unwanted sexual advances.

Ten focus group participants identified multiple minority statuses as an intervening condition. The following quote exemplifies how the different layers of minority statuses affected the support that LGBTQ people received around sexual violence:

> I was talking to a friend of mine who does HIV outreach work, and he was telling me that he met a handful of homeless transwomen of color but they could only stay so long at the shelter because of the racism in the shelter. Like I cannot live there because I got call the n-word too many times and because there are White supremacists walking up and down the street.

Focus group participants described the gaps in services in great detail, such as (a) limited LGBTQ-friendly health care services, (b) lack of adequate training at agencies around LGBTQ issues, (c) limited medical access, and (d) intake forms that are not LGBTQ-friendly. One participant shared her thoughts about some of the problems with intake questionnaires at local social service/medical settings: "Intake forms are very rigid. You have to write down your sex, and a lot of times there is not an option for someone to put down a name different than their legal name."

Survey respondents described other gaps and barriers to services:

> I think many agencies are less LGBTQ-friendly than they realize, simply by mostly talking about heterosexual relationships.

When it comes to getting help, it is not automatically assumed that all providers will be welcoming. This can make it harder to take necessary steps.

Finally, focus group participants identified the degree of outness and the stage of transition for a transgendered person as an intervening condition for the phenomenon because some people might match in appearance more closely with the gender into which they are transitioning and therefore not be questioned in the same way as someone who does not easily pass as the gender into which they are transitioning. Similarly, focus group participants noted that when LGBTQ people are not out, it can be assumed that they are mostly associating with heterosexual people and therefore have no one to talk to if they are sexually assaulted within the LGBTQ community. For example, one participant made the following statement:

> I would want to know if the person was out for the simple fact that if the person is not out and say they meet someone on the Internet that sexually violates them, then who do they have to come back to? They don't want to tell their heterosexual friends that they met someone on the Internet who raped them. So you would want to know how comfortable they are with themselves as this will influence their ability to ask for help.

Current strategies to deal with sexual violence. In light of the context and intervening conditions described above, focus group participants reported that they believed the LGBTQ community had employed the following strategies to deal with sexual violence in the LGBTQ community: (a) minimizing behaviors, (b) taking precautions, (c) avoidance, and (d) staying within the LGBTQ community. Several focus group participants stated that they felt the LGBTQ community was doing things to

minimize the recognition and impact of sexual violence by encouraging silence, rationalizing the violence, or joking about it.

Other focus group participants talked about precautions that they and others around them take to try and stay safe, like gaining more weight so that they might feel less vulnerable or targeted. Six focus group participants described the use of avoidance by the LGBTQ community as a strategy for dealing with sexual violence within the community. For example, one focus group participant said, "I think that there is definitely the sense that while people understand sexual violence can happen; they really don't think it will." Another focus group participant said, "I have heard of some gay people being assaulted, but it is not really discussed because maybe folks don't really think it happens." Finally, many focus group participants reported that discussing sexual violence within the LGBTQ community is an emerging strategy.

Consequences. The strategies used to deal with sexual violence in the LGBTQ community were not without consequences. The consequences that focus group participants mentioned most often were (a) guilt for sharing, (b) protect with secrecy, (c) feeling trapped, (d) increased isolation and feeling cut off, (e) victim blaming, (f) lack of support, and (g) self-degradation. These consequences are illustrated in the following quotes:

> I think a lot of the themes we have talked about deal with isolation and people having space. Eugene is a small city, and then in the queer community the space keeps getting smaller and . . . continually . . . smaller in different aspects. So part of it is about not wanting to lose support when you are already facing so much crap. How do you find people to even reach out to?

> The community is smaller and already struggling with so much oppression that any negative press is unwanted; thus, rape

and intimate partner violence is sometimes hushed up since the very idea of LGBTQ relations themselves is controversial in our society.

I think it's harder for us to talk about the bad things that happen in our community, which makes it even harder to find a solution.

Recommended strategies. An overwhelming majority of focus group participants emphasized the need for sexual diversity and sensitivity training across many sectors of society. Training should raise awareness about the impact of sexual minority status overall as well as its influence specific to sexual violence. Many focus group participants also remarked that training of this nature should be ongoing and would demonstrate commitment to justice among agency and community leaders. Training, many remarked, would lead to needed increased competencies among service providers: "Competent services are needed. Agencies need to educate and train staff on LGBTQ needs." Another participant stated, "Education to care providers about what abuse looks like in queer relationships, as well as the unique health needs of queer individuals, queer positive counseling, and availability of therapists is needed." Several others remarked that mainstream education should incorporate LGBTQ needs: "Better sex education that includes LGBTQ issues is needed. It [the curriculum] should be more open about sexual violence; teach it in classes." And "LGBTQ persons should be included in general, and as a part of any conversation around sexual violence."

Other strategies recommended by focus group participants were (a) to understand violence in the larger context, (b) cooperative protection, and (c) increasing awareness with events. In terms of understanding violence in the larger context, focus group participants reported feeling that sexual violence should not be viewed in isolation but instead be viewed as being within larger cultural influences. One participant stated:

The sexual violence stuff is not separate from the entire culture. So you have to look at what it means to grow up male in our culture. There is something, just something about that. What is the whole thing that is driving this violence?

Seven focus group participants introduced the concept of "cooperative protection," which meant a strategy of facilitating connection to, and responsibility for, each other's neighbors as illustrated in the following quote:

And I think the need is, again, cooperative protection. That is one of the first things I realized 50 years ago that we had to make friends with our neighbors in our [LGBTQ] community in order to protect ourselves. What is needed is awareness that it is your responsibility to reach out and make solid connections within your small community.

Several survey participants extended the concept of cooperative protection and argued that society and agencies must develop a good understanding of sexual violence and LGBTQ needs and issues: "For LGBTQ survivors to feel safe reaching out, there needs to be somewhere they have heard about previously which they know understands LGBTQ issues as well as sexual assault."

Finally, many focus group participants recommended a strategy for increasing awareness about sexual assault against LGBTQ people through community events. They gave multiple examples of events that already take place within the larger community and also provided suggestions for other events. For example, one participant made the following recommendation:

I went to a drag show that was here last year, and there was a really big turnout of not just gay people but heterosexual people as well. I think that it is not only a time to come together and do fun events but also a chance to address facts. Address things that are going on in your community because nobody wants to go to a simple LGBTQ meeting. I mean people have other things to do. But people will take the time to do something fun. An event where people can say, "Hey, let's get together, pull together and realize that sexual violence is out there in our community, so let's voice it out. If this has happened to you, let it be known."

Several survey participants believed that a key function of community events is to promote LGBTQ-safe services:

Advertising that there are places and people in the first place who can and will help. There is a need for a higher profile for helping agencies that makes it clear that they have services specifically available to the LGBTQ community. Nobody knows these places exist or if they are safe.

Additionally, survey respondents had much to share about what they identified as the key characteristics, skills, and behaviors of an ideal health care provider. These characteristics included openness to diversity and valuing a diverse staff, an openness and awareness of the needs of LGBTQ community members, and a guiding belief that sexual assaults happen to queer people. Some of the behaviors and skills that survey respondents hoped that an ideal health care provider would have included the following: using language that is nonheterosexual (not assuming heterosexuality), obtaining accurate knowledge on sexual violence in the queer community, networking their practices into the gay community, posting queer-friendly symbols in the front office, continuing education and providing culturally sensitive trainings with a commitment to applying the knowledge, offering real and unbiased information about where to seek help, examining knowledge of their own privilege and baggage and then reexamining it, and understanding and working to overcome

the barriers that prevent and discourage LGBTQ people from reporting violence.

Discussion

This exploratory study investigated the experiences and needs of LGBTQ survivors of sexual violence from the perspective of individuals who perceived themselves as familiar with the LGBTQ community. Several limitations should be considered. For instance, it is not known whether these findings represent the views of the majority of individuals who are familiar with and sensitive to the needs of the LGBTQ community. And certainly everything that could be said about the issues and needs of LGBTQ sexual assault survivors—even among the participants in this single study—is not captured in this data set. In addition, the data are largely one-dimensional; they do not tease out the many similarities and differences within the LGBTQ community. Despite these limitations, this exploratory study supports several previous assertions in the literature and provides a focal point for further examination.

The findings of this study closely match the existing literature with regard to (a) emphasis placed on overall discrimination and misunderstanding toward and about the LGBTQ community and the impact of those factors on sexual violence response, intervention, and prevention; (b) sexual violence not generally being discussed in the LGBTQ community, perhaps largely because of the need to protect the community from additional discrimination; and (c) associated gaps and barriers in services for LGBTQ persons. Many survey and focus group participants, for example, reported that sexual violence is a problem in the LGBTQ community and believe that the problem is exacerbated by social conditions that force silence, breed denial, and thwart the development of and access to LGBTQ-friendly services.

Although 94% of survey participants agreed or strongly agreed that sexual violence is a problem in society overall and 72% agreed or strongly agreed that sexual violence is a problem in the LGBTQ community, many were not familiar with local efforts to prevent sexual violence in the LGBTQ community, and many (41.5%) believed or strongly believed that open dialogue specific to sexual violence in the LGBTQ community is not occurring locally.

This study also supports the ongoing need to understand the multiple identities held by members of the LGBTQ community and the impact of those identities on access to services, community relations, and sexual violence risk. As described by the NRCDV (2007), "LGBT people are not members of a monolithic community or unified culture. Each lesbian, gay, bisexual or trans individual holds membership in many overlapping communities that face similar as well as very different issues" (p. 1). In the survey portion of this study, for example, the largest between-groups differences emerged around gender and victimization status. Compared to their male and transgender counterparts, females were 2.8 times more likely to have used SASS services or to know someone who has, 3.1 times more likely to be aware of LGBTQ-friendly services for survivors of sexual violence, and 2.1 times more likely to see sexual violence as a problem in our society. Moreover, female respondents were 1.6 times more likely to see sexual violence as a problem in the local community, 1.4 times more likely to be interested in working for sexual violence prevention, and 0.6 times *less* likely to feel that local ER staff are well equipped to handle incidents of sexual violence in the LGBTQ community. Victimization status was also associated with significant differences. For example, when compared with non-survivors, survivors of sexual assault were 1.8 times more likely to see sexual violence as a problem in the local community.

Barriers to services expressed by participants also closely matched the existing literature (Bieschke et al., 2007; Kenagy, 2005; Lombardi, 2001). For instance, participants believed that members of the LGBTQ community cannot assume that services are LGBTQ safe and friendly, that services are not properly tailored for members of the LGBTQ community (e.g., services for males, inclusive language), and that cultural oppression and sanctioning of sexual minorities enforce silence. Finally, participants offered many recommendations, ranging from sweeping and foundational changes (e.g., reduce oppression of sexual minorities and eliminate the conditions that contribute to sexual violence) to feasible and immediately applicable ideas. Pragmatic recommendations included, among others, LGBTQ awareness training across health care provider and social service curricula, inclusive language in agency paperwork, surveillance and advertising of organizations that are sensitive to the needs of the LGBTQ community, and recognition that agencies and agency staff are often not as LGBTQ friendly as they may believe.

Survey and focus group participants in this study highlighted the importance of changing attitudes about the LGBTQ community, increasing access to LGBTQ-friendly services, and developing and implementing LGBTQ-sensitive training protocols for key social and health service delivery systems. Research that evaluates the impact of training modules on provider knowledge, attitudes, and behavior is needed. Ristock (2005), for example, argued that cultural competency training should include same-sex issues, including domestic and sexual violence, and that LGBTQ-friendly practices should be incorporated into mainstream systems. We support this important recommendation and urge the use of program evaluation and participatory action research methods (e.g., Israel, Schultz, Parker, & Becker, 2000) toward measuring the impact of these efforts.

Notes

1. Many sexual minority people do not identify with any one of these labels.

2. The definition of same-sex sexual assault is the same as heterosexual sexual assault, with the exception that same-sex sexual assault involves a perpetrator of the same gender.

3. This study investigated sexual violence service issues for the LGBTQ population and same-sex couples. The researchers did not assume that all sexual victimization occurred in the context of same-sex relationships. For instance, a lesbian woman may have been sexually assaulted by a male relative and not by her female partner in adulthood.

4. Pilot survey data are not included in the survey data.

References

Anfara, V. A., Brown, K. M., & Mangione, T. L. (2002). Qualitative analysis on stage: Making the research process more public. *Educational Researcher, 31*(7), 28–38.

Balsam, K. F., Rothblum, E. D., & Beauchaine, T. P. (2005). Victimization over the life span: A comparison of lesbian, gay, bisexual, and heterosexual siblings. *Journal of Consulting and Clinical Psychology, 3*, 477–487.

Barret, B., & Logan, C. (2002). *Counseling gay men and lesbians: A practice primer.* Pacific Grove, CA: Brooks/Cole.

Basile, K. C. (2002). Prevalence of wife rape and other intimate partner sexual coercion in a nationally representative sample of women. *Violence & Victims, 17*, 511–524.

Berrill, K. (1990). Anti-gay violence and victimization in the United States: An overview. *Journal of Interpersonal Violence, 5*, 274–294.

Bieschke, K. J., Perez, R. M., & DeBord, K. A. (2007). *Handbook of counseling and psychotherapy with lesbian, gay, bisexual and transgender clients* (2nd ed.). Washington, DC: American Psychological Association.

Catalano, S. M. (2004). *Criminal victimization, 2003.* Washington, DC: U.S. Department of Justice, Office of Justice Programs.

Creswell, J. W. (2003). *Research design: Qualitative, quantitative, and mixed methods approaches* (2nd ed.). Thousand Oaks, CA: Sage.

Cruz, J. M. (2003). "Why doesn't he just leave?" Gay male domestic violence and the reasons victims stay. *Journal of Men's Studies, 11*, 309–324.

Duncan, D. F. (1990). Prevalence of sexual assault victimization among heterosexual and gay/lesbian university students. *Psychological Reports, 66*, 65–66.

Girshick, L. B. (2002). No sugar, no spice: Reflections on research on woman-to-woman sexual violence. *Violence Against Women, 8*, 1500–1520.

Heidt, J. M., Marx, B. P., & Gold, S. D. (2005). Sexual revictimization among sexual minorities: A preliminary study. *Journal of Traumatic Stress, 18*, 533–540.

Hickson, F. C. I., Davies, P. M., Hunt, A. J., Weatherburn, P., McManus, T. J., & Coxon, A. P. M. (1994). Gay men as victims of non-consensual sex. *Archives of Sexual Behavior, 23*, 281–284.

Hosmer, D. W., & Lemeshow, S. (2000). *Applied logistic regression* (2nd ed.). New York: Wiley.

Human Rights Campaign. (n.d.). *Transgender basics.* Retrieved July 9, 2007, from http://www.hrc.org/Template.cfm?Section=Transgender_Basics

Israel, B., Schultz, A., Parker, E., & Becker, A. (2000, April/May). *Community-based participatory research: Engaging communities as partners in health research.* Paper presented at the 4th Annual Conference, Community-Campus Partnerships for Health, Washington, DC.

Kenagy, G. P. (2005). Transgender health: Findings from two needs assessment studies in Philadelphia. *Health & Social Work, 30*, 19–26.

Kilpatrick, D. G. (March, 2002). *Making sense of rape in America: Where do the numbers come from and what do they mean?* Paper presented at the Violence Against Women Supplement Meeting, Centers for Disease Control and Prevention, Atlanta, GA.

Kilpatrick, D. G., & Ruggiero, K. J. (2003). *Rape in Oregon: A report to the state.* Charleston, SC: National Violence Against Women Prevention Research Center, Medical University of South Carolina.

Kilpatrick, D. G., & Ruggiero, K. J. (2004). *Making sense of rape in America: Where do the numbers come from and what do they mean?* Retrieved January 17, 2008, from http://new.vawnet.org/Assoc_Files_VAWnet/MakingSenseofRape.pdf

Logan T. K., Cole, J., & Shannon, L. (2007). A mixed-methods examination of sexual coercion and degradation among women in violent relationships who do and do not report forced sex. *Violence & Victims, 22*, 71–94.

Lombardi, E. (2001). Enhancing transgender health care. *American Journal of Public Health, 91*, 869–872.

Mendez, J. M. (1996). Serving gays and lesbians of color who are survivors of domestic violence. In C. M. Renzetti & C. H. Miley (Eds.), *Violence in gay and lesbian domestic partnerships* (pp. 51–59). New York: Harrington Park Press.

Merlis, S., & Linville, D. (2004, September). *A community's response to lesbian domestic violence.* Paper presented at the Annual Meeting of the American Association for Marriage and Family Therapy, Atlanta, GA.

Merrill, G. S., & Wolfe, V. (2000). Battered gay men: An exploration of abuse, help-seeking and why they stay. *Journal of Homosexuality, 39,* 1–30.

Myers, J. L., & Well, A. D. (2001). *Research design and statistical analysis.* Mahwah, NJ: Lawrence Erlbaum.

National Resource Center on Domestic Violence. (2007). *LGBT communities and domestic violence: Information and resources.* Harrisburg, PA: Author.

Pagano, R. R. (1995). *Understanding statistics in the behavioral sciences* (7th ed.). Belmont, CA: Wadsworth/Thomson.

Renzetti, C. M. (1998). Violence and abuse in lesbian relationships: Theoretical and empirical issues. In R. K. Bergen (Ed.), *Issues in intimate violence* (pp. 117–128). Thousand Oaks, CA: Sage.

Renzetti, C. M. (2001). Violence in lesbian and gay relationships. In C. M. Renzetti, J. L. Edelson, & R. K. Bergen (Eds.), *Sourcebook on violence against women* (pp. 285–293). Thousand Oaks, CA: Sage.

Ristock, J. L. (2001). Decentering heterosexuality: Responses of feminist service counselors to abuse in lesbian relationships. *Women & Therapy, 23*(3), 59–72.

Ristock, J. L. (2003). Exploring dynamics of abusive lesbian relationships: Preliminary analysis of a multisite, qualitative study. *American Journal of Community Psychology, 31,* 329–341.

Ristock, J. L. (2005). *Relationship violence in lesbian/ gay/bisexual/transgender/queer communities: Moving beyond a gender-based framework.* Violence Against Women Online Resources, Office for Violence Against Women. Available at http://www.mincava.umn.edu/documents/lgbtqviolence/lgbtqviolence.html

Strauss, A., & Corbin, J. (1990). *Basics of qualitative research.* Newbury Park, CA: Sage.

Tjaden, P., & Thoennes, N. (2000). *Consequences of violence against women: Research report.* Washington, DC: National Institute of Justice and the Centers for Disease Control and Prevention.

Tjaden, P., Thoennes, N., & Allison, C. J. (1999). Comparing violence over the life span in samples of same-sex and opposite-sex cohabitants. *Violence & Victims, 14,* 413–425.

Tonnies, F. (1887). *Gemeinschaft und gesellschaft* [Community and society] (C. P. Loomis, Ed. & Trans.). New York: Harper & Row.

Vaid, U. (1995). *Virtual equality: The mainstreaming of gay and lesbian liberation.* New York: Anchor Books.

Velleman, P. F., & Wilkinson, L. (1993). Nominal, ordinal, interval, and ratio typologies are misleading. *American Statistician, 47,* 65–72.

CHAPTER 17

Normative Misperceptions of Abuse Among Perpetrators of Intimate Partner Violence

Clayton Neighbors, Denise D. Walker, Lyungai F. Mbilinyi, Allison O'Rourke, Jeffrey L. Edleson, Joan Zegree, and Roger A. Roffman

This article evaluates normative misperceptions of domestic abuse behaviors among male perpetrators of intimate partner violence (IPV). In other domains, individuals engaging in a variety of behaviors (e.g., gambling, substance use, disordered eating) have been consistently shown to overestimate the extent to which others also engage in these behaviors. The magnitude of misperception has often been associated with severity of behavior, and correction of normative misperception has been successfully applied in prevention and treatment. The primary aim of this research was to evaluate the applicability and potential clinical utility of this approach among male IPV perpetrators.

IPV Perpetration

The magnitude of adverse consequences of IPV on its victims has been well documented by several national surveys (Henneberg, 2000; Straus & Gelles, 1990; Tjaden & Thoennes, 2000). A variety of treatment programs (Batterer Intervention Programs [BIPs]) have been implemented in the past three decades to help adult men recognize and end their abusive behavior. Many of these BIPs have been evaluated; however, most have not used experimentally controlled designs. Varying methods from one program to another have led to mixed and often uninterpretable findings. Reviews of the few evaluation studies that have used experimentally controlled designs have

Neighbors, C., Walker, D. D., Mbilinyi, L. F., O'Rourke, A., Edleson, J. L., Zegree, J., & Roffman, R. A. (2010). Normative misperceptions of abuse among perpetrators of IPV. *Violence Against Women, 16,* 370–386.

335

found small positive effects or inconclusive results on the effectiveness of one program over another (Babcock, Green, & Robie, 2004; Bennett & Williams, 2001; Feder & Wilson, 2005; Gondolf, 2004). These mixed and modest findings of domestic violence treatment for IPV perpetrators magnify the urgency and need to incorporate novel and innovative treatment approaches, evaluated by experimentally controlled research designs.

Social Norms

In the broadest sense, social norms can be defined as implicit or explicit rules regarding the appropriateness of behavior (Sherif, 1936). As such, social norms form the basis for what is considered appropriate versus inappropriate behavior. Social norms have been more precisely defined as being of two distinct types: descriptive and injunctive norms (Cialdini, Kallgren, & Reno, 1991). Whereas injunctive norms refer to the perceived or actual approval or disapproval of a given behavior, descriptive norms, the focus of the present article, refer to the perceived or actual prevalence of a given behavior. The distinction between perceived versus actual norms is a critical distinction given that our perceptions of others' attitudes and behaviors have a greater influence on our behavior relative to others' actual attitudes and behaviors, of which we often have no direct knowledge (Lewin, 1943; Neighbors, Dillard, Lewis, Bergstrom, & Neil, 2006).

IPV perpetration injunctive social norms, manifested by laws and policies against IPV, have existed for several decades (Salazar, Baker, Price, & Carlin, 2003; Taylor & Sorenson, 2005). Despite the public's general awareness of these laws and IPV's negative impact on family members, violence continues to occur and is often not reported to law enforcement (Taylor & Sorenson, 2005). Moreover, researchers have found perceived informal sanctions (e.g., potential loss of one's partner; loss of respect from

friends and loved ones) to be more effective in deterring violence than perceived criminal penalties (Smithey & Straus, 2003; Williams & Hawkins, 1992).

Perpetrators may to some extent be unaware that their behavior is "outside the norm." They tend to justify their abuse based on assumptions of others' behaviors or general acceptance of violence toward women. Researchers have found a strong relationship between perpetration of violence and acceptance or justification of violence or hostility toward women (Holtzworth-Munroe, Meehan, Herron, & Rehamn, 2000; Taylor & Sorenson, 2004). Although recent intervention studies have begun to investigate misperceptions of men's traditional gender roles (Beatty, Syzdek, & Bakkum, 2006), research has yet to directly evaluate misperceptions of descriptive IPV norms. Several researchers have pointed to the need for interventions to directly impact men's perceptions of other men's use of violence as an intervention strategy (Fabiano, Perkins, Berkowitz, Linkenbach, & Stark, 2003; Taylor & Sorenson, 2004). However, application of social norms approaches to IPV may be premature without first empirically documenting that misperceptions exist in relation to IPV norms and that they are associated with behavior (Lewis & Neighbors, 2006).

Although social norms have been less widely investigated with respect to IPV, they have been examined more extensively in association with other behaviors, especially in college student populations. Findings have consistently shown that people tend to overestimate norms for problematic behaviors, and this is especially true among individuals who engage in those behaviors. Furthermore, estimates of problematic behaviors are positively correlated with the extent to which individuals engage in those behaviors. These findings have been documented with respect to alcohol use (Baer, Stacy, & Larimer, 1991; Borsari & Carey, 2001; Lewis & Neighbors, 2004), marijuana and other drug use (Kilmer et al., 2006), risky sexual behavior (Chia & Gunther, 2006; Lewis, Lee, Patrick, & Fossos, 2007), body image concerns and disordered eating behavior (Bergstrom, Neighbors, & Lewis, 2004; Bergstrom, Neighbors, & Malheim, 2009), and gambling (Larimer & Neighbors, 2003; Neighbors et al., 2007). Intervention and treatment approaches that have been successful in changing perceived norms have been relatively successful in changing behavior, especially drinking behavior (Borsari & Carey, 2000; Chan, Neighbors, Gilson, Larimer, & Marlatt, 2007; Cunningham, Humphreys, & Koski-Jannes, 2000; Cunningham, Wild, Bondy, & Lin, 2001; Lewis & Neighbors, 2007; Neighbors, Larimer, & Lewis, 2004; Neighbors, Lewis, Bergstrom, & Larimer, 2006).

Normative data have also been an essential component of motivational enhancement therapy (MET) for the early intervention and treatment of risky behaviors such as alcohol and drug abuse (Miller & Rollnick, 2002). MET is an adaptation of motivational interviewing (Miller & Rollnick, 2002) developed as a client-centered method of communication for helping to resolve ambivalence and motivate change. MET consists of assessment of the risky behavior followed by a personalized session using motivational interviewing to offer feedback on the results of that assessment. Because perpetrators of domestic violence often struggle with motivation to change their behavior, engage in treatment, and complete treatment, motivational interviewing and MET have been identified as promising approaches for the application of IPV perpetration intervention (Roffman, Edleson, Neighbors, Mbilinyi, & Walker, 2008).

The primary objective of the present research was to evaluate the potential applicability of social norms approaches to IPV by evaluating whether normative misperceptions exist in relation to IPV norms and whether perceived IPV norms are associated with behavior. Specific aims of this article include (a) providing base rate norms for the prevalence of violent behaviors perpetrated by men based on estimates derived from the National Violence Against Women Survey (NVAWS); (b) evaluating whether male IPV perpetrators

overestimate the prevalence of violent behaviors; (c) evaluating the relationship between normative misperceptions of IPV and violent behavior. More specifically, we aimed to evaluate whether men who engage in more IPV differ from men who engage in less IPV in their perceptions of violence among other men; and (d) discussing the clinical application of perceived norms in treating IPV perpetrators.

Method

Participants were screened from 348 male callers who responded to various forms of advertising media, including radio and newspaper ads, flyers distributed throughout the community, and referrals from professionals and friends. Each caller completed two anonymous or confidential screening phone calls to determine his eligibility to participate in the project. Eligibility criteria included behaving abusively toward an intimate partner in the past 90 days, using substances in the past 90 days, not currently being adjudicated in a domestic abuse-related court matter, not having been arrested in the past 90 days for domestic abuse or a substance use charge, and not currently participating in IPV or substance abuse treatment.

Current engagement in domestic abuse behaviors was assessed using the Revised Conflict Tactics Scale (CTS2; Straus, Hamby, Boney-McCoy, & Sugarman, 1996). During screening, each caller was asked about his lifetime behaviors and past 90-day behaviors from the injury, physical violence, sexual violence, and psychological abuse scales of the CTS2. Callers who reported engaging in at least one behavior in the past 90 days and one nonpsychological behavior in their lifetime were eligible to participate in the project.

Eligible callers who completed the screening process were scheduled to complete a baseline assessment by telephone prior to randomization. Participants had the right to refuse to answer any or all of these questions. Of the 348 callers, 124 were found eligible to participate in the study and completed a baseline assessment. The 124 participants identified their race as follows: White (63%), African American (16%), Asian/Asian American (5%), American Indian (4%), Multiracial (2%), and Other (4%). The age distribution of participants was 18 to 30 (25.00%), 31 to 40 (29.03%), 41 to 50 (31.45%), and 51+ (14.52%). Eligible callers were demographically similar to ineligible callers; however, the present sample included a higher proportion of White and older men than would be expected in a larger/more representative sample of IPV perpetrating men.

Measures

Perceived norms were assessed by a questionnaire constructed for the present study. Participants were asked to estimate the percentage of men who have ever engaged in the following seven behaviors with their partners: throwing something at their partner that could hurt; pushing, grabbing, or shoving their partner; slapping or hitting their partner; choking their partner; beating up their partner; threatening their partner with a gun; and making their partner have sex with them or "give in" to sex when their partner did not want to. Internal consistency reliability among the seven items was high (a = .92).

Abusive behavior was assessed using a modified version of the CTS2 (Straus et al., 1996). The scale was modified to assess the frequency of violent behaviors perpetrated over the past 90 days. Psychological abuse was assessed with eight items (e.g., insulted or swore at partner; destroyed something that belonged to partner). All participants reported engaging in one or more forms of psychological abuse at least once over the past 90 days. The score for psychological abuse was thus computed as the sum of the eight items in which participants reported the number of times they had engaged in each behavior over the past 90 days with scores for all items capped at a maximum of 90

(a = .80). Physical violence including injurious behavior was assessed with 18 items (e.g., slammed partner against wall; partner had a broken bone from a fight with participant). Frequency counts were relatively low for these behaviors with 62% of the sample reporting no physical assault or injurious behaviors over the past 90 days. Thus, the score for this variable was computed as the sum of dichotomously coded items indicating whether they had engaged in each of the 18 behaviors over the past 90 days (a = .78). Sexual assault was assessed with seven items (e.g., insisted on sex when partner did not want to; used force to make partner have oral/anal sex). Given the relatively low frequency of these behaviors (i.e., 18% of participants reported engaging in one or more sexual assault behaviors in the past 90 days), this variable was also initially scored as the sum of dichotomously coded items indicating whether they had engaged in each act over the past 90 days (a = .34). Due to the unacceptable reliability of these items as a scale, we subsequently elected to score sexual assault as a binary variable with 0 indicating "no acts on any sexual assault item" and 1 indicating "one or more acts on any of the sexual assault items."

Base Rate Norms for Adult IPV Perpetration

Careful consideration was employed in choosing a source for estimating base rate norms for the prevalence of these violent behaviors. The two most relevant databases available are the NVAWS (Tjaden & Thoennes, 2000) and the National Family Violence Survey (NFVS; Straus & Gelles, 1990). We ultimately elected to base norms on the NVAWS for several reasons. First, the NVAWS was more recent (1995 vs. 1985). Second, the NFVS was limited to married, cohabiting, or recently separated or divorced adults, thus excluding many intimate relationships that may contain violence that do not fall into any of these categories. Similarly, the NFVS was limited to heterosexual relationships, thus excluding homosexual relationships. Finally, the NVAWS assessed reports of victimization, and domestic violence research has found victim reports of abuse to be more accurate than abusers' self-reports of abuse.

Funded by the National Institute of Justice and Centers for Disease Control and Prevention, the NVAW telephone survey collected data on a nationally representative sample of 8,000 women and 8,000 men regarding their experiences with rape, physical assault, and stalking. Although prevalence and incidence rates were based on victimization and not perpetration of violent acts, respondents were asked about the perpetrator's gender and type of relationship (e.g., intimate partnership). The NVAWS used a modified version of the CTS2 (Straus et al., 1996) to ask respondents about various types of violent acts they may have endured (see Table 17.1).

By using information on the perpetrator's gender, type of relationship, and decennial 2000 Census data, we were able to estimate the percentage of adult men who have ever engaged (lifetime) in physical assault and rape against female and/or male intimate partners. We first calculated the number of women and men who had been victimized at some point in their lifetime by an intimate partner by multiplying the percentage of the NVAWS sample who had experienced that type of violence by the number of adult women and men (18 years of age and older) in the population. We adjusted these numbers by the percentage of the women (93%) and men (86%) who were victimized by men. We then combined the number of women and men who were victimized by men, and divided that number by the population of adult men, reaching an estimated percentage of men who victimize women and men. Although these calculations are based on the assumption that all the male and female victims were abused by different male perpetrators, they are arguably the best estimates available given a lack of a nationally representative survey directly asking

men about their own perpetration of violent acts toward their intimate partners.

Results

A series of one-sample t tests were conducted to evaluate the accuracy of IPV perpetrators' perceptions of the prevalence of specific behaviors. Perceptions were compared with estimated population values derived from the National Database as described above. Effect size d was calculated as the difference between the mean of the perceived norm and the estimated population value divided by the standard deviation of the perceived norm (Cohen, 1988). By convention, effect sizes in the range of .2, .5, and .8 are considered small, medium, and large, respectively (Cohen, 1992). Distributions for all variables were examined for significant departure from normality. Both t tests and correlations have been consistently described as being robust to moderate departures from normality (e.g., Cohen, Cohen, West, & Aiken, 2003). With the exception of the perceived norm for threatening a partner with a gun, the distributions of perceptions did not approach extreme departure (Kline, 1998) from normality (all skewness and kurtosis values were within the +2 to −2 range). The distribution of the perceived norm for threatening a partner with a gun was positively skewed (2.47) and leptokurtic (6.73), suggesting caution in interpreting the results of the one-sample t test for this variable.

Results of one-sample t tests indicated that IPV perpetrators overestimated the prevalence rates of all seven behaviors on which perceived norms were assessed. Moreover, men overestimated the percentage of men who had ever thrown something at a partner to hurt, $t(123) = 7.61$, $p < .001$, $d = .68$; punched, grabbed, or shoved a partner, $t(123) = 5.51$, $p < .001$, $d = .49$; slapped or hit a partner, $t(123) = 3.01$, $p < .01$, $d = .27$; choked a partner, $t(123) = 6.17$, $p < .001$, $d = .55$; beat up a partner, $t(123) = 4.71$, $p < .001$, $d = .42$; threatened a partner with a gun, $t(123) = 4.13$, $p < .001$, $d = .37$; and made a partner have sex when

Table 17.1 Calculations of Base Rate Norms for Adult IPV Male Perpetration

Type of Violence	Women Victimized (%; n = 8,000)	No. of Women Victimized (108,133,727 Women >18)[a]	93% of the Women Were Victimized by Men	Men Victimized (%; n = 8,000)	No. of Men Victimized (100,994,367 Men 18)[a]	86% of the Men Were Victimized by Men	Total Women and Men Victimized by Men	Percentage of Men who Victimize Women and Men (100,994,367 Men > 18 Years Old)[a]
Threw something	8.1	8,758,832	8,145,714	4.4	4,443,752	3,821,627	11,967,341	11.85 (12%)
Pushed, grabbed, shoved	18.1	19,572,204	18,202,150	5.4	5,453,695	4,690,178	22,892,328	22.67 (23%)
Slap, hit	16.0	17,301,396	16,090,298	5.5	5,554,690	4,777,033	20,867,331	20.67 (21%)
Choked	6.1	6,596,157	6,134,426	0.5	504,972	434,276	6,568,702	6.50 (7%)
Beat up	8.5	9,191,367	8,547,971	0.6	605,966	521,131	9,069,102	8.98 (9%)
Threatened with gun	3.5	3,784,680	3,519,752	0.4	403,977	347,420	3,867,172	3.83 (4%)
Raped	7.7	8,326,297	7,743,456	0.3	302,983	260,565	8,004,021	7.93 (8%)

NOTE: IPV = intimate partner violence

Number based on U.S. population aged 18 years and older, U.S. Census Bureau, 2000, Decennial Census (100%)

they did not want to, $t(121) = 6.81, p < .001, d = .62$. Figure 17.1 presents means and standard errors for perceived norms relative to actual estimates.

To evaluate whether normative misperceptions were associated with IPV behaviors, we first calculated variables representing the discrepancy between participants' perceptions and actual norms for each of the seven specific behaviors by subtracting the actual norm as derived from the NVAWS data and the estimates provided by participants. The distributions of these discrepancy variables, henceforth referred to as normative misperceptions, mirrored the distributions for the perceived norms variables reported above. Normative misperceptions of threatening a partner with a gun considerably violated the normality assumption, and for the purposes of correlation analyses we used a constant (5) log transformation on this variable, which substantially reduced skewness (.74) and kurtosis (−.58). The distributions of the IPV

variables did not approach extreme departure from normality for physical violence, including injurious behavior or sexual assault (skewness and kurtosis values were within the +2 to −2 range), but did for psychological abuse (skewness = 2.47; kurtosis = 5.59). For the latter variable, we performed a constant (5) log transformation that considerably reduced skewness (1.38) and kurtosis (1.01).

Table 17.2 presents means and standard deviations for perceived norms and normative misperceptions. Table 17.3 presents means and standard deviations for IPV categories. Table 17.4 presents correlations of normative misperceptions for each specific behavior as well as the mean of the normative misperceptions with psychological abuse; physical violence, including injurious behavior; and sexual violence. Overall results indicate positive associations between perceived norms and IPV, with strongest associations for psychological abuse.

Figure 17.1   Normative Misperceptions of Violent Behaviors by IPV-Perpetrating Men

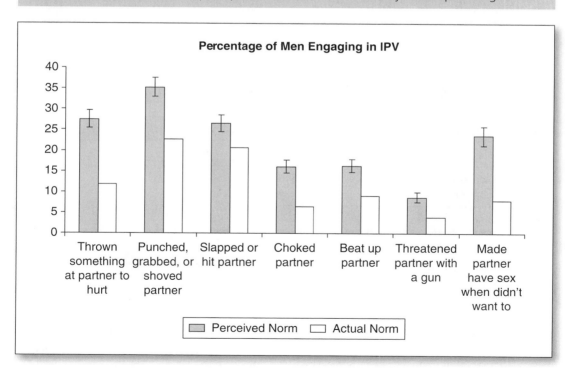

NOTE: IPV = intimate partner violence

Table 17.2   Means and Standard Deviations for Perceived Norms and Normative Misperceptions

Norm	Perceived Norm (%)		Actual Norm (% from NVAWS)	Normative Misperception
	M	**SD**		
Thrown something at partner to hurt (11.85)	27.55	22.98	11.85	15.70
Punched, grabbed, or shoved partner (22.67)	35.26	25.45	22.67	12.64
Slapped or hit partner (20.67)	26.56	21.78	20.67	5.89
Choked partner (6.50)	16.06	17.24	6.50	9.56
Beat up partner (8.98)	16.28	17.28	8.98	7.30
Threatened partner with a gun (3.83)	8.69	13.09	3.83	4.86
Made partner have sex when they did not want to (7.93)	23.57	25.34	7.93	15.70

NOTE: NVAWS = National Violence Against Women Survey. For the transformed normative misperception variable "threatened partner with a gun" used in the correlation analysis $M = 1.69$, $SD = 1.03$.

Table 17.3   Means and Standard Deviations for IPV Categories

IPV Category	**M**	**SD**
Psychological abuse	7.75	12.31
Physical violence including injurious behavior	5.10	3.42
Sexual assault	0.44	0.50

NOTE: IPV = intimate partner violence. For the transformed psychological abuse variable used in the correlation analysis $M = 1.69$, $SD = 1.03$.

Discussion

The present research evaluated the potential utility of providing social norms feedback to IPV perpetrating men. The logic for the application of personalized normative feedback as it has been applied in other domains can be described as follows: If perceptions of the prevalence of a given behavior influence one's own behavior (i.e., perceiving a given behavior as more common

Table 17.4　Correlations Between Normative Misperceptions and IPV

Normative Misperception Assault	Psychological Abuse	Physical Violence/Injury	Sexual
Thrown something at partner to hurt	.32***	.28**	.13
Punched, grabbed, or shoved partner	.24**	.28**	.12
Slapped or hit partner	.34***	.30***	.15
Choked partner	.44***	.29**	.14
Beat up partner	.38***	.34***	.16
Threatened partner with a gun	.33***	.26**	.14
Made partner have sex when they did not want to	.18*	.01	.22*

$*p < .05.$ $**p < .01.$ $***p < .001.$

["normal"] is associated with greater likelihood of engaging in the behavior) and one overestimates the prevalence of that behavior, then correcting this misperception should reduce the behavior. This research provides support for the first two components of this logic applied to IPV perpetrating men. Results indicated that IPV perpetrating men overestimated the prevalence of seven specific violent behaviors and that their perceptions/misperceptions were associated with their behavior. Moreover, the more they overestimated the more they themselves reported engaging in psychological abuse and physical violence, including injurious behavior. Alternatively, men who reported engaging in more psychological abuse and physical violence, including injurious behavior, held greater normative misperceptions of IPV related to men who reported engaging less in these behaviors. With respect to sexual assault, the association was more specific. Engaging in sexual assault was associated with normative misperceptions of sexual assault but was not associated with normative misperceptions of other IPV behaviors. Similarly, overestimating the prevalence of sexual assault was associated with greater likelihood of engaging in sexual

assault and psychological abuse but not other forms of physical violence.

This research was conducted in the context of considering MET as a means of reaching substance-using, IPV-perpetrating men and motivating them to take steps toward changing their behavior. Correction of normative misperceptions has been an important part of this approach for other behaviors. The primary objectives of this research were to provide evidence for the potential utility of this approach by evaluating whether IPV perpetrating men overestimate the prevalence of IPV behaviors and to evaluate the relationship between perceived IPV norms and IPV behavior. As described below, we also wished to disseminate estimates for actual norms and to describe how they might be used therapeutically with IPV perpetrators in the context of MET and other related approaches (Roffman et al., 2008).

The normative data published here are directly applicable and can be implemented in the context of treatment efforts to motivate behavior change in this population. As found here, men who are engaging in IPV tend to overestimate how often those behaviors are engaged in by other men. Allowing clients to examine and discuss the normative data can have several positive outcomes. First, becoming aware of the actual rates of these behaviors in society can provide objective data that suggest engaging in violence toward an intimate partner is outside the norm of what others do and thus is a less desirable behavior. Second, observing that his own perceptions of the rates of violence are exaggerated can provide the impetus for an engaging discussion on why his perceptions might be high. This is an opportunity for the client to learn that we tend to believe that others engage in the same behaviors we do. As IPV is often a taboo topic, it can be difficult to gauge what others are doing. In addition, one's own experience and family history can affect perceptions of behavioral norms. For example, if a client witnessed IPV as a child, he may overestimate the proportions of others who engage in those behaviors. Third, correcting normative misperceptions may motivate a client to change his behavior.

What would feedback on normative misperceptions look like in a clinical setting? Figure 17.2 is an example of the type of normative data feedback that we have provided in our ongoing clinical trial. A graph is provided that displays a bar representing the estimated actual percentage of men who have engaged in these behaviors; the other bar represents a hypothetical client's estimate of the frequency of this behavior. The counselor introduces these data by saying, "We asked you to estimate the prevalence of a number of domestic violence-related behaviors. Here are your estimates compared with the actual percentages of men who have engaged in these behaviors. The data represented here came from the NVAWS that polled 8,000 men and 8,000 women across the United States on violence in their intimate relationships. The participants in this survey were assured their responses would remain confidential and they were urged to respond truthfully, so we have confidence these numbers are representative of the violence that is occurring within the United States. What do you make of this?" The client is provided an opportunity to ask questions about the data and

to discuss his thoughts. It is typical for men to be surprised that their estimates of the proportion of men who engage in IPV are higher than the actual proportion of men who engage in IPV. Counselors often reflect this surprise and provide additional information: "You are surprised that you overestimated how many other men do these things. It's very common for people to believe that everyone else does the same things they do. This may be because we tend to surround ourselves with people who have similar interests, beliefs, or attitudes as ours. This can make it easy for us to incorrectly assume that our behavior is more typical than it actually is. The important thing you are seeing here is that fewer men do these things than you thought."

A second technique is to highlight the violent behaviors the client reported. In this way, specific attention can be placed on the personal relevance of these norms to the participant, and the participant gains an awareness of how infrequently the violence he has engaged in is happening in other relationships. For example, a counselor might review the normative data from the survey in the following way: "You estimated that 27% of men have thrown something at their partner to hurt. The actual rate of this behavior is 12%. This is one of the items that you reported doing to your partner. What do you make of these numbers?"

Personalizing this feedback with the participants' own reports of violent behavior must be done delicately, using the full spirit of motivational interviewing (including collaboration, evocation, and autonomy supporting). Reactions to this information are likely to vary considerably, including interest and surprise (ideally), apathetic disregard, justification, and/or disbelief and challenging the credibility of the data. For example, suppose an individual estimates that 25% of men have slapped or hit their partner. In being informed that the actual norm is 20%, a given individual may perceive this as a relatively large percentage of men, providing some justification—"Lots of men (one in five) slap their partners from time to time"—rather than

Figure 17.2 Example of Personalized Normative Feedback

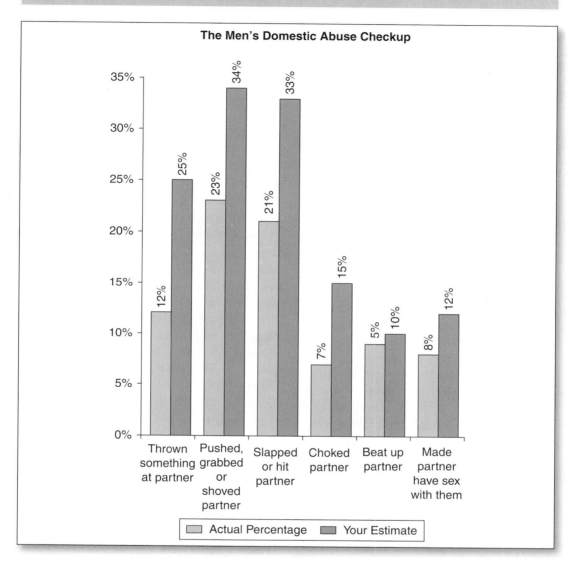

responding with surprise and discomfort at being in the 20% minority. A skilled MET therapist might use this as an opportunity to present a complex reflection, for example, "You've expressed some ambivalence about your behavior toward your partner, and it's comforting to know you aren't the only one." Relatedly, the magnitude of discrepancy is likely to vary considerably across behaviors and individuals. Dramatic discrepancies are more likely to result in correction of normative misperceptions, but even accurate estimations (or discrepancies of only one or two percentage points) provide the opportunity to discuss societal norms regarding the behavior. As with any therapeutic technique, efficacy is likely to be influenced by the skills of the provider. If there is a hint of disgust, confrontation, or judgment in the delivery of this type of feedback, the participant is likely to defend or minimize his actions. Moreover, such a tone can destroy rapport. Damaging the therapeutic relationship or eliciting defensiveness from the client is unlikely to produce an environment conducive to change.

Limitations and Conclusions

To our knowledge, this research represents the first study that has evaluated normative misperceptions of abusive behaviors in men who are perpetrators of IPV. There are several limitations that warrant consideration in interpreting the findings. Additional research is necessary to evaluate the generalizability of these results given the sample characteristics.

Data were drawn from a relatively small sample of substance-using, IPV-perpetrating men volunteering for a research study advertised as an opportunity for them to talk with someone about their behavior. Another limitation of this work is the difficulty in verification of actual norms. As detailed in the measures section, we elected to use the NVAWS for a variety of reasons, including its size, recency, inclusiveness, and emphasis on victims' reports. Nevertheless, it is important to note that the norms we calculated are estimates. In addition, the absence of men who do not engage in IPV from the sample precludes our ability to suggest that men who engage in IPV differ in their normative perceptions from men who do not engage in IPV. However, the results do suggest that perpetrating men who engage in more IPV differ from men who engage in less IPV in their perceptions of violence among other men.

A further limitation is that data were cross-sectional and preclude inferences regarding the causal direction between perceived norms and behavior. It is unclear the extent to which overestimating the prevalence of domestic abuse may influence an individual's behavior versus the reverse; men who engage in domestic abuse may justify their behavior by assuming it is more common than it is. It is plausible that both directions may be operating simultaneously, as has been found in other longitudinal research examining temporal precedence of the norms/behavior relationship in other contexts (Neighbors, Dillard, et al., 2006). Additional research evaluating IPV norms and behavior over time would allow more direct evaluation of this issue. Another issue worthy of additional attention is the specificity of the referent in normative feedback. This research focuses on national norms for men in the United States. However, consistent with social impact theory (Latane, 1981) and social identity theory (Tajfel & Turner, 1986), emerging evidence in other domains suggests that more specific/subcultural referent groups might have more influence in normative feedback, and this may be more true for some subgroups than others (e.g., Borsari & Carey, 2003; Lewis & Neighbors, 2007; Neighbors et al., 2007). Thus, additional work considering more specific normative referent groups in the context of IPV perpetration may prove useful. Nevertheless, the preliminary documentation that IPV perpetrating men overestimate the national prevalence of domestic violence and that their estimates are significantly and positively correlated with their own behavior provides an important first step in understanding and applying normative feedback in motivating behavior change.

Declaration of Conflicting Interests

The authors declared no potential conflicts of interest with respect to the authorship and/or publication of this article.

Funding

The authors disclosed receipt of the following financial support for the research and/or authorship of this article: Preparation of this manuscript was supported in part by the National Institute on Drug Abuse Grant R01DA017873.

References

Babcock, J. C., Green, C. E., & Robie, C. (2004). Does batterers' treatment work? A meta-analytic review of domestic violence treatment. *Clinical Psychology Review, 23,* 1023–1053.

Baer, J. S., Stacy, A., & Larimer, M. (1991). Biases in the perception of drinking norms among college students. *Journal of Studies on Alcohol, 52,* 580–586.

Beatty, A., Syzdek, M., & Bakkum, A. (2006). The Saint John's Experience Project: Challenging men's perceptions of normative gender role conflict. *Journal of Men's Studies, 14,* 322–336.

Bennett, L., & Williams, O. J. (2001). *Controversies and recent studies of batterer intervention effectiveness.* Harrisburg, PA: National Electronic Network on Violence Against Women (VAWnet, PCADV/NRCDV). Available from http://www.vawnet.org

Bergstrom, R. L., Neighbors, C., & Lewis, M. A. (2004). Do men find "bony" women attractive? Consequences of misperceiving opposite sex perceptions of attractive body image. *Body Image, 1,* 183–191.

Bergstrom, R. L., Neighbors, C., & Malheim, J. E. (2009). Media comparisons and threats to body image: Seeking evidence of self-affirmation. *Journal of Social and Clinical Psychology, 28,* 264–280.

Borsari, B., & Carey, K. B. (2000). Effects of a brief motivational intervention with college student drinkers. *Journal of Consulting and Clinical Psychology, 68,* 728–733.

Borsari, B., & Carey, K. B. (2001). Peer influences on college drinking. *Journal of Substance Abuse, 13,* 391–424.

Borsari, B., & Carey, K. B. (2003). Descriptive and injunctive norms in college drinking: A meta-analytic integration. *Journal of Studies on Alcohol, 64,* 331–341.

Chan, K. K., Neighbors, C., Gilson, M., Larimer, M. E., & Marlatt, G. A. (2007). Epidemiological trends in drinking by age and gender: Providing normative feedback to adults. *Addictive Behaviors, 32,* 967–976.

Chia, S. C., & Gunther, A. C. (2006). How media contribute to misperceptions of social norms about sex. *Mass Communication and Society, 9,* 301–320.

Cialdini, R. B., Kallgren, C. A., & Reno, R. R. (1991). A focus theory of normative conduct: A theoretical refinement and reevaluation of the role of norms in human behavior. *Advances in Experimental Social Psychology, 24,* 201–234.

Cohen, J. (1988). *Statistical power analysis for the behavioral sciences.* San Diego, CA: Academic Press.

Cohen, J. (1992). A power primer. *Psychological Bulletin, 112,* 155–159.

Cohen, J., Cohen, P., West, S. G., & Aiken, L. S. (2003). *Applied multiple regression/correlation analysis for the behavioral sciences* (3rd ed.). Mahwah, NJ: Lawrence Erlbaum.

Cunningham, J. A., Humphreys, K., & Koski-Jannes, A. (2000). Providing personalized assessment feedback for problem drinking on the Internet: A pilot project. *Journal of Studies on Alcohol, 61,* 794–798.

Cunningham, J. A., Wild, T. C., Bondy, S. J., & Lin, E. (2001). Impact of normative feedback on problem drinkers: A small-area population study. *Journal of Studies on Alcohol, 62,* 228–233.

Fabiano, P. M., Perkins, W., Berkowitz, A., Linkenbach, J., & Stark, C. (2003). Engaging men as social justice allies in ending violence against women: Evidence for a social norm approach. *Journal of American College Health, 52,* 105–112.

Feder, L., & Wilson, D. B. (2005). A meta-analytic review of court-mandated batterer intervention programs: Can courts affect abusers' behavior? *Journal of Experimental Criminology, 1,* 239–262.

Gondolf, E. W. (2004). Evaluating batterer counseling programs. *Aggression and Violent Behavior, 9,* 605–631.

Henneberg, M. (2000). *Bureau of Justice Statistics 2000: At a glance.* (Publication No. NCJ183014). Washington, DC: U.S. Department of Justice, Bureau of Justice Statistics.

Holtzworth-Munroe, A., Meehan, J. C., Herron, K., & Rehamn, U. (2000). Testing the Holtzworth-Munroe and Stuart (1994) batterer typology. *Journal of Consulting and Clinical Psychology, 68,* 1000–1019.

Kilmer, J. R., Walker, D. D., Lee, C. M., Palmer, R. S., Mallett, K. A., Fabiano, P., et al. (2006).

Misperceptions of college student marijuana use: Implications for prevention. *Journal of Studies on Alcohol, 67,* 277–281.

Kline, R. B. (1998). *Principles and practice of structural equation modeling.* New York: Guilford.

Larimer, M. E., & Neighbors, C. (2003). Normative misperceptions and the impact of descriptive and injunctive norms on college student gambling. *Psychology of Addictive Behaviors, 17,* 225–243.

Latane, B. (1981). The psychology of social impact. *American Psychologist, 36,* 343–356.

Lewin, K. (1943). Defining the "field at a given time." *Psychological Review, 50,* 292–310.

Lewis, M. A., Lee, C. M., Patrick, M. E., & Fossos, N. (2007). Gender-specific normative misperceptions of risky sexual behavior and alcohol-related risky sexual behavior. *Sex Roles, 57,* 81–90.

Lewis, M. A., & Neighbors, C. (2004). Gender-specific misperceptions of college student drinking norms. *Psychology of Addictive Behaviors, 18,* 334–339.

Lewis, M. A., & Neighbors, C. (2006). Social norms approaches using descriptive drinking norms education: A review of the research on personalized normative feedback. *Journal of American College Health, 54,* 213–218.

Lewis, M. A., & Neighbors, C. (2007). Optimizing personalized normative feedback: The use of gender-specific referents. *Journal of Studies on Alcohol and Drugs, 68,* 228–237.

Miller, W. R., & Rollnick, S. (2002). *Motivational interviewing* (2nd ed.). New York: Guilford.

Neighbors, C., Dillard, A. J., Lewis, M. A., Bergstrom, R. L., & Neil, T. A. (2006). Normative misperceptions and temporal precedence of perceived norms and drinking. *Journal of Studies on Alcohol, 67,* 290–299.

Neighbors, C., Larimer, M. E., & Lewis, M. A. (2004). Targeting misperceptions of descriptive drinking norms: Efficacy of a computer-delivered personalized normative feedback intervention. *Journal of Consulting and Clinical Psychology, 72,* 434–447.

Neighbors, C., Lewis, M. A., Bergstrom, R. L., & Larimer, M. E. (2006). Being controlled by normative influences: Self-determination as a moderator of a normative feedback alcohol intervention. *Health Psychology, 25,* 571–579.

Neighbors, C., Lostutter, T. W., Whiteside, U., Fossos, N., Walker, D. D., & Larimer, M. E. (2007).

Injunctive norms and problem gambling among college students. *Journal of Gambling Studies, 23,* 259–273.

Roffman, R. A., Edleson, J. L., Neighbors, C., Mbilinyi, L., & Walker, D. (2008). The Men's Domestic Abuse Checkup: A protocol for reaching the non-adjudicated and untreated man who batters and abuses substances. *Violence Against Women, 14,* 589–605.

Salazar, L. F., Baker, C. K., Price, A. W., & Carlin, K. (2003). Moving beyond the individual: Examining the effects of domestic violence policies on social norms. *American Journal of Community Psychology, 32,* 253–264.

Sherif, M. (1936). *The psychology of social norms.* New York: Harper.

Smithey, M., & Straus, M. A. (2003). Primary prevention of intimate partner violence. In H. Kury & J. Obergfell-Fuchs (Eds.), *Crime prevention: New approaches* (pp. 239–276). The Max Planck Institute. Mainz, Germany: Weisser Ring.

Straus, M., & Gelles, R. (1990). *Physical violence in American families—Risk factors and adaptations to violence in 8,145 families.* New Brunswick, NJ: Transaction Publishers.

Straus, M. A., Hamby, S. L., Boney-McCoy, S., & Sugarman, D. B. (1996). The Revised Conflict Tactics Scales (CTS2): Development and preliminary psychometric data. *Journal of Family Issues, 17,* 283–316.

Tajfel, H., & Turner, J. C. (1986). The social identity theory of inter-group behavior. In S. Worchel & L. W. Austin (Eds.), *Psychology of intergroup relations* (pp. 7–24). Chicago: Nelson-Hall.

Taylor, C. A., & Sorenson, S. B. (2004). Injunctive social norms of adults regarding teen dating violence. *Journal of Adolescent Health, 34,* 468–479.

Taylor, C. A., & Sorenson, S. B. (2005). Community-based norms about intimate partner violence: Putting attributions of fault and responsibility into context. *Sex Roles, 53,* 573–589.

Tjaden, P., & Thoennes, N. (2000). *Full report of the prevalence, incidence, and consequences of violence against women.* Washington, DC: Office of Justice Programs, U.S. Department of Justice.

Williams, K. R., & Hawkins, R. (1992). Wife assault, costs of arrest, and the deterrence process. *Journal of Research in Crime and Delinquency, 29,* 292–310.

CHAPTER 18

Danger Zone

Battered Mothers and Their Families in Supervised Visitation

Tracee Parker, Kellie Rogers, Meghan Collins, and Jeffrey L. Edleson

The crises represented by domestic violence and its immediate aftermath are the primary focus of current interventions with battered women and their families. Services focus on crisis telephone support, safe shelter, police response, and legal advocacy within the criminal justice system. Yet, there is considerable evidence that battering continues even after couples have separated (Hardesty, 2002; Jaffe, Lemon, & Poisson, 2002). Fleury, Sullivan, and Bybee (2000) found that more than one third (36%) of the 135 battered women they studied were reassaulted during separation from their perpetrators. Leighton (1989) found that a quarter of the 235 Canadian battered women he interviewed reported threats by a perpetrator during child visitations.

In many cases of adult domestic violence, the court will assign continued contact between a child and his or her noncustodial parent. Contact may range from informal, unsupervised visits to highly structured and professionally supervised visitation in centers set up for this purpose. Kernic, Monary-Ernsdorff, Kopsell, and Holt (2005) found in a study of 257 selected divorce cases with documented domestic violence that in only 23.6% of these cases was information about the domestic violence submitted into evidence. However, the courts did restrict fathers' access in 71.2% of the cases with evidence or allegations of domestic violence compared to only 17.5% of cases without such evidence or allegations. Judges specifically assigned supervised visitation in 25.6% of cases with substantiated domestic

Parker, T., Rogers, K., Collins, M., & Edleson, J. L. (2008). Danger zone: Battered mothers and their families in supervised visitation. *Violence Against Women, 14,* 1313–1325.

AUTHORS' NOTE: The views expressed in this article are solely the responsibility of the authors and do not necessarily represent the official views of the City of Kent. The authors wish to thank Monica Cruz of the Safe Havens Visitation Center for her contributions to this article.

violence compared to only 4.6% of the time when there was no evidence or allegation of domestic violence. Thoennes and Pearson (1999) found that 82% of court officers responding in their national survey favored supervised visitation when violence was alleged between parents. Clear in these data is the fact that even with evidence of domestic violence the courts are reluctant to cut off contact between a violent parent and his or her children.

Supervised visitation programs have developed rapidly across the United States. The services offered can include child exchange, off-site supervision, telephone contact, multifamily group visitation, one-on-one sessions, and therapeutic supervision (Center for Families, Children and the Courts, 2000; Thoennes & Pearson, 1999). The SVCs were initially developed as a way to permit parents to spend time with children who were placed outside the home due to child abuse or neglect, but the uses of such programs have expanded to include a wider range of problems, such as domestic violence, parental mental illness, substance abuse, threat of abduction, and reinitiating contact between parents and their children.

The Center for Families, Children and the Courts (2000) had reported that domestic violence is a key issue that brings families to California's SVCs. The use of SVCs in cases of domestic violence has increased for a number of reasons, including the National Council of Juvenile and Family Court Judges' (1994) effort to promote a model code regarding domestic violence over the past decade. The model code suggested states adopt a rebuttable presumption statute presuming it is not in the best interest of a child for a parent who perpetrates domestic violence to be given sole or joint custody of the child. Almost half of the states have now adopted such legislation (see Dunford-Jackson, 2004). Studying the effects of rebuttable presumption laws, Morrill, Dai, Dunn, Sung, and Smith (2005) found that in states with such laws judges were significantly more likely (69%) to assign structured visitation for noncustodial parent contact with a child than in states without such provisions (54%).

Although SVCs aim to facilitate safety for families experiencing domestic violence, violence may continue even when structured and supervised visitation or exchanges are in place. The murder of Melanie Edwards and her 2-year-old daughter, Carli, by Melanie's estranged husband, Carlton, as they left a supervised visitation program in the Seattle area in December 1998 (Barker, 1998) illustrates many concerns about continued abuse and safety during visitation and exchanges. Sadly, though Melanie had taken many precautions, including selling her car to buy one that her husband would be less likely to notice or track, Carlton was still able to use the court-ordered contact point to carry out the ultimate act of domestic violence. He waited for Melanie after his scheduled visit with Carli and then shot and killed both Melanie and Carli outside the supervised visitation center (SVC). Although murders like these are extreme and somewhat rare, continued abuse during supervised visitation is common. A survey of 14 Canadian supervised visitation programs showed that even in these highly controlled settings abuse continues (Park, Peterson-Badali, & Jenkins, 1997).

The National Council of Juvenile and Family Court Judges (1994, 1999) has responded to situations like that of the Edwards family by cautioning that supervised visitation be provided only when safety and security measures are taken and staff are well trained in the unique dangers raised by domestic violence perpetrators. Some supervised visitation programs are taking steps to enhance security for families experiencing domestic violence. Suggested security measures include closer supervision of domestic violence-related visitations by trained staff, staggered arrival and departure times, separate entrances for mothers and fathers, escorts to cars, and center's access to police through direct electronic connections (Park et al., 1997).

This article describes some of the key lessons we learned over 18 months of planning and then the subsequent 18 months of implementation at a SVC developed specifically to serve families for whom adult domestic violence was the primary reason for referral. We found that many dangers continued for battered mothers and their children when using our center. In this article, we outline the major issues that arose during our first year and a half in operation as well as our responses to them. Our experiences are organized around five major themes: (a) battered women's experiences in supervised visitation, (b) how battering continues during supervised visitation, (c) how rules at the SVC evolved over the first 18 months of implementation, (d) the importance of well-trained visit monitors, and (e) the need to embed SVCs within a larger context of coordinated community responses to domestic violence.

City of Kent's Safe Havens Visitation Center

The Safe Havens Supervised Visitation and Safe Exchange Initiative was begun by the Department of Justice's Office on Violence Against Women (OVW) in 2002 to explore how supervised visitation services might be changed to account for the unique safety issues surrounding domestic violence and access to children. The City of Kent, WA, was selected as one of four demonstration sites (along with Chicago; Santa Clara County, CA; and the state of Michigan) and received funding in January 2003 to plan and implement a state-of-the-art supervised visitation and exchange center. Collaborative partners included the King County Superior Court, King County Coalition Against Domestic Violence, Washington State Coalition Against Domestic Violence, the Young Women's Christian Association (YWCA) of Seattle and South King County, Chaya (a program for South Asian battered women), and Communities Against Rape and Abuse. In January 2005, after 18 months of extensive planning and preparation, the Safe Havens Visitation Center opened its doors for business. The center is currently fully grant funded and

serves only those families in which one parent needs protection from the other due to a history of domestic violence.

The mission of the Kent Safe Havens Visitation Center is to provide a safe, accessible, and culturally sensitive supervised visitation and exchange program for families affected by domestic violence, sexual assault, child abuse, and stalking. Our SVC aims to increase safety for victims of domestic violence and decrease opportunities for further abuse regardless of which parent is designated as the nonresidential party. We define domestic violence as a pattern of behaviors and ongoing threats to safety that one person uses to dominate, control, and/or coerce another person through physical, emotional, and sexual abuse.

Battered Mothers in Supervised Visitation

Our SVC staff has extensive experience in working with victims of domestic violence in advocacy settings. Because women usually see advocates as their allies and a source of support, we were surprised to discover that many mothers bringing their children to the SVC were angry or confused about the court-ordered visitation and highly distrustful of us. We were often viewed as part of a court system, and some feared the program was structured more to meet the needs of the visiting fathers than those of the women and children. Sometimes, these views were reinforced by previous experiences with other SVCs, where the intake process might only include interviews with the noncustodial parent and little interaction with the mother. We also quickly came to understand that most of the mothers bringing children to the center did not necessarily define themselves as battered women and were not utilizing community-based domestic violence advocacy services even though it seemed clear they could benefit from such services.

The SVC staff decided that changes were needed to better meet the needs of custodial mothers. We tried to make the mothers' waiting area more friendly and useful for those who prefer to stay on-site during visits. We added a comfortable couch, a lending library, and a computer terminal with Internet access. More importantly, we also made an effort to reach out to the mothers in a more systematic way. We made sure to frequently check in with mothers, often having one staff member spend the full visit hour sitting with a waiting mother and simply listening. We purposefully tried to have many different staff members check in with each mother throughout the duration of her time using the center. This helped the mother understand that all of the staff knew her family history and encouraged her to express her concerns as needed. However, we struggled with the fine line between being supportive and leading her to view us as her advocates. We were committed to providing excellent visitation services that take into account ongoing battering, and to do so we had to be very clear about the limitations of our role. We felt we could not act as advocates and maintain our credibility within the legal community. Instead, we worked diligently to connect the clients we served with other providers who could truly assist them in getting their needs met.

As a result of these experiences, we see SVCs as a location that offers great opportunity to provide advocacy for battered women. Most of these mothers are dealing with the complex issues of reconstructing their lives after separation from their children's father. Some, but not all, mothers are in need of postseparation advocacy services that may not necessarily be immediate and crisis oriented but rather focused on defending or asserting their rights as parents, repairing damage to the mother-child relationship that is often undermined by abusive partners, and developing a stable and safe environment for themselves and their children.

The SVCs are generally not equipped to offer extensive advocacy services to battered mothers. One solution might be to co-locate advocates at SVCs, so that during their children's visits with noncustodial fathers the mothers can receive advocacy services. Co-located advocates from another agency (rather than on-staff advocates) would permit confidential services and avoid potential conflicts of interest. This model would have the added benefit of developing a more coordinated response and provide mothers with easier access to other services. For example, several of the mothers bringing their children to our SVC were in the midst of financial decline. Many had to increase work hours or take second jobs to make ends meet. Some had been suddenly thrown into the work force with no strong experience and were receiving minimal wages. Finding time to meet with an advocate can be viewed as just another hassle. We found that many mothers use their time at the SVC to work on their parenting plans, fill out court paperwork, or review the stacks of brochures and information they collected. This could be a perfect time to meet with an advocate and receive meaningful assistance and emotional support.

How Men Who Batter Continue Their Abuse During Supervised Visitation

During our first 18 months in operation, we were consistently surprised and awed by the battering tactics we witnessed at the SVC. Within a month of opening our doors, we realized how easily our program could become part of the batterer's methods to control his victim, despite our extensive experience and training. From the very first contact with a family ordered to the SVC, it is essential that staff be consistent in the messages conveyed. For example, fathers often called our center to schedule an intake as ordered by court, but they spent the majority of the call trying to figure out if our staff had already spoken with the other parent, what she told us, what her plans were, and the schedule of her intake. Many would call a second or third time, attempting to talk with different staff members in an effort to gain more or different information. We quickly discovered that any inconsistency on our part would be used against the other parent. As a result, very early we developed a staff communication log to track all interactions with clients and implemented weekly case consultation meetings to discuss every family we served. These efforts proved to be invaluable in strategizing how to increase safety for mothers and children and decrease opportunities for fathers to use SVC staff as informants.

Simply scheduling the first visit becomes a battering tactic with many of the fathers we are serving. For example, many will complete the intake process and repeatedly insist that they will do anything to see their children as soon as possible and are available anytime. Quite commonly, when a first visit appointment is offered, these same men will ask for a different time, accept, and then cancel at the last minute, stating they are looking for another provider or demand a time slot they know the other parent can't accommodate followed by a threat to file contempt charges against her if she does not bring the child as ordered. Once services begin, fathers often try to send messages to the other parent through their children in very subtle and, in fact, quite brilliant ways. For example, one father had been violating his protection order by calling his estranged wife's cell phone and leaving her messages that she should come back to him. When she changed her number, his behavior at the center also changed. At his next visit, instead of playing with his children, he became sullen and withdrawn, causing his children to ask why he was mad at them. He came to his next supervised visit wearing excessive cologne and, at the end of the visit, during his goodbye hugs, managed to rub his neck all over the kids so they reeked of his scent. This was a very effective way of making sure his estranged wife would be reminded of him throughout the rest of the day.

In another case, a father brought in a specialty coffee drink to his visit. Staff assumed the drink was for him; however, when the visit started he gave it to his 3-year-old son. At the end of the visit, when staff brought the child and the drink out to the waiting mother, she was visibly shaken.

She explained that during their relationship, this man forbade her or her child to have caffeine, chocolate, or sugar with the exception of this particular drink, which she was only allowed when she was behaving in a manner he deemed as acceptable. This was the drink the child brought to her from the supervised visit reminding her that he was still very much in control of their lives.

Evolving Rules at the SVC

The examples above provide a glimpse into why clear and consistent guidelines and behavioral expectations are critical in dealing with the issues and challenges that arise during supervised visitation. We began services with some very broad guidelines about arrival and departure, scheduling, and visit behavior, based on the assumption that if we had too many specific rules we would be forced to bend them more frequently. However, almost immediately every vague expectation was challenged, and we discovered that any inconsistency on our part was used to split staff and undermine our credibility. We reacted by discarding our philosophy of flexibility and adding more rules. However, this proved only to increase the perception of an adversarial relationship between clients and staff, thereby leading to a much more hostile environment and potentially increasing danger for all of us. Sadly, we found ourselves in a power struggle with many of our clients as we tried to catch them, and they tried to figure out ways to get around our rules.

As a result, we have come full circle as an agency on this issue and now work to be clearer with each client from the very beginning. This means explaining that we are here to keep adults and children safe in and around the SVC, before, during, and after visits and that every intervention is based on these goals. We work to be responsive as opposed to reactive. For example, when the father (in one of the examples mentioned earlier) rubbed cologne all over his children, our reaction was to post notices in both waiting rooms asking all clients to refrain from wearing colognes and perfumes in the visitation area. However, when we were able to step back from the situation and respond rationally, we realized we needed to simply discuss our concerns in a respectful manner with the father in question. We have come to accept that we cannot create a one-size-fits-all program. Each family comes to us with different issues and circumstances. Some clients require more time and energy than others, and we must be ready and able to explain what the expectations for the client are, both verbally and in writing.

The Importance of Well-Trained and Skillful Monitors

Being clear and consistent from the beginning requires well-trained and skillful visit monitors. Over the past 3 years, we have toured other SVCs across the nation, attended multiple institutes and conferences specific to domestic violence and supervised visitation, and participated in several think tanks focused on documentation of contacts with families and promising practices for building partnerships with advocates, judges, and court personnel. We have had endless discussions and debates about the role of supervised visitation providers and read visitation notes by visit monitors from other non-Safe Havens programs that seem to dismiss battering altogether. These notes have become excellent learning tools.

For example, one visit monitor's report from a local, non-Safe Havens center described an incident where a visiting father and his children were walking back to the program center from an off-site visit to a nearby park when the father stopped at his car, reached in, and retrieved roses and a card for the mother. This visit monitor read the card, documented that she did not see anything of concern, and so allowed the children to accept the gift. This may seem benign if the monitor views his or her role as simply documenting interactions and activities of the visit. However, in this particular case, the custodial parent and children had a lifetime order for protection resulting from serious domestic violence, stalking, and threats of murder and abduction. Viewed through the lens of domestic violence, this scene is fraught with potential danger. The father could have easily abducted the children when he walked them to his car, he could have pulled out a weapon, or the card and flowers could have delivered a threatening message only the mother would understand. Visit monitors need to be conscientious at all times of potential risks to physical and emotional safety of mothers and their children and be willing to react quickly and effectively.

Monitors also have the difficult task of intervening. Under the best of circumstances, it is difficult to confront people about negative behavior. Add to this the context of domestic violence, where visiting fathers have been court mandated to supervised visitation. At our SVC, many were not enrolled in any kind of intervention programs and had seldom been held accountable for their actions. Well-trained monitors can intervene in a way that does not make children feel responsible for the behavior of their parent and that models how conflict can be dealt with in a safe way. For example, we have worked with several families in which it has been common practice for the batterer to drill their children for information about the other parent to find out where they go, who they talk to, and the like. This may lead a child to feel disloyal to one parent or the other or to feel responsible for negative consequences that might arise from offering such information. At our SVC, when a visiting parent attempts to get information from the child, we offer a quick and simple reminder that he is here just to visit his children and not to talk about the mom. Another example is when visiting parents try to force their children to have more physical contact than the children are comfortable with; for instance, they may want to whisper something to them or embrace them as they begin to sob. A skilled monitor should notice when children are pulling away or trying to divert dad's attention elsewhere and can direct him to other activities.

Many fathers see SVC staff as adversaries regardless of our efforts to demonstrate neutrality. Monitors must weigh the benefits of intervening in the moment versus having a discussion with the parent after a visit. This is a fine line that must be walked at all times. In some visits, the act of intervening by the monitor is seen as aggressive and can escalate the visiting parent's behavior, thereby increasing the danger level for everyone. For some fathers, a nonverbal intervention with the promise for an explanation after the visit is all that is needed. There are others, however, who require verbal interventions, and sometimes a visit must be terminated until the batterer learns to cease their inappropriate and abusive behaviors in the visitation setting. Thinking through which interventions are most effective for which parent can be extremely difficult in the best of situations. Add to this the myriad of personalities and possibly threatening behavior, and it becomes clear why the monitor must be an individual who is confident and grounded in his or her understanding of the dynamics of domestic violence, has had good training in multiple arenas and solid experience in providing direct service to battered women, and is supported by peers, the court, and others in the domestic violence community.

Continuous staff debriefing and dialogue are essential to self-care. This includes learning to shake it off, finding humor where we can, connecting with other supervised visitation providers, and frequent and public acknowledgement for a job well done.

The other side of the coin is that many batterers see the monitor and their role as an opportunity for getting a good parenting report to give to the court. This is perhaps one of the more typical ways in which fathers use their children to continue to batter the mother. As Bancroft and Silverman (2002) suggested, battering fathers make every effort to look good when under supervision. Fathers often tell us at intake that they

have been the primary caregiver for the children, all the way from feeding them to changing diapers to taking them to the doctor. During visits, many will bring snacks and offer to play games or ask to help with homework. Although this is a positive product of supervised visitation, it has no bearing on whether this type of interaction would occur in another setting. Nor does it relate to whether the batterer has stopped battering. Unfortunately, visitation supervisors who do not take battering and domestic violence allegations into account often write glowing reports about the noncustodial parent's visits. These reports can then be used by the father in court as proof that he is a great father and should be allowed unsupervised access to his children. Often the courts, impressed by such positive findings, will agree and subsequently change orders to permit him more access to his children. It is then that battering may continue unimpeded.

A perfect example of this occurred at our SVC. We had one visiting parent who was a delight to supervise. He often brought picnic lunches to the visit and would set up the visiting area with lots of games and activities for his young child during the visit. Then we overheard him tell another visiting parent that he was having his child's mother followed night and day; he was facing a criminal stalking charge at the time. Per our SVC's policy regarding threats to safety, we informed the mother of his comment and then informed him that we had done so. He was furious. He stated that he did not see how that had anything to do with his fathering and that he was expecting a good assessment from us. We reminded him that we did not provide parenting assessments and from then on his visits changed completely. He rarely spoke to the child during visits and stopped setting up games altogether. Within a month, he stopped showing up at appointed times and then stopped scheduling visits.

When domestic violence is the primary reason for referral to supervised visitation, we believe that it is altogether inappropriate to offer parenting evaluations based on the visitation itself. It has been our experience that most fathers assume that we are going to provide reports on their parenting to the court. As demonstrated above, the quality of the visits can change significantly when batterers clearly understand that the SVC will not provide written parenting evaluations or recommendations to the court. In addition, it is imperative to remember that nonproblematic visits do not indicate safety for the mother and children between visits. We have no way of knowing if the batterer has indeed stopped his abusive behavior, and his use of positive behaviors during supervised visits may be yet another tactic to gain an advantage over the mother.

Embedding Supervised Visitation Within a Coordinated Response

One of the more problematic aspects of providing this service has been the realization that there is not a strong network among systems-based services for men who batter to make serious change in their behaviors and attitudes. We are committed to modeling compassion, empathy, and kindness, though at the same time being very direct and open about battering tactics. However, many of the fathers using our services have been ordered to use the SVC by a civil court and are not enrolled in batterer intervention programs. If they are enrolled in such a program, they often choose one that does not have a meaningful connection to the domestic violence advocacy community or a visible commitment to holding batterers accountable. For example, one batterer intervention program facilitator called us to ask how the visits were going for one of the men also enrolled in his program. He stated he was preparing to write a report on behalf of his client recommending a move to unsupervised visitation. This facilitator had never seen the children in question.

We have also come to realize how little battered women's advocates and supervised visitation providers know about each other's services. In fact, when we initially began this project, as

advocates we were aware of only one other supervised visitation provider in our area. As we have become more entrenched in this service arena and women have begun to request our program, we have learned of multiple supervised visitation providers—private, for-profit, and not-for-profit—that exist in our community. To our knowledge, none of these programs is actively connected to domestic violence services or advocacy programs.

It is critically important to develop and nurture a partnership between the domestic violence advocacy community and SVCs. The SVCs should be part of a coordinated community response that includes women's advocates, batterers' intervention providers, law enforcement, family law attorneys, judges, social workers, child advocates, and probation officers. Through dialogue, cross-training, and collaboration, we can increase safety for battered women and children and perhaps begin to collectively hold batterers accountable for their abusive behaviors.

Finally, attorneys and judges are an important part of a community's response. Whether attorneys are representing men who batter or battered women, they need more education about postseparation battering tactics, including how SVCs can be helpful or harmful. As a practical matter, attorneys tend to be involved in helping their clients select particular SVC programs when there is such a choice. An attorney knowledgeable about domestic violence and choices among SVCs could help a client connect to a preferred program and understand its benefits and limitations. In addition, attorneys should strive to help clients articulate any safety concerns for themselves or their children to aid the court in making decisions that increase safety and accountability. For example, a battered woman might develop a parenting plan that outlines certain steps that need to be completed before visitation is increased or made less restrictive, such as successful completion of a perpetrator treatment program, no violations of protective orders for a specified length of time, and consistent compliance with court recommendations.

Parenting plans might include phases of parenting time that progress as various conditions are met by the batterer. By extension, better-informed attorneys can indirectly increase the court's awareness of SVCs that have taken the extra steps necessary to safeguard battered mothers and their children. Direct education of the judiciary about postseparation battering tactics and the impact of domestic violence on children is also an important step in achieving safe outcomes for mothers and children. Similarly, educating attorneys and judges about why SVCs should not make parenting assessments or recommendations and who is competent to report back to the court about the batterer's parenting could prevent further abuse and possible tragedy for children or their parents.

Conclusion

Our experience leads us to the following conclusions:

- Battered mothers do not always see SVCs as an ally for their safety, and we must better organize services to support them.
- Battering may continue in explicit and more subtle ways, even during supervised visits and the interactions surrounding them, requiring vigilance on the part of SVC staff.
- Clear, consistent, and documented communication from the beginning of contact with all parties is essential when working with domestic violence perpetrators.
- Well-trained and skillful monitors who are extremely sensitive to the issues of domestic violence and strategies of perpetrators are the critical component of success for SVCs working with these families.
- Successful SVCs must be a part of a larger, coordinated community response to domestic violence that allows battered mothers, their children, and violent fathers to access the array of services and interventions necessary to achieve safe families.

These points cannot be stressed enough. Battered mothers using SVCs come with complex safety planning needs that are many times unmet. This situation presents an opportunity for advocacy services that are desperately needed and could be available in SVCs through collaborative arrangements with battered women's service providers. In addition, abusive behavior on the part of the violent men continues in subtle ways, for example, through the use of perfume or coffee cups, and extreme ways, such as in the case of Melanie and Carli Edwards. These behaviors require clear and consistent rules governing child contact. Continuing abuse during child visits and the need for clear and consistent rules require highly skilled SVC staff who are informed, united, and vigilant with regard to interventions and who communicate clearly with all parties involved.

Given the full spectrum of ways abuse can continue at SVCs, there is a great need for the SVC community to reach out to and work with the domestic violence advocacy community to increase physical and emotional safety during visitations and exchanges. A strong and mutually respectful working relationship between SVCs, local courts, and the domestic violence advocacy community must be a priority for all partners in a coordinated response to domestic violence that ensures safety for mothers and their children.

References

Bancroft, L., & Silverman, J. G. (2002). *The batterer as parent.* Thousand Oaks, CA: Sage.

Barker, K. (1998). Killer "lived and breathed" his estranged wife's terror. *Seattle Times.* Retrieved January 15, 2001, from http://www.seattletimes.com

Center for Families, Children and the Courts. (2000). *Supervised visitation: A look at the research literature (research update).* San Francisco: Author.

Dunford-Jackson, B. L. (2004). The role of family courts in domestic violence: The U.S. experience. In P. G. Jaffe, L. L. Baker, & A. J. Cunningham (Eds.), *Protecting children from domestic violence: Strategies for community intervention* (pp. 8–28). New York: Guilford.

Fleury, R. E., Sullivan. C. M., & Bybee, D. I. (2000). When ending the relationship does not end the violence. *Violence Against Women, 6*, 1363–1383.

Hardesty, J. L. (2002). Separation assault in the context of postdivorce parenting. *Violence Against Women, 8*, 597–625.

Jaffe, P. G., Lemon, N. K. D., & Poisson, S. E. (2002). *Child custody and domestic violence: A call for safety and accountability.* Thousand Oaks, CA: Sage.

Kernic, M. A., Monary-Ernsdorff, D. J., Koepsell, J. K., & Holt, V. L. (2005). Children in the crossfire: Child custody decisions among couples with a history of intimate partner violence. *Violence Against Women, 11*, 991–1021.

Leighton, B. (1989). *Spousal abuse in metropolitan Toronto: Research report on the response of the criminal justice system* (*Report No. 1989-02*). Ottawa, ON: Solicitor General of Canada.

Morrill, A. C., Dai, J., Dunn, S., Sung, I., & Smith, K. (2005). Child custody and visitation decisions when the father has perpetrated violence against the mother. *Violence Against Women, 11*, 1076–1107.

National Council of Juvenile and Family Court Judges. (1994). *Model code on domestic and family violence.* Reno, NV: Author.

National Council of Juvenile and Family Court Judges. (1999). *Effective intervention in domestic violence and child maltreatment: Guidelines for policy and practice.* Reno, NV: Author.

Park, N. W., Peterson-Badali, M., & Jenkins, J. M. (1997). An evaluation of supervised Access I: Organizational issues. *Family and Conciliation Courts Review, 35*, 37–55.

Thoennes, N., & Pearson, J. (1999). Supervised visitation: A profile of providers. *Family and Conciliation Courts Review, 37*, 460–477.

CHAPTER 19

Factors Associated With Engagement in a Police-Advocacy Home Visit Intervention to Prevent Domestic Violence

Carla Smith Stover, Anna M. Rainey,
Miriam Berkman, and Steven Marans

According to the National Violence Against Women Survey, 5.3 million intimate partner victimizations of women more than 18 years old occur in the United States each year, resulting in 2 million injuries (Centers for Disease Control and Prevention, 2003). Twenty-eight percent of female homicides committed in a given year are at the hands of intimate partners (see Bachman & Saltzman, 1995). Battering is a significant direct and indirect risk factor for various physical health problems frequently seen in health care settings, and intimate partner violence (IPV) is one of the most common causes of injury to women (Rand, 1997). In addition to these health and safety concerns for women, it is estimated that between 10 and 17.8 million children witness domestic violence in the United States each year (McDonald, Jouriles, Ramisetty-Mikler, Caetano, & Green, 2006; Silvern et al., 1995; Straus & Gelles, 1990). These children are at increased risk for a wide range of immediate and long-term emotional and behavioral difficulties (Carlson, 2000; Edleson, 1999; Graham-Berman & Levendosky, 1998; Kolbo, 1996). Given the staggering prevalence and consequences of IPV, substantial efforts have been devoted to the development of intervention programs for

Stover, C. S., Rainey, A. M., Berkman, M., & Marans, S. (2008). Factors associated with engagement in a police-advocacy home-visit intervention to prevent domestic violence. *Violence Against Women, 14,* 1430–1450.

victims, child witnesses, and perpetrators of IPV, using various approaches within the criminal justice, mental health, social services, and grassroots advocacy systems.

Research in recent years has focused on evaluating the impact of these interventions on rates and patterns of repeat violence, various measures of victim and child emotional and physical well-being, and patterns of service use and satisfaction (Graham-Berman & Edleson, 2001; Stover, 2005). Despite the wide array of services and programs available for IPV victims, their children, and the abusers, most efforts to reduce IPV recidivism have met with limited success (Maxwell, Garner, & Fagen, 2001; Shepard, 2005; Stover, 2005). Victims' engagement in services and programs specifically designed for their use is quite variable, and many services for battered women and their children are underused (Fugate, Landis, Riordan, Naureckas, & Engel, 2005). Given the enormous cost of intervention and advocacy services for IPV, it is important to determine factors that are associated with engagement in a specific intervention model and to understand what makes an intervention a good fit for a particular family or community. This article examines demographic and IPV incident factors that may be associated with engagement in a domestic violence intervention program developed at the Yale University Child Study Center. The intervention and its context will first be described, followed by a summary of relevant research on IPV victims' engagement with police and other services to provide a context for the questions addressed in the current study.

Context of the Domestic Violence Home Visit Intervention Program

The current study took place in New Haven, Connecticut, a small city (approximately 123,000 residents) characterized by a high rate of poverty and ethnic diversity: The 2000 census reports 43.6% Caucasian residents, 37.4% African American, 21.4% Hispanic or Latino, 3.9% Asian, 0.4% American Indian, 0.1% Pacific Islander; 20.5% of city residents live below the poverty line. Police in New Haven investigate an average of 2,000 cases of IPV each year, with approximately 50% of police reports noting the presence of children at the incident (New Haven Department of Police Service, personal communication, 2006).

Connecticut statutes mandate arrest in every family violence case in which there is probable cause that a crime involving physical injury, assault, or threat resulting in fear of violence was committed (Conn. Gen. Stat., § 46b–38a[2]). Although responding patrol officers retain some discretion in deciding what crime to charge, they may not dispose of a case by informal noncriminal processes if there is reason to believe that IPV did take place. Officers have no authority to decline prosecution based on a victim's request or their own belief that the family would be better served by intervention outside the criminal justice system. Police are discouraged from arresting both parties to a domestic dispute, but dual arrests are sometimes required by the mandatory arrest statute (Conn. Gen. Stat., § 46b–38b[b]; Davies, Eppler-Epstein, & Walsh-Hart, 2004).

This study also took place in the context of the New Haven Police Department's commitment to a philosophy of community-based policing. Unlike traditional, 911-driven policing approaches, which rely on rapid police response by officers who do not necessarily have any previous or continuing relationship with the community in which the event occurred, community policing emphasizes crime prevention and problem-solving efforts by officers who are familiar with the neighborhoods where they are commonly assigned. Officers develop ongoing alliances with community residents, groups, and institutions through actions such as walking beats and school-based activities (Fridell, 2002a; Geller, 1991; Goldstein, 1990). Studies indicate that this mode of policing increases public comfort and willingness to call the police (Fridell, 2002b). In community policing settings, officers who respond to acute IPV calls are more likely to be familiar to the parties, either from prior calls for domestic disputes or from other neighborhood contacts. In addition, officers' conception of their role as problem solvers may generate more comprehensive efforts to understand and address complex patterns of violence rather than isolated incidents (see, e.g., Anderson & Herman, 2002; Fremont Police Department, 1997; Police Executive Research Forum, 2003).

The Domestic Violence Home Visit Intervention (DVHVI) was developed in 2000, with support of the U.S. Justice Department Office on Violence Against Women, by a closely collaborating team of police supervisors, mental health clinicians, and advocates, as an enhancement of police service to IPV victims and their families in New Haven. The project grew out of the larger Child Development-Community Policing Program, which is a partnership between the New Haven Department of Police Service and the Yale Child Study Center (Marans, Adnopoz, & Berkman et al., 1995; Marans, Berkowitz, & Cohen, 1998; Marans & Cohen, 1993; Marans, Murphy, & Berkowitz, 2002). The cornerstone of the DVHVI is a neighborhood-based home visit follow-up project staffed by teams of patrol officers and clinically informed domestic violence advocates. Unlike first-responding officers, who come to a family's home at a moment of acute crisis with a mandate to investigate and arrest, officers involved in the DVHVI project return to the home after the crisis for the purpose of monitoring and addressing continuing safety concerns and providing the family with information, liaison to community resources, and assistance in dealing with some of the underlying problems that led to the violent incident. The DVHVI was intended to bring together police officers, who have essential knowledge of available criminal justice remedies and the communities where victims live, with advocates and mental health clinicians, who have additional expertise and resources for addressing legal, practical, and psychological issues that may undermine the safety of the family.

Description of the Intervention Program

Detectives in the Police Department's Domestic Violence Unit identify households where an intimate partner assault has been reported. These cases are then reviewed by the DVHVI clinical team, which includes domestic violence advocates and licensed clinical social workers. Following this review, cases are assigned to police-advocate teams to receive the DVHVI. Home visits take place as soon as possible after the violent event, usually within 72 hr of the reported incident. Visits are conducted during early evening hours when families are most likely to be home. Police officers participating in the project are community-based patrol officers regularly assigned to the neighborhood where the follow-up visits are taking place and are familiar with neighborhood issues, resources, and many local residents. They have received specialized training in the effects of violence exposure on children and child development. Officers are paired with advocates, who are trained in basic domestic violence issues, crisis intervention, and child development principles and familiar with local domestic violence law, criminal justice processes, and social service resources, and who are clinically supervised by Child Study Center faculty members. Follow-up home visits are intended to monitor victim safety, improve victims' understanding and enforcement of court orders, increase access to information and basic services (e.g., 911 phone, shelters, food assistance), and provide psychological screening, acute psychological support, and access to treatment for victims and their children (see Table 19.1). The DVHVI focuses attention on children's experiences and needs with the goal of engaging mothers who might decline assistance for themselves.

Table 19.1   Description of DVHVI Service Types

DVHVI Service Variable	Description of Services Included
Safety	Development of a safety plan, 911 emergency phone provided, shelter or alternative housing information
Police	Expedited warrant, arrest of perpetrator at the time of visit due to outstanding warrant or violation of a protective order
Legal	Explanation of a protective order, help with a temporary restraining order, court advocacy
Psychoeducation	Educational materials and/or discussion of the impact of domestic violence for victims and their children
Crisis mental health	Adult mental health screening, child mental health screening, crisis intervention
Follow-up	Additional home visit or appointment with advocate provided after the initial outreach visit

NOTE: DVHVI = Domestic Violence Home Visit Intervention.

Officers introduce the visits as a police activity based on the department's commitment to furthering the safety of battered women and the well-being of their children. Advocates maintain a log documenting the specific services provided at every visit and the amount of time spent. As noted above, the DVHVI builds on community policing practice. The model increases officers' personal attention to the safety needs of IPV victims, which makes it consistent with current efforts to improve coordination of criminal justice responses to domestic violence (Shepard & Pence, 1999). The DVHVI also builds on client-directed, comprehensive community-based advocacy models that have demonstrated increases in battered women's safety and well-being (Bybee & Sullivan 2005; Sullivan, Bybee, & Allen, 2002). The collaborative strategy is in keeping with other current approaches to IPV intervention, which seek to increase safety for women and children by coordinating the efforts of multiple service systems that traditionally operate independently and potentially at cross purposes (Allen, Bybee, & Sullivan, 2004; Gwinn & Strack, 2006; Lecklitner, Malik, Aaron, & Lederman, 1999). The DVHVI model is unique in the degree to which it integrates police intervention with battered women's advocacy and a focus on children. Because the DVHVI encompasses both enhanced law enforcement and outreach advocacy, it is important to examine the available research on IPV victims' use and feelings about police and social service interventions in cases of domestic violence to help understand possible factors related to victims' engagement in the intervention.

Factors Related to the Use of Police Services and Satisfaction With the Police

Previous research has examined the impact of demographic and situational variables on battered women's use of the criminal justice system, including police, to end violence in their relationships. Demographic variables, including race, ethnicity, socioeconomic status, age, and marital status have been investigated, as have situational variables, such as severity of the current violent incident, history of previous violence, history of prior police contact, the victim's desires regarding the criminal justice outcome, economic dependence of victim on perpetrator, and substance abuse by either party. There is significant variation in the findings of these studies with regard to demographic variables; however, multiple studies report that African American women are more likely than Caucasian women to seek help from police (Bachman & Coker, 1995; Hutchison, 2003; Lipsky, Caetano, Field, & Larkin, 2006). Lipsky et al. (2006) found no difference in police use between Hispanic and Caucasian women, though others have found higher and lower rates of police calls among other Hispanic samples. Some studies find higher rates of police use among women living in poverty (Hutchison, 2003), whereas others find women's employment to be associated with increased intention to seek help from police (Fleury-Steiner, Bybee, Sullivan, Belknap, & Melton, 2006). Situational factors, including severity of abuse, use of weapons, and substance abuse by the offender, have been more consistently associated with police use (Fleury-Steiner et al., 2006; Hutchison, 2003).

Studies of general community attitudes have consistently shown that minority groups are less trusting of and feel unfairly treated by the police (Garafolo, 1977; Huang & Vaughn, 1996; Tyler & Huo, 2002). Studies of IPV populations have yielded more varied results. For example, Yegidis and Berman Renzy (1994) found that female victims of IPV from a shelter sample had positive reactions to the police, except African American participants, who all rated the police as unhelpful. In contrast, Apsler, Cummins, and Carl (2003) found no relationship between ethnic background and helpfulness ratings of the police in a community sample of IPV victims. Instead,

they found that age had a curvilinear relationship with respect to satisfaction ratings. Youngest and oldest IPV victims were the most satisfied with police interventions. Other studies from community samples found a wide variation in responses to police, ranging from mostly negative (Erez & Belknap, 1998) to very positive (Martin, 1997). A study by Wiist and McFarlane (1998), in which they interviewed a monolingual Spanish-speaking sample, found more than half of the women reporting that the police were effective in reducing the violence in their relationships.

These studies also found a correlation between positive ratings and receiving helpful services. Apsler et al. (2003) found that women were more satisfied with police if they felt the officers listened to their wishes at the time of the incident either in terms of arrest of the perpetrator or provision of other services. Women in this sample were the least satisfied if they did not want help obtaining counseling by police and were given this help anyhow, whereas women who wanted and received help with counseling gave the police the highest possible rating. Similarly, a recent investigation of women's intention to recontact the police for help in the event of repeat violence found that women were more likely to call the police again if their previous experiences with police and prosecution had been positive (e.g., if they received requested information from police, if they did not feel pressured, and if the outcome of the case was consistent with their wishes; Fleury-Steiner et al., 2006).

Factors Associated With Engagement in Social Services and Treatment

Researchers have also examined factors associated with IPV victims' engagement in a variety of social, physical, and mental health interventions. In general service use studies, Hispanic and Asian families have been found less likely to engage in mental health services than African American or Caucasian families (Sue, Zane, & Young, 1994), and African American clients are more likely to drop out of treatment prematurely (Sue, 1991). Other studies have found that African Americans are less likely than Caucasians to turn to traditional and specialized mental health services for personal problems (Alvidrez, 1999; Cooper-Patric et al., 1999; Ford & Cooper, 1995; Neighbors, 1988), and they are more likely to be dissatisfied and less likely to use services in the future, even when controlling for other demographic factors such as gender and socioeconomic status (Diala et al., 2000).

In specific studies of IPV victims' use of services, race and ethnicity remain significant factors. El-Khoury et al. (2004) found that African American women were much less likely to use mental health services than Caucasians to deal with IPV and instead were more likely to use prayer, regardless of the severity of the IPV experienced. A recent study by Lipsky et al. (2006) found that Hispanic IPV victims were significantly less likely to use health care and social services than African American or Caucasian victims. Other studies have found the severity of violence experienced by women and the status of their relationship with their abusive partner to be the two strongest predictors of service usage by battered women. A higher severity of violence leads to increased help seeking, whereas a continued relationship with the partner leads to a decrease in service usage (Dutton, Goodman, & Bennett, 1999).

Understanding the factors that are associated with IPV victims' use of and satisfaction with police and social services offered to them is important to aid in the cost-effective use of resources. The DVHVI program that is the focus of this study received referrals for all domestic violence incidents in five participating police districts in New Haven, CT. Police-advocate teams attempted home visits for each referral, making multiple visits to the same residence if they did not find women at home. Determining demographic and incident-specific information

that may lead to use of services offered can allow for modification of the intervention to better serve the community. A clinical record review was undertaken to determine if any information provided in referral police reports or by clinical advocates in their service logs was associated with engagement in the DVHVI services.

Method

Participants and Case Selection

The data for the present study were gathered from police reports and intervention records related by DVHVI advocates. A sample of 406 domestic violence cases that were referred for the DVHVI program were available for analysis, representing all reported cases from five police districts participating in the DVHVI program in New Haven, CT, during an 18-month period (beginning January 1, 2004, and ending July 30, 2005). Although the intervention originated in 2000, January of 2004 marked the onset of standardized clinical data collection, resulting in the availability of systematic intervention data. To meet study criteria, a case needed to include a victim being referred to the DVHVI for the first time within the 18-month sampling period. This required the exclusion of all cases with prior contact (i.e., any victim contact with the intervention team before January of 2004 or any victims with repeat cases within the data set). Accurate collection of case recidivism was not possible because police report data were provided for only 5 of the 10 police districts in New Haven for a population that is largely transitory (e.g., moving in and out of police districts). Consequently, because the intervention was conducted in only half of the city's districts, the research team had no way of tracking incidents that occurred outside of the intervention districts, generating unrepresentative repeat cases. In addition, 12 cases were removed because the perpetrator was never charged with a crime. This resulted in exclusion of 82 reported incidents; frequencies revealed that only 5 cases involved victims of Asian ethnicity; 3 cases involved same-sex partners; and 15 cases involved male victims. Therefore, these cases were excluded, making the sample heterosexual intimate partners with female victims only. Lastly, insufficient information resulted in the elimination of 1 case. In addition to accounts of the various services provided to the victim, the final sample ($N = 301$ cases) included descriptive information on the perpetrator, the victim, and the IPV incident gleaned from police reports.

Sample Demographics

The demographic characteristics of the sample are presented in Table 19.2. In accordance with the ethnic makeup of the intervention districts, the vast majority of individuals in this sample were of African American (56.5%) or Hispanic (35.2%) descent. The ages of the victims ranged from 16 to 58 ($M = 29.74$, $SD = 7.56$), with perpetrator ages ranging from 17 to 75 ($M = 31.86$, $SD = 8.68$). The number of children present at the time of the domestic incident ranged from zero to four ($M = 0.84$, $SD = 0.41$).

Procedures

Measurement. Police-reported criminal charges were initially coded into four distinct categories based on type of crime: property crimes, personal crimes, child-related crimes, and police interference (see Table 19.3). Each of these variables was coded according to the severity of the crime (based on the crime definitions and penalty scale contained in the Connecticut criminal statutes (Conn. Gen. Stat., tit. 53a). Police in the

Table 19.2   Demographics of Study Sample

Variable	Victims Referred (n = 301)	Victims With DVHVI Team Contact (n = 204)
Ethnicity		
African American	147 (48.8%)	88 (43.1%)
Caucasian	31 (10.3%)	24 (11.8%)
Hispanic	123 (40.9%)	92 (45.1)
Relationship status		
Married or living together	144 (47.8%)	97 (47.5%)
Dating or ex-partners	157 (52.2%)	107 (52.5%)
Injured at incident	137 (45/5%)	94 (46.1%)
Substance abuse at incident	118 (39.2%)	82 (40.2%)
Weapon used at incident	46 (15.3%)	31 (15.2%)
Limited English proficiency	31 (10.3%)	24 (11.8%)

NOTE: DVHVI = Domestic Violence Home Visit Intervention.

intervention districts reported few incidents of property crimes, child-related crimes, or police interference (21.3%, 19.1%, and 13.5% of the cases, respectively, had charges in these categories). The most common property crime fell under the "criminal mischief (1st and 2nd degree) [i.e., vandalism] and/or trespassing" grouping ($n = 54$, or 16.2%), whereas "custodial interference and/or risk of injury to a minor" was the most frequently reported child-related grouping ($n = 63$, or 18.9%). Under the police interference variable, reports were nearly split between the "interference with 911 and/or interference with an officer" grouping ($n = 18$, or 5.4%), and the "violation of a protective or restraining order" grouping ($n = 27$, or 8.1%). As for personal crimes, police reported 137 (41.1%) instances of charges for disorderly conduct, breach of peace, or harassment 2nd degree; and 93 (27.9%) instances of assault 3rd degree (i.e., without weapon or serious injury), unlawful restraint 1st degree, stalking 1st degree, harassment 1st degree, or threatening 1st degree.

To provide a continuous variable to describe the severity of charges, the scores for each of the four charge categories were summed to create a total incident severity composite score. The numerical values were assigned according to the severity of charges in each category (see Table 19.3) and then summed. For example, if the perpetrator was charged with criminal mischief 1st degree, breach of peace, and interference with an officer the total severity score for that case would equal 4, on a scale of 1 to 12 (12 being the most severe). Furthermore, if the perpetrator had more than one charge under any category, only the highest level of crime was coded; no case had more than one charge under the same level of severity (e.g., burglary 1st degree and arson 1st degree). Nearly half of the sample cases (42.2%) had severity scores of 1 or 2, indicating a low level of severity and lack of physical violence.

Ethnicity of victims, advocates, and officers was of particular interest. Therefore, cases were coded for ethnic match between advocate and victim, and officer and victim. The DVHVI

teams include one Caucasian advocate and one Hispanic (Spanish-speaking) advocate. Sixty-three cases contained a Hispanic-Hispanic ethnic match and 11 cases included a Caucasian-Caucasian match. Of the 45 Hispanic ethnic match cases, 24 of the victims spoke limited English. Seventy-nine victims' ethnicities matched those of the assigned DVHVI police officer. Of those, 20 were African American, 55 were Hispanic, and only 4 were Caucasian officer-victim matches. Ethnic match variables were collapsed into dichotomies to provide sufficient numbers of ethnic match cases for analyses.

Description of hypothesis variables and analysis plan. The goal of this study was to determine which demographic and incident variables may predict engagement in the DVHVI services. Outcome variables of interest include whether the team is able to make contact with the victim, amount of time spent with the victim, and number and type of DVHVI service components provided (see Table 19.1).

Given the large number of possible demographic and IPV incident-related factors that might have been used as independent or predictor variables, preliminary chi-square and t tests were conducted to determine bivariate differences in victims with DVHVI team contact and those without on the independent variables of interest. These variables included victim age, ethnicity, relationship with the perpetrator (married vs. unmarried), victim's number of children, severity of charges, whether the victim sustained any injuries at the time of the incident (binary variable), use of a weapon at the time of the incident (binary), and substance abuse at the time of the incident (binary variable that may include use of alcohol, drugs, or both by either party at the time of the incident). Variables that were found to be significantly different between the DVHVI contact groups or were thought to be important variables based on existing literature (e.g., severity of the IPV incident) were then entered into a binomial logistic regression using the entire sample of 301 cases to determine

Table 19.3 Scoring Criteria for Criminal Charges

Score	Property Crimes	Personal Crimes	Child-Related Crimes	Police Interference
0	No charges	No charges	No charges	No charges
1	Criminal mischief 2/3, trespassing	Disorderly conduct, breach of peace, harassment 2	Custodial interference 2	Interference with 911 or officer's duties
2	Criminal mischief 1, burglary 2/3, or arson	Threatening 2, stalking 2/3	Custodial interference 1, risk of injury to a minor	Violation of protective or restraining order
3	Burglary 1, arson 1	Reckless endangerment, unlawful restraint 2	NA	NA
4	NA	Assault 3, unlawful restraint 1, stalking 1, or threatening 1	NA	NA
5	NA	Assault 1 or 2, sexual assault, rape, kidnapping	NA	NA

NOTE: Charge severity was categorized with reference to the definitions contained in the Connecticut criminal code (Conn. Gen. Stat., tit. 53a). Connecticut statutes list some crimes that may occur in several degrees, e.g., assault. For these crimes, the lowest degree refers to the most severe crime (e.g., Assault 1). Charges coded in the current study were those initially charged by police at the time of the incident and not as subsequently modified by prosecutor or court.

which demographic and IPV incident variables predicted whether DVHVI teams were able to make contact with victims.

Next, multivariate multiple regression analyses were used to examine the subset of cases with victim contact ($n = 204$). Demographic (ethnicity, English language proficiency, and number of children), team (victim-advocate and victim-officer ethnic match), and incident predictor variables (severity of charges) were entered into the equation to assess their relationship to the DVHVI service criterion variables of (a) total time spent with the victim and (b) total number of different types of services provided by the DVHVI team (as described in Table 19.1).

Lastly, a subsequent multivariate multiple regression was used to look at factors that may have predicted engagement in those components of the DVHVI that were used the least frequently.

Results

Descriptive Information on the DVHVI Services Provided to the Sample

According to the advocates' accounts, 67.8% ($n = 204$) of the referred cases were contacted at least once by a DVHVI team. The intervention teams were unable to make contact with the remaining 32.2% ($n = 97$) of the cases, despite repeated attempts. Of those cases that received team contact, the mean time spent on the case was 35 min (see Table 19.4); however, the range of time spent on the cases was quite variable. DVHVI

teams reported providing the following services to victims at the time of the home visit (see Table 19.1 for descriptions): safety planning (95.6%), legal information and assistance (93.6%), psycho-education (91.7%), crisis mental health services (44.6%), and police services (17.2%).

Table 19.4 Descriptive Statistics of Hypothesis Variables for Cases With Team Contact ($n = 204$)

Variable	M	Mdn	SD	Minimum	Maximum
Total minutes spent with victim	35.06	25	39.69	0	280
Severity of charges	3.20	3	1.94	1	11
DVHVI services provided	8.02	8	2.90	1	19
DVHVI follow-up services	0.95	0	1.40	0	7

NOTE: DVHVI = Domestic Violence Home Visit Intervention.

Table 19.5 Chi-Square and t Test to Compare DVHVI Contact vs. Noncontact Cases ($n < 301$)

Variable	df	χ^2	t	p
Relationship status	1	0.02	–	.88
Hispanic ethnicity	1	4.70*	–	.03
Substance abuse	1	0.26	–	.61
Weapon use at incident	1	0.00	–	.96
Limited English proficiency	1	1.47	–	.23
Injury (yes/no)	1	0.00	–	.96
No. of children	296	–	1.97*	.05
No. of injuries	299	–	−0.56	.58
Severity of charges	299	–	−0.088	.93
Victim age	299	–	−0.916	.36

NOTE: DVHVI = Domestic Violence Home Visit Intervention. Empty cells with dashes indicate NA.

*$p < .05$.

Factors Associated With DVHVI Teams Making Initial Contact With Victims

Preliminary chi-square and t tests revealed significant differences between women who received the intervention and those who did not with respect to Hispanic ethnicity and number of children (see Table 19.5). These variables were used as predictors in subsequent logistical regression modeling in addition to substance abuse and injuries at the time of the incident.

No incident variables (victim injuries or substance abuse at the time of the incident) were significantly associated with victim contact. However, Hispanic ethnicity of the victim ($b = -.556$, $p = .036$) and number of victim's children ($b = .226$, $p = .07$) were associated with DVHVI team contact at the initial visit (see Table 19.6).

Factors Associated With Engagement in DVHVI Service Following Team Contact

Multivariate multiple regression analyses were computed to determine the predictive value of ethnicity, English proficiency, victim-advocate ethnic match, victim-officer ethnic match, severity of charges, substance abuse, and number of children on the "bundle" of outcome variables (time spent with victim and number of DVHVI services provided). Victim-advocate ethnic match (Pillias's trace = .040, $p = .02$) and total number of children (Pillias's trace = .038, $p = .027$) significantly predicted the outcome variables. Severity of charges also showed a trend in prediction (Pillias's trace = .027, $p = .079$). The model accounted for 7.4% of the variance in home visit services provided and 11.5% of the variance in total time spent with the victim. When looking at between-subjects effects, advocate-victim ethnic match and severity of charges were significant predictors of the amount of time spent with the victim, $F(1, 197) = 7.68$, $p = .006$, and $F(1, 197) = 5.16$, $p = .024$, respectively, whereas total number of children was the only significant predictor of the number of home visit services provided, $F(1, 197) = 5.91$, $p = .016$. Advocate-victim ethnic match showed a trend in predicting total number of services provided (see Table 19.6). Hispanic women who were served by the Hispanic advocate received the most time on the case and were provided with a broader range of services than those who did not have an advocate-victim ethnic match.

Table 19.6   Logistic Regression for DVHVI Team Contact ($n < 310$)

Predictors	B	SE B	p
Hispanic ethnicity	−0.56*	0.25	.04
No. of children	0.23†	0.13	.08
Victim injuries	0.03	0.26	.91
Substance abuse	−0.04	0.26	.88
Age	0.00	0.02	.91

NOTE: DVHVI = Domestic Violence Home Visit Intervention.

*$p < .05$. †$p < .10$.

Factors Associated With Service Components and Follow-Up

As described above, police and crisis mental health services were provided to a limited number of participants, with 48% of victims receiving any follow-up after the initial DVHVI visit. Only 21% of victims received a follow-up home visit from the team and 7% scheduled a future appointment with the advocate alone. Other follow-up services included phone check-in, DVHVI team contact with court-based advocacy, or other service providers for the victim. To help understand which cases received less frequent service components, a multivariate multiple regression was used entering the same variables described previously as predictors and using police services, crisis mental health services, and total follow-up services as criterion variables. Results revealed an overall effect for severity of charges (Pillias's trace = .40, $p = .05$) and advocate-victim ethnic match (Pillias's trace = .70, $p = .003$) on the set of criterion variables. Between-subjects analyses revealed that police-victim ethnic match predicted follow-up services, whereas advocate-victim ethnic match resulted in less crisis mental health services and more police services (see Table 19.7).

Table 19.7   Multivariate Multiple Regression: Factors Associated With Time Spent on Case and Number of Services Provided ($n < 204$)

Variable	df	F	p
Total DVHVI service components provided			
Substance abuse	1	0.96	.33
Police-victim ethnic match	1	0.14	.71
Advocate-victim ethnic match	1	2.71	.11
Hispanic ethnicity	1	0.11	.74
Limited English proficiency	1	0.95	.33
Severity	1	1.49	.22
No. of children	1	7.09**	.009
Error		189	(8.06)
Total time spent with victim			
Substance abuse	1	0.00	.98
Police-victim ethnic match	1	0.13	.72
Advocate-victim ethnic match	1	7.91**	.005
Hispanic ethnicity	1	0.09	.76
Limited English proficiency	1	0.58	.45
Severity	1	5.16*	.02
No. of children	1	0.72	.40
Error		190	(1,445.96)

NOTE: DVHVI = Domestic Violence Home Visit Intervention.

$^*p < .05.$ $^{**}p < .01.$

Lastly, to better understand factors related to whether victims received a follow-up home visit from the DVHVI team, a binary logistic regression was computed. Number of children ($b = .320$, $p = .03$) significantly predicted a follow-up visit, with a trend for severity of charges ($b = .169$, $p = .07$). No other demographic or case-related variables were associated with a follow-up team visit (see Table 19.8).

Table 19.8 Factors Associated With Police and Crisis Mental Health and Follow-Up Services ($n < 204$)

Variable	df	F	p
DVHVI police services			
Substance abuse	1	0.11	.50
Police-victim ethnic match	1	0.00	.97
Advocate-victim ethnic match	1	3.79*	.05
Hispanic ethnicity	1	0.12	.73
Severity	1	0.00	.96
Limited English proficiency	1	0.14	.71
No. of children	1	0.22	.64
Error		189	(.246)
DVHVI crisis mental health services			
Substance abuse	1	0.20	.66
Police-victim ethnic match	1	0.18	.72
Advocate-victim ethnic match	1	10.10**	.002
Hispanic ethnicity	1	3.06†	.08
Severity	1	3.78†	.07
Limited English proficiency	1	4.91†	.07
No. of children	1	0.96	.32
Error		189	(1.472)
DVHVI follow-up services			
Substance abuse	1	0.06	.81
Police-victim ethnic match	1	0.3.38†	.07
Advocate-victim ethnic match	1	1.73	.20

(Continued)

(Continued)

Variable	df	F	p
Hispanic ethnicity	1	0.46	.50
Severity	1	4.17*	.04
Limited English proficiency	1	0.04	.88
No. of children	1	0.93	.34
Error		189	(1.742)

NOTE: DVHVI = Domestic Violence Home Visit Intervention.

*$p < .05$. **$p < .01$. †$p < .10$.

Discussion

The variables related to service engagement in this sample of IPV cases referred to the DVHVI program at the Yale University Child Study Center were ethnicity (of the victim, advocate, and officer), severity of IPV charges, and number of children. Surprisingly, the use of weapons, injuries sustained, and substance use at the time of the incident were all unrelated to whether victims chose to use services offered by the DVHVI teams. Ethnicity had the strongest relationship to service engagement, with an ethnic match between the victim and advocate accounting for the most significant variance in time spent with victim. Ethnic match with the police officer was nonsignificant for time with victim but was associated with increased follow-up services. Hispanic women who were served by a Hispanic, Spanish-speaking advocate were most engaged with the advocate. This seems likely because of language barriers. A Spanish-speaking advocate may have been able to provide clarity to a victim about her rights, and gained further information about the severity of the incident and the woman's feeling of safety beyond what might have been gathered at the time of the incident from police officers alone, who may have had limited Spanish-language proficiency or ability to communicate with the victim. This is consistent with other studies that have found that non-English-speaking women have felt disadvantaged when attempting to communicate their experiences to the police (Wolf, Ly, Hobart, & Kernic, 2003). Spanish-speaking victims may also have had greater need for the advocate's help in multiple domains as language barriers impinged on their ability to access needed resources for their families.

It was surprising that there was not a significant statistical difference in the amount of time spent on cases involving Hispanic women of limited English proficiency and those Hispanic women identified as English-speaking. It may be that Hispanic women in general used the services of the Hispanic advocate and officer teams because they were more comfortable speaking their native language and they felt that the advocate could help address the cultural and institutional barriers they face in dealing with the criminal justice system and other service providers.

Given that this study did not include examination of African American women who were served by an African American advocate, it is impossible to determine if this finding would hold for ethnic match for other groups. This would be a valuable addition to the study given that previous studies have found African American women dissatisfied with both police and mental health services. Ethnic match and Spanish language proficiency for advocate-officer teams were important factors for Hispanic Spanish-speaking women. This is an important finding given that Hispanic women, especially those with low acculturation, have been found to have the lowest use of health care and social services following an incident of IPV—lower than African American and Caucasian women (Lipsky et al., 2006). Improving engagement in services and outcomes for Hispanic women may be one of the most important outcomes of the DVHVI intervention.

Although it was not possible to examine an ethnic match for the victim and advocate for African American women, the ethnic match of the officer and victim was analyzed. This match did not improve engagement for African American women. This may be related to other studies' findings that African American IPV victims have negative feelings toward the police (Yegidis & Berman Renzy, 1994) or that African Americans are less trusting of police in general (Garafolo, 1977; Huang & Vaughn, 1996; Tyler & Huo, 2002). The finding may also be related to the fact that advocates and not officers provided most DVHVI services following initial introductions and safety screening. Therefore, client engagement was determined more by women's comfort with the advocate than by their affinity for the officer.

Substance use and injuries sustained by the victim were unrelated to service engagement. Given that more severe cases are likely to repeat (Babcock & Steiner, 1999; Hilton et al., 2004; Shepard, Falk, & Elliot, 2002), increased time spent on these cases would be appropriate. Yet these victims were not more likely to engage in DVHVI services. These findings along with a lack of association between relationship status and engagement in services were consistent with an earlier study by Apsler et al. (2003). It is important to note that this sample contained a large number of minor cases of IPV. Forty-three percent of the cases had severity scores of 2 or below, indicating that they were minor arguments without injuries, property damage, or involving

children. This skewed sample may not provide enough variability in severity to truly understand the impact of case severity or injuries on service engagement.

The percentage of women who wanted follow-up services from the team was low (29%). This was even lower than the 38% of victims in other studies who reported wanting help with counseling following an IPV incident (Apsler et al., 2003; Crowell & Burgess, 1996). The reasons for this are unclear. A possible explanation for the low number of women who requested a follow-up is that because of the low severity of most cases, few women were in need of advocacy beyond the initial visit. In addition, because the DVHVI uses outreach visits to offer services to women who have not identified themselves as in need of help, a lower rate of service acceptance can be expected.

Limitations

This study relied solely on the DVHVI team and police records for data. Women were not directly interviewed. This reliance on clinical and police reports does not allow for a direct understanding from victims about the reasons for engagement in the DVHVI. Relying on police reports to provide information such as number of children, substance abuse, and injuries is also limited given that the information available may be inadequate or victims and/or perpetrators may provide false information to police at the time of the incident. Owing to the nature of data collection after provision of the DVHVI service, it was not possible to control for ethnic match or other service variables. Future studies could include ethnic match of officers and advocates for a broader range of victims.

Future Directions

This article is the first in a series that will evaluate the DVHVI. The next step in understanding the significance of the DVHVI will require interviewing women directly about their experiences with the DVHVI teams; this process is currently under way. This will provide valuable information about women's interpretations of the intervention and what aspects they find helpful, in addition to what other services are offered or provided to them via other avenues. It will also provide an opportunity to build on previous studies, which demonstrate that battered women's decisions regarding where and when to seek help are complex ones, informed by many variables, including such subjective factors as previous experiences being listened to and heard, feeling comfortable, and receiving the help they need.

Overall, the current study suggests that interventions targeting IPV victims must bear in mind the ethnicity and language proficiency of the victims in the community they are serving when considering staffing and implementation of interventions. This intervention model, when provided by Spanish-speaking advocate-officer teams, seems to be beneficial to Hispanic, Spanish-speaking women and should be considered for implementation in these communities.

References

Allen, N., Bybee, D. I., & Sullivan, C. M. (2004). Battered women's multitude of needs: Evidence supporting the need for comprehensive advocacy. *Violence Against Women, 10,* 1015–1035.

Alvidrez, J. (1999). Ethnic variations in mental health attitudes and service use among low income African American, Latina, and European American young women. *Community Mental Health Journal, 35,* 515–530.

Anderson, D., & Herman, S. (2002). First response to domestic violence. In *Bringing victims into community policing: A police guide to initial response* (pp. 35–50). Washington, DC: United States Department of Justice, COPS Office.

Apsler, R., Cummins, M. R., & Carl, S. (2003). Perceptions of the police by female victims of domestic partner violence. *Violence Against Women, 9,* 1318–1335.

Babcock, J. C., & Steiner, R. (1999). The relationship between treatment, incarceration, and recidivism of battering: A program evaluation of Seattle's coordinated community response to domestic violence. *Journal of Family Psychology, 13,* 46–59.

Bachman, R., & Coker, A. L. (1995). Police involvement in domestic violence: The interactive effects of victim injury, offender's history and race. *Violence and Victims, 10,* 91–106.

Bachman, R., & Saltzman, L. E. (1995). *Violence against women: Estimates of the redesigned survey.* Washington, DC: U.S. Department of Justice, Office of Justice Programs.

Bybee, D., & Sullivan, C. M. (2005). Predicting re-victimization of battered women 3 years after exiting a shelter program. *American Journal of Community Psychology, 36,* 85–96.

Carlson, B. E. (2000). Children exposed to intimate partner violence: Research findings and implications for intervention. *Trauma, Violence and Abuse, 1,* 321–342.

Centers for Disease Control and Prevention. (2003). *Costs of intimate partner violence against women in the United States: Executive summary.* Atlanta, GA: Author.

Connecticut General Statutes, §§ 46b–38a(2)–38b(b); title 53a (2006).

Cooper-Patrick, L., Gallo, J., Powe, N., Steinwachs, D., Eaton, W., & Ford, D. (1999). Mental health service utilization by African Americans and Whites: The Baltimore epidemiologic catchment area follow-up. *Medical Care, 37,* 1034–1045.

Crowell, N. A., & Burgess, A. W. (Eds.). (1996). *Understanding violence against women.* Washington, DC: National Academy Press.

Davies, J. M., Eppler-Epstein, S. D., & Walsh-Hart, K. (2004). *A guide to Connecticut's family violence laws* (4th ed.). Hartford: Connecticut Coalition Against Domestic Violence, Inc.

Diala, C., Muntaner, C., Walrath, C., Nickerson, K., LaVeist, T., & Leaf, P. (2000). Racial differences in attitudes toward professional mental health care and in the use of services. *American Journal of Orthopsychiatry, 70,* 455–464.

Dutton, M. A., Goodman, L. A., & Bennett, L. (1999). Court-involved battered women's responses to violence: The role of psychological, physical, and sexual abuse. *Violence and Victims, 14,* 89–104.

Edleson, J. L. (1999). Children's witnessing of adult domestic violence. *Journal of Interpersonal Violence, 14,* 839–870.

El-Khoury, M., Dutton, M. A., Goodman, L. A., Engel, L., Belamaric, R., & Murphy, M. (2004). Ethnic differences in battered women's formal help-seeking strategies: A focus on health, mental health, and spirituality. *Cultural Diversity and Ethnic Minority Psychology, 10,* 383–393.

Erez, E., & Belknap, J. (1998). In their own words: Battered women's assessment of the criminal processing system's responses. *Violence and Victims, 13,* 251–268.

Fleury-Steiner, R., Bybee, D., Sullivan, D., Belknap, R., & Melton, H. (2006). Contextual factors impacting battered women's intentions to reuse the criminal legal system. *Journal of Community Psychology, 34,* 327–342.

Ford, E., & Cooper, R. (1995). Implications of race/ethnicity for health and health care use. *Health Services Research, 30,* 237–252.

Fremont Police Department. (1997). *Domestic violence revictimization prevention: Improving police response to repeat calls of domestic violence.* Problem Oriented Policing Library. Retrieved October 13, 2008, from http://www.popcenter.org/library/awards/goldstein/1997/97-17(F)

Fridell, L. (2002a). The defining characteristics of community policing. In L. Fridell & M. A. Wycoff (Eds.), *Community policing: The past, present and future* (pp. 3–12). Washington, DC: Annie E. Casey Foundation and Police Executive Research Forum.

Fridell, L. (2002b). The results of three national surveys on community policing. In L. Fridell & M. A. Wycoff (Eds.), *Community policing: The past, present and future* (pp. 39–48). Washington, DC: Annie E. Casey Foundation and Police Executive Research Forum.

Fugate, M., Landis, L., Riordan, K., Naurekas, S., & Engel, B. (2005). Barriers to domestic violence help seeking. *Violence Against Women, 11,* 290–310.

Garafolo, J. (1977). *Public opinion about crime: The attitudes of victims and nonvictims in selected cities.* Washington, DC: Government Printing Office.

Geller, W. (Ed.). (1991). *Local government police management.* Washington, DC: International City/County Management Association.

Goldstein, H. (1990). *Problem-oriented policing.* Philadelphia: Temple University Press.

Graham-Bermann, S. A., & Edleson, J. L. (Eds.). (2001). *Domestic violence in the lives of children: The future of research, intervention, and social policy.* Washington, DC: American Psychological Association.

Graham-Berman, S. A., & Levendosky, A. A. (1998). Traumatic stress symptoms in children of battered women. *Journal of Interpersonal Violence, 13,* 111–128.

Gwinn, C., & Strack, G. (2006). *Hope for hurting families: Creating family justice centers across America.* Volcano, CA: Volcano Press.

Hilton, Z. N., Harris, G. T., Rice, M. E., Lang, C., Cormier, C., & Lines, K. (2004). A brief actuarial assessment for prediction of wife assault recidivism: The Ontario Domestic Assault Risk Assessment. *Psychological Assessment, 16,* 267–275.

Huang, W. S. W., & Vaughn, M. S. (1996). Support and confidence: Public attitudes toward police. In D. J. Flanagan & D. R. Longmire (Eds.), *Americans view crime and justice: A national public opinion survey* (pp. 31–45). Thousand Oaks, CA: Sage.

Hutchison, I. W. (2003). Substance use and abused women's utilization of the police. *Journal of Family Violence, 18,* 93–106.

Kolbo, J. R. (1996). Risk and resilience among children exposed to family violence. *Violence and Victims, 11,* 113–128.

Lecklitner, G. L., Malik, N. M, Aaron, S. M., & Lederman, C. S. (1999). Promoting safety for abused children and battered mothers: Miami-Dade county's model dependency court intervention program. *Child Maltreatment, 4,* 175–82.

Lipsky, S., Caetano, R., Field, C., & Larkin, G. (2006). The role of intimate partner violence, race and ethnicity in help-seeking behaviors. *Ethnicity and Health, 11,* 81–100.

Marans, S., Adnopoz, J., & Berkman, M., Esserman, D., MacDonald, D., Nagler, S., et al. (1995). *The police-mental health partnership: A community-based response to urban violence.* New Haven, CT: Yale University Press.

Marans, S., Berkowitz, S. J., & Cohen, D. J. (1998). Police and mental health professionals: Collaborative responses to the impact of violence on children and families. *Child and Adolescent Psychiatric Clinicians of North America, 7,* 635–651.

Marans, S., & Cohen, D. (1993). Children and inner-city violence: Strategies for intervention. In L. Leavitt & N. Fox (Eds.), *Psychological effects of war and violence on children* (pp. 281–301). Hillsdale, NJ: Lawrence Erlbaum.

Marans, S., Murphy, R. A., & Berkowitz, S. J. (2002). Police-mental health responses to children exposed to violence: The child development-community policing program. In M. Lewis (Ed.), *Child and adolescent psychiatry: A comprehensive textbook* (3rd ed., pp. 1406–1416). Baltimore: Lippincott Williams & Wilkins.

Martin, M. E. (1997). Policy promise: Community policing and domestic violence victim satisfaction. *Policing: An International Journal of Police Strategies & Management, 20,* 519–531.

Maxwell, C. D., Garner, J. H., & Fagan, J. A. (2001). *The effects of arrest on intimate partner violence: New evidence from the Spouse Assault Replication Program.* Washington, DC: National Institute of Justice.

McDonald, R., Jouriles, E. N., Ramisetty-Mikler, S., Caetano, R., & Green, C. E. (2006). Estimating the number of American children living in partner-violent families. *Journal of Family Psychology, 20,* 137–142.

Neighbors, H. W. (1988). Needed research on the epidemiology of mental disorders in Black Americans. In A. O. Harrison, J. S. Jackson, C. Munday, & N. B. Bleiden (Eds.), *A search for understanding: The Michigan Research Conference on Mental Health Services for Black Americans* (pp. 49–60). Detroit, MI: Wayne State University Press.

Police Executive Research Forum. (2003). Domestic violence intervention in Charlotte-Mecklenburg. *Problem Solving Quarterly, 16*(1), 1–4.

Rand, M. R. (1997). *Violence-related injuries treated in hospital emergency departments.* Washington, DC: U.S. Department of Justice, National Institute of Justice.

Shepard, M. (2005). Twenty years of progress in addressing domestic violence: An agenda for the next 10. *Journal of Interpersonal Violence, 20,* 436–441.

Shepard, M., Falk, D. R., & Elliot, B. A. (2002). Enhancing coordinated community responses to

reduce recidivism in cases of domestic violence. *Journal of Interpersonal Violence, 1,* 551–569.

Shepard, M., & Pence, E. (Eds.). (1999). *Coordinated community response to domestic violence: Lessons from the Duluth model.* Thousand Oaks, CA: Sage.

Silvern, L., Karyl, J., Waelde, L., Hodges, W. F., Starek, J., Heidt, E., et al. (1995). Retrospective reports of parental partner abuse: Relationships to depression, trauma symptoms and self-esteem among college students. *Journal of Family Violence, 10,* 177–202.

Stover, C. S. (2005). Domestic violence research: What have we learned and where do we go from here? *Journal of Interpersonal Violence, 20,* 448–454.

Straus, M. A., & Gelles, R. J. (Eds.). (1990). *Physical violence in American families: Risk factors and adaptations to violence in 8,145 families.* New Brunswick, NJ: Transaction.

Sue, S. (1991). Ethnicity and culture in psychological research and practice. In J. D. Goodchilds (Ed.), *Psychological perspectives on human diversity* (pp. 47–85). Washington, DC: American Psychological Association.

Sue, S., Zane, N., & Young, K. (1994). Research on psychotherapy with culturally diverse populations. In A. E. Bergin & S. L. Garfield (Eds.), *Handbook of psychotherapy and behavior change* (4th ed., pp. 783–817). New York: John Wiley.

Sullivan, C. M., Bybee, D. I., & Allen, N. E. (2002). Findings from a community-based program for battered women and their children. *Journal of Interpersonal Violence, 17,* 915–936.

Tyler, T. R., & Huo, Y. J. (2002). *Trust in the law: Encouraging public cooperation with the police and courts.* New York: Russell Sage.

Wiist, W. H., & McFarlane, J. (1998). Utilization of police by abused pregnant Hispanic women. *Violence Against Women, 4,* 677–693.

Wolf, M. E., Ly, U., Hobart, M. A., & Kernic, M. A. (2003). Barriers to seeking police help for intimate partner violence. *Journal of Family Violence, 18,* 121–129.

Yegidis, B. L., & Berman Renzy, R. (1994). Battered women's experiences with a preferred arrest policy. *Affilia, 9,* 60–70.

CHAPTER 20

Partnering With Community-Based Organizations to Reduce Intimate Partner Violence

Tina Bloom, Jennifer Wagman, Rebecca Hernandez, Nan Yragui, Noelia Hernandez-Valdovinos, Marie Dahlstrom, and Nancy Glass

This article describes successful strategies employed by a partnership of academic researchers and community-based organizations (CBOs) to develop a workplace intimate partner violence (IPV) intervention for Latinas. We share recommendations to build such partnerships for improved quality of research, including strategies for building a partnership plan, sharing leadership, challenging academic culture and infrastructure, partnering with the expertise of bicultural or bilingual researchers and community health workers, being accountable to CBOs and the target population, and engaging the larger community. Although our study focused on abused Latinas, we believe these recommendations are useful for researchers that are (a) planning research addressing sensitive issues, (b) strategizing to identify and locate immigrant and minority participants who have not traditionally taken part in research, and/or (c) developing approaches for building and maintaining research partnerships with CBOs.

Bloom, T., Wagman, J., Hernandez, R., Yragui, N., Hernandez-Valdovinos, N., Dahlstrom, M., & Glass, N. (2009). Partnering with community-based organizations to reduce intimate partner violence. *Hispanic Journal of Behavioral Sciences, 31,* 224–257.

AUTHORS' NOTE: The research was supported by funding from the National Institutes of Health/National Institutes for Nursing Research R01 NR08771-04 (PI: N. Glass 9/04–5/09). We acknowledge and thank the community-based organizations, *promotoras de salud,* and community leaders who supported this research through their extensive social networks and their commitment to the health of the community. We would also like to thank the survivors who participated in the study by sharing their experiences, time, and expertise.

Background

IPV against women is an important public health problem associated with injury, physical and mental health sequelae, disabilities, and death (Campbell, 2002; Garcia-Moreno et al., 2006; Glass, Dearwater, & Campbell, 2001; Grisso et al., 1999; Kyriacou et al., 1999; Lipsky, Caetano, Field, & Bazargan, 2004; Sutherland, Bybee, & Sullivan, 2002; Walton-Moss, Manganello, Frye, & Campbell, 2005). IPV is a significant concern among U.S. Latinas, with past-year incidence reports ranging from 10.5% to 18.7% (Hazen & Soriano, 2007; Ingram, 2007; Lown & Vega, 2000; Neff, Holaman, & Schluter, 1995; Office on Women's Health, 2001; Ratner, 1993; Sorenson, Upchurch, & Shen, 1996; Straus & Smith, 1990; Torres, 1991). In population-based data, 21% of Latinas report lifetime physical assault, and 7.9% report intimate partner rape (Tjaden & Thoennes, 2000).

Most IPV intervention studies have not focused on abused minority women (Klevens, 2007; Lee, Thompson, & Mechanic, 2002; West, Kantor, & Jasinski, 1998) and have been tied to the use of formal services, such as health care clinics, law enforcement, criminal justice, community-based domestic violence programs, and welfare agencies (Crenshaw, 1994; Donnelly, Cook, van Ausdale, & Foley, 2005; Lee et al., 2002; Liang, Goodman, Tummala-Narra, & Weintraub, 2005; West et al., 1998). Abused Latinas typically underuse such formal resources (Bauer, Rodriguez, Quiroga, & Flores-Ortiz, 2000; Ingram, 2007), often due to fear, distrust, and/or cultural and language barriers (Crenshaw, 1994; Denham et al., 2007; Ingram, 2007; Rivera, 1994; West et al., 1998). To effectively develop resources for abused Latinas, we must include their voices in intervention research and engage and collaborate with CBOs that serve them.

Community-Based Participatory Research (CBPR) Approach

The CBPR approach is widely used for intervention research in public health, nursing, and medicine. This dialogic, collaborative approach intentionally blurs the line between "researcher" and "researched." CBPR begins with a topic of importance to the community, such as violence against women, and combines scientific knowledge generation with actions to end the violence (Israel, Eng, Schulz, & Parker, 2005; Israel, Schulz, Parker, & Becker, 1998; Savage et al., 2006). In this approach, CBOs can have a meaningful influence on the design, implementation, and interpretation of research (Israel et al., 2005). CBPR benefits communities by increasing knowledge, skills, and credibility for CBO members; raises community awareness of health issues; and limits the possibility that research findings have unintended consequences for the community. Likewise, collaborating with CBOs helps academics reach wary and "invisible" communities (Israel et al., 2005). Notwithstanding these benefits of partnership, there are also challenges, discussed later in this article.

Method

Study Setting and Objectives

This Oregon-based CBPR project, "Community Partnered Response to Intimate Partner Violence," is funded by NIH/National Institute for Nursing Research (NINR). It began in September 2004 and is currently in its fifth and final year (estimated completion date of May 2009). The team includes researchers from the Johns Hopkins University (JHU) School of Nursing and Oregon Health & Sciences University (OHSU) School of Nursing and community partners from Volunteers of America Home Free (VOA) and Hacienda Community Development Corporation (CDC). These two CBOs provide services to Oregon's Latino population. VOA provides domestic violence advocacy services, with bilingual, bicultural outreach services in the Latino community. Hacienda CDC develops affordable supportive housing for Latino families and builds a *comunidad viva*, or "living" connected community with educational and social activities for residents.

Oregon has relatively few racial and ethnic minorities. However, the Latino population, which is primarily Mexican American (U.S. Census Bureau, 2000), grew by 144% between 1990 and 2000, compared to the national average of 57.9% (Cai, 2003). Since research has shown that Latinas underuse formal IPV-related services, our research partnership aimed to evaluate the impact of taking domestic violence interventions to Latinas in the workplace. The mission of the workplace intervention is to increase Latinas' access and use of IPV support services by incorporating the provision of culturally appropriate resources into their daily routines. Participation of abused Latinas was foundational to developing an effective intervention. Without our CBO partnerships, we would have had limited access to Latinas through traditional settings in a state where 8% of the population is Latino.

The Women's Health Survey

We conducted a Women's Health Survey (WHS) with Latina IPV survivors from September 2004 to May 2006 to inform intervention development. An informed consent process was undertaken with all participants. All study materials and protocols were reviewed and approved by the JHU and OHSU institutional review boards (IRBs).

CBO research staff conducted all components of the WHS, including recruitment, informed consent, and data collection. CBO research staff included Latina domestic violence advocates and *promotoras de salud* ("community health workers"; Swider, 2002). These staff provided health, wellness, and violence services in the community prior to study partnership, working as advocates, clinic outreach workers, batterer treatment program facilitator/outreach workers, parent trainers, and mental health workers. Promotoras are trusted in the Latino communities where they work or volunteer (Larkey et al., 2002; McQuiston & Uribe, 2001; Ramos, May, & Ramos, 2001). As such, their involvement in our

study helped convey that the research is of value to Latinas, that the researchers are trustworthy (Larkey et al., 2002), and that the overall study is *recomendado* ("recommended") by the promotora.

CBO staff received training in research conduct and scientific methods and approaches. Promotoras and advocates discussed and helped refine guidelines for how to introduce the study, maintain privacy and safety, reduce nonresponse, and assist participants to access needed services. These important team members linked us to immigrant Latino communities, including rural communities and grassroots networks, and organized and facilitated 1-day interview sessions across the state, so that the voices of rural abused Latinas could be included. Participants were recruited from our partner CBOs and a network of other CBOs offering parenting classes, postpartum depression groups, women's leadership program, and welfare and job-ready support groups.

Safety is a primary concern in IPV research, and we collaboratively developed safety protocols and trainings that included safety strategies for participants and interviewers and covered a variety of circumstances (e.g., if abusive partner showed up during the interview). Protocols were reviewed and amended as needed and provided an opportunity for interviewers to debrief and support each other. All participants were provided with resource referrals, safety planning, and connection to advocacy as needed. We also developed an algorithm to follow if a woman became distressed during the interview and needed ongoing support, and we provided ongoing training about child abuse reporting. In addition, our team included a bilingual/bicultural domestic violence advocate available to participants after interviews.

Participants

WHS participants were female, age 18 or older, spoke English or Spanish, had been physically or sexually abused by a partner in the past year, and had been employed and/or enrolled in school within the previous 6 months. Participants were compensated $20, and the interviews typically lasted 1 to 2 hours. Interviews were conducted in safe and convenient locations determined by participants and assessed abusers' interference with women's employment, the type of workplace support for IPV she received, and the type of support she wanted.

Measures

After completing demographics (age, ethnicity, born in or immigrated to United States, income) and an acculturation measure (Marin SASH), we used the Work/School Abuse Scale to ask about violence experienced at work. The Work/School Abuse Scale has two subscales (abuser behaviors, which prevent the woman from getting to work or school, and those that interfere with her participation once she is there; Riger, Ahrens, & Blickenstaff, 2000). Each subscale is made up of six questions (e.g., "During your relationship in the past six months has your partner ever come to work to harass you?") to which the respondent answers 0 (*no*) or 1 (*yes*). In addition, we used the Social Support Desired From Supervisor scale, developed and piloted in an earlier phase of this study, to examine workplace support desired and received by women. Eighteen items were based in part on qualitative interviews conducted with survivors, employees, and supervisors in Oregon. A sample item is, "Gave me paid time off to deal with my abusive relationship"; respondents were asked to indicate (*yes* or *no*) whether they (a) desired each type of support and (b) received each type of support in the workplace.

Results

Participants

Latina participants (*n* = 114, 54.5% of the total sample) were primarily Mexican American,

ranging in age from 18 to 62 years (*M* = 34.6, *SD* = 8.4). Approximately half (46.8%) had not completed high school. Participants ranged from foreign-born, monolingual, and recently immigrated (0–10 years) women to U.S.-born bilingual second- and third-generation Mexican American women. The average Marin SASH score was 8.25 on a range of possible scores from 5 to 25, with higher scores indicating greater acculturation (Marin, Sabogal, Marin, Otero-Sabogal, & Perez-Stable, 1987). Many women reported significant interference with work due to abuser behaviors. For example, 27.4% of respondents reported that their abuser sabotaged the car so she could not go to work or threatened her to make her leave work (32.4%). Workplace support was typically low; while half (50.9%) reported they had told their supervisor about the abuse, they received less than half (45%) of the support they wanted, for example, confidentiality, flexibility in work schedule or hours, or information about company policy related to domestic violence.

The Workplace Intervention

Findings from the WHS informed the development of the intervention, particularly the degree to which abuser behaviors interfered with an abused woman's ability to get to work, do her job, and keep her job and the type of support women received and desired at work. The team, including both academic and CBO partners, met many times to share and interpret WHS findings and devise the intervention. In these meetings, the principal investigator presented findings and sought input from all team members regarding the meaning of the findings and implications for intervention until a consensus was reached regarding next steps. The perspectives and expertise of CBO partners were privileged in these discussions. Subsequently, a workplace-based IPV intervention for supervisors was collaboratively created, evaluated, and revised, using an interactive computer-based training approach.

Discussion

In this study, the partnership of academic researchers with CBOs using a CBPR approach was critical to successfully include the voices of vulnerable, abused Latinas of relatively low acculturation in the development of an IPV intervention. In the section to follow, we provide six recommendations for overcome the challenges to maintaining such partnerships.

Recommendation 1: Develop a Written Partnership Plan at the Outset of the Study

A clear and agreed-upon partnership plan outlines goals, rights, responsibilities, and roles and commits all partners to a long-term respectful collaboration where everyone benefits. Without such a plan, partnerships are prone to struggle with confusion about the purpose, goals, and strategies of the partnership; low levels of interpersonal trust and accountability; unclear benefits of partnership; and a lack of advance planning for returning findings to the community. We suggest the plan should specify that meetings be collaborative and co-led, have an agenda, observe rules of discussion, and be documented with minutes or recordings if appropriate.

Academic partners must be continually mindful of historical and inherent power imbalances between communities and academia, ensuring equal power for decision making and treating CBOs as full partners, with fair and full compensation. Benefits to CBOs described in the partnership plan may include financially supporting and mentoring CBO staff to attend or present at conferences, providing adjunct faculty positions to CBO staff, and training to build research capacity at the CBO. Our plan pays CBOs for their time and expertise, including indirect administrative costs (approximately 10%–15% of the CBO's study budget).

This plan should acknowledge that conflict is inevitable, providing steps for resolution and rules of engagement that keep lines of communication open. In addition, as there is little program development and evaluation research conducted with marginalized populations such as abused minority women, CBOs typically have limited access to research findings. Thus, many CBOs struggle when competing for funding. The partnership plan should thus outline coauthorship plans and data access for CBO partners.

Recommendation 2: Share Leadership and Power

In our study, partner CBOs conducted all components of the WHS, including recruitment, informed consent, and data collection with abused women. A common pitfall in partnerships is unshared division of power and leadership, usually when academics are unwilling to relinquish control. Lack of leadership sharing impedes trust and prevents the development of deeper connections and research capacity within CBOs. Shared leadership and power with the CBO *and* continuous evaluation of the partnership for assessment of who is in the best position to lead is critical. As federal agencies increasingly recognize community expertise, partners may also consider using the multiple principal investigator (PI) option when submitting a CBPR application, with academic and CBO co-PIs to strengthen the application for funding.

When CBOs and their staff have the stability, experience, and capacity, it may be logical to position the CBO as the study lead, with the academic institution as a subcontractor.

This may be especially appropriate and cost-effective with recruitment and data collection strategies where the majority of work in conducted at the CBO. Academic institutions often have an off-campus project indirect rate approximately 20% lower than the on-campus rate. This also typically results in an increased percentage of grant funds going to the research activities and CBO partners. An investigator who is willing to negotiate with their institution for a reduced indirect rate for off-campus research activities is often viewed by the CBO as an advocate for respectful and equitable partnership.

Recommendation 3: Challenge Academic Culture and Regulations

Inherent power imbalances between large resource-rich academic institutions and resource-limited CBOs can inhibit partnership and research capacity. For example, processes (e.g., human subjects training, timing, and procedures for subcontracts) can lack transparency and are often created for the ease of the university, rather than what works best for community partners.

This challenge can be mitigated by prioritizing the values and needs of the community. Academics can mentor CBO staff in the language, culture, and politics of academia and be prepared to creatively revise or challenge academic culture and regulations to accommodate CBO needs. For example, we invited the university's sponsored projects staff to partnership meetings to discuss subcontract and invoice components required to receive timely payment, which had the added benefit of connecting university and CBO staff face to face. Further, we collaborated with the university IRB to develop an interactive group human subjects training program in Spanish to meet the needs of the IRB and the CBO, providing computers and translators for promotoras and advocates to access training.

Recommendation 4: Partner With Bilingual, Bicultural Researchers and Community Health Workers

We devoted a great deal of time and care to navigating language barriers, another challenge of academic-CBO partnerships involving English-speaking researchers and non-English-speaking target populations. Such barriers introduce recruitment bias (since they limit the ability to reach certain communities) and response bias (since respondents might not fully understand or might differentially interpret questions). It is imperative to involve bilingual and bicultural staff members who can assure that the study is culturally and linguistically appropriate, will be endorsed by the community, and avoids major mistakes in translation of sensitive issues, such as the language to define sexual violence.

Recommendation 5: Demonstrate Accountability to the CBO and Target Population

In any IPV project, it is important that interviews validate vulnerable women's experiences, provide information about IPV, and communicate the message that women are not alone. Accountability to participants is a requirement of ethical research, and upholding such standards is crucial to maintaining the CBO's status and credibility within the community.

Borrowing from previous guidelines, we recommend that explicit attention be paid to women's needs for convenience, comfort, and advocacy; a supportive and nonjudgmental approach; and allowing time and space for participants to develop trust in the researchers before being asked sensitive questions (Clayson, Castaneda, Sanchez, & Brindis, 2002). We accommodated women's schedules and transportation difficulties, meeting anywhere women wished to meet that was safe (e.g., her home, a park, a friend's house) and providing transportation and child care if needed. Often, interview sessions were held at community settings where women were already comfortable such as churches, schools, and community program offices, where we provided a relaxed atmosphere with an opportunity to visit and obtain advocacy and resource referral.

Accountability also lies in the obligation to return research results to the community. The expertise of CBO partners guides the production of findings and dissemination in ways that are culturally competent, accessible, and useful to communities. We recommend (a) allowing CBOs to include interview questions to evaluate their existing services and client satisfaction and (b) inviting participants to voluntarily provide safe contact information to receive study findings. In our study, we also conducted community presentations of findings to varied audiences including parent groups, provider service groups, unions, employee assistance programs, and informal groups of women in the community.

Recommendation 6: Engage With the Larger Community to Raise Awareness and Support

In our study, we participated in community events, such as statewide Latino leadership and health conferences, and promoted the work of our partner organizations, providing brochures on IPV and community resources in Spanish and English. We also attended community fairs, fundraising events, community college classrooms, Head Start programs, English as a Second Language programs, and churches to share study information in English and Spanish. One research staff member participated in a fund-raising 5K run to support supported the MDJ Foundation, a Latino men's foundation to prevent IPV. Academics must recognize that they cannot be detached from the community or simply "work through" partner CBOs. Successful partnership and addressing difficult issues such as IPV require supporting the mission of partner CBOs *and* their collaborators through active involvement and actual representation. Academics should take advantage of every opportunity to support community partners and to be involved in the larger community.

Conclusion

In this article, we provide an overview of a CBPR project to develop and implement a culturally and linguistically appropriate intervention that takes services and resources for abused Latinas to the workplace. Our academic-CBO partnership was critical to locating and interviewing abused Latinas who have not been included in previous intervention research. Our team learned several lessons that we considered vital to building and maintaining effective partnerships, and the six recommendations we offer emerged from an engaged and ongoing process of CBPR. Through this collaborative work, we found that the strategies we recommend in this article allowed us to build a sustainable community of academics and CBOs working together.

References

Bauer, H. M., Rodriguez, M. A., Quiroga, S. S., & Flores-Ortiz, Y. G. (2000). Barriers to health care for abused Latina and Asian immigrant women. *Journal of Health Care for the Poor & Underserved, 11*(1), 33–44.

Cai, Q. (2003, December). *Oregon's population change: 1990–2000.* Portland, OR: Population Research Center, Portland State University.

Campbell, J. C. (2002). Health consequences of intimate partner violence. *Lancet, 359*(9314), 1331–1336.

Clayson, Z. C., Castaneda, X., Sanchez, E., & Brindis, C. (2002). Unequal power—changing landscapes: Negotiations between evaluation stakeholders in Latino communities. *American Journal of Evaluation, 23*(1), 33–44.

Crenshaw, K. W. (1994). Mapping the margins: Intersectionality, identity politics, and violence against women of color. In M. A. Fineman & R. Mykitiuk (Eds.), *The public nature of private violence* (pp. 93–118). New York: Routledge.

Denham, A. C., Frasier, P. Y., Hooten, E. G., Belton, L., Newton, W., Gonzalez, P., et al. (2007). Intimate partner violence among Latinas in eastern North Carolina. *Violence Against Women, 13*(2), 123–140.

Donnelly, D. A., Cook, K. J., van Ausdale, D., & Foley, L. (2005). White privilege, color blindness, and services to battered women. *Violence Against Women, 11*(1), 6–37.

Garcia-Moreno, C., Jansen, H. A., Ellsberg, M., Heise, L., Watts, C. H., & WHO Multi-Country Study on Women's Health and Domestic Violence Against Women Study Team. (2006). Prevalence of intimate partner violence: Findings from the WHO multi-country study on women's health and domestic violence. *Lancet, 368*(9543), 1260–1269.

Glass, N., Dearwater, S., & Campbell, J. (2001). Intimate partner violence screening and intervention: Data from eleven Pennsylvania and California community hospital emergency departments. *Journal of Emergency Nursing, 27*(2), 141–149.

Grisso, J. A., Schwarz, D. F., Hirschinger, N., Sammel, M., Brensinger, C., Santanna, J., et al. (1999). Violent injuries among women in an urban area. *New England Journal of Medicine, 341*(25), 1899–1905.

Hazen, A. L., & Soriano, F. I. (2007). Experiences with intimate partner violence among Latina women. *Violence Against Women, 13*(6), 562–582.

Ingram, E. M. (2007). A comparison of help seeking between Latino and non-Latino victims of intimate partner violence. *Violence Against Women, 13*(2), 159–171.

Israel, B. A., Eng, E., Schulz, A. J., & Parker, E. A. (2005). *Methods in community-based participatory research for health*. San Francisco: Jossey–Bass.

Israel, B. A., Schulz, A. J., Parker, E. A., & Becker, A. B. (1998). Review of community-based research: Assessing partnership approaches to improve public health. *Annual Review in Public Health, 19,* 173–202.

Klevens, J. (2007). An overview of intimate partner violence among Latinos. *Violence Against Women, 13*(2), 111–122.

Kyriacou, D. N., Anglin, D., Taliaferro, E., Stone, S., Tubb, T., Linden, J. A., et al. (1999). Risk factors for injury to women from domestic violence. *New England Journal of Medicine, 341*(25), 1892–1898.

Larkey, L. K., Staten, L. K., Ritenbaugh, C., Hall, R. A., Buller, D. B., Bassford, T., et al. (2002). Recruitment of Hispanic women to the Women's Health Initiative: The case of Embajadoras in Arizona. *Controlled Clinical Trials, 23*(3), 289–298.

Lee, R. K., Thompson, V. L., & Mechanic, M. B. (2002). Intimate partner violence and women of color: A call for innovations. *American Journal of Public Health, 92*(4), 530–534.

Liang, B., Goodman, L., Tummala-Narra, P., & Weintraub, S. (2005). A theoretical framework for understanding help-seeking processes among survivors of intimate partner violence. *American Journal of Community Psychology, 36*(1–2), 71–84.

Lipsky, S., Caetano, R., Field, C. A., & Bazargan, S. (2004). Violence-related injury and intimate partner violence in an urban emergency department. *Journal of Trauma-Injury Infection & Critical Care, 57*(2), 352–359.

Lown, E. A., & Vega, W. (2000). Prevalence and predictors of physical partner abuse among Mexican American women. *American Journal of Public Health, 91,* 441–445.

Marin, G., Sabogal, F., Marin, B. V., Otero-Sabogal, R., & Perez-Stable, E. J. (1987). Development of a short acculturation scale for Hispanics. *Hispanic Journal of Behavioral Sciences, 9*(2), 183–205.

McQuiston, C., & Uribe, L. (2001). Latino recruitment and retention strategies: Community-based HIV prevention. *Journal of Immigrant Health, 3*(2), 97–105.

Neff, J. A., Holaman, B., & Schluter, T. D. (1995). Spousal violence among Anglos, Blacks, and Mexican Americans: The role of demographic variables, psychosocial predictors and alcohol consumption. *Journal of Family Violence, 10,* 1–21.

Office on Women's Health. (2001). *Women's health issues: An overview*. Washington, DC: Department of Health and Human Services.

Ramos, I. N., May, M., & Ramos, K. S. (2001). Environmental health training of promotoras in colonias along the Texas-Mexico border. *American Journal of Public Health, 91*(4), 568–570.

Ratner, P. (1993). The incidence of wife abuse and mental health status in abused wives in Edmonton, Alberta. *Canadian Journal of Public Health, 84,* 246–249.

Riger, S., Ahrens, A., & Blickenstaff, A. (2000). Measuring interference with employment and education reported by women with abusive partners: Preliminary data. *Violence and Victims, 15*(2), 161–172.

Rivera, J. (1994). Domestic violence against Latinas by Latino males: An analysis of race, national origin, and gender differentials. *Boston College Third World Law Journal, 14,* 231–251.

Savage, C. L., Xu, Y., Lee, R., Rose, B. L., Kappesser, M., & Anthony, J. A. (2006). A case study in the use of community-based participatory research in public health nursing. *Public Health Nursing, 23*(5), 472–478.

Sorenson, S. B., Upchurch, D., & Shen, H. (1996). Violence and injury in marital arguments: Risk patterns and gender differences. *American Journal of Public Health, 86,* 35–40.

Straus, M. A., & Smith, C. (1990). *Physical violence in American families.* New Brunswick, NJ: Transaction.

Sutherland, C. A., Bybee, D. I., & Sullivan, C. M. (2002). Beyond bruises and broken bones: The joint effects of stress and injuries on battered women's health. *American Journal of Community Psychology, 30*(5), 609–636.

Swider, S. M. (2002). Outcome effectiveness of community health workers: An integrative literature review. *Public Health Nursing, 19*(1), 11–20.

Tjaden, P., & Thoennes, N. (2000). *Extent, nature, and consequences of physical violence: Findings from the National Violence Against Women Survey.* Washington, DC: National Institute of Justice and Centers for Disease Control and Prevention.

Torres, S. A. (1991). Comparison of wife abuse between two cultures: Perceptions, attitudes, nature, and extent. *Issues in Mental Health Nursing, 12,* 113–131.

U.S. Census Bureau. (2000, May). *Profiles of general demographic characteristics: Oregon.* Washington, DC: Author.

Walton-Moss, B. J., Manganello, J., Frye, V., & Campbell, J. C. (2005). Risk factors for intimate partner violence and associated injury among urban women. *Journal of Community Health, 30*(5), 377–389.

West, C. M., Kantor, G. K., & Jasinski, J. L. (1998). Sociodemographic predictors and cultural barriers to help-seeking behavior by Latina and Anglo American battered women. *Violence and Victims, 13*(4), 361–375.

CHAPTER 21

The Violence Against Women Campaigns in Latin America

New Feminist Alliances

Sally Cole and Lynne Phillips

I s the backlash against gender-sensitive policies a global phenomenon? In this article, we urge caution on this point, drawing inspiration from current events in Latin America. We consider how international efforts to prevent violence against women have been taken up in proactive and skillful ways through the collaboration of international organizations and nation-states and by expanding and evolving women's movements in the region. We argue that international, national, and regional coalitions and alliances have been central to the success of efforts to combat violence against women. Specifically, we argue that the push for the development of democratic citizenship in Latin America has articulated possibilities for bringing awareness of violence against women to a public that has been encouraged (as "civil society") to engage with social justice issues—including gender equity—and to collaborate on multiple

fronts. On the basis of movement documents and interviews conducted in Brazil and Ecuador in 2007,[1] we show how efforts to bring issues of violence against women to a wide audience have helped not only to denormalize and deprivatize gender violence but to revitalize feminism as part of a broad front to build progressive societies.

It is sometimes assumed by scholars that the particular experience of political and economic change in Europe and North America has resonance throughout the world. It might be presumed, for example, that because human rights and citizenship approaches to violence against women do not have political cachet in Europe and North America, they would not be constructive for other nations. Yet there is increasing evidence that although the women's movement struggles to stay alive as neoliberal cutbacks work slowly to starve women's organizations and policies in Canada, the United States, and Britain,

Cole, S., & Phillips, L. (2008). The violence against women campaigns in Latin America. *Feminist Criminology, 3,* 145–168.

there are active and vibrant women's movements in other countries from which lessons can be learned (Erwin, 2006; Stanko, 2004; Thayer, 2000; Weldon, 2002).

The complex relationship between the women's movement and efforts to combat violence against women has been examined by feminist researchers for more than two decades. In the early 1980s, Kathleen Tierney (1982) analyzed the role of professional movements in transforming wife beating into a "social problem" in the United States, noting that wife beating had gone "from a subject of private shame and misery to an object of public concern" (p. 210) in less than 10 years. Her groundbreaking research challenged sociological assumptions about why problems became "social" and set the stage for further study by suggesting that a range of factors (such as resource mobilization, movement flexibility, and the media) can determine the success of movement efforts to bring attention to "battered women." However, even in this early period, Tierney (1982) argued that there may be costs to taking a social problem approach to violence against women, as the issue increasingly becomes channeled into social service-oriented programmes and cleansed of its more radical demands for social transformation. This latter point was usefully taken up by Gillian Walker (1990), who investigated how violence against women in Canada came to be defined by government legislation and policing agencies during the 1980s; wife beating was absorbed into concerns about "family violence" and "domestic assault." Walker's theoretical approach focuses on how a broad range of conceptual practices are tied to state power (or "relations of ruling," in Dorothy Smith's lexicon), and how this is a process in which we are all incorporated, not just "the battered wife." In this way, Walker is able to define violence against women in broad terms (since "'we women' [are] all battered to some degree by a sexist system," p. 46) and hints that this approach may be of strategic value when feminists make demands of the state to support women's issues.

Although these are important arguments that continue to play a role in how we come to understand efforts to combat violence against women today, it is important to bear in mind that they were framed before the upsurge and spread of globalization and what are today recognized as transnational social movements (e.g., see Basu, 1995; Ferree & Tripp, 2006; Keck & Sikkink, 1998; Moghadam, 2005; Waller & Marcos, 2005). As many scholars have noted, neither globalization nor neoliberalism have made the state irrelevant (Hindess, 2004; Sassen, 2006), but they have reshaped politics and our political relationships to the state in the 21st century. Virtually all of the literature examining feminist political interaction with this new terrain notes the considerable success in bringing global and national attention to women's issues—with international communication technologies, the United Nations (UN) conferences, the World Social Forum, and new economic and political opportunities being identified as important factors in this success.

Yet a familiar matter of concern that haunts this interaction has been the problem of co-optation, and the related theme of the depoliticization of feminist movements; indeed some authors explain the current decline in feminist political activity in terms of the extensive co-optation of feminist ideas and activists into governmental projects.[2] Our position on this question is that analysts need to be careful in comparing the appearance of feminist politics engaged in two *different* political, economic, and social contexts. For politics are always shaped by the contexts within which they operate and, in engaging with the contradictory and contentious "context" of globalization, feminism has no doubt changed as well. For this position, we find support in the work of Sylvia Walby (2002) who, instead of lamenting the disappearance of debates about men's oppression of women on the global stage, investigates the strengths of a feminism that takes advantage of a universal human rights regime to promote the issue of violence against women. Walby places this shift *in context*, arguing that

The discourse of women's rights as human rights has a powerful resonance in the new global context. While traditionally this political discourse has been associated with a liberal feminism too meek to make a difference, this is, today, an inappropriate understanding. Rather, it is a discourse that is strategically utilized by collectively organized women, in the context of developing powerful transnational political institutions. Globalization is being used creatively as a new framing for feminist politics. (p. 549)

From this perspective, the state is still important—at the very least to ensure a legal and policing framework conducive to combating violence against women—but it is only "one node in a wider network of relevant political forums" (Walby, 2002, p. 550).[3] Moreover, because globalization is in part a *product* of feminist transnational politics and because in seeking new coalitions in campaigns against violence, feminism has learned hard lessons about the importance of diversity, the issue of working *with* difference remains an integral part of, rather than erased from, this new form of feminist politics. For our purposes, the important point is that the extent to which feminist alliances are fostered (and multiple feminisms engaged) for an issue like violence against women depends on a particular constellation of global, national, and regional contexts.

This is why it is important to note that Latin America currently appears to be treading unusual political waters compared to other regions in the international landscape: whereas countries such as the United States, Canada, Australia, and France are currently governed by conservative neoliberal leaders, the electorate in an increasing number of Latin American countries have been voting for more progressive candidates with explicit platforms to develop alternative economic and political futures for the region. In this article we concentrate on two of these countries, Brazil and Ecuador, to show how the success of

the violence against women campaigns in reframing public discourse has depended on strategic political alliances at diverse scales.[4]

Occupying a territory the size of the continental United States, Brazil has a population of nearly 190 million people living predominantly in urban industrial centers: Rio de Janeiro, population 9 million; São Paulo, population 18 million; and a dozen other cities that have populations of greater than 1 million people. Following several short-term presidencies in the early years of democratization after the fall of the military regime in 1985, President Fernando Henrique Cardoso and the Party of the Brazilian Democratic Movement (1994–2002) stabilized the economy introducing the new currency, the *real*, and bringing inflation under control. At this time, second-wave feminists played a strong and visible role in the building of democracy in Brazil (Alvarez, 1990). Known as the "lipstick lobby" (*lobby do baton*), their campaign for gender equality was supported in the establishment of the National Council for the Rights of Women in 1985 and affirmed in the first democratic constitution in 1988. Additional support came with the establishment in Brasília, by the United Nations in 1992, of the United Nations Development Fund for Women (UNIFEM) office responsible for the Southern Cone countries: Brazil, Argentina, Chile, Uruguay, and Paraguay.

Feminists were also active in the building of the Workers' Party, establishing discussion groups to ensure that gender issues were on the party agenda. A prominent slogan of Party feminists proclaimed that "Without women there is no socialism" (*Sem as mulheres não há socialismo*). In 2002, the first national-level Workers' Party government under Luís Inácio da Silva (Lula) was elected; the government was reelected for a second term in 2006. Lula's presidency has actively sought to fulfill promises made to its women and feminist supporters as well as to implement commitments Brazil made during and following the United Nations 4th World Conference on Women held in Beijing in 1995 and the terms of the international conventions the country had previously formally ratified: the Convention on the Elimination of All Forms of Discrimination Against Women in 1985 and the Inter-American Convention on the Prevention, Punishment and Eradication of Violence Against Women in 1995. The government follows an explicit policy of transversalism (*transversalidade*) to integrate gender issues in programs and policy making across the government and to initiate dialogue and develop participatory mechanisms for consultation with civil society.[5] In 2003, Lula created the Special Secretariat for Policy for Women (SPM) with ministerial powers linked to the president's office. The government transformed the existing National Council for the Rights of Women into a presidential advisory body with representation from diverse sectors of civil society, including women in the union movement; the World March for Women; the Movement of Rural Women Workers; the Association of Brazilian Women, which brings together delegates from each of the 26 states; and the Brazilian Lesbian League. The Lula government has also sponsored a series of national conferences on a wide variety of issues affecting women.[6]

Brazil is an important example because the country is emerging in the region as an innovator and leader in alternative democratic political and economic associations and practices, including the Landless Peoples' Movement, the World March of Women, and participatory municipal budgets. Brazil hosted the World Social Forum in 2001 and 2003 and the fourth conference of the global peasant movement, La Vía Campesina, in 2004. Brazil has also been a leader in the region in ending the silence around violence against women. In 1995, the country had hosted the Inter-American Convention on the Prevention, Punishment and Eradication of Violence Against Women in the city of Belém in the northern state of Pará. In 2006, with the ratification of the Maria da Penha Law (no. 11.340), Brazil established violence against women as a criminal offence. In its name the law immortalizes Maria da Penha, a poor woman who was left a paraplegic

through abuse at the hands of her husband; she had campaigned for more than two decades to have him convicted. On the signing of the law, the Minister for the Special Secretariat for Policy for Women, Nilcéa Freire, reflected that the 20-year struggle of Maria da Penha and women like her "transformed pain into struggle and resistance, tragedy into solidarity" (*transformou dor em luta, tragédia em solaridade*). The Maria da Penha Law finally overturned the traditional Brazilian proverb: *Entre marido e mulher não se mete a colher* (Between husband and wife, don't interfere [lit. don't place a spoon]). The slogan of the violence against women campaign in Brazil is, *Em briga de marido e mulher, vamos meter a colher* (In violence between husband and wife, we will intervene [lit. we will place a spoon]). No longer is conjugal violence considered a private affair; it is now the responsibility of all citizens (Special Secretariat for Policy for Women, 2006, 2007).

Ecuador is a smaller country than Brazil with a diverse but relatively small population of approximately 12 million and a fragile economy based primarily on oil and banana exports. Ecuador has experienced considerable political and economic instability throughout much of its transition from military rule in 1979. The last decade has been especially characterized by nationwide protests against strict structural adjustment and neoliberal policies, particularly with the expansion and consolidation of the country's indigenous movements and other social movements, including a nascent women's movement. No president has completed a full term in office since 1996. During this time, the United Nations and other international development organizations have been important for providing a modicum of continuity and support to the country through social and economic programmes, including through the work of the office of the United Nations Development Fund for Women, UNIFEM, responsible for the Andean region (Bolivia, Ecuador, Peru, and Venezuela) and established in Quito, Ecuador, in 1991. It is noteworthy that the National Council for Women, CONAMU, was established in 1997 as a partial governmental body that would provide an effective structural basis for supporting women's issues throughout this time period. For example, it was due to the alliances of UNIFEM, CONAMU, and the women's movement that Ecuador formally recognized the equality of women as a right in its 1998 Constitution. Building on such alliances with transnational feminist networks also formed the basis for Ecuador hosting the Encuentro de Mujeres de las Americas in 2002 (held in Cuenca, Ecuador, to develop proposals for the World Social Forum held in Porto Alegre, Brazil, in 2003) and the first Social Forum of the Americas, held in Quito in 2004.

The election of Rafael Correa as the nation's president in 2006 has marked something of a shift in electoral politics. Correa did not come from a traditional political party and drew his support from a broad alliance of progressive groups, including indigenous movements, workers' movements, and middle-class citizens antipathetic to the extensive corruption of the traditional political system. Describing his platform as "21st-century socialism," Correa faces heavy pressure from the International Monetary Fund, the World Bank, and the government of the United States to follow his predecessors by committing to neoliberal free trade agreements on one hand and from his broad base of supporters who demand that Ecuador not be "a colony of the United States" (Zibechi, 2007, p. 2) on the other. Within this new context, a presidential decree was signed in September 2007 that establishes the struggle against gender violence as a specific state policy with budget support. Following the practice of transversalism, President Correa's national plan for the elimination of gender-based violence will be implemented across four ministries—education, health, government, and economic and social inclusion—and will include, among other things, a new national registry system of cases of violence, an integrated system of protection, and faster access to justice for victims of violence (United Nations Development Fund for Women, 2007). Although the women's

movement, CONAMU, and UNIFEM mark this as a significant historical event—the culmination of their efforts over the last two decades—there remains some concern about Correa's decision to reopen the 1998 Constitution to establish among other things a legal framework for renegotiating the country's relations with multinational corporations and banks. On the other hand, as clarified in this article, there seems little doubt that the strategic coalitions of women's organizations and movements in the nation will reemerge to ensure that the rights won in the 1998 Constitution are maintained and extended.

In the remainder of this article, we examine three confluent efforts to combat violence against women in Brazil and Ecuador: (a) the international offices of the United Nations, specifically the two subregional offices of UNIFEM in Latin America, the Andean office located in Quito, Ecuador, and the Southern Cone office located in Brasília, Brazil; (b) the government approach in these two countries, as represented by the offices established for women's issues, CONAMU, the National Council for women in Ecuador and SPM, the Special Secretariat for Policy for Women in Brazil; and (c) transnational feminist networks—represented by the Network of Women Transforming the Economy, REMTE, which has links to other social movements active in Latin America.

Our argument draws on the idea that the outcome of any social change exercise, including efforts to eradicate violence against women, is always shaped by a specific assemblage of resources, strategies, and practices within specific moral and political spaces. It situates itself in the literature concerned to explore, with a critical eye, the potential of global, national, and local collaborations to create alternatives to neoliberal global capitalism (Bennett, 2001; Desmarais, 2007; Faria, 2003; Gibson-Graham, 2006; León, 2005; Merry, 2006; Tsing, 2005). Within this literature, the relationships between global and local scales have been theorized in terms of how international ideas about human rights and gender violence can be "translated" in positive ways by local cultures (Merry, 2006) and how the effectiveness of international, national, and local collaborations around social issues does not depend on the existence of homogeneous interest groups but on a politics of working with difference (Tsing, 2005; Walby, 2002). At the same time, feminist activists are making conceptual contributions to framing public discourse on violence against women, particularly through creative alliances with antineoliberal globalization movements in many parts of the world such as La Vía Campesina and the World Social Forum and in coalitions against free trade (Desmarais, 2007; Faria, 2003; Vargas, 2003). In this article, we focus on the work and alliance building of activists in the Latin American REMTE. In developing alternatives to neoliberal globalization and in their collaborations on multiple fronts, they have not only initiated actions and campaigns but have also reframed public discourse on violence against women through a radical critique of the economy and of the relations on which many forms of violence depend. As a contribution to these academic and activist efforts, we hope to demonstrate in the following sections the efficacy of combating violence against women through attention to diverse alliances and different scales.

Violence Against Women and the United Nations

In this section we suggest that the efforts associated with the United Nations, in the form of the Beijing Declaration and Platform for Action as well as other international and regional initiatives to prevent violence against women, have been central both in moving violence against women out of the private and into the public arena in Latin America and in providing opportunities for feminist initiatives to transform public space around issues related to violence against women.

In 1995, the United Nations 4th World Conference on Women in Beijing brought together women's groups from around the world to build an international coalition to take action for equality, development, and peace (for a Latin American account, see Alvarez et al., 2002). The main outcome of the conference was a document referred to as the Beijing Declaration and Platform for Action (the Beijing Platform) that outlined 12 critical areas of concern preventing the achievement of these goals, one of which was violence against women.

The Beijing Platform undertook an extensive "diagnosis" of violence against women and identified 44 actions to be taken primarily by governments to combat violence against women. These actions range from adopting appropriate legislation and providing shelters and other services to protect and support victims to developing media campaigns and educational programs in schools and workplaces to prevent violence against women. The UN asked all national governments of member states to complete a questionnaire, in 2000, about their efforts to address the Beijing Platform 5 years later (Beijing +5) and again, in 2004, with the additional consideration of the United Nations Millennium Development Goals. The Millennium Development Goals, established in 2000 with specific goals to be reached by 2015, constitute a massive international effort to reignite interest in and financial support for development issues. Only one of the nine goals, MDG 3, considers the specific theme of advancing gender equality and women's empowerment; however, its target is limited to improving women's participation in the education sector and it is silent on violence against women and other important women's issues. Feminist activists have reacted strongly to this eclipsing of women's issues.

The widely held position throughout Latin America is that the Millennium Development Goals should in no way diminish the international agreements made in Beijing and through the Convention on the Elimination of All Forms of Discrimination Against Women, where language about the importance of eliminating violence against women is made clear (see Lara, 2006). Recognition of the centrality of violence against women to MDG 3 has also been introduced through the reports coming from the Millennium Project, which was launched as a 3-year project to identify the best strategies for meeting the Millennium Development Goals with the help of 10 task forces, one of which was the Task Force on Education and Gender Equality. This task force not only recommended adding two additional targets for MDG 3 but suggested three additional indicators for assessing whether the targets were being met, one of which is the prevalence of domestic violence (see United Nations Development Fund for Women, 2002, p. 52). At the 2005 World Summit, which took stock of the progress toward the Millennium Development Goals, it was noted that "Heads of State and Government identified violence against women as one key factor that has to be addressed in order to achieve gender equality and achieve the Millennium Development Goals" (Heyzer, 2006).

International and national organizations and movements pressured the United Nations regarding the silence and lack of progress on violence against women. In 1993 the UN General Assembly had passed a Declaration on the Elimination of Violence against Women (A/res/48/104) and in 1999 had declared November 25 as the International Day for the Elimination of Violence Against Women. After its Declaration on the Millennium Development Goals, the Assembly began addressing the question of violence against women on an annual basis (see United Nations, 2003, 2004, 2005, 2006). In 2004 it adopted a specific resolution on the elimination of domestic violence against women and in early 2007 it accepted a strongly worded and comprehensive resolution to intensify efforts to eliminate all forms of violence against women, broadening the discussion to include "all forms of gender-based violence" (A/res/61/143). To quote:

> [The General Assembly] Strongly condemns all acts of violence against women and girls, whether these acts are perpetrated by the State, by private persons or by non-State actors, calls for the elimination of all forms

of gender-based violence in the family, within the general community and where perpetrated or condoned by the State, and stresses the need to treat all forms of violence against women and girls as a criminal offence, punishable by law. (United Nations, 2007, p. 3)

The 2007 resolution, based on an extensive report written by then-UN Secretary-General Koffi Annan (2006), recognizes the importance of diverse strategies to combat violence against women, given the intersection of gender with other factors, and it acknowledges the great diversity in women's unequal status based on

> nationality, ethnicity, religion or language, indigenous women, migrant women, stateless women, women living in underdeveloped, rural or remote communities, homeless women, women in institutions or in detention, women with disabilities, elderly women, widows and women who are otherwise discriminated against. (Annan, 2006, p. 4)

The resolution points to the need for the creation of training programs about gender-based violence for a wide range of social groups, including health workers, teachers, the police, the military, judges, and community leaders. It also encourages men and boys "to speak out strongly against violence against women." It specifically notes the importance of integrating efforts to eliminate gender-based violence in national action and development plans, "including those supported by international cooperation" (Annan, 2006, p. 3), which would include the Millennium Development Goals, though they are not specifically mentioned.

The UN's 2007 resolution followed on the heels of an international campaign, the 16 Days of Activism against Gender Violence.[7] The campaign in 2006 had specifically mobilized organizations around the world to answer Koffi Annan's call for response on issues related to gender-based violence. The range and number of actions organized throughout Latin America during the 2006 16 Days of Activism Campaign (United Nations Development Fund for Women, 2006) is an example of the skillful way women's movements in the region choose to engage with the international level to press for change at times when it may have particular resonance. For its part, although the UN was responsible for promoting public awareness in many countries around the world, it still had to be prodded to take more serious action against violence against women as an integral aspect of its own declarations on gender equality and human rights.

Koffi Annan's report drew from a country-by-country report prepared by the UN Special Rapporteur on Violence Against Women, Radhika Coomaraswamy (Special Rapporteur on Violence Against Women, 2003). This 379-page report outlines the international, regional, and national progress of countries from around the world between 1994 and 2003 and identifies remaining issues of concern. In her review of the Latin American region, Coomaraswamy notes the important work of the Organization of American States' Inter-American Commission on Human Rights and the Special Rapporteurship on the Rights of Women, established in 1994. With Beijing in mind, the mandate of the Rapporteur was to identify the laws and practices that discriminated against women in the Americas (Latin America and the Caribbean, Canada, and the United States) and to make recommendations for further action. This same year, the Organization of American States adopted the Inter-American Convention on the Prevention, Punishment and Eradication of Violence against Women (known as the Convention of Belém do Pará), which recognizes violence against women as a product of gender-based discrimination. The Convention is now widely ratified by member states of the Organization of American States and "reflects a regional consensus on the need to recognize the gravity of the problem of violence against women and to take concrete steps to eradicate it" (Special Rapporteur on Violence Against Women, 2003, p. 183).[8] In addition, the Convention provides a regional mechanism for victims of violence who allege unfair treatment by their domestic legal systems or judiciaries. Cases from Brazil, Mexico, Chile, and Peru have highlighted the obligation of governments to prosecute and punish all perpetrators of gender-based violence, including the military and other security forces. We mention the Report of the UN Special Rapporteur on Violence Against Women not only because of its extensive international evaluation of violence against women and its impact on government policies in Latin America but because of its role in providing otherwise marginalized organizations spaces for change. Coomaraswamy herself reports that "more than its impact on Governments, the role of the Special Rapporteur has been raised and taken into consideration by NGOs, feminists, and the women's movement throughout the region. The UN Special Rapporteur on Violence Against Women has contributed to make the demands and proposals from the women's groups more visible and [has] made it possible to discuss with the Governments" (Special Rapporteur on Violence Against Women, 2003, p. 182).

UNIFEM, the UN Development Fund for Women, which has regional offices on every continent, has recognized violence against women as part of its work since its founding in 1976, but the Beijing Platform provided particular support for its activities. In 1995, UNIFEM was given the mandate to carry out the recommendations of the Beijing Platform and specifically to strengthen its activities around eradicating violence against women (General Assembly resolution 50/166). A year later, UNIFEM's Trust Fund in Support of Actions to Eliminate Violence against Women was established as international financial support for such initiatives. It is to be noted that the participation of Latin American feminists in previous United Nations conferences had been relatively weak (Alvarez et al., 2002) but with the highlighting of violence against women in the preconference process leading to the Beijing conference, there was now convergence with the issue that had been a major mobilizing force for feminists in the region. As a result of this mobilization and the continuing frustration associated with advancing these issues at the national level in the early 1990s, Latin American participation and interest in UN programs greatly increased.

Interviews in the Quito office of UNIFEM responsible for the Andean region confirmed the importance of UN-sponsored campaigns against violence against women in Latin America.

> We did a campaign from this office for all of Latin America and the Caribbean on the theme of violence against women and human rights. . . . We produced written material, we went to the television stations, to the Press. In the end it was a fantastic thing because as a result of that campaign certain laws were proposed in Latin America countries and many women parliamentarians were empowered with that and began to fight in their parliaments for revisions to the laws they had. It was [also] gratifying to see men represented on the panels acknowledging the fact that they have a patriarchal attitude and how they are not really contributing to its eradication, [to recognize] for example, that violence against women is a social scar. Or to have seated on a panel the captain of the National Selection Soccer team of Ecuador, to see him seated there saying "I am committed. I have a Foundation in which we are working on combating violence and I believe that we should abolish it." That he is saying it, a *futbolista*, famous in the country [especially] since Ecuador went to the World Cup, but that he is saying it there, seated with other men, and they acknowledged that they were not doing enough, that they have to change, and that . . . well, they are saying it on a panel but in addition you can see an attitude, in the sense of having a Foundation, and they are working on it. It's not that they are simply sitting there and, "ciao," they go. Or [another example is] a television channel comes up to you and says

> "Look, señora, we want to collaborate with you during all of 2007; work with us to have a sustainable campaign on the theme of violence." That television channel said that to [us] last year and it was they who called *us*. . . . To see people who have violent attitudes, seated at the table and saying things like that, or a television channel that makes such an offer without asking for one cent, it is very gratifying. It summarizes many things, all the work that the office does.

A widespread sentiment inside and outside UN offices in Latin America is that such campaigns have made a significant difference for the public acknowledgment of violence against women, although, as we will show, different organizations and movements bring different interpretations as to why violence against women is an important issue. For a UNIFEM officer in the Ecuador office, for example, violence against women is important because it is costly, economically, to national development:

> Violence has gone from being a private problem to being a public problem. For some UN agencies, it is a problem of public health. For our case, in UNIFEM, it is an obstacle to development. We take it as a theme of development because violence affects all aspects of life in the country. Studies done by BID [Inter-American Development Bank] show how much an abused woman costs the state, because she can't go to work, because she doesn't produce . . . and this decreases the economic income of the country.

Both the Andean and Southern Cone UNIFEM regional offices work extensively with a range of women's groups in their respective subregions, and particularly with what the UN calls national women's "machineries": the National Council on Women, CONAMU, in Ecuador and the Special Secretariat for Policy for Women, SPM, in Brazil. Both of these state agencies were created in part as responses to the recommendations of the

Convention on the Elimination of All Forms of Discrimination Against Women, widely recognized as an international bill of rights for women and signed by both Brazil and Ecuador before the Beijing Conference took place.

National Women's Machineries and Violence Against Women

In this section we discuss the national-level approaches of Brazil and Ecuador to combating violence against women and outline the role of state agencies in these efforts. We argue that post-1995 international and regional efforts to target violence against women provided a strong context in which legal and other changes could be implemented and, in countries where there was a strong interest in mobilizing citizens for democratic change, helped to open spaces for deeper and broader analyses of and action on issues of gender-based violence.

After visiting Brazil in 1996, the UN Special Rapporteur on Violence Against Women expressed concerns about Brazil's urban-focused activities that left large areas of the country at the margins of reforms and legally unprotected. In her report, the Special Rapporteur also noted that immunity in cases of "honour crimes" still persisted in practice and that few shelters were provided for victims of violence (Special Rapporteur on Violence Against Women, 2003, pp. 190–191). However, since 2003, Brazil has been building unique institutional mechanisms for addressing the concerns of all Brazilian women and is concentrating on developing *participative* and *transversal* mechanisms to ensure that women's concerns are integrated into policy development across all government agencies (Brazil, 2004). President Lula has created three interconnected special secretariats that have ministerial status and are linked directly with the President's Office: the Special Secretariat for Policy for Women, the Special Secretariat for the Promotion of Policies on Racial Equality, and the Special Secretariat for Human Rights. The government has also made

clear that participative discussions are central to the way in which gender, race, and human rights issues will be treated by the government. One of the key responsibilities of the Special Secretariat for Policy for Women, SPM, is to articulate relations with civil society through maintaining dialogue with social movements. The first National Plan for Policies for Women (Plano Nacional de Políticas para as Mulheres) in 2006 was the result of extensive consultation by the SPM with civil society through the participatory organization of the 2004 National Conference on Policies for Women, which mobilized 120,000 women in preconferences held in each of Brazil's 26 states and at the national conference held in Brasília. The government also established the Inter-Ministerial Working Group, which involves civil society participation to ensure the development of better laws and social conditions for dealing with domestic violence. The Inter-Ministerial Working Group defines violence against women as a violation of human rights and maintains that "all women, independently of class, race, ethnicity, sexual orientation, income, culture, educational background, age or religion have the right to live free of violence, denounce anyone who assaults them and seek assistance from the Public Authorities" (Brazil, 2004, p. 15). Councils for women's rights, which began at the national level with the establishment of the National Council for the Rights of Women in 1985, have now been created throughout the country at the municipal and state levels (Brazil, 2004, p. 26). The specific accomplishments of the Brazilian government regarding gender-based violence include legal changes incorporated in the Maria da Penha Law passed in 2006 that established violence against women as a criminal offence; support for shelters and other medical and psychological services, including the establishment in 2005 of a free national 24-hour hotline, Ligue 180, to assist women victims of violence; capacity building in and expansion of women's police stations, with a total of 339 stations by 2004; and training of personnel in institutions dealing with violence against women (Brazil, 2004, p. 14).

A feminist member of the Workers' Party—active in the women's movement since the 1980s—whom we interviewed in Brasília in 2007 where she now works in the Special Secretariat for Policy for Women, credits the campaign against violence against women with providing the model for the transversal approach that the Lula government now takes to formulating wider policy for gender and race equity in Brazil. She also underscored that it is as a result of feminist campaigns that violence against women is no longer viewed as a private issue and is now understood as a question of women's citizenship and as a reflection of women's status.

Within the government, violence against women is seen as a violation against the human rights of women, as a problem of public security, as a question of justice, [and] as a very serious problem of public health . . . if we had relied on the government, many of the advances we have seen would not have happened without the women's movement. . . . The Maria da Penha Law—a law that deals with violence against women—would never have happened without the historic role of feminists but it is also necessary to have governments genuinely committed to implementation. . . . This is one of the major advances of this government. For example, the government already worked within the international Convention of the Elimination of All Forms of Discrimination Against Women. But the Ministry of Justice worked in isolation. The Ministry of Health worked in isolation. Those working with a draft law for women victims of sexual violence—rape—worked isolated in one area. . . . There was no coordination. It was a problem of the government of the time. Once the government began to see violence against women as a problem of health, a problem of violation of human rights, a problem of public security, a problem of justice, coordination became possible . . . gender equality policy must be . . . throughout the government.

It was this observation that led to the policy of transversalism that the Brazilian government now follows.

Ecuador's written response to the United Nations' request for progress on the Beijing Platform was developed in a Report prepared by CONAMU, the country's National Council for Women. The Report comments that although Ecuador's political problems have been an obstacle to significant achievements (with "three governments in five years, and the consequent debilitation of democratic institutions," National Council for Women, 2004, p. 4), there has been some progress in developing institutional mechanisms for addressing women's issues. Not only was CONAMU created "as the oversight organ for government policies with a gender perspective" (2004, p. 4), the National Congressional Committee on Women and the Family was given the status of a Specialized Permanent Commission (1998) and an Office of the Assistant Director for Women and Children was created within the *Defensoria del Pueblo*. CONAMU also developed several Equal Opportunity Plans (see National Council for Women, 2005) that one CONAMU official we interviewed described as intimately connected to the issues of women at the grassroots level:

[W]e developed a participative process for developing the Equal Opportunity Plan. This plan was constructed by elevating the agendas of diverse women in all the country, and it permitted us to go almost everywhere [in the country] to know about their demands. What we have done is to position the Equal Opportunity Plan as a state policy. . . . This Plan was not constructed here, but from women from many places. From there they posed their agendas, from there we have direct contacts, and from there we have constructed it collectively with them.

In this sense, CONAMU understands its work as creating spaces to mobilize (*capacitar*) local issues. Its unique structure, distinct from Brazil's, has advantages and disadvantages. It does not operate as a ministry ("We are not an organism that executes directly like a ministry") but comprises both governmental appointments and positions filled by women's organizations. The weakness of this kind of institutional structure is that it is vulnerable to the whims of changing governments, but its strength lies in the capacity of its civil society members to push for change beyond the establishment of policies to ensure that these policies are applied and function effectively.

Much of the progress on violence against women in Ecuador relates to developing legal support and counseling for women in the form of Women and Family Commissariats (later to come under the umbrella of the Gender Directorate within the Ministry of the Interior) and changing laws, especially around domestic violence. With continual pressure from women's organizations around the country, from CONAMU within the government itself and through UNIFEM from the international arena, violence against women has remained on public radar despite political and economic crises. Like UNIFEM officers, feminists at CONAMU also consider it significant that violence is now viewed as a public issue in Ecuador, but unlike UNIFEM officers, CONAMU officials—like feminists at SPM in Brazil—understand and work toward eliminating violence against women as a public health issue:

> To first make visible intrafamilial violence, and later other types of gender violence, to put it on the public agenda and have the Ecuadorian state take it on as a public health issue and, therefore, to generate policies for its eradication, fixing a series of elements, has also been important. Because, before this, violence against women was considered natural, normal, as part of life that women had to accept. Not anymore.

Unlike the pre-1995 years, therefore, gender-related violence now figures prominently on the public agenda and is formally recognized in the country's legal structures (National Council for Women, 2004, 2005). Still, the political instabilities have taken a toll on progress, as the constant changes in all branches of government make it difficult to train personnel in issues around gender-based violence and even to publish regulations regarding how offences are to be handled by the Women and Family Commissariats. Moreover, according to the country's Criminal Code, domestic violence could still be classified as a misdemeanor (*contravención*) rather than a crime (National Council for Women, 2004, p. 17). To make matters worse, although the new Correa government has undertaken positive initiatives such as doubling the Bono de Vivienda, or "poverty voucher," for the unemployed, it is in the process of undermining the structural independence of CONAMU by placing it in a newly created governmental unit, the National Secretariat for Citizen Participation, along with organizations representing other "vulnerable groups" such as indigenous people, blacks, and coastal peasants. Although CONAMU is fighting hard to maintain its strong position in defining government policy, this move by the current government may prove to have negative consequences on a system that has effectively buoyed and pushed forward women's issues under extremely difficult economic and political circumstances (Lind, 2005; Silva, 2005). The irony here is that the past successes of Ecuador's CONAMU in effecting gendered citizenship participation, confirmed by women working within social movements within the country, as we see below, may be undermined by a new secretariat ostensibly aimed at "citizen participation."

Regional Women's Movements: Violence Against Women and the Possibility of "Another World"

One of the characteristics of the terrain of feminisms in Latin America is that feminist movements have played key roles in building the new democracies in the region. As a result, many feminists have been integrated as civil servants into the new government structures that have been created to develop policies to address women's concerns. There is great debate among Latin American feminists about whether or not this inevitably constitutes co-optation and there have emerged new divisions among feminists who are variously labeled *autónomas*, *institucionalizadas*, or *popular*—autonomous, institutionalized, or grassroots (Alvarez, 1999; Alvarez et al., 2002). Nonetheless, because of this historical process, there is also a great deal of fluidity between the women's movements and the government owing to informal networks of friendship and previous experience of working together in various campaigns, notably campaigns against gender-based violence. Every person we interviewed, at all levels—international, national government, and regional movement—identified violence against women as the focal point for bringing together women in diverse contexts and with diverse backgrounds and goals to work together. In Ecuador, violence against women was described as the issue that provided continuity for feminists through years of political instability. In Brazil, violence against women was identified as the issue that was able to bring together women otherwise divided by deep divisions of race, region, and income inequality and the issue that helped to crystallize the Lula government's transversal approach to gender equality.

Our case study of a regional-level, transnational, women's movement is REMTE. REMTE sees women's rights as inextricably tied to questions of economic justice and gender equality. For REMTE, campaigns to end violence against women are an integral part of campaigns against neoliberal globalization and of the work to build "another world," another—more just—globalization in which violence against women will be obsolete. REMTE feminists ally with peasant, antiglobalization, and popular women's movements to articulate a unified critique of globalization and are especially concerned with

the potential impacts on women of the proposed Free Trade Zone of the Americas. In the REMTE context, violence against women is broadly defined to comprise—in addition to domestic violence and rape—the retrenching of gender inequality and gender violence evident in the commoditization of women in the beauty industry, the expansion of global sexual tourism, and the discursive framing of "flexible," unregulated employment as women's "freedom" to participate in the labour force. Less concerned with lobbying and affecting government policy, REMTE focuses its efforts on popular education, building the women's movement, and ensuring that a radical feminist critique is present in antiglobalization movements (see Alvarez, 2004, p. 202; Diaz, 2007; Faria, 2003).

The mobilization of Latin American feminists working for gender equality through economic transformation has a long history prior to the founding of REMTE in 1997. Discussions had been taking place at the Feminist Encuentros since 1981.[9] In the 1990s, Flora Tristan, a women's group in Peru working on small-scale income-generating projects, had begun to work with the idea of *economia solidária* (the solidarity economy) as both an anticapitalist critique and a project of building an alternative economy.[10] Informal discussions of what was then called "popular economy" had taken place among Latin American feminists at the parallel alternative NGO conference that had occurred alongside the United Nations Conference in Beijing in 1995. These discussions were continued at a workshop "The Globalization of Neoliberalism and Economic Justice for Women" at the 7th Feminist Encuentro in Chile in 1996. A year later in Lima, a seminar-workshop was organized to discuss the impact of structural adjustment programs on women. At the end of this meeting, REMTE—the Network of Women Transforming the Economy—was formally founded. The founding members were women's organizations in Chile, Colombia, Mexico, Nicaragua, and Peru. By 2007, the Network comprised feminist organizations in 11 Latin American countries including

REMTE-Ecuador and REF, the Feminism and Economy Network, in Brazil. It is a transnational network that has built on and reinforces previously existing women's networks and organizations at national and grassroots levels. REMTE works to make visible the links between the macroeconomy and women's lives and is especially concerned to develop critical analysis and popular education around the impact of free trade on women (Diaz, 2007). Coordination of the Network rotates among the participating national organizations and is currently based in São Paulo, Brazil, where REMTE has allied its activities with the much larger transnational feminist movement, the World March of Women, with which it shares office space. The World March of Women was founded in Montreal, Quebec, in 1998 where it was based until 2007 when its international coordination was moved to Brazil. The March is a transnational feminist movement that works at local and international levels and within other social movements to focus on women's everyday lives and specifically the roots of the poverty and violence women experience.[11] REMTE and the World March of Women work in alliance to ensure that women's issues and a gender critique are in place in the agendas, workshops, campaigns, and declarations of the World Social Forum, the anti-Free Trade campaign and other "mixed" (i.e., with men) movement spaces in which they are active. In Brazil, they also work together on the presidential advisory councils for policy for women and for policy on the solidarity economy and on the organizing committee for the National Conferences on Policy for Women in 2004 and 2007.

Our interviews with activists in REMTE member organizations in both Ecuador and Brazil underlined the strategic role the issue of violence against women has played in mobilizing women and developing experiences of collaboration and leadership that many are now bringing to other issues such as land reform and minimum wage legislation. In the words of REMTE's coordinator: "Our urgent task is to link the fight against violence against women with the global

struggle against neoliberal capitalism" (Faria, 2005, p. 28; our translation). REMTE is simultaneously engaged in building a feminist movement around a critique of neoliberal globalization that has retrenched class, race, and gender inequality to produce new forms of violence against women and in coalition building to ensure that violence against women is addressed within the antiglobalization and other alternative social movements.

In Brazil, REMTE and its ally, the World March of Women, are monitoring the postlegislation trajectory of the Maria da Penha Law. Although on one hand they respond to the Maria da Penha law as an important victory of the feminist movement's campaign against violence against women, on the other hand, REMTE and the World March of Women remind that the legislation presents new challenges to fight the gender inequality that lies at the base of gender violence:

> Violence against women is one of the main expressions of male dominance. . . . It is not possible to reduce violence only with punitive legislation . . . for women not to suffer violence it is necessary to fight for action in education and policies of prevention. . . . To combat violence, both policies and social transformation are needed. . . . To not only interrupt, but to prevent violence against women, it is necessary to understand the roots that sustain it. . . . With the deepening of neoliberalism there has been an increase in machismo and violence. So we must always relate the battle against violence against women to the global struggle against capitalism that is machista, racist, and homophobic. (The World March of Women, 2007, p. 3)

In Ecuador, REMTE views the maintenance of links between the women's movements and CONAMU (The National Council of Women) as crucial to yielding concrete consequences in the approval of a new constitution that for the first time in 1998 incorporated women's rights in a wide range of areas, including health, education, and work (Foro Nacional Permanente de la Mujer Ecuatoriana, 2002; Silva, 2005). UNIFEM, CONAMU, and the National Permanent Forum of Ecuadorian Women, all of which were strategically linked to women's organizations and movements in the country, were central to this constitutional outcome. According to a member of REMTE in Ecuador, CONAMU stands out as a significant "profile" that kept feminist issues alive: "[CONAMU] has been a space that, in the midst of all these [political and economic] irregularities, has been getting stronger, consolidating, taking a more radical line. It is within the structure of the state, but it has a discourse that goes beyond the rest of the state. In that sense, it has been a good bridge for many things." REMTE-Ecuador has focused on linking with local women in peasant, indigenous, and urban-based unions and connecting their concerns with the national agenda, with international organizations such as La Vía Campesina and the World Social Forum, and with regional efforts such as the campaign against the Free Trade for the Americas Agreement and the Regional Conferences on Latin American and Caribbean Women organized by the UN's Economic Commission for Latin America and the Caribbean.[12] REMTE's coordinator in Ecuador summarizes the Network's strategic approach when describing the rationale for their participation in the World Social Forum: "Our vision is that feminism runs throughout the shared agenda of the Forum. We don't come to *dispute*, we come to *construct* a feminist vision from our proposal that another world is possible."

In sum, the orientation of the alternative women's movements in the region, as represented here by REMTE, has been to make alliances with diverse organizations, movements and campaigns and to bring women's issues to the forefront at every opportunity in these encounters: "The idea is to look for a meeting point (*un punto de encuentro*) and to construct a shared discourse." Linking the eradication of violence against women to the need for broader social and economic transformations, REMTE aligns with social movements engaged in struggles for land reform and women's rights to land, the plight of rural women who are often isolated in abusive situations and remote from urban-based shelters and support, and poor women. At the same time, REMTE, through its participation in the World Social Forum and anti-free trade movements, infuses these public spaces with a feminist, anticapitalist critique. In this sense, REMTE works "with and across difference" (Walby, 2002, p. 541), including building coalitions with indigenous organizations, Afro-descendent communities, popular women's groups, male activists, unions, and others in its efforts to build feminism into alternative ways of living. As indicated in REMTE's campaigns against the objectification of women in the transnational beauty industry and sexual tourism, the strategy has been to draw out connections between the violence of neoliberal globalization and violence against women and then to move forward with conscious efforts to create more hopeful scenarios by realigning the axes of gender and economy.

Conclusion

In this article we have identified a political moment in which there has been dynamic collaboration between international, national, and regional movements on the issue of gender-based violence on one hand and developing democracies that have instigated greater citizen engagement with public issues on the other. This moment has produced a positive effect on public awareness of violence against women. How things will move on from this hopeful moment—how this collaborative opportunity will unfold—is unclear, since a withdrawal of support or shift in allegiances on the part of any of the interested parties could make a radical difference in the effectiveness of this collaboration for combating violence against women. But this example does point to the importance of building political alliances at international, national, and regional scales on an issue such as violence against women, despite different ways of framing the issue of gender violence. In addition, it points to the centrality of all three scales to successful outcomes. Although it cannot be said that violence against women is disappearing in Latin America today, it is an accomplishment that considerably more positive public and discursive spaces have been created for moving forward on violence against women as a result of the strategic work and transversal approaches of feminists and their supporters at all scales in this period of democratic development.

Our mapping of the multiple and different efforts to combat violence against women in Latin America highlights the importance of maintaining broad definitions of a given political project to accommodate a broad coalition of potential support. Given that some groups interpreted gender-based violence as a health issue whereas others viewed it as a development issue, and still others understood it to be a product of a powerful economic system, an oppositional "politics of difference" could have easily emerged in this case. Instead, the importance of strategic coalitions across difference was recognized as central to having violence against women successfully recognized as a global, regional, and national issue for which serious attention and resources were necessary. This recognition emerged in a particular historical conjuncture in which women's movements had battled authoritarian and/or corrupt regimes and, in emerging from them sought new spaces for their political projects. Although some might accuse women's organizations and movements of being co-opted in their efforts here—by the state, by the UN, by men's groups—we hope to have shown that it is much more useful to translate these efforts as hopeful moments of strategic unity—of feminist politics in the current era of globalization—to address a crucial social and economic issue.

Notes

1. The data in this article derive from document analysis and from fieldwork in Ecuador and Brazil. Interviews were conducted by the authors in Spanish, Portuguese, and English with feminists working on women's issues in the United Nations Development Fund for Women (UNIFEM) and in the state agencies for women in both national governments (the National Council for Women, CONAMU, in Ecuador and the Secretariat for Policy for Women, SPM, in Brazil) and with activists in each country who are developing a feminist alternative to neoliberal capitalism through the Network of Women Transforming the Economy (REMTE). Interviews were taped. All translations are ours. In this research, we focus on the experience and expertise of urban state feminists and activists. In previous research we have (separately) conducted field research that focused on rural women, households, and gender politics in marginalized areas: Phillips in coastal Ecuador and Cole in northeast Brazil.

2. Drogus and Stewart-Gambino (2005) take on, and ultimately challenge, this argument for the cases of Brazil and Chile.

3. It is clear that Walby is not unaware of the limitations of a rights discourse, but she challenges the argument that a rights discourse necessarily leads to individualistic and divisive outcomes (Walby, 2002, p. 548).

4. We began our project comparing Brazil and Ecuador not only because these are the locations in which we have prior experience conducting feminist ethnographic research, but because these two countries house the two subregional offices of the United Nations Development Fund for Women, UNIFEM, in South America.

5. Transversalism refers to the political practice of seeking connections, creating dialogue, and generating relationships across sectors. According to Nira Yuval-Davis the term transversal politics is "used both descriptively, referring to political activities and organizing that have been taking place in a variety of locations, and normatively, as a model of political activism that is worth following" (2006, p. 280). She traces the idea of transversal politics to autonomous left politics in Bologna in the 1970s. For Yuval-Davis, transversalism

is replacing identity politics and is foundational to what has become a global feminist "epistemological community" through processes such as the UN conferences where feminists from the "South" were the most organized and innovative: "Anyone who took part in transversal politics of feminists across the borders and boundaries of ethnic and national conflicts would know that the processes of change have radically affected women on both sides and have often created such common epistemological communities" (Yuval-Davis, 2006, p. 285). In Brazil, the convergence of transversalism as political practice of both feminist activists and the current Workers' Party government is an auspicious moment in the history of Latin American feminisms.

6. Since coming into office in the fall of 2002, the Lula government has sponsored 36 national conferences on numerous themes—more than all previous governments combined. Brazilian political theorist Céli Pinto (2007) describes the conference process as the creation of a unique "public co-managed space," what she calls "a medium-range public." Regarding the two National Conferences for Policy for Women held in 2004 and 2007, Pinto says that the conferences cannot be understood simply as an official state program because what takes place when thousands of women are mobilized from different societal levels and regions cannot be predicted.

7. In 1991, the U.S.-based Center for Women's Global Leadership, headed by Charlotte Bunch, launched the 16 Days of Activism against Gender Violence campaign to establish violence against women as a violation of human rights. It focuses international attention on violence against women during the 16 days between November 25, the date selected and observed as International Day Against Violence Against Women by the 4th Feminist Encuentro in Mexico in 1987 (in commemoration of a group of sisters in the Dominican Republic who were killed in 1961), and International Human Rights Day on December 10. In 1999, the United Nations declared November 25 the International Day for the Elimination of Violence against Women. 16 Days is an annual international campaign that, since its inception, has involved more than 1,000 organizations and 130 countries (see Center for Women's Global Leadership, 2007). Each year it establishes themes, proposes actions, and prepares online information kits in multiple languages for use by women's organizations and media during the 16-day period. It monitors and annually updates information on the progress (or lack of progress) individual national governments are making toward eliminating violence against women. 16 Days is both a virtual forum through which information, activities, and strategies are globally shared and a center that develops tools for ensuring that governments implement the promises they have made to eliminate violence against women.

8. It is noted in this report that in contrast to Latin America, "the North American relationship with the Inter-American system is fairly negative. Canada and the United States of America have not ratified the American Convention [on Human Rights] and do not recognize the jurisdiction of the [Inter-American] Commission [on Human Rights] and Court. However, the Commission is still competent to receive complaints against Canada and the United States . . . under the 1949 American Declaration of the Rights and Duties of Man, and there are a few cases currently pending" (Special Rapporteur on Violence Against Women, 2003, p. 210).

9. For accounts of the earlier Feminist Encuentros in Latin America, see Miller (1991) and Stephen (1997). Alvarez et al. (2002) discuss the debates of the Encuentros that took place in 1993 (El Salvador), 1996 (Chile), and 1999 (Dominican Republic) and point to the significance of the Encuentros for the development of Latin American feminism. Miller notes that one of the two resolutions passed at the first Encuentro in Colombia in 1981 was "to initiate an international campaign protesting violence against women" (1991, p. 215).

10. See Gibson-Graham (2006) for a discussion of the idea of solidarity economy as a perspective that refuses "capitalocentrism" and seeks to "resocialize" economic relations. The solidarity economy is diverse and plural, sees people as the primary resource, and makes visible other forms of economic activity based on the "fugitive energies" of caring, social concern, and collectivity (p. 24).

11. The World March of Women held its 1st International Meeting in 1998 in Montreal, Quebec, and its 6th International Meeting in Lima, Peru, in 2006 where 59 delegates from 29 countries and the Native Women's Network of the Americas participated. At the 2006 meeting the March identified "four areas of action that will allow us to deepen our initial commitment to fighting poverty and violence: peace and demilitarization; violence as a tool to control women's bodies and lives; work/employment and pay equity; and the common good and food sovereignty"

(World March of Women, 2006). The March actively maintains alliances with the alternative antiglobalization movement through its participation in the World Social Forum, the Social Movements International Network, and the organization of a Forum on Food Sovereignty in partnership with La Vía Campesina. At the Lima meeting, the International Secretariat of the March was transferred from Quebec to Brazil.

12. For example, REMTE-Ecuador participated in the Meeting of Networks for the Continental Campaign against the Free Trade for the Americas Agreement held in Quito in 2002 and in the 10th Regional Conference on Latin American and Caribbean Women of the UN's Economic Commission for Latin America and the Caribbean held in Quito in August 2007.

References

Alvarez, S. (1990). *Engendering democracy in Brazil: Women's movements in transition politics.* Princeton, NJ: Princeton University Press.

Alvarez, S. (1999). The Latin American feminist NGO "boom." *International Feminist Journal of Politics, 1*(2), 181–209.

Alvarez, S. (with Faria, N., & Nobre, M.). (2004). Another (also feminist) world is possible: Constructing transnational spaces and global alternatives from the movements. In J. Sen, A. Anand, A. Escobar, & P. Waterman (Eds.), *World Social Forum: Challenging empires* (pp. 199–206). New Delhi: Viveka Foundation.

Alvarez, S., Friedman, E., Beckman, E., Blackwell, M., Chinchilla, N. S., Lebon, N., et al. (2002). Encountering Latin American and Caribbean feminisms. *Signs, 28*(2), 537–579.

Annan, K. (2006). *In-depth study on all forms of violence against women.* New York: United Nations.

Basu, A. (Ed.). (1995). *The challenge of local feminisms: Women's movements in global perspective.* Boulder, CO: Westview.

Bennett, J. (2001). *The enchantment of modern life: Attachments, crossings and ethics.* Princeton, NJ: Princeton University Press.

Brazil. (2004). *Brazil's response to the "Questionnaire on the application of the Beijing Platform for Action (1995) and the results of the twenty-third period of the extraordinary sessions of the General Assembly (2000)."* United Nations Division for the Advancement of Women. Retrieved from http://www.un.org/womenwatch/daw/Review/responses/BRAZIL-English.pdf

Center for Women's Global Leadership. (2007). *About the 16 Days.* Retrieved February 13, 2008, from www.cwgl.rutgers.edu

Desmarais, A. A. (2007). *La vía campesina: Globalization and the power of peasants.* Halifax, Canada: Fernwood.

Diaz, C. A. (2007). *Building bridges between feminism and resistance to free trade: The experience of the Latin American network of women transforming the economy.* Unpublished master's thesis, Département de Science Politique, Université de Montréal.

Drogus, C. A., & Stewart-Gambino, H. (2005). *Activist faith: Grassroots women in democratic Brazil and Chile.* University Park: Pennsylvania State University Press.

Erwin, P. E. (2006). Exporting U.S. domestic violence reforms: An analysis of human rights frameworks and U.S. "best practices." *Feminist Criminology, 1*(3), 188–206.

Faria, N. (Ed.). (2003). *Construir la igualdad: debates feministas en el foro social mundial* [To construct equality: Feminist debates in the World Social Forum]. Lima, Peru: Latin American Network of Women Transforming the Economy.

Faria, N. (2005). Para a eradicação da violência doméstica e sexual. In A. Semprevivas (Ed.), *Feminismo e luta das mulheres: Analises e debates* [Feminism and the struggle of women: Analyses and debates] (pp. 23–29). São Paulo, Brazil: Sempreviva Organização Feminista.

Ferree, M. A., & Tripp, A. M. (Eds.). (2006). *Global feminism: Transnational women's activism, organizing, and human rights.* New York: New York University Press.

Foro Nacional Permanente de la Mujer Ecuatoriana. (2002). *Base política.* Quito, Ecuador: Author.

Gibson-Graham, J. K. (2006). *A postcapitalist politics.* Minneapolis: University of Minnesota Press.

Heyzer, N. (2006). *Investment in proven strategies needed to end violence against women.* United Nations Development Fund for Women press statement for the International Day for the Elimination of Violence against Women, November 22, 2006.

Hindess, B. (2004). Liberalism: What's in a name? In W. Larner & W. Walters (Eds.), *Global governmentality* (pp. 23–39). London: Routledge.

Keck, M., & Sikkink, K. (1998). *Activists beyond borders: Advocacy networks in international politics.* Ithaca, NY: Cornell University Press.

Lara, S. (2006). *Las metas del milenio y la igualdad de género: El caso de Ecuador* [The millennium goals and gender equality: The case of Ecuador]. Santiago de Chile, Chile: CEPAL.

León, I. (Ed.). (2005). *Women in resistance: Experiences, visions and proposals.* Quito, Ecuador: Agencia Latino Americana da Información.

Lind, A. (2005). *Gendered paradoxes: Women's movements, state restructuring, and global development in Ecuador.* University Park: Pennsylvania State University Press.

Merry, S. E. (2006). *Human rights and gender violence: Translating international law into local justice.* Chicago: University of Chicago Press.

Miller, F. (1991). *Latin American women and the search for social justice.* Hanover, NH: University Press of New England.

Moghadam, V. (2005). *Globalizing women: Transnational feminist networks.* Baltimore: Johns Hopkins University Press.

National Council for Women. (2004). *Questionnaire to governments on implementation of the Beijing Platform for Action (1995) and the outcome of the twenty-third special session of the General Assembly (2000).* Quito, Ecuador: Author.

National Council for Women. (2005). *Plan de igualdad de oportunidades de las mujeres Ecautorianas* [Plan of equal opportunities for Ecuadorian women]. Quito, Ecuador: Author.

Pinto, C. R. J. (2007, September 5–8). *Brazil's national conferences: A "medium-range" public?* Paper presented at the Latin American Studies Association Meetings, Montreal, Quebec, Canada.

Sassen, S. (2006). *Territory, authority, rights: From medieval to global assemblages.* Princeton, NJ: Princeton University Press.

Silva, E. (Ed.). (2005). *Identidad y Ciudadanía de las Mujeres* [The identity and citizenship of women]. Quito, Ecuador: Ediciones Abya-Yala.

Special Rapporteur on Violence Against Women. (2003). *Integration of the human rights of women and the gender perspective: Violence against women. Report of the Special Rapporteur on violence against women, its causes and consequences. Addendum 1: International, regional and national developments in the area of violence against women, 1994–2003.* New York: United Nations Commission on Human Rights, E/CN.4/2003/75/Add1.

Special Secretariat for Policy for Women. (2006). *Memória 2003–2006* [Memoirs, 2003–2006]. Brasília, Brazil: Secretaria Especial de Políticas para as Mulheres.

Special Secretariat for Policy for Women. (2007). *Lei Maria da Penha. Lei no 11.340 de 7 de agosto de 2006. Coíbe a violência domestica e familiar contra a mulher* [The Maria da Penha Law. Law no. 11.340 of August 7, 2006. Restraining familial and domestic violence against women]. Brasília, Brazil: Presidência da República.

Stanko, B. (2004). A tribute to 10 years of knowledge. *Violence Against Women, 10*(12), 1395–1400.

Stephen, L. (1997). *Women and social movements in Latin America: Power from below.* Austin: University of Texas.

Thayer, M. (2000). Traveling feminisms: From embodied women to engendered citizenship. In M. Burawoy, J. A. Blum, S. George, Z. Gille, T. Gowan, L. Haney, et al. (Eds.), *Global ethnography* (pp. 203–233). Berkeley: University of California Press.

Tierney, K. J. (1982). The battered women movement and the creation of the wife beating problem. *Social Problems, 29*(3), 207–220.

Tsing, A. L. (2005). *Friction: An ethnography of global connection.* Princeton, NJ: Princeton University Press.

United Nations. (2003). *Elimination of all forms of violence against women, including crimes identified in the outcome document of the 23rd special session of the General Assembly, titled "Women 2000: Gender equality, development and peace for the 21st century."* Resolution adopted by the General Assembly, Fifty-seventh session, 57/181.

United Nations. (2004). *In-depth study on all forms of violence against women.* Resolution adopted by the General Assembly, Fifty-eighth session, 58/185.

United Nations. (2005). *Elimination of all forms of violence against women, including crimes identified in the outcome document of the 23rd special session of the General Assembly, titled "Women 2000: Gender equality, development and peace for the 21st century.* Resolution adopted by the General Assembly, fifty-ninth session, 59/167.

United Nations. (2006). *In-depth study on all forms of violence against women.* Resolution adopted by the General Assembly, sixtieth session, 60/136.

United Nations. (2007). *Intensification of efforts to eliminate all forms of violence against women.* Resolution adopted by the General Assembly, sixty-first session, A/res/61/143.

United Nations Development Fund for Women. (2002). *Progress of the world's women.* New York: Author.

United Nations Development Fund for Women. (2006). *Not a minute more: November 25th and 16 Days of activism against gender violence.* Available at www.unifem.org/campaigns/november25.

United Nations Development Fund for Women. (2007, September 10). La Lucha contra la violencia de género es ya política de Estado en Ecuador desde el 10 de Septiembre de 2007. *Archivos Noticias.* Available from the United Nations Development Fund for Women Web site.

Vargas, V. (2003). Feminism, globalization and the global justice and solidarity movement. *Cultural Studies, 17*(6), 905–920.

Walby, S. (2002). Feminism in a global era. *Economy and Society, 31*(4), 533–557.

Walker, G. (1990). *Family violence and the women's movement: The conceptual politics of struggle.* Toronto: University of Toronto Press.

Waller, M., & Marcos, S. (Eds.). (2005). *Dialogue and difference: Feminisms challenge globalization.* New York: Palgrave.

Weldon, S. L. (2002). *Protest, policy, and the problem of violence against women: A cross-national comparison.* Pittsburgh, PA: University of Pittsburgh Press.

World March of Women. (2006). Editorial. *World March of Women Newsletter 9*(2), 1–2.

The World March of Women. (2007). *Jornal da marcha.* São Paulo, Brazil: Sempreviva Organização Feminista.

Yuval-Davis, N. (2006). Human/women's rights and feminist transversal politics. In M. Ferree & A. Tripp (Eds.), *Global feminism: Transnational women's activism, organizing, and human rights* (pp. 275–295). New York: New York University Press.

Zibechi, R. (2007). *Ecuador's prolonged instability. Americas program report.* Silver City, NM: International Relations Center.

Index

About the Editors

Raquel Kennedy Bergen is a professor and chair of the Department of Sociology at Saint Joseph's University in Philadelphia, Pennsylvania. She is the author or coauthor of numerous scholarly publications and seven books on violence against women including *Wife Rape: Understanding the Response of Survivors and Service Providers;* and *Issues in Intimate Violence.* With Claire Renzetti and Jeffrey Edleson she edited *Sourcebook on Violence Against Women* and *Violence Against Women: Classic Statements.* She has served as a member of the Pennsylvania State Ethics Commission since 2004 when she was appointed by Governor Edward G. Rendell. She has volunteered as an advocate for battered women and sexual assault survivors for the past 21 years. Her current research explores women's experiences of sexual and physical violence during pregnancy.

Jeffrey L. Edleson is a professor in the University of Minnesota School of Social Work and director of the Minnesota Center Against Violence and Abuse (www .mincava.umn.edu). He is one of the world's leading authorities on children exposed to domestic violence and has published more than 100 articles and 10 books on domestic violence, group work, and program evaluation.

Claire M. Renzetti is the Judi Conway Patton Endowed Chair for Studies of Violence Against Women in the Center for Research on Violence Against Women, and Professor of Sociology at the University of Kentucky. She is editor of the international, interdisciplinary journal, *Violence Against Women;* coeditor with Jeffrey Edleson of the Interpersonal Violence book series for Oxford University Press; and editor of the Gender, Crime and Law book series for Northeastern University Press. She has authored or edited 16 books as well as numerous book chapters and articles in professional journals. Much of her research has focused on the violent victimization experiences of economically marginalized women living in public housing developments. She is currently conducting an ethnography of a faith-based organization involved in anti-trafficking work as well as a survey of nongovernmental organizations that provide services to domestic sex trafficking victims.